THE GOLFERS GUIDE
to Ireland

By
Dermot Gilleece

D1381615

© Travel Publishing L

Published by:
Travel Publishing Ltd
7a Apollo House, Calleva Park
Aldermaston, Berks, RG7 8TN

ISBN 1-902-00749-2

© Travel Publishing Ltd

First Published: 2000

Printing by: Ashford Press, Gosport

Maps by: © MAPS IN MINUTES ™ (2000)

Editor: Dermot Gillece

Cover Design: Lines & Words, Aldermaston

Photographs courtesy of © Bord Fáilte - Irish Tourist Board and © Northern Irish Tourist Board

Foreword

By universal consent Ireland is one of the World's most attractive destinations for the travelling golfer. There are nearly 400 golf clubs in Ireland offering a wide variety of links, parkland, and heathland terrains. Most are set in the beautiful and often stunning inland and coastal scenery for which Ireland is famous. The quality of the courses is reflected in the increasing number of world class tournaments being held in Ireland and by the selection of the K Club in County Kildare as the venue for the Ryder Cup in 2005.

Well over 200,000 overseas visitors play golf in Ireland each year and a large proportion emanate from Britain, the European mainland and the U.S.A. But visitors to the "Emerald Isle" are offered much more than pleasurable games of golf. Ireland is blessed with stunning un-spoilt scenery and a truly relaxed pace of life whilst its inhabitants offer the visitor the most genuine of friendly welcomes. Combining this with Ireland's fascinating mix of history, myth and legend, plus the many places of interest, ensures that most golfers return home with not only fond memories of rounds of golf but also a deep affection for Ireland's scenery and people.

The Golfers Guide to Ireland is very much a comprehensive guide to playing 18-hole golf in the 32 counties (plus Dublin and Belfast) but it also offers the golfer an insight into the scenery, places of interest and people. In addition it provides the golfing visitor with details of over 400 places to stay, eat and drink all of which have been linked to the nearest golf courses. It is therefore the ideal guide for planning every aspect of a golfing trip to Ireland.

We are indebted to Dermot Gilleece (golf correspondent of the Irish Times) for writing the knowledgeable introductions to golf in each county (including recommended golf course itin-eraries for those golfers who wish to experience a variety of golfing terrains) and for his stimulating personal reviews of over 80 golf courses throughout Ireland. However in providing brief details about the scenery, places of interest and people in Ireland he will, we hope, encour-age the golfing visitor to explore the truly wonderful country beyond the 18 holes. We would also like to thank Bord Failte and the golf courses themselves for providing the many wonderful photographs contained in the guide. Finally during the course of researching the locations of the golf clubs in Ireland we found *The Complete Road Atlas of Ireland* by Ordnance Survey an indispensable companion and a worthwhile investment!

We hope you enjoy reading and using *The Golfers Guide to Ireland*. We are always inter-ested to receive readers' comments on the contents of the book, on the golf courses covered (or not covered) and of course on the places to stay, eat and drink. This will help us refine and improve the future editions. Enjoy your golf!

County Map of Ireland

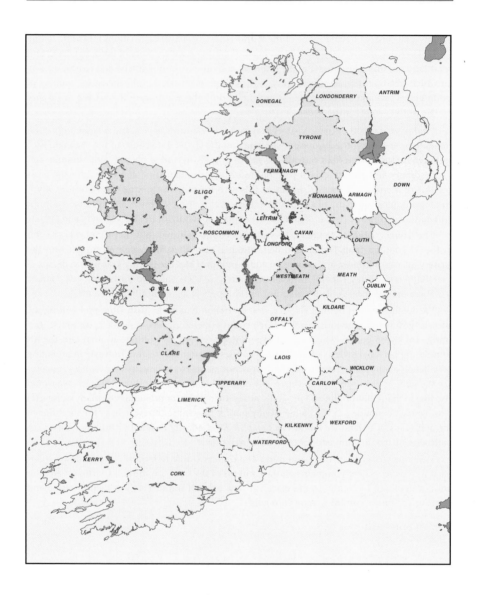

Contents

This page is intentionally blank

How to Use

The Golfers Guide to Ireland has been specifically designed as an easy-to-use guide so there is no need for complicated instructions. However the reader may find the following guidelines helpful in planning the perfect golfing holiday.

CHOOSING WHERE TO PLAY GOLF IN IRELAND

The golfing information for each county (or geographical grouping of counties where there are a limited number of golf courses) may be found as "chapters" in Section I of the guide where the counties are presented in *alphabetical* order. Use the *Contents Page* to find the county of your choice. Each "chapter" contains a review of golf in the county, useful information for players on each golf club and detailed reviews of selected courses. Use this information to decide where to play. Whether you are individuals or a society we do recommend that you contact the Golf Club in advance to avoid disappointment. The telephone number, fax number and email address (where available) may be found under each golf club listing.

GOLFING ITINERARIES

If you wish to experience the varied terrains (links, parkland or heathland) on offer in Ireland without travelling long distances during your golfing holiday you should refer to the list of recommended golfing itineraries prepared by Dermott Gilleece. This can be found on the next page.

CHOOSING WHERE TO STAY, EAT AND DRINK

When you have decided on the golf courses you wish to play simply refer to the list of places to stay, eat and drink found after each golf course. Use the *reference number* beside each listed entry to find more information (including a photograph) on the places of your choice in Section II of the guide. The telephone number, fax number and email address (where available) is listed for each place should you wish to make a booking

INTERNATIONAL CALLING

All telephone numbers throughout the guide are shown with local dialling codes. Please note that for *Northern Ireland* numbers callers from outside the United Kingdom should first dial the country code of 00 44 followed by the number shown in the guide with the leading zero dropped. For numbers in the *Republic of Ireland* the country code is 00 353 and again the leading zero should be dropped prior to dialling the number shown.

LOCAL CURRENCY

All prices quoted in the guide are in *local currency*. Thus for the Republic of Ireland prices are expressed in *Irish punts (pounds)* and for Northern Ireland in *Pounds sterling*.

This page is intentionally blank

Golfing Itineraries

For those golfers who want to enjoy a variety of golfing experiences in Ireland (links, parkland, heathland for example) during their visit without travelling the length and breadth of the island Dermot Gilleece recommends you select a group from the following combination of courses:

ANTRIM AND DERRY:

Galgorm Castle, Stakis Park, Ballycastle, Royal Portrush, Portstewart, Roe Park, Castlerock.

DERRY AND NORTH DONEGAL:

City of Derry, Ballyliffin, Letterkenny, Rosapenna.

SOUTH DONEGAL, SLIGO AND NORTH MAYO:

Donegal, County Sligo, Strandhill , Enniscrone, Belmullet (Carne)

MID-MAYO AND GALWAY:

Claremorris, Westport, Connemara, Bearna, Galway Bay.

CLARE:

Lahinch, Woodstock, Ennis, Shannon.

LIMERICK AND NORTH KERRY:

Adare Golf Club, Newcastle West, Tralee, Ballybunion, Killarney.

SOUTH KERRY AND WEST CORK:

Waterville, Bantry Bay, Old Head of Kinsale, Kinsale.

CORK CITY AND WEST WATERFORD:

Fota Island, Cork GC, West Waterford, Gold Coast, Tramore.

EAST WATERFORD AND SOUTH WEXFORD:

Waterford Municipal, Faithlegg, Rosslare, St. Helen's Bay.

WICKLOW:

The European Club, Druids Glen, Powerscourt, Tulfarris, Rathsallagh.

NORTH DUBLIN:

Portmarnock, Portmarnock Links, The Island, Hollytown, Royal Dublin.

WEST DUBLIN AND EAST KILDARE:

Hermitage, Luttrellstown Castle, The K Club, Curragh.

KILDARE, CARLOW AND KILKENNY:

Kilkea Castle, Carlow, Mount Wolseley, Mount Juliet.

TIPPERARY AND NORTH CORK:

Roscrea, Ballykisteen, Charleville, Clonmel.

OFFLAY, LAOIS, WESTMEATH AND ROSCOMMON:

Tullamore, Esker Hills, The Heath, Mullingar, Athlone, Glasson, Roscommon.

MEATH AND LOUTH:

Headfort, Laytown, and Bettystown, County Louth, Seapoint, Dundalk.

CAVAN, FERMANAGH, TYRONE, ARMAGH AND MONAGHAN:

Slieve Russell, Enniskillen, Dungannon, County Armagh, Nuremore.

SOUTH DOWN:

Warrenpoint, Royal County Down, Kilkeel, Downpatrick.

NORTH DOWN AND BELFAST:

Clandeboye, Belvoir Park, Malone, Royal Belfast, Knock.

We do hope you enjoy playing at these golf clubs but please do not hesitate to send us your own recommendations on the ideal combination of courses to play. We look forward to hearing from you!

x

This page is intentionally blank

Accommodation, Food and Drink

Contents - Republic of Ireland

This page is intentionally blank

CLARE

It is doubtful if anybody projected the essence of Clare golf better than the late Brud Slattery, who was secretary/manager of Lahinch GC from 1954 to 1984. While remembering his easy charm, those fortunate enough to know him would also recall a beguiling eccentricity which, happily, continues to characterise the natives of this fascinating county.

Stories about Slattery are legion, and one I particularly like concerned his reaction on hearing that a golfing neighbour of his had gone to the great fairway in the sky. Remarkable for a

Spanish Point, Co Clare

native of rural Ireland, Brud never read newspaper obituaries and relied on his family to keep him informed of such matters. Anyway, when his son Austin informed him of the neighbour's demise, Brud thought for a moment before commenting somberly: "Wasn't it a terrible pity he had to pass away without curing that dreadful slice of his." His upbringing, during the 1920s and 1930s was probably very similar to that of Peadar Skerritt, a member of a famous Clare golfing family. Skerritt recalled: "It was impossible not to play golf in Lahinch in my youth. I started at the age of eight. Clubs were hard to come by and the only hope of getting one was by caddying, when you could play in the evening with them."

Lahinch is in West Clare, where members of the Black Watch regiment were drawn to the local duneland to indulge skills acquired in their native Scotland. And the area is soon to be enhanced by another splendid links, at Doonbeg, courtesy of American investment and the design skills of Greg Norman. Indeed some local historians claim that the Blackwatch Regiment were attracted to Doonbeg as a possible site before deciding on Lahinch as an ideal location to established the county's first golf club, in 1892, which they did with the help of merchant princes from Limerick. In the event, the county now has a splendid contrast of golfing terrain from the links of Lahinch, Spanish Point and Kilkee on the west coast, to Kilrush and Shannon GC on the Shannon Estuary and on to the further parkland stretches of Ennis, Woodstock and East Clare.

Clare has been described as a peninsula on a grand scale. This derives from it having its only land link is with Co Galway at its north-east boundary. Otherwise, the county is surrounded by water. On the east is Lough Derg, the biggest and most beautiful of the Shannon lakes, and the lower Shannon itself; on the south is the broad sweep of the Shannon Estuary, spreading like an inland sea, and on the west is the wild Atlantic. So it is that the county combines picturesque scenery and a variety of sea-scapes from the desolate Loop Head

The Burren, Co Clare

to the charming beaches of Kilkee, Milltown Malbay and Lahinch, culminating in the majestic Cliffs of Moher and the unique uplands of the famous Burren, with its lunar landscapes and rare flora. Another leading tourist attraction is the Aillwee Cave, about two miles from Ballyvaughan. A relatively recent discovery, it was only in 1944 that a local farmer, Jack McCann, found the entry. Now, accessibility from Ballyvaughan, Lisdoonvarna and Galway has led to its development as the only cave among the many in the Burren region, which visitors can explore easily, without pot-holing expertise or equipment.

The county takes its name from the Gaelic "An Clar", meaning a level surface or plane. This is certainly true of the central area, from north to south. On either side of this level backbone, however, the land is ribbed with higher terrain, from Slieve Elva and Mount Callan in the west, to Slieve Aughty and the Bernagh mountains to the east. Though natives of Dover would, no doubt, strongly argue the point, the Cliffs of Moher are thought to offer some of the most magnificent stretches of cliff scenery in these islands. Rising to about 650 feet above the Atlantic, they extend for five miles from Hag's Head to O'Brien's Tower. Yet the locals can often be rather blase about their stunning impact on the tourist. Like the Liscannor publican who, on being asked by an American visitor what he thought of the famous Cliffs, replied philosophically: "Begob isn't it great they're there, all the same. Otherwise we'd all be drowned."

Shannon Airport, situated beside the Estuary, due south of the county-town of Ennis, offers tremendous access for the overseas tourist. Indeed many golfing visitors to Ireland, especially from the US, take the option of landing at Shannon from where their first stop is Lahinch GC,

Cliffs of Moher, Co Clare

before they head south to the Kerry courses. Others take the option of easing their game into shape on the fine, championship-standard course at Shannon GC. And while in the Shannon area, they have the opportunity of savouring rather special banquets and entertainments at the medieval castles of Bunratty, Knappogue and Dunguaire, and traditional Irish music in the local pubs, quite apart from fun-filled festivals. These are the attractions which prompted Tom Watson, when travelling from Ballybunion to Lahinch in the summer of 1999, to go by van, rather than a considerably quicker helicopter. "You don't meet the local people in the air," he explained with a smile.

From a golfing standpoint, the appeal of the eastern side of the county has been greatly enhanced by the development of East Clare GC. This is located at the village of Bodyke, only a short drive from Lough Derg, where there are attractive boat trips on the Shannon which, incidentally, is the longest river in these islands.

One of the most famous characters at Lahinch around the time of World War II, was an Ennistymon butcher named Mick O'Loughlin, known to his many golfing friends as "Mickey the Meat" (pronounced mate). During a crucial foursomes match they played together for Lahinch, his partner, Brud Slattery, suggested he should use a wedge for a particular approach shot. To which O'Loughlin made the classic reply: "Sorry Slattery. That shot is not in my programme." By way of contrast, Clare can justifiably claim to be able to offer the tourist a rich programme of almost limitless variety.

Location of Golf Courses

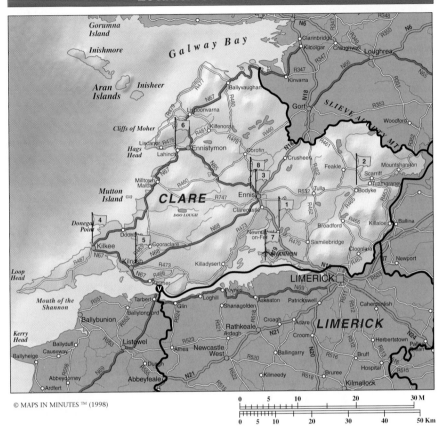

© MAPS IN MINUTES ™ (1998)

0   5   10   20   30 M

0   5   10   20   30   40   50 Km

1. **Dromoland Castle Golf Club,** Newmarket-on-Fergus   6
2. **East Clare Golf Club,** Coolreagh   6
3. **Ennis Golf Club,** Ennis   7
4. **Kilkee Golf Club,** Kilkee   8
5. **Kilrush Golf Club,** Kilrush   8
6. **Lahinch Golf Club,** Lahinch   9
7. **Shannon Golf Club,** Shannon   10
8. **Woodstock Golf Club,** Ennis   11

Dromoland Castle

Dromoland Castle, Newmarket-on-Fergus,
Co Clare

Tel: 061 368144

Sec/Manager:	John O'Halloran
Professional:	Philip Murphy
Directions:	I mile North of Newmarket-on-Fergus. On right hand side of N18
Type of Course:	Parkland
Date Founded:	1961
No of Holes:	18
Length:	6254 yds (5719 mtrs)
Par:	71
SSS:	71
Green Fees:	Weekdays: £23 Weekends & Bank Holidays: £25
Visitors:	Welcome: Any time Book in advance
Societies:	Welcome: Any Day Special concessions: Contact club for details
Facilities:	Chipping/Putting Area, Practice Area, Golf Clubs for hire, Trolley hire, Electric Buggy hire, Bar, Restaurant, Swimming Pool

Accommodation, Food and Drink

Reference numbers below refer to detailed
information provided in section 2

Accommodation

Magowna House Hotel, Inch, Ennis, Co Clare
Tel: 065 6839009 A fine modern house offering comfortable Accommodation in 10
en suite rooms. Bar and restaurant.   117
Moyville, Ennis, Co Clare
Tel: 065 6828278 A smart modern house with 4 spacious B&B rooms, all en suite.
Delightful hostess, good parking, tv lounge, nice garden.   114
Newpark House, Ennis, Co Clare
Tel: 065 6821233 Six en suite bedrooms, some with canopied beds. 300-year-old
house set in 50 acres of parkland. Dinner by arrangement.   112
The Baron McQ's, Ennis, Co Clare
Tel: 065 6824608 Delightful location among the lanes of Ennis for a hostelry
offering modest, well-kept bedrooms, bar, all-day snack menu.   119

Villa Nova, Ennis, Co Clare
Tel: 065 6828570 Cheerful modern bungalow with four en suite B&B rooms and a
large rear garden. On the N85 road towards Lahinch.   118

Food and Drink

Fanny O'Dea's, Lissycasey, Co Clare
Tel: 065 6834143 Ireland's oldest family-run pub, a great place for a drink,
wholesome bar food, Irish music and the craic.   113
Magowna House Hotel, Inch, Ennis, Co Clare
Tel: 065 6839009 A fine modern house offering comfortable Accommodation in 10
en suite rooms. Bar and restaurant.   117
Ruby Tuesdays, 9 Merchants Square, Ennis, Co Clare
Tel: 065 6840474 Bright, informal, good-value restaurant with a long menu of
popular dishes. House wine, or bring your own (no corkage).
The Baron McQ's, Ennis, Co Clare
Tel: 065 6824608 Delightful location among the lanes of Ennis for a hostelry
offering modest, well-kept bedrooms, bar, all-day snack menu.   119

East Clare

East Clare Golf Club, Coolreagh, Bodyke,
Co Clare

Tel: 061 921322

A year after its official opening, East Clare played
host to the West of Ireland Seniors Classic in
August 1998, when England's John Morgan captured the title. Eight holes from an original
nine-hole layout were in play in late 1993 the
designer, Arthur Spring, went on to complete a
course of outstanding quality.

Among the first to test it was the venerable
Christy O'Connor Snr, who contributed 14 pars

in a local team event. Later, he repaired to
Smyth's Village Hotel in nearby Feacle, where a
celebration was in full swing to mark the launch
of a book on the Tulla Ceili Band.

Reached down a secluded by-road a few miles
from Scariff, the course was the brainchild of
local society golfers who acquired a charming
site set in beautiful surroundings. For instance,
the seventh tee has the backdrop of classic
bogland which proud locals will tell you "would
take the eyes out of your head when the heather's in full bloom."

Very little earth was moved but Spring made
excellent, strategic use of water. There are 11

lakes, each of which has its own family of ducks, including the one fronting the short 17th where the green contains a devilish, diagonal slope.

The meat of the course is the stretch of four holes from the seventh to the 10th, including the short, 144-yard eighth which is an absolute gem. And the challenge is maintained to a testing, closing hole where a drive over water, though not especially long, is still sufficient to concentrate the mind.

Sec/Manager:	Paul Nesbitt
Professional:	None
Directions:	On the R352 from Ennis to Scarrif turn left just past the village of Bodyke
Type of Course:	Parkland
Date Founded:	1991
No of Holes:	18
Length:	6476 yds (5922 mtrs)
Par:	71
SSS:	71
Green Fees:	Weekdays: £13 Weekends & Bank Holidays; £15
Visitors:	Welcome: Any time Pay & Play
Societies:	Welcome: Any time Pay & Play
Facilities:	Chipping/Putting Area, Practice Area, Golf Clubs for hire, Trolley hire, Electric Buggy hire, Restaurant

Accommodation, Food and Drink

Reference numbers below refer to detailed information provided in section 2

Accommodation

Fort View House, Kinvara, Co Galway
Tel: 091 637147 Six spacious bedrooms in a modern Bed & Breakfast bungalow with an equestrian centre next door. Immaculate throughout. 260

Magowna House Hotel, Inch, Ennis, Co Clare
Tel: 065 6839009 A fine modern house offering comfortable Accommodation in 10 en suite rooms. Bar and restaurant. 117

Moyville, Ennis, Co Clare
Tel: 065 6828278 A smart modern house with 4 spacious B&B rooms, all en suite. Delightful hostess, good parking, tv lounge, nice garden. 114

Newpark House, Ennis, Co Clare
Tel: 065 6821233 Six en suite bedrooms, some with canopied beds. 300-year-old house set in 50 acres of parkland. Dinner by arrangement. 112

The Baron McQ's, Ennis, Co Clare
Tel: 065 6824608 Delightful location among the lanes of Ennis for a hostelry offering modest, well-kept bedrooms, a bar, an all-day snack menu. 119

Villa Nova, Ennis, Co Clare
Tel: 065 6828570 Cheerful modern bungalow with four en suite B&B rooms and a large rear garden. On the N85 road towards Lahinch. 118

Food and Drink

Magowna House Hotel, Inch, Ennis, Co Clare
Tel: 065 6839009 A fine modern house offering comfortable Accommodation in 10 en suite rooms. Bar and restaurant. 117

Ruby Tuesdays, 9 Merchants Square, Ennis, Co Clare
Tel: 065 6840474 Bright, informal, good-value restaurant with a long menu of popular dishes. House wine, or bring your own (no corkage).

The Baron McQ's, Ennis, Co Clare
Tel: 065 6824608 Delightful location among the lanes of Ennis for a hostelry offering modest, well-kept bedrooms, a bar, all-day snack menu. 119

The Blackthorn, Gort, Co Galway
Tel/Fax: 091 632127 Gort's premier pub/restaurant, winner of national awards. Food is served all day, with seafood and steaks the specialities. 264

Ennis

Ennis, Drumbiggle, Ennis, Co Clare
Tel: 065 6824074

Sec/Manager:	John Normoyle
Professional:	Martin Ward
Directions:	Signposted in Ennis, 1 mile West of town centre.
Type of Course:	Parkland
Date Founded:	1912
No of Holes:	18
Length:	6115 yds (5592 mtrs)
Par:	71
SSS:	71
Green Fees:	£18 all week
Visitors:	Welcome: Any time
Societies:	Welcome: Prior booking
Facilities:	Chipping/Putting Area, Golf Clubs for hire, Trolley hire, Bar, Restaurant

Accommodation, Food and Drink

Reference numbers below refer to detailed information provided in section 2

Accommodation

Carraig House, Liscannor, Co Clare
Tel/Fax: 065 7081260 Peace, seclusion and outstanding views in a fine modern B&B a short walk from a fishing village. All rooms en suite. 124

Castle View Lodge, Lahinch, Co Clare
Tel: 065 7081648 Six en suite bedrooms in a modern house an easy walk from the centre of the village. Overlooks Lahinch golf courses. 128

Craggy Island, Ardeamush, Doolin, Co Clare
Tel: 065 7074595 A welcoming family-run Bed & Breakfast house on the edge of the Burren. All rooms en suite. Great views, great walking. 127

Cullinan's Restaurant & Guest House, Doolin, Co Clare
Tel: 065 7074183 e-mail: cullinans@eircom.net Six-room guest house (all rooms en suite) and restaurant serving à la carte dinners from a wide-ranging modern menu.

Glasha Meadows, Doolin, Co Clare
Tel: 065 7074443 Six en suite bedrooms in a family-run B&B on the coast road into Doolin, a village famous for its traditional Irish music. 126

Magowna House Hotel, Inch, Ennis, Co Clare
Tel: 065 6839009 A fine modern house offering comfortable Accommodation in 10 en suite rooms. Bar and restaurant. 117

Moyville, Ennis, Co Clare
Tel: 065 6828278 A smart modern house with 4 spacious B&B rooms, all en suite.

Delightful hostess, good parking, tv lounge, nice garden. 114

Mulcarr House, Lahinch, Co Clare

Tel: 065 7081123 A striking modern house with four high-quality Bed & Breakfast rooms. Superb views. Also self-catering nearby. 111

Newpark House, Ennis, Co Clare

Tel: 065 6821233 Six en suite bedrooms, some with canopied beds. 300-year-old house set in 50 acres of parkland. Diinner by arrangement. 112

O'Looney's Seafood Restaurant, Lahinch, Co Clare

Tel: 065 70814 A cheerful seafood restaurant on the seafront. Seafood platter, poached salmon, surf burger, fish & chips. The owner also has a guesthouse.

The Baron McQ's, Ennis, Co Clare

Tel: 065 6824608 Delightful location among the lanes of Ennis for a hostelry offering modest, well-kept bedrooms, a bar, an all-day snack menu. 119

The Shamrock Inn Hotel, Lahinch, Co Clare

Tel: 065 7081700 A lovely family-run hotel on the main street, with ten spacious, well-presented rooms, bar and restaurant. 115

Tudor Lodge, Lahinch, Co Clare

Tel: 065 7081270 Four well-appointed bedrooms, all en suite, in a modern house with a real home-from-home feel. 116

Tullamore Farmhouse, Kilshanny, Ennistymon, Co Clare

Tel: 065 7071187 Six en suite rooms in an elegant modern Bed & Breakfast house with award-winning breakfasts and great views. 110

Villa Nova, Ennis, Co Clare

Tel: 065 6828570 Cheerful modern bungalow with four en suite B&B rooms and a large rear garden. On the N85 road towards Lahinch. 118

Food and Drink

Cullinan's Restaurant & Guest House, Doolin, Co Clare

Tel: 065 7074183 e-mail: cullinans@eircom. net Six-room guest house (all rooms en suite) and restaurant serving à la carte dinners from a wide-ranging modern menu.

Fanny O'Dea's, Lissycasey, Co Clare

Tel: 065 6834143 Ireland's oldest family-run pub, a great place for a drink, wholesome bar food, Irish music and the craic. 113

Magowna House Hotel, Inch, Ennis, Co Clare

Tel: 065 6839009 A fine modern house offering comfortable Accommodation in 10 en suite rooms. Bar and restaurant. 117

O'Looney's Seafood Restaurant, Lahinch, Co Clare

Tel: 065 70814 A cheerful seafood restaurant on the seafront. Seafood platter, poached salmon, surf burger, fish & chips. The owner also has a guesthouse.

Ruby Tuesdays, 9 Merchants Square, Ennis, Co Clare

Tel: 065 6840474 Bright, informal, good-value restaurant with a long menu of popular dishes. House wine, or bring your own (no corkage).

The Baron McQ's, Ennis, Co Clare

Tel: 065 6824608 Delightful location among the lanes of Ennis for a hostelry offering modest, well-kept bedrooms, a bar, all-day snack menu. 119

The Shamrock Inn Hotel, Lahinch, Co Clare

Tel: 065 7081700 A lovely family-run hotel on the main street, with ten spacious, well-presented rooms, bar and restaurant. 115

Kilkee

Kilkee Golf Club, East End, Kilkee, Co Clare
Tel: 065 905 6048

Sec/Manager:	Paddy McInerny
Professional:	None
Directions:	Half mile northwest of Kilkee
Type of Course:	Links & Parkland
Date Founded:	1941
No of Holes:	18
Length:	6481 yds (5928 mtrs)
Par:	71
SSS:	71
Green Fees:	£20 All week

Visitors:	Welcome: Prior booking advisable
Societies:	Welcome: Apply in writing
Facilities:	Practice Area, Golf Clubs for hire, Trolley hire, Bar, Restaurant

Accommodation, Food and Drink

Reference numbers below refer to detailed information provided in section 2

Accommodation

Carraig House, Liscannor, Co Clare

Tel/Fax: 065 7081260 Peace, seclusion and outstanding views in a fine modern B&B a short walk from a fishing village. All rooms en suite. 124

Castle View Lodge, Lahinch, Co Clare

Tel: 065 7081648 Six en suite bedrooms in a modern house an easy walk from the centre of the village. Overlooks Lahinch golf courses. 128

Cois Na Sionna, Killimer, Co Clare

Tel: 065 9053073 Four well-appointed en suite bedrooms in a striking modern B&B house opposite the Killimer car ferry across the Shannon estuary. 123

Craggy Island, Ardeamush, Doolin, Co Clare

Tel: 065 7074595 A welcoming family-run Bed & Breakfast house on the edge of the Burren. All rooms en suite. Great views, great walking. 127

Fortfield Farm, Donail, Killimer, Co Clare

Tel: 065 9051457 Superior B&B guest Accommodation in a large modern house on a farm with an agricultural zoo. Five rooms, three en suite. 121

Glasha Meadows, Doolin, Co Clare

Tel: 065 7074443 Six en suite bedrooms in a family-run B&B on the coast road into Doolin, a village famous for its traditional Irish music. 126

Mulcarr House, Lahinch, Co Clare

Tel: 065 7081123 A striking modern house with four high-quality Bed & Breakfast rooms. Superb views. Also self-catering nearby. 111

Tudor Lodge, Lahinch, Co Clare

Tel: 065 7081270 Four well-appointed en suite bedrooms in a modern house with a real home-from-home feel. 116

Tullamore Farmhouse, Kilshanny, Ennistymon, Co Clare

Tel: 065 7071187 Six en suite rooms in an elegant modern Bed & Breakfast house with award-winning breakfasts and great views. 110

Westcliff House, Kilkee, Co Clare

Tel: 065 9056108 An imposing 1840s town house with seven letting bedrooms, five en suite. Lovely views over Moore Bay. 120

Food and Drink

Fanny O'Dea's, Lissycasey, Co Clare

Tel: 065 6834143 Ireland's oldest family-run pub, a great place for a drink, wholesome bar food, Irish music and the craic. 113

Kelly's Bar & Restaurant, Kilrush, Co Clare

Tel: 065 9051811 A popular bar and restaurant offering a good range of Food and Drink & traditional and modern music. 125

The Haven Arms, Kilrush, Co Clare

Tel: 065 9051267 A prime site in town for a family-run pub-restaurant with award-winning food, a good range of drinks and regular impromptu live music. 122

The Shamrock Inn Hotel, Lahinch, Co Clare

Tel: 065 7081700 A lovely family-run hotel on the main street, with ten spacious, well-presented rooms, bar and restaurant. 115

Kilrush

Kilrush Golf Club, Parknamoney, Kilrush, Co Clare
Tel: 065 905 1138

Sec/Manager:	Mr. Dennis Nagle
Professional:	Sean O'Connor
Directions:	Half mile north east of Kilrush off the N68 to Ennis

Type of Course: Parkland
Date Founded: 1934
No of Holes: 18
Length: 5736 yds (5985 mtrs)
Par: 70
SSS: 69
Green Fees: £18 Midweek £20 Weekend
Visitors: Welcome
Societies: Welcome: Book in advance
Facilities: Chipping/Putting Area, Practice Area, Driving Range, Golf Clubs for hire, Trolley hire, Bar, Restaurant

Accommodation, Food and Drink

Reference numbers below refer to detailed information provided in section 2

Accommodation

Castle View House, Carrig Island, Co Kerry
Tel/Fax: 068 43304 Six bedrooms, all en suite, in a neat, modern house close to the Tarbert/Killimer car ferry. B&B; dinner by arrangement. 301

Cois Na Sionna, Killimer, Co Clare
Tel: 065 9053073 Four well-appointed en suite bedrooms in a striking modern B&B house opposite the Killimer car ferry across the Shannon estuary. 123

Fortfield Farm, Donail, Killimer, Co Clare
Tel: 065 9051457 Superior B&B guest Accommodation in a large modern house on a farm with an agricultural zoo. Five rooms, three en suite. 121

Greenfields Farmhouse, Asdee, Listowel, Co Kerry
Tel: 068 41233 Three double bedrooms for B&B, one en suite. On the Tarbert/ Ballybunion road. Access, Mastercard, Visa.

Westcliff House, Kilkee, Co Clare
Tel: 065 9056108 An imposing 1840s town house with seven letting bedrooms, five en suite. Lovely views over Moore Bay. 120

Food and Drink

Fanny O'Dea's, Lissycasey, Co Clare
Tel: 065 6834143 Ireland's oldest family-run pub, a great place for a drink, wholesome bar food, Irish music and the craic. 113

Kelly's Bar & Restaurant, Kilrush, Co Clare
Tel: 065 9051811 A popular bar and restaurant offering a good range of food and drink & traditional and modern music. 125

The Haven Arms, Kilrush, Co Clare
Tel: 065 9051267 A prime site in town for a family-run pub-restaurant with award-winning food, a good range of drinks and impromptu live music. 122

The Shamrock Inn Hotel, Lahinch, Co Clare
Tel: 065 7081700 A lovely family-run hotel on the main street, with ten spacious, well-presented rooms, bar and restaurant. 115

Lahinch

Lahinch (Old Course), Lahinch, Co Clare

Tel: 065 70 81003

Before heading off to Carnoustie for the 1999 British Open, Greg Norman visited Lahinch GC for the first time. A 7.40am start with his son Gregory, could be seen as a broadening of the Shark's education of links terrain, prior to his involvement in a major Co Clare project at Doonbeg.

"I really enjoyed Lahinch," said Norman, reflecting, no doubt, on his more successful shots, like a drive of 285 yards down the long second,

where he successfully avoided the cavernous traps. He was especially taken with some of its decidedly quirky holes, like the long fifth, known as the "Klondyke", where the second is totally blind, and the short sixth, "The Dell", which is a mid-iron also into the unknown.

Old Tom Morris did the original links layout in 1893, but it was later remodelled by Alister MacKenzie, whose trademark, tiered greens are still in evidence there. Indeed it remains very much a traditional, out-and-back links, in the Prestwick mould, and those suggesting it should be otherwise, would do so at their peril.

When the US Walker Cup team used it for warm-up practice prior to the 1991 Walker Cup at Portmarnock, leading member Phil Mickelson was so impressed that he declared it his favourite of all links courses. Set on the Atlantic coast, it is renowned for its characters, invariably ready to regale the unwitting visitor with tales of rare golfing exploits.

The second, Castle course, is very much a short, holiday stretch by comparison with its celebrated neighbour.

Sec/Manager: Alan Riordan
Professional: Robert McCavery
Directions: 2 miles West of Ennistimon off the N67

Old Course

Type of Course: Beachside
Date Founded: 1893
No of Holes: 18
Length: 6696 yds (6123 mtrs)
Par: 72
SSS: 73
Green Fees: £60

Castle Course

Type of Course: Links
Date Founded: 1893
No of Holes: 18
Length: 5594 yds (5115 mtrs)
Par: 70
SSS: 70
Green Fees: £30

Visitors:	Welcome: Any time
Societies:	Welcome: Ring Sec. Office in Advance
Facilities:	Chipping/Putting Area, Practice Area, Golf Clubs for hire, Trolley hire, Bar, Restaurant, Caddy service by arrangement

Accommodation, Food and Drink

Reference numbers below refer to detailed
information provided in section 2

Accommodation

Carraig House, Liscannor, Co Clare
Tel/Fax: 065 7081260 Peace, seclusion and outstanding views in a fine modern B&B a short walk from a fishing village. All rooms en suite.   124

Castle View Lodge, Lahinch, Co Clare
Tel: 065 7081648 Six en suite bedrooms in a modern house an easy walk from the centre of the village. Overlooks Lahinch golf courses.   128

Cois Na Sionna, Killimer, Co Clare
Tel: 065 9053073 Four well-appointed en suite bedrooms in a striking modern B&B house opposite the Killimer car ferry across the Shannon estuary.   123

Craggy Island, Ardeamush, Doolin, Co Clare
Tel: 065 7074595 A welcoming family-run Bed & Breakfast house on the edge of the Burren. All rooms en suite. Great views, great walking.   127

Cullinan's Restaurant & Guest House, Doolin, Co Clare
Tel: 065 7074183 e-mail: cullinans@eircom.net Six-room guest house (all rooms en suite) and restaurant serving à la carte dinners from a wide-ranging modern menu.

Glasha Meadows, Doolin, Co Clare
Tel: 065 7074443 Six en suite bedrooms in a family-run B&B on the coast road into Doolin, a village famous for its traditional Irish music.   126

Magowna House Hotel, Inch, Ennis, Co Clare
Tel: 065 6839009 A fine modern house offering comfortable Accommodation in 10 en suite rooms. Bar and restaurant.   117

Moyville, Ennis, Co Clare
Tel: 065 6828278 A smart modern house with 4 spacious B&B rooms, all en suite. Delightful hostess, good parking, tv lounge, nice garden.   114

Mulcarr House, Lahinch, Co Clare
Tel: 065 7081123 A striking modern house with four high-quality Bed & Breakfast rooms. Superb views. Also self-catering available.   111

O'Looney's Seafood Restaurant, Lahinch, Co Clare
Tel: 065 70814 A cheerful seafood restaurant on the seafront. Seafood platter, poached salmon, surf burger, fish & chips. The owner also has a guesthouse.

The Shamrock Inn Hotel, Lahinch, Co Clare
Tel: 065 7081700 A lovely family-run hotel on the main street, with ten spacious, well-presented rooms, bar and restaurant.   115

Tudor Lodge, Lahinch, Co Clare
Tel: 065 7081270 Four well-appointed bedrooms, all en suite, in a modern house with a real home-from-home feel.   116

Tullamore Farmhouse, Kilshanny, Ennistymon, Co Clare
Tel: 065 7071187 Six en suite rooms in an elegant modern Bed & Breakfast house with award-winning breakfasts and great views.   110

Villa Nova, Ennis, Co Clare
Tel: 065 6828570 Cheerful modern bungalow with four en suite B&B rooms and a large rear garden. On the N85 road towards Lahinch.   118

Food and Drink

Cullinan's Restaurant & Guest House, Doolin, Co Clare
Tel: 065 7074183 e-mail: cullinans@eircom.net Six-room guest house (all rooms en suite) and restaurant serving à la carte dinners from a wide-ranging modern menu.

Kelly's Bar & Restaurant, Kilrush, Co Clare
Tel: 065 9051811 A popular bar and restaurant offering a good range of Food and Drink & traditional and modern music.   125

Magowna House Hotel, Inch, Ennis, Co Clare
Tel: 065 6839009 A fine modern house offering comfortable Accommodation in 10 en suite rooms. Bar and restaurant.   117

O'Looney's Seafood Restaurant, Lahinch, Co Clare
Tel: 065 70814 A cheerful seafood restaurant on the seafront. Seafood platter, poached salmon, surf burger, fish & chips. The owner also has a guesthouse.

The Haven Arms, Kilrush, Co Clare
Tel: 065 9051267 A prime site in town for a family-run pub-restaurant with award-winning food, a good range of drinks and impromptu live music.   122

The Shamrock Inn Hotel, Lahinch, Co Clare
Tel: 065 7081700 A lovely family-run hotel on the main street, with ten spacious, well-presented rooms, bar and restaurant.   115

Shannon

Shannon, Shannon Airport, Shannon, Co Clare

Tel: 061 471849 (Pro: 061 471551)

Sec/Manager:	Michael Corry
Professional:	Artie Pyke
Directions:	Half a mile South of Shannon Airport
Type of Course:	Parkland
Date Founded:	1966
No of Holes:	18
Length:	6874 yds (6285 (mtrs)
Par:	72
SSS:	72
Green Fees:	Weekdays: £25 Weekends & Bank Holidays: £30
Visitors:	Welcome: Prior booking required
Societies:	Welcome: Booking required
Facilities:	Practice Area, Golf Clubs for hire, Trolley hire, Bar, Restaurant, Caddy service by arrangement

Accommodation, Food and Drink

Reference numbers below refer to detailed
information provided in section 2

Accommodation

Fortfield Farm, Donail, Killimer, Co Clare
Tel: 065 9051457 Superior B&B guest Accommodation in a large modern house on a farm with an agricultural zoo. Five rooms, three en suite.   121

Magowna House Hotel, Inch, Ennis, Co Clare
Tel: 065 6839009 A fine modern house offering comfortable Accommodation in 10 en suite rooms. Bar and restaurant.   117

Moyville, Ennis, Co Clare
Tel: 065 6828278 A smart modern house with 4 spacious B&B rooms, all en suite. Delightful hostess, good parking, tv lounge, nice garden.   114

Newpark House, Ennis, Co Clare
Tel: 065 6821233 Six en suite bedrooms, some with canopied beds, in a 300-year-old house set in 50 acres of parkland. Full breakfast; dinner by arrangement.   112

The Baron McQ's, Ennis, Co Clare
Tel: 065 6824608 Delightful location among the lanes of Ennis for a hostelry offering moist, well-kept bedrooms, a bar, all-day snack menu.   119

Villa Nova, Ennis, Co Clare
Tel: 065 6828570 Cheerful modern bungalow with four en suite B&B rooms and a large rear garden. On the N85 road towards Lahinch.   118

Food and Drink

Fanny O'Dea's, Lissycasey, Co Clare
Tel: 065 6834143 Ireland's oldest family-run pub, a great place for a drink, wholesome bar food, Irish music and the craic.   113

Hanratty's Hotel, Limerick, Co Limerick
Tel: 061 410999 A prime location off Limerick's main street for a 200-year-old family-run hotel with 22 well-appointed en suite bedrooms and a fine restaurant. 381

Magowna House Hotel, Inch, Ennis, Co Clare
Tel: 065 6839009 A fine modern house offering comfortable Accommodation in 10 en suite rooms. Bar and restaurant.   117

Ruby Tuesdays, 9 Merchants Square, Ennis, Co Clare
Tel: 065 6840474 Bright, informal, good-value restaurant with a long menu of popular dishes. House wine, or bring your own (no corkage).
The Baron McQ's, Ennis, Co Clare
Tel: 065 6824608 Delightful location among the lanes of Ennis for a hostelry offering modest, well-kept bedrooms, a bar, all-day snack menu.   119

Woodstock

Woodstock Golf & Country Club, Shanaway Road, Ennis, Co Clare

Tel: 065 6829463

After playing Ballybunion for the first time, Tom Watson suggested that it was a place where prospective golf architects "should live and play, before they build golf courses." Arthur Spring did the master's bidding .... and then designed the delightful Woodstock course on the outskirts of Ennis, Co Clare.

Owned by Christy and Sheelagh Guerin, it is set on a generous site of 160 acres, where the limestone-based rolling terrain offers admirable, natural drainage. Woodstock is both a members' club and a pay-and-play facility.

Opened in September 1993, the project is about to expand significantly this year with the opening of a £3.5 million (pounds), 55-bedroom hotel, along with high-quality housing. All of which reflects the confidence of the owners in the potential of a challenging layout of championship standard.

Clever routing and expert use of natural and man-made features, compensate for relatively few bunkers. As a spectacular design feature, however, Spring created a two-and-a-half acre lake where the River Inch defines the southern boundary of the course. It and its connecting streams have produced four truly memorable holes - the short sixth (197 yards), the formidable, par-four seventh (410), the short eighth (215) and the short 11th (171).

Woodstock is still a very young course which will not be seen at its best until the 5,000 planted trees, ranging from maple and oak to ash and lime, are mature. In its current state, however, it remains a very fine challenge, particularly appealing for the fact that it is user-friendly.

Sec/Manager:	Anne Marie Russell
Professional:	None
Directions:	Approx. two miles from Ennis on the left off the N85 Lahinch Road
Type of Course:	Parkland
Date Founded:	1994
No of Holes:	18
Length:	6429 yds (5879 mtrs)
Par:	71
SSS:	71
Green Fees:	Weekdays: £23 Weekends & Bank Holidays: £28
Visitors:	Welcome: Book in advance
Societies:	Welcome: Concessions for groups, contact club for details
Facilities:	Practice Area, Golf Clubs for hire, Trolley hire, Electric Buggy hire, Bar, Restaurant, Caddy service by arrangement

Accommodation, Food and Drink

Reference numbers below refer to detailed
information provided in section 2

Accommodation

Cullinan's Restaurant & Guest House, Doolin, Co Clare

Tel: 065 7074183 e-mail: cullinans@eircom.net Six-room guest house (all rooms en
suite) and restaurant serving à la carte dinners from a wide-ranging modern menu.

Magowna House Hotel, Inch, Ennis, Co Clare

Tel: 065 6839009 A fine modern house offering comfortable Accommodation in 10
en suite rooms. Bar and restaurant.   117

Moyville, Ennis, Co Clare

Tel: 065 6828278 A smart modern house with 4 spacious B&B rooms, all en suite.
Delightful hostess, good parking, tv lounge, nice garden.   114

Newpark House, Ennis, Co Clare

Tel: 065 6821233 Six en suite bedrooms, some with canopied beds, in a 300-year-
old house set in 50 acres of parkland. Full breakfast; dinner by arrangement. 112

O'Looney's Seafood Restaurant, Lahinch, Co Clare

Tel: 065 70814 A cheerful seafood restaurant on the seafront. Seafood platter,
poached salmon, surf burger, fish & chips. The owner also has a guesthouse.

The Baron McQ's, Ennis, Co Clare

Tel: 065 6824608 Delightful location among the lanes of Ennis for a hostelry
offering modest, well-kept bedrooms, a bar, all-day snack menu.   119

The Shamrock Inn Hotel, Lahinch, Co Clare

Tel: 065 7081700 A lovely family-run hotel on the main street, with ten spacious,
well-presented rooms, bar and restaurant.   115

Villa Nova, Ennis, Co Clare

Tel: 065 6828570 Cheerful modern bungalow with four en suite B&B rooms and a
large rear garden. On the N85 road towards Lahinch.   118

Food and Drink

Cullinan's Restaurant & Guest House, Doolin, Co Clare

Tel: 0657074183 e-mail: cullinans@eircom.net Six-room guest house (all rooms en
suite) and restaurant serving à la carte dinners from a wide-ranging modern menu.

Fanny O'Dea's, Lissycasey, Co Clare

Tel: 065 6834143 Ireland's oldest family-run pub, a great place for a drink,
wholesome bar food, Irish music and the craic.   113

Magowna House Hotel, Inch, Ennis, Co Clare

Tel: 065 6839009 A fine modern house offering comfortable accommod in 10
ensuite rooms. Bar and restaurant.   117

O'Looney's Seafood Restaurant, Lahinch, Co Clare

Tel: 065 70814 A cheerful seafood restaurant on the seafront. Seafood platter,
poached salmon, surf burger, fish & chips. The owner also has a guesthouse.

Ruby Tuesdays, 9 Merchants Square, Ennis, Co Clare

Tel: 065 6840474 Bright, informal, good-value restaurant with a long menu of
popular dishes. House wine, or bring your own (no corkage).

The Baron McQ's, Ennis, Co Clare

Tel: 0656824608 Delightful location among the lanes of Ennis for a hostelry offering
modest, well-kept bedrooms, a bar, an all-day snack menu.   119

The Shamrock Inn Hotel, Lahinch, Co Clare

Tel: 065 7081700 A lovely family-run hotel on the main street, with ten spacious,
well-presented rooms, bar and restaurant.   115

CORK

Golf's remarkable facility for building enduring bonds of friendship, was illustrated beautifully in the development of the Lee Valley course in Co Cork. As it happens, this is one of the most recent of Cork's 30 courses, making it Ireland's second most populous county, from a golfing standpoint.

Anyway, as we have noted elsewhere in this book, Christy O'Connor Jnr will long be remembered for the wonderful climax to his Ryder Cup match against Fred Couples at The Belfry in 1989. In the circumstances, with Couples failing miserably to make a par at the final hole, one would have imagined it as an incident he would dearly wish to forget. Yet, when O'Connor invited the American to play him once more in an exhibition match to mark the opening of Lee Valley, Couples immediately agreed. So it was that a few short years later, O'Connor was in a position to guarantee an auspicious launch to a course he himself had designed.

Indeed golf in the so-called "Rebel County" is much about personalities and they didn't come any bigger than Jimmy Bruen, whose career lit up the annals of both the Muskerry and Cork clubs, to which he was attached. First mention of him was in a local newspaper report of May 1934, which reported: "A valued correspondent tells me that Master Bruen, aged 13 of that place of universal output, Cork, shapes like a golfing prodigy. His golf is long, accurate and well controlled. If he progresses as he is doing now, he will be an amateur champion at an early age." It went on: "It would be difficult for a good eight-handicap player to beat him today. We welcome Master Bruen heartily, in fact to tell the truth, we have been hoping for someone like him to appear. Provided his father restrains his efforts and makes him aim at well-controlled play, he may yet produce not a prodigy, but what Ireland has long been due to give us, namely a real champion. We have, and have had, real champions, but the modern generation has not supplied them so far."

As it happened, Bruen was given a handicap of six when he joined Muskerry as a 15-year-old. Within a few weeks, he was playing off scratch, having collected several pieces of silverware in the meantime. And the correspondent's wishes for him were more than realised, in victories in the British Boys', British Amateur and Irish Close championships. They still talk reverentially about Bruen down around Cork and, indeed, further afield. But the Cork GC at Little Island has long since ceased to be the focal point of golf in the county, especially since the development of the stunning Old Head of Kinsale. Further west, towards the border with Kerry, the county has also acquired a charming, 18-hole holiday venue in the extended course at Bantry Bay.

But the Old Head seems destined to spearhead a tremendous upsurge in golf tourism in the Cork area, so broadening the appeal of the south-west region. For instance, instead of travelling directly to Dublin after savouring the established Kerry links, visitors are now taking in the Old Head as a key element of their itinerary. During a visit I made there last winter, angry Atlantic breakers were crashing off the cliff face in gale-force winds of 60mph. It seemed anything other than ideal weather for a helicopter ride, but the opportunity of seeing the Old Head from the air, was too good

Sunrise at Old Head, Co Cork

to miss. As it happened, the craft, a six-seater Augusta 109, was remarkably stable. So, thoughts of a mouth-covering brown-paper bag never crossed my mind as we swooped over the famous promontory. There was a perfect view of the new green at the fourth and mounding for the final routing of the majestic 17th. And there was the new, raised tee at the long 12th, as recommended by David Duval, one of six celebrated visitors the previous July. But the exercise had more serious intent than sightseeing, delightful though that was. In fact it was a rehearsal for the introduction of so-called Heligolf to this country.

Having experienced Heliskiing in Canada, John O'Connor, who owns the Old Head with his brother Patrick, felt it was ideally suited to golf. "The way it works in Canada is that you stay in a remote lodge in the Rockies and are then ferried by chopper to the top of a mountain," he said. "After skiing down the slope, the chopper then picks you up at the bottom." O'Connor has since leased the £1.5 million chopper, along with a rota of pilots, for operation at the Old Head and the craft will be based either at the club or at Cork Airport, from where clients will be ferried wherever they wish. Upwards of 100 helicopter flights into the Old Head were made

Cobh Harbour, Co Cork

during the 1999 season including a flight carrying golfers Tiger Woods, Duval, Mark O'Meara, Lee Janzen, Stuart Appleby and the late Payne Stewart. It means reducing a 40-minute road trip from Cork Airport to six minutes, while clients can then fly on to Shannon in 20 minutes, or to Waterville in 30 minutes and Killarney in 20 minutes. Portmarnock can be reached in an hour. "I have no doubt it will be cost-effective," said O'Connor, who is charging his clients £1,000 per hour for the privilege.

Golf is to be found in every area of the county, but the new course at Fota Island, designed by O'Connor and Peter McEvoy, has the added appeal of a neighbouring Wildlife Park. So, after mum and dad have endulged their love of the Royal and Ancient game, the children can be entertained to the sight of giraffes, kangaroos and oryx grazing peacefully, while peacocks and penguins flutter busily before their feet. The Arboretum is one of the finest in the country, beautifully informal in its layout, with exotic trees from all parts of the world, merging almost seamlessly with indigenous plants. Outsiders, no doubt envious of all the treasures the southern county has to offer, will suggest that members are unlikely to clutter the fairways of Little Island at the weekend "for fear people might think they didn't own a yacht." And one can understand these little envious asides, given that the Royal Cork Yacht Club, based at Crosshaven, has the distinction of being the oldest in the world. It was founded in 1720 as the "Water Club of the Harbour of Corke (stet)", and later moved its headquarters to Crosshaven. We are told that under the original rules, no admiral was permitted to bring "more than two dishes of meat for the entertainment of the club .... nor more than two dozen wine to his treat ... except when my Lords the judges are invited." Could this have been the origin of that well-loved ironic phrase, "sober as a judge"? Anyway, the door is always open to visiting yachtsmen, who are welcome to use the modern marina. And just upriver from the clubhouse is Drake's Pool where, according to legend, Francis Drake sought refuge from a Spanish coastal patrol.

Further east, visitors to Youghal GC will have the opportunity of seeing a much photographed waterfront, where the movie "Moby Dick", starring Gregory Peck as Captain Ahab, was shot during the 1950s. Elsewhere in the county is Kanturk, a market town set astride the Dalua and Allow rivers and which gained honorable mention in Spenser's the "Faerie Queene". And Kinsale, with its harbour and superb restaurants, is acknowledged as one of the most picturesque and fashionable resorts in the south-west.

Finally, once cannot depart this hugely interesting county, without mention of Skibbereen, the thriving "capital" of West Cork. Its newspaper is "The Southern Star", successor to "The Skibbereen Eagle", which gained international notoriety as a result of a thundering editorial at the turn of the 19th century. The leader ended with the dire warning: "The Skibbereen Eagle has its eye on the Czar of Russia." More recently, the county has had its eye focused more profitably on an ever-increasing tourist industry.

Location of Golf Courses

© MAPS IN MINUTES ™ (1998)

```
0     5    10         20          30 M
├┼┼┼┼┼┼┤────┼──────────┼
0     5   10    20    30    40    50 Km
```

9 **Bandon Golf Club**, Bandon   16

10 **Bantry Bay Golf Club**, Bantry Bay   16

11 **Charleville Golf Club**, Charleville   17

12 **Cork Golf Club**, Little Island, Cork   18

13 **Douglas Golf Club**, Douglas   19

14 **East Cork Golf Club**, Midleton   20

15 **Fermoy Golf Club**, Fermoy   20

16 **Fernhill Golf Club**, Carrigaline   21

17 **Fota Island Golf Club**, Carrigtwohill   21

18 **Harbour Point Golf Club**, Little Island, Cork   22

19 **Kanturk Golf Club**, Kanturk   23

20 **Kinsale Golf Club**, Kinsale   24

21 **Lee Valley Golf Club**, Ovens   24

22 **Macroom Golf Club**, Macroom   25

23 **Mahon Golf Club**, Blackrock   26

24 **Mallow Golf Club**, Mallow   26

25 **Mitchelstown Golf Club**, Mitchelstown   27

26 **Monkstown Golf Club**, Monkstown   27

27 **Muskerry Golf Club**, Carrigrohane   27

28 **Old Head of Kinsale Golf Club**, Kinsale   28

29 **Skibbereen & West Carbery Golf Club**, Skibbereen   29

30 **Youghal Golf Club**, Youghal   29

Bandon

Castlebernard, Bandon, Co Cork
Tel: 023 41111

Sec/Manager:	Jacintha Kennedy
Professional:	Paddy O'Boyle
Directions:	1 mile southwest of Bandon off the N71 to Clonakilley
Type of Course:	Parkland
Date Founded:	1909
No of Holes:	18
Length:	6191 yds (5663 mtrs)
Par:	70
SSS:	70
Green Fees:	£20 Midweek £28 Weekend
Visitors:	Welcome: Any day except Wednesday
Societies:	Welcome: Any time except Wednesday Prior booking at weekends from March – October
Facilities:	Chipping/Putting Area, Practice Area, Golf Clubs for hire, Trolley hire, Bar, Restaurant, Caddy service by arrangement

Accommodation, Food and Drink

Reference numbers below refer to detailed
information provided in section 2

Accommodation

An Cuasán, Macroom, Co Cork
Tel: 026 40018 A fine country house enjoying a tranquil setting in spacious mature gardens. The six bedrooms all have en suite facilities; some have balconies to make the most of the views. 160

An Garrán Coír, Castlefreke, Clonakilty, Co Cork
Tel: 023 48236 Comfortable Bed & Breakfast Accommodation in lovely relaxing surroundings. Great views. Great breakfasts. 187

An Súgán, Clonakilty, Co Cork
Tel: 023 33498 100-cover pub-restaurant specialising in seafood. B&B in adjacent Strand House, also self-catering cottages. 170

Little Acre, Skibbereen, Co Cork
Tel/Fax: 028 22528 Bed and Breakfast Accommodation in a handsome detached house on the N71. Easy walk to town. 183

Rosalithir Farm Cottage, Rosscarbery, Co Cork
Tel: 023 48136 Self-catering Accommodation in a renovated farmhouse in a private garden on a working farm. B&B next door. 185

Rosalithir, Rosscarbery, Co Cork
Tel: 023 48136 Bed and Breakfast Accommodation in four very spacious en suite bungalow rooms. Self-catering available next door. 184

Springfield House, Rathbarry, Clonakilty, Co Cork
Tel/Fax: 023 40622 Select farmhouse Bed and Breakfast Accommodation. Rooms en suite. Home cooking a speciality. Self-catering also available. 181

Victoria Hotel, Macroom, Co Cork
Tel: 026 41082 Fax: 026 42148 On the main square of a town that's famous for its castle, the Victoria is a fine base for tourists and sportsmen. 16 rooms, all en suite. Restaurant & bar menus 141

Woodleigh, Carrigadrohid, Macroom, Co Cork
Tel: 026 48119 Plain and simple home-from-home Accommodation in a semi-detached house with a conservatory and gardens. The owners have four letting bedrooms, all en suite, with tvs. 171

Food and Drink

An Súgán, Clonakilty, Co Cork
Tel: 023 33498 100-cover pub-restaurant specialising in seafood. B&B in adjacent Strand House, also self-catering cottages. 170

Bernard's Bar, Skibbereen, Co Cork
Tel: Bar and restaurant in the middle of town - the only licensed premises in Skibbereen. Day-long food service. 162

De Barra, Clonakilty, Co Cork
Tel: 023 33381 A cheerful pub with its own folk club and traditional Irish music. 149

Victoria Hotel, Macroom, Co Cork
Tel: 026 41082 Fax: 026 42148 On the main square of a town that's famous for its castle, the Victoria is a fine base for tourists and sportsmen. 16 rooms, all en suite. Restaurant & bar menus 141

Bantry Bay

Bantry, West Cork
Tel: 027 50579

Overseas visitors have long been raving about the charms of West Cork and it seems the locals are determined to spoil them entirely. Overlooking Bantry Bay, they have recently extended their course from nine to 18 holes through the design skills of Christy O'Connor Jnr.

The entire course is set on parkland which stretches to the Atlantic, flanked by the mountains of the Beara Peninsula to the north and Sheep's Head and the Mizen to the south. It's a breathtaking location, where the landscape can change almost by the minute.

From the new front nine, blue mussel lines are to be seen bobbing in choppy waters, gathering a harvest for the local factory and ultimately for a lucrative market abroad. And in terms of scenery and terrain, these holes offer a delightful contrast to the original nine, designed by Eddie Hackett in 1975.

The extension became possible when, in the winter of 1993-1994, an anonymous benefactor gave the club two small sites, totalling a modest one and a half acres. This was the key in that when added to a leased site of 35 acres and a further 15 acres acquired in seperate deals, it constituted an integrated site, extending out to the road.

Up to recent years, golfing visitors to the extreme south-west of Cork, tended to gravitate towards Glengarriff (founded in 1936) and Skibbereen (1905). But Bantry Bay GC is now acknowledged as an important tourist attraction, apart from meeting the recreational needs of the local community.

Sec/Manager:	Liz O'Shea
Professional:	None
Directions:	2 miles North of Bantry off the N71 Glengarruf Road.
Type of Course:	Parkland
Date Founded:	1975
No of Holes:	18
Length:	6463 yds (5910 mtrs)
Par:	71
SSS:	70
Green Fees:	£20
Visitors:	Welcome: Contact club for details
Societies:	Welcome: Book in Advance Concessions for groups of 12 plus
Facilities:	Chipping/Putting Area, Golf Clubs for hire, Trolley hire, Electric Buggy hire, Bar, Restaurant

Accommodation, Food and Drink

Reference numbers below refer to detailed information provided in section 2

Accommodation

An Cuasán, Macroom, Co Cork
Tel: 026 40018 A fine country house enjoying a tranquil setting in spacious mature gardens. The six bedrooms all have en suite facilities; some have balconies to make the most of the views. 160

Cooligreenane House, Inchigeela, Co Cork
Tel: 026 49344 At scenically set Cooligreenane House there are three bedrooms, farmhouse breakfasts and private access to coarse fishing. Rose Cottage and Tigh Mhuire offer self catering. 163

Hill Top Farm, Cill-na-Martra, Macroom, Co Cork
Tel: 026 40154 A lovely secluded setting in the hills between Macroom and Killarney. The house has extensive gardens and a large conservatory. Four bedrooms, full breakfasts, packed lunches, evening meals by arrangement. 165

Little Acre, Skibbereen, Co Cork
Tel/Fax: 028 22528 Bed and Breakfast Accommodation in a handsome detached house on the N71. Easy walk to town. 183

Rosalithir Farm Cottage, Rosscarbery, Co Cork
Tel: 023 48136 Self-catering Accommodation in a renovated farmhouse in a private garden on a working farm. B&B next door. 185

Rosalithir, Rosscarbery, Co Cork
Tel: 023 48136 Bed and Breakfast Accommodation in four very spacious en suite bungalow rooms. Self-catering available next door. 184

Sallyport House, Kenmare, Co Kerry
Tel: 064 42066 web: sallyporthouse.com An elegant country house set in ten acres of lawns and trees overlooking the harbour and the bay. Five antique-furnished bedrooms with either king- or queen-size beds and capacious en suite bathrooms. One has a four-poster. 293

Springfield House, Rathbarry, Clonakilty, Co Cork
Tel/Fax: 023 40622 Select farmhouse Bed and Breakfast Accommodation. Rooms en suite. Home cooking a speciality. Self-catering also available. 181

The Brambles, Kenmare, Co Kerry
Tel: 064 41712 e-mail: brambles@eircom.net Bed and Breakfast Accommodation at Gortamullen. 4 en suite rooms with king-size beds. Licensed bar.

The Wander Inn, Kenmare, Co Kerry
Tel: 064 42700 True Irish hospitality in a town-centre hostelr. A hearty breakfast, lunch and dinner are served in the restaurant, and in the evening everyone shares in the craic in the bar. The hotel has 11 bedrooms, all en suite. 295

Willow Lodge, Kenmare, Co Kerry
Tel: 064 42301 Built in the grounds of a nunnery and just a few minutes' walk from the centre of town, Willow Lodge has a lounge, dining room and five en suite bedrooms, each named after a tree and each with its own individual appeal and charm. 291

Woodleigh, Carrigadrohid, Macroom, Co Cork
Tel: 026 48119 Plain and simple home-from-home Accommodation in a semi-detached house with a conservatory and gardens. The owners have four letting bedrooms, all en suite, with tvs. 171

Ardmore House, Kenmare, Co Kerry
Tel/Fax: 064 41406 Bed and Breakfast Accommodation on the Killarney Road. 1 single, 3 doubles, 2 family rooms, all en suite.

Food and Drink

Bernard's Bar, Skibbereen, Co Cork
Tel: 028 21772 Bar and restaurant in the middle of town - the only licensed premises in Skibbereen. Day-long food service. 162

Café Indigo, Kenmare, Co Kerry
Tel: 064 42356/7 Award winning restaurant, grill and late night bar serving traditional Irish, Mediterranean and European cuisine.

De Barra, Clonakilty, Co Cork
Tel: 023 33381 A cheerful pub with its own folk club and traditional Irish music. 149

The Square Pint, Kenmare, Co Kerry
Tel: 064 42357 One of Ireland's leading live traditional music venues. Convivial pub serving excellent bar food 7 days a week. Late night licence.

The Wander Inn, Kenmare, Co Kerry
Tel: 064 42700 True Irish hospitality in a town-centre hostelr. A hearty breakfast, lunch and dinner are served in the restaurant, and in the evening everyone shares in the craic in the bar. The hotel has 11 bedrooms, all en suite. 295

Charleville

Charleville Golf Club, Smiths Road, Ardmore, Charleville, Co Cork

Tel: 063 81257

Its location, close to the Limerick border - the local railway station is actually in Co Limerick - makes Charleville GC a highly desirable venue for societies. Indeed the connection with their westerly neighbours is emphasised by the fact that as many as 40 per cent of the club's mem-

bers come from the Limerick area. Charleville has undergone a particularly interesting course development over the years. When the present club was formed in 1945, they had a nine-hole stretch. Then it became 12, before a major milestone was reached in 1981 when it was extended to 18.

More recently, they had the pleasure of outstripping most of their Munster rivals, through the acquisition of further land, giving them a total of 191 acres and 27 holes, which offer tremendous flexibility in accommodating green-fee traffic. So it is hardly surprising that they are seeking a significant increase in their turnover this season.

Whether on a weekday or at weekends, greenfees won't exceed £20 (pounds), which represents splendid value, given the fine work done by agromonist Eddie Connaughton in recent years. Apart from designing the new nine, he has provided the greens with a beautiful covering of bent and fescue grasses.

Not short on characters, locals talk with affection of Michael "The Hiker" McCarthy - he got his sobriquet from appearing in a local production of John B Keane's "The Year of the Hiker" - and the work he did in developing the course. Visitors will have much to remember about Charleville.

Sec/Manager:	Matt Keane
Professional:	David A Keating
Directions:	2 miles West of Charleville off the R515 to Newtownshandrum
Type of Course:	Parkland
Date Founded:	1941
No of Holes:	18
Length:	6244 yds (5709 mtrs)
Par:	71
SSS:	69
Green Fees:	Weekdays: £45 Weekends & Bank Holidays: £50
Visitors:	Welcome: Prebooking required
Societies:	Welcome: Contact Club for details
Facilities:	Driving Range, Golf Clubs for hire, Trolley hire, Electric Buggy hire, Bar, Restaurant

Accommodation, Food and Drink

Reference numbers below refer to detailed information provided in section 2

Accommodation

An Bothar Pub, Cuas, Dingle, Co Kerry
Tel: 066 9155342 Pub, restaurant and Accommodation in a lovely secluded setting on the road to Brandon Creek on the Dingle Peninsula. 304

Ashford, Templeglantine, Co Limerick
Tel: 069 84001/84311 A distinguished modern redbrick house in its own beautiful grounds. Five en suite B&B rooms. Fine furnishings and fittings. 383

Deebert House, Kilmallock, Co Limerick
Tel: 063 98106 Five letting bedrooms, including a family room, in a splendid Georgian house set in award-winning gardens. Restaurant. 382

Glanworth Mill, Glanworth, Co Cork
Tel: 025 38555 A country inn with a great sense of history: a restored watermill with 10 en suite bedrooms, a Norman castle, an ancient bridge. 161

Springfort Hall Hotel, Mallow, Co Cork
Tel: 022 21278 Fax: 022 21557 50 en suite bedrooms in an 18th-century manor house 4 miles north of Mallow. Restaurant. Fishing. 150

Food and Drink

Deebert House, Kilmallock, Co Limerick
Tel: 063 98106 Five letting bedrooms, including a family room, in a splendid Georgian house set in award-winning gardens. Restaurant. 382

Glanworth Mill, Glanworth, Co Cork
Tel: 025 38555 A country inn with a great sense of history: a restored watermill with 10 en suite bedrooms, a Norman castle, an ancient bridge. 161

Leen's Hotel, Abbeyfeale, Co Limerick
Tel: 068 31121 Fax: 068 32550 A family-run hotel with 19 en suite bedrooms and a restaurant serving generous helpings of local produce. 384

Springfort Hall Hotel, Mallow, Co Cork
Tel: 022 21278 Fax: 022 21557 50 en suite bedrooms in an 18th-century manor house 4 miles north of Mallow. Restaurant. Fishing. 150

The Castle Inn, Buttevant, Co Cork
Tel: 022 23044 A bar and 40-cover restaurant with a strong local following. Good menu with daily specials; pub games. 182

The Four Winds, Charleville, Co Cork
Tel: 063 89285 A welcoming bar and restaurant occupying a prominent corner site on the N20. Food served from noon till 3. 176

Cork

Cork Golf Club, Little Island, Co Cork

Tel: 021 353451/353037/ 353263

During the period from 1937 to 1940, the great Jimmy Bruen played 47 competitive rounds at Cork GC in figures of 100 under fours. And in 1941 alone, when Bruen was a mere 21-year-old

with a handicap of plus four, he carded 19 rounds in the sixties, including a sparkling 64.

But the club at Little Island, which was founded in 1888, has claims to fame other than the remarkable exploits of its best-known member. It happens to be among the elite group of courses worldwide, to have been designed by the celebrated British architect, Alister MacKenzie.

When MacKenzie arrived at Little Island in 1924, he was accompanied by Jack Fleming, a native of Tuam, Co Galway, who would later make quite a name for himself in course design on the west coast of the US. In the event, we are informed that while working at Cork GC, he travelled each day by sidecar from Blarney, where he stayed in Crowley's Bar.

Much of MacKenzie's work remains in evidence on a charming parkland stretch which has played host to several important events over the years. Among them was the Jeyes Professional Tournament captured by Christy O'Connor Snr with 276 in 1964 and the Carrolls International, which Neil Coles won with 269, a year later.

The course is notable for its large, tiered greens, which are a MacKenzie trademark. And it culminates in a forbidding scretch of par fours, starting with the 434-yard 14th, where the green is situated closeby the clubhouse.

Sec/Manager:	Matt Sands
Professional:	Peter Hickey
Directions:	5 miles East of Cork City. Turn right off the N25 to Little Island: Course is signposted.
Date Founded:	1888
No of Holes:	18
Length:	6632 yds (6064 mtrs)
Par:	72
SSS:	72
Green Fees:	Weekdays: £45 Weekends & Bank Holidays: £50
Visitors:	Welcome: Not Thursday: Saturday & Sunday a.m. only
Societies:	Welcome: Pre-booking required
Facilities:	Chipping/Putting Area, Practice Area, Golf Clubs for hire, Trolley hire, Bar, Restaurant

Accommodation, Food and Drink

Reference numbers below refer to detailed information provided in section 2

Accommodation

Ashgrove Lodge, Cobh, Co Cork
Tel/Fax: 021 812483 Superior self-catering Accommodation in a superbly modernised coach house near the sea, with a castle in the grounds. 157

Glebe House, Cobh, Co Cork
Tel/Fax: 021 811373 Four spacious bedrooms, all with bath and shower en suite, in a house in the centre of Cobh Island. 148

Glenview House, Midleton, Co Cork
Tel: 021 631680 Fax: 021 634680 Family-run Georgian house set in 20 private acres. En suite bedrooms with king-size beds. B&B or self-catering. 143

Ibis Hotel, Dunkettle, Co Cork
Tel: 021 354354 Fax: 021 354202 100 en suite bedrooms in a well-equipped up-to-the-minute chain hotel at the Lee Tunnel roundabout. Full restaurant menu; lounge bar. 175

Lough Mahon House, Tivoli, Co Cork
Tel: 021 502142 Fax: 021 501804 Seven bedrooms offering various permutations in a huge early-Victorian house. Easy parking. Close to Cork city centre. 145

Lynwen Lodge, Midleton, Co Cork
Tel: 021 631934 Bed and full Irish breakfast in a large, well-appointed house on the N25. Evening meals by arrangement. 144

Spanish Point, Ballycotton, Co Cork
Tel: 021 646177 Fax: 021 646179 Speciality seafood restaurant with well-equipped en suite bedrooms in a dramatic clifftop setting. Own beach. Sea fishing. 178

The Bosun, Monkstown, Co Cork
Tel: 021 842172/842006 Fax: 021 842008 En suite Accommodation, restaurant and bars in purpose-built premises overlooking the River Lee. Seafood a speciality. 156

The Brambles, Midleton, Co Cork
Tel/Fax: 021 633758 Up-to-date B&B Accommodation in 5 en suite rooms 15 minutes from Cork, just off N25. Wheelchair accessible. 140

Westfield House, Ballincollig, Co Cork
Tel: 021 871824 Fax: 021 877415 A large detached villa, built in 1974, standing by the N22. Four double rooms, three en suite. Tv. Parking. 152

Food and Drink

Ibis Hotel, Dunkettle, Co Cork
Tel: 021 354354 Fax: 021 354202 100 en suite bedrooms in a well-equipped up-to-the-minute chain hotel at the Lee Tunnel roundabout. Full restaurant menu; lounge bar. 175

Spanish Point, Ballycotton, Co Cork
Tel: 021 646177 Fax: 021 646179 Speciality seafood restaurant with well-equipped en suite bedrooms in a dramatic clifftop setting. Own beach. Sea fishing. 178

The Bosun, Monkstown, Co Cork
Tel: 021 842172/842006 Fax: 021 842008 En suite Accommodation, restaurant and bars in purpose-built premises overlooking the River Lee. Seafood a speciality. 156

The Old Thatch, Killeagh, Co Cork
Tel: 024 95116/95108 A remarkable long, low thatched pub in the same family for 300& years. Bags of history and character. Food served 12-8.30. 146

Trade Winds, Cobh, Co Cork
Tel: 021 813754 An elegant, civilised restaurant in a Victorian building overlooking the sea. Seafood a speciality. Fine wines accompany the fine food. 153

Douglas

Douglas, Co Cork
Tel: 021 895297

Sec/Manager:	Brian Barrett
Professional:	Gary Nicholson
Directions:	Half mile east of Doublas village off the N28 from Cork
Type of Course:	Parkland

Date Founded:	1910
No of Holes:	18
Length:	6529 yds (5972 mtrs)
Par:	72
SSS:	71
Green Fees:	£35 Midweek £42 Weekends
Visitors:	Welcome: Any time except Tuesday
Societies:	Welcome: Except Tuesday. Telephone in advance
Facilities:	Chipping/Putting Area Practice Area, Golf Clubs for hire, Trolley hire, Bar, Restaurant

Accommodation, Food and Drink

Reference numbers below refer to detailed
information provided in section 2

Accommodation

Ashlee Lodge, Tower, Blarney, Co Cork

Tel: 021 385346 Fax: 021 385726 A striking Mediterranean-style bungalow set in prize-winning landscaped. Six bedrooms. Good breakfast menu. Packed lunches on request.   167

Coolim, Tower, Blarney, Co Cork

Tel: 021 382848 A large modern house with Scandinavian look - lots of pin. The three bedrooms all have en suite facilities. Breakfast is served with home-made bread and pancakes.   158

Ibis Hotel, Dunkettle, Co Cork

Tel: 021 354354 Fax: 021 354202 100 en suite bedrooms in a well-equipped up-to-the-minute chain hotel at the Lee Tunnel roundabout. Full restaurant menu; lounge bar.   175

Phelans Woodview House, Blarney, Co Cork

Tel: 021 385197 The restaurant has a full drinks licence for diners and guests. Accommodation comprises 8 bedrooms, all en suite, with tvs. Private car park.   154

Shannonpark House, Carrigaline, Co Cork

Tel: 021 372091 Mobile: 087 2942307 6 en suite rooms in a spacious bungalow with large garden. Handy for car ferry, airport and Cork city.   155

Food and Drink

Eco Douglas, Douglas, Co Cork

Tel: 021 892522 Fax: 021 895354 web: eCoie Highclass 80-cover restaurant with full drinks licence. Excellent choice of dishes of world-wide influence, ditto wine list. 166

Ibis Hotel, Dunkettle, Co Cork

Tel: 021 354354 Fax: 021 354202 100 en suite bedrooms in a well-equipped up-to-the-minute chain hotel at the Lee Tunnel roundabout. Full restaurant menu; lounge bar.   175

Phelans Woodview House, Blarney, Co Cork

Tel: 021 385197 The restaurant has a full drinks licence for diners and guests. Accommodation comprises 8 bedrooms, all en suite, with tvs. Private car park. 154

East Cork

**East Cork Golf Club, Gortacrue, Midleton,
Co Cork
Tel: 021 631687**

Sec/Manager:	Maurice Maloney
Professional:	Dan McFarland
Directions:	2 miles North of Midleton off the R626
Type of Course:	Parkland
Date Founded:	1969
No of Holes:	18
Length:	6314 yds (5774 mtrs)
Par:	69

SSS:	67
Green Fees:	£15
Visitors:	Welcome: Any day
Societies:	Welcome: Prebooking required
Facilities:	Chipping/Putting Area, Practice Area, Driving Range, Golf Clubs for hire, Trolley hire, Restaurant, Caddy service by arrangement

Accommodation, Food and Drink

Reference numbers below refer to detailed
information provided in section 2

Accommodation

Ashgrove Lodge, Cobh, Co Cork

Tel/Fax: 021 812483 Superior self-catering Accommodation in a superbly modernised coach house near the sea, with a castle in the grounds.   157

Ballyvolane House, Castlelyons, Co Cork

Tel: 025 36349 Fax: 025 36781 Superior Accommodation in an 18th-century mansion. B&B, evening meals by arrangement. Also self-catering cottage. Fishing.   173

Glebe House, Cobh, Co Cork

Tel/Fax: 021 811373 Four spacious bedrooms, all with bath and shower en suite, in a house in the centre of Cobh Island.   148

Glenview House, Midleton, Co Cork

Tel: 021 631680 Fax: 021 634680 Family-run Georgian house set in 20 private acres. Six bedrooms with king-size beds. B&B or self-catering.   143

Lynwen Lodge, Midleton, Co Cork

Tel: 021 631934 Bed and full Irish breakfast in a large, well-appointed house on the N25. Evening meals by arrangement.   144

Roseville, Youghal, Co Cork

Tel: 024 92571 Bed & Breakfast in a distinctive late 18th-century house on the N25. 4 double rooms and a twin. Very friendly.   142

Spanish Point, Ballycotton, Co Cork

Tel: 021 646177 Fax: 021 646179 Speciality seafood restaurant with well-equipped en suite bedrooms in a dramatic clifftop setting. Own beach. Sea fishing.   178

Springmount House, Fermoy, Co Cork

Tel: 025 31623 Seven twin-bedded rooms, a double & a family room in a very modern house on the N8. B&B; packed lunches.   151

The Brambles, Midleton, Co Cork

Tel/Fax: 021 633758 Up-to-date B&B Accommodation in 5 en suite rooms 15 minutes from Cork, just off N25. Wheelchair accessible.   140

Food and Drink

Coakley's Bar, Youghal, Co Cork

Tel: 024 93161 Liam Coakley's convivial pub in an 1820s building in the centre of town. Good cheer and good drinking.   169

Spanish Point, Ballycotton, Co Cork

Tel: 021 646177 Fax: 021 646179 Speciality seafood restaurant with well-equipped en suite bedrooms in a dramatic clifftop setting. Own beach. Sea fishing.   178

The Old Thatch, Killeagh, Co Cork

Tel: 024 95116/95108 A remarkable long, low thatched pub in the same family for 300& years. Bags of history and character. Food served 12-8.30.   146

Trade Winds, Cobh, Co Cork

Tel: 021 813754 An elegant, civilised restaurant in a Victorian building overlooking the sea. Seafood a speciality. Fine wines accompany the fine food.   153

Fermoy

**Fermoy Golf Club, Corrin, Fermoy, Co Cork
Tel: 025 32694/31472**

Sec/Manager:	None
Professional:	Brian Moriarty
Directions:	2 miles South of Fermoy on the N8 road to Cork

Type of Course:	Heathland
Date Founded:	1893
No of Holes:	18
Length:	6119 yds (5596 mtrs)
Par:	70
SSS:	70
Green Fees:	Weekdays: £13 Weekends & Bank Holidays: £16
Visitors:	Welcome: Contact Club for details
Societies:	Welcome: Book in Advance
Facilities:	Chipping/Putting Area, Practice Area, Driving Range, Golf Clubs for hire, Trolley hire, Electric Buggy hire, Bar, Restaurant

Accommodation, Food and Drink

Reference numbers below refer to detailed information provided in section 2

Accommodation

Ballyvolane House, Castlelyons, Co Cork

Tel: 025 36349 Fax: 025 36781 Superior Accommodation in an 18th-century mansion. B&B, evening meals by arrangement. Also self-catering cottage. Fishing.   173

Birch Hill House, Grenagh, Blarney, Co Cork

Tel: 021 886106 A grand and imposing grey-painted farmhouse, part of a working dairy and beef farm B&B Accommodation is in six rooms. Overlooks the River Martin, where trout fishing is available.   174

Glanworth Mill, Glanworth, Co Cork

Tel: 025 38555 A country inn with a great sense of history: a restored watermill with 10 en suite bedrooms, a Norman castle, an ancient bridge.   161

Springfort Hall Hotel, Mallow, Co Cork

Tel: 022 21278 Fax: 022 21557 50 en suite bedrooms in an 18th-century manor house 4 miles north of Mallow. Restaurant. Fishing.   150

Springmount House, Fermoy, Co Cork

Tel: 025 31623 Seven twin-bedded rooms, a double & a family room in a very modern house on the N8. B&B; packed lunches.   151

Food and Drink

Glanworth Mill, Glanworth, Co Cork

Tel: 025 38555 A country inn with a great sense of history: a restored watermill with 10 en suite bedrooms, a Norman castle, an ancient bridge.   161

Ibis Hotel, Dunkettle, Co Cork

Tel: 021 354354 Fax: 021 354202 100 en suite bedrooms in a well-equipped up-to-the-minute chain hotel at the Lee Tunnel roundabout. Full restaurant menu; lounge bar.   175

Springfort Hall Hotel, Mallow, Co Cork

Tel: 022 21278 Fax: 022 21557 50 en suite bedrooms in an 18th-century manor house 4 miles north of Mallow. Restaurant. Fishing.   150

The Castle Inn, Buttevant, Co Cork

Tel: 022 23044 A bar and 40-cover restaurant with a strong local following. Good menu with daily specials; pub games.   182

Fernhill

Fernhill Golf & Country Club, Carrigaline, Co Cork

Tel: 021 372226/373103

Sec/Manager:	Phil Aherne
Professional:	None
Directions:	3 miles West of Ringaskiddy off the N28 to Cork
Type of Course:	Parkland
Date Founded:	1994

No of Holes:	18
Length:	6241 yds(5707 mtrs)
Par:	69
SSS:	69
Green Fees:	Weekdays: £9 & after 11am £11 Weekends: £14
Visitors:	Welcome: Pay & Play
Societies:	Welcome: Advance Booking
Facilities:	Chipping/Putting Area, Practice Area, Golf Clubs for hire, Bar, Restaurant, Caddy service by arrangement

Accommodation, Food and Drink

Reference numbers below refer to detailed information provided in section 2

Accommodation

Lough Mahon House, Tivoli, Co Cork

Tel: 021 502142 Fax: 021 501804 Seven bedrooms offering various permutations in a huge early-Victorian house. Easy parking. Close to Cork city centre.   145

Quayside House, Kinsale, Co Cork

Tel: 021 772188 Fax: 021 772664 Family-run B&B guest house by the harbour, with well-equipped en suite bedrooms. Gourmet restaurants nearby.   164

Shannonpark House, Carrigaline, Co Cork

Tel: 021 372091 Mobile: 087 2942307 6 en suite rooms in a spacious bungalow with large garden. Handy for car ferry, airport and Cork city.   155

Westfield House, Ballincollig, Co Cork

Tel: 021 871824 Fax: 021 877415 A large detached villa, built in 1974, standing by the N22. Four double rooms, three en suite. Tv. Parking.   152

Food and Drink

Eco Douglas, Douglas, Co Cork

Tel: 021 892522 Fax: 021 895354 web: eCoie Highclass 80-cover restaurant with full drinks licence. Excellent choice of dishes of world-wide influence, ditto wine list. 166

Ibis Hotel, Dunkettle, Co Cork

Tel: 021 354354 Fax: 021 354202 100 en suite bedrooms in a well-equipped up-to-the-minute chain hotel at the Lee Tunnel roundabout. Full restaurant menu; lounge bar.   175

The Bosun, Monkstown, Co Cork

Tel: 021 842172/842006 Fax: 021 842008 En suite Accommodation, restaurant and bars in purpose-built premises overlooking the River Lee. Seafood a speciality.   156

Fota Island

Fota Island Golf Club, Carrigtwohill, Co Cork

Tel: 021 883700

Situated on an 800-acre estate in Cork Harbour, Fota Island retains its arboretum, semi-tropical gardens and wildlife park. But since 1994, it has

also become familiar as the site of a fine, park-land test of golf, reflecting the combined design skills of Peter McEvoy and Christy O'Connor Jnr.

Significant drainage problems and difficulties with some excessively sloping greens, became evident when the Smurfit Irish Professional Championship was staged there in 1997. Since then, the property has been acquired by Mount Juliet's owners, Killeen Investments, for an understood outlay of £4.5 million.

The success of Mount Juliet was clearly crucial to the deal in that it permitted the secondment of Jeff Howes and Aidan O'Hara to take care of remedial work. Major remodelling at Fota has been carried out by Howes, who worked as design co-ordinator and on-course manager for Jack Nicklaus during the construction of Mount Juliet. Meanwhile, greens superintendent O'Hara took care of agronomy.

As part of the work, all of the fairways have been re-drained, stripped of meadowgrass and re-seeded to the highest standards with creeping bent, the same as in the tees and greens. And all 18 greens have been rebuilt along with an entirely new, short 13th hole.

Major, infrastructural developements in the Cork City area, notably the Jack Lynch Tunnel, greatly enhance Fota's attractiveness as a major tournament venue. Given the quality of the work by Howes and O'Hara, one suspects it won't be long before its potential is put to the test.

Sec/Manager:	Kevin Mulcahy
Professional:	Kevin Morris
Directions:	Half a mile from Cobh exit off N25. 9 miles East of Cork
Type of Course:	Parkland
Date Founded:	1993
No of Holes:	18
Length:	6888 yds (6298 mtrs)
Par:	71
SSS:	73
Green Fees:	Monday - Thursday: £45 Friday - Sunday: £55
Visitors:	Welcome: Any day, Check restrictions with Club

Societies:	Welcome: Contact in Advance
Facilities:	Chipping/Putting Area, Practice Area, Driving Range, Golf Clubs for hire, Electric Buggy hire, Bar, Restaurant, Caddy service by arrangement

Accommodation, Food and Drink

Reference numbers below refer to detailed information provided in section 2

Accommodation

Ashgrove Lodge, Cobh, Co Cork
Tel/Fax: 021 812483 Superior self-catering Accommodation in a superbly modernised coach house near the sea, with a castle in the grounds.   157

Glebe House, Cobh, Co Cork
Tel/Fax: 021 811373 Four spacious bedrooms, all with bath and shower en suite, in a house in the centre of Cobh Island.   148

Glenview House, Midleton, Co Cork
Tel: 021 631680 Fax: 021 634680 Family-run Georgian house set in 20 private acres. En suite bedrooms with king-size beds. B&B or self-catering.   143

Ibis Hotel, Dunkettle, Co Cork
Tel: 021 354354 Fax: 021 354202 100 en suite bedrooms in a well-equipped up-to-the-minute chain hotel at the Lee Tunnel roundabout. Full restaurant menu; lounge bar.   175

Lough Mahon House, Tivoli, Co Cork
Tel: 021 502142 Fax: 021 501804 Seven bedrooms offering various permutations in a huge early-Victorian house. Easy parking. Close to Cork city centre.   145

Lynwen Lodge, Midleton, Co Cork
Tel: 021 631934 Bed and full Irish breakfast in a large, well-appointed house on the N25. Evening meals by arrangement.   144

Spanish Point, Ballycotton, Co Cork
Tel: 021 646177 Fax: 021 646179 Speciality seafood restaurant with well-equipped en suite bedrooms in a dramatic clifftop setting. Own beach. Sea fishing.   178

The Bosun, Monkstown, Co Cork
Tel: 021 842172/842006 Fax: 021 842008 En suite Accommodation, restaurant and bars in purpose-built premises overlooking the River Lee. Seafood a speciality.   156

The Brambles, Midleton, Co Cork
Tel/Fax: 021 633758 Up-to-date B&B Accommodation in 5 en suite rooms 15 minutes from Cork, just off N25. Wheelchair accessible.   140

Food and Drink

Ibis Hotel, Dunkettle, Co Cork
Tel: 021 354354 Fax: 021 354202 100 en suite bedrooms in a well-equipped up-to-the-minute chain hotel at the Lee Tunnel roundabout. Full restaurant menu; lounge bar.   175

Spanish Point, Ballycotton, Co Cork
Tel: 021 646177 Fax: 021 646179 Speciality seafood restaurant with well-equipped en suite bedrooms in a dramatic clifftop setting. Own beach. Sea fishing.   178

The Bosun, Monkstown, Co Cork
Tel: 021 842172/842006 Fax: 021 842008 En suite Accommodation, restaurant and bars in purpose-built premises overlooking the River Lee. Seafood a speciality.   156

The Old Thatch, Killeagh, Co Cork
Tel: 024 95116/95108 A remarkable long, low thatched pub in the same family for 300& years. Bags of history and character. Food served 12-8.30.   146

Trade Winds, Cobh, Co Cork
Tel: 021 813754 An elegant, civilised restaurant in a Victorian building overlooking the sea. Seafood a speciality. Fine wines accompany the fine food.   153

Harbour Point

Harbour Point Golf Club, Clash, Little Island, Co Cork

Tel: 021 353094

Sec/Manager:	Niamh O'Connell

Professional:	Morgan O'Donovan
Directions:	5 miles East of Cork City turn right off the N25 to Little Island: Course is signposted
Type of Course:	Parkland
Date Founded:	1991
No of Holes:	18
Length:	6738 yds (6162 mtrs)
Par:	72
SSS:	72
Green Fees:	Weekdays: £23 Weekends: £26 Early Bird: £16
Visitors:	Welcome: Any Day
Societies:	Welcome: Pre-booking required
Facilities:	Chipping/Putting Area, Practice Area, Driving Range, Golf Clubs for hire, Trolley hire, Electric Buggy hire, Bar, Restaurant, Caddy service by arrangement

Accommodation, Food and Drink

Reference numbers below refer to detailed information provided in section 2

Accommodation

Ashgrove Lodge, Cobh, Co Cork
Tel/Fax: 021 812483 Superior self-catering Accommodation in a superbly modernised coach house near the sea, with a castle in the grounds. 157

Glebe House, Cobh, Co Cork
Tel/Fax: 021 811373 Four spacious bedrooms, all with bath and shower en suite, in a house in the centre of Cobh Island. 148

Glenview House, Midleton, Co Cork
Tel: 021 631680 Fax: 021 634680 Family-run Georgian house set in 20 private acres. En suite bedrooms with king-size beds. B&B or self-catering. 143

Ibis Hotel, Dunkettle, Co Cork
Tel: 021 354354 Fax: 021 354202 100 en suite bedrooms in a well-equipped up-to-the-minute chain hotel at the Lee Tunnel roundabout. Full restaurant menu; lounge bar. 175

Lough Mahon House, Tivoli, Co Cork
Tel: 021 502142 Fax: 021 501804 Seven bedrooms offering various permutations in a huge early-Victorian house. Easy parking. Close to Cork city centre. 145

Lynwen Lodge, Midleton, Co Cork
Tel: 021 631934 Bed and full Irish breakfast in a large, well-appointed house on the N25. Evening meals by arrangement. 144

The Bosun, Monkstown, **Co Cork**
Tel: 021 842172/842006 Fax: 021 842008 En suite Accommodation, restaurant and bars in purpose-built premises overlooking the River Lee. Seafood a speciality. 156

The Brambles, Midleton, Co Cork
Tel/Fax: 021 633758 Up-to-date B&B Accommodation in 5 en suite rooms 15 minutes from Cork, just off N25. Wheelchair accessible. 140

Food and Drink

Ibis Hotel, Dunkettle, Co Cork
Tel: 021 354354 Fax: 021 354202 100 en suite bedrooms in a well-equipped up-to-the-minute chain hotel at the Lee Tunnel roundabout. Full restaurant menu; lounge bar. 175

The Bosun, Monkstown, Co Cork
Tel: 021 842172/842006 Fax: 021 842008 En suite Accommodation, restaurant and bars in purpose-built premises overlooking the River Lee. Seafood a speciality. 156

The Old Thatch, Killeagh, Co Cork
Tel: 024 95116/95108 A remarkable long, low thatched pub in the same family for 300& years. Bags of history and character. Food served 12-8.30. 146

Trade Winds, Cobh, Co Cork
Tel: 021 813754 An elegant, civilised restaurant in a Victorian building overlooking the sea. Seafood a speciality. Fine wines accompany the fine food. 153

Kanturk

Kanturk Golf Club, Fairy Hill, Kanturk, Co Cork
Tel: 029 50534

Sec/Manager:	Tony McAuliffe
Professional:	None
Directions:	1 mile South of Kantruk off the R579 to Banteer
Type of Course:	Parkland
Date Founded:	1973
No of Holes:	18
Length:	6044 yds (5527 mtrs)
Par:	72
SSS:	70
Green Fees:	Weekdays: £12 Weekends & Bank Holidays: £15
Visitors:	Welcome: Not Wednesday
Societies:	Welcome: Special concessions, Contact Club for details
Facilities:	Chipping/Putting Area, Golf Clubs for hire, Trolley hire, Bar, (Restaurant, by arrangement)

Accommodation, Food and Drink

Reference numbers below refer to detailed information provided in section 2

Accommodation

Birch Hill House, Grenagh, Blarney, Co Cork
Tel: 021 886106 A grand and imposing grey-painted farmhouse, part of a working dairy and beef farm B&B Accommodation is in six rooms. Overlooks the River Martin, where trout fishing is available. 174

Bohernamona House, Courtbrack, Blarney, Co Cork
Tel: 021 385181 Fax: 021 382443 The welcome is warm and the beds comfortable in this strikingly designed modern. There are five letting bedrooms, large gardens and plenty of parking space. 179

Clonfert, Fossa, Killarney, Co Kerry
Tel: 064 31459 B&B Accommodation in 5 en suite double rooms. 9 golf courses within a few miles. No credit cards.

Hill Top Farm, Cill-na-Martra, Macroom, Co Cork
Tel: 026 40154 A lovely secluded setting in the hills between Macroom and Killarney. The house has extensive gardens and a large conservatory. Four bedrooms, full breakfasts, packed lunches, evening meals by arrangement. 165

Springfort Hall Hotel, Mallow, Co Cork
Tel: 022 21278 Fax: 022 21557 50 en suite bedrooms in an 18th-century manor house 4 miles north of Mallow. Restaurant. Fishing. 150

The Laune & Taylor's, Killarney, Co Kerry

Tel: 064 32772 Fax: 064 37908 'Wine, dine & stay' in the centre of Killarney. En suite bedrooms; breakfast till noon; lunch and a full à la carte 3 till 10.　306

Victoria Hotel, Macroom, Co Cork

Tel: 026 41082 Fax: 026 42148 On the main square of a town that's famous for its castle, the Victoria is a fine base for tourists and sportsmen. 16 rooms, all en suite. Restaurant & bar menus　141

Food and Drink

Springfort Hall Hotel, Mallow, Co Cork

Tel: 022 21278 Fax: 022 21557 50 en suite bedrooms in an 18th-century manor house 4 miles north of Mallow. Restaurant. Fishing.　150

The Castle Inn, Buttevant, Co Cork

Tel: 022 23044 A bar and 40-cover restaurant with a strong local following. Good menu with daily specials; pub games.　182

The Four Winds, Charleville, Co Cork

Tel: 063 89285 A welcoming bar and restaurant occupying a prominent corner site on the N20. Food served from noon till 3.　176

The Laune & Taylor's, Killarney, Co Kerry

Tel: 064 32772 Fax: 064 37908 'Wine, dine & stay' in the centre of Killarney. En suite bedrooms; breakfast till noon; lunch and a full à la carte 3 till 10.　306

Victoria Hotel, Macroom, Co Cork

Tel: 026 41082 Fax: 026 42148 On the main square of a town that's famous for its castle, the Victoria is a fine base for tourists and sportsmen. 16 rooms, all en suite. Restaurant & bar menus　141

Kinsale

**Kinsale Golf Club, Farrangalway, Kinsale,
Co Cork**

Tel: 021 774722

Sec/Manager:	Pat Murray
Professional:	Ger Broderick
Directions:	2 miles from Kinsale off the R600 to Cork
Type of Course:	Parkland
Date Founded:	1912
No of Holes:	18 (plus 9 hole course)
Length:	7227 yds (6609 mtrs)
Par:	71
SSS:	71
Green Fees:	Monday - Thursday: £22 Friday - Sunday incl. Bank Holidays: £27
Visitors:	Welcome: Booking at weekends required
Societies:	Welcome: Pre-booking required.
Facilities:	Practice Area, Golf Clubs for hire, 5, Electric Buggy hire, Bar, Restaurant, Caddy service by arrangement

Accommodation, Food and Drink

Reference numbers below refer to detailed
information provided in section 2

Accommodation

An Garrán Coír, Castlefreke, Clonakilty, Co Cork

Tel: 023 48236 Comfortable Bed & Breakfast Accommodation in lovely relaxing surroundings. Great views. Great breakfasts.　187

An Súgán, Clonakilty, Co Cork

Tel: 023 33498 100-cover pub-restaurant specialising in seafood. B&B in adjacent Strand House, also self-catering cottages.　170

Quayside House, Kinsale, Co Cork

Tel: 021 772188 Fax: 021 772664 Family-run B&B guest house by the harbour, with well-equipped en suite bedrooms. Gourmet restaurants nearby.　164

Shannonpark House, Carrigaline, Co Cork

Tel: 021 372091 Mobile: 087 2942307 6 en suite rooms in a spacious bungalow with large garden. Handy for car ferry, airport and Cork city.　155

Food and Drink

An Súgán, Clonakilty, Co Cork

Tel: 023 33498 100-cover pub-restaurant specialising in seafood. B&B in adjacent Strand House, also self-catering cottages.　170

De Barra, Clonakilty, Co Cork

Tel: 023 33381 A cheerful pub with its own folk club and traditional Irish music. 149

Eco Douglas, Douglas, Co Cork

Tel: 021 892522 Fax: 021 895354 web: eCoie Highclass 80-cover restaurant with full drinks licence. Excellent choice of dishes of world-wide influence, ditto wine list. 166

The Bosun, Monkstown, Co Cork

Tel: 021 842172/842006 Fax: 021 842008 En suite Accommodation, restaurant and bars in purpose-built premises overlooking the River Lee. Seafood a speciality. 156

Lee Valley

Lee Valley, Clashanure, Ovens, Co Cork

Tel: 021 7331721

Sec/Manager:	John O'Reilly
Professional:	John Savage
Directions:	10 miles West of Cork City on N22
Type of Course:	Parkland
Date Founded:	1993
No of Holes:	18
Length:	6725 yds (6149 mtrs)
Par:	72
SSS:	72
Green Fees:	Weekdays: £29 Weekends incl. Bank Holidays: £32 Nov - Mar: Weekdays £20 Weekends £25
Visitors:	Welcome: Book in advance especially at weekends
Societies:	Welcome: Book in Advance
Facilities:	Chipping/Putting Area, Driving Range, Golf Clubs for hire, 5, Electric Buggy hire, Bar, Restaurant, Caddy service by arrangement

Accommodation, Food and Drink

Reference numbers below refer to detailed
information provided in section 2

Accommodation

An Cuasán, Macroom, Co Cork

Tel: 026 40018 A fine country house enjoying a tranquil setting in spacious mature gardens. The six bedrooms all have en suite facilities; some have balconies to make the most of the views.　160

Bohernamona House, Courtbrack, Blarney, Co Cork

Tel: 021 385181 Fax: 021 382443 The welcome is warm and the beds comfortable in this strikingly designed modern. There are five letting bedrooms, large gardens and plenty of parking space.　179

Cooligreenane House, Inchigeela, Co Cork

Tel: 026 49344 At scenically set Cooligreenane House there are three bedrooms, farmhouse breakfasts and private access to coarse fishing. Rose Cottage and Tigh Mhuire offer self catering.　163

Coolim, Tower, Blarney, Co Cork

Tel: 021 382848 A large modern house with Scandinavian look - lots of pin. The three bedrooms all have en suite facilities. Breakfast is served with home-made bread and pancakes.　158

Hill Top Farm, Cill-na-Martra, Macroom, Co Cork

Tel: 026 40154 A lovely secluded setting in the hills between Macroom and Killarney. The house has extensive gardens and a large conservatory. Four bedrooms, full breakfasts, packed lunches, evening meals by arrangement.   165

Hillview House, Killard, Blarney, Co Cork

Tel: 021 385161 An attractive house with lots of character and a setting of peaceful, colourful gardens and grounds. 4 bedrooms, sun lounge and large private car park. Help with itineraries and warm hospitality.   172

Maranatha Country House, Tower, Blarney, Co Cork

Tel/Fax: 021 385102 Outstanding Accommodation in a distinguished 1880's Victorian home nestled in 27 acres of lawns and gardens. The six en suite bedrooms are nothing short of stunning.   177

Phelans Woodview House, Blarney, Co Cork

Tel: 026 385197 The restaurant has a full drinks licence for diners and guests. Accommodation comprises 8 bedrooms, all en suite, with tvs. Private car park.   154

Victoria Hotel, Macroom, Co Cork

Tel: 026 41082 Fax: 026 42148 On the main square of a town that's famous for its castle, the Victoria is a fine base for tourists and sportsmen. 16 rooms, all en suite. Restaurant & bar menus   141

Westfield House, Ballincollig, Co Cork

Tel: 021 871824 Fax: 021 877415 A large detached villa, built in 1974, standing by the N22. Four double rooms, three en suite. Tv. Parking.   152

Woodleigh, Carrigadrohid, Macroom, Co Cork

Tel: 026 48119 Plain and simple home-from-home Accommodation in a semi-detached house with a conservatory and gardens. The owners have four letting bedrooms, all en suite, with tvs.   171

Food and Drink

Blairs Inn, Cloghroe, Blarney, Co Cork

Tel: 021 381470 A typical Irish country pub in a secluded riverside position. The cuisine puts an Irish twist on international dishes. The fish is freshly landed at Dingle and Kenmare and terrific Irish stew.   159

Phelans Woodview House, Blarney, Co Cork

Tel: 021 385197 The restaurant has a full drinks licence for diners and guests. Accommodation comprises 8 bedrooms, all en suite, with tvs. Private car park.   154

Victoria Hotel, Macroom, Co Cork

Tel: 026 41082 Fax: 026 42148 On the main square of a town that's famous for its castle, the Victoria is a fine base for tourists and sportsmen. 16 rooms, all en suite. Restaurant & bar menus   141

Macroom

Macroom Golf Club, Lackaduve, Macroom, Co Cork

Tel: 026 41072

Sec/Manager:	Leo Goold
Professional:	None
Directions:	Entrance through Castle gates in centre of Macroom
Type of Course:	Parkland
Date Founded:	1924

No of Holes:	18
Length:	6095 yds (5574 mtrs)
Par:	72
SSS:	70
Green Fees:	Weekdays: £15 Weekends: £18
Visitors:	Welcome: Booking essential
Societies:	Welcome: Pre-book in advance
Facilities:	Chipping/Putting Area, Golf Clubs for hire, Trolley hire, Electric Buggy hire, Bar, Restaurant

Accommodation, Food and Drink

Reference numbers below refer to detailed information provided in section 2

Accommodation

An Cuasán, Macroom, Co Cork

Tel: 026 40018 A fine country house enjoying a tranquil setting in spacious mature gardens. The six bedrooms all have en suite facilities; some have balconies to make the most of the views.   160

Birchwood, kilgarvin, Cokerry

Tel: 064 85473 Fax: 065 85570 Spacious B&B Accommodation in 2 en suite double rooms and three en suite triples. AA 4 diamonds. No credit cards.

Bohernamona House, Courtbrack, Blarney, Co Cork

Tel: 021 385181 Fax: 021 382443 The welcome is warm and the beds comfortable in this strikingly designed modern. There are five letting bedrooms, large gardens and plenty of parking space.   179

Cooligreenane House, Inchigeela, Co Cork

Tel: 026 49344 At scenically set Cooligreenane House there are three bedrooms, farmhouse breakfasts and private access to coarse fishing. Rose Cottage and Tigh Mhuire offer self catering.   163

Darby O'Gill's, Lissivigeen, Co Cork

Tel: 064 34168 Fax: 064 36794 Country house hotel with charming en suite bedrooms. Irish cuisine in the evening, lunches in the lounge bar. Darts, rings and cards.   308

Hill Top Farm, Cill-na-Martra, Macroom, Co Cork

Tel: 026 40154 A lovely secluded setting in the hills between Macroom and Killarney. The house has extensive gardens and a large conservatory. Four bedrooms, full breakfasts, packed lunches, evening meals by arrangement.   165

Hillview House, Killard, Blarney, Co Cork

Tel: 021 385161 An attractive house with lots of character and a setting of peaceful, colourful gardens and grounds. 4 bedrooms, sun lounge and large private car park. Help with itineraries and warm hospitality.   172

Mills Inn, Ballyvourney, Macroom, Co Cork

Tel: 026 45237 Fax: 026 45454 Set in landscaped gardens 20 miles from Killarne, this is one of the oldest and finest inns in Ireland. 12 rooms, all en suite. Seafood speciality restaurant.   147

Springfield House, Rathbarry, Clonakilty, Co Cork

Tel/Fax: 023 40622 Select farmhouse Bed and Breakfast Accommodation. Rooms en suite. Home cooking a speciality. Self-catering also available.   181

Victoria Hotel, Macroom, Co Cork

Tel: 026 41082 Fax: 026 42148 On the main square of a town that's famous for its castle, the Victoria is a fine base for tourists and sportsmen. 16 rooms, all en suite. Restaurant & bar menus   141

Woodleigh, Carrigadrohid, Macroom, Co Cork

Tel: 026 48119 Plain and simple home-from-home Accommodation in a semi-detached house with a conservatory and gardens. The owners have four letting bedrooms, all en suite, with tvs.   171

Food and Drink

Darby O'Gill's, Lissivigeen, Co Cork

Tel: 064 34168 Fax: 064 36794 Country house hotel with charming en suite bedrooms. Irish cuisine in the evening, lunches in the lounge bar. Darts, rings and cards.   308

Mills Inn, Ballyvourney, Macroom, Co Cork

Tel: 026 45237 Fax: 026 45454 Set in landscaped gardens 20 miles from Killarne, this is one of the oldest and finest inns in Ireland. 12 rooms, all en suite. Seafood speciality restaurant.   147

Victoria Hotel, Macroom, Co Cork
Tel: 026 41082 Fax: 026 42148 On the main square of a town that's famous for its castle, the Victoria is a fine base for tourists and sportsmen. 16 rooms, all en suite. Restaurant & bar menus   141

Mahon

Mahon Golf Club, Skehard Road, Blackrock, Co Cork
Tel: 021 294280

Sec/Manager:	T. O'Connor
Professional:	None
Directions:	On outskirts of Cork City. 1 mile past Douglas off N28
Type of Course:	Parkland
Date Founded:	1980
No of Holes:	18
Length:	5264 yds (4818 mtrs)
Par:	68
SSS:	66
Green Fees:	Weekdays: £12 Weekends & Bank Holidays: £13
Visitors:	Welcome: Not Friday, Saturday, Sunday a.m. only.
Societies:	Welcome: Any time Pre-booking required
Facilities:	Chipping/Putting Area, Golf Clubs for hire, 5, Bar, Caddy service by arrangement

Accommodation, Food and Drink

Reference numbers below refer to detailed information provided in section 2

Accommodation

Ashlee Lodge, Tower, Blarney, Co Cork
Tel: 021 385346 Fax: 021 385726 A Mediterranean-style bungalow in prize-winning landscaped. 6 bedrooms. Good breakfast menu. Packed lunches on request.   167

Coolim, Tower, Blarney, Co Cork
Tel: 021 382848 A large modern house with Scandinavian look - lots of pin. The three bedrooms all have en suite facilities. Breakfast is served with home-made bread and pancakes.   158

Hillview House, Killard, Blarney, Co Cork
Tel: 021 385161 An attractive house with lots of character and a setting of peaceful, colourful gardens and grounds. 4 bedrooms, sun lounge and large private car park. Help with itineraries and warm hospitality.   172

Phelans Woodview House, Blarney, Co Cork
Tel: 021 385197 The restaurant has a full drinks licence for diners and guests. Accommodation comprises 8 bedrooms, all en suite, with tvs. Private car park.   154

Westfield House, Ballincollig, Co Cork
Tel: 021 871824 Fax: 021 877415 A large detached villa, built in 1974, standing by the N22. Four double rooms, three en suite. Tv. Parking.   152

Food and Drink

Blairs Inn, Cloghroe, Blarney, Co Cork
Tel: 021 381470 A typical Irish country pub in a secluded riverside position. The cuisine puts an Irish twist on international dishes. The fish is freshly landed at Dingle and Kenmare and terrific Irish stew.   159

Eco Douglas, Douglas, Co Cork
Tel: 021 892522 Fax: 021 895354 eCoie Highclass 80-cover restaurant with full drinks licence. Excellent choice of dishes of world-wide influence, ditto wine list.   166

Phelans Woodview House, Blarney, Co Cork
Tel: 021 385197 The restaurant has a full drinks licence for diners and guests. Accommodation comprises 8 bedrooms, all en suite, with tvs. Private car park.   154

Mallow

Mallow Golf Club, Ballyellis, Mallow, Co Cork
Tel: 022 21145

Sec/Manager:	Irene Howell
Professional:	Sean Conway
Directions:	1 mile South West of Mallow off the road to Killavullen
Type of Course:	Parkland
Date Founded:	1947
No of Holes:	18
Length:	6517 yds (5960 mtrs)
Par:	72
SSS:	72
Green Fees:	Weekdays: £20 Weekends & Bank Holidays: £25
Visitors:	Welcome: Not Tuesday, Restrictions at weekends, Ring in advance
Societies:	Welcome: Book in Advance
Facilities:	Chipping/Putting Area, Practice Area, Golf Clubs for hire, Trolley hire, Electric Buggy hire, Bar, Restaurant, Caddy service by arrangement

Accommodation, Food and Drink

Reference numbers below refer to detailed information provided in section 2

Accommodation

Ashlee Lodge, Tower, Blarney, Co Cork
Tel: 021 385346 Fax: 021 385726 A Mediterranean-style bungalow in prize-winning landscaped. Six bedrooms. Good breakfast menu. Packed lunches on request.   167

Ballyvolane House, Castlelyons, Co Cork
Tel: 025 36349 Fax: 025 36781 Superior Accommodation in an 18th-century mansion. B&B, evening meals by arrangement. Also self-catering cottage. Fishing.   173

Birch Hill House, Grenagh, Blarney, Co Cork
Tel: 021 886106 A grand and imposing grey-painted farmhouse, part of a working dairy and beef farm B&B Accommodation is in six rooms. Overlooks the River Martin, where trout fishing is available.   174

Glanworth Mill, Glanworth, Co Cork
Tel: 025 38555 A country inn with a great sense of history: a restored watermill with 10 en suite bedrooms, a Norman castle, an ancient bridge.   161

Hillview House, Killard, Blarney, Co Cork
Tel: 021 385161 An attractive house with lots of character and a setting of peaceful, colourful gardens and grounds. 4 bedrooms, sun lounge and large private car park. Help with itineraries and warm hospitality.   172

Maranatha Country House, Tower, Blarney, Co Cork
Tel/Fax: 021 385102 Outstanding Accommodation in a distinguished 1880's Victorian home nestled in 27 acres of lawns and gardens. The six en suite bedrooms are nothing short of stunning.   177

Springfort Hall Hotel, Mallow, Co Cork
Tel: 022 21278 Fax: 022 21557 50 en suite bedrooms in an 18th-century manor house 4 miles north of Mallow. Restaurant. Fishing.   150

Springmount House, Fermoy, Co Cork
Tel: 025 31623 Seven twin-bedded rooms, a double & a family room in a very modern house on the N8. B&B; packed lunches.   151

Food and Drink

Blairs Inn, Cloghroe, Blarney, Co Cork
Tel: 021 381470 A typical Irish country pub in a secluded riverside position. The cuisine puts an Irish twist on international dishes. The fish is freshly landed at Dingle and Kenmare and terrific Irish stew.   159

Glanworth Mill, Glanworth, Co Cork
Tel: 025 38555 A country inn with a great sense of history: a restored watermill
with 10 en suite bedrooms, a Norman castle, an ancient bridge.   161
Springfort Hall Hotel, Mallow, Co Cork
Tel: 022 21278 Fax: 022 21557 50 en suite bedrooms in an 18th-century manor
house 4 miles north of Mallow. Restaurant. Fishing.   150
The Castle Inn, Buttevant, Co Cork
Tel: 022 23044 A bar and 40-cover restaurant with a strong local following. Good
menu with daily specials; pub games.   182

Mitchelstown

Mitchelstown, Co Cork
Tel: 025 24072

Sec/Manager:	Tony Lewis
Professional:	None
Directions:	Half mile North West of Michelstown off the N8 to Limerick
Type of Course:	Parklands
Date Founded:	1908
No of Holes:	18
Length:	5643 yds (5160 mtrs)
Par:	67
SSS:	
Green Fees:	£12 Weekdays £15 Weekends
Visitors:	Welcome: except Ladies Day Wednesday
Societies:	Welcome: Weekdays only, Book in advance
Facilities:	Chipping/Putting Area, Practice Area, Bar, Restaurant

Accommodation, Food and Drink

Reference numbers below refer to detailed
information provided in section 2

Accommodation

Ballyvolane House, Castlelyons, Co Cork
Tel: 025 36349 Fax: 025 36781 Superior Accommodation in an 18th-century mansion.
B&B, evening meals by arrangement. Also self-catering cottage. Fishing.   173
Deebert House, Kilmallock, Co Limerick
Tel: 063 98106 Five letting bedrooms, including a family room, in a splendid
Georgian house set in award-winning gardens. Restaurant.   382
Glanworth Mill, Glanworth, Co Cork
Tel: 025 38555 A country inn with a great sense of history: a restored watermill
with 10 en suite bedrooms, a Norman castle, an ancient bridge.   161
Springmount House, Fermoy, Co Cork
Tel: 025 31623 Seven twin-bedded rooms, a double & a family room in a very
modern house on the N8. B&B; packed lunches.   151

Food and Drink

Deebert House, Kilmallock, Co Limerick
Tel: 063 98106 Five letting bedrooms, including a family room, in a splendid
Georgian house set in award-winning gardens. Restaurant.   382
Glanworth Mill, Glanworth, Co Cork
Tel: 025 38555 A country inn with a great sense of history: a restored watermill
with 10 en suite bedrooms, a Norman castle, an ancient bridge.   161
The Castle Inn, Buttevant, Co Cork
Tel: 022 23044 A bar and 40-cover restaurant with a strong local following. Good
menu with daily specials; pub games.   182
The Four Winds, Charleville, Co Cork
Tel: 063 89285 A welcoming bar and restaurant occupying a prominent corner site
on the N20. Food served from noon till 3.   176

Monkstown

Monkstown Golf Club, Parkgariffe,
Monkstown, Co Cork
Tel: 021 841376

Sec/Manager:	Jim Long
Professional:	Batt Murphy
Directions:	7 miles Ssouth East of Cork City off the R610
Type of Course:	Parkland
Date Founded:	1908
No of Holes:	18
Length:	6199 yds (5668 mtrs)
Par:	70
SSS:	69
Green Fees:	Monday - Thursday: £23 Friday - Sunday: £26
Visitors:	Welcome: Booking essential
Societies:	Welcome: Essential to book in advance
Facilities:	Chipping/Putting Area, Practice Area, Golf Clubs for hire, Trolley hire, Bar, Restaurant

Accommodation, Food and Drink

Reference numbers below refer to detailed
information provided in section 2

Accommodation

Quayside House, Kinsale, Co Cork
Tel: 021 772188 Fax: 021 772664 Family-run B&B guest house by the harbour, with
well-equipped en suite bedrooms. Gourmet restaurants nearby.   164
Shannonpark House, Carrigaline, Co Cork
Tel: 021 372091 Mobile: 087 2942307 6 en suite rooms in a spacious bungalow
with large garden. Handy for car ferry, airport and Cork city.   155
The Bosun, Monkstown, Co Cork
Tel: 021 842172/842006 Fax: 021 842008 En suite Accommodation, restaurant and
bars in purpose-built premises overlooking the River Lee. Seafood a speciality.   156

Food and Drink

Eco Douglas, Douglas, Co Cork
Tel: 021 892522 Fax: 021 895354 web: eCoie Highclass 80-cover restaurant with full
drinks licence. Excellent choice of dishes of world-wide influence, ditto wine list.   166
Ibis Hotel, Dunkettle, Co Cork
Tel: 021 354354 Fax: 021 354202 100 en suite bedrooms in a well-equipped up-to-
the-minute chain hotel at the Lee Tunnel roundabout. Full restaurant menu; lounge
bar.   175
The Bosun, Monkstown, Co Cork
Tel: 021 842172/842006 Fax: 021 842008 En suite Accommodation, restaurant and
bars in purpose-built premises overlooking the River Lee. Seafood a speciality.   156

Muskerry

Muskerry Golf Club, Carrigrohane, Co Cork
Tel: 021 385297

Sec/Manager:	Joe Moyniham
Professional:	Martin Lehane
Directions:	Off the R617 3 miles South West of Blarney to the North West of Cork

Type of Course:	Parkland
Date Founded:	1897
No of Holes:	18
Length:	6327 yds (5786 mtrs)
Par:	71
SSS:	70
Green Fees:	Monday - Thursday: £23 Friday - Sunday: £26
Visitors:	Welcome: Book in Advance
Societies:	Welcome: Book in advance
Facilities:	Chipping/Putting Area, Practice Area, Golf Clubs for hire, Trolley Hire, Bar, Restaurant

Old Head of Kinsale

Kinsale, Co Cork
Tel: 021 778444

Accommodation, Food and Drink

Reference numbers below refer to detailed
information provided in section 2

Accommodation

Ashlee Lodge, Tower, Blarney, Co Cork

Tel: 021 385346 Fax: 021 385726 A Mediterranean-style bungalow set in prize-winning landscaped. Six bedrooms. Good breakfast menu. Packed lunches on request. 167

Birch Hill House, Grenagh, Blarney, Co Cork

Tel: 021 886106 A grand and imposing grey-painted farmhouse, part of a working dairy and beef farm B&B Accommodation is in six rooms. Overlooks the River Martin, where trout fishing is available. 174

Bohernamona House, Courtbrack, Blarney, Co Cork

Tel: 021 385181 Fax: 021 382443 The welcome is warm and the beds comfortable in this strikingly designed modern. There are five letting bedrooms, large gardens and plenty of parking space. 179

Coolim, Tower, Blarney, Co Cork

Tel: 021 382848 A large modern house with Scandinavian look - lots of pin. The three bedrooms all have en suite facilities. Breakfast is served with home-made bread and pancakes. 158

Hillview House, Killard, Blarney, Co Cork

Tel: 021 385161 An attractive house with lots of character and a setting of peaceful, colourful gardens and grounds. 4 bedrooms, sun lounge and large private car park. Help with itineraries and warm hospitality. 172

Maranatha Country House, Tower, Blarney, Co Cork

Tel/Fax: 021 385102 Outstanding Accommodation in a distinguished 1880's Victorian home nestled in 27 acres of lawns and gardens. The six en suite bedrooms are nothing short of stunning. 177

Phelans Woodview House, Blarney, Co Cork

Tel: 021 385197 The restaurant has a full drinks licence for diners and guests. Accommodation comprises 8 bedrooms, all en suite, with tvs. Private car park. 154

Westfield House, Ballincollig, Co Cork

Tel: 021 871824 Fax: 021 877415 A large detached villa, built in 1974, standing by the N22. Four double rooms, three en suite. Tv. Parking. 152

Food and Drink

Blairs Inn, Cloghroe, Blarney, Co Cork

Tel: 021 381470 A typical Irish country pub in a secluded riverside position. The cuisine puts an Irish twist on international dishes. The fish is freshly landed at Dingle and Kenmare and terrific Irish stew. 159

Eco Douglas, Douglas, Co Cork

Tel: 021 892522 Fax: 021 895354 web: eCoie Highclass 80-cover restaurant with full drinks licence. Excellent choice of dishes of world-wide influence, ditto wine list. 166

Ibis Hotel, Dunkettle, Co Cork

Tel: 021 354354 Fax: 021 354202 100 en suite bedrooms in a well-equipped up-to-the-minute chain hotel at the Lee Tunnel roundabout. Full restaurant; lounge bar. 175

Phelans Woodview House, Blarney, Co Cork

Tel: 021 385197 The restaurant has a full drinks licence for diners and guests. Accommodation comprises 8 bedrooms, all en suite, with tvs. Private car park. 154

Built on a 216-acre promontory, jutting out into the Atlantic, the Old Head of Kinsale was opened in the summer of 1997. With stunning views, taking in 300 feet of rugged rock-face, its awe-inspiring setting makes it arguably the most dramatic golf course in the world.

Overhead, wonderfully noisy birds outdo each other in spectacular flight. Cormorants, guillemots and peregrine falcons, the varieties would test even the most knowledgeable birdwatcher as they swoop along the cliff-face before disappearing into one of the caves, only to reappear on the opposite side of the Head.

The site of 150 acres is of parkland texture. And the fact that as many as nine of the holes are by the sea, reflects the challenge which the location presented to the four designers - Ron Kirby, Patrick Merrigan, Joe Carr and Eddie Hackett - who had an input into the par-72 lay-out of 6,652 yards.

As many as 41 different routings were attempted, before being satisfied they had got it right. The upshot is that six holes, from the second to the short seventh, are sited to the left of the access road to the lighthouse, while the remaining 12 and the practice ground occupy the space to the right.

Prior to the 1999 British Open, it had six distinguished visitors - Tiger Woods, David Duval, Mark O'Meara, Lee Janzen, Stuart Appleby and the late Payne Stewart - who enjoyed the challenge enormously. But the Old Head promises a fascinating experience for golfers of all standards.

Sec/Manager:	J O'Brien
Professional:	D Murray
Directions:	From Kinsale follow the R600 and R604 to Old Head then signposted to Course
Type of Course:	Links
Date Founded:	1997
No of Holes:	18
Length:	6700 yds (6126 mtrs)
Par:	72
SSS:	73
Green Fees:	£120
Visitors:	Welcome: Book in Advance
Societies:	Welcome: Book in Advance, Special rates for groups over 24
Facilities:	Chipping/Putting Area, Practice Area, Driving Range, Golf Clubs for hire, Trolley Hire, Electric Buggy Hire, Bar, Restaurant

Accommodation, Food and Drink

Reference numbers below refer to detailed information provided in section 2

Accommodation

An Garrán Coír, Castlefreke, Clonakilty, Co Cork
Tel: 023 48236 Comfortable Bed & Breakfast Accommodation in lovely relaxing surroundings. Great views. Great breakfasts. 187

An Súgán, Clonakilty, Co Cork
Tel: 023 33498 100-cover pub-restaurant specialising in seafood. B&B in adjacent Strand House, also self-catering cottages. 170

Quayside House, Kinsale, Co Cork
Tel: 021 772188 Fax: 021 772664 Family-run B&B guest house by the harbour, with well-equipped en suite bedrooms. Gourmet restaurants nearby. 164

Rosalithir, Rosscarbery, Co Cork
Tel: 023 48136 Bed and Breakfast Accommodation in four very spacious en suite bungalow rooms. Self-catering available next door. 184

Food and Drink

An Súgán, Clonakilty, Co Cork
Tel: 023 33498 100-cover pub-restaurant specialising in seafood. B&B in adjacent Strand House, also self-catering cottages. 170

Bernard's Bar, Skibbereen, Co Cork
Tel: Bar and restaurant in the middle of town - the only licensed premises in Skibbereen. Day-long food service. 162

De Barra, Clonakilty, Co Cork
Tel: 023 33381 A cheerful pub with its own folk club and traditional Irish music. 149

Skibbereen & West Carbery

Skibbereen & West Carbery, Licknavar, Skibbereen, Co Cork

Tel: 028 21227

Sec/Manager:	Shannon Silvernale
Professional:	None
Directions:	2 miles South West of Skibbereen off the R595 to Baltimore
Type of Course:	Parkland
Date Founded:	1935

No of Holes:	18
Length:	5773 yds (5279 mtrs)
Par:	71
SSS:	69
Green Fees:	Weekdays: £18 Weekends & Bank Holidays: £20
Visitors:	Welcome: Advance Booking Required
Societies:	Welcome: Contact Club in Advance
Facilities:	Chipping/Putting Area, Practice Area, Golf Clubs for hire, Trolley hire, Electric Buggy hire, Bar, Restaurant, Caddy service by arrangement

Accommodation, Food and Drink

Reference numbers below refer to detailed information provided in section 2

Accommodation

An Garrán Coír, Castlefreke, Clonakilty, Co Cork
Tel: 023 48236 Comfortable Bed & Breakfast Accommodation in lovely relaxing surroundings. Great views. Great breakfasts. 187

An Súgán, Clonakilty, Co Cork
Tel: 023 33498 100-cover pub-restaurant specialising in seafood. B&B in adjacent Strand House, also self-catering cottages. 170

Cooligreenane House, Inchigeela, Co Cork
Tel: 026 49344 At scenically set Cooligreenane House there are three bedrooms, farmhouse breakfasts and private access to coarse fishing. Rose Cottage and Tigh Mhuire offer self catering. 163

Little Acre, Skibbereen, Co Cork
Tel/Fax: 028 22528 Bed and Breakfast Accommodation in a handsome detached house on the N71. Easy walk to town. 183

Rosalithir Farm Cottage, Rosscarbery, Co Cork
Tel: 023 48136 Self-catering Accommodation in a renovated farmhouse in a private garden on a working farm. B&B next door. 185

Rosalithir, Rosscarbery, Co Cork
Tel: 023 48136 Bed and Breakfast Accommodation in four very spacious en suite bungalow rooms. Self-catering available next door. 184

Springfield House, Rathbarry, Clonakilty, Co Cork
Tel/Fax: 023 40622 Select farmhouse Bed and Breakfast Accommodation. Rooms en suite. Home cooking a speciality. Self-catering also available. 181

Food and Drink

An Súgán, Clonakilty, Co Cork
Tel: 023 33498 100-cover pub-restaurant specialising in seafood. B&B in adjacent Strand House, also self-catering cottages. 170

Bernard's Bar, Skibbereen, Co Cork
Tel: 028 21772 Bar and restaurant in the middle of town - the only licensed premises in Skibbereen. Day-long food service. 162

De Barra, Clonakilty, Co Cork
Tel: 023 33381 A cheerful pub with its own folk club and traditional Irish music. 149

Youghal

Youghal Golf Club, Knockavery, Youghal, Co Cork

Tel: 024 92787

Sec/Manager:	Margaret O'Sullivan
Professional:	Liam Burns
Directions:	Overlooking Youghal to the West of the town centre
Type of Course:	Meadowland
Date Founded:	1898

No of Holes:	18
Length:	6174 yds (5646 mtrs)
Par:	70
SSS:	69
Green Fees:	Weekdays: £18 Weekends: £20
Visitors:	Welcome: Any Day except Wednesday
Societies:	Welcome: Prebooking essential
Facilities:	Chipping/Putting Area, Golf Clubs for hire, Trolley hire, Electric Buggy hire, Bar, Restaurant, Caddy service by arrangement

Accommodation, Food and Drink

Reference numbers below refer to detailed
information provided in section 2

Accommodation

Carn-na-Radharc, Youghal, Co Cork

Tel: 024 92703 Four B&B bedrooms, 2 en suite. Private car park. Tea/coffee on
arrival. Quiet setting, great views.   168

Roseville, Youghal, Co Cork

Tel: 024 92571 Bed & Breakfast in a distinctive late 18th-century house on the N25.
4 double rooms and a twin. Very friendly.   142

Spanish Point, Ballycotton, Co Cork

Tel: 021 646177 Fax: 021 646179 Speciality seafood restaurant with well-equipped
en suite bedrooms in a dramatic clifftop setting. Own beach. Sea fishing.   178

Walter Raleigh Hotel, Youghal, Co Cork

Tel: 024 92011/92314 Fax: 024 93560 40 rooms, including 15 Executives, all en
suite, on the seafront. Victorian elegance, space, full menus.   180

Food and Drink

Coakley's Bar, Youghal, Co Cork

Tel: 024 93161 Liam Coakley's convivial pub in an 1820s building in the centre of
town. Good cheer and good drinking.   169

Spanish Point, Ballycotton, Co Cork

Tel: 021 646177 Fax: 021 646179 Speciality seafood restaurant with well-equipped
en suite bedrooms in a dramatic clifftop setting. Own beach. Sea fishing.   178

The Old Thatch, Killeagh, Co Cork

Tel: 024 95116/95108 A remarkable long, low thatched pub in the same family for
300& years. Bags of history and character. Food served 12-8.30.   146

Walter Raleigh Hotel, Youghal, Co Cork

Tel: 024 92011/92314 Fax: 024 93560 40 rooms, including 15 Executives, all en
suite, on the seafront. Victorian elegance, space, full menus.   180

DONEGAL

Experts estimate that there are only 150 high-quality links courses in the world, of which 39 are to be found in Ireland. By this they mean pure links, not the American idea of such terrain as characterised by Pebble Beach, which would more accurately be described as parkland by the sea. Of the 39 Irish links, the greatest number happen to be in County Donegal. It can boast no fewer than eight - Ballyliffin, Murvagh, Dunfanaghy, Greencastle, Narin and Portnoo, North West, Portsalon and Rosapenna - which, as it happens, is 47 per cent of the county's population of 17 courses. Those 17 are: Ballybofey and Stranorlar, Ballyliffin, Buncrana, Bundoran, Cloughaneely, Cruit Island, Donegal (Murvagh), Dunfanaghy, Gweedore, Greencastle, Letterkenny, Narin and Portnoo, North West, Otway, Portsalon, Redcastle and Rosapenna. So, if the tourist wishes to experience the greatest variety of links terrain in a single county in Ireland, Donegal is the place to go.

In an effort at creating a greater awareness of this fact, Bord Failte brought the Irish Women's Open to the Glashedy Links at Ballyliffin in 1998 when, sadly, it had to be curtailed to 54-holes because of adverse weather. Interestingly, the championship went from there to the parkland terrain of Letterkenny for its 1999 staging. As things turned out, it resulted in a splendid triumph for the French player Sandrine Mendiburu, who won a four-way play-off with Laura Davies, Spain's Raquel Carriedo and Germany's Elisabeth Esterl. The course, which was designed on a shoestring budget by Eddie Hackett, is notable for not having any sand bunkers, but its main attraction lies in its location.

Mount Errigal, Co Donegal

Situated where the Swilly River opens out into the formidable Lough of that name, Letterkenny can provide an ideal base from which to play the courses of north Donegal. And when the Women's Open came to a splendid conclusion, one club official summed up the feelings of all concerned when he said: "The challenge was thrown down to us and we delivered. That's something to be proud of." Indeed it was a formidable challenge for a modest club. Apart from a major upgrading of their course, they had to find £75,000 as their contribution to the tournament fund. In the meantime, they set themselves a five-year plan of course development under the guidance of agronomist Eddie Connaughton. It is envisaged that drainage problems on the lower 11 holes will be solved by a lake between the fourth and sixth holes.

While in Letterkenny, there is the opportunity of visiting the County Museum which is located in a fine, old building, once part of the local workhouse. It contains a fascinating display of artefacts from the stone age to the medieval period and from the recent history and folk life of the county. Outside the town is the Colmcille Heritage Centre which celebrates the life and times of the saint with lavish displays of illuminated manuscripts. Perhaps it is the impact of their majestic environment, but whatever the reason, the locals like to think of things on a grand scale. So the tourist is recommended to go to the far north of the county, find a wild headland - of which there are many - and then look out at 3,000 miles of wild Atlantic.

As it happens, Donegal is undoubtedly one of Ireland's most beautiful counties. Ruggedly traversed with a pattern of mountains, moors and inland waters, its long and much-indented coastline has been carved into intricate patterns by the ravages of the ocean. It is a striking landscape which remains relatively unaffected by the passage of time. And the people, while renowned for their husbandry, are also famous for their warmth and hospitality. In the recent past, the county was considered somewhat remote for serious golf tourism, but the development of airports at Derry and Sligo has changed the picture dramatically. And few can deny the unique appeal of the Innishowen Peninsula, with the glorious links terrain of North West (near Buncrana), Ballyliffin and Greencastle.

Buncrana is the principal town on the peninsula, boasting three miles of sandy beach and a delightful, traditional golfing challenge. The name of the town is derived from the Gaelic meaning "Foot of the River" and one of its delights is

Silver Strand, Co Donegal

a walk under beech, maple and lime trees beside the brown waters of the River Crana. By the six-arched bridge is the square keep of the 15th century Buncrana Castle, where the Irish patriot, Wolfe Tone (1763-1798) was brought after his capture in 1798. Meanwhile, the Crana River is noted for its salmon and it adorns Swan Park, a haven of peace for the stroller.

Then, on the western side of Lough Swilly, one can savour the delights of Portsalon, Rosapenna and Dunfanaghy. While at Dunfanaghy, the tourist is recommended to make the scenic drive around Horn Head and visit McSwiney's Gun, a natural blow-hole which can create the effect of a loud explosion when the tide rushes in at certain times. Outside the town is the Dunfanaghy Workhouse, where the Great Famine is remembered. Dunfanaghy is also a major centre for brown trout anglers. And as a special bonus, it is reputed to be the only place in Ireland where the corncrake can be heard in its natural habitat.

Narin and Portnoo is on the extreme west coast while the remaining links, Murvagh is further south. Indeed Bundoran could also qualify as a links, though a number of its holes are parkland in texture. On making the journey to Narin and Portnoo, the golfer passes through the Gaelic-speaking area of the county and the charming village of Glenties, which gets its name from Na Gleanta, the Gaelic for glens. Not surprisingly, Glenties lies at the point of two

Glecolumbkille Folk Village, Co Donegal

glens as they converge into a wide valley. Two rivers also meet at this point and the generous, surrounding trees create the image of an oasis. Glenties has retained much of its 19th century character, as is evidenced in the late Georgian courthouse and nearby market house. North of the village, the Fintown Railway promises what the eminent playwright Brian Friel describes as: "a unique journey along the shore of a lake as grand as any in Switzerland or in Minnesota."

In the south of the county, venerable locals will recall days in the early 1950s when they saw Christy O'Connor Snr hit shots on the strand at Bundoran, honing skills that would later conquer Europe. Though it is relatively short by modern standards, the course at Bundoran remains a delightful challenge, with the middle holes from the seventh to the 12th, playing alongside the Atlantic coast. Locals claim their town is an ideal seaside resort with something for everyone. Indeed it is a popular centre for brown trout and salmon anglers, for surfers and swimmers and for those with a taste for lively evenings.

The essence of Donegal is looking down a mighty glen from the top of a corkscrew hill and feeling almost dizzy as the landscape plunges away. It is marvelling at a solitary sheep negotiating a seemingly impossible slope, or rounding a corner of a country lane and suddenly seeing stunning headlands thrust into the ocean. And it is about links golf, unrivalled in its variety.

Location of Golf Courses

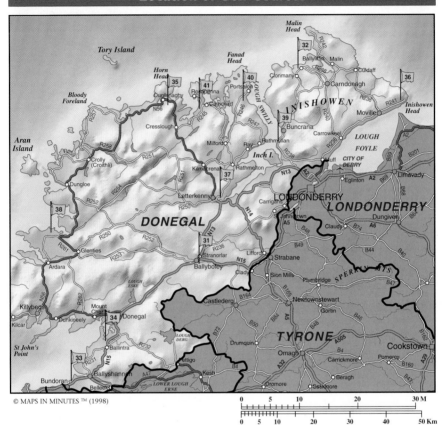

© MAPS IN MINUTES ™ (1998)

Ballybofey & Stranorlar

Ballybofey & Stranorlar, The Glebe,
Stranorlar, Co Donegal
Tel: 074 31093

Sec/Manager:	Alex Harkin
Professional:	None
Directions:	Between Ballbofey and Stranorlar off the N13 to Donegal
Type of Course:	Parkland
Date Founded:	1958
No of Holes:	18
Length:	5903 yds (5399 mtrs)
Par:	68
SSS:	68
Green Fees:	£15 Weekdays £18 Weekends
Visitors:	Welcome: Except Monday (Ladies Day)
Societies:	Welcome: Weekdays, Prior booking at weekends
Facilities:	Chipping/Putting Area, Practice Area, Golf Clubs for hire, Trolley hire, Bar, Restaurant

Accommodation, Food and Drink

Reference numbers below refer to detailed
information provided in section 2

Accommodation

Beechwood House, Londonderry, Co Londonderry
Tel: 028 7126 4900 A block of stables has been converted into self-contained self-catering Accommodation in five chalets which together can sleep 20 in comfort. Everything is provided for families and groups. 921

Dirgefield House, Ballybofey, Co Donegal
Tel: 074 32775 Six en suite Bed & Breakfast rooms in a beautiful house on the main road half a mile from the centre of Ballybofey. 200

Fir Trees Hotel, Strabane, Co Tyrone
Tel: 028 7138 2382 A bright, practical modern complex on the outskirts of town, with 25 well-equipped en suite bedrooms, a restaurant and bar-bistro. 895

The Coast Road Guest House, Mount Charles, Co Donegal
Tel: 073 35018 Two double (1 en suite), 1 twin (en suite), 1 single. Tv and tea/Coffee making facilities. Central heating. Packed lunches on request.

Food and Drink

Badger's, Londonderry, Co Londonderry
Tel/Fax: 028 7136 0763 Three floors of bars and restaurant. Lunchtime specials and the Sunday carvery are particularly popular. 920

Fir Trees Hotel, Strabane, Co Tyrone
Tel: 028 7138 2382 A bright, practical modern complex on the outskirts of town, with 25 well-equipped en suite bedrooms, a restaurant and bar-bistro. 895

The Harbour Restaurant, Donegal, Co Donegal
Tel: 073 21703 Fax: 073 22697 Family-owned-and-run restaurant with views of the quays. Seafood and steaks among the specialities. 201

Ballyliffen

Ballyliffin Golf Club (Old Links Course),
Clonmany, Inishown, Co Donegal
Tel: 077 76119

On visiting the Ballyliffin Old Links in 1993, Nick Faldo described it as the most natural course he had ever played. We are informed it was a glorious June day, when seals basked off Glashedy

Rock and the sea off Pollan Strand was as blue as the Bay of Naples.

Two years later came the opening of the neighbouring Glashedy Links, designed by Pat Ruddy and Tom Craddock. Taking its name from the Glashedy Rock offshore, it completes a complex of 365 acres which, as it happens, is the same area as Augusta National.

But the terrain could hardly be more contrasting. Ballyliffin is characterised by spectacular duneland, bordered on one side by the North

Atlantic and inland by picturesque hills and mountains. Located on the majestic Inishowen Peninsula, the viability of the golf development has been greatly enhanced from a tourist standpoint by its proximity to Derry Airport.

In the event, for a £1 million (pound) investment, the club were presented with a links built on a truly heroic scale. The designers' challenge was to extract a worthy layout from a truly magnificent area of wild duneland and their success was endorsed by competitors such as Laura Davies discovered when the 1998 Irish Women's Open was played there.

As the Nobel Prize winning MP from neighbouring Derry, John Hume, acknowledged: "I suspect many players may find it hard to tear themselves away from Ballyliffin ..... after all, there are now 36 very special reasons for staying." Just so.

Sec/Manager:	Cecil Doherty
Professional:	None
Directions:	Six miles from Cardonagh on the R238

Old Course

Type of Course:	Links
Date Founded:	1947
No of Holes:	18
Length:	6612 yds (6046 mtrs)
Par:	71
SSS:	72
Green Fees:	Weekdays: £21 Weekends & Bank Holidays: £ 24

Glashedy

Type of Course:	Links
Date Founded:	1995
No of Holes:	18
Length:	6466 yds (5912 mtrs)
Par:	72
SSS:	71
Green Fees:	Weekdays: £30 Weekends & Bank Holidays: £ 35

Visitors:	Welcome: Phone to check availability
Societies:	Welcome: Prebooking required
Facilities:	Chipping/Putting Area, Practice Area, Driving Range, Golf Clubs for hire, Trolley hire, Electric Buggy hire, Bar, Restaurant, Caddy service by arrangement

Accommodation, Food and Drink

Reference numbers below refer to detailed information provided in section 2

Accommodation

Banks of the Faughan Motel, Campsie, Co Londonderry
Tel/Fax: 028 7186 0242 Twelve bedrooms, seven with en suite. City of Derry Airport is a very short drive away, and there are several golf and leisure centres nearby. Groups of up to 25 can be accommodated. 918

Beechwood House, Londonderry, Co Londonderry
Tel: 028 7126 4900 A block of stables has been converted into self-contained self-catering Accommodation in five chalets which together can sleep 20 in comfort. Everything is provided for families and groups. 921

The Inn at the Cross, Londonderry, Co Londonderry
Tel: 028 71301 480 Fax: 02871 301940 Views over the countryside to the Faughan river valley. Bedrooms are all en suite. Varied menus, with both à la carte and table d'hote options, in the Fireside Restaurant; less formal eating in Sally Elliot's Bar. 919

The Strand Hotel, Ballyliffin, Inishowen, Co Donegal
Tel: 077 76107 Fax: 077 76486 A friendly, well-run hotel located beside two of Ireland's leading golf courses. Midweek and weekend golf breaks a speciality. 204

Food and Drink

Badger's, Londonderry, Co Londonderry
Tel/Fax: 028 7136 0763 Three floors of bars and restaurant. Lunchtime specials and the Sunday carvery are particularly popular. 920

The Inn at the Cross, Londonderry, Co Londonderry
Tel: 028 7130 1480 Fax: 028 7130 1394 Views over the countryside to the Faughan river valley. Bedrooms are all en suite. Varied menus, with both à la carte and table d'hote options, in the Fireside Restaurant; less formal eating in Sally Elliot's Bar. 919

The Strand Hotel, Ballyliffin, Inishowen, Co Donegal
Tel: 077 76107 Fax: 077 76486 A friendly, well-run hotel located beside two of Ireland's leading golf courses. Midweek and weekend golf breaks a speciality. 204

Bundoran

Bundoran Golf Club, Bundoran, Co Donegal
Tel: 072 41302

Sec/Manager:	John McGagh
Professional:	David Robinson
Directions:	25 miles North of Sligo off the N15 coast road.

Type of Course:	Links
Date Founded:	1894
No of Holes:	18
Length:	6123 yds (5599 mtrs)
Par:	70
SSS:	70
Green Fees:	Weekdays: £18 Weekends & Bank Holidays: £22
Visitors:	Welcome: Any Day except Sunday
Societies:	Welcome: Pre-booking required
Facilities:	Chipping/Putting Area, Practice Area, Golf Clubs for hire, Trolley hire, Electric Buggy hire, Bar, Caddy service by arrangement, Hotel/ Accommodation on site

Accommodation, Food and Drink

Reference numbers below refer to detailed information provided in section 2

Accommodation

Atlantic View House, Bundoran, Co Donegal
Tel: 072 41403 Bed & Breakfast Accommodation in a two-storey town house with ocean views. Owners are keen golfers. 203

Glenview B&B, Strandhill Road, Sligo, Co Sligo
Tel: 071 70401/62457 Modern Bed & Breakfast establishment a mile from Sligo town. Four en suite bedrooms with tv and central heating. 512

Hotel Carlton, Belleek, Co Fermanagh
Tel: 028 6865 8282 19 en suite bedrooms in a handsomely renovated hotel in the centre of a pottery town on the banks of Lough Erne. 874

Moohans Fiddlestone, Belleek, Co Fermanagh
Tel: 028 6865 8008 Traditional pub and licensed guesthouse in the centre of town.
Five en suite bedrooms with tv. Bar with snacks. 876

Portnason House, Ballyshannon, Co Donegal
Tel : 072 52016 Fax: 072 31739 A Georgian house of real character, set in extensive
grounds and offering B&B Accommodation in 10 spacious en suite bedrooms. 202

The Coast Road Guest House, Mount Charles, Co Donegal
Tel: 073 35018 Two double (1 en suite), 1 twin (en suite), 1 single. Tv and tea/
Coffee making facilities. Central heating. Packed lunches on request.

The Railway Hotel, Enniskillen, Co Fermanagh
Tel: 028 6632 2084 19 individually appointed bedrooms in a carefully renovated
Victorian hotel on the Omagh road just away from the centre. 875

Food and Drink

Hotel Carlton, Belleek, Co Fermanagh
Tel: 028 6865 8282 19 en suite bedrooms in a handsomely renovated hotel in the
centre of a pottery town on the banks of Lough Erne. 874

Moohans Fiddlestone, Belleek, Co Fermanagh
Tel: 028 686 58008 Traditional pub and licensed guesthouse in the centre of town.
Five en suite bedrooms with tv. Bar with snacks. 876

The Harbour Restaurant, Donegal, Co Donegal
Tel: 073 21703 Fax: 073 22697 Family-owned-and-run restaurant with views of the
quays. Seafood and steaks among the specialities. 201

The Railway Hotel, Enniskillen, Co Fermanagh
Tel: 028 6632 2084 19 individually appointed bedrooms in a carefully renovated
Victorian hotel on the Omagh road just away from the centre. 875

Donegal (Murvagh)

**Donegal Golf Club, Murvagh, Laghey,
Ballintra, Co Donegal**

Tel: 073 34054

After completing the design of Waterville and
Connemara, Eddie Hackett embarked on his
third links project. And it was to be on a simi-
larly grand scale, on a promontary in Donegal
Bay, overlooked by the picturesque town of
Mountcharles.

The links at Murvagh, stretches to a formidable 7,213 yards off the back tees and can become
a fearsome challenge when the wind rises. So it
was small wonder that when the Irish Women's
Closed went there in 1979, big-hitting Mary
McKenna captured the title.

Isolated from the rest of the mainland by a
thick belt of woodland, the site is spectacular by
any standards. But as the designer recalled with
crushing simplicity: "The greens are on natural
sites: only the levels of some were adjusted by

hand. All I had to do was to develop the course
on what nature provided."

Hackett was especially pleased with the short
fifth, which measures 191 yards off the back tee.
The plateau green has Donegal Bay as a backdrop and with disaster beckoning on all sides,
some members argued that it was too severe. But
Hackett got his way.

Donegal GC was founded in 1960 as a modest nine-hole establishment on lands donated
by the Temple family, close to the town at
Tullyscullion. But the prospect of a move to
Murvagh, albeit four miles further away, was too
good to pass up. So Hackett was given yet another opportunity to flex his muscles, as he had
done at Waterville. And the outcome is stunning.

Sec/Manager:	John McBride
Professional:	Leslie Robinson
Directions:	6 miles South of Donegal on the N15
Type of Course:	Links
Date Founded:	1960
No of Holes:	18
Length:	6827 yds (6243 mtrs)
Par:	73
SSS:	73
Green Fees:	Monday - Thursday: £25 Friday - Sunday & Bank Hols: £30
Visitors:	Welcome: Any Day except Monday, Restrictions at weekends
Societies:	Welcome: Prebooking required
Facilities:	Chipping/Putting Area, Practice Area, Golf Clubs for hire, Trolley hire, Electric Buggy hire, Bar, Restaurant

Accommodation, Food and Drink

Reference numbers below refer to detailed
information provided in section 2

Accommodation

Atlantic View House, Bundoran, Co Donegal
Tel: 072 41403 Bed & Breakfast Accommodation in a two-storey town house with
ocean views. Owners are keen golfers. 203

Dirgefield House, Ballybofey, Co Donegal
Tel: 074 32775 Six en suite Bed & Breakfast rooms in a beautiful house on the
main road half a mile from the centre of Ballybofey. 200

Portnason House, Ballyshannon, Co Donegal
Tel : 072 52016 Fax: 072 31739 A Georgian house of real character, set in extensive
grounds and offering B&B Accommodation in 10 spacious en suite bedrooms. 202

The Coast Road Guest House, Mount Charles, Co Donegal
Tel: 073 35018 Two double (1 en suite), 1 twin (en suite), 1 single. Tv and tea/
Coffee making facilities. Central heating. Packed lunches on request.

Food and Drink

Hotel Carlton, Belleek, Co Fermanagh
Tel: 028 6865 8282 19 en suite bedrooms in a handsomely renovated hotel in the
centre of a pottery town on the banks of Lough Erne. 874

Moohans Fiddlestone, Belleek, Co Fermanagh
Tel: 028 6865 8008 Traditional pub and licensed guesthouse in the centre of town.
Five en suite bedrooms with tv. Bar with snacks. 876

The Harbour Restaurant, Donegal, Co Donegal
Tel: 073 21703 Fax: 073 22697 Family-owned-and-run restaurant with views of the
quays. Seafood and steaks among the specialities. 201

Dunfanaghy

Dunfanaghy Golf Club, Kill, Dunfanaghy, Donegal

Tel: 074 36335

Sec/Manager:	Hanette Moffitt
Professional:	None
Directions:	1 mile South East of Dunfanaghy off the N56 to Lettterkenny
Type of Course:	Links
Date Founded:	1906
No of Holes:	18
Length:	5540 yds (5066 mtrs)
Par:	68
SSS:	66
Green Fees:	Weekdays: £14 Weekends & Bank Holidays: £17
Visitors:	Welcome: Book in Advance
Societies:	Welcome: Prebooking required
Facilities:	Chipping/Putting Area, Golf Clubs for hire, Trolley hire, Electric Buggy hire, Bar, Caddy service by arrangement

Accommodation, Food and Drink

Reference numbers below refer to detailed information provided in section 2

Accommodation

Coastguard Holiday Cottages, Downings, Co Donegal
Tel: 074 25660/25666 Fax: 074 24788 Three-bedroomed self-catering cottages in a magnificent setting of beaches, coves and mountains. Great views, great walking. 206

Mevagh House, Carrigart, Co Donegal
Tel: 074 55693/55512 En suite rooms with tv in a Bed and Breakfast on the B245 five minutes walk from the town. 205

The Inn at the Cross, Londonderry, Co Londonderry
Tel: 028 7130 1480 Fax: 028 7130 1394 Views over the countryside to the Faughan river valley. Bedrooms are all en suite. Varied menus, with both à la carte and table d'hote options, in the Fireside Restaurant; less formal eating in Sally Elliot's Bar. 919

The Strand Hotel, Ballyliffin, Inishowen, Co Donegal
Tel: 077 76107 Fax: 077 76486 A friendly, well-run hotel located beside two of Ireland's leading golf courses. Midweek and weekend golf breaks a speciality. 204

Food and Drink

Badger's, Londonderry, Co Londonderry
Tel/Fax: 028 7136 0763 Three floors of bars and restaurant. Lunchtime specials and the Sunday carvery are particularly popular. 920

The Inn at the Cross, Londonderry, Co Londonderry
Tel: 028 7130 1480 Fax: 028 7130 1394 Views over the countryside to the Faughan river valley. Bedrooms are all en suite. Varied menus, with both à la carte and table d'hote options, in the Fireside Restaurant; less formal eating in Sally Elliot's Bar. 919

The Strand Hotel, Ballyliffin, Inishowen, Co Donegal
Tel: 077 76107 Fax: 077 76486 A friendly, well-run hotel located beside two of Ireland's leading golf courses. Midweek and weekend golf breaks a speciality. 204

Greencastle

Greencastle Golf Club, Greencastle, Inishowen, Co Donegal

Tel: 077 81013

Sec/Manager:	Sam Sterritt
Professional:	None
Directions:	From Londonderry follow A2, then R238 past Corrawheel to Malville. Then follow R241 to Greencastle
Type of Course:	Links
Date Founded:	1892
No of Holes:	18
Length:	5698 yds (5211 mtrs)
Par:	69
SSS:	69
Green Fees:	Weekdays: £12 Weekends & Bank Holidays: £18
Visitors:	Welcome: Phone in Advance to check closure dates
Societies:	Welcome: Prebooking required
Facilities:	Practice Area, Bar, Restaurant, Caddy service by arrangement

Accommodation, Food and Drink

Reference numbers below refer to detailed information provided in section 2

Accommodation

Banks of the Faughan Motel, Campsie, Co Londonderry
Tel/Fax: 028 7186 0242 Twelve bedrooms, seven with en suite. City of Derry Airport is a very short drive away, and there are several golf and leisure centres nearby. Groups of up to 25 can be accommodated. 918

Beechwood House, Londonderry, Co Londonderry
Tel: 028 7126 4900 A block of stables has been converted into self-contained self-catering Accommodation in five chalets which together can sleep 20 in comfort. Everything is provided for families and groups. 921

The Inn at the Cross, Londonderry, Co Londonderry
Tel: 028 7130 1480 Fax: 028 7130 1394 Views over the countryside to the Faughan river valley. Bedrooms are all en suite. Varied menus, with both à la carte and table d'hote options, in the Fireside Restaurant; less formal eating in Sally Elliot's Bar. 919

The Strand Hotel, Ballyliffin, Inishowen, Co Donegal
Tel: 077 76107 Fax: 077 76486 A friendly, well-run hotel located beside two of Ireland's leading golf courses. Midweek and weekend golf breaks a speciality. 204

Food and Drink

Badger's, Londonderry, Co Londonderry
Tel/Fax: 028 7136 0763 Three floors of bars and restaurant. Lunchtime specials and the Sunday carvery are particularly popular. 920

The Inn at the Cross, Londonderry, Co Londonderry
Tel: 028 7130 1480 Fax: 028 7130 1394 Views over the countryside to the Faughan river valley. Bedrooms are all en suite. Varied menus, with both à la carte and table d'hote options, in the Fireside Restaurant; less formal eating in Sally Elliot's Bar. 919

The Strand Hotel, Ballyliffin, Inishowen, Co Donegal
Tel: 077 76107 Fax: 077 76486 A friendly, well-run hotel located beside two of Ireland's leading golf courses. Midweek and weekend golf breaks a speciality. 204

Letterkenny

Letterkenny Golf & Social Club, Barnhill, Letterkenny, County Donegal

Tel: 074 21150

Sec/Manager:	Barry Ramsay
Professional:	None
Directions:	2 miles North of town on Rathmelton Road
Type of Course:	Parkland by riverside
Date Founded:	1913

No of Holes:	18
Length:	6239 yds (5704 mtrs)
Par:	70
SSS:	71
Green Fees:	Weekdays: £15 Weekends: £20
Visitors:	Welcome: Any Day except Tuesday and Wednesday evenings
Societies:	Welcome: Special concessions, Prebooking required
Facilities:	Practice Area, Bar, Restaurant, Caddy service by arrangement

Accommodation, Food and Drink

Reference numbers below refer to detailed information provided in section 2

Accommodation

Coastguard Holiday Cottages, Downings, Co Donegal
Tel: 074 25660/25666 Fax: 074 24788 Three-bedroomed self-catering cottages in a magnificent setting of beaches, coves and mountains. Great views, great walking. 206

Dirgefield House, Ballybofey, Co Donegal
Tel: 074 32775 Six en suite Bed & Breakfast rooms in a beautiful house on the main road half a mile from the centre of Ballybofey. 200

Fir Trees Hotel, Strabane, Co Tyrone
Tel: 028 7138 2382 A bright, practical modern complex on the outskirts of town, with 25 well-equipped en suite bedrooms, a restaurant and bar-bistro. 895

Mevagh House, Carrigart, Co Donegal
Tel: 074 55693/55512 En suite rooms with tv in a Bed and Breakfast on the B245 five minutes walk from the town. 205

The Inn at the Cross, Londonderry, Co Londonderry
Tel: 028 7130 1480 Fax: 028 7130 1394 Views over the countryside to the Faughan river valley. Bedrooms are all en suite. Varied menus, with both à la carte and table d'hote options, in the Fireside Restaurant; less formal eating in Sally Elliot's Bar. 919

Food and Drink

Badger's, Londonderry, Co Londonderry
Tel/Fax: 028 7136 0763 Three floors of bars and restaurant. Lunchtime specials and the Sunday carvery are particularly popular. 920

Fir Trees Hotel, Strabane, Co Tyrone
Tel: 028 7138 2382 A bright, practical modern complex on the outskirts of town, with 25 well-equipped en suite bedrooms, a restaurant and bar-bistro. 895

The Inn at the Cross, Londonderry, Co Londonderry
Tel: 028 7130 1480 Fax: 028 7130 1394 Views over the countryside to the Faughan river valley. Bedrooms are all en suite. Varied menus, with both à la carte and table d'hote options, in the Fireside Restaurant; less formal eating in Sally Elliot's Bar. 919

Narin & Portnoo

Narin & Portnoo Golf Club, Narin, Portnoo, Co Donegal

Tel: 075 45107

Sec/Manager:	Enda Bonner (Secretary) Sean Murphy (Manager)
Professional:	None
Directions:	6 miles North of Ardara off the R261
Type of Course:	Links
Date Founded:	1930
No of Holes:	18
Length:	5820 yds (5322 mtrs)
Par:	69
SSS:	68
Green Fees:	Weekdays: £17 Weekends: £20

Visitors:	Welcome: Booking advisable at weekends
Societies:	Welcome: Contact Club for details
Facilities:	Practice Area, Bar, Restaurant, Caddy service by arrangement

Accommodation, Food and Drink

Reference numbers below refer to detailed information provided in section 2

Accommodation

Coastguard Holiday Cottages, Downings, Co Donegal
Tel: 074 25660/25666 Fax: 074 24788 Three-bedroomed self-catering cottages in a magnificent setting of beaches, coves and mountains. Great views, great walking. 206

Hotel Carlton, Belleek, Co Fermanagh
Tel: 028 8865 8282 19 en suite bedrooms in a handsomely renovated hotel in the centre of a pottery town on the banks of Lough Erne. 874

Mevagh House, Carrigart, Co Donegal
Tel: 074 55693/55512 En suite rooms with tv in a Bed and Breakfast on the B245 five minutes walk from the town. 205

Moohans Fiddlestone, Belleek, Co Fermanagh
Tel: 028 8865 8008 Traditional pub and licensed guesthouse in the centre of town. Five en suite bedrooms with tv. Bar with snacks. 876

The Coast Road Guest House, Mount Charles, Co Donegal
Tel: 073 35018 Two double (1 en suite), 1 twin (en suite), 1 single. Tv and tea/ Coffee making facilities. Central heating. Packed lunches on request.

Food and Drink

Hotel Carlton, Belleek, Co Fermanagh
Tel: 028 8865 8282 19 en suite bedrooms in a handsomely renovated hotel in the centre of a pottery town on the banks of Lough Erne. 874

Moohans Fiddlestone, Belleek, Co Fermanagh
Tel: 028 8865 8008 Traditional pub and licensed guesthouse in the centre of town. Five en suite bedrooms with tv. Bar with snacks. 876

The Harbour Restaurant, Donegal, Co Donegal
Tel: 073 21703 Fax: 073 22697 Family-owned-and-run restaurant with views of the quays. Seafood and steaks among the specialities. 201

North West

North West Golf Club, Lisfannon, Fahan, Co Donegal

Tel: 077 61027

Sec/Manager:	Dudley Coyle
Professional:	Seamus McBriarty
Directions:	1 mile south of Buncrana on the R238 to Londonderry
Type of Course:	Links
Date Founded:	1891
No of Holes:	18
Length:	6239 yds (5704 mtrs)
Par:	70
SSS:	70
Green Fees:	Weekdays: £15 Weekends & Bank Holidays: £20
Visitors:	Welcome: Any Day except Wednesday, Weekend restrictions
Societies:	Welcome: Prebooking required
Facilities:	Chipping/Putting Area, Practice Area, Trolley hire, Bar, Restaurant, plus Beach facilities

Accommodation, Food and Drink

Reference numbers below refer to detailed
information provided in section 2

Accommodation

Banks of the Faughan Motel, Campsie, Co Londonderry

Tel/Fax: 028 7186 0242 Twelve bedrooms, seven with en suite. City of Derry Airport is a very short drive away, and there are several golf and leisure centres nearby. Groups of up to 25 can be accommodated. 918

Beechwood House, Londonderry, Co Londonderry

Tel: 028 7126 4900 A block of stables has been converted into self-contained self-catering Accommodation in five chalets which together can sleep 20 in comfort. Everything is provided for families and groups. 921

The Inn at the Cross, Londonderry, Co Londonderry

Tel: 028 7130 1480 Fax: 028 7130 1394 Views over the countryside to the Faughan river valley. Bedrooms are all en suite. Varied menus, with both à la carte and table d'hote options, in the Fireside Restaurant; less formal eating in Sally Elliot's Bar. 919

The Strand Hotel, Ballyliffin, Inishowen, Co Donegal

Tel: 077 76107 Fax: 077 76486 A friendly, well-run hotel located beside two of Ireland's leading golf courses. Midweek and weekend golf breaks a speciality. 204

Food and Drink

Badger's, Londonderry, Co Londonderry

Tel/Fax: 028 7136 0763 Three floors of bars and restaurant. Lunchtime specials and the Sunday carvery are particularly popular. 920

The Inn at the Cross, Londonderry, Co Londonderry

Tel: 028 7130 1480 Fax: 028 7130 1394 Views over the countryside to the Faughan river valley. Bedrooms are all en suite. Varied menus, with both à la carte and table d'hote options, in the Fireside Restaurant; less formal eating in Sally Elliot's Bar. 919

The Strand Hotel, Ballyliffin, Inishowen, Co Donegal

Tel: 077 76107 Fax: 077 76486 A friendly, well-run hotel located beside two of Ireland's leading golf courses. Midweek and weekend golf breaks a speciality. 204

Portsalon

Portsalon Golf Club, Fanad, Letterkenny, Co Donegal

Tel: 077 61027

Sec/Manager:	Peter Doherty
Professional:	None
Directions:	20 miles North of Letterkenny on the Western shore of Lough Swilly off the R246
Type of Course:	Links
Date Founded:	1891
No of Holes:	18
Length:	5879 yds (5376 mtrs)
Par:	69
SSS:	68
Green Fees:	Weekdays: £18 Weekends & Bank Holidays: £22
Visitors:	Welcome: Ring in advance
Societies:	Welcome: Contact Club for details
Facilities:	Chipping/Putting Area, Trolley hire, Electric Buggy hire, Bar, Restaurant

Accommodation, Food and Drink

Reference numbers below refer to detailed
information provided in section 2

Accommodation

Coastguard Holiday Cottages, Downings, Co Donegal

Tel: 074 25660/25666 Fax: 074 24788 Three-bedroomed self-catering cottages in a

magnificent setting of beaches, coves and mountains. Great views, great walking. 206

Mevagh House, Carrigart, Co Donegal

Tel: 074 55693/55512 En suite rooms with tv in a Bed and Breakfast on the B245 five minutes walk from the town. 205

The Inn at the Cross, Londonderry, Co Londonderry

Tel: 028 7130 1480 Fax: 028 7130 1394 Views over the countryside to the Faughan river valley. Bedrooms are all en suite. Varied menus, with both à la carte and table d'hote options, in the Fireside Restaurant; less formal eating in Sally Elliot's Bar. 919

The Strand Hotel, Ballyliffin, Inishowen, Co Donegal

Tel: 077 76107 Fax: 077 76486 A friendly, well-run hotel located beside two of Ireland's leading golf courses. Midweek and weekend golf breaks a speciality. 204

Food and Drink

Badger's, Londonderry, Co Londonderry

Tel/Fax: 028 7136 0763 Three floors of bars and restaurant. Lunchtime specials and the Sunday carvery are particularly popular. 920

The Inn at the Cross, Londonderry, Co Londonderry

Tel: 028 7130 1480 Fax: 028 7130 1394 Views over the countryside to the Faughan river valley. Bedrooms are all en suite. Varied menus, with both à la carte and table d'hote options, in the Fireside Restaurant; less formal eating in Sally Elliot's Bar. 919

The Strand Hotel, Ballyliffin, Inishowen, Co Donegal

Tel: 077 76107 Fax: 077 76486 A friendly, well-run hotel located beside two of Ireland's leading golf courses. Midweek and weekend golf breaks a speciality. 204

Rosapenna

Rosapenna Golf Club, Downings, Co Donegal

Tel: 074 55301

One can just imagine the excitement of Old Tom Morris on discovering the site of what was to become the Rosapenna links. We are informed that having been employed by Lord Leitrim to lay out a nine-hole course "in the neighbourhood of the Manor House" he was struck by the beauty of the scenery closeby.

"The Sportsmans Holiday Guide" of 1897, reported that "with his prophetic instinct, he predicted before long the redcoats would be seen driving the gutta over its fine slopes." As it happened, Morris did, in fact, lay out a course there.

So it was that the Rosapenna GC was formed in 1895 in a sheltered site on the Rossgull Peninsula, midway between Mulroy and Sheephaven Bays and in the shadow of spectacularly rugged mountains. In 1906, Harry Vardon suggested some new holes "to compensate for the new, rubber-core ball." Then came James Braid, with further modifications.

In 1990, the present owners, Frank and Hilary Casey, commissioned Eddie Hackett to build

eight new holes which might ultimately be integrated with the so-called Valley 10. Meanwhile, the old wooden hotel, built in the Norwegian style, burned to the ground in 1962 and has since been replaced by a modern structure to which an indoor leisure facility was added recently.

In an overall site of 800 acres, Rosapenna currently have 26 holes in play. But a full, second 18, laid out in magnificent duneland by Pat Ruddy and incorporating the Hackett holes, is due to be officially opened in 2001.

Sec/Manager:	Frank Casey
Professional:	None
Directions:	2 miles West of Carrickart off the R245; 25 miles North of Letterkenny
Type of Course:	Links
Date Founded:	1895
No of Holes:	18
Length:	6254 yds (5719 mtrs)
Par:	70
SSS:	71
Green Fees:	Weekdays; £22 Weekends & Bank Holidays: £27
Visitors:	Welcome: Contact in Advance
Societies:	Welcome: Book in Advance
Facilities:	Chipping/Putting Area, Driving Range, Trolley hire, Electric Buggy hire, Bar, Restaurant, plus 4 Star Hotel & Facilities

Accommodation, Food and Drink

Reference numbers below refer to detailed
information provided in section 2

Accommodation

Coastguard Holiday Cottages, Downings, Co Donegal
Tel: 074 25660/25666 Fax: 074 24788 Three-bedroomed self-catering cottages in a magnificent setting of beaches, coves and mountains. Great views, great walking. 206

Mevagh House, Carrigart, Co Donegal
Tel: 074 55693/55512 En suite rooms with tv in a Bed and Breakfast on the B245 five minutes walk from the town. 205

The Inn at the Cross, Londonderry, Co Londonderry
Tel: 028 7130 1480 Fax: 028 7130 1394 Views over the countryside to the Faughan river valley. Bedrooms are all en suite. Varied menus, with both à la carte and table d'hote options, in the Fireside Restaurant; less formal eating in Sally Elliot's Bar. 919

The Strand Hotel, Ballyliffin, Inishowen, Co Donegal
Tel: 077 76107 Fax: 077 76486 A friendly, well-run hotel located beside two of Ireland's leading golf courses. Midweek and weekend golf breaks a speciality. 204

Food and Drink

Badger's, Londonderry, Co Londonderry
Tel/Fax: 028 7136 0763 Three floors of bars and restaurant. Lunchtime specials and the Sunday carvery are particularly popular. 920

The Inn at the Cross, Londonderry, Co Londonderry
Tel: 028 7130 1480 Fax: 028 7130 1394 Views over the countryside to the Faughan river valley. Bedrooms are all en suite. Varied menus, with both à la carte and table d'hote options, in the Fireside Restaurant; less formal eating in Sally Elliot's Bar. 919

The Strand Hotel, Ballyliffin, Inishowen, Co Donegal
Tel: 077 76107 Fax: 077 76486 A friendly, well-run hotel located beside two of Ireland's leading golf courses. Midweek and weekend golf breaks a speciality. 204

DUBLIN

When the Canada Cup was staged at Portmarnock in 1960, Ireland had quite a modest golfing population in 200 clubs, most of which had nine-hole courses. But, as the Golfing Union of Ireland president, Dr Billy O'Sullivan, said at the time: "What we lack in numbers we make up in enthusiasm." In the official programme for the Canada Cup, Pat Ward-Thomas, golf correspondent of the then "Manchester Guardian", wrote: "There are often arguments as to the greatest courses in the home countries, but no one would dispute Portmarnock's right to a place in the first few." He went on: "It may not have the charm of Newcastle, the tailored perfection and superbly precise design of Muirfield, or the ageless sublety of St Andrews - rather is it a bold place for strong men, demanding length and a rare degree of control. Its problems are severe but straightforward; there are no blind shots to the greens and few from the tees; there are no great changes of level and yet there is never unwavering flatness. Many of its holes follow shallow valleys which suggest, but assuredly do not give, protection from the wind."

Were he alive today, Ward-Thomas would hardly credit the dramatic changes that have taken place in golfing life in the Portmarnock area, indeed in Dublin in general, due to the enthusi-

Halfpenny Bridge, Dublin

asm to which Dr O'Sullivan referred. For instance, where the North Dublin village had only the 27 holes of the Portmarnock club at the time of the Canada Cup, it is now within walking distance of no fewer than 72 holes. Eighteen of these are at Portmarnock Links, situated alongside its venerable neighbour, and the remaining 27 are at Beechwood, where Malahide moved in 1991. As a contrast with the other two establishments, Malahide is traditional parkland. And interestingly, the course was designed by Eddie Hackett, the one-time resident professional at Portmarnock. It is a fine venue with a splendidly-appointed clubhouse and an admirably progressive membership.

Officially, there are 19 courses within the boundaries of Dublin City. These are: Carrickmines, Castle, Clontarf, Deer Park, Edmondstown, Elm Green, Elm Park, Foxrock, Grange, Hazel Grove, Howth, Kilmashogue, Milltown, Newlands, Rathfarnham, Royal Dublin, St Anne's, Stackstown and Sutton. But the boundaries of the city are changing almost every year, which means that several other clubs, including Portmarnock, Malahide and the excellent St Margaret's GC, are likely to be added to that list. Anyway, the 31 courses in County Dublin are: Balbriggan, Balcarrick, Ballinascorney, Beaverstown, Beech Park, CityWest, The Open Centre, Corrstown, Donabate, Dublin Mountain, Dun Laoghaire, Forrest Little, Glencullen, Hermitage, Hollywood Lakes, The Island, Killiney, Kilternan, Lucan, Luttrellstown Castle, Malahide, Portmarnock, Rush, St Margaret's, Skerries, Slade Valley, Swords, Turvey, Westmanstown and Woodbrook.

One of the most interesting Dublin establishments is Clontarf GC which holds the unique distinction of being the club located closest to the centre of any capital city in the world.

Founded in 1912, it is, in fact, less than two miles from the centre of Dublin City. Other Dublin clubs will be familiar as the nursery or current home of some of Ireland's most distinguished golfers. For instance, it is impossible to seperate Christy O'Connor Snr from Royal Dublin where, incidentally, there is a special room named in his honour with photographs of his 10 successive Ryder Cup appearances. A similar room at Portmarnock GC honours Harry Bradshaw. And more recently, we have come to associate Grange GC with European Tour player Paul McGinley and Stackstown with Padraig Harrington, both of whom teamed up to capture the World Cup for Ireland at Kiawah Island in 1997.

Meanwhile, the main developments on the south and west sides of the city have been at CityWest and Luttrellstown Castle. CityWest, situated about eight miles out on the N7 to Naas, is a particularly impressive set-up, given that it includes an on-site hotel, a health and leisure centre and a MacGregor Golf Academy, quite apart from a par-70, championship-standard golf course, designed by Christy O'Connor Jnr. England's Alison Nicholas captured the Irish Women's Open there in 1996. Since then, O'Connor has designed a further 18 which is expected to be fully in play in 2001. It will be shorter than the main course, with a par of 65.

This is among a number of pay-and-play facilities in the Dublin area. The north side is admirably served by the 36-hole complex at Deer Park, the 27 holes at Hollystown and the 18-holes at Portmarnock Links and The Open Centre. Then there is the Elmgreen course on the west side at Castleknock. But all of the members' clubs take green-fees, though there are normally restrictions at weekends.

In keeping with the country's booming economy, Dublin is one of the fastest-growing cities in Europe and is proving to be especially popular with weekend visitors from Britain. Like many other European cities, it owes its origins and name to water. The confluence of fresh water from the rivers Liffey, Poddle, Dodder and Tolka and the natural sea harbour, were the genesis of the city. The first indication of a settlement beside the Liffey is in Ptolemy's map of 140 AD, which shows a place called Eblana. Centuries later, it was the flooding of the Liffey which necessitated the building of a ford from boughs and hurdles. This caused it to be named the town of the hurdle ford, Baile Atha Cliath, which remains the Gaelic name for Dublin to this day. The sea facilitiated the arrival of the marauding Vikings in the ninth century. They traded from The Black Pool, an area above the Liffey where Dublin Castle now stands.

Harry Street, Dublin

In Gaelic, this is Duth-Linn which eventually evolved into Dublin. Over 150 years later, the sea brought another foreign power with the arrival of the Normans in 1169, by which stage the city had walls. But the defences were no match for the highly-skilled army of Strongbow, the Earl of Pembroke. Thus was established English control which would last in Dublin for over 700 years.

A reflection of the tremendous investment of recent years is the International Financial Centre on Custom House Quay and the development of Temple Bar, quite apart from the dramatic increase in the number of hotels, many of them reasonably priced and geared for tourism. It is fascinating that as one of the oldest parts of the city, Temple Bar has become the new cultural quarter of Dublin. An exciting renewal scheme has transformed the area into a home for a wide variety of cultural centres, including the Irish Film Centre, the Temple Bar Gallery and Studios, and The Ark, a theatre and arts centre for children. With its 18th century cobbled streets pedestrianised, there is always some exciting activity in Temple Bar, ranging from jazz and rock festivals to street theatre and a public art programme. Indeed Dubliners are now taking fresh pride in a wonderful heritage which gave the world such celebrated writers as Nobel Prize winners, William Butler Yeats and Samuel Beckett, along with Oscar Wilde, James Joyce, Sean O'Casey and Brendan Behan. And there is pride in the modern achievements of film-makers such as Jim Sheridan and Neil Jordan, in the film-acting skills of Gabriel Byrne and in the revival of Irish dancing as exemplified in Riverdance.

And always, there is the Dubliner's wonderfully mischievous sense of humour, often self-deprecating. Like the water-dominated Anna Livia memorial in O'Connell St, known as "The Floozie in the Jacuzzi" and the bronze statue of a buxom Molly Malone with her wheelbarrow of cockles and mussels at the corner of Suffolk St, known as "The Dish with the Fish." In the heart of the city is Trinity College, established in 1591 by Queen Elizabeth I. Jonathan Swift, Bram Stoker, Wilde and Beckett are among the famous writers who studied there, while two of its most famous alumni are commemorated by statues of Edmund Burke and Oliver Goldsmith, which flank the front gate. Then, down O'Connell St, is the General Post Office, which was the scene of the heaviest fighting during the Easter Rising of 1916 when many of the surrounding buildings were destroyed. The GPO itself was extensively rebuilt in the 1920s, after independence, and it is readily identifiable by the three stone figures above the ionic portico, representing Mercury, Hibernia and Fidelity.

Killiney Bay, Co Dublin

There is a wonderful, self-confidence these days about Dubliners and their city, and in the way the old has merged with the new. And the same is true of their golfing facilities. Tourist officials can only hope that impressions are as positive as those which remained with Ward-Thomas after he had travelled over from Britain for the Dunlop Masters at Portmarnock in 1959. Later, in an article for the magazine "Country Life", his closing paragraph served as a beautiful epilogue to a great event. He wrote: "The following morning, Portmarnock was a wilderness of deserted tents and savage rain and I thought of the transience of such things. All the tireless organisation and hard work, the really excellent scoreboards, the capable stewarding, the clamour, the excitement and the heroics, all gone. Then in the twilight, as the aircraft climbed over the city towards the dark sea, there was one last glimpse of that noble links, at peace once more on its lonely peninsula, of the little red clubhouse of Sutton across the estuary, a drive and a brassie from the house of Carr (the golfer Joe Carr), and I knew that these were days which would not be forgotten."

Location of Golf Courses

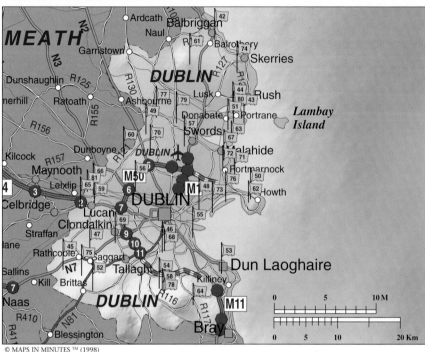

© MAPS IN MINUTES ™ (1998)

Balbriggan

Balbriggan Golf Club, Blackhall, Balbriggan, Co Dublin

Tel: 01 8412229 / 8412173

Sec/Manager:	Michael O'Halloran
Professional:	None
Directions:	1 mile South of Ballbriggan off the N1 Dublin to Belfast road
Type of Course:	Parkland
Date Founded:	1945
No of Holes:	18
Length:	6476 yds (5922 mtrs)
Par:	71
SSS:	71
Green Fees:	£18.
Visitors:	Welcome: Book in advance
Societies:	Welcome: By application to the Secretary / Manager
Facilities:	Chipping/Putting Area, Practice Area Trolley hire, Electric Buggy hire, Bar, Restaurant

Accommodation, Food and Drink

Reference numbers below refer to detailed information provided in section 2

Accommodation

Annesbrook, Duleek, Co Meath
Tel: 041 9823293 A classic 18th-century porticoed country house in ten acres of grounds. Ten en suite rooms for Bed & Breakfast & dinner menu. 447

St Gobnaits, Drogheda, Co Louth
Tel: 041 9837844 A detached house by the N1, with four en suite B&B rooms. One kilometre from town centre, close to golf courses and beaches. 403

The Hawthorn Hotel, Swords, Co Dublin
Tel: 01 8401308 A charming ten-bedroomed hotel on the bustling main street. Super rooms, excellent Food and Drink, warm, efficient staff. 247

Woodview Farmhouse, Skerries, Co Dublin
Tel: 01 8491528 Irish hospitality at its best in a secluded farmhouse offering B&B Accommodation & evening meals by request. 244

Food and Drink

Annesbrook, Duleek, Co Meath
Tel: 041 9823293 A classic 18th-century porticoed country house in ten acres of grounds. Ten en suite rooms for Bed & Breakfast & dinner menu. 447

Monasterboice Inn, Monasterboice, Co Louth
Tel: 041 9837383 An excellent restaurant and bar with a real Irish feel. Steaks a speciality. Located on the main Dublin-Belfast road (N1). 400

The Hawthorn Hotel, Swords, Co Dublin
Tel: 01 8401308 A charming ten-bedroomed hotel on the bustling main street. Super rooms, excellent Food and Drink, warm, efficient staff. 247

Balcarrick

Balcarrick Golf Club, Corballis, Donabate, Co Dublin

Tel: 01 8436957 / 8436228

Sec/Manager:	Joan Byrne

Professional:	Stephen Rayfus
Directions:	Right off the R126 at Donabate then follow signposts
Type of Course:	Parkland
Date Founded:	1972
No of Holes:	18
Length:	6495 yds (5940 mtrs)
Par:	73
SSS:	72
Green Fees:	Weekdays: £17 Weekends & Bank Holidays: £25
Visitors:	Welcome: Contact in advance
Societies:	Welcome: Contact in advance
Facilities:	Practice Area, Trolley hire, Bar, Restaurant

Accommodation, Food and Drink

Reference numbers below refer to detailed information provided in section 2

Accommodation

Estuary House, Malahide, Co Dublin
Tel: 01 8900242 A striking modern brick-built house with four high-quality Bed & Breakfast rooms, most with sea views. 221

Pebble Mill, Kinsealy, Co Dublin
Tel/Fax: 01 8461792 A fine residence in its own grounds just outside Malahide. Three B&B rooms, all en suite. 245

Woodview Farmhouse, Skerries, Co Dublin
Tel: 01 8491528 Irish hospitality at its best in a secluded farmhouse offering B&B Accommodation & evening meals by request. 244

Food and Drink

Gibneys, Malahide, Co Dublin
Tel: 01 8450606 Period appeal aplenty in a grand old pub run by a golfing family. Food from quick snacks to the full works. 226

The Golf Links, Portmarnock, Co Dublin
Tel: 01 8460129 Portmarnock's only pub, overlooking the bay and the golf links. Good-value menu, well-chosen wines. 238

White Sands Hotel, Portmarnock, Co Dublin
Tel: 01 8460003 Thirty-two rooms in a long, low, modern hotel overlooking the sea and the golf course. Executive rooms available. 241

Beaverstown

Beaverstown Golf Club, Beaverstown, Donabate, Co Dublin

Tel: 01 8436439

Sec/Manager:	Frank Ward
Professional:	None
Directions:	Through Donabate on the R126 towards Portraine then follow signposts
Type of Courmtrs	Parkland
Date Founded:	1985
No of Holes:	18
Length:	6423 yds (5874 mtrs)
Par:	71
SSS:	70
Green Fees:	Weekdays: £20 Weekends & Bank Holidays: £25.
Visitors:	Welcome: Avoid Wed, Sat, Sun.

Societies: Welcome: Special concessions, contact club for details

Facilities: Chipping/Putting Area, Practice Area Trolley hire, Bar, Restaurant

Accommodation, Food and Drink

Reference numbers below refer to detailed information provided in section 2

Accommodation

Estuary House, Malahide, Co Dublin
Tel: 01 8900242 A striking modern brick-built house with four high-quality Bed & Breakfast rooms, most with sea views. 221

Pebble Mill, Kinsealy, Co Dublin
Tel/Fax: 01 8461792 A fine residence in its own grounds just outside Malahide. Three B&B rooms, all en suite. 245

Woodview Farmhouse, Skerries, Co Dublin
Tel: 01 8491528 Irish hospitality at its best in a secluded farmhouse offering B&B Accommodation & evening meals by request. 244

Food and Drink

Gibneys, Malahide, Co Dublin
Tel: 01 8450606 Period appeal aplenty in a grand old pub run by a golfing family. Food from quick snacks to the full works. 226

The Golf Links, Portmarnock, Co Dublin
Tel: 01 8460129 Portmarnock's only pub, overlooking the bay and the golf links. Good-value menu, well-chosen wines. 238

White Sands Hotel, Portmarnock, Co Dublin
Tel: 01 8460003 Thirty-two rooms in a long, low, modern hotel overlooking the sea and the golf course. Executive rooms available. 241

Beech Park

Beech Park Golf Club, Johnstown, Rathcoole, Co Dublin

Tel: 01 4580010/4580522

Sec/Manager:	Brian Kiely
Professional:	None
Directions:	Two miles from Rathcoole village off road to Kilkeel
Type of Course:	Parkland
Date Founded:	1973
No of Holes:	18
Length:	6626 yds (5730 mtrs)
Par:	72
SSS:	70
Green Fees:	£25.
Visitors:	Welcome: Weekdays only
Societies:	Welcome: Mon. Thurs. Fri. only, Book in advance
Facilities:	Chipping/Putting Area, Practice Area, Trolley hire, Bar, Restaurant

Accommodation, Food and Drink

Reference numbers below refer to detailed information provided in section 2

Accommodation

Emmerdale, Firhouse Road, Dublin, Co Dublin
Tel: 01 4516270 Three en suite Bed & Breakfast rooms in a modern but old-style cottage set in landscaped gardens. 224

Monaghan's Harbour Hotel, Naas, Co Kildare
Tel: 045 879145 A real home from home feel in a family-run hotel with well-equipped bedrooms, restaurant, coffee shop and bar. 349

Straffan Bed & Breakfast, Straffan, Co Kildare
Tel: 01 6272386 Four en suite bedrooms in an attractive new bungalow with a garmtrslong enough to practice that swing. 350

The Old Forge, Saggart, Co Dublin
Tel: 01 4589226 Six B & B rooms (three en suite) and a self-contained section to sleep five in a row of 18th-century houses. 242

Food and Drink

Monaghan's Harbour Hotel, Naas, Co Kildare
Tel: 045 879145 A real home from home feel in a family-run hotel with well-equipped bedrooms, restaurant, coffee shop and bar. 349

Rushes, Fairr een Street, Naas, Co Kildare
Tel: 045 898400 Classic bar food in Rushes and international cuisine in its neighbour Cicero on a prime site in Naas. Steaks a speciality. 343

The Manor Inn, Naas, Co Kildare
Tel: 045 897471 Warmth, hospitality and good food in a smartly modernised pub on the main street of Naas. Lots of racing memorabilia. 347

Castle

Castle Golf Club, Woodside Drive, Rathfarnham, Dublin 14

Tel: 01 4904207

Sec/Manager:	L. Blackburne
Professional:	D. Kinsella
Directions:	Off the Rathfarnham Road
Type of Course:	Parkland
Date Founded:	1913
No of Holes:	18
Length:	6144 yds (5653 mtrs)
Par:	70
SSS:	70
Green Fees:	Weekdays: £37
Visitors:	Welcome: Weekdays only
Societies:	Welcome: Book in advance
Facilities:	Chipping/Putting Area, Practice Area, Trolley hire, Bar, Restaurant

Accommodation, Food and Drink

Reference numbers below refer to detailed information provided in section 2

Accommodation

Butlers Town House, Ballsbridge, Dublin 4, Co Dublin
Tel: 01 6674022 20 air-conditioned en suite bedrooms in a beautifully restored Victorian town house. Secure car parking. 239

Eglington Manor, 83 Eglinton Road, Donnybrook, Dublin 4
Tel: 01 2693273 Fax: 01 2697527 A handsome Victorian building is now a very comfortable guest house with eight superior en suite bedrooms with tv and phone. 224

Emmerdale, Firhouse Road, Dublin, Co Dublin
Tel: 01 4516270 Three en suite Bed & Breakfast rooms in a modern but old-style cottage set in landscaped gardens. 224

Glenveagh Town House, Ballsbridge, Dublin 4, Co Dublin
Tel: 01 6684612 A stunning late-Victorian town house, now offering superb Bed & Breakfast Accommodation in 13 en suite bedrooms with tv and telephone. 249

McMenamins, Donnybrook, Co Dublin
Tel: 01 4974405 Five en suite Bed & Breakfast rooms with tv and phone in a centrally located but very peaceful period house. 231

Food and Drink

Fagan's, Lower Drumcondra Road, Dublin 9, Co Dublin

Tel: 01 8375309 One of the great Victorian pubs, with bags of atmosphere, a lunchtime carvery and evening à la carte. 232

The Brian Boru, Glasnevin, Dublin 9, Co Dublin

Tel: 01 8304527 Public house and restaurant in a grand building dating from the 1850s. Conservatory, beer garden, spacious car park. 223

The Playwright Inn, Blackrock, Co Dublin

Tel: 01 2885155 A renowned multi-award-winning pub with the longest thatched roof in Europe. Great Food and Drink, great entertainment. 250

Walters, Dun Laoghaire, Co Dublin

Tel: 01 2807442 Elegant, trendy bar-café-restaurant serving anything from a coffee or a drink to a three-course meal. 229

CityWest

Citywest Hotel Conference Centre & Golf Resort, Saggart, Co Dublin

Tel: 01 4588566

Sec/Manager:	Eddie Jones
Professional:	'The McGregor Golf Academy' with four Professionals
Directions:	From Dublin follow N7 and turn left along N82 towards Saggart
Type of Course:	Parkland
Date Founded:	1994
No of Holes:	18
Length:	7317 yds (6691mtrs)
Par:	70
SSS:	72
Green Fees:	Weekdays: £25 Weekends & Bank Holidays: £30
Visitors:	Welcome:: Book in advance
Societies:	Welcome:: Book in advance
Facilities:	Chipping/Putting Area, Practice Area, Driving Range, Golf Clubs for hire, Trolley hire, Electric Buggy hire, Bar, Restaurant, Caddy service by arrangement, plus Leisure Centre in the Hotel

Accommodation, Food and Drink

Reference numbers below refer to detailed information provided in section 2

Accommodation

Emmerdale, Firhouse Road, Dublin, Co Dublin

Tel: 01 4516270 Three en suite Bed & Breakfast rooms in a modern but old-style cottage set in landscaped gardens. 224

Monaghan's Harbour Hotel, Naas, Co Kildare

Tel: 045 879145 A real home from home feel in a family-run hotel with well-equipped bedrooms, restaurant, coffee shop and bar. 349

Straffan Bed & Breakfast, Straffan, Co Dublin

Tel: 01 6272386 Four en suite bedrooms in an attractive new bungalow with a garden long enough to practice that swing. 350

The Old Forge, Saggart, Co Dublin

Tel: 01 4589226 Six B & B rooms (three en suite) and a self-contained section to sleep fmtrsin a row of 18th-century houses. 242

Food and Drink

Monaghan's Harbour Hotel, Naas, Co Kildare

Tel: 045 879145 A real home from home feel in a family-run hotel with well-equipped bedrooms, restaurant, coffee shop and bar. 349

Rushes, Fairgreen Street, Naas, Co Kildare

Tel: 045 898400 Classic bar food in Rushes and international cuisine in its neighbour Cicero on a prime site in Naas. Steaks a speciality. 343

The Manor Inn, Naas, Co Kildare

Tel: 045 897471 Warmth, hospitality and good food in a smartly modernised pub on the main street of Naas. Lots of racing memorabilia. 347

Clontarf

Clontarf Golf Club, Donnycarney House, Malahide Road, Dublin 3

Tel: 01 8331892

Sec/Manager:	Brian Curran
Professional:	Joe Craddock
Directions:	From Custom House Quay in City Centre follow signs for Clontarf & Howth. At Farmers Park turn left into Malahide Road, Golf Course is ¾ mile on right hand side.
Type of Course:	Parkland
Date Founded:	1912
No of Holes:	18
Length:	5814 yds (5317 mtrs)
Par:	69
SSS:	68
Green Fees:	Weekdays: £26 Weekends & Bank Holidays: £35.
Visitors:	Welcome: Any Day, Contact Club in advance
Societies:	Welcome: Tuesday & Friday, Contact Club in advance
Facilities:	Chipping/Putting Area, Golf Clubs for hire, Trolley hire, Bar, Restaurant

Accommodation, Food and Drink

Reference numbers below refer to detailed information provided in section 2

Accommodation

Arranmore House, Lower Drumcondra Road, Dublin 9

Tel: 01 8300009 Four en suite guest rooms in a Bed & Breakfast house in a Victorian terrace. Off-street parking. 222

Butlers Town House, Ballsbridge, Dublin 4, Co Dublin

Tel: 01 6674022 20 air-conditioned en suite bedrooms in a beautifully restored Victorian town house. Secure car parking. 239

Glenveagh Town House, Ballsbridge, Dublin 4, Co Dublin

Tel: 01 6684612 A stunning late-Victorian town house, now offering superb Bed & Breakfast Accommodation in 13 en suite bedrooms with tv and telephone. 249

Hedigan's Guest House, Clontarf, Dublin 3, Co Dublin
Tel: 01 8531663 A fine redbrick mansion with many splendid features. B&B
Accommodation in 15 en suite bedrooms including mini-suites.   251

Pebble Mill, Kinsealy, Co Dublin
Tel/Fax: 01 8461792 A fine residence in its own grounds just outside Malahide.
Three B&B rooms, all en suite.   245

Food and Drink

Fagan's, Lower Drumcondra Road, Dublin 9, Co Dublin
Tel: 01 8375309 One of the great Victorian pubs, with bags of atmosphere, a
lunchtime carvery and evening à la carte.   232

The Playwright Inn, Blackrock, Co Dublin
Tel: 01 2885155 A renowned multi-award-winning pub with the longest thatched roof
in Europe. Great Food and Drink, great entertainment.   250

Walters, Dun Laoghaire, Co Dublin
Tel: 01 2807442 Elegant, trendy bar-café-restaurant serving anything from a coffee
or a drink to a three-course meal.   229

The Brian Boru, Glasnevin, Dublin 9, Co Dublin
Tel: 01 8304527 Public house and restaurant in a grand building dating from the
1850s. Conservatory, beer garden, spacious car park.   223

Corrstown

Corrstown Golf Club, Kilsallaghan, Co Dublin
Tel: 01 8640533

Sec/Manager:	Jason Kelly
Professional:	Pat Gittens
Directions:	North West of Dublin Airport. Half mile South of Kilsallaghan off the R122
Type of Course:	Parkland
Date Founded:	1992
No of Holes:	18 (plus 9)
Length:	6645 yds (6077 mtrs)
Par:	72
SSS:	71
Green Fees:	Weekdays: £20 Weekends & Bank Holidays: £25
Visitors:	Welcome: Any Day, Restrictions at weekends, Prior Booking required
Societies:	Welcome: Special concessions, Contact club in advance
Facilities:	Chipping/Putting Area, Practice Area, Trolley hire, Electric Buggy hire, Bar, Restaurant

Accommodation, Food and Drink

Reference numbers below refer to detailed
information provided in section 2

Accommodation

Annesbrook, Duleek, Co Meath
Tel: 041 9823293 A classic 18th-century porticoed country house in ten acres of
grounds. Ten en suite rooms for Bed & Breakfast & dinner menu.   447

Killeentierna House, Dunshaughlin, Co Meath
Tel: 01 8259722 Five Bed & Breakfast rooms, one of family size, in a modern
residence on the Dublin side of Dunshaughlin.   433

The Evergreens, Ashbourne, Co Meath
Tel: 01 8352392 A lovely bungalow just outside the village provides Bed & Breakfast
Accommodation in four rooms (three en suite). Tv lounge.   442

The Hawthorn Hotel, Swords, Co Dublin
Tel: 01 8401308 A charming ten-bedroomed hotel on the bustling main street. Super
rooms, excellent Food and Drink, warm, efficient staff.   247

The Old Workhouse, Dunshaughlin, Co Meath
Tel/Fax: 01 8259251 Civilised living in a sympathetically restored 1840s building.
Four cosy double bedrooms (2 en suite, 2 with private bathroom). Country house
cooking.

Food and Drink

Annesbrook, Duleek, Co Meath
Tel: 041 9823293 A classic 18th-century porticoed country house in ten acres of
grounds. Ten en suite rooms for Bed & Breakfast & dinner menu.   447

Gibneys, Malahide, Co Dublin
Tel: 01 8450606 Period appeal aplenty in a grand old pub run by a golfing family.
Foodmtrsm quick snacks to the full works.   226

The Hawthorn Hotel, Swords, Co Dublin
Tel: 01 8401308 A charming ten-bedroomed hotel on the bustling main street. Super
rooms, excellent Food and Drink, warm, efficient staff.   247

Deer Park

Deer Park Hotel & Golf Courses, Howth, Co Dublin
Tel: 01 8322624

Sec/Manager:	David Tighe
Professional:	None
Directions:	From Custom House Quay in the City Centre follow signs for Howth along the coast road. From Sutton take the Howth road. Golf course on the right handside before reaching Howth

Deer Park

Type of Course:	Parkland
Date Founded:	1974
No of Holes:	18
Length:	6830 yds (6245 mtrs)
Par:	72
SSS:	71
Green Fees:	Weekdays: £10 Weekends & Bank Holidays: £12.25

Grace O'Malley

Type of Course:	Parkland
Date Founded:	1974
No of Holes:	18
Length:	6503 yds ((5946 mtrs)
Par:	72
SSS:	70
Green Fees:	Weekdays: £10 Weekends & Bank Holidays: £12.25
Visitors:	Welcome: Restrictions, Ring in advance
Societies:	No Societies
Facilities:	Chipping/Putting Area, Golf Clubs for hire, Trolley hire, plus Hotel facilities

Accommodation, Food and Drink

Reference numbers below refer to detailed
information provided in section 2

Accommodation

Gleann-na-Smol, Howth, Co Dublin
Tel: 01 8322936 Personal service in a family-run B&B renowned for its hospitality. 5

en suite rooms include a triple. 243

Marine Hotel, Sutton Cross, Dublin 13, Co Dublin

Tel: 01 8390000 A superior hotel offering high standards of Accommodation, service and food. Great views, too. 220

Roselea, Portmarnock, Co Dublin

Tel: 01 8460117 Two double rooms and two twins, all en suite, in a bungalow set in spacious gardens and lawns. 233

Southdale, Portmarnock, Co Dublin

Tel/Fax: 01 8463760 Four en suite bedrooms in a striking modern B&B house close to the seafront and Portmarnock Golf Club. 240

Steiermark, Portmarnock, Co Dublin

Tel/Fax: 01 8462032 A detached villa with four excellent Bed & Breakfast rooms, sea views and a setting opposite the golf course. 237

White Sands Hotel, Portmarnock, Co Dublin

Tel: 01 8460003 Thirty-two rooms in a long, low, modern hotel overlooking the sea and the golf course. Executive rooms available. 241

Food and Drink

Marine Hotel, Sutton Cross, Dublin 13, Co Dublin

Tel: 01 8390000 A superior hotel offering high standards of Accommodation, service and food. Great views, too. 220

The Bloody Stream, Howth, Co Dublin

Tel: 01 8395076 Howth's busiest pub-restaurant, with 100 covers, beer garden, live music and bags of atmosphere. Seafood a speciality. 234

White Sands Hotel, Portmarnock, Co Dublin

Tel: 01 8460003 Thirty-two rooms in a long, low, modern hotel overlooking the sea and the golf course. Executive rooms available. 241

Donabate

Donabate Golf Club, Balcarrick, Donabate, Co Dublin

Tel: 01 8436346

Sec/Manager:	Brian Judd
Professional:	Hugh Jackson
Directions:	Right off the R126 at Donabate then follow signposts
Type of Course:	Parkland
Date Founded:	1925
No of Holes:	18
Length:	5704 yds (5215 mtrs)
Par:	70
SSS:	69
Green Fees:	£25 per round
Visitors:	Welcome: Any Day, Restrictions at weekends, Contact Club in advance
Societies:	Welcome: Special concessions, Contact Club for details
Facilities:	Chipping/Putting Area, Practice Area, Golf Clubs for hire, Trolley hire, Electric Buggy hire, Bar, Restaurant

Accommodation, Food and Drink

Reference numbers below refer to detailed information provided in section 2

Accommodation

Estuary House, Malahide, Co Dublin

Tel: 01 8900242 A striking modern brick-built house with four high-quality Bed & Breakfast rooms, most with sea views. 221

Pebble Mill, Kinsealy, Co Dublin

Tel/Fax: 01 8461792 A fine residence in its own grounds just outside Malahide. Three B&B rooms, all en suite. 245

The Hawthorn Hotel, Swords, Co Dublin

Tel: 01 8401308 A charming ten-bedroomed hotel on the bustling main street. Super rooms, excellent Food and Drink, warm, efficient staff. 247

Food and Drink

Gibneys, Malahide, Co Dublin

Tel: 01 8450606 Period appeal aplenty in a grand old pub run by a golfing family. Food from quick snacks to the full works. 226

The Golf Links, Portmarnock, Co Dublin

Tel: 01 8460129 Portmarnock's only pub, overlooking the bay and the golf links. Good-value menu, well-chosen wines. 238

The Hawthorn Hotel, Swords, Co Dublin

Tel: 01 8401308 A charming ten-bedroomed hotel on the bustling main street. Super rooms, excellent Food and Drink, warm, efficient staff. 247

Dublin Mountain

Dublin Mountain, Gortlum, Brittas, Co Dublin

Tel: 0145 82570

Sec/Manager:	Pat O'Rourke
Professional:	None
Directions:	1 mile east of Brittan off the R114 to Tallaght
Type of Course:	Parklands
Date Founded:	1993
No of Holes:	18
Length:	6161 yds (5635 mtrs)
Par:	70
SSS:	69
Green Fees:	Weekdays: £9 Weekends £10
Visitors:	Welcome: Tuesday to Saturday
Societies:	Welcome: No restrictions, Book in advance
Facilities:	Practice Area, Trolley hire

Accommodation, Food and Drink

Reference numbers below refer to detailed information provided in section 2

Accommodation

Emmerdale, Firhouse Road, Dublin, Co Dublin

Tel: 01 4516270 Three en suite Bed & Breakfast rooms in a modern but old-style cottage set in landscaped gardens. 224

Glenveagh Town House, Ballsbridge, Dublin 4, Co Dublin

Tel: 01 6684612 A stunning late-Victorian town house, now offering superb Bed & Breakfast Accommodation in 13 en suite bedrooms with tv and telephone. 249

The Old Forge, Saggart, Co Dublin

Tel: 01 4589226 Six B & B rooms (three en suite) and a self-contained section to sleep five in a row of 18th-century houses. 242

Food and Drink

Ashley Bed & Breakfast, Clane, Co Kildare

Tel/Fax: 045 868533 Three en suite B&B rooms in a neat self-contained unit by the main house. Rural setting on the road from Clane to Celbridge. 348

Monaghan's Harbour Hotel, Naas, Co Kildare

Tel: 045 879145 A real home from home feel in a family-run hotel with well-equipped bedrooms, restaurant, coffee shop and bar. 349

The Manor Inn, Naas, Co Kildare

Tel: 045 897471 Warmth, hospitality and good food in a smartly modernised pub on the main street of Naas. Lots of racing memorabilia. 347

Dun Laoghaire

Dun Laoghaire Golf Club, Eglinton Park,
Tivoli Road, Dun Laoghaire
Tel: 01 2803196

Sec/Manager:	Dennis Peacock
Professional:	Owen Mulhall
Directions:	7 miles South of Dublin City. Half mile from Dun Laoghaire Town Centre
Type of Course:	Parkland
Date Founded:	1910
No of Holes:	18
Length:	5793 yds (5298 mtrs)
Par:	69
SSS:	68
Green Fees:	£30 per day
Visitors:	Welcome : Any Day, Restrictions at weekends, Contact Club in advance
Societies:	Welcome: Special concessions, Contact Club for details
Facilities:	Chipping/Putting Area, Practice Area, Golf Clubs for hire, Trolley hire, Bar, Restaurant

Accommodation, Food and Drink

Reference numbers below refer to detailed
information provided in section 2

Accommodation

Ariemond, Dun Laoghaire, Co Dublin

Tel: 01 2801664 Five Bed & Breakfast rooms, three en suite, two with private baths, in a lovely house two minutes walk from the centre. 235

Brookville, 91 Monkstown Road, Monkstown Village, Co Dublin

Tel: 01 2809436 A townhouse Bed & Breakfast with four en suite rooms including a triple. Loads of pubs and restaurants nearby.

Ferry House, Dun Laoghaire, Co Dublin

Tel: 01 2808301 Four en suite Bed & Breakfast rooms in a handsome town house an easy walk from the centre of Dun Laoghaire. 228

Ophira, Dun Laoghaire, Co Dublin

Tel/Fax: 01 2800997 Town-centre Bed & Breakfast Accommodation in a mid-19th century house. Four en suite bedrooms. Tv lounge. 225

The Kingston Hotel, Dun Laoghaire, Co Dublin

Tel: 01 2801810 Fifty-three well-equipped en suite bedrooms – singles, doubles, twins and triples – in a family-run hotel on the seafront. 236

Food and Drink

The Kingston Hotel, Dun Laoghaire, Co Dublin

Tel: 01 2801810 Fifty-three well-equipped en suite bedrooms – singles, doubles, twins and triples – in a family-run hotel on the seafront. 236

The Playwright Inn, Blackrock, Co Dublin

Tel: 01 2885155 A renowned multi-award-winning pub with the longest thatched roof in Europe. Great Food and Drink, great entertainment. 250

Walters, Dun Laoghaire, Co Dublin

Tel: 01 2807442 Elegant, trendy bar-café-restaurant serving anything from a coffee or a drink to a three-course meal. 229

Edmondstown

Edmondstown Golf Club, Edmondstown,
Dublin 16

Tel: 01 4931082

Sec/Manager:	Ray Maertin
Professional:	A. Crofton
Directions:	From Junction 11 of M50 follow signs for Knocklyon and Ballyboden. In Ballyboden take the Edmondstown Road south. Golf Course in on left handside
Type of Course:	Parkland
Date Founded:	1944
No of Holes:	18
Length:	6193 yds (5663 mtrs)
Par:	70
SSS:	70
Green Fees:	Weekdays: £30 Weekends and Bank Holidays: £35
Visitors:	Welcome
Societies:	Special concessions
Facilities:	Practice Area, Golf Clubs for hire, Trolley hire, Electric Buggy hire, Bar, Restaurant

Accommodation, Food and Drink

Reference numbers below refer to detailed
information provided in section 2

Accommodation

Eglington Manor, 83 Eglington Road, Donnybrook, Dublin 4, Co Dublin

Tel: 01 2693273 Fax: 01 2697527 A handsome Victorian building is now a very comfortable guest house with eight superior en suite bedrooms with tv and phone.

Emmerdale, Firhouse Road, Dublin, Co Dublin

Tel: 01 4516270 Three en suite Bed & Breakfast rooms in a modern but old-style cottage set in landscaped gardens. 224

McMenamins, Donnybrook, Co Dublin

Tel: 01 4974405 Five en suite Bed & Breakfast rooms with tv and phone in a centrally located but very peaceful period house. 231

Summerhill House Hotel, Enniskerry, Co Wicklow

Tel: 01 2867928 Fifty-seven bright, spacious airy bedrooms with en suite facilities, tv and telephone in a friendly, well-situated hotel. 668

Woodland Court Hotel, Southern Cross, Bray, Co Wicklow

Tel: 01 2760258 Sixty five en suite bedrooms with all the modern comforts in a characterful hotel at the southern end of the town. Restaurant and lounge. 667

Food and Drink

Summerhill House Hotel, Enniskerry, Co Wicklow

Tel: 01 2867928 Fifty-seven bright, spacious airy bedrooms with en suite facilities, tv and telephone in a friendly, well-situated hotel. 668

The Playwright Inn, Blackrock, Co Dublin

Tel: 01 2885155 A renowned multi-award-winning pub with the longest thatched roof in Europe. Great Food and Drink, great entertainment. 250

Woodland Court Hotel, Southern Cross, Bray, Co Wicklow

Tel: 01 2760258 Sixty five en suite bedrooms with all the modern comforts in a characterful hotel at the southern end of the town. Restaurant and lounge. 667

Elm Park

Elm Park Golf Club, Nutley House, Nutley
Lane, Donnybrook, Dublin 4
Tel: 01 2692650

Sec/Manager:	Adrian McCormack

Professional:	Seamus Green
Directions:	From City Centre follow signs to Dun Laoghaire and In Merrion Village turn right into Nutley Lane. Golf Course is on the lefthand side
Type of Course:	Parkland
Date Founded:	1924
No of Holes:	18
Length:	5422 yds (4957 mtrs)
Par:	69
SSS:	69
Green Fees:	Weekdays £40 Weekends & Bank Holidays £50
Visitors:	Welcome: Ring in advance
Societies:	Welcome: Contact Club for details
Facilities:	Chipping/Putting Area, Practice Area, Driving Range, Golf Clubs for hire, Trolley hire, Electric Buggy hire, Bar, Restaurant, Caddy service by arrangement

Accommodation, Food and Drink

Reference numbers below refer to detailed information provided in section 2

Accommodation

Ariemond, Dun Laoghaire, Co Dublin

Tel: 01 2801664 Five Bed & Breakfast rooms, three en suite, two with private baths, in a lovely house two minutes walk from the centre.   235

Brookville, 91 Monkstown Road, Monkstown Village, Co Dublin

Tel: 01 2809436 A townhouse Bed & Breakfast with four en suite rooms including a triple. Loads of pubs and restaurants nearby.

Butlers Town House, Ballsbridge, Dublin 4, Co Dublin

Tel: 01 6674022 20 air-conditioned en suite bedrooms in a beautifully restored Victorian town house. Secure car parking.   239

Eglington Manor, 83 Eglington Road, Donnybrook, Dublin 4

Tel: 01 2693273 Fax: 01 2697527 A handsome Victorian building is now a very comfortable guest house with eight superior en suite bedrooms with tv and phone.

Ferry House, Dun Laoghaire, Co Dublin

Tel: 01 2808301 Four en suite Bed & Breakfast rooms in a handsome town house an easy walk from the centre of Dun Laoghaire.   228

Glenveagh Town House, Ballsbridge, Dublin 4, Co Dublin

Tel: 01 6684612 A stunning late-Victorian town house, now offering superb Bed & Breakfast Accommodation in 13 en suite bedrooms with tv and telephone.   249

Lucan Spa Hotel, Lucan, Co Dublin

Tel: 01 6280494 Hotel with bar, bistro and restaurant. Superbly appointed en suite bedrooms Scenic waks, National Stud and Championship Golf Courses all close.   255

McMenamins, Donnybrook, Co Dublin

Tel: 01 4974405 Five en suite Bed & Breakfast rooms with tv and phone in a centrally located but very peaceful period house.   231

Ophira, Dun Laoghaire, Co Dublin

Tel/Fax: 01 2800997 Town-centre Bed & Breakfast Accommodation in a mid-19th century house. Four en suite bedrooms. Tv lounge.   225

The Kingston Hotel, Dun Laoghaire, Co Dublin

Tel: 01 2801810 Fifty-three well-equipped en suite bedrooms – singles, doubles, twins and triples – in a family-run hotel on the seafront.   236

Food and Drink

Fagan's, Lower Drumcondra Road, Dublin 9, Co Dublin

Tel: 01 8375309 One of the great Victorian pubs, with bags of atmosphere, a lunchtime carvery and evening à la carte.   232

Lucan Spa Hotel, Lucan, Co Dublin

Tel: 01 6280494 Hotel with bar, bistro and restaurant. Superbly appointed en suite bedrooms Scenic waks, National Stud and Championship Golf Courses all close.   255

The Brian Boru, Glasnevin, Dublin 9, Co Dublin

Tel: 01 8304527 Public house and restaurant in a grand building dating from the 1850s. Conservatory, beer garden, spacious car park.   223

The Kingston Hotel, Dun Laoghaire, Co Dublin

Tel: 01 2801810 Fifty-three well-equipped en suite bedrooms – singles, doubles, twins and triples – in a family-run hotel on the seafront.   236

The Playwright Inn, Blackrock, Co Dublin

Tel: 01 2885155 A renowned multi-award-winning pub with the longest thatched roof in Europe. Great Food and Drink, great entertainment.   250

Walters, Dun Laoghaire, Co Dublin

Tel: 01 2807442 Elegant, trendy bar-café-restaurant serving anything from a coffee or a drink to a three-course meal.   229

Elmgreen

Elmgreen Golf Club, Castleknock, Dublin 15
Tel: 01 8200797

Sec/Manager:	None
Professional:	Paul McGahan
Directions:	From Junction 6 of M50 take Navin Road towards Dublin Centre. At first roundabout turn into Dunsink Road, Golf Course is on the right handside
Type of Course:	Parkland
Date Founded:	1994
No of Holes:	18
Length:	5796 yds (5299 mtrs)
Par:	71
SSS:	68
Green Fees:	Weekdays: £13 Weekends & Bank Holidays: £19
Visitors:	Welcome: Book in advance
Societies:	Welcome: Contact Club in advance
Facilities:	Chipping/Putting Area, Driving Range, Golf Clubs for hire, Trolley hire

Accommodation, Food and Drink

Reference numbers below refer to detailed information provided in section 2

Accommodation

Hedigan's Guest House, Clontarf, Dublin 3, Co Dublin

Tel: 01 8531663 A fine redbrick mansion with many splendid features. B&B Accommodation in 15 en suite bedrooms including mini-suites.   251

The Milestone, Lucan, Co Dublin

Tel: 01 6241818 Four Bed & Breakfast rooms, all en suite, in a large modern detached house surrounded by beautiful lawns.   227

Willo's, Lucan Village, Co Dublin

Tel /Fax: 01 6283365 Seven letting rooms in a pleasant Bed & Breakfast house near the village centre, 15 minutes' drive fron Dublin City.   230

Food and Drink

Fagan's, Lower Drumcondra Road, Dublin 9, Co Dublin

Tel: 01 8375309 One of the great Victorian pubs, with bags of atmosphere, a lunchtime carvery and evening à la carte.   232

The Brian Boru, Glasnevin, Dublin 9, Co Dublin

Tel: 01 8304527 Public house and restaurant in a grand building dating from the 1850s. Conservatory, beer garden, spacious car park.   223

The Golf Links, Portmarnock, Co Dublin

Tel: 01 8460129 Portmarnock's only pub, overlooking the bay and the golf links. Good-value menu, well-chosen wines.   238

The Hawthorn Hotel, Swords, Co Dublin

Tel: 01 8401308 A charming ten-bedroomed hotel on the bustling main street. Super rooms, excellent Food and Drink, warm, efficient staff.   247

Forest Little

Forest Little Golf Club, Cloghran, Co Dublin

Tel: 01 8401183

Sec/Manager:	A. J. Greany
Professional:	Tony Judd
Directions:	Half mile North of Dublin Airport off the N1
Type of Course:	Parkland
Date Founded:	1940
No of Holes:	18
Length:	6413 yds (5865 mtrs)
Par:	70
SSS:	70
Green Fees:	£25
Visitors:	Welcome: Contact Club in advance
Societies:	Welcome: Restrictions, Contact Club in advance
Facilities:	Chipping/Putting Area, Practice Area, Golf Clubs for hire, Trolley hire Bar, Restaurant

Accommodation, Food and Drink

Reference numbers below refer to detailed information provided in section 2

Accommodation

Cedar House, Swords, Co Dublin
Tel: 01 8402757 Bed & Breakfast Accommodation in a modern house not far from the town centre. Packed lunches available. 248

Pebble Mill, Kinsealy, Co Dublin
Tel/Fax: 01 8461792 A fine residence in its own grounds just outside Malahide. Three B&B rooms, all en suite. 245

The Hawthorn Hotel, Swords, Co Dublin
Tel: 01 8401308 A charming ten-bedroomed hotel on the bustling main street. Super rooms, excellent Food and Drink, warm, efficient staff. 247

Willowbrook House, Swords, Co Dublin
Tel: 01 8403843 Five en suite B&B rooms in a modern villa with superb gardens. Easy walk to Swords town centre. 246

Food and Drink

Gibneys, Malahide, Co Dublin
Tel: 01 8450606 Period appeal aplenty in a grand old pub run by a golfing family. Food from quick snacks to the full works. 226

The Golf Links, Portmarnock, Co Dublin
Tel: 01 8460129 Portmarnock's only pub, overlooking the bay and the golf links. Good-value menu, well-chosen wines. 238

The Hawthorn Hotel, Swords, Co Dublin
Tel: 01 8401308 A charming ten-bedroomed hotel on the bustling main street. Super rooms, excellent Food and Drink, warm, efficient staff. 247

Grange

Grange Golf Club, Whitechurch Road, Rathfarnham, Dublin 16

Tel: 01 4932889

Sec/Manager:	J. A. O'Donaghue
Professional:	Barry Hamill

Directions:	From Junction 11 of M50 follow signs for Knockllyon and Ballyboden. At Ballyboden take Taylors Lane to junction with Whitechurch Road, Golf Course is opposite the junction.
Type of Course:	Parkland
Date Founded:	1910
No of Holes:	18 (plus 6 holes)
Length:	6058 yds (5540 mtrs)
Par:	69
SSS:	70
Green Fees:	Weekdays: £35 Weekends & Bank Holidays: £45
Visitors:	Welcome: Weekdays except Tues & Wed. pm, Weekend restrictions.
Societies:	Welcome: Contact the Club in writing
Facilities:	Chipping/Putting Area, Practice Area, Trolley hire, Bar, Restaurant

Accommodation, Food and Drink

Reference numbers below refer to detailed information provided in section 2

Accommodation

Eglington Manor, 83 Eglington Road, Donnybrook, Dublin 4
Tel: 01 2693273 Fax: 01 2697527 A handsome Victorian building is now a very comfortable guest house with eight superior en suite bedrooms with tv and phone.

Emmerdale, Firhouse Road, Dublin, Co Dublin
Tel: 01 4516270 Three en suite Bed & Breakfast rooms in a modern but old-style cottage set in landscaped gardens. 224

McMenamins, Donnybrook, Co Dublin
Tel: 01 4974405 Five en suite Bed & Breakfast rooms with tv and phone in a centrally located but very peaceful period house. 231

Summerhill House Hotel, Enniskerry, Co Wicklow
Tel: 01 2867928 Fifty-seven bright, spacious airy bedrooms with en suite facilities, tv and telephone in a friendly, well-situated hotel. 668

Woodland Court Hotel, Southern Cross, Bray, Co Wicklow
Tel: 01 2760258 Sixty five en suite bedrooms with all the modern comforts in a characterful hotel at the southern end of the town. Restaurant and lounge. 667

Food and Drink

Summerhill House Hotel, Enniskerry, Co Wicklow
Tel: 01 2867928 Fifty-seven bright, spacious airy bedrooms with en suite facilities, tv and telephone in a friendly, well-situated hotel. 668

The Playwright Inn, Blackrock, Co Dublin
Tel: 01 2885155 A renowned multi-award-winning pub with the longest thatched roof in Europe. Great Food and Drink, great entertainment. 250

Woodland Court Hotel, Southern Cross, Bray, Co Wicklow
Tel: 01 2760258 Sixty five en suite bedrooms with all the modern comforts in a characterful hotel at the southern end of the town. Restaurant and lounge. 667

Hermitage

Hermitage Golf Club, Ballydowd, Lucan, Co Dublin

Tel: 01 6268491

Irish teams have reason to hold Hermitage high in their affections in the light of extremely rewarding experiences there. It was the scene of a European Women's Amateur Championship triumph in 1979 and of the European Youths' Championship five years later.

Date Founded:	1905
No of Holes:	18
Length:	6609 yds (6044 mtrs)
Par:	71
SSS:	71
Green Fees:	£34
Visitors:	Welcome: Restricted hours, Contact Club in advance
Societies:	Welcome: Weekdays, Contact Club in advance
Facilities:	Chipping/Putting Area, Practice Area, Driving Range, Trolley hire, Bar, Restaurant, Caddy service by arrangement

Accommodation, Food and Drink

Reference numbers below refer to detailed
information provided in section 2

Accommodation

Ballygoran Lodge, Maynooth, Co Kildare
Tel: 01 6291860 A striking modern villa 1 mile from Maynooth, with four en suite
B&B rooms and a suite with a mini-gym. 342

Lucan Spa Hotel, Lucan, Co Dublin
Tel: 01 6280494 Hotel with bar, bistro and restaurant. Superbly appointed en suite
bedrooms Scenic waks, National Stud and Championship Golf Courses all close. 255

Ophira, Dun Laoghaire, Co Dublin
Tel/Fax: 01 2800997 Town-centre Bed & Breakfast Accommodation in a mid-19th
century house. Four en suite bedrooms. Tv lounge. 225

Straffan Bed & Breakfast, Straffan, Co Kildare
Tel: 01 6272386 Four en suite bedrooms in an attractive new bungalow with a
garden long enough to practice that swing. 350

The Hawthorn Hotel, Swords, Co Dublin
Tel: 01 8401308 A charming ten-bedroomed hotel on the bustling main street. Super
rooms, excellent Food and Drink, warm, efficient staff. 247

The Kingston Hotel, Dun Laoghaire, Co Dublin
Tel: 01 2801810 Fifty-three well-equipped en suite bedrooms — singles, doubles,
twins and triples — in a family-run hotel on the seafront. 236

The Milestone, Lucan, Co Dublin
Tel: 01 6241818 Four Bed & Breakfast rooms, all en suite, in a large modern
detached house surrounded by beautiful lawns. 227

Food and Drink

Fagan's, Lower Drumcondra Road, Dublin 9, Co Dublin
Tel: 01 8375309 One of the great Victorian pubs, with bags of atmosphere, a
lunchtime carvery and evening à la carte. 232

Lucan Spa Hotel, Lucan, Co Dublin
Tel: 01 6280494 Hotel with bar, bistro and restaurant. Superbly appointed en suite
bedrooms Scenic waks, National Stud and Championship Golf Courses all close. 255

Ophira, Dun Laoghaire, Co Dublin
Tel/Fax: 01 2800997 Town-centre Bed & Breakfast Accommodation in a mid-19th
century house. Four en suite bedrooms. Tv lounge. 225

The Hawthorn Hotel, Swords, Co Dublin
Tel: 01 8401308 A charming ten-bedroomed hotel on the bustling main street. Super
rooms, excellent Food and Drink, warm, efficient staff. 247

The Manor Inn, Naas, Co Kildare
Tel: 045 897471 Warmth, hospitality and good food in a smartly modernised pub on
the main street of Naas. Lots of racing memorabilia. 347

The Irish women's line-up on that occasion contained such prominent names as Mary McKenna and Maureen Madill while the youths event will be remembered for a dramatic, tie-hole victory in the final by John McHenry.

Situated in west Dublin about six miles from the city centre, Hermitage has the most charming location, sweeping down to the River Liffey. It is also characterised by an abundance of mature trees which place a premium on accuracy off the tee while a recent development has a major water feature left of the green at the re-shaped second.

Founded in 1905 as a nine-hole layout, Hermitage has always been highly regarded by Irish professionals as a searching examination. Indeed Ian Woosnam was among visiting professionals who enjoyed it during the Christy O'Connor Pro-Am, though from a championship standpoint, its overall length of 6,609 yards has been rendered somewhat modest by modern equipment.

Still, players of all standards are captivated by the 142-yard 10th hole, played from an elevated tee, down to a green nestling close to the bank of the Liffey. And the river becomes an even more dominant feature of the long, 539-yard 11th, where a watery grave awaits the drive or second shot which happened to take an unintended left to right trajectory.

Sec/Manager:	Tom Spelman
Professional:	Simon Byrne
Directions:	On the North Eastern outskirts of Lucan Village off the N4 Lucan Road from Dublin
Type of Course:	Parkland

Hollystown

Hollystown Golf Club, Hollystown, Dublin 15
Tel: 01 8207444

One of Dublin's most popular pay-and-play courses, Hollystown extended their facilities to

which can be adapted for corporate functions or conferences.

In 1997, it gained the rare distinction for a pay-and-play facility of being chosen by the GUI to play host to the Leinster Youths' Championship, won by Ricky Elliott. Meanwhile, club, buggy and trolley hire are deliberately pitched at reasonable prices, so as to reflect the owner's dictum of quality golf at an affordable outlay. And the expansion of the playing facilities clearly added to its appeal.

Sec/Manager:	Oliver Barry
Professional:	Mark Callan
Directions:	From junction 5 of M50 follow N2 towards Ashbourne. Turn left into R121 and follow for 2 miles to golf course.
Type of Course:	Parkland
Date Founded:	1992
No of Holes:	18 (plus 9 holes)
Length:	7066 yds (6501 mtrs)
Par:	71
SSS:	71
Green Fees:	Weekdays: £15 Weekends & Bank Holidays: £20
Visitors:	Welcome: Book in advance
Societies:	Welcome: Book in advance
Facilities:	Chipping/Putting Area, Practice Area, Driving Range, Golf Clubs for hire, Trolley hire, Electric Buggy hire, Bar, Restaurant

27 holes in August 1999. The brainchild of businessman Oliver Barry, it was launched in 1992 closeby the N2 in North Dublin.

The original layout, measuring over 7,000 yards off the back tees, was designed by Eddie Hackett. But the additional nine is the work of resident course superintendent, Joe Bedford and the 27 holes have now been split into the yellow, blue and red nines.

This offers the management the use of three distinct 18-hole combinations, largely similar in character. Indeed the running order of certain holes has been changed to achieve the ultimate flexibility. And both designers have used the natural features of a fine, parkland site - streams, lakes and mature trees - to excellent effect.

A strong golf challenge is splendidly complemented by the new pavilion, which offers some delightful panoramic views, including the 558-yard, par-five finishing hole on the blue course. Then there is the Hollystown Suite on the first floor, which provides a spacious dining area

Accommodation, Food and Drink

Reference numbers below refer to detailed information provided in section 2

Accommodation

Annesbrook, Duleek, Co Meath
Tel: 041 9823293 A classic 18th-century porticoed country house in ten acres of grounds. Ten en suite rooms for Bed & Breakfast & dinner menu.   447

Killeentierna House, Dunshaughlin, Co Meath
Tel: 01 8259722 Five Bed & Breakfast rooms, one of family size, in a modern residence on the Dublin side of Dunshaughlin.   433

The Evergreens, Ashbourne, Co Meath
Tel: 01 8352392 A lovely bungalow just outside the village provides Bed & Breakfast Accommodation in four rooms (three en suite). Tv lounge.   442

The Old Workhouse. Dunshaughlin, Co Meath
Tel/Fax: 01 8259251 Civilised living in a sympathetically restored 1840s building. Four cosy double bedrooms (2 en suite, 2 with private bathroom). Country house cooking.

Wellington Court Hotel, Trim, Co Meath
Tel: 046 31516 Excellent Accommodation and facilities in a comfortable hotel on the Summerhill road (R158). 18 en suite bedrooms with tv and phone.   449

Food and Drink

Annesbrook, Duleek, Co Meath
Tel: 041 9823293 A classic 18th-century porticoed country house in ten acres of grounds. Ten en suite rooms for Bed & Breakfast & dinner menu.   447

The Haggard Inn, Trim, Co Meath
Tel: 046 31110 Restaurant, carvery and bar food in an atmospheric 19th-century hostelry. Traditional music Friday and Saturday.   440

Wellington Court Hotel, Trim, Co Meath
Tel: 046 31516 Excellent Accommodation and facilities in a comfortable hotel on the Summerhill road (R158). 18 en suite bedrooms with tv and phone.   449

Hollywood Lakes

Hollywood Lakes Golf Club, Ballyboughal, Co Dublin

Tel: 01 8433407

Sec/Manager: Austin Brogan
Professional: None
Directions: 12 miles North of Dublin Airport. Take N1 North and turn left at The Five Roads. Golf Course is two and a half miles from the turn off on the left handside
Type of Course: Parkland
Date Founded: 1991
No of Holes: 18
Length: 6870 yds (6281 mtrs)
Par: 72
SSS: 72
Green Fees: Weekdays: £19 Weekends & Bank Holidays: £24
Visitors: Welcome: Book in advance
Societies: Welcome: Special concessions, contact club for details
Facilities: Chipping/Putting Area, Practice Area, Trolley hire, Electric Buggy hire, Bar, Restaurant, plus (Golf Clubs for hire, can be booked in advance)

Accommodation, Food and Drink

Reference numbers below refer to detailed information provided in section 2

Accommodation

Annesbrook, Duleek, Co Meath
Tel: 041 9823293 A classic 18th-century porticoed country house in ten acres of grounds. Ten en suite rooms for Bed & Breakfast & dinner menu. 447

St Gobnaits, Drogheda, Co Louth
Tel: 041 9837844 A detached house by the N1, with four en suite B&B rooms. One kilometre from town centre, close to golf courses and beaches. 403

The Hawthorn Hotel, Swords, Co Dublin
Tel: 01 8401308 A charming ten-bedroomed hotel on the bustling main street. Super rooms, excellent Food and Drink, warm, efficient staff. 247

Woodview Farmhouse, Skerries, Co Dublin
Tel: 01 8491528 Irish hospitality at its best in a secluded farmhouse offering B&B Accommodation & evening meals by request. 244

Food and Drink

Annesbrook, Duleek, Co Meath

Tel: 041 9823293 A classic 18th-century porticoed country house in ten acres of grounds. Ten en suite rooms for Bed & Breakfast & dinner menu. 447

Monasterboice Inn, Monasterboice, Co Louth
Tel: 041 9837383 An excellent restaurant and bar with a real Irish feel. Steaks a speciality. Located on the main Dublin-Belfast road (N1). 400

The Hawthorn Hotel, Swords, Co Dublin
Tel: 01 8401308 A charming ten-bedroomed hotel on the bustling main street. Super rooms, excellent Food and Drink, warm, efficient staff. 247

Howth

Howth Golf Club, St. Fintan's, Carrickbrack Road, Sutton, Dublin 13

Tel: 01 8323055

Sec/Manager: Ann MacNeice
Professional: John McGuirk
Directions: From Custom House Quay in City Centre follow signs for Howth along the coast road. From Sutton turn left into Greenfield Road towards St. Finians into Carrickbrack Road. Golf Course is on the left handside just past St. Finians
Type of Course: Moorland
Date Founded: 1911
No of Holes: 18
Length: 6202 yds (5672 mtrs)
Par: 71
SSS: 69
Green Fees: £27
Visitors: Welcome: Any Day except Wednesday
Societies: Welcome: Special concessions, Contact Club for details

Facilities: Chipping/Putting Area, Practice Area, Trolley hire, Bar

Accommodation, Food and Drink

Reference numbers below refer to detailed information provided in section 2

Accommodation

Gleann-na-Smol, Howth, Co Dublin
Tel: 01 8322936 Personal service in a family-run B&B renowned for its hospitality. 5 en suite rooms include a triple. 243

Marine Hotel, Sutton Cross, Dublin 13, Co Dublin
Tel: 01 8390000 A superior hotel offering high standards of Accommodation, service and food. Great views, too. 220

Roselea, Portmarnock, Co Dublin
Tel: 01 8460117 Two double rooms and two twins, all en suite, in a bungalow set in spacious gardens and lawns. 233

Southdale, Portmarnock, Co Dublin
Tel/Fax: 01 8463760 Four en suite bedrooms in a striking modern B&B house close to the seafront and Portmarnock Golf Club. 240

Steiermark, Portmarnock, Co Dublin
Tel/Fax: 01 8462032 A detached villa with four excellent Bed & Breakfast rooms, sea views and a setting opposite the golf course. 237

White Sands Hotel, Portmarnock, Co Dublin
Tel: 01 8460003 Thirty-two rooms in a long, low, modern hotel overlooking the sea and the golf course. Executive rooms available. 241

Food and Drink

Marine Hotel, Sutton Cross, Dublin 13, Co Dublin
Tel: 01 8390000 A superior hotel offering high standards of Accommodation, service and food. Great views, too. 220

The Bloody Stream, Howth, Co Dublin
Tel: 01 8395076 Howth's busiest pub-restaurant, with 100 covers, beer garden, live music and bags of atmosphere. Seafood a speciality. 234

The Golf Links, Portmarnock, Co Dublin
Tel: 01 8460129 Portmarnock's only pub, overlooking the bay and the golf links. Good-value menu, well-chosen wines. 238

White Sands Hotel, Portmarnock, Co Dublin
Tel: 01 8460003 Thirty-two rooms in a long, low, modern hotel overlooking the sea and the golf course. Executive rooms available. 241

Island

Island Golf Club, Corballis, Donabate, Co Dublin

Tel: 01 8436462

On first playing The Island in the Irish PGA Championship in 1999, Darren Clarke pronounced it to be: "A fanstastic links which tests every club in the bag." And it should be noted that this wasn't the assessment of a generous winner: Clarke was beaten for the title by Royal Dublin's Neil Manchip.

Founded in 1890 by a syndicate of Dublin businessmen, The Island is a quaint, Irish misnomer in that the course is actually on a peninsula. Its name derived from it being most easily accessible by boat from the village of Malahide, but an inland entrance became more appropriate after the clubhouse was relocated 25 years ago.

In preparation for the club's centenary in 1990, the course was radically remodelled, to

splendid effect. Many of its more irritating blind shots were eliminated and with an extended, overall length of 6,646 yards, it became a far more demanding test for longer hitters.

Since then, the clubhouse has also been entirely refurbished and work is in progress on reconstructing the 10th and 11th holes, as part of ongoing development plans. Meanwhile, the course is highly regarded for the quality of its devilishly tricky greens, which are a fitting legacy to the expertise of long-time greenkeeper, the late Paddy Caul.

Cecil Barcroft, the earliest Irish golf architect, descibed it as having "grand, bold sandhills, small and exceedingly good putting greens, often invisible to the approacher." Apart from the bonus of less blindness, much of that assessment of a delightful challenge, still remains valid.

Sec/Manager:	John Finn
Professional:	Kevin Kelliher
Directions:	3 miles East of Swords. Take R126 off the N1 North of Swords and follow signs
Type of Course:	Links
Date Founded:	1890
No of Holes:	18
Length:	6646 yds (6078 mtrs)
Par:	72
SSS:	72
Green Fees:	1st May to 31st Oct: Weekdays £60 Weekends & Bank Holidays £70; 1st Nov. to 30th Apr: Weekdays £50 Weekends & Bank Holidays £60
Visitors:	Welcome: Contact Club in advance
Societies:	Welcome: Special concessions, Contact Club for details
Facilities:	Chipping/Putting Area, Practice Area, Golf Clubs for hire, Trolley hire, Bar, Restaurant, Caddy service by arrangement

Accommodation, Food and Drink

Reference numbers below refer to detailed information provided in section 2

Accommodation

Estuary House, Malahide, Co Dublin
Tel: 01 8900242 A striking modern brick-built house with four high-quality Bed & Breakfast rooms, most with sea views. 221

Pebble Mill, Kinsealy, Co Dublin
Tel/Fax: 01 8461792 A fine residence in its own grounds just outside Malahide. Three B&B rooms, all en suite. 245

White Sands Hotel, Portmarnock, Co Dublin
Tel: 01 8460003 Thirty-two rooms in a long, low, modern hotel overlooking the sea and the golf course. Executive rooms available. 241

Food and Drink

Gibneys, Malahide, Co Dublin
Tel: 01 8450606 Period appeal aplenty in a grand old pub run by a golfing family. Food from quick snacks to the full works. 226

The Golf Links, Portmarnock, Co Dublin
Tel: 01 8460129 Portmarnock's only pub, overlooking the bay and the golf links. Good-value menu, well-chosen wines. 238

White Sands Hotel, Portmarnock, Co Dublin
Tel: 01 8460003 Thirty-two rooms in a long, low, modern hotel overlooking the sea and the golf course. Executive rooms available. 241

Kilternan

Kilternan Golf & Country Club, Enniskerry Road, Kilternan, Co Dublin

Tel: 01 2955559

Sec/Manager:	Jimmy Kinsella
Professional:	Garry Hendley
Directions:	4 miles North West of Bray off the R117 near to Kilternan
Type of Course:	Parkland
Date Founded:	1988
No of Holes:	18
Length:	5906 yds (5400 mtrs)
Par:	68
SSS:	67
Green Fees:	Weekdays: £18 Weekends & Bank Holidays: £22

Visitors:	Welcome: Book in advance
Societies:	Welcome: Contact Club for details
Facilities:	Chipping/Putting Area, Practice Area, Golf Clubs for hire, Trolley hire, Electric Buggy hire, Bar, Restaurant, plus full menu bar food. Full hotel facilities, use of leisure facilities available in hotel. Half price Green Fees for hotel guests

Accommodation, Food and Drink

Reference numbers below refer to detailed information provided in section 2

Accommodation

Brookville, 91 Monkstown Road, Monkstown Village, Co Dublin
Tel: 01 2809436 A townhouse Bed & Breakfast with four en suite rooms including a triple. Loads of pubs and restaurants nearby.

Ferry House, Dun Laoghaire, Co Dublin
Tel: 01 2808301 Four en suite Bed & Breakfast rooms in a handsome town house an easy walk from the centre of Dun Laoghaire. 228

Ophira, Dun Laoghaire, Co Dublin
Tel/Fax: 01 2800997 Town-centre Bed & Breakfast Accommodation in a mid-19th century house. Four en suite bedrooms. Tv lounge. 225

Summerhill House Hotel, Enniskerry, Co Wicklow
Tel: 01 2867928 Fifty-seven bright, spacious airy bedrooms with en suite facilities, tv and telephone in a friendly, well-situated hotel. 668

Woodland Court Hotel, Southern Cross, Bray, Co Wicklow
Tel: 01 2760258 Sixty five en suite bedrooms with all the modern comforts in a characterful hotel at the southern end of the town. Restaurant and lounge. 667

Food and Drink

Summerhill House Hotel, Enniskerry, Co Wicklow
Tel: 01 2867928 Fifty-seven bright, spacious airy bedrooms with en suite facilities, tv and telephone in a friendly, well-situated hotel. 668

Walters, Dun Laoghaire, Co Dublin
Tel: 01 2807442 Elegant, trendy bar-café-restaurant serving anything from a coffee or a drink to a three-course meal. 229

Woodland Court Hotel, Southern Cross, Bray, Co Wicklow
Tel: 01 2760258 Sixty five en suite bedrooms with all the modern comforts in a characterful hotel at the southern end of the town. Restaurant and lounge. 667

Lucan

Lucan Golf Club, Celbridge Road, Lucan, Co Dublin

Tel: 01 6282106

Sec/Manager:	Tom O'Donnell
Professional:	None
Directions:	10 miles from Dublin City. West of Lucan Village off the N4 towards Maynooth
Type of Course:	Parkland
Date Founded:	1897
No of Holes:	18
Length:	6439 yds (5888 mtrs)
Par:	71
SSS:	71
Green Fees:	Weekdays only £25
Visitors:	Welcome: Mon. Tues. Fri. Wed. to 1.00pm
Societies:	Welcome: Special concessions, Contact Club for details

Facilities: Chipping/Putting Area, Golf Clubs for hire, Trolley hire, Electric Buggy hire, Bar, Restaurant, Caddy service by arrangement

Accommodation, Food and Drink

Reference numbers below refer to detailed information provided in section 2

Accommodation

Ballygoran Lodge, Maynooth, Co Kildare
Tel: 01 6291860 A striking modern villa 1 mile from Maynooth, with four en suite B&B rooms and a suite with a mini-gym.   342

Lucan Spa Hotel, Lucan, Co Dublin
Tel: 01 6280494 Hotel with bar, bistro and restaurant. Superbly appointed en suite bedrooms Scenic waks, National Stud and Championship Golf Courses all close.   255

Ophira, Dun Laoghaire, Co Dublin
Tel/Fax: 01 2800997 Town-centre Bed & Breakfast Accommodation in a mid-19th century house. Four en suite bedrooms. Tv lounge.   225

Straffan Bed & Breakfast, Straffan, Co Kildare
Tel: 01 6272386 Four en suite bedrooms in an attractive new bungalow with a garden long enough to practice that swing.   350

The Hawthorn Hotel, Swords, Co Dublin
Tel: 01 8401308 A charming ten-bedroomed hotel on the bustling main street. Super rooms, excellent Food and Drink, warm, efficient staff.   247

The Milestone, Lucan, Co Dublin
Tel: 01 6241818 Four Bed & Breakfast rooms, all en suite, in a large modern detached house surrounded by beautiful lawns.   227

Willo's, Lucan Village, Co Dublin
Tel /Fax: 01 6283365 Seven letting rooms in a pleasant Bed & Breakfast house near the village centre, 15 minutes' drive fron Dublin City.   230

Food and Drink

Fagan's, Lower Drumcondra Road, Dublin 9, Co Dublin
Tel: 01 8375309 One of the great Victorian pubs, with bags of atmosphere, a lunchtime carvery and evening à la carte.   232

Lucan Spa Hotel, Lucan, Co Dublin
Tel: 01628 0494 Hotel with bar, bistro and restaurant. Superbly appointed en suite bedrooms Scenic waks, National Stud and Championship Golf Courses all close.   255

Ophira, Dun Laoghaire, Co Dublin
Tel/Fax: 01 2800997 Town-centre Bed & Breakfast Accommodation in a mid-19th century house. Four en suite bedrooms. Tv lounge.   225

The Hawthorn Hotel, Swords, Co Dublin
Tel: 01 8401308 A charming ten-bedroomed hotel on the bustling main street. Super rooms, excellent Food and Drink, warm, efficient staff.   247

The Manor Inn, Naas, Co Kildare
Tel: 045 897471 Warmth, hospitality and good food in a smartly modernised pub on the main street of Naas. Lots of racing memorabilia.   347

Luttrellstown

Luttrellstown Castle Golf Club, Castleknock, Dublin 15

Tel: 01 8089988

Pop fans will be familiar with Luttrellstown Castle as the place where Victoria Adams, aka Posh Spice, and David Beckham celebrated their highly-publicised nuptials in 1999. And the castle, dating back to 1436, was also where Irish tournament professional Paul McGinley and his English wife, Allison Shapcott, had their wedding reception.

The club is a totally separate operation and from a strictly golfing standpoint, the location,

seven miles west of Dublin, is more noted as a fine parkland test in delightful surroundings. Situated closeby the River Liffey, it actually overlooks the lower holes on the neighbouring Hermitage course.

Situated in a 560-acre estate, the course was designed by Portmarnock member Nick Bielenberg whose objective was an acceptable challenge for the average, handicap player. He achieved this through generous fairways and the non-threatening use of water hazards.

The venue is also notable for its spacious, wooden clubhouse, built in the style of a French chateau and officially opened in 1995. And it has already played host to an important championship, with the staging of the Irish Women's Open of 1997, which attracted a top-quality international field and was won by Patricia Meunier Lebouc of France.

With an overall length of 7,021 yards off the back tees, the par fives are especially testing. But the par fours can also be quite demanding, expecially the 392-yard seventh, which is arguably the most dangerous. The problems there are presented by out of bounds on the left off the tee and water off the mid-iron approach.

Sec/Manager:	None
Professional:	Edward Doyle
Directions:	From Junction 6 of the M50 follow signs to Castleknock and Carpenterstown. Golf Course 1 mile West of Carpenterstown
Type of Course:	Parkland
Date Founded:	1993
No of Holes:	18
Length:	7021 yds (6420 mtrs)
Par:	72
SSS:	73
Green Fees:	Weekdays: £50 Weekends & Bank Holidays: £55
Visitors:	Welcome: Book in advance
Societies:	Welcome: Special concessions, Contact Club for details
Facilities:	Chipping/Putting Area, Practice Area, Driving Range, Golf Clubs for hire, Trolley hire, Electric Buggy hire, Bar, Restaurant, Caddy service by arrangement

Accommodation, Food and Drink

Reference numbers below refer to detailed
information provided in section 2

Accommodation

Ballygoran Lodge, Maynooth, Co Kildare
Tel: 01 6291860 A striking modern villa 1 mile from Maynooth, with four en suite
B&B rooms and a suite with a mini-gym. 342

Lucan Spa Hotel, Lucan, Co Dublin
Tel: 01 6280494 Hotel with bar, bistro and restaurant. Superbly appointed en suite
bedrooms Scenic waks, National Stud and Championship Golf Courses all close. 255

Ophira, Dun Laoghaire, Co Dublin
Tel/Fax: 01 2800997 Town-centre Bed & Breakfast Accommodation in a mid-19th
century house. Four en suite bedrooms. Tv lounge. 225

Straffan Bed & Breakfast, Straffan, Co Kildare
Tel: 01 6272386 Four en suite bedrooms in an attractive new bungalow with a
garden long enough to practice that swing. 350

The Hawthorn Hotel, Swords, Co Dublin
Tel: 01 8401308 A charming ten-bedroomed hotel on the bustling main street. Super
rooms, excellent Food and Drink, warm, efficient staff. 247

The Milestone, Lucan, Co Dublin
Tel: 01 6241818 Four Bed & Breakfast rooms, all en suite, in a large modern
detached house surrounded by beautiful lawns. 227

Willo's, Lucan Village, Co Dublin
Tel /Fax: 01 6283365 Seven letting rooms in a pleasant Bed & Breakfast house near
the village centre, 15 minutes' drive fron Dublin City. 230

Food and Drink

Fagan's, Lower Drumcondra Road, Dublin 9, Co Dublin
Tel: 01 8375309 One of the great Victorian pubs, with bags of atmosphere, a
lunchtime carvery and evening à la carte. 232

Lucan Spa Hotel, Lucan, Co Dublin
Tel: 01 6280494 Hotel with bar, bistro and restaurant. Superbly appointed en suite
bedrooms Scenic waks, National Stud and Championship Golf Courses all close. 255

Ophira, Dun Laoghaire, Co Dublin
Tel/Fax: 01 2800997 Town-centre Bed & Breakfast Accommodation in a mid-19th
century house. Four en suite bedrooms. Tv lounge. 225

The Hawthorn Hotel, Swords, Co Dublin
Tel: 01 8401308 A charming ten-bedroomed hotel on the bustling main street. Super
rooms, excellent Food and Drink, warm, efficient staff. 247

The Manor Inn, Naas, Co Kildare
Tel: 045 897471 Warmth, hospitality and good food in a smartly modernised pub on
the main street of Naas. Lots of racing memorabilia. 347

Malahide

Malahide Golf Club, Beechwood, The Grange,
Malahide, Co Dublin
Tel: 01 8461611

Sec/Manager:	None
Professional:	David Barton
Directions:	1 mile South of Malahide off the R106 coast road near Portmarnock
Type of Course:	Parkland
Date Founded:	1892
No of Holes:	18 plus 9
Length:	6290 yds (5752 mtrs)
Par:	70
SSS:	70
Green Fees:	Weekdays: £35 Weekends & Bank Holidays: £50
Visitors:	Welcome: Weekdays no restrictions Weekends by prior arrangement

Societies:	Welcome: Contact the Club in advance
Facilities:	Chipping/Putting Area Golf Clubs for hire, Trolley hire, Bar, Restaurant, Caddy service by arrangement

Accommodation, Food and Drink

Reference numbers below refer to detailed
information provided in section 2

Accommodation

Cedar House, Swords, Co Dublin
Tel: 01 8402757 Bed & Breakfast Accommodation in a modern house not far from
the town centre. Packed lunches available. 248

Estuary House, Malahide, Co Dublin
Tel: 01 8900242 A striking modern brick-built house with four high-quality Bed &
Breakfast rooms, most with sea views. 221

Pebble Mill, Kinsealy, Co Dublin
Tel/Fax: 01 8461792 A fine residence in its own grounds just outside Malahide.
Three B&B rooms, all en suite. 245

Roselea, Portmarnock, Co Dublin
Tel: 01 8460117 Two double rooms and two twins, all en suite, in a bungalow set in
spacious gardens and lawns. 233

Southdale, Portmarnock, Co Dublin
Tel/Fax: 01 8463760 Four en suite bedrooms in a striking modern B&B house close
to the seafront and Portmarnock Golf Club. 240

Steiermark, Portmarnock, Co Dublin
Tel/Fax: 01 8462032 A detached villa with four excellent Bed & Breakfast rooms, sea
views and a setting opposite the golf course. 237

The Hawthorn Hotel, Swords, Co Dublin
Tel: 01 8401308 A charming ten-bedroomed hotel on the bustling main street. Super
rooms, excellent Food and Drink, warm, efficient staff. 247

White Sands Hotel, Portmarnock, Co Dublin
Tel: 01 8460003 Thirty-two rooms in a long, low, modern hotel overlooking the sea
and the golf course. Executive rooms available. 241

Willowbrook House, Swords, Co Dublin
Tel: 01 8403843 Five en suite B&B rooms in a modern villa with superb gardens.
Easy walk to Swords town centre. 246

Food and Drink

Gibneys, Malahide, Co Dublin
Tel: 01 8450606 Period appeal aplenty in a grand old pub run by a golfing family.
Food from quick snacks to the full works. 226

The Golf Links, Portmarnock, Co Dublin
Tel: 01 8460129 Portmarnock's only pub, overlooking the bay and the golf links.
Good-value menu, well-chosen wines. 238

The Hawthorn Hotel, Swords, Co Dublin
Tel: 01 8401308 A charming ten-bedroomed hotel on the bustling main street. Super
rooms, excellent Food and Drink, warm, efficient staff. 247

White Sands Hotel, Portmarnock, Co Dublin
Tel: 01 8460003 Thirty-two rooms in a long, low, modern hotel overlooking the sea
and the golf course. Executive rooms available. 241

Milltown

Milltown Golf Club, Lower Churchtown
Road, Dublin 14
Tel: 01 4976090

Sec/Manager:	David Dalton
Professional:	John Harnett
Directions:	3 miles South of Dublin City. From Raneleigh take Sandford Road to Clonskeagh and Milltown. At Clonskeagh turn right into Milltown

Road. After 1 mile turn left into Lower Churchtown Road. Golf Course is on right hand side

Type of Course:	Parkland
Date Founded:	1907
No of Holes:	18
Length:	6165 yds (5638 mtrs)
Par:	71
SSS:	69
Green Fees:	Weekdays only: £35
Visitors:	Welcome: Weekdays only, Contact in advance
Societies:	Welcome: Special concessions, Contact Club for details
Facilities:	Chipping/Putting Area, Golf Clubs for hire, Trolley hire, Restaurant, Caddy service by arrangement

Accommodation, Food and Drink

Reference numbers below refer to detailed information provided in section 2

Accommodation

Brookville, 91 Monkstown Road, Monkstown Village, Co Dublin
Tel: 01 2809436 A townhouse Bed & Breakfast with four en suite rooms including a triple. Loads of pubs and restaurants nearby.

Butlers Town House, Ballsbridge, Dublin 4, Co Dublin
Tel: 01 6674022 20 air-conditioned en suite bedrooms in a beautifully restored Victorian town house. Secure car parking.   239

Eglington Manor, 83 Eglington Road, Donnybrook, Dublin 4,
Tel: 01 2693273 Fax: 01 2697527 A handsome guest house with eight superior en suite bedrooms with tv and phone.

Glenveagh Town House, Ballsbridge, Dublin 4, Co Dublin
Tel: 01 6684612 A stunning late-Victorian town house, now offering superb Bed & Breakfast Accommodation in 13 en suite bedrooms with tv and telephone.   249

McMenamins, Donnybrook, Co Dublin
Tel: 01 4974405 Five en suite Bed & Breakfast rooms with tv and phone in a centrally located but very peaceful period house.   231

Food and Drink

Fagan's, Lower Drumcondra Road, Dublin 9, Co Dublin
Tel: 01 8375309 One of the great Victorian pubs, with bags of atmosphere, a lunchtime carvery and evening à la carte.   232

The Playwright Inn, Blackrock, Co Dublin
Tel: 01 2885155 A renowned multi-award-winning pub with the longest thatched roof in Europe. Great Food and Drink, great entertainment.   250

Walters, Dun Laoghaire, Co Dublin
Tel: 01 2807442 Elegant, trendy bar-café-restaurant serving anything from a coffee or a drink to a three-course meal.   229

Newlands

Newlands, Clondalkin, Dublin 22
Tel: 01459 3157

Sec/Manager:	Mr. A. O'Neill
Professional:	Karl O'Donnell
Directions:	From Dublin take the N7 south west to Newlands Cross Junction. Turn left 50 metres along Belgard Road. Course is on the right hand side
Type of Course:	Parkland
Date Founded:	1923
No of Holes:	18

Length:	5897 mtrs 6184 yds
Par:	71
SSS:	70
Green Fees:	£35
Visitors:	Welcome: no restrictions a.m, Ladies Day Tuesday, Advisable to book in advance
Societies:	Welcome: Contact Club in advance
Facilities:	Chipping/Putting Area, Practice Area, Golf Clubs for hire, Trolley hire, Electric Buggy hire, Bar, Restaurant

Accommodation, Food and Drink

Reference numbers below refer to detailed information provided in section 2

Accommodation

Emmerdale, Firhouse Road, Dublin, Co Dublin
Tel: 01 4516270 Three en suite Bed & Breakfast rooms in a modern but old-style cottage set in landscaped gardens.   224

Monaghan's Harbour Hotel, Naas, Co Kildare
Tel: 045 879145 A home from home feel in a family-run hotel with well-equipped bedrooms, restaurant, coffee shop and bar.   349

The Old Forge, Saggart, Co Dublin
Tel: 01 4589226 Six B & B rooms (three en suite) and a self-contained section to sleep five in a row of 18th-century houses.   242

Food and Drink

Monaghan's Harbour Hotel, Naas, Co Kildare
Tel: 045 879145 A real home from home feel in a family-run hotel with well-equipped bedrooms, restaurant, coffee shop and bar.   349

Rushes, Fairgreen Street, Naas, Co Kildare
Tel: 045 898400 Classic bar food in Rushes and international cuisine in its neighbour Cicero on a prime site in Naas. Steaks a speciality.   343

The Manor Inn, Naas, Co Kildare
Tel: 045 897471 Warmth, hospitality and good food in a smartly modernised pub on the main street of Naas. Lots of racing memorabilia.   347

Open Golf Centre

The Open Golf Centre, Newtown Road, St. Margaret's, Co Dublin
Tel: 01 8640324

Sec/Manager:	Graham Bettie
Professional:	R. Yates
Directions:	Half a mile North of Junction 5 of the M50 off N2
Type of Course:	Parkland
Date Founded:	1993
No of Holes:	18 (plus 9)
Length:	6570 yds (6007 mtrs) Main Course
Par:	71
SSS:	69
Green Fees:	Weekdays: £9.50 Weekends & Bank Holidays: £13.50
Visitors:	Welcome: Any Day, Prior Booking required
Societies:	Welcome: Prior booking essential
Facilities:	Chipping/Putting Area, Practice Area, Driving Range, Golf Clubs for hire, Trolley hire

Accommodation, Food and Drink

Reference numbers below refer to detailed
information provided in section 2

Accommodation

Annesbrook, Duleek, Co Meath

Tel: 041 9823293 A classic 18th-century porticoed country house in ten acres of
grounds. Ten en suite rooms for Bed & Breakfast & dinner menu.   447

Killeentierna House, Dunshaughlin, Co Meath

Tel: 01 8259722 Five Bed & Breakfast rooms, one of family size, in a modern
residence on the Dublin side of Dunshaughlin.   433

The Evergreens, Ashbourne, Co Meath

Tel: 01 8352392 A lovely bungalow just outside the village provides Bed & Breakfast
Accommodation in four rooms (three en suite). Tv lounge.   442

The Hawthorn Hotel, Swords, Co Dublin

Tel: 01 8401308 A charming ten-bedroomed hotel on the bustling main street. Super
rooms, excellent Food and Drink, warm, efficient staff.   247

The Old Workhouse. Dunshaughlin, Co Meath

Tel/Fax: 01 8259251 Civilised living in a sympathetically restored 1840s building.
Four cosy double bedrooms (2 en suite, 2 with private bathroom). Country house
cooking.

Food and Drink

Annesbrook, Duleek, Co Meath

Tel: 041 9823293 A classic 18th-century porticoed country house in ten acres of
grounds. Ten en suite rooms for Bed & Breakfast & dinner menu.   447

Gibneys, Malahide, Co Dublin

Tel: 01 8450606 Period appeal aplenty in a grand old pub run by a golfing family.
Food from quick snacks to the full works.   226

The Hawthorn Hotel, Swords, Co Dublin

Tel: 01 8401308 A charming ten-bedroomed hotel on the bustling main street. Super
rooms, excellent Food and Drink, warm, efficient staff.   247

Portmarnock

Portmarnock Golf Club, Portmarnock, Co
Dublin

Tel: 01 8462968

Universally acknowledged as one of the truly
great links courses, Portmarnock is situated on a
tongue of shallow duneland north of Dublin
City. Its quality and location have made it a
splendid venue for some of the game's great
events, from the British Amateur of 1949, to the
Canada Cup in 1960 and the 1991 Walker Cup,
quite apart from 12 stagings of the revived Irish
Open.

The Canada Cup was especially notable for
providing the newly-crowned US Open champion, Arnold Palmer, with his first taste of links
golf. As it happened, he and partner Sam Snead
captured the trophy for the US, and Palmer's
rapid learning skills were later reflected in successive British Open triumphs in 1961 and 1962.

Founded in 1894, the championship course
offers a classic, traditional challenge, which
moved the celebrated golf writer, Bernard Dar-
win, to comment: "I know of no greater finish
in the world than that of the last five holes at
Portmarnock ..." And Tom Watson remarked on
its fairness, devoid as it is of "tricks or nasty sur-
prises."

This standard is mirrored in an additional
nine, designed by the distinguished British architect, Fred Hawtree, whose holes are woven
seamlessly within the championship layout.

Within the curve of the coastline formed by
Howth peninsula, it offers stunning views of Ireland's Eye and Lambay Island, rising sharply
from deep waters. But above all, there is the
charm of its delightful turf, the wildness, the
solitude of the sandhills and the sea, and the
ever-present challenge of the wind.

Sec/Manager:	John Quigley
Professional:	Joey Purcell
Directions:	1 mile South of Portmarnock down a private road
Type of Course:	Links
Date Founded:	1894
No of Holes:	18 (plus 9)
Length:	6956 yds (6361 mtrs)
Par:	72
SSS:	74
Green Fees:	Weekdays (exc. Wed.): £75 Weekends and Bank Holidays: £95
Visitors:	Welcome: Restrictions at weekends, Enquire in advance
Societies:	Welcome: Contact in writing
Facilities:	Chipping/Putting Area, Practice Area, Driving Range, Golf Clubs for hire, Trolley hire, Electric Buggy hire Bar, Restaurant

Accommodation, Food and Drink

Reference numbers below refer to detailed
information provided in section 2

Accommodation

Cedar House, Swords, Co Dublin

Tel: 01 8402757 Bed & Breakfast Accommodation in a modern house not far from
the town centre. Packed lunches available.   248

Estuary House, Malahide, Co Dublin

Tel: 01 8900242 A striking modern brick-built house with four high-quality Bed &
Breakfast rooms, most with sea views.   221

Gleann-na-Smol, Howth, Co Dublin

Tel: 01 8322936 Personal service in a family-run B&B renowned for its hospitality. 5
en suite rooms include a triple.   243

Marine Hotel, Sutton Cross, Dublin 13, Co Dublin
Tel: 01 8390000 A superior hotel offering high standards of Accommodation, service
and food. Great views, too.   220
Pebble Mill, Kinsealy, Co Dublin
Tel/Fax: 01 8461792 A fine residence in its own grounds just outside Malahide.
Three B&B rooms, all en suite.   245
Roselea, Portmarnock, Co Dublin
Tel: 01 8460117 Two double rooms and two twins, all en suite, in a bungalow set in
spacious gardens and lawns.   233
Southdale, Portmarnock, Co Dublin
Tel/Fax: 01 8463760 Four en suite bedrooms in a striking modern B&B house close
to the seafront and Portmarnock Golf Club.   240
Steiermark, Portmarnock, Co Dublin
Tel/Fax: 01 8462032 A detached villa with four excellent Bed & Breakfast rooms, sea
views and a setting opposite the golf course.   237
The Hawthorn Hotel, Swords, Co Dublin
Tel: 01 8401308 A charming ten-bedroomed hotel on the bustling main street. Super
rooms, excellent Food and Drink, warm, efficient staff.   247
White Sands Hotel, Portmarnock, Co Dublin
Tel: 01 8460003 Thirty-two rooms in a long, low, modern hotel overlooking the sea
and the golf course. Executive rooms available.   241
Willowbrook House, Swords, Co Dublin
Tel: 01 8403843 Five en suite B&B rooms in a modern villa with superb gardens.
Easy walk to Swords town centre.   246

Food and Drink

Gibneys, Malahide, Co Dublin
Tel: 01 8450606 Period appeal aplenty in a grand old pub run by a golfing family.
Food from quick snacks to the full works.   226
Marine Hotel, Sutton Cross, Dublin 13, Co Dublin
Tel: 01 8390000 A superior hotel offering high standards of Accommodation, service
and food. Great views, too.   220
The Bloody Stream, Howth, Co Dublin
Tel: 01 8395076 Howth's busiest pub-restaurant, with 100 covers, beer garden, live
music and bags of atmosphere. Seafood a speciality.   234
The Golf Links, Portmarnock, Co Dublin
Tel: 01 8460129 Portmarnock's only pub, overlooking the bay and the golf links.
Good-value menu, well-chosen wines.   238
The Hawthorn Hotel, Swords, Co Dublin
Tel: 01 8401308 A charming ten-bedroomed hotel on the bustling main street. Super
rooms, excellent Food and Drink, warm, efficient staff.   247
White Sands Hotel, Portmarnock, Co Dublin
Tel: 01 8460003 Thirty-two rooms in a long, low, modern hotel overlooking the sea
and the golf course. Executive rooms too.   241

Portmarnock Links

Portmarnock Hotel & Golf Links, Strand Road, Portmarnock, County Dublin

Tel: 01 8461800

In an area where patrons once parked their cars while attending the Irish Open at majestic Portmarnock GC, Bernhard Langer, three times

winner of that particular title, turned his hand to golf-course design. And the result of his endeavours may be savoured at what is now known as Portmarnock Hotel and Golf Links - "where nothing is overlooked but the sea."

Essentially, the area is an extension of the shallow duneland of its celebrated neighbour. Where the Links is concerned, however, the design has delivered a much tighter, 6,815-yard layout, distinguished by some wickedly difficult pot bunkers.

Once the property of Jameson's, the famous Irish distilling family, it is now owned by a consortium of businessmen including Mark McCormack of IMG and Dr Tony O'Reilly of Columbia Investments. And it has proved to be a resounding success, especially with visitors from the UK.

The site is steeped in history, which explains the presence of horizontal lines towards the edges of the stone tee-markers. This is ancient Ogham writing, dating back to second-century druids. It was also the diocese of St Marnock, who lent his name to the area before achieving the same impact at Kilmarnock, having emigrated to Scotland.

One of the Jameson's, Annie, married Guiseppe Marconi, the inventor of the wireless. And in more recent times, the Australian aviator, Charles Kingsford Smith, took off from Portmarnock strand in June 1930, with his Irish navigator, Captain Saul, en route to Newfoundland, which they reached thirty one and a half hours later.

Sec/Manager:	Moira Cassidy
Professional:	None
Directions:	On the outskirts of Portmarnock to the north east of Dublin City
Type of Course:	Links

Date Founded:	1996
No of Holes:	18
Length:	6815 yds (6232 mtrs)
Par:	71
SSS:	73
Green Fees:	Weekdays: £60 Weekends & Bank Holidays:: £60
Visitors:	Welcome: Ring in advance
Societies:	Welcome: Book in advance
Facilities:	Chipping/Putting Area, Practice Area, Golf Clubs for hire, Trolley hire, Bar, Restaurant, Caddy service by arrangement

Accommodation, Food and Drink

Reference numbers below refer to detailed
information provided in section 2

Accommodation

Cedar House, Swords, Co Dublin
Tel: 01 8402757 Bed & Breakfast Accommodation in a modern house not far from
the town centre. Packed lunches available. 248

Estuary House, Malahide, Co Dublin
Tel: 01 8900242 A striking modern brick-built house with four high-quality Bed &
Breakfast rooms, most with sea views. 221

Gleann-na-Smol, Howth, Co Dublin
Tel: 01 8322936 Personal service in a family-run B&B renowned for its hospitality. 5
en suite rooms include a triple. 243

Marine Hotel, Sutton Cross, Dublin 13, Co Dublin
Tel: 01 8390000 A superior hotel offering high standards of Accommodation, service
and food. Great views, too. 220

Pebble Mill, Kinsealy, Co Dublin
Tel/Fax: 01 8461792 A fine residence in its own grounds just outside Malahide.
Three B&B rooms, all en suite. 245

Roselea, Portmarnock, Co Dublin
Tel: 01 8460117 Two double rooms and two twins, all en suite, in a bungalow set in
spacious gardens and lawns. 233

Southdale, Portmarnock, Co Dublin
Tel/Fax: 01 8463760 Four en suite bedrooms in a striking modern B&B house close
to the seafront and Portmarnock Golf Club. 240

Steiermark, Portmarnock, Co Dublin
Tel/Fax: 01 8462032 A detached villa with four excellent Bed & Breakfast rooms, sea
views and a setting opposite the golf course. 237

The Hawthorn Hotel, Swords, Co Dublin
Tel: 01 8401308 A charming ten-bedroomed hotel on the bustling main street. Super
rooms, excellent Food and Drink, warm, efficient staff. 247

White Sands Hotel, Portmarnock, Co Dublin
Tel: 01 8460003 Thirty-two rooms in a long, low, modern hotel overlooking the sea
and the golf course. Executive rooms available. 241

Willowbrook House, Swords, Co Dublin
Tel: 01 8403843 Five en suite B&B rooms in a modern villa with superb gardens.
Easy walk to Swords town centre. 246

Food and Drink

Gibneys, Malahide, Co Dublin
Tel: 01 8450606 Period appeal aplenty in a grand old pub run by a golfing family.
Food from quick snacks to the full works. 226

Marine Hotel, Sutton Cross, Dublin 13, Co Dublin
Tel: 01 8390000 A superior hotel offering high standards of Accommodation, service
and food. Great views, too. 220

The Bloody Stream, Howth, Co Dublin
Tel: 01 8395076 Howth's busiest pub-restaurant, with 100 covers, beer garden, live
music and bags of atmosphere. Seafood a speciality. 234

The Golf Links, Portmarnock, Co Dublin
Tel: 01 8460129 Portmarnock's only pub, overlooking the bay and the golf links.
Good-value menu, well-chosen wines. 238

The Hawthorn Hotel, Swords, Co Dublin
Tel: 01 8401308 A charming ten-bedroomed hotel on the bustling main street. Super
rooms, excellent Food and Drink, warm, efficient staff. 247

White Sands Hotel, Portmarnock, Co Dublin
Tel: 01 8460003 Thirty-two rooms in a long, low, modern hotel overlooking the sea
and the golf course. Executive rooms available. 241

Royal Dublin

Royal Dublin Golf Course, Dollymount,
Dublin 3
Tel: 01 8336346

In the northern suburbs of Dublin, Captain Bligh
of the infamous "Bounty", left the marine engi-
neering legacy of a breakwater known locally as
the Bull Wall. For its part, nature left the Bull
Island, which is home to the Royal Dublin and
St Annes golf clubs.

Having been founded in Phoenix Park in 1885,
Royal Dublin had a short stay at Sutton before
its final move to Dollymount. The members
chose very wisely, finding themselves a marvellous stretch of shallow duneland only five miles
from the City centre.

Their wisdom was also evident in having the
celebrated British architect, Harry Colt, re-design
the layout after World War One, when the British Military used the course as a musketry range.

Later, it was considered good enough to stage the "old" Irish Open in 1931, 1936 and 1950. And it then became the scene of some stirring battles between Seve Ballesteros and Bernhard Langer when the revived Irish Open was staged there from 1983 to 1985.

It is also famous as the home club of Christy O'Connor Snr, revered by the members, not least for his stunning finish of eagle-birdie-eagle, when capturing the Carrolls International Tournament there in 1966. Repeating such an exploit would now be appreciably tougher, however, since the 18th was reduced to a par four.

With an old style, "out and in" layout, the course is normally at its most testing on the homeward journey into the prevailing wind. But it remains a fine challenge, whatever the conditions.

Sec/Manager:	John A. Lamb
Professional:	Leonard Owens
Directions:	4 miles from City Centre. From Custom House Quay follow signs for Howth along the coast road. Just past Clontarf turn right into Bull Wall. Golf Course is on the left hand side.
Type of Course:	Links
Date Founded:	1885
No of Holes:	18
Length:	6594 yds (6030 mtrs)
Par:	73
SSS:	73
Green Fees:	Weekdays: £65 Weekends & Bank Holidays: £80
Visitors:	Welcome: Not Wednesday & Saturday, Restrictions at other times, Contact Club for details
Societies:	Welcome: Contact Club in writing or phone
Facilities:	Chipping/Putting Area, Practice Area, Driving Range, Golf Clubs for hire Trolley hire, Bar, Restaurant

Accommodation, Food and Drink

Reference numbers below refer to detailed information provided in section 2

Accommodation

Arranmore House, Lower Drumcondra Road, Dublin 9, Co Dublin
Tel: 01 8300009 Four en suite guest rooms in a Bed & Breakfast house in a Victorian terrace. Off-street parking.   222

Hedigan's Guest House, Clontarf, Dublin 3, Co Dublin
Tel: 01 8531663 A fine redbrick mansion with many splendid features. B&B Accommodation in 15 en suite bedrooms including mini-suites.   251

Marine Hotel, Sutton Cross, Dublin 13, Co Dublin
Tel: 01 8390000 A superior hotel offering high standards of Accommodation, service and food. Great views, too.   220

Roselea, Portmarnock, Co Dublin
Tel: 01 8460117 Two double rooms and two twins, all en suite, in a bungalow set in spacious gardens and lawns.   233

Steiermark, Portmarnock, Co Dublin
Tel/Fax: 01 8462032 A detached villa with four excellent Bed & Breakfast rooms, sea views and a setting opposite the golf course.   237

Food and Drink

Fagan's, Lower Drumcondra Road, Dublin 9, Co Dublin
Tel: 01 8375309 One of the great Victorian pubs, with bags of atmosphere, a lunchtime carvery and evening à la carte.   232

Marine Hotel, Sutton Cross, Dublin 13, Co Dublin
Tel: 01 8390000 A superior hotel offering high standards of Accommodation, service and food. Great views, too.   220

The Bloody Stream, Howth, Co Dublin
Tel: 01 8395076 Howth's busiest pub-restaurant, with 100 covers, beer garden, live music and bags of atmosphere. Seafood a speciality.   234

The Brian Boru, Glasnevin, Dublin 9, Co Dublin
Tel: 01 8304527 Public house and restaurant in a grand building dating from the 1850s. Conservatory, beer garden, spacious car park.   223

Skerries

Skerries Golf Club, Hacketstown, Skerries, Co Dublin

Tel: 01 8491567

Sec/Manager:	Aiden Burns
Professional:	Jimmy Kinsella
Directions:	1 mile South of Skerries off the R127
Type of Course:	Parkland
Date Founded:	1905
No of Holes:	18
Length:	6667 yds (6097 mtrs)
Par:	73
SSS:	72
Green Fees:	Weekdays: £25 Weekends & Bank Holidays: £30
Visitors:	Welcome: Weekdays only
Societies:	Welcome: Contact Club for details
Facilities:	Practice Area Bar, Restaurant

Accommodation, Food and Drink

Reference numbers below refer to detailed information provided in section 2

Accommodation

Annesbrook, Duleek, Co Meath
Tel: 041 9823293 A classic 18th-century porticoed country house in ten acres of grounds. Ten en suite rooms for Bed & Breakfast & dinner menu.   447

St Gobnaits, Drogheda, Co Louth
Tel: 041 9837844 A detached house by the N1, with four en suite B&B rooms. One kilometre from town centre, close to golf courses and beaches.   403

The Hawthorn Hotel, Swords, Co Dublin
Tel: 01 8401308 A charming ten-bedroomed hotel on the bustling main street. Super rooms, excellent Food and Drink, warm, efficient staff.   247

Woodview Farmhouse, Skerries, Co Dublin
Tel: 01 8491528 Irish hospitality at its best in a secluded farmhouse offering B&B Accommodation & evening meals by request.   244

Food and Drink

Annesbrook, Duleek, Co Meath
Tel: 041 9823293 A classic 18th-century porticoed country house in ten acres of grounds. Ten en suite rooms for Bed & Breakfast & dinner menu.   447

Gibneys, Malahide, Co Dublin
Tel: 01 8450606 Period appeal aplenty in a grand old pub run by a golfing family. Food from quick snacks to the full works.   226

The Hawthorn Hotel, Swords, Co Dublin
Tel: 01 8401308 A charming ten-bedroomed hotel on the bustling main street. Super rooms, excellent Food and Drink, warm, efficient staff.   247

Slade Valley

Slade Valley Golf Club, Lynch Park, Brittas, Co Dublin

Tel: 01 4582183

Sec/Manager:	Pat Maguire
Professional:	John Dignam
Directions:	2 miles North of Brittas off the N81
Type of Course:	Parkland
Date Founded:	1970
No of Holes:	18
Length:	5892 yds (5388 mtrs)
Par:	69
SSS:	68
Green Fees:	Weekdays: £17 Weekends & Bank Holidays: £25
Visitors:	Welcome: Contact Club for details
Societies:	Welcome: Contact Club in writing or phone
Facilities:	Chipping/Putting Area, Golf Clubs for hire Trolley hire, Bar, Restaurant Caddy service by arrangement

Accommodation, Food and Drink

Reference numbers below refer to detailed information provided in section 2

Accommodation

Emmerdale, Firhouse Road, Dublin, Co Dublin

Tel: 01 4516270 Three en suite Bed & Breakfast rooms in a modern but old-style cottage set in landscaped gardens. 224

Monaghan's Harbour Hotel, Naas, Co Kildare

Tel: 045 879145 A real home from home feel in a family-run hotel with well-equipped bedrooms, restaurant, coffee shop and bar. 349

Straffan Bed & Breakfast, Straffan, Co Dublin

Tel: 01 6272386 Four en suite bedrooms in an attractive new bungalow with a garden long enough to practice that swing. 350

The Old Forge, Saggart, Co Dublin

Tel: 01 4589226 Six B & B rooms (three en suite) and a self-contained section to sleep five in a row of 18th-century houses. 242

Food and Drink

Monaghan's Harbour Hotel, Naas, Co Kildare

Tel: 045 879145 A real home from home feel in a family-run hotel with well-equipped bedrooms, restaurant, coffee shop and bar. 349

Rushes, Fairgreen Street, Naas, Co Kildare

Tel: 045 898400 Classic bar food in Rushes and international cuisine in its neighbour Cicero on a prime site in Naas. Steaks a speciality. 343

The Manor Inn, Naas, Co Kildare

Tel: 045 897471 Warmth, hospitality and good food in a smartly modernised pub on the main street of Naas. Lots of racing memorabilia. 347

St Anne's

St. Annes Golf Club, North Bull Island Nature Reserve, North Bull Island, Dublin 5

Tel: 01 8336471

Sec/Manager:	Shirley Sleator
Professional:	P .Skerritt

Directions:	5 miles from City Centre. From Custom House Quay follow signs for Howth along the coast road. Just past Dollymount turn right into Causeway Road. Golf Course is on the left hand side
Type of Course:	Links
Date Founded:	1921
No of Holes:	18
Length:	6199 yds (5669 mtrs)
Par:	70
SSS:	70
Green Fees:	Weekdays: £30 Weekends & Bank Holidays: £40
Visitors:	Welcome: Contact Club for details
Societies:	Welcome: Special concessions, Contact Club for details
Facilities:	Chipping/Putting Area, Trolley hire, Electric Buggy hire, Bar, Restaurant

Accommodation, Food and Drink

Reference numbers below refer to detailed information provided in section 2

Accommodation

Arranmore House, Lower Drumcondra Road, Dublin 9

Tel: 01 8300009 Four en suite guest rooms in a Bed & Breakfast house in a Victorian terrace. Off-street parking. 222

Gleann-na-Smol, Howth, Co Dublin

Tel: 01 8322936 Personal service in a family-run B&B renowned for its hospitality. 5 en suite rooms include a triple. 243

Hedigan's Guest House, Clontarf, Dublin 3, Co Dublin

Tel: 01 8531663 A fine redbrick mansion with many splendid features. B&B Accommodation in 15 en suite bedrooms including mini-suites. 251

Marine Hotel, Sutton Cross, Dublin 13, Co Dublin

Tel: 01 8390000 A superior hotel offering high standards of Accommodation, service and food. Great views, too. 220

Food and Drink

Marine Hotel, Sutton Cross, Dublin 13, Co Dublin

Tel: 01 8390000 A superior hotel offering high standards of Accommodation, service and food. Great views, too. 220

The Bloody Stream, Howth, Co Dublin

Tel: 01 8395076 Howth's busiest pub-restaurant, with 100 covers, beer garden, live music and bags of atmosphere. Seafood a speciality. 234

The Golf Links, Portmarnock, Co Dublin

Tel: 01 8460129 Portmarnock's only pub, overlooking the bay and the golf links. Good-value menu, well-chosen wines. 238

St Margaret's

St. Margaret's Golf & Country Club, St. Margaret's, Co Dublin

Tel: 01 8640400

Sec/Manager:	Tony Judge
Professional:	None
Directions:	West of Dublin Airport. 1 mile North of St. Margaret's off the R122
Type of Course:	Parkland
Date Founded:	1992
No of Holes:	18
Length:	6917 yds (6344 mtrs)

Par:	72
SSS:	71
Green Fees:	Monday – Wednesday: £40 Thursday & Sunday: £45 Friday, Saturday & Bank Holidays: £50
Visitors:	Welcome: Contact Club for details
Societies:	Welcome: Special concessions, Contact Club in writing or phone
Facilities:	Chipping/Putting Area, Practice Area, Driving Range, Golf Clubs for hire, Trolley hire, Electric Buggy hire, Bar, Restaurant

Accommodation, Food and Drink

Reference numbers below refer to detailed information provided in section 2

Accommodation

Arranmore House, Lower Drumcondra Road, Dublin 9
Tel: 01 8300009 Four en suite guest rooms in a Bed & Breakfast house in a Victorian terrace. Off-street parking. 222

Cedar House, Swords, Co Dublin
Tel: 01 8402757 Bed & Breakfast Accommodation in a modern house not far from the town centre. Packed lunches available. 248

The Evergreens, Ashbourne, Co Meath
Tel: 01 8352392 A lovely bungalow just outside the village provides Bed & Breakfast Accommodation in four rooms (three en suite). Tv lounge. 442

The Hawthorn Hotel, Swords, Co Dublin
Tel: 01 8401308 A charming ten-bedroomed hotel on the bustling main street. Super rooms, excellent Food and Drink, warm, efficient staff. 247

Willowbrook House, Swords, Co Dublin
Tel: 01 8403843 Five en suite B&B rooms in a modern villa with superb gardens. Easy walk to Swords town centre. 246

Food and Drink

Gibneys, Malahide, Co Dublin
Tel: 01 8450606 Period appeal aplenty in a grand old pub run by a golfing family. Food from quick snacks to the full works. 226

The Golf Links, Portmarnock, Co Dublin
Tel: 01 8460129 Portmarnock's only pub, overlooking the bay and the golf links. Good-value menu, well-chosen wines. 238

The Hawthorn Hotel, Swords, Co Dublin
Tel: 01 8401308 A charming ten-bedroomed hotel on the bustling main street. Super rooms, excellent Food and Drink, warm, efficient staff. 247

Stackstown

Stackstown Golf Club, Kellystown Road, Rathfarnham, Dublin 16
Tel: 01 4942338

Sec/Manager:	Kieran Lawler
Professional:	Michael Kavanach
Directions:	From Junction 11 of M50 follow signs for Knocklyon & Ballyboden. At Ballyboden take Taylors Lane past Grange Golf Course and Marley Park. At the next major crossroads go straight ahead to Kellystown Road. Golf Course on the right hand side
Type of Course:	Hilly Parkland
Date Founded:	1975
No of Holes:	18
Length:	6509 yds (5952 mtrs)

Par:	72
SSS:	68
Green Fees:	Weekdays: £16 Weekends & Bank Holidays: £20
Visitors:	Welcome: Mon - Friday preferred
Societies:	Welcome: Contact Club in advance
Facilities:	Bar, Restaurant

Accommodation, Food and Drink

Reference numbers below refer to detailed information provided in section 2

Accommodation

Ariemond, Dun Laoghaire, Co Dublin
Tel: 01 2801664 Five Bed & Breakfast rooms, three en suite, two with private baths, in a lovely house two minutes walk from the centre. 235

Emmerdale, Firhouse Road, Dublin, Co Dublin
Tel: 01 4516270 Three en suite Bed & Breakfast rooms in a modern but old-style cottage set in landscaped gardens. 224

Summerhill House Hotel, Enniskerry, Co Wicklow
Tel: 01 2867928 Fifty-seven bright, spacious airy bedrooms with en suite facilities, tv and telephone in a friendly, well-situated hotel. 668

The Kingston Hotel, Dun Laoghaire, Co Dublin
Tel: 01 2801810 Fifty-three well-equipped en suite bedrooms – singles, doubles, twins and triples – in a family-run hotel on the seafront. 236

Woodland Court Hotel, Southern Cross, Bray, Co Wicklow
Tel: 01 2760258 Sixty five en suite bedrooms with all the modern comforts in a characterful hotel at the southern end of the town. Restaurant and lounge. 667

Food and Drink

Summerhill House Hotel, Enniskerry, Co Wicklow
Tel: 01 2867928 Fifty-seven bright, spacious airy bedrooms with en suite facilities, tv and telephone in a friendly, well-situated hotel. 668

The Brian Boru, Glasnevin, Dublin 9, Co Dublin
Tel: 01 8304527 Public house and restaurant in a grand building dating from the 1850s. Conservatory, beer garden, spacious car park. 223

The Kingston Hotel, Dun Laoghaire, Co Dublin
Tel: 01 2801810 Fifty-three well-equipped en suite bedrooms – singles, doubles, twins and triples – in a family-run hotel on the seafront. 236

Woodland Court Hotel, Southern Cross, Bray, Co Wicklow
Tel: 01 2760258 Sixty five en suite bedrooms with all the modern comforts in a characterful hotel at the southern end of the town. Restaurant and lounge. 667

Swords

Swords Golf Course, Balheary Ave, Swords, Co Dublin
Tel: 01 8409819

Sec/Manager:	Orla McGuinness
Professional:	None
Directions:	Two and a half miles North West of Swords off the R125 to Ratoath
Type of Course:	Parkland
Date Founded:	1993
No of Holes:	18
Length:	6203 yds (5673 mtrs)
Par:	71
SSS:	70
Green Fees:	Weekdays: £10 Weekends & Bank Holidays: £14
Visitors:	Welcome: Telephone to book
Societies:	Welcome: Contact in Advance

Facilities: Chipping/Putting Area, Golf Clubs for hire, Trolley hire

Accommodation, Food and Drink

Reference numbers below refer to detailed information provided in section 2

Accommodation

Annesbrook, Duleek, Co Meath

Tel: 041 9823293 A classic 18th-century porticoed country house in ten acres of grounds. Ten en suite rooms for Bed & Breakfast & dinner menu. 447

Cedar House, Swords, Co Dublin

Tel: 01 8402757 Bed & Breakfast Accommodation in a modern house not far from the town centre. Packed lunches available. 248

The Evergreens, Ashbourne, Co Meath

Tel: 01 8352392 A lovely bungalow just outside the village provides Bed & Breakfast Accommodation in four rooms (three en suite). Tv lounge. 442

The Hawthorn Hotel, Swords, Co Dublin

Tel: 01 8401308 A charming ten-bedroomed hotel on the bustling main street. Super rooms, excellent Food and Drink, warm, efficient staff. 247

Willowbrook House, Swords, Co Dublin

Tel: 01 8403843 Five en suite B&B rooms in a modern villa with superb gardens. Easy walk to Swords town centre. 246

Food and Drink

Duleek, Co Meath

Tel: 041 9823293 A classic 18th-century porticoed country house in ten acres of grounds. Ten en suite rooms for Bed & Breakfast & dinner menu. 447

Gibneys, Malahide, Co Dublin

Tel: 01 8450606 Period appeal aplenty in a grand old pub run by a golfing family. Food from quick snacks to the full works. 226

The Hawthorn Hotel, Swords, Co Dublin

Tel: 01 8401308 A charming ten-bedroomed hotel on the bustling main street. Super rooms, excellent Food and Drink, warm, efficient staff. 247

Turvey

Turvey Golf Club, Turvey Avenue, Donabate, Co Dublin

Tel: 01 8435169

Sec/Manager:	Teresa McDermot
Professional:	None
Directions:	1 mile east of Dunabate off the R126 to Portraine
Type of Course:	Parklands
Date Founded:	1994
No of Holes:	18
Length:	6600 yds 6935 mtrs
Par:	71
SSS:	72
Green Fees:	Weekdays £E20 Weekends £24
Visitors:	Welcome: No restrictions
Societies:	Welcome: Weekdays and afternoons at Weekends
Facilities:	Practice Area, Trolley hire, Bar, Restaurant, Caddy service by arrangement, Hotel/Accommodation on site

Accommodation, Food and Drink

Reference numbers below refer to detailed information provided in section 2

Accommodation

Estuary House, Malahide, Co Dublin

Tel: 01 8900242 A striking modern brick-built house with four high-quality Bed & Breakfast rooms, most with sea views. 221

Pebble Mill, Kinsealy, Co Dublin

Tel/Fax: 01 8461792 A fine residence in its own grounds just outside Malahide. Three B&B rooms, all en suite. 245

Woodview Farmhouse, Skerries, Co Dublin

Tel: 01 8491528 Irish hospitality at its best in a secluded farmhouse offering B&B Accommodation & evening meals by request. 244

Food and Drink

Gibneys, Malahide, Co Dublin

Tel: 01 8450606 Period appeal aplenty in a grand old pub run by a golfing family. Food from quick snacks to the full works. 226

The Golf Links, Portmarnock, Co Dublin

Tel: 01 8460129 Portmarnock's only pub, overlooking the bay and the golf links. Good-value menu, well-chosen wines. 238

White Sands Hotel, Portmarnock, Co Dublin

Tel: 01 8460003 Thirty-two rooms in a long, low, modern hotel overlooking the sea and the golf course. Executive rooms available. 241

Westmanstown

Westmanstown Golf Club & Sports Centre, Westmanstown, Clonsilla, Dublin 15

Tel: 01 8205817

Sec/Manager:	John Joyce
Professional:	None
Directions:	2 miles North East of Lucan. From Junction 7 of M50 take N4 into Lucan. In Lucan turn right into Lower Lucan Road over the River Liffey. After three quarters of a mile turn left. Golf Course on the left hand side of road
Type of Course:	Parkland
Date Founded:	1988
No of Holes:	18
Length:	6395 yds (5848 mtrs)
Par:	71
SSS:	70
Green Fees:	Weekdays £25 Weekends & Bank Holidays £30
Visitors:	Welcome: Contact Club in advance
Societies:	Welcome: Special concessions, Contact Club for details
Facilities:	Chipping/Putting Area, Practice Area, Trolley hire, Electric Buggy hire, Bar, Restaurant

Accommodation, Food and Drink

Reference numbers below refer to detailed information provided in section 2

Accommodation

Ballygoran Lodge, Maynooth, Co Kildare

Tel: 01 6291860 A striking modern villa 1 mile from Maynooth, with four en suite B&B rooms and a suite with a mini-gym. 342

Lucan Spa Hotel, Lucan, Co Dublin

Tel: 01 6280494 Hotel with bar, bistro and restaurant. Superbly appointed en suite bedrooms Scenic waks, National Stud and Championship Golf Courses all close. 255

Ophira, Dun Laoghaire, Co Dublin

Tel/Fax: 01 2800997 Town-centre Bed & Breakfast Accommodation in a mid-19th century house. Four en suite bedrooms. Tv lounge. 225

Straffan Bed & Breakfast, Straffan, Co Kildare

Tel: 01 6272386 Four en suite bedrooms in an attractive new bungalow with a garden long enough to practice that swing. 350

The Hawthorn Hotel, Swords, Co Dublin

Tel: 01 8401308 A charming ten-bedroomed hotel on the bustling main street. Super rooms, excellent Food and Drink, warm, efficient staff. 247

The Milestone, Lucan, Co Dublin

Tel: 01 6241818 Four Bed & Breakfast rooms, all en suite, in a large modern detached house surrounded by beautiful lawns. 227

Willo's, Lucan Village, Co Dublin

Tel /Fax: 01 6283365 Seven letting rooms in a pleasant Bed & Breakfast house near the village centre, 15 minutes' drive fron Dublin City. 230

Food and Drink

Fagan's, Lower Drumcondra Road, Dublin 9, Co Dublin

Tel: 01 8375309 One of the great Victorian pubs, with bags of atmosphere, a lunchtime carvery and evening à la carte. 232

Lucan Spa Hotel, Lucan, Co Dublin

Tel: 01 6280494 Hotel with bar, bistro and restaurant. Superbly appointed en suite bedrooms Scenic waks, National Stud and Championship Golf Courses all close. 255

Ophira, Dun Laoghaire, Co Dublin

Tel/Fax: 01 2800997 Town-centre Bed & Breakfast Accommodation in a mid-19th century house. Four en suite bedrooms. Tv lounge. 225

The Hawthorn Hotel, Swords, Co Dublin

Tel: 01 8401308 A charming ten-bedroomed hotel on the bustling main street. Super rooms, excellent Food and Drink, warm, efficient staff. 247

The Manor Inn, Naas, Co Kildare

Tel: 045 897471 Warmth, hospitality and good food in a smartly modernised pub on the main street of Naas. Lots of racing memorabilia. 347

GALWAY

On a hill beside the Derrygrimlagh Bog near Clifden, is a rather special monument. Shaped like the wing of a plane, it commemorates the historic happening, more than 80 years ago, when two transatlantic aviators became the 20th century's first, notable international visitors to Co Galway. Since then, the acknowledged heart of the West of Ireland has become a haven for tourists. And recent developments have made it especially attractive to golfers, who, while treading its fairways, will quickly come to know the exploits of Christy O'Connor Snr and his nephew, Christy Jnr, the county's most illustrious golfing sons.

Their activities are some way removed from those of intrepid pilot, Captain John Alcock, and his navigator, Lt Arthur Brown, who flew a Vickers Vimy 1,900 miles from Newfoundland to

Connemara in six hours and 12 minutes, at a speed of 120mph. By the time not-so-firm ground had been reached at the end of their journey, they had flown into history. Historic achievements are also attributed to the O'Connors. For instance, Christy Snr became the first professional golfer from these islands to win a four-figure tournament cheque when he captured the top prize of £1,000 in the Swallow Penfold Tournament in 1955. Fifteen years later, the same player won a world-record first prize of £25,000 in the John Player Classic at Hollinwell, Notts, a victory which was to have a suitably notable postscript. And in 1973 at Muirfield, he became the first player from either side of the Atlantic to make 10 successive Ryder Cup appearances.

For his part, Christy Jnr achieved a spectacular Ryder Cup victory over Fred Couples in the 1989 Ryder Cup matches at The Belfry, where a two-iron approach of 229 yards to within five feet of the 18th flag, became one of the most celebrated shots in the history of the tournament. Then, in July 1999, he became the first Irish winner of the British Senior Open at Royal Portrush. Both players were born 24 years apart at Knocknacarra, a small townland out-

Derryclare Lake, Connemara, Co Galway

side Galway City on the way to Connemara. Through the years, they have become closely identified with their native county, where Christy Jnr has had the considerable satisfaction of designing two golf courses - the outstanding development at Galway Bay and the more modest members' club at Gort, where he once had a home.

A measure of the county's ties to the Royal and Ancient game is that in 1984, when Galway City had its quincentennial, one of the more prominent celebrations was an international Golf Classic at Galway GC, where Scotland's Gordon Brand Jnr captured the title from a field which included Ian Woosnam and Sandy Lyle. The county's courses are: Athenry, Barna, Connemara, Connemara Isles, Galway GC, Galway Bay G and CC, Glenro Abbey, Loughrea, Mountbellew, Oughterard, Portumna, Tuam and Gort. These courses exemplify beautifully, the way the traditional and the modern have come to sit comfortably together in all aspects of Galway life.

The city itself grew up around a castle built by the De Burgo family in the 13th century, though local historians decided that it didn't get

Eyre Square, Galway City

its charter until two centuries later. By then, strong links had been established with France and Spain, leading to prosperity for the local merchant families. In all, 14 families effectively controlled the city and they became known as the "Tribes of Galway."

Traces of a rich medieval past are still very much in evidence. For instance, there is Lynch's Castle on Shop Street, with its gargoyle, carved coat of arms and stone mullioned windows. And it remains in daily use as a bank. Then there is St Nicholas Collegiate Church where, according to legend, Christopher Columbus prayed before setting out for the New World. Further down the street are the remains of the old city wall and the Spanish Arch, so named because of the city's trading links with Spain. A major part of the wall can also be seen in Eyre Square Shopping Centre, where it becomes the focal point of the overall design. With a population of nearly 60,000 it is a vibrant, cosmopolitan city with a thriving commercial and cultural community. And the recent introduction of pedestrianisation has amplified the medieval nature of its streets, so encouraging the visitor to explore the ancient landmarks on foot.

One of my most interesting, recent trips in the West, was by car from Enniscrone GC to Connemara GC. Along the way, I passed the magnificent Kylemore Abbey which was built for £1.5 million in 1868 by business magnate Mitchell Henry for his wife Margaret. Now home to the Irish Benedictine Nuns, it incorporates the remarkable, miniature cathedral, known locally as the Gothic church. Its exterior of dark limestone contrasts with the light, ornately-carved sandstone of the interior, while marble columns in three colours add to the overall richness of the design. I also got a view of the actual field near Leenane, which became the centre-piece of the movie "The Field" for which Richard Harris in the main role of Bull McCabe received an Academy Award nomination. Though the movie was adapted from the play of the same name by Kerry's John B Keane, it was shot entirely in the heart of Connemara.

Roundstone Harbour, Connemara, Co Galway

Maam Cross is known locally as the Picadilly of Connemara - and with good reason. A hive of activity, it is where the Annual Bogman's Ball is held every February and where, in October, Connemara ponies are bought and sold, along with other livestock and such diverse items as farmyard equipment, carpets and reading glasses. Given the huge expanse of Lough Corrib and the county's Atlantic coast, it is hardly surprising that Galway should be a paradise for anglers of all tastes. It is also a haven for students of the native, Gaelic language, which is still spoken throughout Connemara and on the Aran Islands of Inishmore, Inishmaan and Inisheer in Galway Bay. Galway is also famous for its International Oyster Festival, held every September. And the unitiated are advised that opening an oyster is a task which takes practice and patience as well as two basic tools - a tea towel and a small knife with a strong blade.

In November 1970, when he was still undecided what to do with his record cheque for £25,000, Christy O'Connor Snr kept an important appointment in his native city. A month before his 46th birthday, he walked proudly behind the Great Mace and the City's Civic Sword, before ascending a dais. There, the freedom of his native city was conferred on him by Mayor Martin Divilly. Joining four Presidents, five cardinals, a Papal Nuncio and a former Mayor of New York, O'Connor had become the 12th Freeman of Galway, in recognition of the eminence he had achieved in golf. And he recalled how, in childhood days by the first green at Galway Golf Club, he had engaged in pitching and putting competitions for pennies.

A city and its golfing son, had both come a long way.

Location of Golf Courses

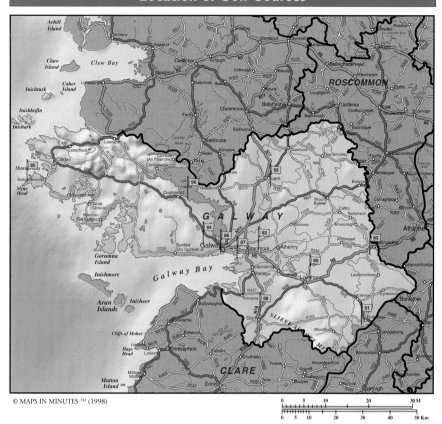

© MAPS IN MINUTES ™ (1998)

Athenry

Athenry Golf Club, Palmerstown, Oranmore, Co Galway

Tel: 091 794466

Sec/Manager:	Padraig Slattery
Professional:	Raymond Ryan
Directions:	5 miles West of Athenry at the junction of the N6 and R348
Type of Course:	Parkland
Date Founded:	1902
No of Holes:	18
Length:	5969 yds (5453 mtrs)
Par:	70
SSS:	70
Green Fees:	Weekdays: £15 Weekends & Bank Holidays: £18
Visitors:	Welcome: Any Day except Sunday
Societies:	Welcome: Contact Secretary for details
Facilities:	Chipping/Putting Area, Practice Area, Driving Range, Golf Clubs for hire, Trolley hire, Electric Buggy hire, Bar, Restaurant

Accommodation, Food and Drink

Reference numbers below refer to detailed information provided in section 2

Accommodation

Ardawn House, Galway, Co Galway

Tel: 091 568833 Fax: 091 563454 City-centre Bed & Breakfast Accommodation in nine en suite bedrooms. The host is captain of the local golf club.   278

Bredagh House, Galway, Co Galway

Tel: 091 770936 Fax: 091 770056 Comfort and convenience in a modern redbrick house a short walk from the beach and the city's attractions.   280

Cill Cuana, Salthill, Galway, Co Galway

Tel: 091 585979 Fax: 091 581772 Five en suite bedrooms in a house very close to Galway Bay and an easy walk from the city centre.   279

Meadow Court Hotel, Loughrea, Co Galway

Tel: 091 841051 Fax: 091 842406 A fine modern hotel with 18 well-appointed en suite bedrooms in landscaped gardens two miles from Loughrea. Restaurant, bars. 270

Teach an Easard, Ballyconneely, Co Galway

Tel/Fax: 095 23560 Six en suite bedrooms in a farmhouse Bed & Breakfast near the coast and just one mile from Connemara Golf Club.   275

Food and Drink

Meadow Court Hotel, Loughrea, Co Galway

Tel: 091 841051 Fax: 091 842406 A fine modern hotel with 18 well-appointed en suite bedrooms in landscaped gardens two miles from Loughrea. Restaurant, bars. 270

The Blackthorn, Gort, Co Galway

Tel/Fax: 091 632127 Gort's premier pub/restaurant, winner of national awards. Food is served all day, with seafood and steaks among the specialities.   264

The Twelve Pins Hotel, Barna Village, Co Galway

Tel: 091 592368 Fax: 091 592485 An 18-bedroomed hotel with restaurant and bar on the Connemara coast road 5 miles from Galway City. All rooms en suite.   273

Ballinasloe

Ballinasloe Golf Club, Rossgloss, Ballinasloe, Co Galway

Tel: 090 542126

Sec/Manager:	Michael S. Kelly
Professional:	Barry Flanagan
Directions:	2 miles from Ballinasloe off the R355 to Portumna
Type of Course:	Parkland
Date Founded:	1894
No of Holes:	18
Length:	6413 yds (5865 mtrs)
Par:	72
SSS:	70
Green Fees:	£12
Visitors:	Welcome: Monday to Saturday
Societies:	Welcome: Special concessions, Contact Club for details
Facilities:	Chipping/Putting Area, Practice Area, Trolley hire, Bar, Restaurant

Accommodation, Food and Drink

Reference numbers below refer to detailed information provided in section 2

Accommodation

Lacken House, Rahara, Athleague, Co Roscommon

Tel/Fax: 090 323449 Choose between B&B in the handsome 1820s manor and self-catering lodges in the grounds. Peaceful rural setting.   523

Meadow Court Hotel, Loughrea, Co Galway

Tel: 091 841051 Fax: 091 842406 A fine modern hotel with 18 well-appointed en suite bedrooms in landscaped gardens two miles from Loughrea. Restaurant, bars. 270

Willmount House, Portumna, Co Galway

Tel: 050 941114 Four en suite double bedrooms in a Georgian (1748) house on a working farm close to Lough Derg. Terrific views.   263

Food and Drink

Meadow Court Hotel, Loughrea, Co Galway

Tel: 091 841051 Fax: 091 842406 A fine modern hotel with 18 well-appointed en suite bedrooms in landscaped gardens two miles from Loughrea. Restaurant, bars. 270

The Beehive, Portumna, Co Galway

Tel: 050 941830 Irish and Italian cuisine in a pleasant oasis just off the main street. Bring your own wine. Last orders 9.30.   267

Willmount House, Portumna, Co Galway

Tel: 050 941114 Four en suite double bedrooms in a Georgian (1748) house on a working farm close to Lough Derg. Terrific views.   263

Bearna

Bearna Golf Club, Corboley, Bearna, Co Galway

Tel: 091 592677

One of the newest courses in Connacht is owned jointly by Galwaymen Pat Donnellan, Sean and Michael Meade and a Mayo business associate,

Length:	6859 yds (6271 mtrs)
Par:	72
SSS:	73
Green Fees:	Weekdays: £25 Weekends & Bank Holidays: £30
Visitors:	Welcome: 7 days a week, Contact Club in advance
Societies:	Welcome: Special concessions, Contact Club for details
Facilities:	Chipping/Putting Area, Golf Clubs for hire, Trolley hire, Electric Buggy hire, Bar, Restaurant, Caddy service by arrangement

Accommodation, Food and Drink

Reference numbers below refer to detailed
information provided in section 2

Accommodation

Ardawn House, Galway, Co Galway
Tel: 091 568833 Fax: 091 563454 City-centre Bed & Breakfast Accommodation in nine en suite bedrooms. The host is captain of the local golf club. 278

Bredagh House, Galway, Co Galway
Tel: 091 770936 Fax: 091 770056 Comfort and convenience in a modern redbrick house a short walk from the beach and the city's attractions. 280

Carna Bay Hotel, Carna, Co Galway
Tel: 095 32255 Fax: 095 32520 A family-run hotel with 26 en suite bedrooms, a dining room (local seafood and Connemara lamb) and fabulous views. 265

Cill Cuana, Salthill, Galway, Co Galway
Tel: 091 585979 Fax: 091 581772 Five en suite bedrooms in a house very close to Galway Bay and an easy walk from the city centre. 279

Lake Hotel, Oughterard, Co Galway
Tel: 091 552275 Fax: 091 552794 Real Irish hospitality in the centre of lovely village. En suite bedrooms with tv and telephone, seafood restaurant, bars. 261

River Walk House, Oughterard, Co Galway
Tel: 091 552788 Eight en suite rooms in a Bed & Breakfast two minutes from the village centre. Great scenery; plenty of sporting activity. 266

The Boat Inn, Oughterard, Co Galway
Tel: 091 552196 Fax: 091 552694 Eleven modern en suite bedrooms in a prime site in the centre of the village. Restaurant with excellent menus; bars; terrace. 276

The Twelve Pins Hotel, Barna Village, Co Galway
Tel: 091 592368 Fax: 091 592485 An 18-bedroomed hotel with restaurant and bar on the Connemara coast road 5 miles from Galway City. All rooms en suite. 273

Food and Drink

Carna Bay Hotel, Carna, Co Galway
Tel: 095 32255 Fax: 095 32520 A family-run hotel with 26 en suite bedrooms, a dining room (local seafood and Connemara lamb) and fabulous views. 265

Lake Hotel, Oughterard, Co Galway
Tel: 091 552275 Fax: 091 552794 Real Irish hospitality in the centre of lovely village. En suite bedrooms with tv and telephone, seafood restaurant, bars. 261

The Boat Inn, Oughterard, Co Galway
Tel: 091 552196 Fax: 091 552694 Eleven modern en suite bedrooms in a prime site in the centre of the village. Restaurant with excellent menus; bars; terrace. 276

The Twelve Pins Hotel, Barna Village, Co Galway
Tel: 091 592368 Fax: 091 592485 An 18-bedroomed hotel with restaurant and bar on the Connemara coast road 5 miles from Galway City. All rooms en suite. 273

Frank O'Gara. Sean Meade and Donnellan will be familiar to followers of Gaelic football as leading lights in the famous Galway teams of the 1960s.

They were prepared to look beyond the county boundary, however, so that full justice would be done to an ambitious golf development on a superb 250-acre site, four and a half miles from Galway City, between the roads to Spiddal and Moycullen. That was why Meade turned to his friend, Bobby Browne of Laytown and Bettystown, to design the layout.

Browne, a familiar figure on the Irish professional scene, used the generous land area to admirable effect, delivering a layout of delightful variety, with all 18 holes offering distinctly different challenges. Indeed only two of the holes on the homeward journey, the 10th and 11th, are in the same direction. The result is a course of outstanding quality and unique character.

Carved out of a typical, Connemara landscape of rock, bog, gorse and heather, it was opened for play in March 1997. And the high-quality greens, built to USGA specifications, would be the envy of far more mature courses.

An especially interesting feature is located at the most westerly end of the course. The intriguingly-named Forbidden Lake, which is known to Gaelic-speaking locals as Loch Toirmeasctha, guards the front of the 13th green, a short but suitably menacing challenge of 132 yards.

Sec/Manager:	Micheal Meade
Professional:	None
Directions:	5 miles West of Galway City off the R336 to Spiddle
Type of Course:	Moorland
Date Founded:	1996
No of Holes:	18

Connemara

Connemara Links, Ballyconneely, Co Galway
Tel: 095 23502

From previous visits to Connemara GC, it would have been difficult to credit that such a glorious

tract of links terrain had been there all the time, awaiting development. Where the outside world was concerned, it was the secret which Eddie Hackett took to his grave three years ago.

The work was completed by his architectural friend, Tom Craddock, who, in November 1998, joined Eddie on fairways in the great beyond. But the legacy of both men is set to become a major asset to Connacht golf, especially when 27 holes are fully operational in 2001.

According to Fr Peter Waldron, secretary of Connemara GC Ltd, the seaside holes, which were opened last August, will combine with the existing back nine as part, ultimately, of a splendid, new championship layout.

Remarkably, there was sufficient space between the existing 10th and 18th for a new, full-blooded, 503-yard par five, with generous areas of rough on either side of the fairway. Even more fortuitously, a large, elevated green is sited directly behind the clubhouse, providing priceless options for 18-hole routings and visitor starting.

Good husbandry is very evident in the running of Connemara GC, not least in the fact that they will complete the new nine holes for the relatively modest, total outlay of £700,000. And when it's done, they will be ready to welcome top quality tournaments in the knowledge that criticism can no longer be directed at the rather flat nature of the opening nine holes.

Sec/Manager:	John McLaughlin
Professional:	Hugh O'Neil
Directions:	4 miles West of Ballyconneely off the R341 from Clifden
Type of Course:	Links
Date Founded:	1973
No of Holes:	18
Length:	6849 yds (6263 mtrs)
Par:	72
SSS:	73
Green Fees:	May - September: £35 October - April: £30
Visitors:	Welcome: Book in advance
Societies:	Welcome: Special concessions, Telephone club for details

Facilities: Chipping/Putting Area, Practice Area, Golf Clubs for hire, Trolley hire, Electric Buggy hire, Bar, Restaurant, Caddy service by arrangement

Accommodation, Food and Drink

Reference numbers below refer to detailed information provided in section 2

Accommodation

Ben View House, Clifden, Co Galway
Tel: 095 21256 Fax: 095 21226 A charming mid 19th-century town house with nine en suite bedrooms for Bed & Breakfast. Same family owners since 1926.   272

Carna Bay Hotel, Carna, Co Galway
Tel: 095 32255 Fax: 095 32520 A family-run hotel with 26 en suite bedrooms, a dining room (local seafood and Connemara lamb) and fabulous views.   265

Clifden Glen, Clifden, Co Galway
Tel: 095 21401 Fax: 095 21818 A holiday village on a private estate just outside Clifden. ApartHotel cottage suites, self-catering lodges, restaurant, pub, tennis.   271

Cregg House, Clifden, Co Galway
Tel: 095 21326 Great views of the beautiful Connemara countryside from a handsome modern Bed & Breakfast house with six en suite bedrooms.   269

Glynsk House Hotel, Cashel Bay, Co Galway
Tel: 095 32279 Fax: 095 32342 A family-run hotel with 12 en suite bedrooms and a seafood restaurant. Glorious setting overlooking Glynsk Bay.   268

Lough Fadda House, Clifden, Co Galway
Tel: 095 21165 Two acres of grounds make an attractive setting for a modern detached house with six en suite bedrooms.   274

Mal Dua House, Clifden, Co Galway
Tel: 095 21171 Fax: 095 21739 Luxury, comfort and hospitality in abundance in a distinguished house in attractive grounds outside Clifden. 14 en suite bedrooms.   281

Roundstone House Hotel, Roundstone, Co Galway
Tel: 095 35864 Fax: 095 35944 Twelve rooms, all en suite, in a family-run hotel in a delightful fishing village. Comfort, care and good food are keynotes.   262

Teach an Easard, Ballyconneely, Co Galway
Tel/Fax: 095 23560 Six en suite bedrooms in a farmhouse Bed & Breakfast near the coast and just one mile from Connemara Golf Club.   275

The Pass Inn, Kylemore, Co Galway
Tel: 095 41141 Fax: 095 41377 Family-run 11-bedroom hotel with restaurant in a beautiful location between the hills and lakes of Connemara.   277

Food and Drink

Carna Bay Hotel, Carna, Co Galway
Tel: 095 32255 Fax: 095 32520 A family-run hotel with 26 en suite bedrooms, a dining room (local seafood and Connemara lamb) and fabulous views.   265

Clifden Glen, Clifden, Co Galway
Tel: 095 21401 Fax: 095 21818 A holiday village on a private estate just outside Clifden. ApartHotel cottage suites, self-catering lodges, restaurant, pub, tennis.   271

Glynsk House Hotel, Cashel Bay, Co Galway
Tel: 095 32279 Fax: 095 32342 A family-run hotel with 12 en suite bedrooms and a seafood restaurant. Glorious setting overlooking Glynsk Bay.   268

Roundstone House Hotel, Roundstone, Co Galway
Tel: 095 35864 Fax: 095 35944 Twelve rooms, all en suite, in a family-run hotel in a delightful fishing village. Comfort, care and good food are keynotes.   262

The Pass Inn, Kylemore, Co Galway
Tel: 095 41141 Fax: 095 41377 Family-run 11-bedroom hotel with restaurant in a beautiful location between the hills and lakes of Connemara.   277

Galway

Galway Golf Club, Blackrock, Galway
Tel: 091 522033

Sec/Manager:	Padraig Fahy
Professional:	Don Wallace

Directions:	3 miles West of Galway Centre in Salthill
Type of Course:	Parkland
Date Founded:	1895
No of Holes:	18
Length:	6360yds (5816 mtrs)
Par:	70
SSS:	71
Green Fees:	Weekdays: £20 Weekends & Bank Holidays: £25
Visitors:	Welcome: Weekdays except Tuesday
Societies:	Welcome: Special concessions, Group rate, Contact Club for details
Facilities:	Chipping/Putting Area, Golf Clubs for hire, Trolley hire

Accommodation, Food and Drink

Reference numbers below refer to detailed information provided in section 2

Accommodation

Ardawn House, Galway, Co Galway
Tel: 091 568833 Fax: 091 563454 City-centre Bed & Breakfast Accommodation in nine en suite bedrooms. The host is captain of the local golf club.   278

Bredagh House, Galway, Co Galway
Tel: 091 770936 Fax: 091 770056 Comfort and convenience in a modern redbrick house a short walk from the beach and the city's attractions.   280

Carna Bay Hotel, Carna, Co Galway
Tel: 095 32255 Fax: 095 32520 A family-run hotel with 26 en suite bedrooms, a dining room (local seafood and Connemara lamb) and fabulous views.   265

Cill Cuana, Salthill, Galway, Co Galway
Tel: 091 585979 Fax: 091 581772 Five en suite bedrooms in a house very close to Galway Bay and an easy walk from the city centre.   279

Lake Hotel, Oughterard, Co Galway
Tel: 091 552275 Fax: 091 552794 Real Irish hospitality in the centre of lovely village. En suite bedrooms with tv and telephone, seafood restaurant, bars.   261

River Walk House, Oughterard, Co Galway
Tel: 091 552788 Eight en suite rooms in a Bed & Breakfast two minutes from the village centre. Great scenery; plenty of sporting activity.   266

The Boat Inn, Oughterard, Co Galway
Tel: 091 552196 Fax: 091 552694 Eleven modern en suite bedrooms in a prime site in the centre of the village. Restaurant with excellent menus; bars; terrace.   276

The Twelve Pins Hotel, Barna Village, Co Galway
Tel: 091 592368 Fax: 091 592485 An 18-bedroomed hotel with restaurant and bar on the Connemara coast road 5 miles from Galway City. All rooms en suite.   273

Food and Drink

Carna Bay Hotel, Carna, Co Galway
Tel: 095 32255 Fax: 095 32520 A family-run hotel with 26 en suite bedrooms, a dining room (local seafood and Connemara lamb) and fabulous views.   265

Lake Hotel, Oughterard, Co Galway
Tel: 091 552275 Fax: 091 552794 Real Irish hospitality in the centre of lovely village. En suite bedrooms with tv and telephone, seafood restaurant, bars.   261

The Boat Inn, Oughterard, Co Galway
Tel: 091 552196 Fax: 091 552694 Eleven modern en suite bedrooms in a prime site in the centre of the village. Restaurant with excellent menus; bars; terrace.   276

The Twelve Pins Hotel, Barna Village, Co Galway
Tel: 091 592368 Fax: 091 592485 An 18-bedroomed hotel with restaurant and bar on the Connemara coast road 5 miles from Galway City. All rooms en suite.   273

Galway Bay

Galway Bay Golf & Country Club, Renville, Oranmore, Co Galway

Tel: 091 790500

Galway Bay GC will always have a special place in the career of Padraig Harrington, because of events there in August 1999. That was when it played host to the West of Ireland Classic in which Harrington, as runner-up, took a major step towards Ryder Cup honours.

The staging of the event was a personal triumph for course designer Christy O'Connor Jnr, a native of the western city. The quality of his work is reflected in the fact that in 1994, only a

year after the course was officially opened, it became the venue for the Irish Professional Championship.

In wild winds sweeping off the Atlantic, Darren Clarke captured the title with a three-under-par aggregate of 285. But Costantino Rocca did considerably better in 1999 in more benign conditions, breaking par in all four rounds to outscore Harrington with a winning total of 276.

Located near the village of Oranmore, seven miles from Galway City, it is essentially parkland by the sea and is bordered on three sides by the Atlantic. The absence of trees leaves it very exposed to the elements and places a high premium on shot-making skills. So, a glance at the nearest Beaufort Scale might be appropriate before venturing forth.

In his design, Junior dedicated one of the holes, the 176-yard par-three 13th to his famous uncle, Christy O'Connor Snr. And since its official opening, the development has been greatly enhanced by a fine hotel to complement the clubhouse, which is one of the finest structures in Irish golf.

Sec/Manager:	Eamonn Meagher
Professional:	Eugene O'Connor
Directions:	3 miles South West of Oranmore off the N6 Galway to Dublin road
Type of Course:	Parkland by the Sea
Date Founded:	1993
No of Holes:	18
Length:	7148 yds (6537 mtrs)
Par:	72
SSS:	73

Green Fees:	Weekdays: £38 Weekends & Bank Holidays: £43
Visitors:	Welcome: Contact in advance
Societies:	Welcome: Special concessions, Contact in advance
Facilities:	Chipping/Putting Area, Practice Area, Driving Range, Golf Clubs for hire, Trolley hire, Electric Buggy hire, Bar, Restaurant, Caddy service by arrangement, plus Hotel

Accommodation, Food and Drink

Reference numbers below refer to detailed information provided in section 2

Accommodation

Ardawn House, Galway, Co Galway
Tel: 091 568833 Fax: 091 563454 City-centre Bed & Breakfast Accommodation in nine en suite bedrooms. The host is captain of the local golf club.   278

Bredagh House, Galway, Co Galway
Tel: 091 770936 Fax: 091 770056 Comfort and convenience in a modern redbrick house a short walk from the beach and the city's attractions.   280

Cill Cuana, Salthill, Galway, Co Galway
Tel: 091 585979 Fax: 091 581772 Five en suite bedrooms in a house very close to Galway Bay and an easy walk from the city centre.   279

Fort View House, Kinvara, Co Galway
Tel: 091 637147 Six spacious bedrooms in a modern Bed & Breakfast bungalow with an equestrian centre next door. Immaculate throughout.   260

The Boat Inn, Oughterard, Co Galway
Tel: 091 552196 Fax: 091 552694 Eleven modern en suite bedrooms in a prime site in the centre of the village. Restaurant with excellent menus; bars; terrace.   276

The Twelve Pins Hotel, Barna Village, Co Galway
Tel: 091 592368 Fax: 091 592485 An 18-bedroomed hotel with restaurant and bar on the Connemara coast road 5 miles from Galway City. All rooms en suite.   273

Food and Drink

The Blackthorn, Gort, Co Galway
Tel/Fax: 091 632127 Gort's premier pub/restaurant, winner of national awards. Food is served all day, with seafood and steaks among the specialities.   264

The Boat Inn, Oughterard, Co Galway
Tel: 091 552196 Fax: 091 552694 Eleven modern en suite bedrooms in a prime site in the centre of the village. Restaurant with excellent menus; bars; terrace.   276

The Twelve Pins Hotel, Barna Village, Co Galway
Tel: 091 592368 Fax: 091 592485 An 18-bedroomed hotel with restaurant and bar on the Connemara coast road 5 miles from Galway City. All rooms en suite.   273

Gort

Gort Golf Club, Castlequarter, Gort, Co Galway
Tel: 091 632244

Sec/Manager:	Sean Devlin
Professional:	None
Directions:	Half mile North of centre of Gort off the N18 to Galway
Type of Course:	Parkland
Date Founded:	1923
No of Holes:	18
Length:	6238 yds (5705 mtrs)
Par:	71
SSS:	69
Green Fees:	£15
Visitors:	Welcome: Advisable to phone

| Societies: | Welcome: Special concessions, Contact Club for details |
| Facilities: | Chipping/Putting Area, Golf Clubs for hire, Trolley hire, Electric Buggy hire, Bar, Restaurant, Caddy service by arrangement |

Accommodation, Food and Drink

Reference numbers below refer to detailed information provided in section 2

Accommodation

Carraig House, Liscannor, Co Clare
Tel/Fax: 065 7081260 Peace, seclusion and outstanding views in a fine modern B&B a short walk from a small fishing village. All rooms en suite.   124

Castle View Lodge, Lahinch, Co Clare
Tel: 065 7081648 Six en suite bedrooms in a well-designed modern house an easy walk from the centre of the village. Overlooks Lahinch golf courses.   128

Craggy Island, Ardeamush, Doolin, Co Clare
Tel: 065 7074595 A welcoming family-run Bed & Breakfast house on the edge of the Burren. All rooms en suite. Great views, great walking.   127

Cullinan's Restaurant & Guest House, Doolin, Co Clare
Tel: 065 7074183 e-mail: cullinans@eircom.net Six-room guest house (all rooms en suite) and restaurant serving à la carte dinners from a wide-ranging modern menu.

Fort View House, Kinvara, Co Galway
Tel: 091 637147 Six spacious bedrooms in a modern Bed & Breakfast bungalow with an equestrian centre next door. Immaculate throughout.   260

Glasha Meadows, Doolin, Co Clare
Tel: 065 7074443 Six en suite bedrooms in a family-run B&B on the coast road into Doolin, a village famous for its traditional Irish music.   126

Meadow Court Hotel, Loughrea, Co Galway
Tel: 091 841051 Fax: 091 842406 A fine modern hotel with 18 well-appointed en suite bedrooms in landscaped gardens two miles from Loughrea. Restaurant, bars.   270

Mulcarr House, Lahinch, Co Clare
Tel: 065 7081123 A striking modern house with four high-quality Bed & Breakfast rooms. Superb views. Also self-catering nearby.   111

Tudor Lodge, Lahinch, Co Clare
Tel: 065 7081270 Four well-appointed bedrooms, all en suite, in a modern house with a real home-from-home feel.   116

Tullamore Farmhouse, Kilshanny, Ennistymon, Co Clare
Tel: 065 7071187 Six en suite rooms in an elegant modern Bed & Breakfast house with award-winning breakfasts and great views.   110

Food and Drink

Cullinan's Restaurant & Guest House, Doolin, Co Clare
Tel: 065 7074183 e-mail: cullinans@eircom.net Six-room guest house (all rooms en suite) and restaurant serving à la carte dinners from a wide-ranging modern menu.

Meadow Court Hotel, Loughrea, Co Galway
Tel: 091 841051 Fax: 091 842406 A fine modern hotel with 18 well-appointed en suite bedrooms in landscaped gardens two miles from Loughrea. Restaurant, bars.270

The Blackthorn, Gort, Co Galway
Tel/Fax: 091 632127 Gort's premier pub/restaurant, winner of national awards. Food is served all day, with seafood and steaks among the specialities.   264

Loughrea

Loughrea Golf Club, Graige, Loughrea, Co Galway
Tel: 091 841049

Sec/Manager:	Danny Hynes
Professional:	None
Directions:	1 mile North of Loughrea on R350 to Bullaun
Type of Course:	Parkland

Date Founded:	1924
No of Holes:	18
Length:	5753 yds (5261 mtrs)
Par:	69
SSS:	67
Green Fees:	£12
Visitors:	Welcome: Any Day, Restrictions may apply on Sunday
Societies:	Welcome: Weekdays, Contact Club in advance
Facilities:	Chipping/Putting Area, Practice Area, Trolley hire, Bar, Restaurant

Accommodation, Food and Drink

Reference numbers below refer to detailed information provided in section 2

Accommodation

Fort View House, Kinvara, Co Galway

Tel: 091 637147 Six spacious bedrooms in a modern Bed & Breakfast bungalow with an equestrian centre next door. Immaculate throughout. 260

Meadow Court Hotel, Loughrea, Co Galway

Tel: 091 841051 Fax: 091 842406 A fine modern hotel with 18 well-appointed en suite bedrooms in landscaped gardens two miles from Loughrea. Restaurant, bars. 270

Willmount House, Portumna, Co Galway

Tel: 050 941114 Four en suite double bedrooms in a Georgian (1748) house on a working farm close to Lough Derg. Terrific views. 263

Food and Drink

Meadow Court Hotel, Loughrea, Co Galway

Tel: 091 841051 Fax: 091 842406 A fine modern hotel with 18 well-appointed en suite bedrooms in landscaped gardens two miles from Loughrea. Restaurant, bars. 270

The Beehive, Portumna, Co Galway

Tel: 050 941830 Irish and Italian cuisine in a pleasant oasis just off the main street. Bring your own wine. Last orders 9.30. 267

The Blackthorn, Gort, Co Galway

Tel/Fax: 091 632127 Gort's premier pub/restaurant, winner of national awards. Food is served all day, with seafood and steaks among the specialities. 264

Willmount House, Portumna, Co Galway

Tel: 050 941114 Four en suite double bedrooms in a Georgian (1748) house on a working farm close to Lough Derg. Terrific views. 263

Oughterard

Oughterard Golf Club, Gorteevagh, Oughterard, Co Galway

Tel: 091 552131

Sec/Manager:	John Waters
Professional:	Michael Ryan
Directions:	15 miles West of Galway City off the N59 two miles East of Oughterard
Type of Course:	Parkland
Date Founded:	1974
No of Holes:	18
Length:	7223 yds (6605 mtrs)
Par:	71
SSS:	69
Green Fees:	£20 per day
Visitors:	Welcome: Book ahead, Restricted playing times subject to availabilty
Societies:	Welcome: Special concessions, Apply to club for details

Facilities:	Chipping/Putting Area, Golf Clubs for hire, Trolley hire, Bar, Restaurant, Caddy service by arrangement, plus Fishing close by

Accommodation, Food and Drink

Reference numbers below refer to detailed information provided in section 2

Accommodation

Ben View House, Clifden, Co Galway

Tel: 095 21256 Fax: 095 21226 A charming mid 19th-century town house with nine en suite bedrooms for Bed & Breakfast. Same family owners since 1926. 272

Carna Bay Hotel, Carna, Co Galway

Tel: 095 32255 Fax: 095 32520 A family-run hotel with 26 en suite bedrooms, a dining room (local seafood and Connemara lamb) and fabulous views. 265

Clifden Glen, Clifden, Co Galway

Tel: 095 21401 Fax: 095 21818 A holiday village on a private estate just outside Clifden. ApartHotel cottage suites, self-catering lodges, restaurant, pub, tennis. 271

Cregg House, Clifden, Co Galway

Tel: 095 21326 Great views of the beautiful Connemara countryside from a handsome modern Bed & Breakfast house with six en suite bedrooms. 269

Glynsk House Hotel, Cashel Bay, Co Galway

Tel: 095 32279 Fax: 095 32342 A family-run hotel with 12 en suite bedrooms and a seafood restaurant. Glorious setting overlooking Glynsk Bay. 268

Lake Hotel, Oughterard, Co Galway

Tel: 091 552275 Fax: 091 552794 Real Irish hospitality in the centre of lovely village. En suite bedrooms with tv and telephone, seafood restaurant, bars. 261

Lough Fadda House, Clifden, Co Galway

Tel: 095 21165 Two acres of grounds make an attractive setting for a modern detached house with six en suite bedrooms. 274

Mal Dua House, Clifden, Co Galway

Tel: 095 21171 Fax: 095 21739 Luxury, comfort and hospitality in abundance in a distinguished house in attractive grounds outside Clifden. 14 en suite bedrooms. 281

River Walk House, Oughterard, Co Galway

Tel: 091 552788 Eight en suite rooms in a Bed & Breakfast two minutes from the village centre. Great scenery; plenty of sporting activity. 266

Roundstone House Hotel, Roundstone, Co Galway

Tel: 095 35864 Fax: 095 35944 Twelve rooms, all en suite, in a family-run hotel in a delightful fishing village. Comfort, care and good food are keynotes. 262

Teach an Easard, Ballyconneely, Co Galway

Tel/Fax: 095 23560 Six en suite bedrooms in a farmhouse Bed & Breakfast near the coast and just one mile from Connemara Golf Club. 275

The Boat Inn, Oughterard, Co Galway

Tel: 091 552196 Fax: 091 552694 Eleven modern en suite bedrooms in a prime site in the centre of the village. Restaurant with excellent menus; bars; terrace. 276

The Pass Inn, Kylemore, Co Galway

Tel: 095 41141 Fax: 095 41377 Family-run 11-bedroom hotel with restaurant in a beautiful location between the hills and lakes of Connemara. 277

The Twelve Pins Hotel, Barna Village, Co Galway

Tel: 091 592368 Fax: 091 592485 An 18-bedroomed hotel with restaurant and bar on the Connemara coast road 5 miles from Galway City. All rooms en suite. 273

Food and Drink

Carna Bay Hotel, Carna, Co Galway

Tel: 095 32255 Fax: 095 32520 A family-run hotel with 26 en suite bedrooms, a dining room (local seafood and Connemara lamb) and fabulous views. 265

Clifden Glen, Clifden, Co Galway

Tel: 095 21401 Fax: 095 21818 A holiday village on a private estate just outside Clifden. ApartHotel cottage suites, self-catering lodges, restaurant, pub, tennis. 271

Glynsk House Hotel, Cashel Bay, Co Galway

Tel: 095 32279 Fax: 095 32342 A family-run hotel with 12 en suite bedrooms and a seafood restaurant. Glorious setting overlooking Glynsk Bay. 268

Lake Hotel, Oughterard, Co Galway

Tel: 091 552275 Fax: 091 552794 Real Irish hospitality in the centre of lovely village. En suite bedrooms with tv and telephone, seafood restaurant, bars. 261

Roundstone House Hotel, Roundstone, Co Galway

Tel: 095 35864 Fax: 095 35944 Twelve rooms, all en suite, in a family-run hotel in a delightful fishing village. Comfort, care and good food are keynotes.   262

The Boat Inn, Oughterard, Co Galway

Tel: 091 552196 Fax: 091 552694 Eleven modern en suite bedrooms in a prime site in the centre of the village. Restaurant with excellent menus; bars; terrace.   276

The Pass Inn, Kylemore, Co Galway

Tel: 095 41141 Fax: 095 41377 Family-run 11-bedroom hotel with restaurant in a beautiful location between the hills and lakes of Connemara.   277

The Twelve Pins Hotel, Barna Village, Co Galway

Tel: 091 592368 Fax: 091 592485 An 18-bedroomed hotel with restaurant and bar on the Connemara coast road 5 miles from Galway City. All rooms en suite.   273

The Beehive, Portumna, Co Galway

Tel: 050 941830 Irish and Italian cuisine in a pleasant oasis just off the main street. Bring your own wine. Last orders 9.30.   267

The Blackthorn, Gort, Co Galway

Tel/Fax: 091 632127 Gort's premier pub/restaurant, winner of national awards. Food is served all day, with seafood and steaks among the specialities.   264

Portumna

Portumna Golf Club, Portumna, Co Galway
Tel: 050 941059

Sec/Manager:	Richard Clarke
Professional:	Richard Clarke
Directions:	2 miles West of Portumna off the R352
Type of Course:	Parkland
Date Founded:	1913
No of Holes:	18
Length:	5986 yds (5474 mtrs)
Par:	68
SSS:	67
Green Fees:	£15 per day
Visitors:	Welcome: Contact Club in advance
Societies:	Welcome: Special concessions, Apply in writing to Club
Facilities:	Practice Area, Trolley hire, Electric Buggy hire, Bar, Restaurant

Tuam

Tuam Golf Club, Barnacurragh, Tuam, Co Galway
Tel: 093 28993

Sec/Manager:	Vincent Gaffney
Professional:	Larry Smyth
Directions:	2 miles South of Tuam off the R347 to Athenry
Type of Course:	Parkland
Date Founded:	1907
No of Holes:	18
Length:	6370 yds (5825 mtrs)
Par:	72
SSS:	70
Green Fees:	£15 per round
Visitors:	Welcome: Any Day except Saturday, Contact Club in advance
Societies:	Welcome: Special concessions, Contact club for details
Facilities:	Chipping/Putting Area, Practice Area, Golf Clubs hire, Trolley hire, Electric Buggy hire, Bar, Restaurant, Caddy service by arrangement

Accommodation, Food and Drink

Reference numbers below refer to detailed information provided in section 2

Accommodation

Annagh Lodge, Coolbawn, Nenagh, Co Tipperary

Tel/Fax: 067 24225 Five comfortably appointed B&B rooms in a period country house on a 200-acre working farm. Dinner by arrangement.   545

Ashley Park House, Ardcroney, Nenagh, Co Tipperary

Tel: 067 38223 Fax: 067 38223 Six twin bedrooms, all en suite, in a handsome early 18th-century residence with a private lake. Bed & Breakfast.   549

Bridget's Bed & Breakfast, Coolbawn, Co Tipperary

Tel: 067 28098 Bed and Breakfast in five en suite rooms in a smart modern bungalow. 5 minutes' walk from Lough Derg.   544

Meadow Court Hotel, Loughrea, Co Galway

Tel: 091 841051 Fax: 091 842406 A fine modern hotel with 18 well-appointed en suite bedrooms in landscaped gardens two miles from Loughrea. Restaurant, bars.270

Otway Lodge, Dromineer, Nenagh, Co Tipperary

Tel: 067 24133/24273 Six-bedroomed B&B guest house (all rooms in suite) on the edge of Lough Derg. Boat hire, fishing trips.   542

Riverrun Cottages, Terryglass, Nenagh, Co Tipperary

Tel: 067 22125 4-star self-catering Accommodation in five units, each sleeping 4. Quiet village setting by Lough Derg.   543

Willmount House, Portumna, Co Galway

Tel: 050 941114 Four en suite double bedrooms in a Georgian (1748) house on a working farm close to Lough Derg. Terrific views.   263

Food and Drink

Meadow Court Hotel, Loughrea, Co Galway

Tel: 091 841051 Fax: 091 842406 A fine modern hotel with 18 well-appointed en suite bedrooms in landscaped gardens two miles from Loughrea. Restaurant, bars.270

Accommodation, Food and Drink

Reference numbers below refer to detailed information provided in section 2

Accommodation

Eskerville, Knock, Co Mayo

Tel: 094 88413 A low-rise Bed & Breakfast house 10 minutes walk from Knock centre. Six bedrooms, four en suite. Scenic location with private gardens.   422

Lake Hotel, Oughterard, Co Galway

Tel: 091 552275 Fax: 091 552794 Real Irish hospitality in the centre of lovely village. En suite bedrooms with tv and telephone, seafood restaurant, bars.   261

The Boat Inn, Oughterard, Co Galway

Tel: 091 552196 Fax: 091 552694 Eleven modern en suite bedrooms in a prime site in the centre of the village. Restaurant with excellent menus; bars; terrace.   276

Valley Lodge, Face Field, Claremorris, Co Mayo

Tel: 094 65180 Five letting rooms offer flexible Accommodation in a modern B&B farmhouse 5 miles outside Claremorris on the Castlebar road (N60).   420

Western Hotel, Claremorris, Co Mayo

Tel: 094 62011 Fax: 094 62838 Main street hotel with 18 en suite bedrooms, busy bars and a restaurant specialising in steaks. Music session Wednesday night.   421

Food and Drink

Lake Hotel, Oughterard, Co Galway

Tel: 091 552275 Fax: 091 552794 Real Irish hospitality in the centre of lovely village. En suite bedrooms with tv and telephone, seafood restaurant, bars.   261

The Boat Inn, Oughterard, Co Galway

Tel: 091 552196 Fax: 091 552694 Eleven modern en suite bedrooms in a prime site in the centre of the village. Restaurant with excellent menus; bars; terrace.   276

Western Hotel, Claremorris, Co Mayo

Tel: 094 62011 Fax: 094 62838 Main street hotel with 18 en suite bedrooms, busy bars and a restaurant specialising in steaks. Music session Wednesday night.   421

KERRY

They take their golf very seriously in Kerry. Which may explain why nobody other than double "major" winner, Mark O'Meara, was considered good enough to warrant an invitation to write the introduction to a recent promotional brochure from South West Ireland Golf (SWING). It is also exemplified in the selection of venerable US architect, Robert Trent Jones, as designer of the second 18 or Cashen Course at Ballybunion and of Arnold Palmer to handle the contract for Tralee's move to the dramatic site at Barrow. Then there is Donald Steel's involvement as designer of the third 18 at Killarney, where another British golfing scribe, Henry Longhurst, contributed to the original layout at Mahony's Point.

Killarney is the hub of most tourist activities in Kerry. And if Viscount Castlerosse had had his way, the visitor would not have felt the need to move further afield. As his lordship, on

whose former lands, incidentally, the golf courses are built, once observed: "When anyone sees Killarney, even if he is the basest heretic, he must believe in God."It is difficult to disagree with him, given nature's extravagance, where charming lakes are complemented by majestic reeks and the texture of the landscape seems to change by the minute. Then, of course, there is the people, who seem to be at their best when performing the role of indulgent host.

Small wonder O'Meara was taken with the place on his first visit in 1998, especially since his forebears, including the O'Learys

Lakes of Killarney, Co Kerry

on his grandmother's side, are of solid Munster stock. "You can imagine what a thrill it was for me to play the wonderful links terrain of the south west of Ireland," he wrote. The American went on: "My good friend, Tiger Woods, joined me on the trip along with Payne Stewart. Our first stop was Waterville, where we had the most enjoyable Texas scramble on that magnificent links. From there we went to Ballybunion. I know Tiger enjoyed it immensely and what better memory could Payne have had than to come away with a hole-in-one on Ballybunion's delightful third hole, a 220-yard par-three.

"From my experience of those links courses, I can well understand the enormous appeal they have for visiting golfers to Ireland. As for my own game, those SWING courses helped me realise the dream of a lifetime - victory in the British Open Championship at Royal Birkdale."

Kerry can boast a delightful mix of parkland and links terrain in the 18-hole stretches at Killarney, Beaufort, Kenmare, Ring of Kerry, Ballybunion, Dooks, Tralee, Waterville, Ceann Sibeal, Ring of Kerry and Killorglin. Then there are the beguiling, nine-hole courses at Castlegregory, Listowel, The Kerries, Parknasilla and Ballyheigue.The philosophy of Kerry tourism was best articulated by Lord Castlerosse when he said: "I do not wish Americans to go away saying that "Killarney has quite a good golf course." It is essential that they should return home, boasters to a man, and shout to all that they have never seen anything so fine as the Killarney Golf Course with its superlative clubhouse."

Against that background, it is rather curious to note that the links courses in Kerry have been relative newcomers to the tourist business. While Killarney was gaining international exposure through such shop windows as the Shell Wonderful World of Golf series, it wasn't until the

1970s that the links courses began to catch up with their esteemed parkland neighbour. That was when the Kerrygold Classic was staged at Waterville, where distinguished Americans, including Doug Ford, Claude Harmon, Gay Brewer, Orville Moody, were joined by other international celebrities such as Tony Jacklin and Roberto de Vicenzo. Still, it was Killarney which gained the distinction of staging the Irish Open in 1991 and 1992, when both titles went to Nick Faldo. But Ballybunion has succeeded in landing the millennium staging of the event in a year in which they can boast none other than Tom Watson as club captain.

It would be the most appalling heresy, however, to suggest that holidaying in Kerry is essentially about golf. That would be to ignore the fretted coastline and deep bays created by the wild Atlantic, quite apart from upper and lower Lough Leane at Killarney; Muckross Lake, Lough Guitane, the River Laune, the Little River Maine and the Brown Flesk River. Further west on the Iveragh Peninsula are Lough Currane, Inny River, Cummeragh River, Sneem River, Caragh Lake, Lough Acoose, Finnihy River and the River Blackwater, as havens of wild brown trout. And for sea anglers, the influential gulf stream with its origins in the Gulf of Mexico, brushes the Kerry coast, bringing with it a mingling of sub-tropical fish with the indigenous blue shark, gurnard, tope, wrasse, pollack, mackerel, plaice, spurdogs, bass, flats, ray, conger, dogfish, whiting and mullet.

We are informed that in the bronze age, people explored the deep bays of the Kerry peninsulas and excavated their mineral wealth. Then there were the early Celtic groups which included the Ciarraighe (hard c, with the gh silent) from which the country got its name. Kerry as we know it today, was defined in 1606. And despite the Great Famine of the 1840s, the high mountains helped to preserve a cultural identity which enhances the richness of the people. It also accounts for the fact that Gaelic is still spoken as a first language along the western fringes of the county, notably around the Dingle Peninsula, which is home to the Ceann Sibeal (Sybil Head) club.

Torc Waterfall, Killarney, Co Kerry

A good base from which to explore this area and the North Kerry Ring, is the county town of Tralee. Containing a variety of 19th century buildings and a beautiful park, Tralee also has The Geraldine Experience, which tells the story of Kerry and of Ireland from earliest times. Of course, it is also home to the annual Rose of Tralee Festival.Valentia Island, linked by a bridge to the mainland at Portmagee, is a substantial island of fascinating character. It boasts the Skellig Experience, which is a heritage centre telling the story of the history and archaelogy of the Skellig Michael's early christian monastery.In Caherdaniel, copper mines were worked over 4,000 years ago and an old butter road runs from the village, which is now part of the Kerry Way walking trail. Then there is Derrynane, the home of Daniel O'Connell, 19th century champion of Catholic Emancipation. Otherwise known as the Liberator, O'Connell has a church dedicated to him in Cahersiveen.

Much is made of the attractions of Killarney - and with good reason. Its National Park comprises over 10,000 hectares, embracing three lakes and an extensive area of natural oak and yew woodland. Then there are the southern European varieties of arbutus, with their flamboyant shows of pink and white flowers and rich, red berries.The Park boundaries also contain Knockreer House, Ross Castle, Muckross Friary, Muckross House, Muckross Traditional Farms, Torc Waterfall, Dinish Island, Derrycunnihy Cascade, Ladies View and other points of interest.

Indeed Kerry can be accurately described as a very beautiful county, a walker's paradise where the central spine of mountains draws the eye of the traveller who can revel in clean crisp air, unsullied by industry. Its largely agricultural inhabitants are noted for their hospitality, their passion for Gaelic football and a deep appreciation of the Royal and Ancient game.

Location of Golf Courses

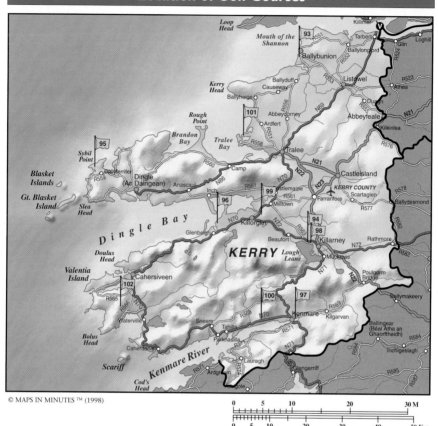

© MAPS IN MINUTES ™ (1998)

Ballybunion

Ballybunion Golf Club, Ballybunion, Co Kerry

Tel: 068 27146

On first viewing the Ballybunion links, Herbert Warren Wind, the doyen of American golf writers, described it as "nothing less than the finest seaside course I have ever seen." Small wonder, against that background, it has become a haven for tourists, especially from the US.

Another American, Tom Watson, sang its praises even more loudly after choosing the Kerry links to fine-tune his game before defending the

British Open title at Royal St George's, in 1981. Later he declared: "After playing Ballybunion for the first time, a man would think that the game of golf originated there."

Watson, who is the millennium captain of the club, went on: "There is a wild look to the place; the long grass covering the dunes that pitch and roll, make it very intimidating. But the contours on the fairways and on the greens are what make it a great course.

"You must play accurate iron shots into the greens, usually to a small target with not a lot of room to miss right or left." When it was chosen to play host to this year's Murphy's Irish Open, Watson added: "With it's unique, vertical dimension, demanding uphill and downhill shots, it was meant to stage such events."

A second course, the Cashen, was designed by Robert Trent Jones. But it is the Old Course will marks Ballybunion as one of the game's truly great venues, where locals talk about the champagne air off the ocean. Quite simply, there is no place like it anywhere in the world.

Sec/Manager:	Jim McKenna
Professional:	Brian O'Callaghan
Directions:	Half mile South of Ballybunion which is on the R551

Old Course

Type of Course:	Links
Date Founded:	1893
No of Holes:	18 Old Course; 18 Cashen Course

Length:	6241 yds (5707 mtrs)
Par:	70
SSS:	71
Green Fees:	£60

Cashen Course

Type of Course:	Links
Date Founded:	n/a
No of Holes:	18
Length:	6260 yds (5724 mtrs)
Par:	72
SSS:	73
Green Fees:	£35

Visitors:	Welcome: Must contact club in advance
Societies:	Welcome: Weekdays only, prior booking required
Facilities:	Chipping/Putting Area, Practice Area, Driving Range, Golf Clubs for hire, Trolley hire Bar, Restaurant, Caddy service by arrangement

Accommodation, Food and Drink

Reference numbers below refer to detailed information provided in section 2

Accommodation

Brook Manor Lodge, Tralee, Co Kerry
Tel: 066 7120406 Fax: 066 7127552 Elegant en suite B&B Accommodation in six luxuriously appointed bedrooms in a secluded country guest house.   290

Castle View House, Carrig Island, Co Kerry
Tel/Fax: 068 43304 Six bedrooms, all en suite, in a neat, modern house close to the Tarbert/Killimer car ferry. B&B; dinner by arrangement.   301

Cois Na Sionna, Killimer, Co Clare
Tel: 065 9053073 Four well-appointed en suite bedrooms in a striking modern B&B house opposite the Killimer car ferry across the Shannon estuary.   123

Fortfield Farm, Donail, Killimer, Co Clare
Tel: 065 9051457 Superior B&B guest Accommodation in a large modern house on a farm with an agricultural zoo. Five rooms, three en suite.   121

Greenfields Farmhouse, Asdee, Listowel, Co Kerry
Tel: 068 41233 Three double bedrooms for B&B, one en suite. On the Tarbert/Ballybunion road. Access, Mastercard, Visa.

Leen's Hotel, Abbeyfeale, Co Limerick
Tel: 068 31121 Fax: 068 32550 A family-run hotel with 19 en suite bedrooms and a restaurant serving generous helpings of local produce.   384

Meadowlands Hotel, Tralee, Co Kerry
Tel: 066 7180444 Fax: 066 7180964 A charming hotel in a landscaped garden just north of Tralee. 24 en suite bedrooms, 3 suites, restaurant and bar.   302

Sallyport House, Kenmare, Co Kerry
Tel: 064 42066 web: sallyporthouse.com An elegant country house set in ten acres of lawns and trees overlooking the harbour and the bay. Five antique-furnished bedrooms with either king- or queen-size beds and capacious en suite bathrooms. One has a four-poster.   293

Tralee Marina Holiday Apartments, Tralee, Co Kerry
Tel: 066 718 1222 web: traleemarina.com 4-star self-catering in 28 apartments in the Marina. Also town houses & apartments & 20 guest house rooms. Major credit cards.

Tralee Townhouse, Tralee, Co Kerry
Tel: 066 7181111 20 bedrooms, including several of family size, in a town house hotel that's handy for all Tralee's attractions.   303

Westcliff House, Kilkee, Co Clare
Tel: 065 9056108 An imposing 1840s town house with seven letting bedrooms, five en suite. Lovely views over Moore Bay.   120

Westward Court, Tralee, Co Kerry
Tel: 066 80081 e-mail: westward@iol.ie Superior budget Accommodation in the

centre of town (Mary Street). 43 modern en suite bedrooms. Restaurant. Private car park. No credit cards.

Food and Drink

Kelly's Bar & Restaurant, Kilrush, Co Clare
Tel: 065 9051811 A popular bar and restaurant offering a good range of Food and Drink & traditional and modern music. 125

Leen's Hotel, Abbeyfeale, Co Limerick
Tel: 068 31121 Fax: 068 32550 A family-run hotel with 19 en suite bedrooms and a restaurant serving generous helpings of local produce. 384

Meadowlands Hotel, Tralee, Co Kerry
Tel: 066 7180444 Fax: 066 7180964 A charming hotel in a landscaped garden just north of Tralee. 24 en suite bedrooms, 3 suites, restaurant and bar. 302

The Haven Arms, Kilrush, Co Clare
Tel: 065 9051267 A prime site in town for a family-run pub-restaurant with award-winning food, a good range of drinks and regular impromptu live music. 122

Westward Court, Tralee, Co Kerry
Tel: 066 80081 e-mail: westward@iol.ie Superior budget Accommodation in the centre of town (Mary Street). 43 modern en suite bedrooms. Restaurant. Private car park. No credit cards.

Beaufort

Beaufort Golf Course, Churchtown, Beaufort, Killarney, Co Kerry

Tel: 064 44440

Sec/Manager:	Colin Kelly
Professional:	Hugh Duggan
Directions:	Seven miles West of Killarney off the N72 towards Killorglin
Type of Course:	Parkland
Date Founded:	1994
No of Holes:	18
Length:	6587 yds (6023 mtrs)
Par:	71
SSS:	72
Green Fees:	Weekdays: £27 Weekends & Bank Holidays; £35
Visitors:	Welcome: Book at weekends
Societies:	Welcome: Special concessions, Advance booking required
Facilities:	Chipping/Putting Area,Practice Area, Golf Clubs for hire,Trolley hire, Electric Buggy hire, Bar, Restaurant, Caddy service by arrangement

Accommodation, Food and Drink

Reference numbers below refer to detailed information provided in section 2

Accommodation

Applecroft House, Woodlawn Road, Killarney, Co Kerry
Tel: 064 32782 e-mail: applecroft@eircom.net Delightful B&B bungalow in neat gardens. 2 double rooms, 3 twin rooms en suite, with tv & hairdryer. Off-street parking. Amex, Visa, Mastercard.

Clonfert, Fossa, Killarney, Co Kerry
Tel: 064 31459 B&B Accommodation in 5 en suite double rooms. 9 golf courses within a few miles. No credit cards.

Crystal Springs, Killarney, Co Cork
Tel: 064 33272 Charming B&B guest house in a quiet setting by a river bank. Fishing. Bureau de change. Wine licence. 299

Darby O'Gill's, Lissivigeen, Co Cork
Tel: 064 34168 Fax: 064 36794 Country house hotel with charming en suite

bedrooms. Irish cuisine in the evening, lunches in the lounge bar. Darts, rings and cards. 308

Hazelwood, Killarney, Co Kerry
Tel/Fax: 064 34363 Bed and Breakfast Accommodation in four double bedrooms and a triple (ideal for families). At Upper Ballyspillane. No credit cards.

Kathleen's Country House, Killarney, Co Kerry
Tel: 064 32810 Fax: 064 32340 An award-winning country guest house of real distinction offering the highest standards of comfort and service. Extensive gardens. No smoking in the bedrooms. 298

Linn Dubh, Aghadoe, Killarney, Co Kerry
Tel: 064 33828 Two triples and three double rooms, all en suite, for B&B Accommodation. Access, Mastercard, Visa.

Meadowlands Hotel, Tralee, Co Kerry
Tel: 066 7180444 Fax: 066 7180964 A charming hotel in a landscaped garden just north of Tralee. 24 en suite bedrooms, 3 suites, restaurant and bar. 302

River Valley Farm House, Killarney, Co Kerry
Tel: 064 32411 Fax: 064 37909 2 twin rooms and two big enough for families, all en suite. B&B. On the Cork Road out of Killarney.

Sika Lodge, Ballydowney, Co Kerry
Tel: 064 36304 Fax: 064 36746 web: kerry-insight.com/sika-lodge/ 6 double bedrooms, all en suite with satellite tv. 5 minutes from Killarney; next to Killarney Golf Club.

St Anthonys Lodge, Killarney, Co Kerry
Tel: 064 31534 Town & Country listed Bed and Breakfast Accommodation on the Cork Road out of Killarney. Double rooms en suite.

The 19th Green, Killarney, Co Cork
Tel: 064 32868 Fax: 064 32637 Family-run guest house with 13 well-equipped bedrooms, car park, putting green. Killarney Golf Club is opposite. 294

The Laune & Taylor's, Killarney, Co Cork
Tel: 064 32772 Fax: 064 37908 'Wine, dine & stay' in the centre of Killarney. En suite bedrooms; breakfast till noon; lunch and a full à la carte 3 till 10. 306

The White House, Kenmare, Co Kerry
Tel: 064 42372 all-in-one Golf & Leisure tours. Groups of 2-7 persons with a choice of 10 plus magnificent golf courses, all within 20 mile. The White House is 2½ miles from Kenmare and Molls Gap. All rooms have mountain views. 296

Woodlands, Killarney, Co Cork
Tel/Fax: 064 31467 Bed & Breakfast Accommodation in 8 en suite bedrooms, half a mile from Killarney Golf Club. 297

Food and Drink

Darby O'Gill's, Lissivigeen, Co Cork
Tel: 064 34168 Fax: 064 36794 Country house hotel with charming en suite bedrooms. Irish cuisine in the evening, plate lunches in the lounge bar. Darts, rings and cards. 308

Meadowlands Hotel, Tralee, Co Kerry
Tel: 066 7180444 Fax: 066 7180964 A charming hotel in a landscaped garden just north of Tralee. 24 en suite bedrooms, 3 suites, restaurant and bar. 302

The Laune & Taylor's, Killarney, Co Kerry
Tel: 064 32772 Fax: 064 37908 'Wine, dine & stay' in the centre of Killarney. En suite bedrooms; breakfast till noon; lunch and a full à la carte 3 till 10. 306

Ceann Sibeal

Ceann Sibeal Golf Club, Ballyoughterach, Ballyferriter, Co Kerry

Tel: 066 9156255/9156408

Sec/Manager:	Steve Fahy
Professional:	Dermot O'Connor
Directions:	9 miles North West of Dingle off the R559
Type of Course:	Links
Date Founded:	1924
No of Holes:	18
Length:	6700 yds (6126 mtrs)

Par:	72
SSS:	71
Green Fees:	£25
Visitors:	Welcome: Prior booking required
Societies:	Welcome: Special concessions, Contact Club for details
Facilities:	Chipping/Putting Area, Trolley hire, Bar, Restaurant

Accommodation, Food and Drink

Reference numbers below refer to detailed information provided in section 2

Accommodation

An Bothar Pub, Cuas, Dingle, Co Kerry

Tel: 066 9155342 Pub, restaurant and Accommodation in a lovely secluded setting on the road to Brandon Creek on the Dingle Peninsula. 304

Greenmount House, Dingle, Co Kerry

Tel: 066 9151414 Fax: 066 9151974 A neat, modern guest house with individually decorated en suite bedrooms. Great views, great breakfasts. 305

Killfountain Farm, Dingle, Co Kerry

Tel: 066 9151389 Six en suite bedrooms in a modern Bed & Breakfast house by Ballyferriter golf course. Golfing breaks a speciality. 307

Meadowlands Hotel, Tralee, Co Kerry

Tel: 066 7180444 Fax: 066 7180964 A charming hotel in a landscaped garden just north of Tralee. 24 en suite bedrooms, 3 suites, restaurant and bar. 302

Tralee Marina Holiday Apartments, Tralee, Co Kerry

Tel: 066 7181222 web: traleemarina.com 4-star self-catering in 28 apartments in the Marina. Also town houses & apartments & 20 guest house rooms. Major credit cards.

Westward Court, Tralee, Co Kerry

Tel: 066 80081 e-mail: westward@iol.ie Superior budget Accommodation in the centre of town (Mary Street). 43 modern en suite bedrooms. Restaurant. Private car park. No credit cards.

Food and Drink

An Bothar Pub, Cuas, Dingle, Co Kerry

Tel: 066 9155342 Pub, restaurant and Accommodation in a lovely secluded setting on the road to Brandon Creek on the Dingle Peninsula. 304

Meadowlands Hotel, Tralee, Co Kerry

Tel: 066 7180444 Fax: 066 7180964 A charming hotel in a landscaped garden just north of Tralee. 24 en suite bedrooms, 3 suites, restaurant and bar. 302

Westward Court, Tralee, Co Kerry

Tel: 066 80081 e-mail: westward@iol.ie Superior budget Accommodation in the centre of town (Mary Street). 43 modern en suite bedrooms. Restaurant. Private car park. No credit cards.

Dooks

Dooks Golf Club, Dooks, Glenbeigh, Co Kerry

Tel: 066 9768205/9768200

Sec/Manager:	D. Mangan
Professional:	None
Directions:	5 miles South West of Killorglin off the N70 coastal road to Glenbeigh
Type of Course:	Links
Date Founded:	1889
No of Holes:	18
Length:	6010 yds (5495 mtrs)
Par:	70
SSS:	68
Green Fees:	£25 per round
Visitors:	Welcome: Contact Club in advance

Societies:	Welcome: Special concessions, Contact Club in advance
Facilities:	Chipping/Putting Area, Trolley hire, Bar, Restaurant

Accommodation, Food and Drink

Reference numbers below refer to detailed information provided in section 2

Accommodation

Aishling House, Waterville, Co Kerry

Tel: 066 947 4247 Bed and Breakfast Accommodation in the main street of Waterville. 4 double bedrooms, all en suite.

An Bothar Pub, Cuas, Dingle, Co Kerry

Tel: 066 9155342 Pub, restaurant and Accommodation in a lovely secluded setting on the road to Brandon Creek on the Dingle Peninsula. 304

Atlantic View, Waterville, Co Kerry

Tel/Fax: 066 947 4335 e-mail: joecurranelect@tinet.ie Sea views at a B&B house with a single and 4 doubles, all en suite. No credit cards.

Brook Manor Lodge, Tralee, Co Kerry

Tel: 066 7120406 Fax: 066 7127552 Elegant en suite B&B Accommodation in six luxuriously appointed bedrooms in a secluded country guest house. 290

Cul Draiochta, Cahersiveen, Co Kerry

Tel/Fax: 066 9473141 e-mail: inugent@esatclear.ie 2 doubles, 2 family rooms all en suite or private. B&B on the N70, great views of Valentia Harbour. Fine base for walking or touring.

Greenmount House, Dingle, Co Kerry

Tel: 066 9151414 Fax: 066 9151974 A neat, modern guest house with individually decorated en suite bedrooms. Great views, great breakfasts. 305

Kathleen's Country House, Killarney, Co Kerry

Tel: 064 32810 Fax: 064 32340 An award-winning country guest house of real distinction offering the highest standards of comfort and service. Extensive gardens. No smoking in the bedrooms. 298

Killfountain Farm, Dingle, Co Kerry

Tel: 066 9151389 Six en suite bedrooms in a modern Bed & Breakfast house by Ballyferriter golf course. Golfing breaks a speciality. 307

Meadowlands Hotel, Tralee, Co Kerry

Tel: 066 7180444 Fax: 066 7180964 A charming hotel in a landscaped garden just north of Tralee. 24 en suite bedrooms, 3 suites, restaurant and bar. 302

O'Grady's Townhouse, Waterville, Co Kerry

Tel: 066 947 4350 Fax: 066 947 4730 Townhouse B&B Accommodation in six bedrooms - four doubles, a twin and a triple for family occupation, all en suite.

Strandview House, Caherciveen, Co Kerry

Tel: 066 947 3315 e-mail: strandviewhse@oceanfree.net B&B in a single, a double and a family room, all en suite, on the scenic Ring of Kerry.

The 19th Green, Killarney, Co Cork

Tel: 064 32868 Fax: 064 32637 Family-run guest house with 13 well-equipped bedrooms, car park, putting green. Killarney Golf Club is opposite. 294

Woodlands, Killarney, Co Cork

Tel/Fax: 064 31467 Bed & Breakfast Accommodation in 8 en suite bedrooms, half a mile from Killarney Golf Club. 297

Food and Drink

An Bothar Pub, Cuas, Dingle, Co Kerry

Tel: 066 9155342 Pub, restaurant and Accommodation in a lovely secluded setting on the road to Brandon Creek on the Dingle Peninsula. 304

Meadowlands Hotel, Tralee, Co Kerry

Tel: 066 7180444 Fax: 066 7180964 A charming hotel in a landscaped garden just north of Tralee. 24 en suite bedrooms, 3 suites, restaurant and bar. 302

Sheilin Seafood Restaurant, Waterville, Co Kerry

Tel: 066 947 4231 A very friendly and relaxed bistro-style restaurant in the town centre. Seafood the speciality, much of it caught in the bay. 300

Kenmare

Kenmare Golf Club, Kenmare, Co Kerry
Tel: 064 41291

Sec/Manager:	Siobhan O'Callaghan
Professional:	None
Directions:	On the southern edge of Kenmare off the N71 to Glengariff
Type of Course:	Parkland
Date Founded:	1903
No of Holes:	18
Length:	6053 yds (5534 mtrs)
Par:	71
SSS:	69
Green Fees:	Weekdays & Saturday: £20 Sundays & Bank Holidays: £25
Visitors:	Welcome: Prior booking required
Societies:	Welcome: Special concessions for 18 or more, Apply to club for details
Facilities:	Chipping/Putting Area, Practice Area, Golf Clubs for hire, Trolley hire, Bar, Caddy service by arrangement

Accommodation, Food and Drink

Reference numbers below refer to detailed information provided in section 2

Accommodation

Ardmore House, Kenmare, Co Kerry
Tel/Fax: 064 41406 Bed and Breakfast Accommodation on the Killarney Road. 1 single, 3 doubles, 2 family rooms, all en suite.

Birchwood, Kilgarvin, Co Kerry
Tel: 064 85473 Fax: 065 85570 Spacious B&B Accommodation in 2 en suite double rooms and three en suite triples. AA 4 diamonds. No credit cards.

Brookvilla, Sneem, Co Kerry
Tel: 064 45172 Quiet Bed and Breakfast Accommodation: 1 double room, 1 twin, 2 family rooms, all en suite. Warm welcome assured. 7 miles from Ring of Kerry and 13 miles from Kenmare. PGA professional, equipment for hire and sale.

Darby O'Gill's, Lissivigeen, Co Cork
Tel: 064 34168 Fax: 064 36794 Country house hotel with charming en suite bedrooms. Irish cuisine in the evening, lunches in the lounge bar. Darts, rings and cards. 308

Linn Dubh, Aghadoe, Killarney, Co Kerry
Tel: 064 33828 Two triples and three double rooms, all en suite, for B&B Accommodation. Access, Mastercard, Visa.

Mills Inn, Ballyvourney, Macroom, Co Cork
Tel: 026 45237 Fax: 026 45454 Set in landscaped gardens 20 miles from Killarne, this is one of the oldest and finest inns in Ireland. 12 rooms, all en suite. Seafood speciality restaurant. 147

O'Donnells of Ashgrove, Kenmare, Co Kerry
Tel: 064 41228 Family-run Bed and Breakfast place with 1 single and 3 en suite double rooms. Visa only.

O'Shea's, Kenmare, Co Kerry
Tel: 064 41498 Thérèse O'Shea's B&B on the Killarney Road out of Kenmare. 2 double rooms, 1 twin, 2 family rooms, all en suite. No credit cards.

Shelburne Lodge, Kenmare, Co Kerry
Tel: 064 41013 Fax: 064 42135 Family-run B&B on the Cork Road out of Kenmare. 9 double bedrooms, all en suite.

The Brambles, Kenmare, Co Kerry
Tel: 064 41712 e-mail: brambles@eircom.net Bed and Breakfast Accommodation at Gortamullen. 4 en suite rooms with king-size beds. Licensed bar.

The Wander Inn, Kenmare, Co Kerry
Tel: 064 42700 True Irish hospitality in a town-centre hostelr. A hearty breakfast, lunch and dinner are served in the restaurant, and in the evening everyone shares in the craic in the bar. The hotel has 11 bedrooms, all en suite. 295

The White House, Kenmare, Co Kerry
Tel: 064 42372 all-in-one Golf & Leisure tours. Groups of 2-7 persons with a choice of 10 plus magnificent golf courses, all within 20 mile. The White House is 2½ miles from Kenmare and Molls Gap. All rooms have mountain views. 296

Willow Lodge, Kenmare, Co Kerry
Tel: 064 42301 Built in the grounds of a nunnery and just a few minutes' walk from the centre of town, Willow Lodge has a lounge, dining room and five en suite bedrooms, each named after a tree and each with its own individual appeal and charm. 291

Food and Drink

Café Indigo, Kenmare, Co Kerry
Tel: 064 42356/7 Award winning restaurant, grill and late night bar serving traditional Irish, Mediterranean and European cuisine.

Darby O'Gill's, Lissivigeen, Co Cork
Tel: 064 34168 Fax: 064 36794 Country house hotel with charming en suite bedrooms. Irish cuisine in the evening, lunches in the lounge bar. Darts, rings and cards. 308

Mills Inn, Ballyvourney, Macroom, Co Cork
Tel: 026 45237 Fax: 026 45454 Set in landscaped gardens 20 miles from Killarne, this is one of the oldest and finest inns in Ireland. 12 rooms, all en suite. Seafood speciality restaurant. 147

Sheilin Seafood Restaurant, Waterville, Co Kerry
Tel: 066 9474231 A very friendly and relaxed bistro-style restaurant in the town centre. Seafood is the speciality, much of it caught in the bay. 300

The Old Dutch Restaurant, Kenmare, Co Kerry
Tel: 064 41449 Dutch-owned restaurant serving Irish and European cuisine. Wine licence. Closed Mondays 1 Oct-1 May.

The Square Pint, Kenmare, Co Kerry
Tel: 064 42357 One of Ireland's leading live traditional music venues. Convivial pub serving excellent bar food 7 days a week. Late night licence.

The Wander Inn, Kenmare, Co Kerry
Tel: 064 42700 True Irish hospitality in a town-centre hostelr. A hearty breakfast, lunch and dinner are served in the restaurant, and in the evening everyone shares in the craic in the bar. The hotel has 11 bedrooms, all en suite. 295

Killarney

Killarney Golf Club, Killarney, Co Kerry
Tel: 064 31034/31242

In June 1999, Killarney GC gained a unique place among Irish clubs when the third 18, designed by Donald Steel, came into play. And a £5 million development will be completed when a new clubhouse of 4,000 square feet, is opened officially in July 2000.

From its foundation in 1893, it could be said that Killarney always had its eye on the ball. For instance, one of the club's earliest ventures was

Length:	6741 yds (6164 mtrs)
Par:	72
SSS:	72
Green Fees:	£43

Killeen

Type of Course:	Parkland
Date Founded:	1968
No of Holes:	18
Length:	7079 yds (6474 mtrs)
Par:	72
SSS:	73
Green Fees:	£43

Lackabane

Type of Course:	Parkland
Date Founded:	1999
No of Holes:	18
Length:	7014 yds (6414 mtrs)
Par:	72
SSS:	72
Green Fees:	£43

Visitors:	Welcome: Contact Club in advance
Societies:	Welcome: Special concessions, Contact Club for details
Facilities:	Chipping/Putting Area, Practice Area, Golf Clubs for hire, Trolley hire Bar, Restaurant, Caddy service by arrangement, plus Sauna & Gym

an exhibition match in 1903 involving the celebrated Scottish professional Sandy Herd and the British Open runner-up of that year, Tom Vardon.

"The Post" later reported: "It speaks well for the enterprise of a small club like Killarney that they were able to provide the golfers of Kerry with such a first-class match." Similar sentiments were expressed when Nick Faldo captured the Irish Open on the Killeen Course in 1991 and 1992.

"When the wind blows off the lake, even the best player in the world will be hard-pressed to break 80. The 18th hole in particular, is one of

the most memorable holes in golf." This was how Gene Sarazen described the Mahony's Point layout, which was designed by Sir Guy Campbell and Henry Longhurst in 1938.

Thirty years later, the premier, Killeen stretch, began to take shape to a design by Eddie Hackett and Dr Billy O'Sullivan. Then came the extention to 54 holes. And the entire complex is summed-up perfectly in the words of Bing Crosby, who described Killarney as "a genuine test in a lovely environment."

Sec/Manager:	Tom Prendergast
Professional:	Tony Coveney
Directions:	Two miles West of Killarney off the N72 to Killorglin

Mahony's Point

Type of Course:	Parkland
Date Founded:	1938
No of Holes:	18

Accommodation, Food and Drink

Reference numbers below refer to detailed information provided in section 2

Accommodation

Applecroft House, Woodlawn Road, Killarney, Co Kerry
Tel: 064 32782 e-mail: applecroft@eircom.net Delightful B&B bungalow in neat gardens. 2 double rooms, 3 twin rooms en suite, with tv & hairdryer. Off-street parking. Amex, Visa, Mastercard.

Clonfert, Fossa, Killarney, Co Kerry
Tel: 064 31459 B&B Accommodation in 5 en suite double rooms. 9 golf courses within a few miles. No credit cards.

Crystal Springs, Killarney, Co Cork
Tel: 064 33272 Charming B&B guest house in a quiet setting by a river bank. Fishing. Bureau de change. Wine licence.   299

Darby O'Gill's, Lissivigeen, Co Cork
Tel: 064 34168 Fax: 064 36794 Country house hotel with charming en suite bedrooms. Irish cuisine in the evening, lunches in the lounge bar. Darts, rings and cards.   308

Hazelwood, Killarney, Co Kerry
Tel/Fax: 064 34363 Bed and Breakfast Accommodation in four double bedrooms and a triple (ideal for families). At Upper Ballyspillane. No credit cards.

Kathleen's Country House, Killarney, Co Kerry
Tel: 064 32810 Fax: 064 32340 An award-winning country guest house of real distinction offering the highest standards of comfort and service. Extensive gardens. No smoking in the bedrooms.   298

Linn Dubh, Aghadoe, Killarney, Co Kerry
Tel: 064 33828 Two triples and three double rooms, all en suite, for B&B Accommodation. Access, Mastercard, Visa.

Mills Inn, Ballyvourney, Macroom, Co Cork
Tel: 026 45237 Fax: 026 45454 Set in landscaped gardens 20 miles from Killarne, this is one of the oldest and finest inns in Ireland. 12 rooms, all en suite. Seafood speciality restaurant.   147

O'Shea's, Kenmare, Co Kerry
Tel: 064 41498 Thérèse O'Shea's B&B on the Killarney Road out of Kenmare. 2 double rooms, 1 twin, 2 family rooms, all en suite. No credit cards.

River Valley Farm House, Killarney, Co Kerry
Tel: 064 32411 Fax: 064 37909 2 twin rooms and two big enough for families, all en suite. B&B. On the Cork Road out of Killarney.

Sallyport House, Kenmare, Co Kerry
Tel: 064 42066 web: sallyporthouse.com An elegant country house set in ten acres of lawns and trees overlooking the harbour and the bay. Five antique-furnished bedrooms with either king- or queen-size beds and capacious en suite bathrooms. One has a four-poster. 293

Sika Lodge, Ballydowney, Co Kerry
Tel: 064 36304 Fax: 064 36746 web: kerry-insight.com/sika-lodge/ 6 double bedrooms, all en suite with satellite tv. 5 minutes from Killarney; next to Killarney Golf Club.

St Anthonys Lodge, Killarney, Co Kerry
Tel: 064 31534 Town & Country listed Bed and Breakfast Accommodation on the Cork Road out of Killarney. Double rooms en suite.

The 19th Green, Killarney, Co Cork
Tel: 064 32868 Fax: 064 32637 Family-run guest house with 13 well-equipped bedrooms, car park, putting green. Killarney Golf Club is opposite. 294

The Laune & Taylor's, Killarney, Co Kerry
Tel: 064 32772 Fax: 064 37908 'Wine, dine & stay' in the centre of Killarney. En suite bedrooms; breakfast till noon; lunch and a full à la carte 3 til 10. 306

The Wander Inn, Kenmare, Co Kerry
Tel: 064 42700 True Irish hospitality in a town-centre hostel. A hearty breakfast, lunch and dinner are served in the restaurant, and in the evening everyone shares in the craic in the bar. The hotel has 11 bedrooms, all en suite. 295

The White House, Kenmare, Co Kerry
Tel: 064 42312 all-in-one Golf & Leisure tours. Groups of 2-7 persons with a choice of 10 plus magnificent golf courses, all within 20 mile. The White House is 2½ miles from Kenmare and Molls Gap. All rooms have mountain views. 296

Willow Lodge, Kenmare, Co Kerry
Tel: 064 42301 Built in the grounds of a nunnery and just a few minutes' walk from the centre of town, Willow Lodge has a lounge, dining room and five en suite bedrooms, each named after a tree and each with its own individual appeal and charm. 291

Woodlands, Killarney, Co Cork
Tel/Fax: 064 31467 Bed & Breakfast Accommodation in 8 en suite bedrooms, half a mile from Killarney Golf Club. 297

Food and Drink

Darby O'Gill's, Lissivigeen, Co Cork
Tel: 064 34168 Fax: 064 36794 Country house hotel with charming en suite bedrooms. Irish cuisine in the evening, lunches in the lounge bar. Darts, rings and cards. 308

Mills Inn, Ballyvourney, Macroom, Co Cork
Tel: 026 45237 Fax: 026 45454 Set in landscaped gardens 20 miles from Killarne, this is one of the oldest and finest inns in Ireland. 12 rooms, all en suite. Seafood speciality restaurant. 147

The Laune & Taylor's, Killarney, Co Kerry
Tel: 064 32772 Fax: 064 37908 'Wine, dine & stay' in the centre of Killarney. En suite bedrooms; breakfast till noon; lunch and a full à la carte 3 till 10. 306

The Wander Inn, Kenmare, Co Kerry
Tel: 064 42700 True Irish hospitality in a town-centre hostel. A hearty breakfast, lunch and dinner are served in the restaurant, and in the evening everyone shares in the craic in the bar. The hotel has 11 bedrooms, all en suite. 295

Killorglin

Killorglin Golf Club, Steelroe, Killorglin, Co Kerry
Tel: 066 9761979

Sec/Manager:	Bill Dodd
Professional:	None
Directions:	2 miles North East of Killorglin off the N70 to Tralee
Type of Course:	Parkland
Date Founded:	1992

No of Holes:	18
Length:	6467 yds (5913 mtrs)
Par:	72
SSS:	71
Green Fees:	Weekdays: £15 Weekends & Bank Holidays: £18
Visitors:	Welcome: Prebooking required
Societies:	Welcome: Contact Club for details
Facilities:	Chipping/Putting Area, Practice Area, Golf Clubs for hire, Trolley hire, Electric Buggy hire, Bar, Restaurant

Accommodation, Food and Drink

Reference numbers below refer to detailed information provided in section 2

Accommodation

An Bothar Pub, Cuas, Dingle, Co Kerry
Tel: 066 9155342 Pub, restaurant and Accommodation in a lovely secluded setting on the road to Brandon Creek on the Dingle Peninsula. 304

Brook Manor Lodge, Tralee, Co Kerry
Tel: 066 7120406 Fax: 066 7127552 Elegant en suite B&B Accommodation in six luxuriously appointed bedrooms in a secluded country guest house. 290

Crystal Springs, Killarney, Co Cork
Tel: 064 33272 Charming B&B guest house in a quiet setting by a river bank. Fishing. Bureau de change. Wine licence. 299

Greenmount House, Dingle, Co Kerry
Tel: 066 9151414 Fax: 066 9151974 A neat, modern guest house with individually decorated en suite bedrooms. Great views, great breakfasts. 305

Hazelwood, Killarney, Co Kerry
Tel/Fax: 064 34363 Bed and Breakfast Accommodation in four double bedrooms and a triple (ideal for families). At Upper Ballyspillane. No credit cards.

Kathleen's Country House, Killarney, Co Kerry
Tel: 064 32810 Fax: 064 32340 An award-winning country guest house of real distinction offering the highest standards of comfort and service. Extensive gardens. No smoking in the bedrooms. 298

Killfountain Farm, Dingle, Co Kerry
Tel: 066 9151389 Six en suite bedrooms in a modern Bed & Breakfast house by Ballyferriter golf course. Golfing breaks a speciality. 307

Meadowlands Hotel, Tralee, Co Kerry
Tel: 066 7180444 Fax: 066 7180964 A charming hotel in a landscaped garden just north of Tralee. 24 en suite bedrooms, 3 suites, restaurant and bar. 302

River Valley Farm House, Killarney, Co Kerry
Tel: 064 32411 Fax: 064 37909 2 twin rooms and two big enough for families, all en suite. B&B. On the Cork Road out of Killarney.

Sika Lodge, Ballydowney, Co Kerry
Tel: 064 36304 Fax: 064 36746 web: kerry-insight.com/sika-lodge/ 6 double bedrooms, all en suite with satellite tv. 5 minutes from Killarney; next to Killarney Golf Club.

St Anthonys Lodge, Killarney, Co Kerry
Tel: 064 31534 Town & Country listed Bed and Breakfast Accommodation on the Cork Road out of Killarney. Double rooms en suite.

The 19th Green, Killarney, Co Cork
Tel: 064 32868 Fax: 064 32637 Family-run guest house with 13 well-equipped bedrooms, car park, putting green. Killarney Golf Club is opposite. 294

The Laune & Taylor's, Killarney, Co Kerry
Tel: 064 32772 Fax: 064 37908 'Wine, dine & stay' in the centre of Killarney. En suite bedrooms; breakfast till noon; lunch and a full à la carte 3 till 10. 306

Tralee Townhouse, Tralee, Co Kerry
Tel: 066 7181111 20 bedrooms, including several of family size, in a town house hotel that's handy for all Tralee's attractions. 303

Woodlands, Killarney, Co Cork
Tel/Fax: 064 31467 Bed & Breakfast Accommodation in 8 en suite bedrooms, half a mile from Killarney Golf Club. 297

Food and Drink

An Bothar Pub, Cuas, Dingle, Co Kerry
Tel: 066 9155342 Pub, restaurant and Accommodation in a lovely secluded setting

on the road to Brandon Creek on the Dingle Peninsula. 304

Meadowlands Hotel, Tralee, Co Kerry
Tel: 066 7180444 Fax: 066 7180964 A charming hotel in a landscaped garden just north of Tralee. 24 en suite bedrooms, 3 suites, restaurant and bar. 302

The Laune & Taylor's, Killarney, Co Kerry
Tel: 064 32772 Fax: 064 37908 'Wine, dine & stay' in the centre of Killarney. En suite bedrooms; breakfast till noon; lunch and a full à la carte 3 till 10. 306

Ring Of Kerry

Ring of Kerry, Templenoe, Kenmare, County Kerry

Tel: 064 6442000

Sec/Manager:	V. Devlin
Professional:	None
Directions:	4 miles west of Kenmore off the N70 to Sneem
Type of Course:	Parkland/Links
Date Founded:	1998
No of Holes:	18
Length:	6923 yds (6330 mtrs)
Par:	72
SSS:	73
Green Fees:	Weekdays: £45 Weekends & Bank Holidays: £45
Visitors:	Welcome: Ring in advance
Societies:	Welcome: Book in advance
Facilities:	Chipping/Putting Area, Golf Clubs for hire, Trolley hire, Electric Buggy hire, Bar, Restaurant, Caddy service by arrangement

Accommodation, Food and Drink

Reference numbers below refer to detailed information provided in section 2

Accommodation

Aishling House, Waterville, Co Kerry
Tel: 066 9474247 Bed and Breakfast Accommodation in the main street of Waterville. 4 double bedrooms, all en suite.

Applecroft House, Woodlawn Road, Killarney, Co Kerry
Tel: 064 32782 e-mail: applecroft@eircom.net Delightful B&B bungalow in neat gardens. 2 double rooms, 3 twin rooms en suite, with tv & hairdryer. Off-street parking. Amex, Visa, Mastercard.

Ardmore House, Kenmare, Co Kerry
Tel/Fax: 064 41406 Bed and Breakfast Accommodation on the Killarney Road. 1 single, 3 doubles, 2 family rooms, all en suite.

Atlantic View, Waterville, Co Kerry
Tel/Fax: 066 9474335 e-mail: joecurranelect@tinet.ie Sea views at a B&B house with a single and 4 doubles, all en suite. No credit cards.

Birchwood, Kilgarvin, Co Kerry
Tel: 064 85473 Fax: 065 85570 Spacious B&B Accommodation in 2 en suite double rooms and three en suite triples. AA 3 diamonds. No credit cards.

Brookvilla, Sneem, Co Kerry
Tel: 064 45172 Quiet Bed and Breakfast Accommodation: 1 double room, 1 twin, 2 family rooms, all en suite. Warm welcome assured. 7 miles from Ring of Kerry and 13 miles from Kenmare. PGA professional, equipment for hire and sale.

Cul Draiochta, Cahersiveen, Co Kerry
Tel/Fax: 066 9473141 e-mail: inugent@esatclear.ie 2 doubles, 2 family rooms all en suite or private. B&B on the N70, great views of Valentia Harbour. Fine base for walking or touring.

O'Donnells of Ashgrove, Kenmare, Co Kerry
Tel: 064 41228 Family-run Bed and Breakfast place with 1 single and 3 en suite

double rooms. Visa only.

O'Grady's Townhouse, Waterville, Co Kerry
Tel: 066 9474350 Fax: 066 9474730 Townhouse B&B Accommodation in six bedrooms - four doubles, a twin and a triple for family occupation, all en suite.

O'Shea's, Kenmare, Co Kerry
Tel: 064 41498 Thérèse O'Shea's B&B on the Killarney Road out of Kenmare. 2 double rooms, 1 twin, 2 family rooms, all en suite. No credit cards.

Sallyport House, Kenmare, Co Kerry
Tel: 064 42066 web: sallyporthouse.com An elegant country house set in ten acres of lawns and trees overlooking the harbour and the bay. Five antique-furnished bedrooms with either king- or queen-size beds and capacious en suite bathrooms. One has a four-poster. 293

Shelburne Lodge, Kenmare, Co Kerry
Tel: 064 41013 Fax: 064 42135 Family-run B&B on the Cork Road out of Kenmare. 9 double bedrooms, all en suite.

Strandview House, Caherciveen, Co Kerry
Tel: 066 9473315 e-mail: strandviewhse@oceanfree.net B&B in a single, a double and a family room, all en suite, on the scenic Ring of Kerry.

The Brambles, Kenmare, Co Kerry
Tel: 064 41712 e-mail: brambles@eircom.net Bed and Breakfast Accommodation at Gortamullen. 4 en suite rooms with king-size beds. Licensed bar.

The Wander Inn, Kenmare, Co Kerry
Tel: 064 42700 True Irish hospitality in a town-centre hostelr. A hearty breakfast, lunch and dinner are served in the restaurant, and in the evening everyone shares in the craic in the bar. The hotel has 11 bedrooms, all en suite. 295

The White House, Kenmare, Co Kerry
Tel: 064 42372 all-in-one Golf & Leisure tours. Groups of 2-7 persons with a choice of 10 plus magnificent golf courses, all within 20 mile. The White House is 2½ miles from Kenmare and Molls Gap. All rooms have mountain views. 296

Willow Lodge, Kenmare, Co Kerry
Tel: 064 42301 Built in the grounds of a nunnery and just a few minutes' walk from the centre of town, Willow Lodge has a lounge, dining room and five en suite bedrooms, each named after a tree and each with its own individual appeal and charm. 291

Food and Drink

Café Indigo, Kenmare, Co Kerry
Tel: 064 42356/7 Award winning restaurant, grill and late night bar serving traditional Irish, Mediterranean and European cuisine.

Sheilin Seafood Restaurant, Waterville, Co Kerry
Tel: 066 9474231 A very friendly and relaxed bistro-style restaurant in the town centre. Seafood is the speciality, much of it caught in the bay. 300

The Old Dutch Restaurant, Kenmare, Co Kerry
Tel: 064 41449 Dutch-owned restaurant serving Irish and European cuisine. Wine licence. Closed Mondays 1 Oct-1May.

The Square Pint, Kenmare, Co Kerry
Tel: 064 42357 One of Ireland's leading live traditional music venues. Convivial pub serving excellent bar food 7 days a week. Late night licence.

The Wander Inn, Kenmare, Co Kerry
Tel: 064 42700 True Irish hospitality in a town-centre hostelr. A hearty breakfast, lunch and dinner are served in the restaurant, and in the evening everyone shares in the craic in the bar. The hotel has 11 bedrooms, all en suite. 295

Tralee

Tralee, West Barrow, Ardfert, Tralee, Co Kerry

Tel: 066 7136379

Having purchased a magnificent site for the relatively modest price of £170,000 officials of the Tralee club knew it deserved to be exploited only by appropriate design skills. And when Arnold Palmer's company produced the only layout which fully developed the site's duneland, he and his chief architect, Ed Seay, were duly handed the contract.

Prior to the move to Barrow in 1983, the club had a nine-hole stretch in the town. With 18-hole Accommodation of splendid quality, however, they have since become one of the premier clubs in the south-west.

It would be difficult to imagine a site more suited to golf-course development. Overlooking the wild Atlantic with a mixture of pastureland, duneland and rugged cliffs, the area was used extensively by the celebrated British director David Lean for the movie "Ryan's Daughter" starring Robert Mitchum and Sarah Miles.

Despite serious problems in getting the greens to thrive, Palmer was justifiably proud of the finished product. The front nine has the feel of parkland by the sea, with the long, 587-yard second hole following the line of the coast as a double dog-leg to the right. Then comes the short third where the cave below the green was featured in Lean's movie.

The homeward journey, which is pure links, offers a fascinating contrast and visitors almost invariably refer to the wickedly difficult, 437-yard 12th, where it seems the only place to land the second shot in on the green. And the short 16th offers stunning views of sea and sand.

Sec/Manager:	Patrick Nugent
Professional:	David Power
Directions:	7 miles north west of Tralee off the R558. Turn right at Spa through Church Hill to Barrow
Type of Course:	Parkland/Links
Date Founded:	1989
No of Holes:	18
Length:	6252 mtrs 6835 yds
Par:	71
SSS:	71
Green Fees:	Weekdays: £40 Weekends £60
Visitors:	Welcome: Except Wednesday & Saturday, Further restrictions at weekends. Contact Club in advance
Societies:	Welcome: Weekdays only, Book in advance
Facilities:	Chipping/Putting Area, Practice Area, Golf Clubs for hire, Trolley hire, Bar, Restaurant, Caddy service by arrangement, Steam room

Accommodation, Food and Drink

Reference numbers below refer to detailed information provided in section 2

Accommodation

An Bothar Pub, Cuas, Dingle, Co Kerry
Tel: 066 9155342 Pub, restaurant and Accommodation in a lovely secluded setting on the road to Brandon Creek on the Dingle Peninsula. 304

Brook Manor Lodge, Tralee, Co Kerry
Tel: 066 7120406 Fax: 066 7127552 Elegant en suite B&B Accommodation in six luxuriously appointed bedrooms in a secluded country guest house. 290

Castle View House, Carrig Island, Co Kerry
Tel/Fax: 068 43304 Six bedrooms, all en suite, in a neat, modern house close to the Tarbert/Killimer car ferry. B&B; dinner by arrangement. 301

Crystal Springs, Killarney, Co Cork
Tel: 064 33272 Charming B&B guest house in a quiet setting by a river bank. Fishing. Bureau de change. Wine licence. 299

Greenmount House, Dingle, Co Kerry
Tel: 066 9151414 Fax: 066 9151974 A neat, modern guest house with individually decorated en suite bedrooms. Great views, great breakfasts. 305

Killfountain Farm, Dingle, Co Kerry
Tel: 066 9151389 Six en suite bedrooms in a modern Bed & Breakfast house by Ballyferriter golf course. Golfing breaks a speciality. 307

Meadowlands Hotel, Tralee, Co Kerry
Tel: 066 7180444 Fax: 066 7180964 A charming hotel in a landscaped garden just north of Tralee. 24 en suite bedrooms, 3 suites, restaurant and bar. 302

Tralee Marina Holiday Apartments, Tralee, Co Kerry
Tel: 066 7181222 web: traleemarina.com 4-star self-catering in 28 apartments in the Marina. Also town houses & apartments & 20 guest house rooms. Major credit cards.

Tralee Townhouse, Tralee, Co Kerry
Tel: 066 7181111 20 bedrooms, including several of family size, in a town house hotel that's handy for all Tralee's attractions. 303

Westward Court, Tralee, Co Kerry
Tel: 066 80081 e-mail: westward@iol.ie Superior budget Accommodation in the centre of town (Mary Street). 43 modern en suite bedrooms. Restaurant. Private car park. No credit cards.

Food and Drink

An Bothar Pub, Cuas, Dingle, Co Kerry
Tel: 066 9155342 Pub, restaurant and Accommodation in a lovely secluded setting on the road to Brandon Creek on the Dingle Peninsula. 304

Meadowlands Hotel, Tralee, Co Kerry
Tel: 066 7180444 Fax: 066 7180964 A charming hotel in a landscaped garden just north of Tralee. 24 en suite bedrooms, 3 suites, restaurant and bar. 302

Westward Court, Tralee, Co Kerry
Tel: 066 80081 e-mail: westward@iol.ie Superior budget Accommodation in the centre of town (Mary Street). 43 modern en suite bedrooms. Restaurant. Private car park. No credit cards.

Waterville

Waterville Golf Club, Ring of Kerry, Waterville, Co Kerry

Tel: 066 9474102

Eddie Hackett would insist that "nature is the best architect." And by way of proving the point, he would follow the lie of the land, siting holes wherever "the Good Lord provided." These were the principles he applied to the design of Waterville, which remains a worthy monument to his memory.

On another occasion, Ireland's most prolific golf-course architect remarked: "I could never break up the earth the way they tell me some

SSS:	74
Green Fees:	All Week: £75; Mon – Thu before 8.00 and after 4.00: £45
Visitors:	Welcome: Prebooking required
Societies:	Welcome: Contact Club direct for details
Facilities:	Chipping/Putting Area, Practice Area, Golf Clubs for hire, Trolley hire, Bar, Restaurant

Accommodation, Food and Drink

Reference numbers below refer to detailed information provided in section 2

Accommodation

Aishling House, Waterville, Co Kerry
Tel: 066 9474247 Bed and Breakfast Accommodation in the main street of Waterville. 4 double bedrooms, all en suite.

Atlantic View, Waterville, Co Kerry
Tel/Fax: 066 9474335 e-mail: joecurranelect@tinet.ie Sea views at a B&B house with a single and 4 doubles, all en suite. No credit cards.

Brookvilla, Sneem, Co Kerry
Tel: 064 45172 Quiet Bed and Breakfast Accommodation: 1 double room, 1 twin, 2 family rooms, all en suite. Warm welcome assured. 7 miles from Ring of Kerry and 13 miles from Kenmare. PGA professional, equipment for hire and sale.

Cul Draiochta, Cahersiveen, Co Kerry
Tel/Fax: 066 9473141 e-mail: inugent@esatclear.ie 2 doubles, 2 family rooms all en suite or private. B&B on the N70, great views of Valentia Harbour. Fine base for walking or touring.

O'Donnells of Ashgrove, Kenmare, Co Kerry
Tel: 064 41228 Family-run Bed and Breakfast place with 1 single and 3 en suite double rooms. Visa only.

O'Grady's Townhouse, Waterville, Co Kerry
Tel: 066 9474350 Fax: 066 947 4730 Townhouse B&B Accommodation in six bedrooms - four doubles, a twin and a triple for family occupation, all en suite.

Strandview House, Caherciveen, Co Kerry
Tel: 066 9473315 e-mail: strandviewhse@oceanfree.net B&B in a single, a double and a family room, all en suite, on the scenic Ring of Kerry.

Food and Drink

Sheilin Seafood Restaurant, Waterville, Co Kerry
Tel: 066 9474231 A very friendly and relaxed bistro-style restaurant in the town centre. Seafood is the speciality, much of it caught in the bay.   300

The Old Dutch Restaurant, Kenmare, Co Kerry
Tel: 064 41449 Dutch-owned restaurant serving Irish and European cuisine. Wine licence. Closed Mondays 1 Oct-1May.

The Square Pint, Kenmare, Co Kerry
Tel: 064 42357 One of Ireland's leading live traditional music venues. Convivial pub serving excellent bar food 7 days a week. Late night licence.

architects do. You disrupt the soil profile and anyway, it's unnatural. Within reason, I try to use what's there, and you can never do with trees what you can do with sand dunes."

His love of links terrain is reflected in a wonderful layout, which played host to the Kerrygold Classic from 1975 to 1977, when Tony Jacklin was among the winners. More recently, it became a favoured hideaway for such leading Americans as Tiger Woods, Mark O'Meara, David Duval, and the late Payne Stewart.

Typical of his approach to a wonderful site was his treatment of the short 12th. "Local contractors told me they weren't going to touch the ground there because Mass was once celebrated in the hollow," he recalled. "And we never touched it. It's plateau green is natural and there is no need of bunkers, which is the best tribute you can pay a hole."

Hackett called Waterville "a beautiful monster." And in all its windswept majesty, there could hardly be a more appropriate description, especially when wild winds sweep in from the Atlantic.

Sec/Manager:	Noel Cronin
Professional:	Liam Higgins
Directions:	1 mile North West of Waterville off the N70 to Cahersiveen
Type of Course:	Links
Date Founded:	1889
No of Holes:	18
Length:	6549 yds (5988 mtrs)
Par:	72

KILDARE

On the Monday morning after the 1989 staging of the Ryder Cup at The Belfry, the then executive director of the PGA, John Lindsay, read out a list of applicants wishing to play host to the event in 1993. There was quite a raising of eyebrows when the list included the Kildare Golf and Country Club, which had yet to be built. The significance of the move, however, was not lost on Irish observers. They knew that Dr Michael Smurfit was simply putting down a marker with a view to landing the grand prize sometime down the road. With the support of the Irish Government, the pay-off comes in 2005 when The K Club will gain the distinction of becoming the first Irish venue to stage the biennial matches against the Americans. And by then, it is expected that the high-profile Straffan facility will have a second course fully operational.

Indeed Kildare is expected to have another major development by that stage. Mark O'Meara and Colin Montgomerie have been commissioned to design complementary courses in the Carton demesne on the outskirts of Maynooth, the town developed around the 12th century castle of the Fitzgerald clan. Once the home of the dukes of Leinster, Carton is dominated by a magnificent, 18th century mansion. At the moment, however, Kildare has 18 courses. They are: Athy, Bodenstown, Castlewarden, Celbridge, Cill Dara, Clane, Clongowes, Craddockstown, Curragh, Highfield, The K Club, Kilkea Castle, Killeen, Knockanally, Leixlip, Naas, Newbridge and Woodlands.

Though it was founded as recently as 1985, Knockanally already has a significant claim to fame through the staging of the Irish International Matchplay Championship. It first took

Fishing on the Liffey, Co Kildare

place in 1987 when England's Brian Waites beat fellow Ryder Cup representative Brian Barnes for the title. Its founder, Noel Lyons, was drawn to the site by the splendid manor house. And it is intriguing that a stunning building was also the key element leading to the development of Kilkea Castle and The K Club.

County Kildare gets its name from St Brigid's monastery, as in Cill Dara, the church beneath the oak tree. Being an inland county, it shares much of its landscape features with its neighbours. The Wicklow Mountains are to the east and the foothills spread westwards to meet the unique plains of the Curragh of Kildare, which extend into the undulating, central lowlands. Three great rivers dominate the county - the Liffey which flows northwards from the Wicklow Mountains to enter the sea at Dublin; the Barrow which forms the border with Laois, and the legendary Boyne, the source of which is beneath the historic hill of Carbury.

Then there are the Grand and Royal canals which traverse the county, the Royal along the northern boundaries and the Grand crossing the county from Lyons in the east to Rathangan and Monasterevan in the west and with a line southwards to join the Barrow navigation at Athy. These waterways are noted for their excellent coarse fishing, while enthusiastis anglers should note that good salmon and brown trout are available on several stretches of the Liffey.

There is also a long-established coarse angling festival held at Prosperous every May.

Mention of the Liffey leads inevitably to Arthur Guinness, founder of the internationally famous brewing company. He was born at Celbridge in 1725 and opened his first brewery at Leixlip in 1756. Three years later he bought the brewery at St James's Gate in Dublin where he began brewing porter, using the incomparable Liffey water. Though it soon quickly became the capital's major industry, the family never severed their links with Kildare. Indeed when Arthur Guinness died in 1803, he was buried at Oughterard, near Kill, and his descendents still live in Leixlip Castle.

The Curragh has a special place in the Kildare life - and with good reason. Its 2,000 hectares make it the largest commonage in Ireland and it has been celebrated since earliest times as a pasture for sheep and as a dwelling and gathering place of prehistoric man. Links with the Anglo-Normans were established there in the 12th century and by the 17th century it had become a noted location for military encampments. In 1855, the British army built a permanent camp on the plains which became the main training camp for their garrison in Ireland. Indeed 20,000 men were based there during the World War I. Since independence, it has been the principal training base for the Irish army and the presence of soldiers has become an important element of the local economy.

It is also home to the Republic's oldest golf club - Curragh GC - and to Donnelly's Hollow, where, the locals would have us believe, the footprints of the famous bare-knuckle fighter, Dan Donnelly are still to be seen. Donnelly, of the remarkably long arms, is reputed to have made them in the arena after defeating the English champion, George Cooper, in 1815. Above everything else, however, the Curragh

Curragh Race Course, Co Kildare

is famous as Ireland's premier racing venue, with 17 racing days each year, including the Irish Classics. Not surprisingly, the race-track is surrounded by some of the country's leading horse-training and breeding establishments. Indeed as many as 1,200 thoroughbreds are in training there at any given time. Among the great names in racing to have bases at the Curragh are the Aga Khan, Sheik Al Maktoum, Kevin Prendergast, Mick O'Toole and Dermot Weld. Appropriately, the headquarters of the Irish Turf Club is located near the Strandhouse and the Irish National Stud and the Racing Apprentice Centre of Education, are based in Kildare town.

Indeed Kildare is steeped in equine activities. There are 14 annual race days at Naas, while the steeplechase course at Punchestown stages the Irish National Hunt Meeting each April, along with major events such as international three-day trials. The Kildare Hunt, one of the longest-established in the country, has its kennels at Naas. And the headquarters of the Kildare Polo Club are in Newbridge. Meanwhile, there are equestrian centres near Castledermot, Celbridge, Clane, Kildare, Kilmeague, Kill, Maynooth, Monasterevin and Naas, and major bloodstock sales are held at Goff's Kildare Paddocks, Kill.

Against that background, it may be no harm to warn the unwary visitor of the formidable practitioners to be found on golf courses throughout County Kildare. They are jockeys and similar employees in the bloodstock industry, who develop remarkable strength in their hands and arms from working horses. One such player was Lillian Behan who, when not working horses for Dick Collins on the Curragh plains, was to be found shooting birdies on the Curragh golf course. And she gained the distinction of capturing the British Women's Matchplay Championship at Ganton in 1985, before going on to play in the historic Curtis Cup triumph at Prairie Dunes, Kansas, a year later. Like others before her and since, she showed golf and horses to be a dynamic combination.

Location of Golf Courses

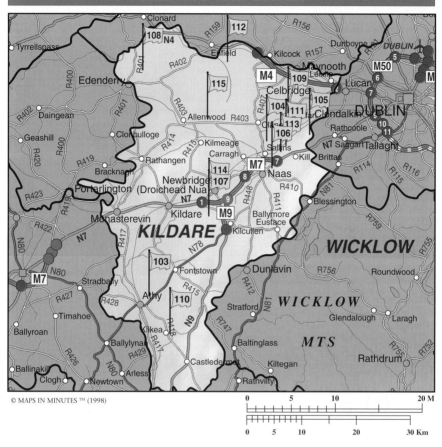

© MAPS IN MINUTES ™ (1998)

| 0 | 5 | 10 | 20 M |

| 0 | 5 | 10 | 20 | 30 Km |

103 **Athy Golf Club,** Athy 94

104 **Bodenstown Golf Club,** Sallins 94

105 **Castlewarden Golf Club,** Castlewarden 94

106 **Craddockstown Golf Club,** Naas 95

107 **Curragh Golf Club,** Curragh 95

108 **Highfield Golf Club,** Carbury 96

109 **K Club Golf Club,** Straffan 97

110 **Kilkea Castle Golf Club,** Castledermot 97

111 **Killeen Golf Club,** Kildare 98

112 **Knockanally Golf Club,** Donadea 99

113 **Naas Golf Club,** Naas 99

114 **Newbridge Golf Club,** Newbridge 100

115 **Woodlands Golf Club,** Naas 100

Athy

Athy Golf Club, Geraldine, Athy, Co Kildare

Tel: 050 731729

Sec/Manager:	Brian Wathorn
Professional:	None
Directions:	1 mile North East of Athy off the N78 to Kildare
Type of Course:	Parkland
Date Founded:	1906
No of Holes:	18
Length:	6340 yds (5797 mtrs)
Par:	71
SSS:	69
Green Fees:	Weekdays: £13 Weekends & Bank Holidays: £17
Visitors:	Welcome: Weekdays, booking advisable
Societies:	Welcome: Special concessions, Contact Club for details
Facilities:	Chipping/Putting Area, Practice Area, Trolley hire Bar, Restaurant

Accommodation, Food and Drink

Reference numbers below refer to detailed information provided in section 2

Accommodation

The Gables, Ryston, Newbridge, Co Kildare

Tel: 045 435330 A super guest house on the banks of the Liffey, with ten en suite bedrooms and a leisure centre (pool, gym, sauna). 351

Woodcourte House, Timolin, Moone, Athy, Co Kildare

Tel: 050 724167 Six spacious bedrooms (two en suite) in a modern B&B house in a picturesque village just off the main N9 Dublin-Kilkenny road. 340

Food and Drink

Gleann-na-Smol, Howth, Co Dublin

Tel: 01 8322936 Personal service in a family-run B&B renowned for its hospitality. 5 en suite rooms include a triple. 243

Swifts, Newbridge, Co Kildare

Tel: 045 433234 All-day menus in Newbridge's trendiest bar, with a long, elegant bar and several spacious lounges. 346

Teach Dolmain, Carlow Town, Co Carlow

Tel: 050 330911 Traditional Irish pub with three bars and two restaurants. A charming setting, great hospitality, fine food and Irish music. 370

The Beams Restaurant, 59 Dublin Street, Carlow Town, Co Carlow

Tel: 050 331824 Restored 18th-century coaching inn offering fine cuisine (seafood a speciality) and an excellent wine list. Tuesday-Saturday evenings.

Bodenstown

Bodenstown Golf Club, Sallins, Co Kildare

Tel: 045 897096

Sec/Manager:	Bernadette Mather
Professional:	None
Directions:	4 miles North of Naas off the R407 Sallins to Clare Road

Old Course

Type of Course:	Parkland
Date Founded:	1973
No of Holes:	18
Length:	6706 yds (6132 mtrs)
Par:	72
SSS:	71
Green Fees:	£12

Lady Hill

Type of Course:	Parkland
Date Founded:	1973
No of Holes:	18
Length:	5772 yds (5278 mtrs)
Par:	72
SSS:	69
Green Fees:	£10
Visitors:	Welcome: Weekdays only
Societies:	Welcome: Contact Club in advance
Facilities:	Chipping/Putting Area, Practice Area, Driving Range, Golf Clubs for hire, Trolley hire Electric Buggy hire, Bar, Restaurant

Accommodation, Food and Drink

Reference numbers below refer to detailed information provided in section 2

Accommodation

Ashley Bed & Breakfast, Clane, Co Kildare

Tel/Fax: 045 868533 Three en suite B&B rooms in a neat self-contained unit by the main house. Rural setting on the road from Clane to Celbridge. 348

Monaghan's Harbour Hotel, Naas, Co Kildare

Tel: 045 879145 A real home from home feel in a family-run hotel with well-equipped bedrooms, restaurant, coffee shop and bar. 349

Straffan Bed & Breakfast, Straffan, Co Kildare

Tel: 01 6272386 Four en suite bedrooms in an attractive new bungalow with a garden long enough to practice that swing. 350

Westown Farm, Johnstown, Naas, Co Kildare

Tel/Fax: 045 897006 Farmhouse Bed & Breakfast Accommodation run by a mother-and-daughter team. Five bedrooms, three of them en suite.

Food and Drink

Monaghan's Harbour Hotel, Naas, Co Kildare

Tel: 045 879145 A real home from home feel in a family-run hotel with well-equipped bedrooms, restaurant, coffee shop and bar. 349

Rushes, Fairgreen Street, Naas, Co Kildare

Tel: 045 898400 Classic bar food in Rushes and international cuisine in its neighbour Cicero on a prime site in Naas. Steaks a speciality. 343

The Manor Inn, Naas, Co Kildare

Tel: 045 897471 Warmth, hospitality and good food in a smartly modernised pub on the main street of Naas. Lots of racing memorabilia. 347

Castlewarden

Castlewarden Golf Club, Castlewarden, Straffan, Co Kildare

Tel: 01 4589254

Sec/Manager:	Pat Sheehan
Professional:	Gerry Egan

Directions:	6 miles North East of Naas off the N7 road to Rathcoole
Type of Course:	Parkland
Date Founded:	1990
No of Holes:	18
Length:	6624 yds (6056 mtrs)
Par:	72
SSS:	70
Green Fees:	Weekdays: £17 Weekends & Bank Holidays: £23
Visitors:	Welcome: Any Day except Tuesday
Societies:	Welcome: Special concessions, Group rates, Contact club for details
Facilities:	Chipping/Putting Area, Practice Area, Trolley hire, Bar, Restaurant

Accommodation, Food and Drink

Reference numbers below refer to detailed information provided in section 2

Accommodation

Ashley Bed & Breakfast, Clane, Co Kildare
Tel/Fax: 045 868533 Three en suite B&B rooms in a neat self-contained unit by the main house. Rural setting on the road from Clane to Celbridge. 348

Ballygoran Lodge, Maynooth, Co Kildare
Tel: 01 6291860 A striking modern villa 1 mile from Maynooth, with four en suite B&B rooms and a suite with a mini-gym. 342

Monaghan's Harbour Hotel, Naas, Co Kildare
Tel: 045 879145 A real home from home feel in a family-run hotel with well-equipped bedrooms, restaurant, coffee shop and bar. 349

Straffan Bed & Breakfast, Straffan, Co Kildare
Tel: 01 6272386 Four en suite bedrooms in an attractive new bungalow with a garden long enough to practice that swing. 350

Food and Drink

Monaghan's Harbour Hotel, Naas, Co Kildare
Tel: 045 879145 A real home from home feel in a family-run hotel with well-equipped bedrooms, restaurant, coffee shop and bar. 349

Rushes, Fairgreen Street, Naas, Co Kildare
Tel: 045 898400 Classic bar food in Rushes and international cuisine in its neighbour Cicero on a prime site in Naas. Steaks a speciality. 343

The Manor Inn, Naas, Co Kildare
Tel: 045 897471 Warmth, hospitality and good food in a smartly modernised pub on the main street of Naas. Lots of racing memorabilia. 347

Craddockstown

Craddockstown Golf Club, Blessington Road, Naas, Co Kildare

Tel: 045 897610

Sec/Manager:	L. A. Wilson
Professional:	None
Directions:	One and a half miles East of Nass town
Type of Course:	Parkland
Date Founded:	1991
No of Holes:	18
Length:	6698 yds (6125 mtrs)
Par:	71
SSS:	70
Green Fees:	Weekdays: £15 Weekends & Bank Holidays: £20

Visitors:	Welcome: Any day, Contact club in advance
Societies:	Welcome: Special concessions, Group rates, Contact club for details
Facilities:	Chipping/Putting Area, Practice Area, Driving Range, Trolley hire, Bar, Restaurant

Accommodation, Food and Drink

Reference numbers below refer to detailed information provided in section 2

Accommodation

Annagh Lodge, Newbridge, Co Kildare
Tel: 045 433518 Nine excellent Bed & Breakfast rooms in a striking modern bungalow on the Dublin side of Newbridge. Sauna, conservatory. 345

Monaghan's Harbour Hotel, Naas, Co Kildare
Tel: 045 879145 A real home from home feel in a family-run hotel with well-equipped bedrooms, restaurant, coffee shop and bar. 349

Westown Farm, Johnstown, Naas, Co Kildare
Tel/Fax: 045 897006 Farmhouse Bed & Breakfast Accommodation run by a mother-and-daughter team. Five bedrooms, three of them en suite.

Food and Drink

Monaghan's Harbour Hotel, Naas, Co Kildare
Tel: 045 879145 A real home from home feel in a family-run hotel with well-equipped bedrooms, restaurant, coffee shop and bar. 349

Rushes, Fairgreen Street, Naas, Co Kildare
Tel: 045 898400 Classic bar food in Rushes and international cuisine in its neighbour Cicero on a prime site in Naas. Steaks a speciality. 343

Swifts, Newbridge, Co Kildare
Tel: 045 433234 All-day menus in Newbridge's trendiest bar, with a long, elegant bar and several spacious lounges. 346

The Manor Inn, Naas, Co Kildare
Tel: 045 897471 Warmth, hospitality and good food in a smartly modernised pub on the main street of Naas. Lots of racing memorabilia. 347

Curragh

The Curragh, Curragh, Co Kildare

Tel: 045 441714

In researching the history of his club, Col Bill Gibson made the discovery that golf was actually played in the area of the Curragh in 1857. The participants were a certain Alexander Love and a Scotsman named David Ritchie, who migrated to the area armed with the golfer's luggage of the time - some gutty balls and a set of hickory-shafted clubs.

Ritchie had been a member of Musselburgh and on arrival at the Curragh, he laid out a course

at a site known as Donnelly's Hollow. The current course was later located closeby and is reputed to have been where the then Prince of Wales lost his virginity to a local wench in a greenkeeper's hut.

In settling for an official foundation in 1883, Gibson was being decidedly conservative. It is clear from his research that the game was played there for some years prior to that. Either way, it remains the oldest club in the Republic.

Remarkably, the club received the royal charter from King George V in 1910, but they have never exercised their right to use it. This has to do with a significant portion of their membershp coming from the Irish Army. Indeed the captaincy alternates between a civilian and a soldier, each year.

Situated on prime heathland on the opposite side of the road from the Curragh Racecourse, where the Irish classics are staged, it stretches to 6,598 yards and is the home club of former British Women's champion, Lillian Behan.

Sec/Manager:	Anne Culliton
Professional:	Gerry Burke
Directions:	3 miles south of Newbridge and the N7 to Kildare off the R413
Type of Course:	Parkland
Date Founded:	1883
No of Holes:	18
Length:	6035 mtrs (6598 yds)
Par:	72
SSS:	71
Green Fees:	Weekdays: £18 Weekends £22
Visitors:	Welcome: Weekdays except Tuesday. Contact Club in advance
Societies:	Welcome: Book in advance, Mon, Wed, Thurs & Fri only
Facilities:	Chipping/Putting Area, Practice Area, Golf Clubs for hire, Trolley hire, Bar, Restaurant

Accommodation, Food and Drink

Reference numbers below refer to detailed information provided in section 2

Accommodation

Annagh Lodge, Newbridge, Co Kildare
Tel: 045 433518 Nine excellent Bed & Breakfast rooms in a striking modern bungalow on the Dublin side of Newbridge. Sauna, conservatory.   345
Bushfield Lodge, Ballymore Eustace, Co Kildare
Tel: 045 864389/864972 A substantial modern house in a quiet rural location, with high-quality en suite bedrooms. Also a cookery school.   344
Monaghan's Harbour Hotel, Naas, Co Kildare
Tel: 045 879145 A real home from home feel in a family-run hotel with well-equipped bedrooms, restaurant, coffee shop and bar.   349

Food and Drink

Monaghan's Harbour Hotel, Naas, Co Kildare
Tel: 045 879145 A real home from home feel in a family-run hotel with well-equipped bedrooms, restaurant, coffee shop and bar.   349
Rushes, Fairgreen Street, Naas, Co Kildare
Tel: 045 898400 Classic bar food in Rushes and international cuisine in its

neighbour Cicero on a prime site in Naas. Steaks a speciality.   343
Swifts, Newbridge, Co Kildare
Tel: 045 433234 All-day menus in Newbridge's trendiest bar, with a long, elegant bar and several spacious lounges.   346
The Manor Inn, Naas, Co Kildare
Tel: 045 897471 Warmth, hospitality and good food in a smartly modernised pub on the main street of Naas. Lots of racing memorabilia.   347

Highfield

Highfield Golf Course, Carbury, Co Kildare
Tel: 040 531021

Sec/Manager:	Margaret Duggan
Professional:	Peter O'Hagan
Directions:	Two and a half miles North East of Edonderry off the R402 to Carbury
Type of Course:	Parkland
Date Founded:	1992
No of Holes:	18
Length:	6277 yds (5739 mtrs)
Par:	72
SSS:	69
Green Fees:	Weekdays: £10 Weekends & Bank Holidays: £14
Visitors:	Welcome: Any Day, Contact Club at weekends
Societies:	Welcome: Contact Club in writing
Facilities:	Chipping/Putting Area, Practice Area, Driving Range, Golf Clubs for hire, Trolley hire, Electric Buggy hire, Bar, Restaurant

Accommodation, Food and Drink

Reference numbers below refer to detailed information provided in section 2

Accommodation

Ballygoran Lodge, Maynooth, Co Kildare
Tel: 01 6291860 A striking modern villa 1 mile from Maynooth, with four en suite B&B rooms and a suite with a mini-gym.   342
Brogans Guest House, Trim, Co Meath
Tel: 046 31237 Family-run guest house famed for its hospitality. 15 en suite bedrooms, tv, telephone. Bar with regular music sessions.   431
Wellington Court Hotel, Trim, Co Meath
Tel: 046 31516 Excellent Accommodation and facilities in a comfortable hotel on the Summerhill road (R158). 18 en suite bedrooms with tv and phone.   449

Food and Drink

The Haggard Inn, Trim, Co Meath
Tel: 046 31110 Restaurant, carvery and bar food in an atmospheric 19th-century hostelry. Traditional music Friday and Saturday.   440
Tyrrells Restaurant, Edenderry, Co Offaly
Tel: 040 532400 An atmospheric restaurant with rough-hewn walls and flagstone floor in the many-acred complex of Ballindoolin House & Gardens.   500
Wellington Court Hotel, Trim, Co Meath
Tel: 046 31516 Excellent Accommodation and facilities in a comfortable hotel on the Summerhill road (R158). 18 en suite bedrooms with tv and phone.   449

K Club

Kildare Hotel & Country Club, The 'K' Club, Straffan, Co Kildare

Tel: 01 6017300

From the time that Fred Daly and Harry Bradshaw dominated the home effort in the Ryder Cup at Wentworth in 1953, there had been an understandable yearning to bring the biennial showpiece to Ireland. But it remained an elusive target, even after 1993 when Portmarnock seemed likely to succeed, only to lose out to The Belfry.

In the meantime, leading Irish company, the Jefferson Smurfit Group, had bought Straffan House and its estate, overlooking the River Liffey in Co Kildare. And with Arnold Palmer as the designer, an outstanding, championship-standard course became the centrepiece of a £30 million development.

From the outset, company chairman Dr Michael Smurfit set himself the target of staging the Ryder Cup. And with the Irish Government showing the way, the prize has been landed for 2005 at The K Club.

It will be a worthy venue, given the overall quality of the development, from the testing, parkland stretch to the practice facilities, luxurious clubhouse and five-star hotel. Invaluable experience has been gained through the annual staging of the Smurfit European Open since 1995 and the venue also played host to the biennial PGA Cup matches in 1992.

Water, which is used liberally throughout the layout, is used to particularly testing effect at the 387-yard 16th. Yet, even stretching to nearly 7,000 yards, The K Club almost yielded the European Tour's first 59 when Darren Clarke narrowly missed out, with a 12-under-par 60, during the 1999 European Open. Not surprisingly, it remains the course record.

Sec/Manager:	Paul Crowe
Professional:	Ernie Jones
Directions:	Off the R403 Clane to Celbridge

	Road at Straffan
Type of Course:	Parkland
Date Founded:	1991
No of Holes:	18
Length:	6829 yds (6244 mtrs)
Par:	72
SSS:	74
Green Fees:	Winter: £75 From 1st April: £140
Visitors:	Welcome: Prebooking required
Societies:	Welcome: Not at weekends and Wednesday afternoon, Contact Club for details
Facilities:	Chipping/Putting Area, Practice Area, Golf Clubs for hire, Trolley hire Bar, Restaurant, Caddy service by arrangement

Accommodation, Food and Drink

Reference numbers below refer to detailed information provided in section 2

Accommodation

Ashley Bed & Breakfast, Clane, Co Kildare
Tel/Fax: 045 868533 Three en suite B&B rooms in a neat self-contained unit by the main house. Rural setting on the road from Clane to Celbridge. 348

Ballygoran Lodge, Maynooth, Co Kildare
Tel: 01 6291860 A striking modern villa 1 mile from Maynooth, with four en suite B&B rooms and a suite with a mini-gym. 342

Monaghan's Harbour Hotel, Naas, Co Kildare
Tel: 045 879145 A real home from home feel in a family-run hotel with well-equipped bedrooms, restaurant, coffee shop and bar. 349

Straffan Bed & Breakfast, Straffan, Co Kildare
Tel: 01 6272386 Four en suite bedrooms in an attractive new bungalow with a garden long enough to practice that swing. 350

Food and Drink

Monaghan's Harbour Hotel, Naas, Co Kildare
Tel: 045 879145 A real home from home feel in a family-run hotel with well-equipped bedrooms, restaurant, coffee shop and bar. 349

Rushes, Fairgreen Street, Naas, Co Kildare
Tel: 045 898400 Classic bar food in Rushes and international cuisine in its neighbour Cicero on a prime site in Naas. Steaks a speciality. 343

The Manor Inn, Naas, Co Kildare
Tel: 045 897471 Warmth, hospitality and good food in a smartly modernised pub on the main street of Naas. Lots of racing memorabilia. 347

Kilkea Castle

Kilkea Castle Golf Club, Kilkea Castle, Castledermot, Co Kildare

Tel: 050 345555

In the delightfully pastoral setting of Kilkea Castle near Castledermot, there are three holes with arguably the greatest card-wrecking potential of any finishing stretch in Irish golf. And one senses the lone piper is warning the unwary competitor of impending doom, as his plaintive note is carried on the wind from the castle courtyard.

As it happens, the piper's function is to deliver a cheery welcome to the day's wedding party at this busy venue, but his presence could also be seen as a nice, traditional touch. Indeed

Kilkea holds the distinction of being the oldest inhabited building of its kind in Ireland, having first been occupied by Sir Walter de Riddleford in 1181.

The course was opened in 1997, 10 years after the castle and an adjoining 22 acres were bought by Irish-American businessman Dave Conway. In the meantime, Conway spent £8 million on expanding and upgrading the project to its present, impressive state.

On the front nine, splendid use has been made of the ubiquitous River Griese, which seems to be an ever-present hazard throughout the layout, even if there are actually 10 holes where it is not in play. So, a high premium is placed on accuracy off the tee.

But what of the fearsome finish? The short 16th combines the hazards of trees and water; the 17th is a dog-leg right where the dreaded river beckons once more off the tee and the 18th is a dog-leg left where a large pond eats menacingly into the fairway.

Sec/Manager:	Adeline Molloy
Professional:	None
Directions:	Three and a half miles North West of Castledermot at Kilkea off the R418 to Athy
Type of Course:	Parkland
Date Founded:	1995
No of Holes:	18
Length:	6701 yds (6128 mtrs)
Par:	70
SSS:	71
Green Fees:	£25
Visitors:	Welcome: Contact Club in advance
Societies:	Welcome: Special concessions, Contact Club for details
Facilities:	Chipping/Putting Area, Practice Area, Golf Clubs for hire, Trolley hire Bar, Restaurant

Accommodation, Food and Drink

Reference numbers below refer to detailed information provided in section 2

Accommodation

Sherwood Park House, Kilbride, Ballon, Co Carlow
Tel: 050 359117 Five en suite rooms in a superb Georgian house on its own working estate. B&B, evening meals on request.   371
The Rafter Dempsey's, Kilkenny, Co Kilkenny
Tel/Fax: 056 22970 17 rooms (13 en suite) in a characterful pub in the heart of the city. Lunch and dinner menus. Live music.   361
Woodcourte House, Timolin, Moone, Athy, Co Kildare
Tel: 050 724167 Six spacious bedrooms (two en suite) in a modern B&B house in a picturesque village just off the main N9 Dublin-Kilkenny road.   340

Food and Drink

Teach Dolmain, Carlow Town, Co Carlow
Tel: 050 330911 Traditional Irish pub with three bars and two restaurants. A charming setting, great hospitality, fine food and Irish music.   370
The Beams Restaurant, 59 Dublin Street, Carlow Town, Co Carlow
Tel: 050 331824 Restored 18th-century coaching inn offering fine cuisine (seafood a speciality) and an excellent wine list. Tuesday-Saturday evenings.
The Rafter Dempsey's, Kilkenny, Co Kilkenny
Tel/Fax: 056 22970 17 rooms (13 en suite) in a characterful pub in the heart of the city. Lunch and dinner menus. Live music.   361

Killeen

Killeen Golf Club, Kill, Co Kildare
Tel: 045 866003

Sec/Manager:	Maurice Kelly
Professional:	None
Directions:	One and a half miles North West of Kill Village off the N7 road from Naas to Dublin
Type of Course:	Parkland
Date Founded:	1981
No of Holes:	18
Length:	6359 yds (5815 mtrs)
Par:	71
SSS:	71
Green Fees:	Weekdays: £17 Weekends & Bank

Holidays: £20

Visitors:	Welcome: Any Day. Check tee-times in advance
Societies:	Welcome: Special concessions, contact Club for details
Facilities:	Chipping/Putting Area, Practice Area, Trolley hire Bar, Restaurant

Accommodation, Food and Drink

Reference numbers below refer to detailed information provided in section 2

Accommodation

Monaghan's Harbour Hotel, Naas, Co Kildare
Tel: 045 879145 A real home from home feel in a family-run hotel with well-equipped bedrooms, restaurant, coffee shop and bar. 349

Straffan Bed & Breakfast, Straffan, Co Kildare
Tel: 01 6272386 Four en suite bedrooms in an attractive new bungalow with a garden long enough to practice that swing. 350

Westown Farm, Johnstown, Naas, Co Kildare
Tel/Fax: 045 897006 Farmhouse Bed & Breakfast Accommodation run by a mother-and-daughter team. Five bedrooms, three of them en suite.

Food and Drink

Monaghan's Harbour Hotel, Naas, Co Kildare
Tel: 045 879145 A real home from home feel in a family-run hotel with well-equipped bedrooms, restaurant, coffee shop and bar. 349

Rushes, Fairgreen Street, Naas, Co Kildare
Tel: 045 898400 Classic bar food in Rushes and international cuisine in its neighbour Cicero on a prime site in Naas. Steaks a speciality. 343

The Manor Inn, Naas, Co Kildare
Tel: 045 897471 Warmth, hospitality and good food in a smartly modernised pub on the main street of Naas. Lots of racing memorabilia. 347

Knockanally

Knockanally Golf Club, Donadea, North Kildare
Tel: 045 869322

Sec/Manager:	Noel Lyons
Professional:	Martin Darcy
Directions:	3 miles off the N4 Kilcock to Innfield road near Newtown
Type of Course:	Parkland
Date Founded:	1985
No of Holes:	18
Length:	6424 yds (5874 mtrs)
Par:	72
SSS:	72
Green Fees:	Weekdays: £20 Weekends & Bank Holidays: £25
Visitors:	Welcome: Any Day, Rrestrictions on Sundays, Telephone in advance
Societies:	Welcome: Special concessions, Apply to club for details
Facilities:	Chipping/Putting Area, Practice Area, Golf Clubs for hire, Trolley hire, Electric Buggy hire, Bar, Restaurant, Caddy service by arrangement

Accommodation, Food and Drink

Reference numbers below refer to detailed information provided in section 2

Accommodation

Ballygoran Lodge, Maynooth, Co Kildare
Tel: 01 6291860 A striking modern villa 1 mile from Maynooth, with four en suite B&B rooms and a suite with a mini-gym. 342

Killeentierna House, Dunshaughlin, Co Meath
Tel: 01 8259722 Five Bed & Breakfast rooms, one of family size, in a modern residence on the Dublin side of Dunshaughlin. 433

The Old Workhouse. Dunshaughlin, Co Meath
Tel/Fax: 01 8259251 Civilised living in a sympathetically restored 1840s building. Four cosy double bedrooms (2 en suite, 2 with private bathroom). Country house cooking.

Wellington Court Hotel, Trim, Co Meath
Tel: 046 31516 Excellent Accommodation and facilities in a comfortable hotel on the Summerhill road (R158). 18 en suite bedrooms with tv and phone. 449

Food and Drink

The Haggard Inn, Trim, Co Meath
Tel: 046 31110 Restaurant, carvery and bar food in an atmospheric 19th-century hostelry. Traditional music Friday and Saturday. 440

Tyrrells Restaurant, Edenderry, Co Offaly
Tel: 040 532400 An atmospheric restaurant with rough-hewn walls and flagstone floor in the many-acred complex of Ballindoolin House & Gardens. 500

Wellington Court Hotel, Trim, Co Meath
Tel: 046 31516 Excellent Accommodation and facilities in a comfortable hotel on the Summerhill road (R158). 18 en suite bedrooms with tv and phone. 449

Naas

Naas Golf Club, Kerdiffstown, Naas, Co Kildare
Tel: 045 897509

Sec/Manager:	Michael Conway
Professional:	None
Directions:	1 mile North of Johnstone off the N7 Nass to Dublin road towards Sallins
Type of Course:	Parkland
Date Founded:	1896
No of Holes:	18
Length:	6189 yds (5660 mtrs)
Par:	71
SSS:	68
Green Fees:	Weekdays: £18 Weekends & Bank Holidays: £24
Visitors:	Welcome: Mon, Wed, Fri and Sat.
Societies:	Welcome: Contact Club in advance
Facilities:	Chipping/Putting Area, Practice Area, Trolley hire, Bar, Restaurant

Accommodation, Food and Drink

Reference numbers below refer to detailed information provided in section 2

Accommodation

Bushfield Lodge, Ballymore Eustace, Co Kildare
Tel: 045 864389/864972 A substantial modern house in a quiet rural location, with high-quality en suite bedrooms. Also a cookery school. 344

Monaghan's Harbour Hotel, Naas, Co Kildare
Tel: 045 879145 A real home from home feel in a family-run hotel with well-equipped be,drooms, restaurant, coffee shop and bar. 349

The Gables, Ryston, Newbridge, Co Kildare

Tel: 045 435330 A super guest house on the banks of the Liffey, with ten en suite bedrooms and a leisure centre (pool, gym, sauna). 351

Westown Farm, Johnstown, Naas, Co Kildare

Tel/Fax: 045 897006 Farmhouse Bed & Breakfast Accommodation run by a mother-and-daughter team. Five bedrooms, three of them en suite.

Food and Drink

Monaghan's Harbour Hotel, Naas, Co Kildare

Tel: 045 879145 A real home from home feel in a family-run hotel with well-equipped bedrooms, restaurant, coffee shop and bar. 349

Rushes, Fairgreen Street, Naas, Co Kildare

Tel: 045 898400 Classic bar food in Rushes and international cuisine in its neighbour Cicero on a prime site in Naas. Steaks a speciality. 343

The Manor Inn, Naas, Co Kildare

Tel: 045 897471 Warmth, hospitality and good food in a smartly modernised pub on the main street of Naas. Lots of racing memorabilia. 347

Newbridge

Newbridge Golf Club, Barrettstown, Newbridge, Co Kildare

Tel: 045 431289

Sec/Manager:	Jamie Stafford
Professional:	None
Directions:	8 miles South West of Naas off M7 on the outskirts of Newbridge
Type of Course:	Parkland
Date Founded:	1995
No of Holes:	18
Length:	6513 yds (5956 mtrs)
Par:	72
SSS:	70
Green Fees:	Weekdays: £10 Weekends & Bank Holidays: £12
Visitors:	Welcome: No restrictions
Societies:	Welcome: Special concessions, Contact Club for details
Facilities:	Chipping/Putting Area, Golf Clubs for hire, Trolley hire, Bar, Restaurant, Caddy service by arrangement

Accommodation, Food and Drink

Reference numbers below refer to detailed information provided in section 2

Accommodation

Annagh Lodge, Newbridge, Co Kildare

Tel: 045 433518 Nine excellent Bed & Breakfast rooms in a striking modern bungalow on the Dublin side of Newbridge. Sauna, conservatory 345

Monaghan's Harbour Hotel, Naas, Co Kildare

Tel: 045 879145 A real home from home feel in a family-run hotel with well-equipped bedrooms, restaurant, coffee shop and bar. 349

The Gables, Ryston, Newbridge, Co Kildare

Tel: 045 435330 A super guest house on the banks of the Liffey, with ten en suite bedrooms and a leisure centre (pool, gym, sauna). 351

Food and Drink

Monaghan's Harbour Hotel, Naas, Co Kildare

Tel: 045 879145 A real home from home feel in a family-run hotel with well-equipped bedrooms, restaurant, coffee shop and bar. 349

Rushes, Fairgreen Street, Naas, Co Kildare

Tel: 045 898400 Classic bar food in Rushes and international cuisine in its

---

neighbour Cicero on a prime site in Naas. Steaks a speciality. 343

Swifts, Newbridge, Co Kildare

Tel: 045 433234 All-day menus in Newbridge's trendiest bar, with a long, elegant bar and several spacious lounges. 346

Woodlands

Woodlands Golf Course, Cooleragh, Coill Dubh, Naas, Co Kildare

Tel: 045 860777

Sec/Manager:	Michael Seery
Professional:	None
Directions:	8 miles North Wet of Naas off the R403 Clane to Allenwood road
Type of Course:	Parkland
Date Founded:	1988
No of Holes:	18
Length:	6572 yds (6010 mtrs)
Par:	72
SSS:	71
Green Fees:	Weekdays: £12 Weekends & Bank Holidays: £15
Visitors:	Welcome: Weekdays, Restrictions at weekend, Contact Club in advance
Societies:	Welcome: Special concessions apply, Contact Club in advance
Facilities:	Chipping/Putting Area, Practice Area, Trolley hire, Bar, Restaurant

Accommodation, Food and Drink

Reference numbers below refer to detailed information provided in section 2

Accommodation

Ashley Bed & Breakfast, Clane, Co Kildare

Tel/Fax: 045 868533 Three en suite B&B rooms in a neat self-contained unit by the main house. Rural setting on the road from Clane to Celbridge. 348

The Gables, Ryston, Newbridge, Co Kildare

Tel: 045 435330 A super guest house on the banks of the Liffey, with ten en suite bedrooms and a leisure centre (pool, gym, sauna). 351

Wellington Court Hotel, Trim, Co Meath

Tel: 046 31516 Excellent Accommodation and facilities in a comfortable hotel on the Summerhill road (R158). 18 en suite bedrooms with tv and phone. 449

Food and Drink

Rushes, Fairgreen Street, Naas, Co Kildare

Tel: 045 898400 Classic bar food in Rushes and international cuisine in its neighbour Cicero on a prime site in Naas. Steaks a speciality. 343

The Manor Inn, Naas, Co Kildare

Tel: 045 897471 Warmth, hospitality and good food in a smartly modernised pub on the main street of Naas. Lots of racing memorabilia. 347

Tyrrells Restaurant, Edenderry, Co Offaly

Tel: 040 532400 An atmospheric restaurant with rough-hewn walls and flagstone floor in the many-acred complex of Ballindoolin House & Gardens. 500

Wellington Court Hotel, Trim, Co Meath

Tel: 046 31516 Excellent Accommodation and facilities in a comfortable hotel on the Summerhill road (R158). 18 en suite bedrooms with tv and phone. 449

KILKENNY, LAOIS & CARLOW

When Christy O'Connor Snr won the ninth of his 10 Irish Professional Championship titles at Carlow GC in 1975, he was fast approaching his 51st birthday. So, it was perhaps little wonder that he vowed it would be the last time for him to play 36 holes of competitive golf on the one day. By his own admission, he enjoyed the challenge of Carlow, with its free-draining, sandy sub-soil. And his nephew, Christy Jnr, would have had similar thoughts about the terrain at Kilkenny GC, after capturing the Carrolls Irish Matchplay Championship there in 1973. Both men have returned to the area in recent years in very different circumstances. For Senior, the assignment was an exhibition match against designer Jack Nicklaus to mark the official opening of the splendid Mount Juliet course in July 1991. And for Junior, there were numerous visits to Tullow during the nineties, to supervise developments on his design of Mount Wolseley.

River Barrow, Co Kilkenny

The area is served by a total of 14 courses, where quality more than compensates for modest quantity. They are: Kilkenny (6) - Callan, Castlecomer, Kilkenny, Mountain View, Mount Juliet, Waterford; Laois (5) - Abbeyleix, The Heath, Mountrath, Portarlington, Rathdowney; Carlow (3) - Borris, Carlow, Mount Wolseley. Even while beating Nicklaus over 18 holes at Mount Juliet, however, it would have been difficult for Senior to visualise the distinguished visitors who would grace that terrain over the ensuing years. Players like Nick Faldo, Tom Watson, Fred Couples, Greg Norman, David Frost, Craig Stadler and John Daly, quite apart from all of the top European players. Meanwhile, Mount Wolseley had the distinction in 1995 of playing host to a special celebration by the Wolseley family, to mark the centenary of the founding of the once famous British motor company. Donal Morrissey, who now owns the property, was more than happy to welcome surviving members of the clan, who travelled from England for a sentimental homecoming.

Kilkenny Castle, Co Kilkenny

Kilkenny is the oldest club in the area, having been founded in 1896. And by way of illustrating their ability to keep abreast of changing times, they can boast a prominent tournament professional in their ranks, now that Gary Murphy has become a card-holding member of the PGA European Tour. Earlier, Murphy had brought honour to the club by capturing the 1992 Irish Amateur Close Championship at Portstewart.

From an historical standpoint, Kilkenny is one of Ireland's most important cities, but it is also noted as the home of fine beer, courtesy of the Smithwick family. So, it is interesting to note that in the spring of 1908, 12 years after the club's institution, a general meeting of the members decided that a site for a 12-months-of-the-year course should be found. That was when a certain James Swithwick entered the picture.

"The Irish Field" reported that as a keen golfer, Smithwick "came forward and offered the present excellent course on very liberal terms." Though the club later moved to its current site in November 1924, the Swithwick connection was clearly invaluable in its development.

It seems entirely logical that golf should flourish in an area steeped in the game of hurling. But the transition is not always as comfortable as observers might imagine. As the brilliant, former Kilkenny hurler, Eddie Keher, remarked recently: "We hurlers make the mistake of trying to hit the ball." All three counties are visited by the River Nore and River Barrow. Indeed the Mount Juliet estate is traversed by the Nore, though Nicklaus avoided it as a design feature, because of its tendency to flood.

De Vesci Monument, Abbeyleix, Co Laois

Laois is especially interesting for being constituted as Queen's County by an act of parliament in 1556, during the reign of Queen Mary. It was pieced together out of various, unrelated Gaelic territories and earlier chiefdoms. After Ireland gained its independence in 1922, however, the county was renamed Laois, or Laoighis (the gh is silent) in memory of the Loigis mercenaries who helped Welsh invaders conquer the province of Leinster. Slieve Bloom, bridging the borders of Offaly and Laois, comprises landscapes full of character, flora and fauna, history and fable. Elsewhere, the village of Ballintubbert will be interesting to visitors as the birthplace of poet laureate, Cecil Day Lewis, father of the Academy Award winning screen actor, Daniel Day Lewis.

They will also delight in Ballyfin House, which is arguably the finest neo-classical house in the country. It was built between 1821 and 1826 in Slieve Bloom sandstone by Sir Charles Coote to a design by Dominic Madden and his son, William Vitruvius. On entering by the tetrastyle ionic portico and through the formal entrance hall, one is confronted by a magnificent suite of rooms. Adjoining the library is a superb Richard Turner conservatory. The grounds were landscaped by Sutherland and include fine trees, vistas, ice caves, a grotto, a serpentine lake, a tower folly and three gate lodges.

Glen Barrow Waterfall, Co Laois

The great heath of Maryborough, present location of The Heath GC, is one of Ireland's most important archaeological sites. It was where the battle of Cainthinc took place in the third century and was home to the stone called Leac Reta, where the seven cantreds of ancient Leix met. More recently, there was 19th century horse-racing and manouevres by the Queen's County Militia. Portlaoise, where the main roads from Dublin, Cork and Limerick converge, is the commercial and principal town and administrative centre of the county. Prior to independence in 1922, it was known at Maryborough, hence the name given to the local heath. Among other things, the county is famous for The Steam Festival at Stradbally. But Laois people also enjoy their golf, when they are not busily engaged in trying to match the hurling standards of their celebrated neighbours from Kilkenny.

Location of Golf Courses

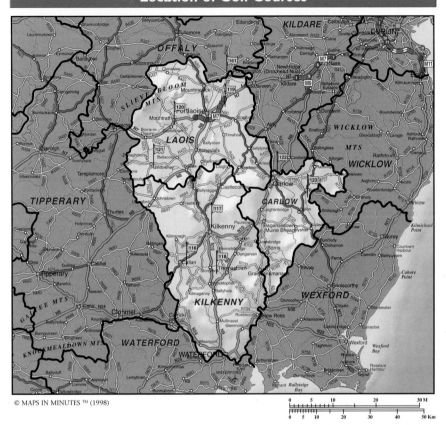

© MAPS IN MINUTES ™ (1998)

Callan

Callan Golf Club, Geraldine, Callan, Co Kilkenny
Tel: 056 25135 / 25949

Sec/Manager:	Mr. Duggan
Professional:	John O'Dwyer
Directions:	1 mile South East of Vallan off the R699 to Knocktopher
Type of Course:	Parkland
Date Founded:	1929
No of Holes:	18
Length:	6400 yds (5852 mtrs)
Par:	72
SSS:	70
Green Fees:	£15
Visitors:	Welcome: Contact Club in advance
Societies:	Welcome: Prior booking required
Facilities:	Chipping/Putting Area, Practice Area, Driving Range, Golf Clubs for hire, Trolley hire, Bar, Restaurant

Accommodation, Food and Drink

Reference numbers below refer to detailed information provided in section 2

Accommodation

Banville's Bed & Breakfast, Kilkenny, Co Kilkenny
Tel: 056 70182 Four bright, homely, en suite double bedrooms in an end-of-terrace house a five-minute walk from the city centre. 366

Berkeley House, Kilkenny, Co Kilkenny
Tel: 056 64848 Ten bright, spacious B&B bedrooms in a dignified house in a classic 18th-century terrace. City-centre location. 362

Chaplins, Castlecomer Road, Kilkenny, Co Kilkenny
Tel: 056 52236 Quality Bed & Breakfast Accommodation in a spacious town house within walking distance of the city centre. Six en suite rooms; plenty of parking space.

Fennessy's Hotel, Clonmel, Co Tipperary
Tel: 052 23680 Fax: 052 23783 Ten-bedroomed hotel offering flexible en suite Accommodation in a prime site off the main street. Leisure centre next door. 554

Grove Farmhouse, Ballycocksuist, Inistioge, Co Kilkenny
Tel: 056 58467 Four generously sized B&B rooms in a 200-year-old country house on a working beef farm. All rooms en suite. 363

The Rafter Dempsey's, Kilkenny, Co Kilkenny
Tel/Fax: 056 22970 17 rooms (13 en suite) in a characterful pub in the heart of the city. Lunch and dinner menus. Live music. 361

Viewmount House, Kilkenny, Co Kilkenny
Tel: 056 62447 Six en suite bedrooms with fine views in a well-appointed country house next to Kilkenny Golf Club. 365

White Oaks, Kilkenny, Co Kilkenny
Tel: 056 63295 Four spacious bedrooms in an immaculate bungalow in a rural setting outside Kilkenny on the N76 Clonmel Road. 360

Food and Drink

Circle of Friends, Inistioge, Co Kilkenny
Tel: 056 58800 High-quality traditional and modern Irish cuisine in a picture-postcard village setting. Open every evening. 364

Fennessy's Hotel, Clonmel, Co Tipperary
Tel: 052 23680 Fax: 052 23783 Ten-bedroomed hotel offering flexible en suite Accommodation in a prime site off the main street. Leisure centre next door. 554

The Rafter Dempsey's, Kilkenny, Co Kilkenny
Tel/Fax: 056 22970 17 rooms (13 en suite) in a characterful pub in the heart of the city. Lunch and dinner menus. Live music. 361

Kilkenny

Kilkenny Golf Club, Glendine, Kilkenny
Tel: 056 65400

Sec/Manager:	Sean O'Neill
Professional:	Noel Leahy
Directions:	1 mile North of Kilkenny off the N77 road to Castlecomer
Type of Course:	Parkland
Date Founded:	1896
No of Holes:	18
Length:	6452 yds (5900 mtrs)
Par:	70
SSS:	71
Green Fees:	Weekdays: £20 Weekends & Bank Holidays: £25
Visitors:	Welcome: Contact Club in advance
Societies:	Welcome: Special concessions, Apply to club for details
Facilities:	Chipping/Putting Area, Practice Area, Golf Clubs for hire, Trolley hire, Electric Buggy hire, Bar, Restaurant, Caddy service by arrangement

Accommodation, Food and Drink

Reference numbers below refer to detailed information provided in section 2

Accommodation

Banville's Bed & Breakfast, Kilkenny, Co Kilkenny
Tel: 056 70182 Four bright, homely, en suite double bedrooms in an end-of-terrace house a five-minute walk from the city centre. 366

Berkeley House, Kilkenny, Co Kilkenny
Tel: 056 64848 Ten bright, spacious B&B bedrooms in a dignified house in a classic 18th-century terrace. City-centre location. 362

Chaplins, Castlecomer Road, Kilkenny, Co Kilkenny
Tel: 056 52236 Quality Bed & Breakfast Accommodation in a spacious town house within walking distance of the city centre. Six en suite rooms; plenty of parking space.

San Giovanni, Castlecomer, Co Carlow
Tel: 0503 40828 Nine bedrooms, seven en suite, in a fine modern house with front and rear gardens. Easy parking, good views. 372

The Rafter Dempsey's, Kilkenny, Co Kilkenny
Tel/Fax: 056 22970 17 rooms (13 en suite) in a characterful pub in the heart of the city. Lunch and dinner menus. Live music. 361

Viewmount House, Kilkenny, Co Kilkenny
Tel: 056 62447 Six en suite bedrooms with fine views in a well-appointed country house next to Kilkenny Golf Club. 365

White Oaks, Kilkenny, Co Kilkenny
Tel: 056 63295 Four spacious bedrooms in an immaculate bungalow in a rural setting outside Kilkenny on the N76 Clonmel Road. 360

Food and Drink

Circle of Friends, Inistioge, Co Kilkenny
Tel: 056 58800 High-quality traditional and modern Irish cuisine in a picture-postcard village setting. Open every evening. 364

Teach Dolmain, Carlow Town, Co Carlow
Tel: 0503 30911 Traditional Irish pub with three bars and two restaurants. A charming setting, great hospitality, fine food and Irish music. 370

The Beams Restaurant, 59 Dublin Street, Carlow, Co Carlow
Tel: 0503 31824 Restored 18th-century coaching inn offering fine cuisine (seafood a speciality) and an excellent wine list. Tuesday-Saturday evenings.

The Rafter Dempsey's, Kilkenny, Co Kilkenny

Tel/Fax: 056 22970 17 rooms (13 en suite) in a characterful pub in the heart of the city. Lunch and dinner menus. Live music. 361

Mount Juliet

Mount Juliet Golf & Country Club, Thomastown, Co Kilkenny

Tel: 056 24725

In the summer of 1986 at Royal Dublin, reigning US Masters champion, Jack Nicklaus, played an exhibition match against Seve Ballesteros. During the project, Tim Mahony, chairman of the sponsoring company, Toyota Ireland, got the idea of a major golf development where Nicklaus would be the course designer. So it was that Mount Juliet was born.

Five years later, in July 1991, Nicklaus played another Irish exhibition, this time against Christy O'Connor Snr, to mark the official opening of Mount Juliet. In the 1,500-acre estate once owned by racehorse breeder Major Victor McCalmont, Nicklaus had created a parkland course worthy of a stunning, pastoral setting, traversed by the River Nore.

For drainage reasons, the Bear resisted the temptation to use the river as a design feature. But he clearly earned his $1.25 million (dollar) fee when the venue was considered good enough, only two years later, to play host to the Irish Open Championship.

That was when Nick Faldo captured the title for a third successive year with a course-record last round of 65 to tie with Jose-Maria Olazabal,

whom he then beat in a play-off. In the process, Faldo declared the creeping bent, sand-based greens to be the best he had played on in Europe that year.

Situated outside Thomastown, Co Kilkenny, Mount Juliet is everything one would expect from a development which Nicklaus views as the flagship of his European operations. And as a bonus, it has a wonderful putting course, the only one of its kind this side of the Atlantic.

Sec/Manager:	Kate Maccann
Professional:	Ted Higgins Jnr.
Directions:	10 miles South of Kilkenny off the N10 from Kilkenny to Waterford or the N9 from Thomastown to Waterford
Type of Course:	Parkland
Date Founded:	1991
No of Holes:	18
Length:	7112 yds (6503 mtrs)
Par:	72
SSS:	72
Green Fees:	Summer: Mon-Thurs £75, Fri-Sun £85 Winter: Mon-Thurs £40, Fri-Sun £50
Visitors:	Welcome: Book ahead
Societies:	Welcome: Special concessions, Contact Club for details
Facilities:	Chipping/Putting Area, Practice Area, Driving Range, Golf Clubs for hire, Trolley hire, Bar, Restaurant, Caddy service by arrangement, Hotel/Accommodation on site

Accommodation, Food and Drink

Reference numbers below refer to detailed information provided in section 2

Accommodation

Arthur's Rest, Arthurstown, Co Wexford
Tel: 051 389192 Fax: 051 389362 A choice between Bed & Breakfast and self-catering Accommodation in a charming house near the Ballyhack car ferry. 651

Ballybro Lodge, Tagoat, Killinick, Co Wexford
Tel/Fax: 053 32333 Five en suite bedrooms in a large detached house run by a golfing couple. Large gardens with varied wildlife. 652

Banville's Bed & Breakfast, Kilkenny, Co Kilkenny
Tel: 056 70182 Four bright, homely, en suite double bedrooms in an end-of-terrace house a five-minute walk from the city centre. 366

Berkeley House, Kilkenny, Co Kilkenny
Tel: 056 64848 Ten well appointed B&B bedrooms in a dignified house in a classic 18th-century terrace. City-centre location. 362

Chaplins, Castlecomer Road, Kilkenny, Co Kilkenny
Tel: 056 52236 Quality Bed & Breakfast Accommodation in a spacious town house within walking distance of the city centre. Six en suite rooms; plenty of parking space.

Glendower House, New Ross, Co Wexford
Tel/Fax: 051 421989 Eight en suite bedrooms in a modern B&B on the main road into town from Wexford. Also evening meals. 650

Grove Farmhouse, Ballycocksuist, Inistioge, Co Kilkenny
Tel: 056 58467 Four generously sized B&B rooms in a 200-year-old country house on a working beef farm. All rooms en suite. 363

The Rafter Dempsey's, Kilkenny, Co Kilkenny
Tel/Fax: 05622970 rooms (13 en suite) in a characterful pub in the heart of the city. Lunch and dinner menus. Live music. 361

Viewmount House, Kilkenny, Co Kilkenny

Tel: 056 62447 Six en suite bedrooms with fine views in a well-appointed country
house next to Kilkenny Golf Club. 365
White Oaks, Kilkenny, Co Kilkenny
Tel: 056 63295 Four spacious bedrooms in an immaculate bungalow in a rural
setting outside Kilkenny on the N76 Clonmel Road. 360

Food and Drink

Circle of Friends, Inistioge, Co Kilkenny
Tel: 056 58800 High-quality traditional and modern Irish cuisine in a picture-
postcard village setting. Open every evening. 364
The Horse & Hound, Ballinaboola, New Ross, Co Wexford
Tel: 051 428323 Restaurant, bar and 12 rooms for Bed & Breakfast in a friendly
family-run hotel on the N25, four miles from New Ross. 653
The Rafter Dempsey's, Kilkenny, Co Kilkenny
Tel/Fax: 056 22970 17 rooms (13 en suite) in a characterful pub in the heart of
the city. Lunch and dinner menus. Live music. 361

Heath

Heath Golf Club, The Heath, Portlaoise, Co Laois

Tel: 050 246533

Golf clubs are rarely shy about highlighting their seniority. In claiming a foundation date as relatively recent as 1930, however, The Heath GC appear content to overlook earlier incarnations.

It seems they could claim to be the seventh oldest club in the country, given that the Queen's County (the pre-Treaty name for Laois) Heath GC was founded in 1889. And historians have established that another club on the site, the Maryboro GC, had an institution date of 1903.

It, too, was situated on "the Great Heath of Maryborough." And "The Golfing Annual of 1894/'95", described an excellent clubhouse "originally the Grand Stand, when races were held on The Heath." As an enduring link with that rich heritage, the present clubhouse is in exactly the same location as the old Grand Stand of 1889.

Meanwhile, as the name suggests, the 6,439-yard, par-71 layout is classic heathland where the hazards can often include wayward sheep. Set in picturesque surroundings, with views of the rolling hills of Co Laois, the course is noted for its splendid drainage, making it a particularly attractive venue during the winter.

The layout includes three lakes, which are situated to the left of the long fourth, off the tee at the par-four fifth and to the right of the tee at the 389-yard 18th. Elsewhere, there are numerous trees, heather and gorse to challenge the accuracy of the player, especially with the driver. This is especially true of the 427-yard 13th, which is a worthy index one.

Sec/Manager:	David O'Brien
Professional:	Eddie Doyle
Directions:	3 miles North East of Portlaoise off the M7
Type of Course:	Parkland -
Date Founded:	1889
No of Holes:	18
Length:	6422 yds (5873 mtrs)
Par:	71
SSS:	70
Green Fees:	Weekdays: £10 Weekends & Bank Holidays: £17
Visitors:	Welcome: Weekdays, Prior booking advisable
Societies:	Welcome: Contact Club in writing
Facilities:	Chipping/Putting Area, Practice Area, Driving Range, Golf Clubs for hire, Trolley hire, Electric Buggy hire, Bar, Restaurant, Caddy service by arrangement

Accommodation, Food and Drink

Reference numbers below refer to detailed
information provided in section 2

Accommodation

Annagh Lodge, Newbridge, Co Kildare
Tel: 045 433518 Nine excellent Bed & Breakfast rooms in a striking modern
bungalow on the Dublin side of Newbridge. Sauna, conservatory. 345
San Giovanni, Castlecomber, Co Carlow
Tel: 0503 40828 Nine bedrooms, seven en suite, in a fine modern house with front
and rear gardens. Easy parking, good views. 372
The Gables, Ryston, Newbridge, Co Kildare
Tel: 045 435330 A super guest house on the banks of the Liffey, with ten en suite
bedrooms and a leisure centre (pool, gym, sauna). 351
Westown Farm, Johnstown, Naas, Co Kildare
Tel/Fax: 045 897006 Farmhouse Bed & Breakfast Accommodation run by a mother-
and-daughter team. Five bedrooms, three of them en suite.

Food and Drink

Swifts, Newbridge, Co Kildare
Tel: 045 433234 All-day menus in Newbridge's trendiest bar, with a long, elegant bar
and several spacious lounges. 346

Teach Dolmain, Carlow Town, Co Carlow

Tel: 0503 30911 Traditional Irish pub with three bars and two restaurants. A charming setting, great hospitality, fine food and Irish music. 370

The Beams Restaurant, 59 Dublin Street, Carlow, Co Carlow

Tel: 0503 31824 Restored 18th-century coaching inn offering fine cuisine (seafood a speciality) and an excellent wine list. Tuesday-Saturday evenings.

The Waterfront, Roscrea, Co Tipperary

Tel: 0505 22431 Family restaurant catering for all tastes. Snacks, full meals, takeaways. Open from 9.30 till 9. 541

Mountrath

Mountrath Golf Club, Knockinina, Mountrath, Co Laois
Tel: 050 232558

Sec/Manager:	John Mulhare
Professional:	None
Directions:	Half a mile South of Mountrath off the N7 Port Laoise to Roscrea road
Type of Course:	Parkland
Date Founded:	1929
No of Holes:	18
Length:	6007 yds (5493 mtrs)
Par:	71
SSS:	69
Green Fees:	IR £12
Visitors:	Welcome: Any Day., Check available tee-times at weekends
Societies:	Welcome: Special concessions, Apply to club for details
Facilities:	Chipping/Putting Area, Practice Area, Trolley hire, Bar, Restaurant

Accommodation, Food and Drink

Reference numbers below refer to detailed information provided in section 2

Accommodation

Berkeley House, Kilkenny, Co Kilkenny

Tel: 056 64848 Ten bright, spacious B&B bedrooms in a dignified house in a classic 18th-century location. City-centre location. 362

San Giovanni, Castlecomber, Co Carlow

Tel: 0503 40828 Nine bedrooms, seven en suite, in a fine modern house with front and rear gardens. Easy parking, good views. 372

The Rafter Dempsey's, Kilkenny, Co Kilkenny

Tel/Fax: 056 22970 17 rooms (13 en suite) in a characterful pub in the heart of the city. Lunch and dinner menus. Live music. 361

Viewmount House, Kilkenny, Co Kilkenny

Tel: 056 62447 Six en suite bedrooms with fine views in a well-appointed country house next to Kilkenny Golf Club. 365

Food and Drink

Teach Dolmain, Carlow Town, Co Carlow

Tel: 0503 30911 Traditional Irish pub with three bars and two restaurants. A charming setting, great hospitality, fine food and Irish music. 370

The Beams Restaurant, 59 Dublin Street, Carlow, Co Carlow

Tel: 0503 31824 Restored 18th-century coaching inn offering fine cuisine (seafood a speciality) and an excellent wine list. Tuesday-Saturday evenings.

The Waterfront, Roscrea, Co Tipperary

Tel: 0505 22431 Family restaurant catering for all tastes. Snacks, full meals, takeaways. Open from 9.30 till 9. 541

Portarlington

Portarlington Golf Club, Garryhinch, Portarlington, Co Laois
Tel: 050 223115

Sec/Manager:	Martin Turley
Professional:	None
Directions:	2 miles South West of Portarlington off the R419 to Port Laoise
Type of Course:	Parkland
Date Founded:	1909
No of Holes:	18
Length:	6421 yds (5872 mtrs)
Par:	71
SSS:	71
Green Fees:	Weekdays: £14 Weekends & Bank Holidays: £17
Visitors:	Welcome: Any Day, Restrictions Tuesday & weekends, Ring in advance
Societies:	Welcome: Special concessions, Apply to club for details
Facilities:	Chipping/Putting Area, Practice Area, Trolley hire, Electric Buggy hire, Bar, Restaurant, Caddy service by arrangement

Accommodation, Food and Drink

Reference numbers below refer to detailed information provided in section 2

Accommodation

Annagh Lodge, Newbridge, Co Kildare

Tel: 045 433518 Nine excellent Bed & Breakfast rooms in a striking modern bungalow on the Dublin side of Newbridge. Sauna, conservatory. 345

The Gables, Ryston, Newbridge, Co Kildare

Tel: 045 435330 A super guest house on the banks of the Liffey, with ten en suite bedrooms and a leisure centre (pool, gym, sauna). 351

Westown Farm, Johnstown, Naas, Co Kildare

Tel/Fax: 045 897006 Farmhouse Bed & Breakfast Accommodation run by a mother-and-daughter team. Five bedrooms, three of them en suite.

Woodcourte House, Timolin, Moone, Athy, Co Kildare

Tel: 0507 24167 Six spacious bedrooms (two en suite) in a modern B&B house in a picturesque village just off the main N9 Dublin-Kilkenny road. 340

Food and Drink

Teach Dolmain, Carlow Town, Co Carlow

Tel: 050 330911 Traditional Irish pub with three bars and two restaurants. A charming setting, great hospitality, fine food and Irish music. 370

The Beams Restaurant, 59 Dublin Street, Carlow Town, Co Carlow

Tel: 050 331824 Restored 18th-century coaching inn offering fine cuisine (seafood a speciality) and an excellent wine list. Tuesday-Saturday evenings.

The Waterfront, Roscrea, Co Tipperary

Tel: 050 522431 Family restaurant catering for all tastes. Snacks, full meals, takeaways. Open from 9.30 till 9. 541

Tyrrells Restaurant, Edenderry, Co Offaly

Tel: 040 532400 An atmospheric restaurant with rough-hewn walls and flagstone floor in the many-acred complex of Ballindoolin House & Gardens. 500

Rathdowney

Rathdowney Golf Club, Coulnaboul West,
Rathdowney, Co Laois
Tel: 050 546170/546166

Sec/Manager:	Mike Munro
Professional:	None
Directions:	Half a mile South East of Rathdowney off the R433 from Abbeyleix
Type of Course:	Parkland
Date Founded:	1930
No of Holes:	18
Length:	6412 yds (5864 mtrs)
Par:	71
SSS:	70
Green Fees:	£12
Visitors:	Welcome: Restrictions on Wednesdays and weekends, Contact Club for tee-times
Societies:	Welcome: Contact Club for details
Facilities:	Chipping/Putting Area, Trolley hire, Bar, Restaurant

Accommodation, Food and Drink

Reference numbers below refer to detailed
information provided in section 2

Accommodation

Berkeley House, Kilkenny, Co Kilkenny
Tel: 056 64848 Ten bright, spacious B&B bedrooms in a dignified house in a classic 18th-century terrace. City-centre location.   362

Chaplins, Castlecomer Road, Kilkenny, Co Kilkenny
Tel: 056 52236 Quality Bed & Breakfast Accommodation in a spacious town house within walking distance of the city centre. Six en suite rooms; plenty of parking space.

Hawthorn View, Thurles, Co Tipperary
Tel: 050 421710 4 en suite Bed & Breakfast rooms in a modern bungalow set back from the N62. Very close to Thurles Golf Course. Equestrian Centre nearby.   540

San Giovanni, Castlecomber, Co Carlow
Tel: 050 340828 Nine bedrooms, seven en suite, in a fine modern house with front and rear gardens. Easy parking, good views.   372

Viewmount House, Kilkenny, Co Kilkenny
Tel: 056 62447 Six en suite bedrooms with fine views in a well-appointed country house next to Kilkenny Golf Club.   365

Food and Drink

Teach Dolmain, Carlow Town, Co Carlow
Tel: 050 330911 Traditional Irish pub with three bars and two restaurants. A charming setting, great hospitality, fine food and Irish music.   370

The Beams Restaurant, 59 Dublin Street, Carlow, Co Carlow
Tel: 050 331824 Restored 18th-century coaching inn offering fine cuisine (seafood a speciality) and an excellent wine list. Tuesday-Saturday evenings.

The Waterfront, Roscrea, Co Tipperary
Tel: 050 522431 Family restaurant catering for all tastes. Snacks, full meals, takeaways. Open from 9.30 till 9.   541

Carlow

Carlow Golf Club, Deerpark, Carlow
Tel: 050 331695

Though Carlow GC has always been highly-rated among Irish lovers of the Royal and Ancient game, its fame spread to the British Midlands as a result of a stunning strokeplay performance on the weekend of October 3rd and 4th, 1981. That was when Peter McEvoy won the Midland Scratch there by the stunning margin of 15 strokes.

His exploits at Carlow became the lead story on the back page of the "Birmingham Post." Indeed a nine-under-par aggregate of 271 was the Englishman's finest-ever scoring over 72 holes, despite three further victories in the event. And, by McEvoy's reckoning, his heroics were achieved on a course which was "more difficult than my figures would suggest."

Carlow was also the scene of a rather special exhibition match in July 1934, involving Joe Kirkwood and no less a figure in the game than Gene Sarazen. Part of deal was that the players would be taken by taxi from Dublin and back, at a cost of three guineas to the club.

But the final bill was somewhat higher, due to the fact that the taxi driver was fined £5 for dangerous driving, having been stopped by gardai on the return journey.

Over the years, this highly-progressive club employed such renowned course architects as Cecil Barcroft, the partnership of J H Taylor and Fred Hawtree, Alister MacKenzie and Tom Simpson. And all the while, the sandy sub-soil has ensured splendid drainage for regular visits from admirers, including Joe Carr and Walker Cup colleague David Sheahan.

Sec/Manager:	Margaret Meaney
Professional:	Andrew Gilbert
Directions:	Two miles North East of Carlow on the N9
Type of Course:	Inland Links
Date Founded:	1899
No of Holes:	18
Length:	6533 yds (5974 mtrs)
Par:	70
SSS:	71
Green Fees:	Weekdays: £28 Weekends & Bank Holidays: £34

Visitors:	Welcome: Contact club in advance
Societies:	Welcome: Special concessions, Contact Club for details
Facilities:	Practice Area, Golf Clubs for hire, Trolley hire, Bar, Restaurant

Accommodation, Food and Drink

Reference numbers below refer to detailed
information provided in section 2

Accommodation

San Giovanni, Castlecomber, Co Carlow
Tel: 050 340828 Nine bedrooms, seven en suite, in a fine modern house with front
and rear gardens. Easy parking, good views. 372

Sherwood Park House, Kilbride, Ballon, Co Carlow
Tel: 050 359117 Five en suite rooms in a superb Georgian house on its own
working estate. B&B, evening meals on request. 371

The Rafter Dempsey's, Kilkenny, Co Kilkenny
Tel/Fax: 056 22970 17 rooms (13 en suite) in a characterful pub in the heart of
the city. Lunch and dinner menus. Live music. 361

Woodcourte House, Timolin, Moone, Athy, Co Kildare
Tel: 050 724167 Six spacious bedrooms (two en suite) in a modern B&B house in a
picturesque village just off the main N9 Dublin-Kilkenny road. 340

Food and Drink

Teach Dolmain, Carlow Town, Co Carlow
Tel: 050 330911 Traditional Irish pub with three bars and two restaurants. A
charming setting, great hospitality, fine food and Irish music. 370

The Beams Restaurant, 59 Dublin Street, Carlow, Co Carlow
Tel: 050 331824 Restored 18th-century coaching inn offering fine cuisine (seafood a
speciality) and an excellent wine list. Tuesday-Saturday evenings.

The Rafter Dempsey's, Kilkenny, Co Kilkenny
Tel/Fax: 056 22970 17 rooms (13 en suite) in a characterful pub in the heart of
the city. Lunch and dinner menus. Live music. 361

Mount Wolseley

**Mount Wolseley Golf & Country Club, Tullow,
Co Carlow**

Tel: 050 351674

Two charming old Wolseley cars, parked in front
of the clubhouse, provide a clear pointer to the
origins of this beautiful stretch of land, 10 miles
from Carlow Town. It was once the home of the
Wolseley family who would later lend their name
to one of the great marques of the British motor
industry.

Officially opened in August 1997, Mount
Wolseley is owned by Donal Morrissey who is
anxious to maintain the motoring link, especially
since the cars ceased production in 1975. And it
has already become a highly desirable destination for the discerning golfer.

Morrissey, was a member of Carlow GC when
Christy O'Connor Jnr was the professional there.
So, after buying the property for £600,000 in
1994, he could think of no architect more suited
for the job. So it was that O'Connor was employed as course designer, a task which he
discharged admirably.

Set on 130 acres only a few hundred yards

from the meandering River Slaney, it is a strong,
spacious layout which will test golfers of all levels. Predictably, O'Connor has made strategic use
of water to focus the mind.

The distinctive clubhouse was once the 19th
century home of Garnet Wolseley and his
younger brother Frederick York, founder of the
motor company. And it is reported that Garnet,
in pursuit of a military career, arranged the tree-
planting on the estate to replicate the troop
formations at the Battle of Waterloo, so as to
ingratiate himself with the Duke of Wellington.

Sec/Manager:	Kathy Walsh
Professional:	Jimmy Bolger
Directions:	2 miles South East of Tullow on the Ardattin Road
Type of Course:	Parkland
Date Founded:	1996
No of Holes:	18
Length:	7106 yds (6497 mtrs)
Par:	72
SSS:	74
Green Fees:	Weekdays: £30 Weekends & Bank Holidays: £35
Visitors:	Welcome: Any time, Check weekend availability with club
Societies:	Welcome: Prior booking required
Facilities:	Chipping/Putting Area, Practice Area, Golf Clubs for hire, Trolley hire, Bar, Restaurant.

Accommodation, Food and Drink

Reference numbers below refer to detailed
information provided in section 2

Accommodation

San Giovanni, Castlecomber, Co Carlow
Tel: 050 340828 Nine bedrooms, seven en suite, in a fine modern house with front
and rear gardens. Easy parking, good views. 372

Sherwood Park House, Kilbride, Ballon, Co Carlow

Tel: 050 359117 Five en suite rooms in a superb Georgian house on its own
working estate. B&B, evening meals on request.   371

The Rafter Dempsey's, Kilkenny, Co Kilkenny

Tel/Fax: 056 22970 17 rooms (13 en suite) in a characterful pub in the heart of
the city. Lunch and dinner menus. Live music.   361

Woodcourte House, Timolin, Moone, Athy, Co Kildare

Tel: 050 724167 Six spacious bedrooms (two en suite) in a modern B&B house in a
picturesque village just off the main N9 Dublin-Kilkenny road.   340

Food and Drink

Teach Dolmain, Carlow Town, Co Carlow

Tel: 050 330911 Traditional Irish pub with three bars and two restaurants. A
charming setting, great hospitality, fine food and Irish music.   370

The Beams Restaurant, 59 Dublin Street, Carlow, Co Carlow

Tel: 050 331824 Restored 18th-century coaching inn offering fine cuisine (seafood a
speciality) and an excellent wine list. Tuesday-Saturday evenings.

The Rafter Dempsey's, Kilkenny, Co Kilkenny

Tel/Fax: 056 22970 17 rooms (13 en suite) in a characterful pub in the heart of
the city. Lunch and dinner menus. Live music.   361

LIMERICK

The popular description of Limerick as a gateway to the south-west, does scant justice to its considerable attractions in its own right, not least as a golfing destination. Granted, it lacks the majestic links terrain of its neighbours, Clare and Kerry, but its splendid parkland courses include one of particular merit.

River Shannon, Co Limerick

Adare Manor and Country Club, where the venerable Robert Trent Jones laid out one of Ireland's most impressive parkland stretches, fulfills two highly significant roles in golfing tourism in the region. With the manor house turned into a superb hotel, it has become an ideal base from which the wealthier tourist can travel to the premier Kerry courses. Then there is the Adare Manor course itself which, in the view of most observers, contains a wonderful back-nine, culminating in the par-five 18th when the competitor encounters the ubiquitous River Maigue for the last time. And as a further delight, the charmingly compact Adare Manor GC is next door.

Limerick's courses also include Abbeyfeale (nine holes), Castletroy, Killeline Park, Castletroy, Limerick, Limerick County, Newcastle West and Rathbane, all of which are parkland. Limerick GC, which had nine locations before moving to its present home at Ballyclough on June 1st 1919, is the home club of the well-known racehorse owner and international financier, J P McManus, once described as "The Sundance Kid", because of his punting exploits at Cheltenham. Through his sponsorship, an international pro-am was held at Limerick GC in 1995 and was repeated in July 2000, when leading American tournament players competed for prize money of £400,000.

Locals are justifiably proud of what they describe as a nicely compact county, roughly rectangular in shape and extending some 50 miles from east to west and 25 miles from north to south. A large part of north, central and east Limerick consists of a fertile, limestone plain, dotted with numerous hills and ridges from where church spires can be picked out as the location of small towns and villages. From available evidence, it would appear that man had established himself in the Lough Gur area of east Limerick as early as 3000 BC. These mesolithic people would have lived on hunting, fishing and other forms of food gathering: the actual production of food was a much later development.

In more recent times the city of Limerick became famous for the two sieges it endured in 1690 and 1691, during the Jacobite-Williamite wars. It was during the first of these sieges that the city's heroic defender, General Patrick Sarsfield, destroyed a great

O'Connell Street, Limerick

convoy of Williamite guns and ammunition in a daring raid on Ballyneety. The Catholic Irish had supported the Jacobite cause and when the war ended in defeat, the Treaty of Limerick was signed in 1691. The actual signing is believed to have taken place on the Treaty Stone, a rough hewn block of masonry which today sits on a pedestal on the opposite side of Thomond Bridge from King John's Castle.

Soldiers came to Limerick in more benign circumstances 200 years later. Indeed the officers of the 2nd Battalion of the Blackwatch Regiment had a key role in the founding of Limerick GC in 1891, before heading off to spread the gospel at Lahinch, a year later. We are informed that the regiment originally came to Ireland in the autumn of 1886, when they were first posted to the Curragh in Co Kildare. In the following year, they moved to Dublin where they became actively involved in the Dublin GC (later Royal Dublin), presenting a medal for a competition which still exists in the club. Then came a move to Belfast, followed by their posting to Limerick.

"The Irish Golfer" of October 1891 reported: "The Limerick Golf Club, which played in the winter over the racecourse and in the summer over the downs of Kilkee (Co Clare), was founded in 1891 by Messrs A W Shaw, M Gavin, Capt Willington and Richard Plummer. The time was favourable for such a movement (develop-ment), for the Blackwatch had just been quartered in Limerick and it numbered several enthusiastic and expert golfers."

Against such a rich, his-toric background, it is hardly surprising that Limerick has much to of-fer the tourist by way of sightseeing. For instance, King John's Castle was built around 1200 and re-mains one of the finest examples of fortified Nor-man architecture in Ireland. The original en-trance, on the north side, is flanked by two towers and retains traces of a

King Johns Castle, Co Limerick

portcullis above it. Excavations of the castle are continuing as part of a new visitor facility. Limerick is very much a sporting city, famous for its rugby clubs, one of which, Garryowen, gave its name to the high punt which is so much a part of the Munster game. Dominated by the River Shannon, it also has a rich tradition in rowing, while its hurlers have tasted some spar-kling successes at national level.

From Limerick County GC at Kilmallock in the south-east, to Newcastle West in the west, naturally, its courses are spread throughout the county. But the visitor has to travel only seven miles outside the city to discover the delights of the Adare courses, which are situated in one of the prettiest villages imaginable.

Location of Golf Courses

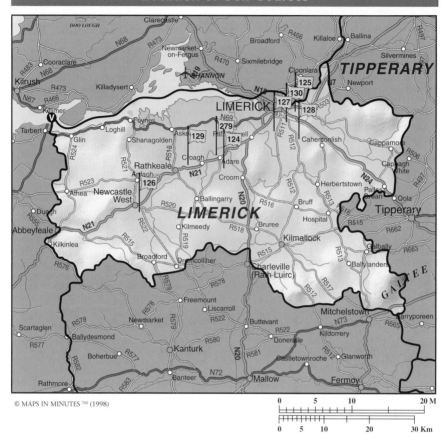

© MAPS IN MINUTES ™ (1998)

```
0        5        10              20 M
|-+-+-+-+-+-+-+-+-+-+-+-+-|
|-+-+-+-+-+-+-|
0     5    10        20        30 Km
```

Adare Golf Club

Adare, Co Limerick

Tel: 061 396566

New Jersey financier, Tom Kane, invested £15 million of his own money in this luxury development, seven miles from Limerick city. In the process, he employed the veteran American architect Robert Trent Jones to design a 7,138-yard, championship-standard course in 230 acres of what was formerly the family estate of the Earl of Dunraven.

Kane's brainchild has been completed to the highest standards, worthy of the extended manor house which is now well-established as a five-star hotel. "It took its toll on me, but I never doubted I'd finish it," said the proud owner.

Admirers of Trent Jones will be familiar with his affection for water as a design feature. Here, the old man really undulged himself by creating a 14-acre lake - the heavy-duty polythene base cost £300,000 - to dominate the front nine.

There are two further lakes, albeit of considerably smaller dimensions, to the right of the 14th green and between tee and green at the short 16th. And a generous purse is reflected in two bridges were built, at a combined cost over £500,000, over the River Maigue which dominates the back nine.

The long, 544-yard 18th, is a worthy finishing hole, with two, isolated trees standing sentinel on the right side of the fairway at a distance of 340 yards from the back tee. Depending on wind direction, the green is reachable in two,

but only after a long-iron or fairway-wood shot, hit diagonally across the river to a wide but shallow target.

Sec/Manager:	Mark Feane
Professional:	B Shaw
Directions:	11 miles south west of Limerick off the N20 to Killarney
Type of Course:	Parkland
Date Founded:	1995
No of Holes:	18
Length:	6557 yds (5995 mtrs)
Par:	72
SSS:	72
Green Fees:	£60 non-members, £50 hotel residents
Visitors:	Welcome: Book in advance
Societies:	Welcome: Anytime by prior arrangement
Facilities:	Chipping/Putting Area, Practice Area, Driving Range, Golf Clubs for hire, Trolley hire, Electric buggy hire, Bar, Restaurant, Caddy service by arrangement, Swimming pool, Sauna, Hotel/Accommodation on site

Accommodation, Food and Drink

Reference numbers below refer to detailed information provided in section 2

Accommodation

Ashford, Templeglantine, Co Limerick
Tel: 069 84001/84311 A distinguished modern redbrick house in its own beautiful grounds. Five en suite B&B rooms. Fine furnishings and fittings. 383

Berkeley Lodge, Adare, Co Limerick
Tel/Fax: 061 396857 Top-quality Bed & Breakfast Accommodation in six superbly appointed en suite bedrooms. Great breakfasts. Also self-catering cottage for 6. 388

Cedar Lodge, Patrickswell, Co Limerick
Tel: 061 355137 Five en suite rooms with tv in a farmhouse-style dwelling in a quiet setting not far from Limerick. Good choice for breakfast. 380

Clonunion House, Adare, Co Limerick
Tel: 061 396657 Farmhouse Accommodation in tranquil surroundings and mature gardens two kilometres from Adare. Four beautiful bedrooms, 3 en suite and 1 with private bathroom. 387

Deebert House, Kilmallock, Co Limerick
Tel: 063 98106 Five letting bedrooms, including a family room, in a splendid Georgian house set in award-winning gardens. Restaurant. 382

Dunraven Arms Hotel, Adare, Co Limerick
Tel: 061 396633 Fax: 061 396541 Established in 1792, this is one of Ireland's greatest country hotels, with 76 beautifully appointed bedrooms and a top-class restaurant. 389

Fort Ann, Patrickswell, Co Limerick
Tel: 061 355162 A beautiful B&B farmhouse in a charming location by the main Limerick-Adare road. Four good-sized en suite bedrooms. 386

Rathkeale House Hotel, Rathkeale, Co Limerick
Tel: 069 63333 Fax: 069 63330 Purpose-built in 1997, the long, low hotel has welcoming family owners, 30 en suite bedrooms, fine restaurant and a lively bar. 391

Food and Drink

Deebert House, Kilmallock, Co Limerick
Tel: 063 98106 Five letting bedrooms, including a family room, in a splendid Georgian house set in award-winning gardens. Restaurant. 382

Dunraven Arms Hotel, Adare, Co Limerick
Tel: 061 396633 Fax: 061 396541 Established in 1792, this is one of Ireland's greatest country hotels, with 76 beautifully appointed bedrooms and a top-class restaurant. 389

Rathkeale House Hotel, Rathkeale, Co Limerick
Tel: 069 63333 Fax: 069 63330 Purpose-built in 1997, the long, low hotel has welcoming family owners, 30 en suite bedrooms, fine restaurant and a lively bar. 391
The Dark Horse, Patrickswell, Co Limerick
Tel: 061 355196 A cheerful pub with a sporting theme, serving great Guinness and day-long snacks. Evening restaurant next door. 385
The Peppercorn, Patrickswell, Co Limerick
Tel: 061 355999 Fine food and fast, friendly service in an intimate restaurant on the main Limerick-Cork road. Open for dinner Tuesday-Sunday. 392
The Wild Geese, Adare, Co Limerick
Tel/Fax: 061 396451 A terrific restaurant in a magnificent row of thatched cottages. Duck is the speciality, also goose and venison on a superb seasonal menu. 390

Adare Manor

Adare, Co Limerick
Tel: 061 396204

Sec/Manager:	Phil Bray
Professional:	J Coyle
Directions:	11 miles south west of Limerick off the N20 to Killarney
Type of Course:	Parkland
Date Founded:	1900
No of Holes:	18
Length:	5764 yds (5271 mtrs)
Par:	70
SSS:	69
Green Fees:	Weekdays: £15 Weekends £20
Visitors:	Welcome: except Thursday Ladies Day
Societies:	Welcome: Anytime by prior arrangement
Facilities:	Chipping/Putting Area, Practice Area, Golf Clubs for hire, Trolley hire, Bar, Restaurant

Accommodation, Food and Drink

Reference numbers below refer to detailed information provided in section 2

Accommodation

Ashford, Templeglantine, Co Limerick
Tel: 069 84001/84311 A distinguished modern redbrick house in its own beautiful grounds. Five en suite B&B rooms. Fine furnishings and fittings. 383
Berkeley Lodge, Adare, Co Limerick
Tel/Fax: 061 396857 Top-quality Bed & Breakfast Accommodation in six superbly appointed en suite bedrooms. Great breakfasts. Also self-catering cottage for 6. 388
Cedar Lodge, Patrickswell, Co Limerick
Tel: 061 355137 Five en suite rooms with tv in a farmhouse-style dwelling in a quiet setting not far from Limerick. Good choice for breakfast. 380
Clonunion House, Adare, Co Limerick
Tel: 061 396657 Farmhouse Accommodation in tranquil surroundings and mature gardens two kilometres from Adare. Four beautiful bedrooms, 3 en suite and 1 with private bathroom. 387
Deebert House, Kilmallock, Co Limerick
Tel: 063 98106 Five letting bedrooms, including a family room, in a splendid Georgian house set in award-winning gardens. Restaurant. 382
Dunraven Arms Hotel, Adare, Co Limerick
Tel: 061 396633 Fax: 061 396541 Established in 1792, this is one of Ireland's greatest country hotels, with 76 beautifully appointed bedrooms and a top-class restaurant. 389
Fort Ann, Patrickswell, Co Limerick
Tel: 061 355162 A beautiful B&B farmhouse in a charming location by the main

Limerick-Adare road. Four good-sized en suite bedrooms. 386
Rathkeale House Hotel, Rathkeale, Co Limerick
Tel: 069 63333 Fax: 069 63330 Purpose-built in 1997, the long, low hotel has welcoming family owners, 30 en suite bedrooms, fine restaurant and a lively bar. 391

Food and Drink

Deebert House, Kilmallock, Co Limerick
Tel: 063 98106 Five letting bedrooms, including a family room, in a splendid Georgian house set in award-winning gardens. Restaurant. 382
Dunraven Arms Hotel, Adare, Co Limerick
Tel: 061 396633 Fax: 061 396541 Established in 1792, this is one of Ireland's greatest country hotels, with 76 beautifully appointed bedrooms and a top-class restaurant. 389
Rathkeale House Hotel, Rathkeale, Co Limerick
Tel: 069 63333 Fax: 069 63330 Purpose-built in 1997, the long, low hotel has welcoming family owners, 30 en suite bedrooms, fine restaurant and a lively bar. 391
The Dark Horse, Patrickswell, Co Limerick
Tel: 061 355196 A cheerful pub with a sporting theme, serving great Guinness and day-long snacks. Evening restaurant next door. 385
The Peppercorn, Patrickswell, Co Limerick
Tel: 061 355999 Fine food and fast, friendly service in an intimate restaurant on the main Limerick-Cork road. Open for dinner Tuesday-Sunday. 392
The Wild Geese, Adare, Co Limerick
Tel/Fax: 061 396451 A terrific restaurant in a magnificent row of thatched cottages. Duck is the speciality, also goose and venison on a superb seasonal menu. 390

Castletroy

Castletroy Golf Club, Castletroy, Co Limerick
Tel: 061 335261

Sec/Manager:	Laurence Hayes
Professional:	None
Directions:	Less than 3 miles from Limerick City Centre off the N7 to Dublin
Type of Course:	Parkland
Date Founded:	1937
No of Holes:	18
Length:	6345 yds (5802 mtrs)
Par:	71
SSS:	71
Green Fees:	Weekdays: £24 Weekends & Bank Holidays: £30
Visitors:	Welcome: Weekday mornings, Restrictions at other times, Contact Club in advance
Societies:	Welcome: Special concessions, Contact Club in advance
Facilities:	Chipping/Putting Area, Practice Area, Golf Clubs for hire, Trolley hire, Electric Buggy hire, Bar, Restaurant, Caddy service by arrangement

Accommodation, Food and Drink

Reference numbers below refer to detailed information provided in section 2

Accommodation

Cedar Lodge, Patrickswell, Co Limerick
Tel: 061 355137 Five en suite rooms with tv in a farmhouse-style dwelling in a quiet setting not far from Limerick. Good choice for breakfast. 380
Fort Ann, Patrickswell, Co Limerick
Tel: 061 355162 A beautiful B&B farmhouse in a charming location by the main Limerick-Adare road. Four good-sized en suite bedrooms. 386

Hanratty's Hotel, Limerick, Co Limerick
Tel: 061 410999 A prime location off Limerick's main street for a 200-year-old family-run hotel with 22 well-appointed en suite bedrooms and a fine restaurant. 381

Food and Drink

Hanratty's Hotel, Limerick, Co Limerick
Tel: 061 410999 A prime location off Limerick's main street for a 200-year-old family-run hotel with 22 well-appointed en suite bedrooms and a fine restaurant. 381

The Dark Horse, Patrickswell, Co Limerick
Tel: 061 355196 A cheerful pub with a sporting theme, serving great Guinness and day-long snacks. Evening restaurant next door. 385

The Peppercorn, Patrickswell, Co Limerick
Tel: 061 355999 Fine food and fast, friendly service in an intimate restaurant on the main Limerick-Cork road. Open for dinner Tuesday-Sunday. 392

Food and Drink

Deebert House, Kilmallock, Co Limerick
Tel: 063 98106 Five letting bedrooms, including a family room, in a splendid Georgian house set in award-winning gardens. Restaurant. 382

Leen's Hotel, Abbeyfeale, Co Limerick
Tel: 068 31121 Fax: 068 32550 A family-run hotel with 19 en suite bedrooms and a restaurant serving generous helpings of local produce. 384

Rathkeale House Hotel, Rathkeale, Co Limerick
Tel: 069 63333 Fax: 069 63330 Purpose-built in 1997, the long, low hotel has welcoming family owners, 30 en suite bedrooms, fine restaurant and a lively bar. 391

The Four Winds, Charleville, Co Cork
Tel: 063 89285 A welcoming bar and restaurant occupying a prominent corner site on the N20. Food served from noon till 3. 176

Killeline

Limerick

Killeline Park Golf & Country Club, Cork Road, Newcastle West, Co Limerick

Tel: 069 61600

Sec/Manager:	None
Professional:	Kevin Dorrian
Directions:	Half a mile South of Newcastle West off the R522 to Dromcolliher
Type of Course:	Parkland
Date Founded:	1938
No of Holes:	18
Length:	6500 yds (5943 mtrs)
Par:	71
SSS:	71
Green Fees:	£15
Visitors:	Welcome: Any Day, Contact Club in advance
Societies:	Welcome: Contact Club for details
Facilities:	Practice Area, Golf Clubs for hire, Trolley hire, Bar, Restaurant

Accommodation, Food and Drink

Reference numbers below refer to detailed information provided in section 2

Accommodation

Ashford, Templeglantine, Co Limerick
Tel: 069 84001/84311 A distinguished modern redbrick house in its own beautiful grounds. Five en suite B&B rooms. Fine furnishings and fittings. 383

Castle View House, Carrig Island, Co Kerry
Tel/Fax: 068 43304 Six bedrooms, all en suite, in a neat, modern house close to the Tarbert/Killimer car ferry. B&B; dinner by arrangement. 301

Deebert House, Kilmallock, Co Limerick
Tel: 063 98106 Five letting bedrooms, including a family room, in a splendid Georgian house set in award-winning gardens. Restaurant. 382

Greenfields Farmhouse, Asdee, Listowel, Co Kerry
Tel: 068 41233 Three double bedrooms for B&B, one en suite. On the Tarbert/Ballybunion road. Access, Mastercard, Visa.

Leen's Hotel, Abbeyfeale, Co Limerick
Tel: 068 31121 Fax: 068 32550 A family-run hotel with 19 en suite bedrooms and a restaurant serving generous helpings of local produce. 384

Rathkeale House Hotel, Rathkeale, Co Limerick
Tel: 069 63333 Fax: 069 63330 Purpose-built in 1997, the long, low hotel has welcoming family owners, 30 en suite bedrooms, fine restaurant and a lively bar. 391

Tralee Townhouse, Tralee, Co Kerry
Tel: 066 7181111 20 bedrooms, including several of family size, in a town house hotel that's handy for all Tralee's attractions. 303

Limerick Golf Club, Ballyclough, Limerick

Tel: 061 414083/415146

Sec/Manager:	Declan McDonogh
Professional:	Lee Harrington
Directions:	3 miles South of Limerick City Centre off the R511
Type of Course:	Parkland
Date Founded:	1891
No of Holes:	18
Length:	6487 yds (5932 mtrs)
Par:	72
SSS:	71
Green Fees:	£22.50
Visitors:	Welcome: Any Day except Tuesday and at weekends.
Societies:	Welcome: Special concessions, Contact Club for details
Facilities:	Chipping/Putting Area, Practice Area, Golf Clubs for hire, Trolley hire, Electric Buggy hire, Bar, Restaurant, Caddy service by arrangement

Accommodation, Food and Drink

Reference numbers below refer to detailed information provided in section 2

Accommodation

Berkeley Lodge, Adare, Co Limerick
Tel/Fax: 061 396857 Top-quality Bed & Breakfast Accommodation in six superbly appointed en suite bedrooms. Great breakfasts. Also self-catering cottage for 6. 388

Cedar Lodge, Patrickswell, Co Limerick
Tel: 061 355137 Five en suite rooms with tv in a farmhouse-style dwelling in a quiet setting not far from Limerick. Good choice for breakfast. 380

Clonunion House, Adare, Co Limerick
Tel: 061 396657 Farmhouse Accommodation in tranquil surroundings and mature gardens two kilometres from Adare. Four beautiful bedrooms, en suite and 1 with private bathroom. 387

Dunraven Arms Hotel, Adare, Co Limerick
Tel: 061 396633 Fax: 061 396541 Established in 1792, this is one of Ireland's greatest country hotels, with 76 beautifully appointed bedrooms and a top-class restaurant. 389

Fort Ann, Patrickswell, Co Limerick
Tel: 061 355162 A beautiful B&B farmhouse in a charming location by the main Limerick-Adare road. Four good-sized en suite bedrooms. 386

Hanratty's Hotel, Limerick, Co Limerick
Tel: 061 410999 A prime location off Limerick's main street for a 200-year-old family-run hotel with 22 well-appointed en suite bedrooms and a fine restaurant. 381

Food and Drink

Dunraven Arms Hotel, Adare, Co Limerick

Tel: 061 396633 Fax: 061 396541 Established in 1792, this is one of Ireland's greatest country hotels, with 76 beautifully appointed bedrooms and a top-class restaurant. 389

Hanratty's Hotel, Limerick, Co Limerick

Tel: 061 410999 A prime location off Limerick's main street for a 200-year-old family-run hotel with 22 well-appointed en suite bedrooms and a fine restaurant. 381

The Dark Horse, Patrickswell, Co Limerick

Tel: 061 355196 A cheerful pub with a sporting theme, serving great Guinness and day-long snacks. Evening restaurant next door. 385

The Peppercorn, Patrickswell, Co Limerick

Tel: 061 355999 Fine food and fast, friendly service in an intimate restaurant on the main Limerick-Cork road. Open for dinner Tuesday-Sunday. 392

The Wild Geese, Adare, Co Limerick

Tel/Fax: 061 396451 A terrific restaurant in a magnificent row of thatched cottages. Duck is the speciality, also goose and venison on a superb seasonal menu. 390

Limerick County

Limerick County Golf & Country Club, Ballyneety, Co Limerick

Tel: 061 351881 e-mail: lcgolf@iol.ie

Sec/Manager:	John Heaton
Professional:	Philip Murphy
Directions:	5 miles South of Limerick City Centre off the R512 to Kilmallock
Type of Course:	Parkland
Date Founded:	1994
No of Holes:	18
Length:	6711 yds (6137 mtrs)
Par:	72
SSS:	74
Green Fees:	Weekdays: £20 Weekends & Bank Holidays: £25
Visitors:	Welcome: Any Day, Prebooking required
Societies:	Welcome: Contact Club in advance
Facilities:	Chipping/Putting Area, Practice Area, Driving Range, Golf Clubs for hire, Trolley hire, Electric Buggy hire, Bar, Restaurant, Caddy service by arrangement, plusJacuzzi & Steam Room

Accommodation, Food and Drink

Reference numbers below refer to detailed information provided in section 2

Accommodation

Berkeley Lodge, Adare, Co Limerick

Tel/Fax: 061 396857 Top-quality Bed & Breakfast Accommodation in six superbly appointed en suite bedrooms. Great breakfasts. Also self-catering cottage for 6. 388

Cedar Lodge, Patrickswell, Co Limerick

Tel: 061 355137 Five en suite rooms with tv in a farmhouse-style dwelling in a quiet setting not far from Limerick. Good choice for breakfast. 380

Dunraven Arms Hotel, Adare, Co Limerick

Tel: 061 396633 Fax: 061 396541 Established in 1792, this is one of Ireland's greatest country hotels, with 76 beautifully appointed bedrooms and a top-class restaurant. 389

Fort Ann, Patrickswell, Co Limerick

Tel: 061 355162 A beautiful B&B farmhouse in a charming location by the main Limerick-Adare road. Four good-sized en suite bedrooms. 386

Hanratty's Hotel, Limerick, Co Limerick

Tel: 061 410999 A prime location off Limerick's main street for a 200-year-old family-run hotel with 22 well-appointed en suite bedrooms and a fine restaurant. 381

Food and Drink

Dunraven Arms Hotel, Adare, Co Limerick

Tel: 061 396633 Fax: 061 396541 Established in 1792, this is one of Ireland's greatest country hotels, with 76 beautifully appointed bedrooms and a top-class restaurant. 389

Hanratty's Hotel, Limerick, Co Limerick

Tel: 061 410999 A prime location off Limerick's main street for a 200-year-old family-run hotel with 22 well-appointed en suite bedrooms and a fine restaurant. 381

The Dark Horse, Patrickswell, Co Limerick

Tel: 061 355196 A cheerful pub with a sporting theme, serving great Guinness and day-long snacks. Evening restaurant next door. 385

The Peppercorn, Patrickswell, Co Limerick

Tel: 061 355999 Fine food and fast, friendly service in an intimate restaurant on the main Limerick-Cork road. Open for dinner Tuesday-Sunday. 392

The Wild Geese, Adare, Co Limerick

Tel/Fax: 061 396451 A terrific restaurant in a magnificent row of thatched cottages. Duck is the speciality, also goose and venison on a superb seasonal menu. 390

Newcastle West

Newcastle West Golf Club, Ardagh, Co Limerick

Tel: 069 76500

With a four-fold increase in membership since they expanded to 18 holes in 1994, Newcastle West GC are among the most progressive clubs in the south-west. The decision to move from the outskirts of the west Limerick town, down the road near the village of Ardagh, was taken in November 1991.

Once a stud-farm owned by racehorse breeder, Col Dick Cripps, the property still has stables which have since been converted into locker rooms downstairs and a bar and restaurant upstairs. And there are plans to link the stables with the main, cut-limestone house by building a first-floor bar, which would overlook the ninth and 18th greens.

The famous Ardagh Chalice, one of Ireland's greatest treasures, was found nearby in 1868 by a Mrs Quinn and her son, who were digging potatoes. Though west Limerick is noted for its heavy land and high rainfall, Rathgoonan is blessed with light, free draining soil.

It also has an abundance of mature, broadleaf trees which prompted locals to recall the words of Bobby Jones about his beloved Augusta National: "It seemed that this land had been lying there for years, just waiting for someone to lay a golf course upon it."

Designer Arthur Spring has given the members a delightfully challenging course in a beautiful, pastoral setting. A suitably optimistic mood is set by a shortish par five where the drive is hit from an elevated tee. After that, a strong variety is maintained through the 6,444 yards, off the back tees.

Sec/Manager:	Patrick Lyons
Professional:	Ger Jones
Directions:	3 miles East of Rathkeale off the N21 to Limerick
Type of Course:	Parkland
Date Founded:	1994
No of Holes:	18
Length:	6444yds (5892 mtrs)
Par:	71
SSS:	72
Green Fees:	£18 per day
Visitors:	Welcome: Any Day, Contact Club for weekend availability
Societies:	Welcome: Special concessions, Contact Club for details
Facilities:	Chipping/Putting Area, Practice Area, Driving Range, Golf Clubs for hire, Trolley hire, Bar, Restaurant, Caddy service by arrangement

Accommodation, Food and Drink

Reference numbers below refer to detailed information provided in section 2

Accommodation

Ashford, Templeglantine, Co Limerick
Tel: 069 84001/84311 A distinguished modern redbrick house in its own beautiful grounds. Five en suite B&B rooms. Fine furnishings and fittings.   383

Clonunion House, Adare, Co Limerick
Tel: 061 396657 Farmhouse Accommodation in tranquil surroundings and mature gardens two kilometres from Adare. Four beautiful bedrooms, 3 en suite and 1 with private bathroom.   387

Hanratty's Hotel, Limerick, Co Limerick
Tel: 061 410999 A prime location off Limerick's main street for a 200-year-old family-run hotel with 22 well-appointed en suite bedrooms and a fine restaurant.381

Leen's Hotel, Abbeyfeale, Co Limerick
Tel: 068 31121 Fax: 068 32550 A family-run hotel with 19 en sulte bedrooms and a restaurant serving generous helpings of local produce.   384

Rathkeale House Hotel, Rathkeale, Co Limerick
Tel: 069 63333 Fax: 069 63330 Purpose-built in 1997, the long, low hotel has welcoming family owners, 30 en suite bedrooms, fine restaurant and a lively bar. 391

Food and Drink

Hanratty's Hotel, Limerick, Co Limerick
Tel: 061 410999 A prime location off Limerick's main street for a 200-year-old family-run hotel with 22 well-appointed en suite bedrooms and a fine restaurant.381

Leen's Hotel, Abbeyfeale, Co Limerick
Tel: 068 31121 Fax: 068 32550 A family-run hotel with 19 en sulte bedrooms and a restaurant serving generous helpings of local produce.   384

Rathkeale House Hotel, Rathkeale, Co Limerick
Tel: 069 63333 Fax: 069 63330 Purpose-built in 1997, the long, low hotel has welcoming family owners, 30 en suite bedrooms, fine restaurant and a lively bar. 391

Rathbane

Rathbane Golf Club, Rathbane, Limerick, Co Limerick

Tel: 061 313655

Sec/Manager:	Jackie Cassidy
Professional:	Noel Cassidy
Directions:	2 miles south of Limerick off the R512 to Kilmallock
Type of Course:	Parkland
Date Founded:	1998
No of Holes:	18
Length:	6201 yds (5671 mtrs)
Par:	70
SSS:	68
Green Fees:	Weekdays: £11, Weekends and BAnk Holidays: £13
Visitors:	Welcome: Any Day
Societies:	Welcome: Contact Club for details
Facilities:	Chipping/Putting Area, Practice Area, Driving Range, Golf Clubs for hire, Trolley hire, Restaurant

Accommodation, Food and Drink

Reference numbers below refer to detailed information provided in section 2

Accommodation

Cedar Lodge, Patrickswell, Co Limerick
Tel: 061 355137 Five en suite rooms with tv in a farmhouse-style dwelling in a quiet setting not far from Limerick. Good choice for breakfast.   380

Fort Ann, Patrickswell, Co Limerick
Tel: 061 355162 A beautiful B&B farmhouse in a charming location by the main Limerick-Adare road. Four good-sized en suite bedrooms.   386

Hanratty's Hotel, Limerick, Co Limerick
Tel: 061 410999 A prime location off Limerick's main street for a 200-year-old family-run hotel with 22 well-appointed en suite bedrooms and a fine restaurant.381

Food and Drink

Hanratty's Hotel, Limerick, Co Limerick
Tel: 061 410999 A prime location off Limerick's main street for a 200-year-old family-run hotel with 22 well-appointed en suite bedrooms and a fine restaurant.381

Monasterboice Inn, Monasterboice, Co Louth
Tel: 041 9837383 An excellent restaurant and bar with a real Irish feel. Steaks a speciality. Located on the main Dublin-Belfast road (N1).   400

The Dark Horse, Patrickswell, Co Limerick
Tel: 061 355196 A cheerful pub with a sporting theme, serving great Guinness and day-long snacks. Evening restaurant next door.   385

The Peppercorn, Patrickswell, Co Limerick
Tel: 061 355999 Fine food and fast, friendly service in an intimate restaurant on the main Limerick-Cork road. Open for dinner Tuesday-Sunday.   392

LOUTH

On April 1st 1922, a golfer known in the US as Pat O'Hara, won the only North and South Professional Open to be played over 54 holes. And two years later, his brother Peter was tied seventh behind Cyril Walker in the US Open at Oakland Hills. As it happened, it took the passage of 77 years for Pat O'Hara's achievement to be emulated by Christy O'Connor Jnr, who became only the second Irishman to win an important professional event in the US, by capturing the State Farm Senior Classic in July 1999. But Peter's US Open performance has yet to be matched, though Darren Clarke came close by finishing in a share of 10th place behind Payne Stewart at Pinehurst No 2 in 1999.

They were, in fact, the O'Hare brothers from Greenore, Co Louth, but on arriving in the New World, they became known by what Americans considered to be the more acceptable Irish name of O'Hara. Another brother, James, remained at home and captured the Irish Professional Championship at Castlerock in 1920. At the time, they had a profound influence on the development of the game in their native county, especially around the Greenore area and in nearby Dundalk. And their legacy has been carried on at professional level by the McGuirk family, of whom Paddy is the current professional at Baltray, and by stalwarts of the amateur game such as the Garveys, Reddans and Gannons.

Carlingford, Co Louth

In fact few Irish counties can boast such a rich tradition in the Royal and Ancient game. And it would be difficult to rival the town of Drogheda and the village of Baltray, four miles away, as a hotbed of golf. It is also an area of considerable importance for its birdlife, which includes ducks, brent geese, black-tailed godwits, terns and ringed plovers. To most visitors, however, Baltray is synonymous with golf. And its international image has been enhanced considerably by having as one of its more prominent residents, the tournament professional, Des Smyth. Though a native of Mornington on the Meath side of the Boyne Estuary, Smyth had no difficulty in gaining acceptance among the golfing elite of Baltray, through his exploits with club and ball. And if that weren't enough, he married the former Vicki Reddan, daughter of Irish Women's champion and Curtis Cup representative, Clarrie Reddan.

Greenore, which gave the O'Hares to the golfing world, has an idyllic location, on the shores of Carlingford Lough. Across the estuary are the majestic Mournes while the Lough itself is one of the country's most important freight and passenger links with the west coast of Britain. Essentially an inland course, designed by Eddie Hackett, Greenore has an undeniable links texture, though its tall pine trees, in play on seven of the holes, are alien to such terrain. Its most famous hole is the par-three 14th, known as the Pig's Back and tucked in between the eighth and 12th, both of which are testing par fours.

St Laurences Gate, Drogheda, Co Louth

County Louth has a total of seven courses - Ardee, Co Louth (Baltray), Dundalk, Greenore, Killinbeg, Seapoint and Townley Hall. Of these, the adjoining links of Baltray and Seapoint undoubtedly represent the focal point of golfing activity in the county. But Louth has much more to offer.

As the smallest county in Ireland, it is known colloqually as the "Wee County", though it stretches from the banks of the Boyne in the south to Moiry Pass in the north. It has been settled from earliest times, evidence of which is to be found in the various burial tombs, ranging in size from the massive Passage graves of the Boyne Valley to the smaller Court Cairns and Dolmens of the Dundalk/Carlingford area. The county takes its name from Lugh, the great pagan god of the ancient Celts. Interestingly, it is a place-name found elsewhere in Europe in Lyons Loudon in France, Leiden in Holland and Liegnitz in Silesia.

Tourist attractions range from the so-called Jumping Church to the Proleek Cromlech. The former is a church ruin in the townland of Millockstown, a mile and a half sourth of Ardee. While no natural explanation is offered as to what caused the church to jump, local folklore has it that a victim of excommunication, was buried within its walls, causing the church to "jump" inwards, to exclude the grave. Excavated in 1953, some fragments of stained-glass windows and a silver penny of Edward III, were recovered. The famous Proleek Cromlech is to be found in the grounds of the Ballymascanlon

Mellifont Abbey, Co Louth

House Hotel, situated outside Dundalk within a mile of the roundabout where the road to Carlingford is linked to the N1. It is a huge, 40-ton capstone of the neolithic period, supported by three very slender pillars. A nearby rectangular gallery grave is believed to date back to the early bronze age.

The Hill of Faughart, three miles north of Dundalk, is one of the great historical sites of north Louth, with its iron-age hill fort, an early Christian ecclesiastical foundation associated with St Brigid, a Norman motte-castle and a medieval church ruin. Faughart stands along the so-called Slighe Midhluachra, the ancient roadway into Ulster, not far from the Moiry Pass which was otherwise known as the Gap of the North. It has been the scene of many notable battles, including the defeat of Edward Bruce, the Scots pretender to the throne of Ireland, in 1315. Though locals like to think of him as having been buried in the graveyard, Bruce's body was in fact quartered and the parts exhibited in various towns in Ireland, while his head was despatched to the King in London.

Faughart was later to be a departure point for English onslaughts on Ulster, the most notable being Mountjoy's passage through the Moiry Pass in 1600. And the last leader to travel that way with battle on his mind, was William of Orange, en route to the River Boyne and what was to become a rather significant meeting with King James. Happily, travellers to the Boyne these days, have more gentle pursuits in mind.

Location of Golf Courses

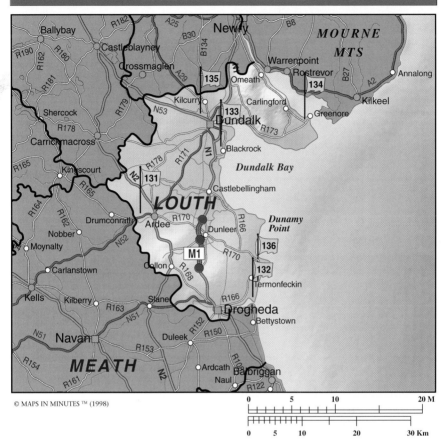

© MAPS IN MINUTES ™ (1998)

Ardee

Ardee Golf Club, Town Parks, County Louth
Tel: 041 685227

Sec/Manager:	Kevin McCarthy
Professional:	None
Directions:	½ mile north west of Ardee off the N52 to Kells
Type of Course:	Parkland
Date Founded:	1911
No of Holes:	18
Length:	6348yds (5805 mtrs)
Par:	70
SSS:	71
Green Fees:	Weekdays: £25 Weekends & Bank Holidays: £30
Visitors:	Welcome: Book in Advance
Societies:	Welcome: Book in Advance
Facilities:	Golf Clubs for hire, Trolley hire, Electric Buggy hire, Bar, Restaurant, Hotel/Accommodation on site

Accommodation, Food and Drink

Reference numbers below refer to detailed
information provided in section 2

Accommodation

Arradale House, Carrickmacross, Co Monaghan
Tel: 042 9661941 Ten en suite bedrooms for full or part board Accommodation on a
working farm in a beautiful setting of woods and lakes.   461

Sillougue House, Drogheda, Co Louth
Tel: 041 9845284 Luxurious B&B Accommodation in a striking modern house on the
main Dublin-Belfast road. 14 beautifully appointed en suite rooms with tv, phone
and hairdryer.   402

St Gobnaits, Drogheda, Co Louth
Tel: 041 9837844 A detached house by the N1, with four en suite B&B rooms. One
kilometre from town centre, close to golf courses and beaches.   403

Teach Cuailgne, Carlasntwon, Kells, Co Meath
Tel/Fax: 046 46621 Four rooms (two en suite) in a detached house in a pleasant
rural setting 3 miles from Kells. Excellent breakfasts.   435

The Heritage, Dundalk, Co Louth
Tel: 042 9335850 Keen golfers run this B&B house in a rural setting 1½ miles from
Dundalk. Five letting bedrooms, 3 en suite.   401

White Gables, Headfort Place, Kells, Co Meath
Tel: 046 40322 Three double rooms and a twin, all en suite, with tv. B&B, packed
lunches on request, dinner by arrangement for parties of 8 or more.   441

Food and Drink

Monasterboice Inn, Monasterboice, Co Louth
Tel: 041 9837383 An excellent restaurant and bar with a real Irish feel. Steaks a
speciality. Located on the main Dublin-Belfast road (N1).   400

County Louth

County Louth Golf Club, Balltray, Co Louth
Tel: 041 9822329

Often referred to as Baltray after the local
townland, this could reasonably be described as
one of Joe Carr's most popular stomping
grounds. It is where he won the East of Ireland

Amateur Strokepllay Championship on no fewer
than 12 occasions, starting with the inaugural
staging in 1941.

Visitors to Co Louth are often surprised that
such a challenging and interesting links should
have a rather modest international profile. The
reason has much to do with its secluded location at the mouth of the River Boyne, where
access is too restricted for major tournament
play.

Noted for the wonderful condition of its
greens and the splendid clubhouse fare, Co
Louth was founded in 1890. The present course,
however, did not come into being until 1938
when the celebrated design team of Tom
Simpson and his assistant Molly Gourlay upgraded the layout.

It has since been modified again, with a fine,
new opening hole situated closer to the clubhouse, while the old first is now the fourth. It
has five par-fives while two loops of nine - an
outward 37 followed by a homeward 36 - give
an overall par of 73.

Especially popular with golfers from Northern Ireland, Co Louth is home to some famous
Irish golfing families, notably the Gannons, the
Reddans and the Smyths. Clarrie Reddan is a
former Curtis Cup player while her son, Barry is
an Irish international who has also been club
captain. A daughter, Vicky, is married to Des
Smyth, the noted Irish tournament professional.

Sec/Manager:	Michael Delany
Professional:	Paddy McGuirk
Directions:	Five miles North East of Drogheda off the R167 on the North bank of the river estuary
Type of Course:	Links
Date Founded:	1892
No of Holes:	18
Length:	6783 yds (6202 mtrs)
Par:	73
SSS:	72
Green Fees:	Weekdays: £50 Weekends & Bank holidays: £60
Visitors:	Welcome: Contact Club in advance
Societies:	Welcome: Special Society Packages, Apply to Club for details

Facilities: Chipping/Putting Area, Practice Area, Golf Clubs for hire, Trolley hire, Electric Buggy hire, Bar, Restaurant, Caddy service by arrangement, plus Tennis & Residential Accommodation

Accommodation, Food and Drink

Reference numbers below refer to detailed information provided in section 2

Accommodation

Sillougue House, Drogheda, Co Louth

Tel: 041 9845284 Luxurious B&B Accommodation in a striking modern house on the main Dublin-Belfast road. 14 beautifully appointed en suite rooms with tv, phone and hairdryer. 402

St Gobnaits, Drogheda, Co Louth

Tel: 041 9837844 A detached house by the N1, with four en suite B&B rooms. One kilometre from town centre, close to golf courses and beaches. 403

Teach Cuailgne, Carlasntwon, Kells, Co Meath

Tel/Fax: 046 46621 Four rooms (two en suite) in a detached house in a pleasant rural setting 3 miles from Kells. Excellent breakfasts. 435

The Headfort Arms Hotel, Kells, Co Meath

Tel: 046 40063 A comfortable, welcoming, family-run hotel with 18 en suite bedrooms with tv and phone. Bistro, carvery, coffee shop, bar and nightclub. 438

White Gables, Headfort Place, Kells, Co Meath

Tel: 046 40322 Three double rooms and a twin, all en suite, with tv. B&B, packed lunches on request, dinner by arrangement for parties of 8 or more. 441

Food and Drink

Blackwater Inn, Kells, Co Meath

Tel: 046 40386 A town-centre pub with stone floor, heavy wooden furniture, live music and a good pint of stout. 443

Monasterboice Inn, Monasterboice, Co Louth

Tel: 041 9837383 An excellent restaurant and bar with a real Irish feel. Steaks a speciality. Located on the main Dublin-Belfast road (N1). 400

The Ground Floor Restaurant, Kells, Co Meath

Tel: 046 49688 A stylish modern restaurant with varied, good-value menus of Irish and International dishes. Full bar licence. 448

The Headfort Arms Hotel, Kells, Co Meath

Tel: 046 40063 A comfortable, welcoming, family-run hotel with 18 en suite bedrooms with tv and phone. Bistro, carvery, coffee shop, bar and nightclub. 438

Dundalk

Dundalk Golf Club, Blackrock, Dundalk, Co Louth

Tel: 042 9321731

Some novel initiatives allied to sound business sense have combined to give Dundalk one of Ireland's finest parkland courses. And it received appropriate approval from a sprinkling of the country's leading amateurs when the national Cups and Shields finals were played there in 1997.

Aware of the limitations of their original layout, officials raffled a yearling colt in 1963 and with the considerable proceeds of £1,500, they bought an additional 27 acres. And after the acquisition of further land, they embarked on a major redevelopment programme.

A new clubhouse and practice ground were constructed and in 1978, the design team of Peter Alliss and Dave Thomas were contracted to

upgrade the course. This was completed two years later when the new layout was officially opened by an exhibition fourball involving Christy O'Connor Snr, Des Smyth, Philip Walton and Ronan Rafferty.

Set out amid mature trees on classic, rolling terrain, the course offers a fine test, especially from the back tees which give it an overall length of 6,736 yards. But the real attraction of the venue lies in its fine conditioning, which is no more than one would expect.

A few years ago, the club inveigled greenkeeper Ollie English from Baltray, where he had wrought wonders with that fine links. And English has showed himself to be equally adept on parkland, judging by the improvements which came about at Dundalk. It is certainly unrecognisable from the modest stretch on which Harry Bradshaw won the Irish Professional Championship in 1953.

Sec/Manager:	Terry Sloane
Professional:	James Cassidy
Directions:	1 mile South of Dundalk off the R172 at Blackrock
Type of Course:	Parkland
Date Founded:	1904
No of Holes:	18
Length:	6736 yds (6160 mtrs)
Par:	72
SSS:	72
Green Fees:	Weekdays: £20 Weekends & Bank Holidays: £24
Visitors:	Welcome: Any Day except Tuesday & Saturday, Contact Club in advance
Societies:	Welcome: Contact Club in advance
Facilities:	Chipping/Putting Area, Practice Area, Golf Clubs for hire, Trolley hire, Bar, Restaurant

Accommodation, Food and Drink

Reference numbers below refer to detailed information provided in section 2

Accommodation

Arradale House, Carrickmacross, Co Monaghan

Tel: 042 9661941 Ten en suite bedrooms for full or part board Accommodation on a working farm in a beautiful setting of woods and lakes. 461

Sillougue House, Drogheda, Co Louth

Tel: 041 9845284 Luxurious B&B Accommodation in a striking modern house on the main Dublin-Belfast road. 14 beautifully appointed en suite rooms with tv, phone and hairdryer. 402

The Heritage, Dundalk, Co Louth

Tel: 042 9335850 Keen golfers run this B&B house in a rural setting 1½ miles from Dundalk. Five letting bedrooms, 3 en suite. 401

Food and Drink

Archways, Kilkeel, Co Down

Tel: 028 41764112 A spacious restaurant with bar and lounge. Daily lunches, evening à la carte; entertainment. 834

Monasterboice Inn, Monasterboice, Co Louth

Tel: 041 9837383 An excellent restaurant and bar with a real Irish feel. Steaks a speciality. Located on the main Dublin-Belfast road (N1). 400

The Kilbroney Bar and Restaurant, Rostrevor, Co Down
Tel: 02841 738390 Town-centre restaurant, bar and beer garden. Food is served all
day, every day from an à la carte menu. 830

Greenore

Greenore Golf Club, Greenore, Co Louth
Tel: 042 9373678/9373212

Sec/Manager:	Roisin Daly
Professional:	None
Directions:	12 miles South East of Newry off R173 and 11 miles North East of Dundalk
Type of Course:	Links and Woodland
Date Founded:	1896
No of Holes:	18
Length:	6514 yds (5956 mtrs)
Par:	71
SSS:	71
Green Fees:	Weekdays: £18 Weekends & Bank Holidays: £25
Visitors:	Welcome: Contact in advance for weekend availability
Societies:	Welcome: Prebooking required
Facilities:	Chipping/Putting Area, Practice Area, Trolley hire, Bar, Restaurant

Accommodation, Food and Drink

Reference numbers below refer to detailed
information provided in section 2

Accommodation

Arradale House, Carrickmacross, Co Monaghan
Tel: 042 9661941 Ten en suite bedrooms for full or part board Accommodation on a
working farm in a beautiful setting of woods and lakes. 461
Sillougue House, Drogheda, Co Louth
Tel: 041 9845284 Luxurious B&B Accommodation in a striking modern house on the
main Dublin-Belfast road. 14 beautifully appointed en suite rooms with tv, phone
and hairdryer. 402
The Heritage, Dundalk, Co Louth
Tel: 042 9335850 Keen golfers run this B&B house in a rural setting 1½ miles from
Dundalk. Five letting bedrooms, 3 en suite. 401

Food and Drink

Archways, Kilkeel, Co Down
Tel: 028 41764112 A spacious restaurant with bar and lounge. Daily lunches, evening
à la carte; entertainment. 834
Monasterboice Inn, Monasterboice, Co Louth
Tel: 041 9837383 An excellent restaurant and bar with a real Irish feel. Steaks a
speciality. Located on the main Dublin-Belfast road (N1). 400
The Kilbroney Bar and Restaurant, Rostrevor, Co Down
Tel: 028 41738390 Town-centre restaurant, bar and beer garden. Food is served all
day, every day from an à la carte menu. 830

Killinbeg

Killinbeg Park Golf Club, Killin Park, Killin,
Dundalk, Co Louth
Tel: 042 9339303

Sec/Manager:	Pat Reynolds
Professional:	None
Directions:	2 miles West off the N53 Dundalk to Castleblayney Road
Type of Course:	Parkland
Date Founded:	1991
No of Holes:	18
Length:	5158 yds (4716 mtrs)
Par:	69
SSS:	65
Green Fees:	Weekdays: £10 Weekends & Bank Holidays: £14
Visitors:	Welcome: Any Day
Societies:	Welcome: Contact club in advance
Facilities:	Golf Clubs for hire, Trolley hire, Bar, Restaurant

Accommodation, Food and Drink

Reference numbers below refer to detailed
information provided in section 2

Accommodation

Arradale House, Carrickmacross, Co Monaghan
Tel: 042 9661941 Ten en suite bedrooms for full or part board Accommodation on a
working farm in a beautiful setting of woods and lakes. 461
Sillougue House, Drogheda, Co Louth
Tel: 041 9845284 Luxurious B&B Accommodation in a striking modern house on the
main Dublin-Belfast road. 14 beautifully appointed en suite rooms with tv, phone
and hairdryer. 402
The Heritage, Dundalk, Co Louth
Tel: 042 9335850 Keen golfers run this B&B house in a rural setting 1½ miles from
Dundalk. Five letting bedrooms, 3 en suite. 401

Food and Drink

Archways, Kilkeel, Co Down
Tel: 028 41764112 A spacious restaurant with bar and lounge. Daily lunches, evening
à la carte; entertainment. 834
Monasterboice Inn, Monasterboice, Co Louth
Tel: 041 9837383 An excellent restaurant and bar with a real Irish feel. Steaks a
speciality. Located on the main Dublin-Belfast road (N1). 400
The Kilbroney Bar and Restaurant, Rostrevor, Co Down
Tel: 028 41738390 Town-centre restaurant, bar and beer garden. Food is served all
day, every day from an à la carte menu. 830

Seapoint

Seapoint Golf Club, Termonfeckin, Drogheda,
County Louth
Tel: 041 9822333

Des Smyth gained a rare distinction in 1995
when he captured an important title on a course
he had designed only six years previously. That
was when Seapoint played host to the Glen
Dimplex Matchplay Tournament in which
Smyth beat Paul McGinley in the final.

Though it borders the Co Louth links, most
of the early holes at Seapoint appear heathland
in character. Indeed it is only on the last four
holes that one encounters the sort of dunes
which characterise the neighbouring stretch. Yet
Smyth insists that the entire course has a sand
base of up to three feet in depth.

Par:	72
SSS:	71
Green Fees:	Weekdays: £25 Weekends & Bank Holidays: £30
Visitors:	Welcome: Book in Advance
Societies:	Welcome: Book in Advance
Facilities:	Golf Clubs for hire, Trolley hire, Electric Buggy hire, Bar, Restaurant, Hotel/Accommodation on site

Accommodation, Food and Drink

Reference numbers below refer to detailed
information provided in section 2

Accommodation

Annesbrook, Duleek, Co Meath
Tel: 041 9823293 A classic 18th-century porticoed country house in ten acres of grounds. Ten en suite rooms for Bed & Breakfast & dinner menu.   447

Castle View House, Slane, Co Meath
Tel: 041 9824510 A lovely chalet-bungalow on an elevated site with a large garden. Five en suite bedrooms including triples.   444

San Giovanni House, Slane, Co Meath
Tel: 041 9824147 Five en suite bedrooms in a large modern Bed & Breakfast house on a mushroom farm near several historic sites.   446

Sillougue House, Drogheda, Co Louth
Tel: 041 9845284 Luxurious B&B Accommodation in a striking modern house on the main Dublin-Belfast road. 14 beautifully appointed en suite rooms with tv, phone and hairdryer.   402

St Gobnaits, Drogheda, Co Louth
Tel: 041 9837844 A detached house by the N1, with four en suite B&B rooms. One kilometre from town centre, close to golf courses and beaches.   403

Food and Drink

Annesbrook, Duleek, Co Meath
Tel: 041 9823293 A classic 18th-century porticoed country house in ten acres of grounds. Ten en suite rooms for Bed & Breakfast & dinner menu.   447

Monasterboice Inn, Monasterboice, Co Louth
Tel: 041 9837383 An excellent restaurant and bar with a real Irish feel. Steaks a speciality. Located on the main Dublin-Belfast road.   400

Ryan's Bar and Restaurant, Navan, Co Meath
Tel/Fax: 046 78333 A smart modern bar and restaurant serving an excellent range of drinks and snacks. The owner is a keen golfer.   432

Declan Branigan, an expert on soil structure, collaborated with Smyth to ensure that Seapoint was built to the highest standards. For his part, Smyth is acknowledged as an eminently sensible designer who produces very playable layouts. And their success can be gauged from the popularity of the venue with visiting players.

Seapoint is located near the village of Termonfeckin, which can be reached from Baltray or from the northern side of Drogheda. Construction began in 1989 and the course was opened for play in 1993 at a time when Ireland was enjoying a major boom in golf-course development.

The course is notable for the quality of its greens and the excellent drainage which makes it an enjoyable challenge, even in wet conditions. And when the competitor is battling to achieve a crucial edge over the finishing stretch,

the testing nature of the cleverly worked duneland can be fully appreciated.

Sec/Manager:	Kevin Carrie
Professional:	David Carroll
Directions:	4 miles north east of Drogheda off the R166 to Clogherhead
Type of Course:	Links
Date Founded:	1993
No of Holes:	18
Length:	6932 yds (6339 mtrs)

MAYO

Looking at a map with Dublin as a starting-point, it seems a long way to travel. But the development of Knock Airport in the heart of the county, with regular flights to the UK and seasonal flights to the Continent, has made Mayo admirably accessible to the tourist with golf or other activities in mind. For those who still prefer to travel by road, there is the prospect of some dramatic changes in scenery, especially if one happens to be heading for the extreme north-western seaboard. There, at Belmullet, is the location of the spectacular Carne links, which has become one of the West's biggest attractions.

Driving from Ballina, the thrill of adventure is sparked by the sight of Ireland's first windfarm, with propellor blades turning lazily in the breeze, while sunlit hills in the distance take on dazzling autumnal shades of brown, gold and light green. Further along the road to Bangor is the electricity power station at Bellacorick, where smoke from its high chimneys drifts skywards. And all the while on the left-hand side, there is the ever-present Owenmore River, until the N59 is abandoned for the R313 and the final run into Belmullet. Approaching the town, Blacksod Bay stretched away to the left, providing the first sight of the Atlantic. From there, it is only a short drive to Carne and its charming clubhouse on elevated ground, overlooking the links.

Mayo is a county of golfing contrasts, from the traditional parkland of Claremorris, Ballina, Ballinrobe and Castlebar, to parkland-by-the-sea at Westport and then the classic duneland of Carne.

Croagh Patrick, Co Mayo

But it has much to offer besides, from game, coarse and sea angling, to charming walks. And, of course, there are the places of pilgrimage. Six miles from Westport, on the Louisburgh road, is Croagh Patrick, rising to a height of 2,510 feet. Overlooking Clew Bay, it is where St Patrick is reputed to have spent the 40 days of Lent in 441 AD, praying and fasting so that he would be successful in his mission to convert Ireland to the Christian faith. Throughout the year, people of all ages and various levels of devotion, make the physically demanding but spiritually rewarding climb to the summit, as they believe Patrick once did. But the last Sunday of July, known as Reek Sunday, is when the main, annual pilgrimage takes place. On that day, as many as 60,000 people from far and wide, make the ascent, starting at Murrisk Abbey. They begin their trek before drawn, with hand-held lights. And when the area is eventually bathed in daylight, there are stunning views of Clew Bay and its reputed 365 islands, one for every day of the year. A recent archaeological survey uncovered a range of ancient sites throughout the mountain and its hinterland. These included fulacht fiadha, which were ancient cooking sites; megalithic tombs, standing stones, burial mounds, ringforts, monastic sites and children's burial grounds.

The other famous place of pilgrimage in Mayo is the Marian Shrine of Knock, which is visited by more than half a million people each year. It commemorates an apparition in 1879, when 15 local people of varying ages reported seeing the Virgin Mary, with St Joseph on her right and

Westport, Co Mayo

St John the Evangelist on her left, his left hand holding an open book, while the right hand was raised as if he were preaching. To the left of St John they saw an altar on which was a lamb, a large cross and hovering angels. And the entire apparition, which they reportedly watched for two hours in pouring rain, took place at the gable of the parish church. As it happens, more and more visitors are using Knock International Airport not only to visit the shrine, but as a gateway to a region of stunning beauty.

Apart from its golf, Mayo can justifiably claim to be a game angler's paradise. The county has four of the great western lakes - Conn, Cullin, Carra and Mask - all of which are renowned for their brown trout. Then there are numerous rivers, along with small, mountain lakes in remote locations. From a sporting standpoint, Westport, with a population of 4,250, offers an ideal holiday base, with extensive accommodation. Designated as one of the Irish Tourist Board's so-called Heritage Towns, it is one of the few planned developments in the country, having been designed by a certain James Wyatt in the 18th century. Its features include an elegant, tree-lined boulevard known as The Mall; the busy, bustling Bridge Street and the town's square, known as The Octagon, where a weekly market is held. Five miles to the south-west is Murrisk, home to the ruin of a 15th century Augistinian Friary, overlooking Clew Bay.

Then, offshore, there is Achill which, measuring 15 miles by 12, is Ireland's largest island. Connected to the mainland by a bridge, it offers magnificent, cliff scenery along with long, sandy beaches, picturesque villages and a wealth of historical monuments. A particularly attractive island village is Keel, where the three miles of sandy beach is known as Trawmore (Gaelic for the big strand). Two miles further on is the village of Dooagh, while Achill's north shore is dominated by Dugort town at the foot of the Slievemore Mountains.

The county is also rich in folklore, especially about Ireland's most notorious woman pirate, Granuaile, or Grace O'Malley, who ruled the waters around Mayo in the 16th century. In fact when

Keem Bay, Achill Island, Co Mayo

the English viceroy, Sir Richard Bingham, began suppressing local chieftains in 1593, Granuaile travelled to London where she sought and gained protection from Queen Elizabeth I. After being given an assurance that she would be left to live in peace, she returned to her beloved Mayo where she died in 1603. In more recent times, emigrants from the county have also been able to realise this ambition, through the new-found strength of the Irish economy.

Location of Golf Courses

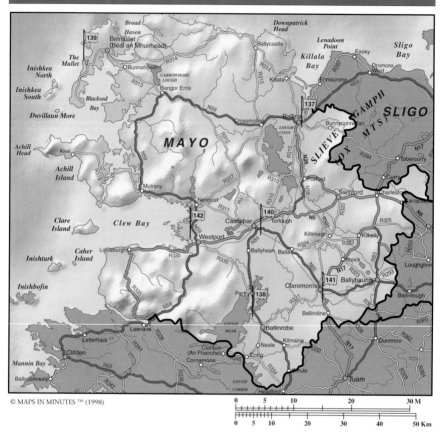

© MAPS IN MINUTES ™ (1998)

Ballina

Ballina Golf Club, Mossgrove, Shanaghy, Ballina, Co Mayo

Tel: 096 21050

Sec/Manager:	Padhreig Connolly
Professional:	None
Directions:	I mile East of Ballina off the R294 to Bunnyconnellan
Type of Course:	Parkland
Date Founded:	1910
No of Holes:	18
Length:	6103 yds (5580 mtrs)
Par:	71
SSS:	69
Green Fees:	1st Oct – 31st March: Weekdays: £12 Weekends & Bank Holidays £16; 1st April-30th Sept : Weekdays: £16 Weekends & Bank Holidays: £IR20
Visitors:	Welcome: Any Day, Restrictions on Sunday. Check availability in advance
Societies:	Welcome: Special concessions, Contact Club for details
Facilities:	Chipping/Putting Area, Practice Area, Golf Clubs for hire, Trolley hire, Electric Buggy hire, Bar, plus (Restaurant, can be booked in advance for societies)

Accommodation, Food and Drink

Reference numbers below refer to detailed information provided in section 2

Accommodation

Ashleam House, Ballina, Co Mayo
Tel: 096 22406 Six letting bedrooms (4 en suite) in a neat Bed & Breakfast house south of Ballina and only yards from the River Moy. 414

Castle Arms Hotel, Enniscrone, Co Sligo
Tel/Fax: 096 36156 A family-run hotel in the heart of Enniscrone. 27 en suite bedrooms with tv and telephone. Restaurant and bar. Seconds from the beach. 511

Cill Aodáin, Kiltimagh, Co Mayo
Tel: 094 81761 A friendly hotel in a small town in the heart of the county. Standard or superior rooms available. Continental and country cuisine. Bar. 424

Claddagh House, Ballina, Co Mayo
Tel: 096 71670 Six bedrooms, all en suite, in a stand-alone Bed & Breakfast establishment on the Sligo road out of Ballina. Easy parking. 410

Downhill Inn, Ballina, Co Mayo
Tel: 096 73444 Fax: 096 73411 A welcoming modern hotel with 45 rooms, all with two beds, en suite bath/shower, tv, telephone. Restaurant, bar, patio, gardens. 413

Enniscoe House, Ballina, Crossmolina, Co Mayo
Tel: 096 31112 A 17th-century house of great charm on the shores of Lough Conn. Six en suite bedrooms, also 3 courtyard apartments. 411

Quignalegan House, Ballina Road, Co Mayo
Tel/Fax: 096 71644 Five en suite bedrooms in a purpose-built modern house with imposing grounds and a huge car park. 412

St Martins, Enniscrone, Co Mayo
Tel: 096 36111 A prime site on the main street for a long, single-storey house offering Bed & Breakfast. Seven en suite rooms. 513

Suncroft, Ballina, Co Mayo
Tel: 096 21573 Excellent modern B&B townhouse in the shadow of the Cathedral. Renowned breakfasts. Popular base for anglers. 423

Food and Drink

Castle Arms Hotel, Enniscrone, Co Sligo
Tel/Fax: 096 36156 A family-run hotel in the heart of Enniscrone. 27 en suite bedrooms with tv and telephone. Restaurant and bar. Seconds from the beach. 511

Cill Aodáin, Kiltimagh, Co Mayo
Tel: 094 81761 A friendly hotel in a small town in the heart of the county. Standard or superior rooms available. Continental and country cuisine. Bar. 424

Downhill Inn, Ballina, Co Mayo
Tel: 096 73444 Fax: 096 73411 A welcoming modern hotel with 45 rooms, all with two beds, en suite bath/shower, tv, telephone. Restaurant, bar, patio, gardens. 413

Lavelle's Erris Bar, Belmullet, Co Mayo
Tel: 097 82222 Fax: 097 81056 A typical Irish pub with bags of atmosphere. Food served all day & high-season restaurant. Coffee shop adjacent. 419

Ballinrobe

Ballinrobe Golf Club, Clooncastle, Balinrobe, County Mayo

Tel: 092 41118

Sec/Manager:	John Feerick
Professional:	David Kearney
Directions:	I mile north west of Ballinrobe off the N84 to Castlebar
Type of Course:	Parkland
Date Founded:	1895
No of Holes:	18
Length:	6609 yds (6043 mtrs)
Par:	73
SSS:	72
Green Fees:	Weekdays: £15 Weekends & Bank Holidays: £18
Visitors:	Welcome: Book in Advance
Societies:	Welcome: Book in Advance
Facilities:	Driving Range, Trolley hire, Electric Buggy hire, Bar, Restaurant

Accommodation, Food and Drink

Reference numbers below refer to detailed information provided in section 2

Accommodation

Eskerville, Knock, Co Mayo
Tel: 094 88413 A low-rise Bed & Breakfast house 10 minutes walk from Knock centre. Six bedrooms, four en suite. Scenic location with private gardens. 422

River Walk House, Oughterard, Co Galway
Tel: 091 552788 Eight en suite rooms in a Bed & Breakfast two minutes from the village centre. Great scenery, plenty of sporting activity. 266

Roundstone House Hotel, Roundstone, Co Galway
Tel: 095 35864 Fax: 095 35944 Twelve rooms, all en suite, in a family-run hotel in a delightful fishing village. Comfort, care and good food are keynotes. 262

St Anthony's, Westport, Co Mayo
Tel: 098 28887 Fax: 098 25172 A manse house built in 1820, now a characterful Bed & Breakfast with six individually-appointed bedrooms. Also self-catering unit. 416

The Boat Inn, Oughterard, Co Galway
Tel: 091 552196 Fax: 091 502694 Eleven modern en suite bedrooms in a prime site in the centre of the village. Restaurant with excellent menus; bars; terrace. 276

Valley Lodge, Face Field, Claremorris, Co Mayo
Tel: 094 65180 Five letting rooms offer flexible Accommodation in a modern B&B farmhouse 5 miles outside Claremorris on the Castlebar road (N60). 420

Western Hotel, Claremorris, Co Mayo
Tel: 094 62011 Fax: 094 62838 Main street hotel with 18 en suite bedrooms, busy bars and a restaurant specialising in steaks. Music session Wednesday night. 421

Food and Drink

Roundstone House Hotel, Roundstone, Co Galway
Tel: 095 35864 Fax: 095 35944 Twelve rooms, all en suite, in a family-run hotel in a delightful fishing village. Comfort, care and good food are keynotes.   262

The Boat Inn, Oughterard, Co Galway
Tel: 091 552196 Fax: 091 502694 Eleven modern en suite bedrooms in a prime site in the centre of the village. Restaurant with excellent menus; bars; terrace.   276

Western Hotel, Claremorris, Co Mayo
Tel: 094 62011 Fax: 094 62838 Main street hotel with 18 en suite bedrooms, busy bars and a restaurant specialising in steaks. Music session Wednesday night.   421

Belmullet (Carne)

Belmullet Golf Club, Belmullet, Co Mayo

Tel: 097 82292

Towering dunes has become something of a cliche in describing links courses but at Carne, the term seems almost inadequate. One's surprise stems from the fact that the terrain, all 270 acres of it, has been revealed to outsiders, only since the official opening of the golf course four years ago.

On entering the clubhouse, there is no doubt about its Gaeltacht (Irish speaking) location. A door marked "Seomra Hackett" leads to the bar and dining area where, over the fireplace at the far end, is a large, framed portrait of Eddie Hackett.

Apparently the course designer would sit at a small table, surveying his handiwork. And it's not difficult to imagine him taking a long, proud look at some of the finest work of his illustrious career. Carne, quite simply, remains the most stunning "discovery" I have made in golf.

There is quite a degree of blindness on the course, much of which could easily be eliminated by modern, earthmoving equipment. But Hackett insisted on maintaining a traditional look, with a level of blindness that's accepted at places such as Lahinch and Royal Co Down.

In the event, the nines at Carne are delightfully contrasting, the outward journey being set against the backdrop of Blacksod Bay, while the homeward loop, with dunes up to 70 feet high, winds it way out to the Atlantic coast and back in again. If Waterville is to be acknowledged as the first, major triumph for Hackett's design skills, Carne must surely rank as a fitting swansong.

Sec/Manager:	Evelyn Keane
Professional:	None
Directions:	On the Mullet Peninsula three miles South West of Belmullet off the R313
Type of Course:	Links
Date Founded:	1925
No of Holes:	18
Length:	6691 yds (6119 mtrs)
Par:	72
SSS:	71
Green Fees:	£ 25 per day
Visitors:	Welcome: Any Day, Check tee-times in advance
Societies:	Welcome: Special concessions, Apply to Club for details
Facilities:	Chipping/Putting Area, Practice Area, Golf Clubs for hire, Trolley hire, Electric Buggy hire, Bar, Restaurant

Accommodation, Food and Drink

Reference numbers below refer to detailed information provided in section 2

Accommodation

Castle Arms Hotel, Enniscrone, Co Sligo
Tel/Fax: 096 36156 A family-run hotel in the heart of Enniscrone. 27 en suite bedrooms with tv and telephone. Restaurant and bar. Seconds from the beach.   511

Downhill Inn, Ballina, Co Mayo
Tel: 096 73444 Fax: 096 73411 A welcoming modern hotel with 45 rooms, all with two beds, en suite bath/shower, tv, telephone. Restaurant, bar, patio, gardens.   413

Drom Caoin, Belmullet, Co Mayo

Tel/Fax: 097 81195 A striking modern house offering a choice of Bed & Breakfast (evening meals with notice) or self-catering Accommodation. Golfing breaks a speciality. 418

Drumshinnagh House, Castlebar, Co Mayo
Tel/Fax: 094 24211 A fine modern B&B house on an elevated site. Seven en suite bedrooms with tv. Private car park. Access for disabled guests. 415

Enniscoe House, Ballina, Crossmolina, Co Mayo
Tel: 096 31112 A 17th-century house of great charm on the shores of Lough Conn. Six en suite bedrooms, also 3 courtyard apartments. 411

Suncroft, Ballina, Co Mayo
Tel: 096 21573 Excellent modern B&B townhouse in the shadow of the Cathedral. Renowned breakfasts. Popular base for anglers. 423

Food and Drink

Castle Arms Hotel, Enniscrone, Co Sligo
Tel/Fax: 096 36156 A family-run hotel in the heart of Enniscrone. 27 en suite bedrooms with tv and telephone. Restaurant and bar. Seconds from the beach. 511

Downhill Inn, Ballina, Co Mayo
Tel: 096 73444 Fax: 096 73411 A welcoming modern hotel with 45 rooms, all with two beds, en suite bath/shower, tv, telephone. Restaurant, bar, patio, gardens. 413

Lavelle's Erris Bar, Belmullet, Co Mayo
Tel: 097 82222 Fax: 097 81056 A typical Irish pub with bags of atmosphere. Food served all day & high-season restaurant. Coffee shop adjacent. 419

Castlebar

Castlebar Golf Club, Hawthorn Avenue, Rocklands, Castlebar, County Mayo
Tel: 094 21649

Sec/Manager:	Enda Lonergan
Professional:	None
Directions:	2 miles south east of Castlebar off the N84 to Ballinrobe
Type of Course:	Parkland
Date Founded:	1910
No of Holes:	18
Length:	6500 yds (5944 mtrs)
Par:	71
SSS:	72
Green Fees:	Weekdays: £20 Weekends & Bank Holidays: £25
Visitors:	Welcome: No visitors on Sundays
Societies:	Welcome: Book in Advance
Facilities:	Chipping/Putting Area, Golf Clubs for hire, Trolley hire, Electric Buggy hire, Bar, Restaurant, Caddy service by arrangement

Accommodation, Food and Drink
Reference numbers below refer to detailed information provided in section 2

Accommodation
Ashleam House, Ballina, Co Mayo
Tel: 096 22406 Six letting bedrooms (4 en suite) in a neat Bed & Breakfast house south of Ballina and only yards from the River Moy. 414

Ben View House, Clifden, Co Galway
Tel: 095 21256 Fax: 095 21226 A charming mid 19th-century town house with nine en suite bedrooms for Bed & Breakfast. Same family owners since 1926. 272

Cill Aodáin, Kiltimagh, Co Mayo
Tel: 094 81761 A friendly hotel in a small town in the heart of the county. Standard or superior rooms available. Continental and country cuisine. Bar. 424

Claddagh House, Ballina, Co Mayo
Tel: 096 71670 Six bedrooms, all en suite, in a stand-alone Bed & Breakfast establishment on the Sligo road out of Ballina. Easy parking. 410

Clifden Glen, Clifden, Co Galway
Tel: 095 21401 Fax: 095 21818 A holiday village on a private estate just outside Clifden. ApartHotel cottage suites, self-catering lodges, restaurant, pub, tennis. 271

Cregg House, Clifden, Co Galway
Tel: 095 21326 Great views of the beautiful Connemara countryside from a handsome modern Bed & Breakfast house with six en suite bedrooms. 269

Drom Caoin, Belmullet, Co Mayo
Tel/Fax: 097 81195 A striking modern house offering a choice of Bed & Breakfast (evening meals with notice) or self-catering Accommodation. Golfing breaks a speciality. 418

Drumshinnagh House, Castlebar, Co Mayo
Tel/Fax: 094 24211 A fine modern B&B house on an elevated site. Seven en suite bedrooms with tv. Private car park. Access for disabled guests. 415

Eskerville, Knock, Co Mayo
Tel: 094 88413 A low-rise Bed & Breakfast house 10 minutes walk from Knock centre. Six bedrooms, four en suite. Scenic location with private gardens. 422

Lough Fadda House, Clifden, Co Galway
Tel: 095 21165 Two acres of grounds make an attractive setting for a modern detached house with six en suite bedrooms. 274

Mal Dua House, Clifden, Co Galway
Tel: 095 21171 Luxury, comfort and hospitality in abundance in a distinguished house in attractive grounds just outside Clifden. 14 en suite bedrooms. 281

Quignalegan House, Ballina Road, Co Mayo
Tel/Fax: 096 71644 Five en suite bedrooms in a purpose-built modern house with imposing grounds and a huge car park. 412

St Anthony's, Westport, Co Mayo
Tel: 098 28887 Fax: 098 25172 A manse house built in 1820, now a characterful Bed & Breakfast with six individually-appointed bedrooms. Also self-catering unit. 416

The Pass Inn, Kylemore, Co Galway
Tel: 095 41141 Fax: 095 41377 Family-run 11-bedroom hotel with restaurant in a beautiful location between the hills and lakes of Connemara. 277

Travellers Friend, Castlebar, Co Mayo
Tel/Fax: 094 23111 Hotel & Theatre complex near the town centre. Well-equipped en suite bedrooms, restaurant, bar, business centre, popular theatre. 417

Valley Lodge, Face Field, Claremorris, Co Mayo
Tel: 094 65180 Five letting rooms offer flexible Accommodation in a modern B&B farmhouse 5 miles outside Claremorris on the Castlebar road (N60). 420

Western Hotel, Claremorris, Co Mayo
Tel: 094 62011 Fax: 094 62838 Main street hotel with 18 en suite bedrooms, busy bars and a restaurant specialising in steaks. Music session Wednesday night. 421

Food and Drink
Cill Aodáin, Kiltimagh, Co Mayo
Tel: 094 81761 A friendly hotel in a small town in the heart of the county. Standard or superior rooms available. Continental and country cuisine. Bar. 424

Clifden Glen, Clifden, Co Galway
Tel: 095 21401 Fax: 095 21818 A holiday village on a private estate just outside Clifden. ApartHotel cottage suites, self-catering lodges, restaurant, pub, tennis. 271

The Pass Inn, Kylemore, Co Galway
Tel: 095 41141 Fax: 095 41377 Family-run 11-bedroom hotel with restaurant in a beautiful location between the hills and lakes of Connemara. 277

Travellers Friend, Castlebar, Co Mayo
Tel/Fax: 094 23111 Hotel & Theatre complex near the town centre. Well-equipped en suite bedrooms, restaurant, bar, business centre, popular theatre. 417

Western Hotel, Claremorris, Co Mayo
Tel: 094 62011 Fax: 094 62838 Main street hotel with 18 en suite bedrooms, busy bars and a restaurant specialising in steaks. Music session Wednesday night. 421

Claremorris

Claremorris Golf Club, Castlemargaret, Claremorris, Co Mayo
Tel: 094 71527

After nearly 80 years as a nine-hole facility, Claremorris GC had the official opening of their new 18 last July. And to ensure that the word spreads far and wide throughout County Mayo and beyond, they have advertised the fact by placing a large bill-board at the entrance to the club driveway on the N17, outside the town.

Tom Craddock, former Walker Cup player turned golf-course designer, did a splendid job of integrating the new holes into the existing, nine-hole layout. But much of the actual physical work was done by the members, men and women who didn't hesitate to help in bringing a major undertaking to a successful conclusion.

Among other things, the club can boast 10 native Swiss as overseas members. Each has paid £1,000 each for the privilege, having been encouraged by a Zurich-based brother of a former club captain.

Apart from the rolling nature of the terrain, there are mature ash and sycamore trees, along with numerous water features provided by tributaries to the River Robe, which borders the course behind the 15th tee. Particularly interesting is

the 440-yard sixth hole, where the tee is on the highest point of the course.

A wonderfully-testing par four, it offers as a bonus, a stunning view of Caltra Hill in the distance, while to the rear is the old Oranmore and Brown estate. And to cap it all, there is the overall quality of the greens which are quite simply outstanding and a credit to the head greenkeeper, Joe Disken.

Sec/Manager:	Willy Feely
Professional:	David Karney
Directions:	2 miles south of Claremorris on the N17 road to Galway
Type of Course:	Parkland
Date Founded:	1927
No of Holes:	18
Length:	6889 yds (6300 mtrs)
Par:	73
SSS:	72
Green Fees:	Weekdays: £15 Weekends & Bank Holidays: £18
Visitors:	Welcome: Weekdays: Contact Club for weekend availability
Societies:	Welcome: Weekdays: Special concessions, Apply to Club for details
Facilities:	Chipping/Putting Area, Practice Area, Golf Clubs for hire, Trolley hire, Electric Buggy hire, Bar, Restaurant

Accommodation, Food and Drink

Reference numbers below refer to detailed information provided in section 2

Accommodation

Cill Aodáin, Kiltimagh, Co Mayo
Tel: 094 81761 A friendly hotel in a small town in the heart of the county. Standard or superior rooms available. Continental and country cuisine. Bar.   424

Drumshinnagh House, Castlebar, Co Mayo
Tel/Fax: 094 24211 A fine modern B&B house on an elevated site. Seven en suite bedrooms with tv. Private car park. Access for disabled guests.   415

Eskerville, Knock, Co Mayo
Tel: 094 88413 A low-rise Bed & Breakfast house 10 minutes walk from Knock centre. Six bedrooms, four en suite. Scenic location with private gardens.   422

St Anthony's, Westport, Co Mayo
Tel: 098 28887 Fax: 098 25172 A manse house built in 1820, now a characterful Bed & Breakfast with six individually-appointed bedrooms. Also self-catering unit.   416

Travellers Friend, Castlebar, Co Mayo
Tel/Fax: 094 23111 Hotel & Theatre complex near the town centre. Well-equipped en suite bedrooms, restaurant, bar, business centre, popular theatre.   417

Valley Lodge, Face Field, Claremorris, Co Mayo
Tel: 094 65180 Five letting rooms offer flexible Accommodation in a modern B&B farmhouse 5 miles outside Claremorris on the Castlebar road (N60).   420

Western Hotel, Claremorris, Co Mayo
Tel: 094 62011 Fax: 094 62838 Main street hotel with 18 en suite bedrooms, busy bars and a restaurant specialising in steaks. Music session Wednesday night.   421

Food and Drink

Cill Aodáin, Kiltimagh, Co Mayo
Tel: 094 81761 A friendly hotel in a small town in the heart of the county. Standard or superior rooms available. Continental and country cuisine. Bar.   424

Travellers Friend, Castlebar, Co Mayo
Tel/Fax: 094 23111 Hotel & Theatre complex near the town centre. Well-equipped en suite bedrooms, restaurant, bar, business centre, popular theatre.   417

Western Hotel, Claremorris, Co Mayo
Tel: 094 62011 Fax: 094 62838 Main street hotel with 18 en suite bedrooms, busy bars and a restaurant specialising in steaks. Music session Wednesday night.   421

Westport

Westport Golf Club, Carrowholly, Westport, Co Mayo
Tel: 098 28262/27070

In 1977, the late stage and movie actor, Robert Shaw, was among an enthusiastic gallery watching the final of the Irish Close Championship. An enthusiastic 14-handicapper, he had a home in nearby Tourmakeady and a visit to Westport on such an auspicious occasion was more than he could resist.

As it happened, the man Shaw fancied for the title, was overhauled in a pulsating climax, which contained as much drama as the actor had ever encountered in pursuit of his craft. Mark Gannon came from five down to tie Tony Hayes and went on to clinch the title in a sudden-death play-off.

The "Close" went back to Westport in 1985 and 1997 and it was where Mary McKenna gained the last of her eight Irish Women's titles in 1989. And all the while, the course adopted the sort of maturity which had been promised by its designer, Fred Hawtree.

Measuring 6,950 yards off the back tees, it can be an extremely demanding test in wet weather, when long irons or fairway woods are frequently

in a player's hands. And wet or dry, a crisp Atlantic breeze seems to be ever-present.

When the celebrated English writer, William Makepeace Thackeray, visited Westport in 1842, he enthused that: "The bay and the reek which sweeps down to the sea and the hundred islands in it, were dressed up in gold and purple and crimson and with the whole, cloudy West in a flame." His words offer a foretaste of a rather special place.

Sec/Manager:	Pat Smyth
Professional:	Alex Mealia
Directions:	2 miles West of Westport Town
Type of Course:	Parkland
Date Founded:	1923
No of Holes:	18
Length:	6653 yds (6083 mtrs)
Par:	73
SSS:	72
Green Fees:	Weekdays: £20 Weekends & Bank Holidays: £25
Visitors:	Welcome: Book in advance
Societies:	Welcome: Society rates available on request Contact Club for details
Facilities:	Chipping/Putting Area, Practice Area, Golf Clubs for hire, Trolley hire, Electric Buggy hire, Bar, Restaurant, Caddy service by arrangement

Accommodation, Food and Drink

Reference numbers below refer to detailed information provided in section 2

Accommodation

Ashleam House, Ballina, Co Mayo
Tel: 096 22406 Six letting bedrooms (4 en suite) in a neat Bed & Breakfast house south of Ballina and only yards from the River Moy.   414

Ben View House, Clifden, Co Galway
Tel: 095 21256 Fax: 095 21226 A charming mid 19th-century town house with nine en suite bedrooms for Bed & Breakfast. Same family owners since 1926.   272

Clifden Glen, Clifden, Co Galway
Tel: 095 21401 Fax: 095 21818 A holiday village on a private estate just outside Clifden. ApartHotel cottage suites, self-catering lodges, restaurant, pub, tennis.   271

Cregg House, Clifden, Co Galway
Tel: 095 21326 Great views of the beautiful Connemara countryside from a handsome modern Bed & Breakfast house with six en suite bedrooms.   269

Drom Caoin, Belmullet, Co Mayo
Tel/Fax: 097 81195 A striking modern house offering a choice of Bed & Breakfast (evening meals with notice) or self-catering Accommodation. Golfing breaks a speciality.   418

Drumshinnagh House, Castlebar, Co Mayo
Tel/Fax: 094 24211 A fine modern B&B house on an elevated site. Seven en suite bedrooms with tv. Private car park. Access for disabled guests   415

Cashel Bay, Co Galway
Tel: 095 32279 Fax: 095 32342 A family-run hotel with 12 en suite bedrooms and a seafood restaurant. Glorious setting overlooking Glynsk Bay.   268

Lough Fadda House, Clifden, Co Galway
Tel: 095 21165 Two acres of grounds make an attractive setting for a modern detached house with six en suite bedrooms.   274

Mal Dua House, Clifden, Co Galway
Tel: 095 21171 Luxury, comfort and hospitality in abundance in a distinguished house in attractive grounds just outside Clifden. 14 en suite bedrooms.   281

Quignalegan House, Ballina Road, Co Mayo
Tel/Fax: 096 71644 Five en suite bedrooms in a purpose-built modern house with

imposing grounds and a huge car park.   412

Roundstone House Hotel, Roundstone, Co Galway

Tel: 095 35864 Fax: 095 35944 Twelve rooms, all en suite, in a family-run hotel in
a delightful fishing village. Comfort, care and good food are keynotes.   262

St Anthony's, Westport, Co Mayo

Tel: 098 28887 Fax: 098 25172 A manse house built in 1820, now a characterful
Bed & Breakfast with six individually-appointed bedrooms. Also self-catering unit. 416

Teach an Easard, Ballyconneely, Co Galway

Tel/Fax: 095 23560 Six en suite bedrooms in a farmhouse Bed & Breakfast near the
coast and just one mile from Connemara Golf Club.   275

The Pass Inn, Kylemore, Co Galway

Tel: 095 41141 Fax: 095 41377 Family-run 11-bedroom hotel with restaurant in a
beautiful location between the hills and lakes of Connemara.   277

Travellers Friend, Castlebar, Co Mayo

Tel/Fax: 094 23111 Hotel & Theatre complex near the town centre. Well-equipped en
suite bedrooms, restaurant, bar, business centre, popular theatre.   417

Food and Drink

Clifden Glen, Clifden, Co Galway

Tel: 095 21401 Fax: 095 21818 A holiday village on a private estate just outside
Clifden. ApartHotel cottage suites, self-catering lodges, restaurant, pub, tennis. 271

Glynsk House Hotel, Cashel Bay, Co Galway

Tel: 095 32279 Fax: 095 32342 A family-run hotel with 12 en suite bedrooms and a
seafood restaurant. Glorious setting overlooking Glynsk Bay.   268

Lavelle's Erris Bar, Belmullet, Co Mayo

Tel: 097 82222 Fax: 097 81056 A typical Irish pub with bags of atmosphere. Food
served all day & high-season restaurant. Coffee shop adjacent.   419

Roundstone House Hotel, Roundstone, Co Galway

Tel: 095 35864 Fax: 095 35944 Twelve rooms, all en suite, in a family-run hotel in
a delightful fishing village. Comfort, care and good food are keynotes.   262

The Pass Inn, Kylemore, Co Galway

Tel: 095 41141 Fax: 095 41377 Family-run 11-bedroom hotel with restaurant in a
beautiful location between the hills and lakes of Connemara.   277

Travellers Friend, Castlebar, Co Mayo

Tel/Fax: 094 23111 Hotel & Theatre complex near the town centre. Well-equipped en
suite bedrooms, restaurant, bar, business centre, popular theatre.   417

MEATH

When the question is posed as to how many courses in Ireland have received the royal charter, the chances of getting the correct answer, are somewhat slim. And with fair justification. For instance, not many observers would be aware that the Curragh GC are entitled to carry the royal prefix, which they received from King George V in 1910. And there are others who would automatically include Royal Tara with the established names of Royal Portrush, Royal Co Down, Royal Belfast and Royal Dublin. But Tara, which now has 27 holes, is different on two counts. It was formerly Bellinter Park, which changed its name to Royal Tara in 1966, when it progressed from nine to 18 holes. And the new name had to do with the seat of ancient Irish kings in

Newgrange Tumulus, Co Meath

County Meath, rather than with British patronage. Which accounts for Meath being known as the "Royal County." And its 12 clubs are: Ashbourne, Black Bush, Co Meath (Trim), Gormanston, Headfort, Kilcock, Laytown and Bettystown, Moor Park, Navan, Royal Tara, South Meath and Summerhill. Of these, the best known are Headfort and Laytown and Bettystown, both of which have played host to prominent, national tournaments.

The importance of historic monuments within the present-day boundaries of Meath, bears rich testimony to the ancient significance of the region. Indeed it is the home of some of Ireland's most important historic sites and monuments, especially Newgrange, from where the winter solstice was televised nationally in December 1999. Beautifully restored, Newgrange is a neolithic passage grave, built around 3200 BC. The passage and chamber, which were discovered

accidentally by road builders in 1699, are within a mound measuring almost 40 feet high and 290 feet in diameter and featuring a 60-foot passageway to a central burial chamber. Remarkably, the corbelled roof of the chamber has remained watertight for over 5,000 years, but the most intriguing feature is the Roof Box. This small opening above a doorway is so precisely aligned as to catch the rays of the rising sun on the morning of the winter solstice, December 21st. From a camera within the chamber, Irish television viewers were treated to stunning pictures of this phenomenon, as a beam of light passed through the Roof Box, down the passageway and illuminated the chamber for about 20 minutes. Then it faded once more before leaving the dead to slumber in darkness for another year.

There are not many hills in Meath, which, in fact, is noted for its plains. But three of them are of major importance - the Hill of Tara, which was the site of the residence of the High Kings of Ireland; the Hill of Slane, where St Patrick is believed to have lit the Paschal Fire, and the Loughcrew Hills near Oldcastle, which contain extensive megalithic tombs. Legend has it that the appearance of flames on the Hill of Slane caused consternation at Tara. Indeed High King Laoghaire was warned by his druids that if the fire (of christianity) were not

Church at the Hill of Tara, Co Meath

stamped out immediately, it would never be extinguished. Anyway, Patrick was brought before the King, whereupon druid priests subjected him to various trials and tests. Eventually, the missionary succeeded in pacifying Laoghaire and, in the process, sowed the seed of Christianity in Ireland. And we are told that he did it through the use of the three-leafed shamrock, as a way of demonstrating the concept of the Holy Trinity, as in three persons - the Father, Son and Holy Ghost - in one God.

Meath is also famous for its horses. Indeed it was where Arkle was trained by Tom Dreaper for his spectacular Gold Cup dominance over Mill House at Cheltenham. So, it is hardly surprising that the county should be the home of prominent courses such as Fairyhouse and Navan, where, incidentally, Arkle won his first race. But the racing calendar also includes a fascinating summer meeting on the strand at Laytown, while the Bellewstown meeting has been in existence for more than 300 years.

The River Boyne enters Meath at Clonard and continues through Trim and Navan before flowing into the Irish Sea at Drogheda. Against the background of bitter divisions in Ulster, it is difficult to think of it as the "Sacred River of Ireland", that is how it's known, historically. In more practical terms, it is famous for its splendid salmon. The southern bank of the Boyne estuary at Mornington, marks the border of Meath and County Louth. It also marks the start of a sandy stretch of beach which has become the long-established seaside resort of Bettystown. It was there that the eighth-century Tara Brooch, one of the finest examples of the goldsmith's art in early, Christian Ireland, was found, in 1850.

As it happens, the adjoining seaside towns of Laytown and Bettystown are combined in the name of Meath's only links. And Headfort GC, soon to be

Site of Battle of the Boyne, Co Meath

extended to a 36-hole facility, takes its name from the former Headfort Demesne, which was built in the mid-18th century by the Taylor family. Indeed "The Irish Field" of 1905 reported that the Marquis of Headfort "has been greatly fascinated by the Royal and Ancient game, and has a private links laid out at his Irish seat in County Meath."

In a way, it seems an entirely natural development, that a county which was once the home of ancient Irish royalty, should have made what has latterly become a thriving, golfing connection.

Location of Golf Courses

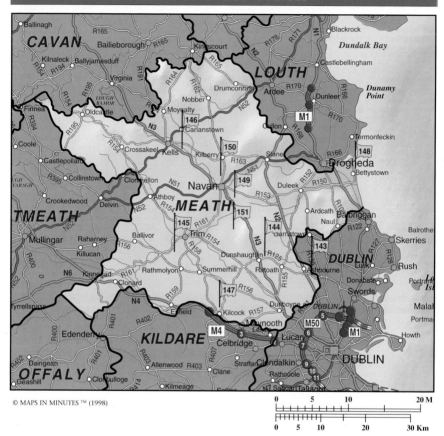

© MAPS IN MINUTES ™ (1998)

Ashbourne

Black Bush

Ashbourne Golf Club, Archerstown.,
Ashbourne, County Meath

Tel: 01 8352005

Black Bush Golf Club, Thomastown,
Dunshaughlin, Co Meath

Tel: 01 8250021

Sec/Manager:	Jim Clancy
Professional:	J Dwyer
Directions:	I mile south east of Ashbourne off the N2 to Dublin
Type of Course:	Parkland
Date Founded:	1991
No of Holes:	18
Length:	6435 yds (5884 mtrs)
Par:	71
SSS:	70
Green Fees:	Weekdays: £20 Weekends & Bank Holidays: £25
Visitors:	Welcome: Book in Advance on Thursdays
Societies:	Welcome: Book in Advance
Facilities:	Chipping/Putting Area, Practice Area, Driving Range, Golf Clubs for hire, Trolley hire, Electric Buggy hire, Bar, Restaurant, Caddy service by arrangement

Sec/Manager:	Seamus Ryan
Professional:	Shane O'Grady
Directions:	I mile East of Dunshaughlin off the R125 Ratoath Road
Type of Course:	Parkland
Date Founded:	1987
No of Holes:	18 (plus 9)
Length:	6644 yds (6075 mtrs)
Par:	72
SSS:	72
Green Fees:	Weekdays: £20 Weekends & Bank Holidays: £25
Visitors:	Welcome: Any Day, Restrictions apply weekdays, Contact Club in advance
Societies:	Welcome: Special concessions, Contact Club for details
Facilities:	Chipping/Putting Area, Practice Area, Driving Range, Golf Clubs for hire, Trolley hire, Electric Buggy hire, Bar, Restaurant

Accommodation, Food and Drink

Reference numbers below refer to detailed
information provided in section 2

Accommodation

Annesbrook, Duleek, Co Meath

Tel: 041 9823293 A classic 18th-century porticoed country house in ten acres of grounds. Ten en suite rooms for Bed & Breakfast & dinner menu. 447

Killeentierna House, Dunshaughlin, Co Meath

Tel: 01 8259722 Five Bed & Breakfast rooms, one of family size, in a modern residence on the Dublin side of Dunshaughlin. 433

The Evergreens, Ashbourne, Co Meath

Tel: 01 8352392 A lovely bungalow just outside the village provides Bed & Breakfast Accommodation in four rooms (three en suite). Tv lounge. 442

The Hawthorn Hotel, Swords, Co Dublin

Tel: 01 8401308 A charming ten-bedroomed hotel on the bustling main street. Super rooms, excellent Food and Drink, warm, efficient staff. 247

The Old Workhouse. Dunshaughlin, Co Meath

Tel/Fax: 01 8259251 Civilised living in a sympathetically restored 1840s building. Four cosy double bedrooms (2 en suite, 2 with private bathroom). Country house cooking.

Food and Drink

Annesbrook, Duleek, Co Meath

Tel: 041 9823293 A classic 18th-century porticoed country house in ten acres of grounds. Ten en suite rooms for Bed & Breakfast & dinner menu. 447

The Hawthorn Hotel, Swords, Co Dublin

Tel: 01 8401308 A charming ten-bedroomed hotel on the bustling main street. Super rooms, excellent Food and Drink, warm, efficient staff. 247

The Loft Restaurant, Navan, Co Meath

Tel: 046 71755 A 70-cover restaurant with a continental feel and a wide-ranging menu that includes popular classics, Oriental flavours and fresh seafood. 430

Accommodation, Food and Drink

Reference numbers below refer to detailed
information provided in section 2

Accommodation

Annesbrook, Duleek, Co Meath

Tel: 041 9823293 A classic 18th-century porticoed country house in ten acres of grounds. Ten en suite rooms for Bed & Breakfast & dinner menu. 447

Killeentierna House, Dunshaughlin, Co Meath

Tel: 01 8259722 Five Bed & Breakfast rooms, one of family size, in a modern residence on the Dublin side of Dunshaughlin. 433

The Evergreens, Ashbourne, Co Meath

Tel: 01 8352392 A lovely bungalow just outside the village provides Bed & Breakfast Accommodation in four rooms (three en suite). Tv lounge. 442

The Old Workhouse. Dunshaughlin, Co Meath

Tel/Fax: 01 8259251 Civilised living in a sympathetically restored 1840s building. Four cosy double bedrooms (2 en suite, 2 with private bathroom). Country house cooking.

Seamroy, Hill of Tara, Dunsany, Co Meath

Tel: 046 25296 Three letting Bed & Breakfast rooms in a house located right beside the historic Hill of Tara and its Visitor Centre. 451

Food and Drink

Banjo Sherlock's, Navan, Co Meath

Tel: 046 74688 A modern concept bar and restaurant among Navan's shops. Sandwiches, snacks, pasta, pizza, grills, sauced dishes. 445

Ryan's Bar and Restaurant, Navan, Co Meath

Tel/Fax: 046 78333 A smart modern bar and restaurant serving an excellent range of drinks and snacks. The owner is a keen golfer. 432

The Loft Restaurant, Navan, Co Meath

Tel: 046 71755 A 70-cover restaurant with a continental feel and a wide-ranging menu that includes popular classics, Oriental flavours and fresh seafood. 430

County Meath

County Meath Golf Club, Newtownmoynagh, Trim, Co Meath

Tel: 046 31463

Sec/Manager:	John McInenery
Professional:	None
Directions:	3 miles South West of Trim on the R160 to Longwood
Type of Course:	Parkland
Date Founded:	1898
No of Holes:	18
Length:	6720 yds (6144 mtrs)
Par:	73
SSS:	72
Green Fees:	Weekdays: £20 Weekends & Bank Holidays: £25
Visitors:	Welcome: Restrictions, Contact Club in advance
Societies:	Welcome: No special concessions, Prebooking required
Facilities:	Chipping/Putting Area, Practice Area, Trolley hire, Bar, Restaurant

Accommodation, Food and Drink

Reference numbers below refer to detailed information provided in section 2

Accommodation

Bondique House, Cullen, Beauparc, Navan, Co Meath
Tel/Fax: 041 9824823 En suite B&B Accommodation in a modern bungalow with private car park and large gardens. Tv lounge. Families welcome.

Brogans Guest House, Trim, Co Meath
Tel: 046 31237 Family-run guest house famed for its hospitality. 15 en suite bedrooms, tv, telephone. Bar with regular music sessions. 431

Dunlair House, Athlumney, Navan, Co Meath
Tel: 046 72551 Four capacious en suite in a large modern house in an acre of grounds. Picturesque setting 10-minute walk from town centre. 436

Seamroy, Hill of Tara, Dunsany, Co Meath
Tel: 046 25296 Three letting Bed & Breakfast rooms in a house located right beside the historic Hill of Tara and its Visitor Centre.

Wellington Court Hotel, Trim, Co Meath
Tel: 046 31516 Excellent Accommodation and facilities in a comfortable hotel on the Summerhill road (R158). 18 en suite bedrooms with tv and phone. 449

Food and Drink

Ryan's Bar and Restaurant, Navan, Co Meath
Tel/Fax: 046 78333 A smart modern bar and restaurant serving an excellent range of drinks and snacks. The owner is a keen golfer. 432

The Haggard Inn, Trim, Co Meath
Tel: 046 31110 Restaurant, carvery and bar food in an atmospheric 19th-century hostelry. Traditional music Friday and Saturday. 440

Wellington Court Hotel, Trim, Co Meath
Tel: 046 31516 Excellent Accommodation and facilities in a comfortable hotel on the Summerhill road (R158). 18 en suite bedrooms with tv and phone. 449

Headfort

Headfort Golf Club, Kells, Co Meath
Tel: 046 40146

One of the most dazzling performances in the history of Irish golf was produced at Headfort in 1980. That was when Des Smyth captured the Dunlop Tournament with a 27-under-par aggregate of 261 to win by no fewer than 16 strokes from second-placed Peter Townsend on a tight course, noted for its variety of mature trees.

Having started with a nine-hole layout, leased from the Marquis of Headfort in 1928, the club are set to expand to 36 holes at a cost of £2.1 million. This became possible through the recent purchase of 240 acres of adjoining land, part of the old Headfort Estate.

Comprising undulating parkland, mature woodland and forest, it straddles the River Blackwater on which there are two beautiful, wooded islands. The new course has been designed by Christy O'Connor Jnr, who is acquiring a reputation as one of the most aesthetically sensitive of modern Irish architects.

A feature of one of the islands which, incidentally were man-made and dug out by hand in the early part of the nineteenth century, is a magnificent collection of Asiatic conifers, assembled by one of the Lords of Headfort. In fact they are considered sufficiently important to be listed by the Botanic Gardens.

Meanwhile, as president of the club from 1961 to 1982, the last Marquis of Headfort, Michael, would have witnessed Smyth's exploits. Now the club is set to enter a new era with potentially the country's most attractive, 36-hole parkland facility, apart from the Killeen and Mahony's Point courses at Killarney.

Sec/Manager:	Brendan McCabe
Professional:	Brendan McGovern
Directions:	1 mile East of Kells off the N3 to Novan
Type of Course:	Parkland
Date Founded:	1928
No of Holes:	18
Length:	6569 yds (6007 mtrs)
Par:	72
SSS:	71
Green Fees:	Weekdays: £21 Weekends & Bank Holidays: £26
Visitors:	Welcome: Any Day except Tuesday, Contact Club in advance
Societies:	Welcome: Contact Club in writing
Facilities:	Chipping/Putting Area, Practice Area, Golf Clubs for hire, Trolley hire, Bar, Restaurant, Caddy service by arrangement

Accommodation, Food and Drink

Reference numbers below refer to detailed information provided in section 2

Accommodation

Castle View House, Slane, Co Meath
Tel: 041 9824510 A lovely chalet-bungalow on an elevated site with a large garden. Five en suite bedrooms including triples. 444

Killyon, Dublin Road, Navan, Co Meath
Tel: 046 71224 The River Boyne runs through the garden of this trim Bed & Breakfast house with ten en suite bedrooms. 437

Royal View House, Bellinter, Navan, Co Meath
Tel: 046 27893 Four en suite bedrooms in a fine modern house in a lovely rural location with front and back gardens. 439

San Giovanni House, Slane, Co Meath
Tel: 041 9824147 Five en suite bedrooms in a large modern Bed & Breakfast house on a mushroom farm near several historic sites. 446

The Headfort Arms Hotel, Kells, Co Meath
Tel: 046 40063 A comfortable, welcoming, family-run hotel with 18 en suite bedrooms with tv and phone. Bistro, carvery, coffee shop, bar and nightclub. 438

White Gables, Headfort Place, Kells, Co Meath
Tel: 046 40322 Three double rooms and a twin, all en suite, with tv. B&B, packed

lunches on request, dinner by arrangement for parties of 8 or more. 441

Teach Cuailgne, Carlasntwon, Kells, Co Meath
Tel/Fax: 046 46621 Four rooms (two en suite) in a detached house in a pleasant rural setting 3 miles from Kells. Excellent breakfasts. 435

Food and Drink

Blackwater Inn, Kells, Co Meath
Tel: 046 40386 A town-centre pub with stone floor, heavy wooden furniture, live music and a good pint of stout. 443

Jack's Railway Bar, Kells, Co Meath
Tel/Fax: 046 40215 A grand pub with log fires in winter and barbecues in the beer garden in summer. Lunchtime carvery; evening meals with notice. Games room. 434

The Evergreens, Ashbourne, Co Meath
Tel: 01 8352392 A lovely bungalow just outside the village provides Bed & Breakfast Accommodation in four rooms (three en suite). Tv lounge. 442

The Ground Floor Restaurant, Kells, Co Meath
Tel: 046 49688 A stylish modern restaurant with varied, good-value menus of Irish and International dishes. Full bar licence. 448

The Loft Restaurant, Navan, Co Meath
Tel: 046 71755 A 70-cover restaurant with a continental feel and a wide-ranging menu that includes popular classics, Oriental flavours and fresh seafood. 430

The Headfort Arms Hotel, Kells, Co Meath
Tel: 046 40063 A comfortable, welcoming, family-run hotel with 18 en suite bedrooms with tv and phone. Bistro, carvery, coffee shop, bar and nightclub. 438

Kilcock

Kilcock Golf Club, Gallow, Kilcock, County Meath
Tel: 01 6284074

Sec/Manager:	Seamus Kelly
Professional:	None
Directions:	4 miles west of Maynooth and ½ mile north of Kilcock off the R125
Type of Course:	Parkland
Date Founded:	1985
No of Holes:	18
Length:	6300yds (5761 mtrs)
Par:	71
SSS:	70
Green Fees:	Weekdays: £11 Weekends & Bank Holidays: £13
Visitors:	Welcome: No restrictions
Societies:	Welcome: Book in Advance
Facilities:	Chipping/Putting Area, Trolley hire, Bar, Restaurant, Caddy service by arrangement

Accommodation, Food and Drink

Reference numbers below refer to detailed information provided in section 2

Accommodation

Killeentierna House, Dunshaughlin, Co Meath
Tel: 01 8259722 Five Bed & Breakfast rooms, one of family size, in a modern residence on the Dublin side of Dunshaughlin. 433

The Old Forge, Saggart, Co Dublin
Tel: 01 4589226 Six B & B rooms (three en suite) and a self-contained section to sleep five in a row of 18th-century houses. 242

The Old Workhouse, Dunshaughlin, Co Meath
Tel/Fax: 01 8259251 Civilised living in a sympathetically restored 1840s building. Four cosy double bedrooms (2 en suite, 2 with private bathroom). Country house cooking.

Wellington Court Hotel, Trim, Co Meath
Tel: 046 31516 Excellent Accommodation and facilities in a comfortable hotel on the Summerhill road (R158). 18 en suite bedrooms with tv and phone. 449

Food and Drink
The Haggard Inn, Trim, Co Meath
Tel: 046 31110 Restaurant, carvery and bar food in an atmospheric 19th-century hostelry. Traditional music Friday and Saturday. 440
Tyrrells Restaurant, Edenderry, Co Offaly
Tel: 0405 32400 An atmospheric restaurant with rough-hewn walls and flagstone floor in the many-acred complex of Ballindoolin House & Gardens. 500
Wellington Court Hotel, Trim, Co Meath
Tel: 046 31516 Excellent Accommodation and facilities in a comfortable hotel on the Summerhill road (R158). 18 en suite bedrooms with tv and phone. 449

Laytown & Bettystown

Laytown & Bettystown Golf Club, Bettystown, Co Meath

Tel: 041 98 27170

On the evening of Sunday, October 16th 1988, Declan Branigan was celebrating a course-record 63 at Laytown and Bettystown, only to be up-staged by his closest golfing friend. Des Smyth made a late arrival from St Andrews, where he had been a member of Ireland's winning team in the Dunhill Cup earlier in the day.

As it happens, that eight-under-par record is now out of date, due to recent revision work on the course done by Smyth and Branigan in their capacity as golf-course architects. They re-de-signed the sixth, seventh and eighth holes, strengthening the layout appreciably.

The course is a traditional links, which is something of an oddity, given its location in Co Meath, which is almost entirely land-locked. In fact it is a stretch of only eight miles, known as the Mornington Dunes, which touches the Irish Sea.

With an overall length of 6,399 yards for a par of 71, the course is relatively short by mod-ern standards. But there is ample compensation in the difficulty which its undulating topogra-phy presents for ball striking with even the short irons. And the test is heightened by strategic bunkering and small greens.

Its products, notably Smyth and Branigan, are wonderful wind players. This was brought home to Smyth's contemporaries early in his European Tour career when he shot what was considered a miraculous 67 in a gale-force wind during the 1980 Jersey Open at La Moye. Mary McKenna captured her sixth Irish Women's title there in 1981.

Sec/Manager:	Helen Finnegan
Professional:	R. J. Brown
Directions:	4 miles East of Drogheda off the R151 North of Bettystown
Type of Course:	Links
Date Founded:	1909
No of Holes:	18
Length:	6399 yds (5852 mtrs)
Par:	71
SSS:	72
Green Fees:	Weekdays: £25 Weekends & Bank Holidays: £30
Visitors:	Welcome: Restrictions weekdays, Limited availability at weekends, Contact Club in advance
Societies:	Welcome: Contact Club for details
Facilities:	Chipping/Putting Area, Practice Area, Golf Clubs for hire, Trolley hire, Bar, Restaurant

Accommodation, Food and Drink
Reference numbers below refer to detailed information provided in section 2

Accommodation
Annesbrook, Duleek, Co Meath
Tel: 041 9823293 A classic 18th-century porticoed country house in ten acres of grounds. Ten en suite rooms for Bed & Breakfast & dinner menu. 447
Sillougue House, Drogheda, Co Louth
Tel: 041 9845284 Luxurious B&B Accommodation in a striking modern house on the main Dublin-Belfast road. 14 beautifully appointed en suite rooms with tv, phone and hairdryer. 402
St Gobnaits, Drogheda, Co Louth
Tel: 041 9837844 A detached house by the N1, with four en suite B&B rooms. One kilometre from town centre, close to golf courses and beaches. 403

Food and Drink
Annesbrook, Duleek, Co Meath
Tel: 041 9823293 A classic 18th-century porticoed country house in ten acres of grounds. Ten en suite rooms for Bed & Breakfast & dinner menu. 447
Monasterboice Inn, Monasterboice, Co Louth
Tel: 041 9837383 An excellent restaurant and bar with a real Irish feel. Steaks a speciality. Located on the main Dublin-Belfast road (N1). 400
Ryan's Bar and Restaurant, Navan, Co Meath
Tel/Fax: 046 78333 A smart modern bar and restaurant serving an excellent range of drinks and snacks. The owner is a keen golfer. 432

Moor Park

Mooretown, Navan, County Meath

Tel: 046 27661

Sec/Manager:	Martin Fagan
Professional:	None

Directions:	3 miles South East of Navan off the N3 to Dublin
Type of Course:	Parkland
Date Founded:	1993
No of Holes:	18
Length:	6400yds (5852 mtrs)
Par:	72
SSS:	69
Green Fees:	Weekdays: £8 Weekends & Bank Holidays: £10
Visitors:	Welcome: No restrictions except Sundays
Societies:	Welcome: No restrictions except Sundays. Book in advance
Facilities:	Golf Clubs for hire, Trolley hire, Caddy service by arrangement

Accommodation, Food and Drink

Reference numbers below refer to detailed information provided in section 2

Accommodation

Annesbrook, Duleek, Co Meath
Tel: 041 9823293 A classic 18th-century porticoed country house in ten acres of grounds. Ten en suite rooms for Bed & Breakfast & dinner menu. 447

Bondique House, Cullen, Beauparc, Navan, Co Meath
Tel/Fax: 041 9824823 En suite B&B Accommodation in a modern bungalow with private car park and large gardens. Tv lounge. Families welcome.

Brogans Guest House, Trim, Co Meath
Tel: 046 31237 Family-run guest house famed for its hospitality. 15 en suite bedrooms, tv, telephone. Bar with regular music sessions. 431

Castle View House, Slane, Co Meath
Tel: 041 9824510 A lovely chalet-bungalow on an elevated site with a large garden. Five en suite bedrooms including triples. 444

Dunlair House, Athlumney, Navan, Co Meath
Tel: 046 72551 Four capacious en suite in a large modern house in an acre of grounds. Picturesque setting 10-minute walk from town centre. 436

Killyon, Dublin Road, Navan, Co Meath
Tel: 046 71224 The River Boyne runs through the garden of this trim Bed & Breakfast house with ten en suite bedrooms. 437

Royal View House, Bellinter, Navan, Co Meath
Tel: 046 27893 Four en suite bedrooms in a fine modern house in a lovely rural location with front and back gardens. 439

San Giovanni House, Slane, Co Meath
Tel: 041 9824147 Five en suite bedrooms in a large modern Bed & Breakfast house on a mushroom farm near several historic sites. 446

Seamroy, Hill of Tara, Dunsany, Co Meath
Tel: 046 25296 Three letting Bed & Breakfast rooms in a house located right beside the historic Hill of Tara and its Visitor Centre.

Teach Cuailgne, Carlasntwon, Kells, Co Meath
Tel/Fax: 046 46621 Four rooms (two en suite) in a detached house in a pleasant rural setting 3 miles from Kells. Excellent breakfasts. 435

The Headfort Arms Hotel, Kells, Co Meath
Tel: 046 40063 A comfortable, welcoming, family-run hotel with 18 en suite bedrooms with tv and phone. Bistro, carvery, coffee shop, bar and nightclub. 438

Wellington Court Hotel, Trim, Co Meath
Tel: 046 31516 Excellent Accommodation and facilities in a comfortable hotel on the Summerhill road (R158). 18 en suite bedrooms with tv and phone. 449

Food and Drink

Banjo Sherlock's, Navan, Co Meath
Tel: 046 74688 A modern concept bar and restaurant among Navan's shops. Sandwiches, snacks, pasta, pizza, grills, sauced dishes. 445

Blackwater Inn, Kells, Co Meath
Tel: 046 40386 A town-centre pub with stone floor, heavy wooden furniture, live music and a good pint of stout. 443

Jack's Railway Bar, Kells, Co Meath
Tel/Fax: 046 40215 A grand pub with log fires in winter and barbecues in the beer garden in summer. Lunchtime carvery; evening meals with notice. Games room. 434

Ryan's Bar and Restaurant, Navan, Co Meath
Tel/Fax: 046 78333 A smart modern bar and restaurant serving an excellent range of drinks and snacks. The owner is a keen golfer. 432

The Ground Floor Restaurant, Kells, Co Meath
Tel: 046 49688 A stylish modern restaurant with varied, good-value menus of Irish and International dishes. Full bar licence. 448

The Headfort Arms Hotel, Kells, Co Meath
Tel: 046 40063 A comfortable, welcoming, family-run hotel with 18 en suite bedrooms with tv and phone. Bistro, carvery, coffee shop, bar and nightclub. 438

The Loft Restaurant, Navan, Co Meath
Tel: 046 71755 A 70-cover restaurant with a continental feel and a wide-ranging menu that includes popular classics, Oriental flavours and fresh seafood. 430

Wellington Court Hotel, Trim, Co Meath
Tel: 046 31516 Excellent Accommodation and facilities in a comfortable hotel on the Summerhill road (R158). 18 en suite bedrooms with tv and phone. 449

Navan

Navan Golf Club, Proudstown, Navan, Co Meath

Tel: 046 72888

Sec/Manager:	Francis Duffy
Professional:	Sean Browne
Directions:	2 miles North of Navan off the R162 to Kilberry
Type of Course:	Parkland
Date Founded:	1997
No of Holes:	18
Length:	6600 yds (6035 mtrs)
Par:	72
SSS:	70
Green Fees:	Weekdays: £15 Weekends & Bank Holidays: £20
Visitors:	Welcome: Contact Club in advance
Societies:	Welcome: Special concessions, Apply to club for details
Facilities:	Chipping/Putting Area, Driving Range, Golf Clubs for hire, Trolley hire, Electric Buggy hire, Bar, Restaurant, Caddy service by arrangement, plus Function Rooms

Accommodation, Food and Drink

Reference numbers below refer to detailed information provided in section 2

Accommodation

Annesbrook, Duleek, Co Meath
Tel: 041 9823293 A classic 18th-century porticoed country house in ten acres of grounds. Ten en suite rooms for Bed & Breakfast & dinner menu. 447

Bondique House, Cullen, Beauparc, Navan, Co Meath
Tel/Fax: 041 9824823 En suite B&B Accommodation in a modern bungalow with private car park and large gardens. Tv lounge. Families welcome.

Brogans Guest House, Trim, Co Meath
Tel: 046 31237 Family-run guest house famed for its hospitality. 15 en suite bedrooms, tv, telephone. Bar with regular music sessions. 431

Castle View House, Slane, Co Meath
Tel: 041 9824510 A lovely chalet-bungalow on an elevated site with a large garden. Five en suite bedrooms including triples. 444

Dunlair House, Athlumney, Navan, Co Meath

Tel: 046 72551 Four capacious en suite in a large modern house in an acre of grounds. Picturesque setting 10-minute walk from town centre.   436

Killyon, Dublin Road, Navan, Co Meath

Tel: 046 71224 The River Boyne runs through the garden of this trim Bed & Breakfast house with ten en suite bedrooms.   437

Royal View House, Bellinter, Navan, Co Meath

Tel: 046 27893 Four en suite bedrooms in a fine modern house in a lovely rural location with front and back gardens.   439

San Giovanni House, Slane, Co Meath

Tel: 041 9824147 Five en suite bedrooms in a large modern Bed & Breakfast house on a mushroom farm near several historic sites.   446

Teach Cuailgne, Carlasntwon, Kells, Co Meath

Tel/Fax: 046 46621 Four rooms (two en suite) in a detached house in a pleasant rural setting 3 miles from Kells. Excellent breakfasts.   435

The Headfort Arms Hotel, Kells, Co Meath

Tel: 046 40063 A comfortable, welcoming, family-run hotel with 18 en suite bedrooms with tv and phone. Bistro, carvery, coffee shop, bar and nightclub.   438

Wellington Court Hotel, Trim, Co Meath

Tel: 046 31516 Excellent Accommodation and facilities in a comfortable hotel on the Summerhill road (R158). 18 en suite bedrooms with tv and phone.   449

White Gables, Headfort Place, Kells, Co Meath

Tel: 046 40322 Three double rooms and a twin, all en suite, with tv. B&B, packed lunches on request, dinner by arrangement for parties of 8 or more.   441

Food and Drink

Banjo Sherlock's, Navan, Co Meath

Tel: 046 74688 A modern concept bar and restaurant among Navan's shops. Sandwiches, snacks, pasta, pizza, grills, sauced dishes.   445

Blackwater Inn, Kells, Co Meath

Tel: 046 40386 A town-centre pub with stone floor, heavy wooden furniture, live music and a good pint of stout.   443

Jack's Railway Bar, Kells, Co Meath

Tel/Fax: 046 40215 A grand pub with log fires in winter and barbecues in the beer garden in summer. Lunchtime carvery; evening meals with notice. Games room.   434

Ryan's Bar and Restaurant, Navan, Co Meath

Tel/Fax: 046 78333 A smart modern bar and restaurant serving an excellent range of drinks and snacks. The owner is a keen golfer.   432

The Ground Floor Restaurant, Kells, Co Meath

Tel: 046 49688 A stylish modern restaurant with varied, good-value menus of Irish and International dishes. Full bar licence.   448

The Loft Restaurant, Navan, Co Meath

Tel: 046 71755 A 70-cover restaurant with a continental feel and a wide-ranging menu that includes popular classics, Oriental flavours and fresh seafood.   430

Wellington Court Hotel, Trim, Co Meath

Tel: 046 31516 Excellent Accommodation and facilities in a comfortable hotel on the Summerhill road (R158). 18 en suite bedrooms with tv and phone.   449

The Headfort Arms Hotel, Kells, Co Meath

Tel: 046 40063 A comfortable, welcoming, family-run hotel with 18 en suite bedrooms with tv and phone. Bistro, carvery, coffee shop, bar and nightclub.   438

Royal Tara

Royal Tara Golf Club, Bellinter, Navan, Co Meath

Tel: 046 25244/25508

Sec/Manager:	Paddy O'Brien
Professional:	Adam Whiston
Directions:	4 miles South of Navan off the N3 to Dublin
Type of Course:	Parkland
Date Founded:	1906
No of Holes:	18 (plus 9)
Length:	6456 yds (5904 mtrs)

Par:	72
SSS:	71
Green Fees:	Weekdays: £20 Weekends & Bank Holidays: £25
Visitors:	Welcome: Any Day except Tuesday, Contact Club in advance
Societies:	Welcome: No special concessions, Prebooking is required
Facilities:	Chipping/Putting Area, Practice Area, Golf Clubs for hire, Trolley hire, Electric Buggy hire, Bar, Restaurant, Caddy service by arrangement

Accommodation, Food and Drink

Reference numbers below refer to detailed information provided in section 2

Accommodation

Bondique House, Cullen, Beauparc, Navan, Co Meath

Tel/Fax: 041 9824823 En suite B&B Accommodation in a modern bungalow with private car park and large gardens. Tv lounge. Families welcome.

Brogans Guest House, Trim, Co Meath

Tel: 046 31237 Family-run guest house famed for its hospitality. 15 en suite bedrooms, tv, telephone. Bar with regular music sessions.   431

Castle View House, Slane, Co Meath

Tel: 041 9824510 A lovely chalet-bungalow on an elevated site with a large garden. Five en suite bedrooms including triples.   444

Dunlair House, Athlumney, Navan, Co Meath

Tel: 046 72551 Four capacious en suite in a large modern house in an acre of grounds. Picturesque setting 10-minute walk from town centre.   436

Killeentierna House, Dunshaughlin, Co Meath

Tel: 01 8259722 Five Bed & Breakfast rooms, one of family size, in a modern residence on the Dublin side of Dunshaughlin.   433

Killyon, Dublin Road, Navan, Co Meath

Tel: 046 71224 The River Boyne runs through the garden of this trim Bed & Breakfast house with ten en suite bedrooms.   437

Royal View House, Bellinter, Navan, Co Meath

Tel: 046 27893 Four en suite bedrooms in a fine modern house in a lovely rural location with front and back gardens.   439

San Giovanni House, Slane, Co Meath

Tel: 041 9824147 Five en suite bedrooms in a large modern Bed & Breakfast house on a mushroom farm near several historic sites.   446

Seamroy, Hill of Tara, Dunsany, Co Meath

Tel: 046 25296 Three letting Bed & Breakfast rooms in a house located right beside the historic Hill of Tara and its Visitor Centre.

The Headfort Arms Hotel, Kells, Co Meath

Tel: 046 40063 A comfortable, welcoming, family-run hotel with 18 en suite bedrooms with tv and phone. Bistro, carvery, coffee shop, bar and nightclub.   438

Wellington Court Hotel, Trim, Co Meath

Tel: 046 31516 Excellent Accommodation and facilities in a comfortable hotel on the Summerhill road (R158). 18 en suite bedrooms with tv and phone.   449

Food and Drink

Banjo Sherlock's, Navan, Co Meath

Tel: 046 74688 A modern concept bar and restaurant among Navan's shops. Sandwiches, snacks, pasta, pizza, grills, sauced dishes.   445

Blackwater Inn, Kells, Co Meath

Tel: 046 40386 A town-centre pub with stone floor, heavy wooden furniture, live music and a good pint of stout.   443

Ryan's Bar and Restaurant, Navan, Co Meath

Tel/Fax: 046 78333 A smart modern bar and restaurant serving an excellent range of drinks and snacks. The owner is a keen golfer.   432

The Evergreens, Ashbourne, Co Meath

Tel: 01 8352392 A lovely bungalow just outside the village provides Bed & Breakfast Accommodation in four rooms (three en suite). Tv lounge.   442

The Haggard Inn, Trim, Co Meath

Tel: 046 31110 Restaurant, carvery and bar food in an atmospheric 19th-century hostelry. Traditional music Friday and Saturday.   440

The Headfort Arms Hotel, Kells, Co Meath

Tel: 046 40063 A comfortable, welcoming, family-run hotel with 18 en suite bedrooms with tv and phone. Bistro, carvery, coffee shop, bar and nightclub.   438

The Loft Restaurant, Navan, Co Meath

Tel: 046 71755 A 70-cover restaurant with a continental feel and a wide-ranging menu that includes popular classics, Oriental flavours and fresh seafood.   430

Wellington Court Hotel, Trim, Co Meath

Tel: 046 31516 Excellent Accommodation and facilities in a comfortable hotel on the Summerhill road (R158). 18 en suite bedrooms with tv and phone.   449

MONAGHAN, CAVAN & LONGFORD

For the most part, golf came late to the Republic's so-called Border counties. Indeed it is interesting to note that while County Cavan now has six clubs, only one of them existed prior to 1928. Similarly, Clones and Rossmore were the only County Monaghan clubs to have been instituted before the country gained independence.

The area of Monaghan/Cavan/Longford has a total of 12 courses. They are: Monaghan - Castleblaney, Clones, Mannan Castle, Nuremore, Rossmore; Cavan - Belturbet, Blacklion, Cabra Castle, Slieve Russell, Virginia; Longford - Co Longford. Significantly, of the 12, only five are 18-hole stretches - Nuremore, Rossmore, Co Cavan, Slieve Russell and Co Longford.

The origins of golf in Cavan were detailed by the indefatigable chronicler, Lionel Hewson, in his monthly magazine "Irish Golf" in January 1930. In it he wrote: "It was in the middle eighties of the last (nineteenth) century that Mr Thomas Lough, afterwards MP for West Islington and Under Secretary for Education in the Campbell Bannerman ministry, laid out a nine-hole course at his Cavan residence. Killynebbar, 10 minutes' walk from the town.

"At first, it was used only by the Lough family and their political visitors from across the Channel, as not for a year or two could any of the local residents be induced to interest themselves in the game. Eventually, however, a sufficient number, probably not more than 20, came together and formed the nucleus of a modest club."

As might be expected, all of the courses in the area are parkland, while incorporating quite a liberal use of water features. For instance, the charming nine-hole stretch at Blacklion is bordered on two sides by Lough McNean; water is in play on five holes at Slieve Russell; Nuremore and Rossmore also carry the threat of a watery grave, while the nine-hole course at Castleblaney overlooks the scenic Lake Muchno. Against that background, it will come as no surprise that water also features prominently among the tourist attractions of the area. For instance, the tree-clad hills of County Cavan conceal a host of sparkling lakes which the visitor will come upon suddenly, thereby adding excitement and enchantment to the journey.

Wild, solitary birds and mammals find a ready home in this remote and unpolluted wilderness. Because of scale, however, the wilderness is never far from picturesque towns and villages, where the pace of life is decidedly leisurely. Two great river systems have their sources here. One is the Shannon, the longest river in these islands, which rises near Glangevlin and flows south for 190 miles before reaching the Atlantic at Limerick. The Erne, which rises east of Lough Gowna, is dominated by three beautiful lakes, Lough Oughter in Co Cavan and Lough Erne, Upper and Lower, in Co Fermanagh. Undisturbed marshland, covering much of Cavan's lake shores, is a haven for snipe, curlew, lapwing, redshank and water rail, while the hen harrier is a colourful hunter among the reed beds. Then there are the sparrowhawk and kestrel which find a home in the wild oak wood near

Rossmore Memorial, Monaghan

Teemore on the Shannon-Erne Waterway. Angling is also a feature of County Monaghan where over 60 water courses provide a wide variety of species, from bream to rudd, tench, roach and perch, along with hybrids. The main centres are Monaghan Town, Carrickmacross, Castleblaney, Clones and Ballybay.

Monaghan Town was incorporated as a parliamentary borough by King James I in 1613. Long before it had become a Scottish Calvinist town, however, it had been home to Celtic and pre-Celtic peoples. Convent Lake, in the grounds of the St Louis Convent, contains a brannog, or fortified lake dwelling, which was a stronghold of the MacMahons, the most powerful chieftains of the area.

Patrick Kavanagh Centre, Inniskeen, Co Monaghan

On the approaches to Inniskeen, there is a signpost indicating where the poet, Patrick Kavanagh, was born in 1904. And an inscription on the wall of the local school captures the perception, isolation and essential loneliness of the artist:

"We are not alone in our loneliness
Others have been here and known
Griefs we thought our special own,
Problems that we could not solve
Lovers that we could not have
Pleasures that we missed by inches ....."

County Longford lies in the Shannon basin and the upper catchment of the Erne. From a vantage point on the summit of Lisduff, the visitor can look north and see a deep, rolling plain stretching out for a distance of up to six miles, bounded by historic Cairn Hill. Right and left of this hill, the county slopes down to a fertile, level plain, beautifully wooded, through which the River Camlin flows to the Shannon. Then, in a north-eastern direction, the rising country about Granard looms up in a succession of hazy hillocks. Lakeland, bogland, pastureland and wetland form the main surface features of County Longford, where the most extensive lakes are Lough Gowna to the north and Lough Kinale, near Granard, both of which form the boundary with County Cavan.For the greater part if its course through Longford, the Shannon appears more like a lake than a river. Lough Forbes is near the north-western boundary and Lough Ree extends southwards from Lanesboro. Among its more important islands are Inchcleraun or Quaker's Island, and Saint's Island, which is now joined to the mainland.

Saints Island, Lough Ree, Co Longford

County Longford, of course, is also the birthplace of Oliver Goldsmith, poet, essayist, novelist and traveller, for whom Dr Samuel Johnson composed the epitaph: "He touched nothing which he did not adorn." Best known for his wonderfully evocative poem "The Deserted Village", for his novel "The Vicar of Wakefield" and for his timeless play "She Stoops to Conquer", Goldsmith first saw the light at Pallas in 1729. His father, Rev Charles Goldsmith, was rector of Forgney, near Ballymahon. The attractions of his native county could hardly be captured better than in these lines from "The Deserted Village": "Sweet Auburn! loveliest village of the plain; where health and plenty cheered the labouring swain, where smiling spring its earliest visit paid, and parting summer's blooms delayed."

Location of Golf Courses

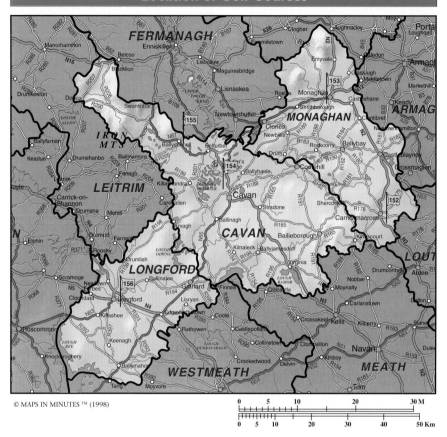

© MAPS IN MINUTES ™ (1998)

Nuremore

Nuremore Golf Club, Nuremore,
Carrickmacross, County Monaghan

Tel: 042 9664016

	off the N2 to Ardee
Type of Course:	Parkland
Date Founded:	1991
No of Holes:	18
Length:	6419 yds (5870 mtrs)
Par:	71
SSS:	69
Green Fees:	Weekdays: £20 Weekends & Bank Holidays: £25
Visitors:	Welcome: Book in advance
Societies:	Welcome: Special Deals, Book in advance
Facilities:	Chipping/Putting Area, Practice Area, Golf Clubs for hire, Trolley hire, Electric Buggy hire, Bar, Restaurant, Caddy service by arrangement, Sauna, Hotel/Accommodation on site

Accommodation, Food and Drink

Reference numbers below refer to detailed
information provided in section 2

Accommodation

Arradale House, Carrickmacross, Co Monaghan
Tel: 042 9661941 Ten en suite bedrooms for full or part board Accommodation on a working farm in a beautiful setting of woods and lakes.   461

Fortsingleton Georgian Mansion, Emyvale, Co Monaghan
Tel: 047 86054 Fourteen en suite bedrooms in a substantial Georgian mansion of exceptional character. Family-run; B&B plus dinner.   460

Glynch House, Newbliss, Co Monaghan
Tel: 047 54045 Five bedrooms, three en suite, on a 200-acre working beef farm just outside the village. B&B, evening meals by arrangement.   463

Riverside House, Cootehill, Co Cavan
Tel/Fax: 049 5552150 Five en suite bedrooms (B&B; dinner by arrangement) in a farm guesthouse. Also a self-catering bungalow for six.   470

The Headfort Arms Hotel, Kells, Co Meath
Tel: 046 40063 A comfortable, welcoming, family-run hotel with 18 en suite bedrooms with tv and phone. Bistro, carvery, coffee shop, bar and nightclub.   438

Food and Drink

Blackwater Inn, Kells, Co Meath
Tel: 046 40386 A town-centre pub with stone floor, heavy wooden furniture, live music and a good pint of stout.   443

Monasterboice Inn, Monasterboice, Co Louth
Tel: 041 9837383 An excellent restaurant and bar with a real Irish feel. Steaks a speciality. Located on the main Dublin-Belfast road (N1).   400

The Ground Floor Restaurant, Kells, Co Meath
Tel: 046 49688 A stylish modern restaurant with varied, good-value menus of Irish and International dishes. Full bar licence.   448

The Headfort Arms Hotel, Kells, Co Meath
Tel: 046 40063 A comfortable, welcoming, family-run hotel with 18 en suite bedrooms with tv and phone. Bistro, carvery, coffee shop, bar and nightclub.   438

Located on the southern side of Carrickmacross, Nuremore was originally a nine-hole course which later became part of a major development including a luxury hotel and leisure complex, conceived by the late owner, Gerry Gilhooly. When work was completed in 1991, it was acknowledged as one of its county's finest amenities.

The typically parkland layout, which has played host to the Ulster Professional Championship, has been modified by David Jones so as to make it less daunting, physically. Its overall length of 6,706 yards off the back tees, incorporates several strong par fours, especially the 474-yard 18th, running parallel to the first.

Interestingly, it originally started with two par fives, the same as Eddie Hackett's design of the Enniscrone links. As part of the Jones modifications, however, the first has been reduced to a long par four, so lowering the overall par to 71 which, incidentally, is the course record held by David Higgins.

Built in two loops of nine, it offers stunning views of the surrounding countryside, while presenting a searching test of golfing skills. In the latter context, there are some forbidding water hazards, created by a lake between the second and fifth holes on the outward journey and by a greater expance on the homeward nine, notably off the tee at the par-four 10th.

Nuremore is a fine example of a new development sympathetic with nature. This is evident on the driveway to the hotel, where motorists are cautioned: "Slow, please. Ducks crossing." And they do, in numbers.

Sec/Manager:	Fergus Lane
Professional:	Maurice Cassidy
Directions:	2 miles south east of Carrickmacross

Rossmore

Rossmore Golf Club, Cootehill Road,
Monaghan, Co Monaghan

Tel: 047 81316

Sec/Manager:	Jimmy McKenna
Professional:	Mark Nicholson
Directions:	2 miles South of Monaghan off the R188 to Cootehill
Type of Course:	Parkland

Date Founded:	1916
No of Holes:	18
Length:	6129 yds (5605 mtrs)
Par:	70
SSS:	68
Green Fees:	£20 per day
Visitors:	Welcome: Ring in advance
Societies:	Welcome: Special concessions, Apply to club for details
Facilities:	Chipping/Putting Area, Golf Clubs for hire, Trolley hire, Bar, Restaurant, plus Driving Range nearby

Accommodation, Food and Drink

Reference numbers below refer to detailed information provided in section 2

Accommodation

Donn Carragh Hotel, Lisnaskea, Co Fermanagh
Tel: 028 67721206 A newly refurbished hotel in the heart of town by Upper Lough Erne. 18 en suite bedrooms with tv and phone. Bar, lounge, restaurant. 871

Fortsingleton Georgian Mansion, Emyvale, Co Monaghan
Tel: 047 86054 Fourteen en suite bedrooms in a substantial Georgian mansion of exceptional character. Family-run; B&B plus dinner. 460

Glynch House, Newbliss, Co Monaghan
Tel: 047 54045 Five bedrooms, three en suite, on a 200-acre working beef farm just outside the village. B&B, evening meals by arrangement. 463

Lennard Arms Hotel, The Diamond, Clones, Co Monaghan
Tel: 047 51075/51530 Family-run hotel just off the market place, with ten bedrooms, a full meal service and secured parking. regular live music. 462

Riverside House, Cootehill, Co Cavan
Tel/Fax: 049 5552150 Five en suite bedrooms (B&B; dinner by arrangement) in a farm guesthouse. Also a self-catering bungalow for six. 470

The Valley Hotel, Fivemiletown, Co Tyrone
Tel: 028 89521505 A modern hotel on the main Belfast-Enniskillen road (A4), with 22 comprehensively equipped en suite bedrooms. Bar, restaurant. 899

Food and Drink

Donn Carragh Hotel, Lisnaskea, Co Fermanagh
Tel: 028 67721206 A newly refurbished hotel in the heart of town by Upper Lough Erne. 18 en suite bedrooms with tv and phone. Bar, lounge, restaurant. 871

Lennard Arms Hotel, The Diamond, Clones, Co Monaghan
Tel: 047 51075/51530 Family-run hotel just off the market place, with ten bedrooms, a full meal service and secured parking. regular live music. 462

The Valley Hotel, Fivemiletown, Co Tyrone
Tel: 028 89521505 A modern hotel on the main Belfast-Enniskillen road (A4), with 22 comprehensively equipped en suite bedrooms. Bar, restaurant. 899

County Cavan

County Cavan, Arnmore House, Drumelis, Cavan, Co Cavan

Tel: 049 4331388

Sec/Manager:	Jim Farher
Professional:	Ciaran Caroll
Directions:	Off the R198 Killeshandra Road one mile North West of Cavan
Type of Course:	Parkland
Date Founded:	1894
No of Holes:	18
Length:	6161 yds (5634 mtrs)
Par:	70

SSS:	69
Green Fees:	Weekdays: £14 Weekends & Bank Holidays; £16
Visitors:	Welcome: Any time
Societies:	Welcome: Any time, Book in advance
Facilities:	Chipping/Putting Area, Practice Area, Driving Range, Golf Clubs for hire, Bar, Restaurant, Caddy service by arrangement

Accommodation, Food and Drink

Reference numbers below refer to detailed information provided in section 2

Accommodation

Breffni Arms Hotel, Arvagh, Co Cavan
Tel: 049 4335127 Family-run hotel, restaurant and leisure centre in the heart of Ireland's Lakelands. 13 en suite bedrooms with tv, phone, computer point. 471

Fortsingleton Georgian Mansion, Emyvale, Co Monaghan
Tel: 047 86054 Fourteen en suite bedrooms in a substantial Georgian mansion of exceptional character. Family-run; B&B plus dinner. 460

Glynch House, Newbliss, Co Monaghan
Tel: 047 54045 Five bedrooms, three en suite, on a 200-acre working beef farm just outside the village. B&B, evening meals by arrangement. 463

Lennard Arms Hotel, The Diamond, Clones, Co Monaghan
Tel: 047 51075/51530 Family-run hotel just off the market place, with ten bedrooms, a full meal service and secured parking. regular live music. 462

Lisnamandra, Crossdoney, Co Cavan
Tel: 049 4337196 Spacious Accommodation in four guest bedrooms, three en suite, on a working dairy farm five miles from Cavan. B&B, light meals. 472

Longford Arms Hotel, Longford, Co Longford
Tel: 043 46296 Comfortable family-run hotel in the main street. Well-appointed Accommodation includes 18 executive rooms with both bath and shower en suite. Coffee shop. 481

Riverside House, Cootehill, Co Cavan
Tel/Fax: 049 5552150 Five en suite bedrooms (B&B; dinner by arrangement) in a farm guesthouse. Also a self-catering bungalow for six. 470

Food and Drink

Bella Pasta, Roosky, Co Roscommon
Tel: 078 6705556 A taste of Italy in an Irish bar complex just yards from the Shannon. Pizza, pasta and many other favourites. 522

Breffni Arms Hotel, Arvagh, Co Cavan
Tel: 049 4335127 Family-run hotel, restaurant and leisure centre in the heart of Ireland's Lakelands. 13 en suite bedrooms with tv, phone, computer point. 471

Lennard Arms Hotel, The Diamond, Clones, Co Monaghan
Tel: 047 51075/51530 Family-run hotel just off the market place, with ten bedrooms, a full meal service and secured parking. regular live music. 462

Longford Arms Hotel, Longford, Co Longford
Tel: 043 46296 Comfortable family-run hotel in the main street. Well-appointed Accommodation includes 18 executive rooms with both bath and shower en suite. Coffee shop. 481

Slieve Russell

The Slieve Russell Golf & Country Club, Ballyconnell, Co Cavan

Tel: 049 9526444

An unwitting visitor to Slieve Russell would be somewhat taken aback to see the slight figure of Catriona McKiernan striding out over the 300-acre site. But the course and its environs happen to be a regular training area for the international marathon champion.

Slieve Russell is the brainchild of Cavan businessman Sean Quinn who amassed considerable wealth through sand and cement companies on both sides of the Border with Northern Ireland. Situated near the small town of Ballyconnell, it comprises a 150-bedroom hotel and a championship-standard golf course designed by Patrick Merrigan.

From the back tees, the layout stretches to 7,013 yards, which made it eminently suitable for the staging of the Smurfit Irish Professional Championship in 1996. That was when Des Smyth captured the title for a sixth time froma strong field which included the holder, Philip Walton, and the 1994 champion, Darren Clarke.

The availability of a plentiful supply of sand and gravel ensured that the course was built to the highest standards, notably where drainage was concerned. And the rolling, parkland layout is notable for the strategic use of water and the undulating nature of the sand-based greens.

It deserves to rank as one of Merrigan's better designs and is especially memorable for the par-five 13th which dog-legs to the left around the shore of Lough Rud. Depending on the amount of water the player is prepared to traverse, the green can be reachable in two, but it is very much a high risk challenge.

Sec/Manager:	P. J. Creamer
Professional:	Liam McCool
Directions:	From Belturbot proceed on N87 towards Ballyconnell. Golf Course is signposted on the right before entering the town.
Type of Course:	Parkland
Date Founded:	1992
No of Holes:	18
Length:	7013 yds (6412 mtrs)
Par:	72
SSS:	72
Green Fees:	Weekdays: £32 Weekends & Bank Holidays: £40.
Visitors:	Welcome: Anytime, Book in advance
Societies:	Welcome: Book in advance
Facilities:	Chipping/Putting Area, Driving Range, Golf Clubs for hire, Trolley hire, Electric Buggy hire, Bar, Restaurant

Accommodation, Food and Drink

Reference numbers below refer to detailed information provided in section 2

Accommodation

Breffni Arms Hotel, Arvagh, Co Cavan
Tel: 049 4335127 Family-run hotel, restaurant and leisure centre in the heart of Ireland's Lakelands. 13 en suite bedrooms with tv, phone, computer point.   471

Donn Carragh Hotel, Lisnaskea, Co Fermanagh
Tel: 028 67721206 A newly refurbished hotel in the heart of town by Upper Lough Erne. 18 en suite bedrooms with tv and phone. Bar, lounge, restaurant.   871

Fortsingleton Georgian Mansion, Emyvale, Co Monaghan
Tel: 047 86054 Fourteen en suite bedrooms in a substantial Georgian mansion of exceptional character. Family-run; B&B plus dinner.   460

Glencarne House, Ardcarne, Carrick-on-Shannon, Co Roscommon
Tel: 079 67013 Four en suite bedrooms in a Bed & Breakfast house on a working beef farm. Close to Lough Key Forest Park.

Glynch House, Newbliss, Co Monaghan
Tel: 047 54045 Five bedrooms, three en suite, on a 200-acre working beef farm just outside the village. B&B, evening meals by arrangement.   463

Lennard Arms Hotel, The Diamond, Clones, Co Monaghan
Tel: 047 51075/51530 Family-run hotel just off the market place, with ten bedrooms, a full meal service and secured parking. regular live music.   462

Lisnamandra, Crossdoney, Co Cavan
Tel: 049 4337196 Spacious Accommodation in four guest bedrooms, three en suite, on a working dairy farm five miles from Cavan. B&B, light meals.   472

Riverside House, Cootehill, Co Cavan
Tel/Fax: 049 5552150 Five en suite bedrooms (B&B); dinner by arrangement) in a farm guesthouse. Also a self-catering bungalow for six.   470

Food and Drink

Breffni Arms Hotel, Arvagh, Co Cavan
Tel: 049 4335127 Family-run hotel, restaurant and leisure centre in the heart of Ireland's Lakelands. 13 en suite bedrooms with tv, phone, computer point.   471

Four Winds, 146 Crankhill Road, Slangford, Ballymena, Co Antrim, BT44 9HA,
Tel: 028 25685360 The Four Winds is the farmhouse for a mixed working farm which offers bed & breakfast Accommodation. The modern building has been recently refurbished and now provides 3 letting rooms, (2 family and 1 double, all with hot and cold).

Lennard Arms Hotel, The Diamond, Clones, Co Monaghan
Tel: 047 51075/51530 Family-run hotel just off the market place, with ten bedrooms, a full meal service and secured parking. regular live music.   462

County Longford

County Longford, Glack, Dublin Road, Longford, Co Longford

Tel: 043 46310

The current strength of the Irish economy has brought about not only a marked increase in the building of new courses, but an upgrading of existing facilities. Co Longford, which dates back to 1900, is a typical example.

Despite having a very attractive, par-70 stretch of 6,080 yards, designed by Eddie Hackett on the Dublin side of the town, they have ambitious plans for expansion. Indeed extensive work was recently completed on the clubhouse at a cost of £80,000.

Plans for a course upgrading on their free-draining, elevated site, were already at an

advanced stage in 1999 when the opportunity arose to purchase 14 acres of adjoining land. So the work, soon to be commenced, will be even more dramatic than originally envisaged.

A dominant feature of the layout is a stream which traverses every fairway from the fourth to the eighth and is also in play at the 18th. Meanwhile, though the earliest records of the club have gone missing, "The Golfing Annual" of 1909/1910 recorded 1900 as the year of institution. Which means that their centenary celebrations coincide rather nicely with the millennium.

Among the interesting revelations in the early history of certain Irish parkland clubs is the nature of the playing season. We are informed that in 1916, the club paid a nominal rent to the Earl of Longford "who also generously provided a small clubhouse," and that "play begins in October and ends on May 1st." Just in time for the grazing season.

Sec/Manager:	Edna Dooley
Professional:	None
Directions:	South East of Longford off the N4 to Dublin
Type of Course:	Parkland
Date Founded:	1894
No of Holes:	18
Length:	6080 yds (5560 mtrs)
Par:	70
SSS:	69
Green Fees:	Weekdays: £12 Weekends & Bank Holidays: £15
Visitors:	Welcome: Any Day, Check tee-times in advance
Societies:	Welcome: Special concessions, Book in advance
Facilities:	Practice Area Golf Clubs for hire, Trolley hire, Electric Buggy hire, Bar, Restaurant

Accommodation, Food and Drink

Reference numbers below refer to detailed information provided in section 2

Accommodation

Breffni Arms Hotel, Arvagh, Co Cavan
Tel: 049 4335127 Family-run hotel, restaurant and leisure centre in the heart of Ireland's Lakelands. 13 en suite bedrooms with tv, phone, computer point. 471

Glencarne House, Ardcarne, Carrick-on-Shannon, Co Roscommon
Tel: 079 67013 Four en suite bedrooms in a Bed & Breakfast house on a working beef farm. Close to Lough Key Forest Park.

Lackan Lodge, Edgeworthstown, Co Longford
Tel: 043 71299 Four guest bedrooms (2 en suite) in a peacefully located modern farmhouse on the Longford side of Edgeworthstown. No smoking. 482

Lisnamandra, Crossdoney, Co Cavan
Tel: 049 4337196 Spacious Accommodation in four guest bedrooms, three en suite, on a working dairy farm five miles from Cavan. B&B, light meals. 472

Longford Arms Hotel, Longford, Co Longford
Tel: 043 46296 Comfortable family-run hotel in the main street. Well-appointed Accommodation includes 18 executive rooms with both bath and shower en suite. Coffee shop. 481

Regans, Market Square, Roscommon, Co Roscommon
Tel: 090 325339/26373 14 en suite bedrooms, day-long restaurant, bar, nightclub and function room - under one roof in the town centre. 524

The Gardens, The Walk, Roscommon, Co Roscommon
Tel/Fax: 090 326828 Four simply-appointed en suite bedrooms in a Bed & Breakfast house near the main roundabout in Roscommon. Parking available.

Viewmount House, Longford, Co Longford
Tel: 043 41919 High-quality Accommodation in a former farmhouse a mile from the town centre. En suite bedrooms, lovely gardens, fine dining. 480

Food and Drink

Bella Pasta, Roosky, Co Roscommon
Tel: 078 6705556 A taste of Italy in an Irish bar complex just yards from the Shannon. Pizza, pasta and many other favourites. 522

Breffni Arms Hotel, Arvagh, Co Cavan
Tel: 049 4335127 Family-run hotel, restaurant and leisure centre in the heart of Ireland's Lakelands. 13 en suite bedrooms with tv, phone, computer point. 471

Cill Aodáin, Kiltimagh, Co Mayo
Tel: 094 81761 A friendly hotel in a small town in the heart of the county. Standard or superior rooms available. Continental and country cuisine. Bar. 424

Chungs Chinese Restaurant, Boyle, Co. Roscommon
Tel: 079 62016 Fax: 079 64949 A Chinese restaurant in the Royal Hotel Boyle, with the usual long à la carte list and set menus for two or more.

Hillside House, Doon, Corrigeenroe, Boyle, Co Roscommon
Tel: 079 66075 Four B&B rooms in an attractive country home beside Lough Key with its forest, fishing and boating. Great views.

Lisroyne Inn, Strokestown, Co Roscommon
Tel: 078 33214 The smartest pub in town - neat and spotless. A warm welcome, good drinking and snacking. 521

Longford Arms Hotel, Longford, Co Longford
Tel: 043 46296 Comfortable family-run hotel in the main street. Well-appointed Accommodation includes 18 executive rooms with both bath and shower en suite. Coffee shop. 481

The Pollard Arms Hotel, Castlepollard, Co Westmeath
Tel: 044 61194 Recently refurbished hotel in the centre of Castlepollard. Fifteen en suite bedrooms, bar, restaurant and function room. 600

Viewmount House, Longford, Co Longford
Tel: 043 41919 High-quality Accommodation in a former farmhouse a mile from the town centre. En suite bedrooms, lovely gardens, fine dining. 480

OFFALY

In 1947, the incomparable Babe Zaharias became the first American winner of the British Women's Matchplay Championship. Four years later, the title went to the Republic of Ireland for the first time - in the possession of Kitty MacCann, a member of the Tullamore club. Offaly can claim other important golfing distinctions. Like the achievement of Birr GC member, Richard Coughlan, who, in 1997, became the first competitor to win simultaneous players' tour cards on both sides of the Atlantic. All of which reflects considerable credit on a county with only five clubs. They are: Birr, Castle Barna, Edenderry, Esker Hills and Tullamore. Of these five, typically parkland stretches, Tullamore and Esker Hills are championship standard. Offaly's location in the heart of Ireland, however, offers easy access by road to a

Shannon Bridge, Co Offaly

wide selection of courses in neighbouring counties. Incidentally, Ms MacCann went on to become one of only 12 Irish players to gain representative honours in the Curtis Cup. Indeed she was a member of the history-making line-up at Muirfield in 1952, when their 5-4 victory brought the trophy to this side of the Atlantic for the first time.

A trip to Birr GC in the south of the county, provides the opportunity of visiting Birr Castle and its magnificent grounds. As the seat of the Earls of Rosse for more than 350 years, it was originally one of the castles of the great O'Carroll Clan. Still a family home, it is open to the public only on special occasions, though the grounds are open throughout the year. Laid out around a lake and along the banks of two adjacent rivers, the demesne is acknowledged as one of the finest and most beautiful ornamental gardens in Europe. Centrepiece is the recently restored Great Telescope, built by the Third Earl of Rosse in the 1840s. Up to 1917, it had the distinction of being the largest in the world. Now, with the same looks and movement as it had 150 years ago, it stands as a monument to the pioneering achievements of the Parsons family, who are honoured in the recently-opened Historic Science Centre. The O'Carroll chieftains date back to the sixth century and are

Clonmacnoise, Co Offaly

associated with as many as 40 castles in south Offaly and north Tipperary. Family strongholds still in existence include the castles of Birr, Leap, Kinnity and Emmel.

The Slieve Bloom mountain range, which extends from neighbouring Laois, has its own environment park which is home to a wide variety of wildlife, including fallow deer, hares, stoats and even wild goats, quite apart from the 65 species of birds which have been spotted there. Nestling at the foot of the mountains is the charming village of Kinnity - with its own pyramid! And just outside the village is Kinnity Castle, a gothic revival castle which has been luxuriously refurbished into a five-star hotel.

To the west, Offaly is bordered by the River Shannon where the town of Banagher, with its extensive marina facilities, is a major base for cruiser hire. A river-bus offers leisurely, scenic tours while the more adventurous may explore the river for themselves by hiring a canoe, complete with camping equipment. Visitors are also welcome at the local squash and tennis courts, while on the west bank of the river, there is an outdoor swimming pool and a pitch-and-putt course. Outside Banagher is Cloghan Castle, the oldest inhabited building of its kind in Ireland, which has been recently restored and is open to the public.

Leap Castle, Co Offaly

"The Irish Times" of May 12th, 1896, reported a match between the golf clubs of Tullamore and Banagher, "over the links of the Tullamore club at Ballykilmurry". The report went on: "Though the weather was inclement, the play was watched with much interest by a number of visitors." We are further informed that Banagher won by 31 holes to nil, which suggests a particularly strong playing membership. Other newspaper reports of the period suggest that the Banagher club was formed in 1894. But within 15 years, a thriving club was "believed to be extinct."

Meanwhile, a visit to the Silver River reserve at Cadamstown, can be the start of a geological journey offering insight into a landscape formed by seas and rivers more than 400 million years ago. The Silver River gorge retains much of the ancient character which attracted its first settlers in about 3000 BC. More recently, the valley has become a haven for students of geology and botany.

Travelling westwards from Cadamstown across Knock Hill, one is confronted by a panoramic view of north and west Offaly and the province of Connacht in the distance. And the road leads on to the ancient village of Balluyboy where, in 1690, King William of Orange and his army of 13,000 men, camped for one night en route to Limerick.

In a county rich in history, reminders of the past are always at hand. And this is especially true of Tullamore GC, where the more venerable members will be only too happy to regale the visitor with the splendid exploits of Kitty MacCann.

Location of Golf Courses

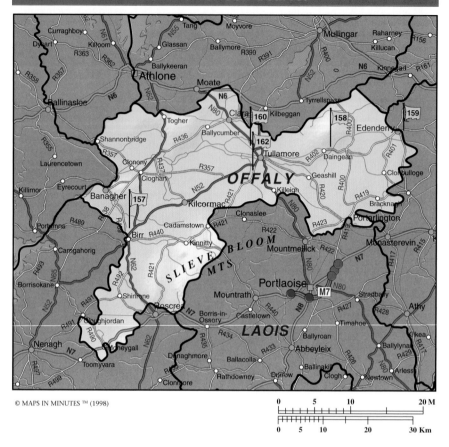

© MAPS IN MINUTES ™ (1998)

Birr

Castle Barna

Birr Golf Club, The Glenns, Birr, Co Offaly
Tel: 050 920082

Castle Barna Golf Club, Daingean, Co Offaly
Tel: 050 653384

Sec/Manager:	Mary O'Gorman
Professional:	None
Directions:	2 miles from Birr off the R439 to Banagher
Type of Course:	Parkland
Date Founded:	1893
No of Holes:	18
Length:	6292 yds (5754 mtrs)
Par:	70
SSS:	70
Green Fees:	Weekdays: £12 Weekends & Bank Holidays: £14
Visitors:	Welcome: Prebooking required, Contact Club in advance
Societies:	Welcome: Contact Club for details
Facilities:	Chipping/Putting Area, Practice Area, Driving Range, Golf Clubs for hire, Trolley hire Bar, Restaurant

Sec/Manager:	Evelyn Mangan
Professional:	None
Directions:	10 miles East of Tullamore
Type of Course:	Parkland
Date Founded:	1994
No of Holes:	18
Length:	6200 yds (5669 mtrs)
Par:	72
SSS:	69
Green Fees:	Weekdays: £10 Weekends & Bank Holidays: £14
Visitors:	Welcome: Ring in advance
Societies:	Welcome: Special concessions, Contact club for details
Facilities:	Chipping/Putting Area, Practice Area, Golf Clubs for hire, Trolley hire, Electric Buggy hire, Bar, Restaurant

Accommodation, Food and Drink

Reference numbers below refer to detailed information provided in section 2

Accommodation

Annagh Lodge, Coolbawn, Nenagh, Co Tipperary
Tel/Fax: 067 24225 Five comfortably appointed B&B rooms in a period country house on a 200-acre working farm. Dinner by arrangement. 545

Ashley Park House, Ardcroney, Nenagh, Co Tipperary
Tel: 067 38223 Fax: 067 38223 Six twin bedrooms, all en suite, in a handsome early 18th-century residence with a private lake. Bed & Breakfast. 549

Bridget's Bed & Breakfast, Coolbawn, Co Tipperary
Tel: 067 28098 Bed and Breakfast in five en suite rooms in a smart modern bungalow. 5 minutes' walk from Lough Derg. 544

Catstone Lodge, Ballymore, Co. Westmeath
Tel: 044 56494 Fax: 044 56196 www.catstone.net Luxurious en suite bedrooms (60 sq m each) in a restored period-style farmhouse. Tv, sitting area, kitchenette. B&B or self-catering.

Otway Lodge, Dromineer, Nenagh, Co Tipperary
Tel: 067 24133/24273 Six-bedroomed B&B guest house (all rooms en suite) on the edge of Lough Derg. Boat hire, fishing trips. 542

Riverrun Cottages, Terryglass, Nenagh, Co Tipperary
Tel: 067 22125 4-star self-catering Accommodation in five units, each sleeping 4. Quiet village setting by Lough Derg. 543

Willmount House, Portumna, Co Galway
Tel: 050 941114 Four en suite double bedrooms in a Georgian (1748) house on a working farm close to Lough Derg. Terrific views. 263

Food and Drink

The Boat Inn, Oughterard, Co Galway
Tel: 091 552196 Fax: 091 502694 Eleven modern en suite bedrooms in a prime site in the centre of the village. Restaurant with excellent menus; bars; terrace. 276

The Waterfront, Roscrea, Co Tipperary
Tel: 050 522431 Family restaurant catering for all tastes. Snacks, full meals, takeaways. Open from 9.30 till 9. 541

Willmount House, Portumna, Co Galway
Tel: 050 941114 Four en suite double bedrooms in a Georgian (1748) house on a working farm close to Lough Derg. Terrific views. 263

Accommodation, Food and Drink

Reference numbers below refer to detailed information provided in section 2

Accommodation

Bloomfield House, Mullingar, Co Westmeath
Tel: 044 40894 Fax: 044 43767 Sixty-five en suite bedrooms, including executive suites, in a high-quality hotel on the Tullamore road (N52) by Lough Ennell. Leisure Club on site. 602

Lake Villa, Grange South, Mullingar, Co Westmeath
Tel: 044 41946 B&B in 2 doubles (1 with an extra bed) and a twin on the Ballymahon road. Tv, telephone. No credit cards.

Lynnbury, Mullingar, Co Westmeath
Tel: 044 48432/40444 Country home Accommodation in a handsome house on the main Tullamore Road, very near the golf course.

Mearescourt House, Rathconrath, Mullingar, Co Westmeath
Tel: 044 55112 Four en suite guest bedrooms, each sleeping up to four, in a magnificent Georgian mansion set in sweeping parkland. Dinner by arrangement. 604

The Fairways, Bloomfield, Mullingar, Co Westmeath
Tel: 044 42584 Four en suite rooms (one family size) with tv in a B&B guest house opposite Mullingar Golf Club.

Food and Drink

Bloomfield House, Mullingar, Co Westmeath
Tel: 044 40894 Fax: 044 43767 Sixty-five en suite bedrooms, including executive suites, in a high-quality hotel on the Tullamore road (N52) by Lough Ennell. Leisure Club on site. 602

Oscars, Mullingar, Co Westmeath
Tel: 044 44909 A charming town-centre restaurant with a cosmopolitan menu catering for all tastes. Full drinks licence. 605

Tyrrells Restaurant, Edenderry, Co Offaly
Tel: 040 532400 An atmospheric restaurant with rough-hewn walls and flagstone floor in the many-acred complex of Ballindoolin House & Gardens. 500

Edenderry

Edenderry Golf Club, Kishavanna, Edenderry, County Offaly
Tel: 040 531072

Sec/Manager:	Niall Dempsey
Professional:	None
Directions:	1½ miles North East of Edenderry off the R402 to Innfield
Type of Course:	Parkland
Date Founded:	1910
No of Holes:	18
Length:	6593 yds (6029 mtrs)
Par:	72
SSS:	72
Green Fees:	Weekdays: £15 Weekends & Bank Holidays: £20
Visitors:	Welcome: Restrictions on Thursdays and weekends, Ring in advance
Societies:	Welcome: Restrictions on Thursdays and weekends, Book in advance
Facilities:	Trolley hire, Bar, Restaurant

Accommodation, Food and Drink

Reference numbers below refer to detailed information provided in section 2

Accommodation

Bloomfield House, Mullingar, Co Westmeath
Tel: 044 40894 Fax: 044 43767 Sixty-five en suite bedrooms, including executive suites, in a high-quality hotel on the Tullamore road (N52) by Lough Ennell. Leisure Club on site.   602

Lake Villa, Grange South, Mullingar, Co Westmeath
Tel: 044 41946 B&B in 2 doubles (1 with an extra bed) and a twin on the Ballymahon road. Tv, telephone. No credit cards.

Lynnbury, Mullingar, Co Westmeath
Tel: 044 48432/40444 Country home Accommodation in a handsome house on the main Tullamore Road, very near the golf course.

Mearescourt House, Rathconrath, Mullingar, Co Westmeath
Tel: 044 55112 Four en suite guest bedrooms, each sleeping up to four, in a magnificent Georgian mansion set in sweeping parkland. Dinner by arrangement. 604

The Fairways, Bloomfield, Mullingar, Co Westmeath
Tel: 044 42584 Four en suite rooms (one family size) with tv in a B&B guest house opposite Mullingar Golf Club.

Food and Drink

Bloomfield House, Mullingar, Co Westmeath
Tel: 044 40894 Fax: 044 43767 Sixty-five en suite bedrooms, including executive suites, in a high-quality hotel on the Tullamore road (N52) by Lough Ennell. Leisure Club on site.   602

Oscars, Mullingar, Co Westmeath
Tel: 044 44909 A charming town-centre restaurant with a cosmopolitan menu catering for all tastes. Full drinks licence.   605

Tyrrells Restaurant, Edenderry, Co Offaly
Tel: 040 532400 An atmospheric restaurant with rough-hewn walls and flagstone floor in the many-acred complex of Ballindoolin House & Gardens.   500

Esker Hills

Esker Hills Golf & Country Club,
Ballykilmurray, Tullamore, Co Offaly
Tel: 050 655999

"On telling people about our course, the usual reaction was that if it's in Offaly, it has to be a bog," said Donal Molloy, one of three brothers who own the Esker Hills development along with a fourth partner. Indeed a cement factory, which they also own, is visible from certain areas of the 150-acre site.

In the event, visitors anticipating bogland couldn't be more wrong. It seems that more than 10,000 years ago, the unique landscape of Offaly was powerfully sculpted by the awesome natural forces of the dying Ice Age.

As the great glaciers retreated, they left in their wake narrow ridges of sand and gravel which were deposited by the streams of water that had once flowed in tunnels beneath the melting ice. These ridges now comprise the majestic Esker Riada, from which the course gets its name.

Course architect, Christy O'Connor Jnr, coped wonderfully well with difficult, severely undulating terrain, two and a half miles outside Tullamore. During the construction stage, he insisted on the minimum of soil disturbance, yet his craftsmanship is such that the driver remains very much in the player's hands.

This is true even of the 307-yard 10th, another one of those "par-three-and-a-half" holes, which are becoming an attractive feature of O'Connor's courses. Meanwhile, excellent, natural drainage is one of the more obvious advantages of the site, as golfing terrain. And as splendid design features, there are the dramatic undulations of valleys and plateaux, along with natural lakes and woodlands.

Sec/Manager:	Donal Malloy
Professional:	None
Directions:	3 miles from Tullamore off the N80 to Clara
Type of Course:	Parkland
Date Founded:	1996
No of Holes:	18
Length:	6669 yds (6098 mtrs)
Par:	71
SSS:	71
Green Fees:	Weekdays: £18 Weekends & Bank Holidays: £24
Visitors:	Welcome: Ring in advance
Societies:	Welcome: Ring in advance
Facilities:	Practice Area, Golf Clubs for hire, Trolley hire, Electric Buggy hire

Accommodation, Food and Drink

Reference numbers below refer to detailed
information provided in section 2

Accommodation

Bloomfield House, Mullingar, Co Westmeath

Tel: 044 40894 Fax: 044 43767 Sixty-five en suite bedrooms, including executive
suites, in a high-quality hotel on the Tullamore road (N52) by Lough Ennell. Leisure
Club on site.   602

Catstone Lodge, Ballymore, Co. Westmeath

Tel: 044 56494 Fax: 044 56196 Luxurious en suite bedrooms (60 sq m each) in a
restored period-style farmhouse. Tv, sitting area, kitchenette. B&B or self-catering.

Lake Villa, Grange South, Mullingar, Co Westmeath

Tel: 044 41946 B&B in 2 doubles (1 with an extra bed) and a twin on the
Ballymahon road. Tv, telephone. No credit cards.

Shelmalier House, Cartrontroy, Athlone, Co Westmeath

Tel: 090 272145 Fax: 090 273190 Quiet Accommodation in seven en suite B&B
rooms with tv and phone. Award-winning breakfasts. Signposted off the N6.   606

Food and Drink

Bloomfield House, Mullingar, Co Westmeath

Tel: 044 40894 Fax: 044 43767 Sixty-five en suite bedrooms, including executive
suites, in a high-quality hotel on the Tullamore road (N52) by Lough Ennell. Leisure
Club on site.   602

Oscars, Mullingar, Co Westmeath

Tel: 044 44909 A charming town-centre restaurant with a cosmopolitan menu
catering for all tastes. Full drinks licence.   605

Tyrrells Restaurant, Edenderry, Co Offaly

Tel: 040 532400 An atmospheric restaurant with rough-hewn walls and flagstone
floor in the many-acred complex of Ballindoolin House & Gardens.   500

Tullamore

**Tullamore Golf Club, Brookfield, Tullamore,
Co Offaly**

Tel: 050 621439

It's not often we learn of golf being introduced
to a town by an army officer on a visit to the
local rectory. But that happens to represent the
origins of Tullamore GC in 1896, when a Colonel R A Craig and a few friends drove their gutty
balls in a field beside the Geashill Road.

The club moved to its present home in
Brookfield in 1926. And 12 years later, when
James Braid was involved in the design of
Mullingar GC in neighbouring Westmeath, he
was inveigled to Tullamore to upgrade the course
to meet the competitive standards of the time.

Approaching their centenary celebrations in
1996, it was felt that a further modification was
appropriate. So it was that leading architect
Patrick Merrigan set about creating seven new
greens, 11 new tees and forming three lakes in a
major reconstruction effort.

Appropriately, Merrigan happens to be a great
admirer of Braid's work, so everthing was done
in sympathy with the old master. The outcome
is a par-70 layout of 6,428 yards where all the
familiar visual attractions of mature woodland
against the backdrop of the Slieve Bloom mountains, have gained a fresh perspective.

Tullamore, where visitors remember the elusive green at the par-four 16th, protected by trees
and water, has always been among the country's leading parkland courses. Indeed Ryder Cup
representative Hugh Boyle won both the Irish
Professional Championship and the Irish Dunlop
tournament there. Now, Merrigan's work makes
it a worthy challenge for the new millennium.

Sec/Manager:	Pat Burns
Professional:	Donagh MacArdle
Directions:	Three miles South of Tullamore off the R421 to Birr
Type of Course:	Parkland
Date Founded:	1886
No of Holes:	18
Length:	6457 yds (5904 mtrs)
Par:	70
SSS:	71
Green Fees:	Weekdays: £20 Weekends & Bank Holidays: £24
Visitors:	Welcome: Any Day, Restrictions on Tuesday and weekends, Book ahead
Societies:	Welcome: Special concessions, Contact Club for details
Facilities:	Chipping/Putting Area, Practice Area, Golf Clubs for hire, Trolley hire, Electric Buggy hire, Bar, Restaurant, Caddy service by arrangement

Accommodation, Food and Drink

Reference numbers below refer to detailed
information provided in section 2

Accommodation

Bloomfield House, Mullingar, Co Westmeath

Tel: 044 40894 Fax: 044 43767 Sixty-five en suite bedrooms, including executive suites, in a high-quality hotel on the Tullamore road (N52) by Lough Ennell. Leisure Club on site. 602

Catstone Lodge, Ballymore, Co. Westmeath

Tel: 044 56494 Fax: 044 56196 www.catstone.net Luxurious en suite bedrooms (60 sq m each) in a restored period-style farmhouse. Tv, sitting area, kitchenette. B&B or self-catering.

Lake Villa, Grange South, Mullingar, Co Westmeath

Tel: 044 41946 B&B in 2 doubles (1 with an extra bed) and a twin on the Ballymahon road. Tv, telephone. No credit cards.

Lynnbury, Mullingar, Co Westmeath

Tel: 044 48432/40444 Country home Accommodation in a handsome house on the main Tullamore Road, very near the golf course.

The Fairways, Bloomfield, Mullingar, Co Westmeath

Tel: 044 42584 Four en suite rooms (one family size) with tv in a B&B guest house opposite Mullingar Golf Club.

Food and Drink

Bloomfield House, Mullingar, Co Westmeath

Tel: 044 40894 Fax: 044 43767 Sixty-five en suite bedrooms, including executive suites, in a high-quality hotel on the Tullamore road (N52) by Lough Ennell. Leisure Club on site. 602

Oscars, Mullingar, Co Westmeath

Tel: 044 44909 A charming town-centre restaurant with a cosmopolitan menu catering for all tastes. Full drinks licence. 605

SLIGO, ROSCOMMON & LEITRIM

"Under Ben Bulben's head
In Drumcliff churchyard Yeats is laid.
An ancestor was rector there
Long years ago ...."

William Butler Yeats was born in Sandymount Avenue, Dublin, before his father abandoned a legal career and emigrated to London in 1867 in the hope of becoming a successful painter. So it was that through an accident of fate, Jack Yeats, the poet's brother, was born in London. The Yeats boys were drawn increasingly, however, to Sligo, where they were made feel truly at home with their maternal grandparents, William and Elizabeth Pollexfen, who moved to Melville, a gracious house on an elevated site with views of Ben Bulmen and Knocknarea.

Later, idyllic summers were spent at Thornhill in Sligo or Moyle Lodge at Rosses Point. And on many an enchanting day, they went boating, swimming, fishing and generally relaxing at Elsinore Lodge, which the poet accorded a place in literature through the lines:

"My name is Henry Middleton
I have a small demesne
A small forgotten house that's set
On a storm-bitten green
I scrub its floors and make my bed
I cook and change my plate
The post and garden-boy alone
Have keys to my old gate."

But the Pollexfens died within six weeks of each other in 1892 and with the death of their son George in 1910, the visits by poet and painter to an area which would have such a profound influence on their respective careers, became less frequent.

W B Yeats once described the Metal Man, which stands sentinel on the narrow channel into Sligo Harbour as "the only Rosses Point man who never told a lie." One can assume that this mischievous observation was born of a deep affection for an area that would become not only the inspiration for some breathtaking verse, but for some rare sporting exploits with club and ball around the County Sligo links at Rosses Point.

On August 2nd, 1895, the "Sligo Independent" reported: "The Golf Club has become quite an established institution at the Point, and from early morn to dewy eve, the Greenlands now resound to the warning cry of "Fore!" and the melodious click of the ball struck straight from the tee. "On the links, occasionally other sounds not quite so tuneful are wafted gently on the breeze, from the depths of some of the numerous bunkers, but we pass lightly over that - 'it's only human nature after all.' We understand that a friendly match against the Bundoran Club will

Tha Harbour, Rosses Point, Co Sligo

probably be played on Wednesday, the 14th instant, when we hope the home team will follow the splendid example set by their confreres of the Polo Club last week, in carrying the Sligo colours to victory." Rosses Point is situated only four miles from Sligo Town, which is noted as a centre of the arts. It is also where the celebrated tenor, Count John McCormack, who was to become arguably the 20th century's finest singer of Handel and Mozart, went from his native Athlone to receive a secondary education on scholarship at Summerhill College.

The area of Sligo/Roscommon/Leitrim contains the relatively few number of 13 courses: Sligo - Ballymote, Co Sligo, Enniscrone, Strandhill, Tubbercurry; Roscommon - Athlone, Ballaghaderreen, Boyle, Castlerea, Roscommon, Strokestown; Leitrim - Ballinamore, Carrick-on-Shannon. But they are rich in quality. It would be difficult to find better links terrain than at Co Sligo (Rosses Point), Enniscrone and Strandhill, while parkland doesn't come any more classi-

cal than at picturesque Athlone GC, overlooking the River Shannon at Hodson Bay. Roscommon GC is also developing an enviable reputation since its extension to 18 holes.

By comparison, golf in Leitrim, comprising two nine-hole courses, is decidedly modest. But the county has much else to offer. Indeed nature has fashioned fantastic shapes in the highlands of north Leitrim, where towering cliffs preside over the beautiful rivers and lakes which adorn the floors of deep, silent valleys. The county stretches a slim neck to Atlantic waters on a narrow band of coastline which touches the County Donegal resort of Bundoran. Nearby Lough Melvin is an angler's paradise and is a shared amenity with County Fermanagh in Northern Ireland.

Further south, Lough Allen, the first of the River Shannon's great lakes, effectively splits the county in two. Broken, rugged countryside and smaller, fish-filled lakes are a feature south of Lough Allen while Carrick-on-Shannon, the county

Glencar Waterfall, Co Leitrim

town, boasts one of the finest pleasure cruiser marinas in Ireland. The Shannon-Erne Waterway, an old canal given a new lease on life, joins the Shannon with Lough Erne. Meanwhile, the towns and villages are rural centres of considerable charm and are used to playing host to the many international anglers who come to enjoy the wild fish in prolific Leitrim waters.

Roscommon, which stretches a compact 62 miles from north to south, offers similar attractions for the discerning fisherman, as one might expect from a county bounded to the east by the River Shannon and to the west by the River Suck. In fact two-thirds of the county is bordered by water, with Lough Key, Lough Gara and Lough Boderg to the north and Lough Ree on the Shannon to the east. As the one-time capital of Connacht, the county gave ancient Ireland its last High King (Ard Ri) and modern Ireland its first President. So, it is hardly surprising that Roscommon, in the heart of the country, treasures its old-world charm where the locals invariably find time to stop and talk. Dr Douglas Hyde, the first President of Ireland and founder of the Gaelic League, is commemorated in an Interpretive Centre halfway between the towns of Ballaghaderreen and Frenchpark, on the N5. Housed in the church where his father was rector, the exhibition acknowledges Hyde's immense contributions to the Irish language and traditions.

Lough Key Forest Park, Co Roscommon

The county museum is to be found in Roscommon Town, where exhibits include a ninth-century inscribed slab from St Coman's foundation and a replica of the Cross of Cong. Closeby is Roscommon jail which had the distinction of a female hangman in the person of "Lady Betty". As a classic Irish solution to an Irish problem, she was a criminal who had her sentence for murder quashed on condition that she carried out the hangman's duties without fee.

Location of Golf Courses

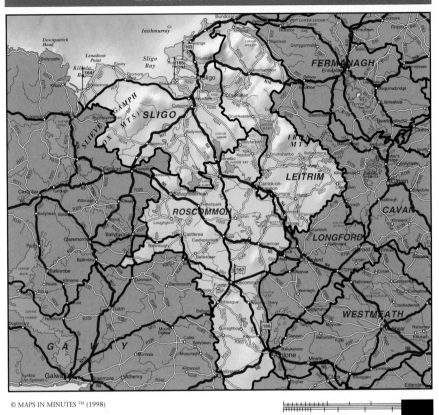

© MAPS IN MINUTES ™ (1998)

County Sligo

County Sligo Golf Club, Rosses Point, Co Sligo

Tel: 071 77186/77134

Joe Carr, 12 times winner of the West of Ireland amateur title at Co Sligo, described its challenge with typical succinctness. "At the risk of being accused of clapping myself on the back, I would suggest its great strength is that it almost invariably produced good winners," said Carr.

He went on: "It is not possible to scramble successfully at Rosses Point: the right golf shots have to be played." And Tom Watson, who visited there with his good friend Byron Nelson in July 1989, made particular mention of the quality of the 14th and 17th holes while describing it as "a magnificent links."

Though the club was founded in 1894, the course as we now know it didn't come into being until 35 years later. That was when the design of distinguished architect Harry Colt, for a fee of forty guineas plus £9.7.0d expenses, came into play, to general acclaim.

Popularly known as Rosses Point, after the village closeby, Co Sligo is being extended to 27 holes, through the construction of an additional nine in wetlands known as Bomore. This work, allied to the re-sodding of 10 greens on the championship layout, caused the West of Ireland Championship to be switched to Enniscrone for the last three years.

The "West" returned to its spiritual home, however, for the millennium. Meanwhile, the club has a regular stream of distinguished visitors, including Manchester United manager, Sir Alex Ferguson, who played there recently with local man Sean Fallon, former assistant manager at Celtic.

Sec/Manager:	Teresa Banks
Professional:	Leslie Robinson
Directions:	5 miles North West of Sligo off the R291
Type of Course:	Links
Date Founded:	1894
No of Holes:	18 (plus 9)
Length:	6608 yds (6043 mtrs)
Par:	71
SSS:	72

Green Fees:	Mon. to Thurs.: £35 Fri. Sat. Sun.: £45
Visitors:	Welcome: Any Day, Contact Club in advance
Societies:	Welcome: Special concessions, Contact Club for details
Facilities:	Chipping/Putting Area, Practice Area, Golf Clubs for hire, Trolley hire, Electric Buggy hire, Bar, Restaurant, Caddy service by arrangement

Accommodation, Food and Drink

Reference numbers below refer to detailed information provided in section 2

Accommodation

Atlantic View House, Bundoran, Co Donegal
Tel: 072 41403 Bed & Breakfast Accommodation in a two-storey town house with ocean views. Owners are keen golfers.   203

Castle Arms Hotel, Enniscrone, Co Sligo
Tel/Fax: 096 36156 A family-run hotel in the heart of Enniscrone. 27 en suite bedrooms with tv and telephone. Restaurant and bar. Seconds from the beach.   511

Glenview B&B, Strandhill Road, Sligo, Co Sligo
Tel: 071 70401/62457 Modern Bed & Breakfast establishment a mile from Sligo town. Four en suite bedrooms with tv and central heating.   512

Hillside House, Doon, Corrigeenroe, Boyle, Co Roscommon
Tel: 079 66075 Four B&B rooms in an attractive country home beside Lough Key with its forest, fishing and boating. Great views.

Portnason House, Ballyshannon, Co Donegal
Tel : 072 52016 Fax: 072 31739 A Georgian house of real character, set in extensive grounds and offering B&B Accommodation in 10 spacious en suite bedrooms.   202

St Martins, Enniscrone, Co Mayo
Tel: 096 36111 A prime site on the main street for a long, single-storey house offering Bed & Breakfast. Seven en suite rooms.   513

The Royal Hotel, Boyle, Co Roscommon
Tel: 079 62016 Sixteen en suite bedrooms in a town centre hotel with a large car park, cosy bars and a riverside restaurant.   520

Food and Drink

Castle Arms Hotel, Enniscrone, Co Sligo
Tel/Fax: 096 36156 A family-run hotel in the heart of Enniscrone. 27 en suite bedrooms with tv and telephone. Restaurant and bar. Seconds from the beach.   511

Fiddlers Creek, Sligo, Co Sligo
Tel: 071 41866 Traditionally appointed bar and restaurant in the town centre. Excellent all-day menu. Live music Wednesday, Thursday and Friday.   510

The Royal Hotel, Boyle, Co Roscommon
Tel: 079 62016 Sixteen en suite bedrooms in a town centre hotel with a large car park, cosy bars and a riverside restaurant.   520

Enniscrone

Enniscrone Golf Club, Enniscrone, Co Silgo

Tel: 096 36297

Last year, Enniscrone celebrated the silver jubilee of their 18-hole status and work is in progress on an additional nine holes, designed by the British architect, Donald Steel. It is no more than one has come to expect from this highly progressive club on Ireland's western seaboard.

In recent years, the club have proved their worth through the successful staging of the Irish Close Championship of 1993, the Irish Women's Close of 1997 and the West of Ireland Championship of 1997, 1998 and 1999. Then

there was the new clubhouse extension which was opened in May 1998.

Fresh from critical acclaim for his design of Waterville, Eddie Hackett was equally proud of his work in extending the original nine to 18 holes in 1974. Typically, his fee was modest and by working with local volunteers, he managed to revamp existing holes and extend the layout for the ridiculously small outlay of less than £5,000.

In the event, the back nine is entirely Hackett's creation and reflects a marvellous empathy with majestic duneland. Memorable holes such as the tricky 10th and more testing par-four 11th and 15th holes, lead on to the utterly charming, par-three 17th.

Set on the shores of Killala Bay, the quality of the terrain prompted a leading architect to describe it as "the last site for a great links course development in the British Isles." And it will be suitably complemented by Steel's design of a £1 million project scheduled to be in play in 2001.

Sec/Manager:	Brian Casey
Professional:	Charles McGoldrick
Directions:	Half mile South of Enniscrone off the R297 to Ballina
Type of Course:	Links
Date Founded:	1918
No of Holes:	18
Length:	6620 yds (6053 mtrs)
Par:	72
SSS:	72
Green Fees:	Weekdays: £26 Weekends & Bank Holidays: £35
Visitors:	Welcome: Any Day, Restrictions on Sunday
Societies:	Welcome: Special concessions, Contact Club for details
Facilities:	Chipping/Putting Area, Practice Area, Driving Range, Golf Clubs for hire, Trolley hire, Electric Buggy hire, Bar, Restaurant, Caddy service by arrangement

Accommodation, Food and Drink

Reference numbers below refer to detailed information provided in section 2

Accommodation

Ashleam House, Ballina, Co Mayo
Tel: 096 22406 Six letting bedrooms (4 en suite) in a neat Bed & Breakfast house south of Ballina and only yards from the River Moy. 414

Castle Arms Hotel, Enniscrone, Co Sligo
Tel/Fax: 096 36156 A family-run hotel in the heart of Enniscrone. 27 en suite bedrooms with tv and telephone. Restaurant and bar. Seconds from the beach. 511

Claddagh House, Ballina, Co Mayo
Tel: 096 71670 Six bedrooms, all en suite, in a stand-alone Bed & Breakfast establishment on the Sligo road out of Ballina. Easy parking. 410

Downhill Inn, Ballina, Co Mayo
Tel: 096 73444 Fax: 096 73411 A welcoming modern hotel with 45 rooms, all with two beds, en suite bath/shower, tv, telephone. Restaurant, bar, patio, gardens. 413

Drom Caoin, Belmullet, Co Mayo
Tel/Fax: 097 81195 A striking modern house offering a choice of Bed & Breakfast (evening meals with notice) or self-catering Accommodation. Golfing breaks a speciality. 418

Enniscoe House, Ballina, Crossmolina, Co Mayo
Tel: 096 31112 A 17th-century house of great charm on the shores of Lough Conn. Six en suite bedrooms, also 3 courtyard apartments. 411

Hillside House, Doon, Corrigeenroe, Boyle, Co Roscommon
Tel: 079 66075 Four B&B rooms in an attractive country home beside Lough Key with its forest, fishing and boating. Great views.

Quignalegan House, Ballina Road, Co Mayo
Tel/Fax: 096 71644 Five en suite bedrooms in a purpose-built modern house with imposing grounds and a huge car park. 412

St Martins, Enniscrone, Co Mayo
Tel: 096 36111 A prime site on the main street for a long, single-storey house offering Bed & Breakfast. Seven en suite rooms. 513

Suncroft, Ballina, Co Mayo
Tel: 096 21573 Excellent modern B&B townhouse in the shadow of the Cathedral. Renowned breakfasts. Popular base for anglers. 423

Food and Drink

Castle Arms Hotel, Enniscrone, Co Sligo
Tel/Fax: 096 36156 A family-run hotel in the heart of Enniscrone. 27 en suite bedrooms with tv and telephone. Restaurant and bar. Seconds from the beach. 511

Downhill Inn, Ballina, Co Mayo
Tel: 096 73444 Fax: 096 73411 A welcoming modern hotel with 45 rooms, all with two beds, en suite bath/shower, tv, telephone. Restaurant, bar, patio, gardens. 413

Fiddlers Creek, Sligo, Co Sligo
Tel: 071 41866 Traditionally appointed bar and restaurant in the town centre. Excellent all-day menu. Live music Wednesday, Thursday and Friday. 510

Lavelle's Erris Bar, Belmullet, Co Mayo
Tel: 097 82222 Fax: 097 81056 A typical Irish pub with bags of atmosphere. Food served all day & high-season restaurant. Coffee shop adjacent. 419

Strandhill

Strandhill Golf Club, Strandhill, Co Sligo
Tel: 071 68188

Sec/Manager:	John Donogue
Professional:	None
Directions:	5 miles West of Sligo City off the R292
Type of Course:	Links
Date Founded:	1931
No of Holes:	18
Length:	6162 yds (5635 mtrs)
Par:	69
SSS:	68
Green Fees:	Weekdays: £25 Weekends & Bank Holidays: £30

Visitors: Welcome: Contact club in advance
Societies: Welcome: Special concessions,
              Contact Club for details
Facilities: Chipping/Putting Area, Practice Area,
              Golf Clubs for hire, Trolley hire,
              Electric Buggy hire, Bar, Restaurant

Accommodation, Food and Drink

Reference numbers below refer to detailed
information provided in section 2

Accommodation

Atlantic View House, Bundoran, Co Donegal

Tel: 072 41403 Bed & Breakfast Accommodation in a two-storey town house with
ocean views. Owners are keen golfers.   203

Castle Arms Hotel, Enniscrone, Co Sligo

Tel/Fax: 096 36156 A family-run hotel in the heart of Enniscrone. 27 en suite
bedrooms with tv and telephone. Restaurant and bar. Seconds from the beach.   511

Claddagh House, Ballina, Co Mayo

Tel: 096 71670 Six bedrooms, all en suite, in a stand-alone Bed & Breakfast
establishment on the Sligo road out of Ballina. Easy parking.   410

Downhill Inn, Ballina, Co Mayo

Tel: 096 73444 Fax: 096 73411 A welcoming modern hotel with 45 rooms, all with
two beds, en suite bath/shower, tv, telephone. Restaurant, bar, patio, gardens.   413

Enniscoe House, Ballina, Crossmolina, Co Mayo

Tel: 096 31112 A 17th-century house of great charm on the shores of Lough Conn.
Six en suite bedrooms, also 3 courtyard apartments.   411

Glenview B&B, Strandhill Road, Sligo, Co Sligo

Tel: 071 70401/62459 Modern Bed & Breakfast establishment a mile from Sligo
town. Four en suite bedrooms with tv and central heating.   512

Hillside House, Doon, Corrigeenroe, Boyle, Co Roscommon

Tel: 079 66075 Four B&B rooms in an attractive country home beside Lough Key
with its forest, fishing and boating. Great views.   515

Portnason House, Ballyshannon, Co Donegal

Tel : 072 52016 Fax: 072 31739 A Georgian house of real character, set in extensive
grounds and offering B&B Accommodation in 10 spacious en suite bedrooms.   202

St Martins, Enniscrone, Co Mayo

Tel: 096 36111 A prime site on the main street for a long, single-storey house
offering Bed & Breakfast. Seven en suite rooms.   513

The Royal Hotel, Boyle, Co Roscommon

Tel: 079 62016 Sixteen en suite bedrooms in a town centre hotel with a large car
park, cosy bars and a riverside restaurant.   520

Food and Drink

Castle Arms Hotel, Enniscrone, Co Sligo

Tel/Fax: 096 36156 A family-run hotel in the heart of Enniscrone. 27 en suite
bedrooms with tv and telephone. Restaurant and bar. Seconds from the beach.   511

Downhill Inn, Ballina, Co Mayo

Tel: 096 73444 Fax: 096 73411 A welcoming modern hotel with 45 rooms, all with
two beds, en suite bath/shower, tv, telephone. Restaurant, bar, patio, gardens.   413

Fiddlers Creek, Sligo, Co Sligo

Tel: 071 41866 Traditionally appointed bar and restaurant in the town centre.
Excellent all-day menu. Live music Wednesday, Thursday and Friday.   510

The Royal Hotel, Boyle, Co Roscommon

Tel: 079 62016 Sixteen en suite bedrooms in a town centre hotel with a large car
park, cosy bars and a riverside restaurant.   520

Athlone

Athlone Golf Club, Hodson Bay, Athlone, Co Roscommon

Tel: 090 292073

A few years after Athlone GC was founded in
1892, its original nine-hole course, which was
built around an old fortification, was described

as "difficult". This is hardly surprising, given that
the hazards are listed as walls, moats, ditches,
roads and the railway.

At a cost of less than £1,000, however, the
club moved to its present location in 1938, and
it could hardly be more pleasing, overlooking
Lough Ree on the River Shannon at Hodson Bay.
Another major step was taken 34 years later at
considerably greater cost.

On August 28th 1972, a new, £41,000 clubhouse, was officially opened, giving Athlone its
status it desired as one of the leading clubs in
Connacht. Since then, it has been used regularly
for GUI competitions, most recently for a highly
successful staging of the All-Ireland Cups and
Shields Finals of 1998.

The club's best-known personality was Jack
O'Sullivan, honorary secretary of the Connacht
Branch GUI for 25 years. A formidable competitor, he scorned the usual handicap calculations
on the first tee. Instead, having watched the op-
position take a few practice swings, he would
turn to his partner and whisper: "I think we can
give these chucks a few up." And he invariably
won.

The feature hole is the 453-yard 16th, a semi-
dogleg left, which hugs the shore of the lake on
the left, while a large oak stands sentinel down
the right. Despite a relatively modest overall
length of 6,529 yards off the back tees, it remains
a formidable test.

Sec/Manager:	Laurence Fagin
Professional:	Martin Quinn
Directions:	4 miles from Athlone off the N61 to Roscommon on the shores of Lough Ree
Type of Course:	Parkland
Date Founded:	1892
No of Holes:	18
Length:	6401 yds (5854 mtrs)
Par:	71
SSS:	71
Green Fees:	Weekdays: £18 Weekends & Public Holidays: £20
Visitors:	Welcome: Any Day, Contact Club for details
Societies:	Welcome: Special concessions, Contact the Club in advance
Facilities:	Chipping/Putting Area, Practice Area, Golf Clubs for hire, Trolley hire, Electric Buggy hire, Bar, Restaurant, Caddy service by arrangement

Accommodation, Food and Drink

Reference numbers below refer to detailed information provided in section 2

Accommodation

Creagduff House, Coosan, Athlone, Co Westmeath
Tel: 090 275891 Two self-catering apartments, each sleeping up to 4, on a 300-year-old estate. Easy parking. Tv. No credit cards.

Catstone Lodge, Ballymore, Co. Westmeath
Tel: 044 56494 Fax: 044 56196 www.catstone.net Luxurious en suite bedrooms (60 sq m each) in a restored period-style farmhouse. Tv, sitting area, kitchenette. B&B or self-catering.

Lisroyne Inn, Strokestown, Co Roscommon
Tel: 078 33214 The smartest pub in town - neat and spotless. A warm welcome, good drinking and snacking. 521

Regans, Market Square, Roscommon, Co Roscommon
Tel: 0903 25339/26373 14 en suite bedrooms, day-long restaurant, bar, nightclub and function room - under one roof in the town centre. 524

The Gardens, The Walk, Roscommon, Co Roscommon
Tel/Fax: 090 326828 Four simply-appointed en suite bedrooms in a Bed & Breakfast house near the main roundabout in Roscommon. Parking available.

Villa St John, Athlone, Co Westmeath
Tel/Fax: 090 292490 Eight bedrooms, five en suite, in a smart modern Bed & Breakfast house half a mile out of Athlone. Large terrace. Easy parking. 601

Food and Drink

Chungs Chinese Restaurant, Boyle, Co. Roscommon
Tel: 079 62016 Fax: 079 64949 A Chinese restaurant in the Royal Hotel Boyle, with the usual long à la carte list and set menus for two or more.

Hillside House, Doon, Corrigeenroe, Boyle, Co Roscommon
Tel: 079 66075 Four B&B rooms in an attractive country home beside Lough Key with its forest, fishing and boating. Great views.

Lisroyne Inn, Strokestown, Co Roscommon
Tel: 078 33214 The smartest pub in town - neat and spotless. A warm welcome, good drinking and snacking. 521

Regans, Market Square, Roscommon, Co Roscommon
Tel: 090 325339/326373 14 en suite bedrooms, day-long restaurant, bar, nightclub and function room - under one roof in the town centre. 524

Roscommon

Roscommon Golf Club, Mote Park, Roscommon, Co Roscommon

Tel: 090 326382

Though progress at Roscommon GC may have been slow, it has been admirably steady, culminating in what are now regarded as among the finest amenities in Connacht. Their championship-standard, 18-hole layout is clearly a far cry from the modest six-hole stretch, which launched golf in the town, back in 1904.

From their original location at Ballingard, they moved to their present home at Moate Park, which was purchased in 1948. But it was more than 40 years later before the opportunity arose to extend to 18 holes.

This was done in 1996 to a design by Eddie Connaughton, who used mature, wooded terrain to excellent effect, so much so that it is virtually impossible to distinguish the new holes from the old. In the process, he achieved a testing, overall length of 6,900 yards off the back tees.

Meanwhile, the members had to endure the trauma of losing their clubhouse through fire in 1995. But with admirable resilience and an overall investment of £1.2 million (pounds), they now have a new, purpose-built clubhouse to complement their extended course.

The charming, pastoral setting contains gentle rather than dramatic inclines, which are seen to interesting effect around the turn. At the north-facing ninth, a par-three of 179 yards, an elevated tee-shot is played to a well-trapped green 20 yards below, where water beckons on the left. Then comes the formidable, 446-yard 10th, which is played uphill all the way, with trees lining both sides of the fairway, to the elevated green.

Sec/Manager:	Cathal McConn
Professional:	None
Directions:	Half mile South East oif Roscommon off the N61 to Athlone
Type of Course:	Parkland
Date Founded:	1904
No of Holes:	18
Length:	6605 yds (6040 mtrs)
Par:	72
SSS:	70
Green Fees:	1st Nov. to 15th March: £10 At other times: £15
Visitors:	Welcome: Any Day, Contact Club for tee-times
Societies:	Welcome: Special concessions, Contact Club for details
Facilities:	Chipping/Putting Area, Practice Area, Trolley hire, Electric Buggy hire, Bar, Restaurant

Accommodation, Food and Drink

Reference numbers below refer to detailed information provided in section 2

Accommodation

Catstone Lodge, Ballymore, Co. Westmeath
Tel: 044 56494 Fax: 044 56196 Luxurious en suite bedrooms (60 sq m each) in a restored period-style farmhouse. Tv, sitting area, kitchenette. B&B or self-catering.

Glencarne House, Ardcarne, Carrick-on-Shannon, Co Roscommon
Tel: 079 67013 Four en suite bedrooms in a Bed & Breakfast house on a working beef farm. Close to Lough Key Forest Park.

Hillside House, Doon, Corrigeenroe, Boyle, Co Roscommon
Tel: 079 66075 Four B&B rooms in an attractive country home beside Lough Key with its forest, fishing and boating. Great views.

Lackan Lodge, Edgeworthstown, Co Longford
Tel: 043 71299 Four guest bedrooms (2 en suite) in a peacefully located modern farmhouse on the Longford side of Edgeworthstown. No smoking.   482

Lacken House, Rahara, Athleague, Co Roscommon
Tel/Fax: 090 323449 Choose between B&B in the handsome 1820s manor and self-catering lodges in the grounds. Peaceful rural setting.   523

Longford Arms Hotel, Longford, Co Longford
Tel: 043 46296 Comfortable family-run hotel in the main street. Well-appointed Accommodation includes 18 executive rooms with both bath and shower en suite. Coffee shop.   481

Regans, Market Square, Roscommon, Co Roscommon
Tel: 090 325339/326373 14 en suite bedrooms, day-long restaurant, bar, nightclub and function room - under one roof in the town centre.   524

The Gardens, The Walk, Roscommon, Co Roscommon
Tel/Fax: 090 326828 Four simply-appointed en suite bedrooms in a Bed & Breakfast house near the main roundabout in Roscommon. Parking available.

The Royal Hotel, Boyle, Co Roscommon
Tel: 079 62016 Sixteen en suite bedrooms in a town centre hotel with a large car park, cosy bars and a riverside restaurant.   520

Viewmount House, Longford, Co Longford
Tel: 043 41919 High-quality Accommodation in a former farmhouse a mile from the town centre. En suite bedrooms, lovely gardens, fine dining.   480

Food and Drink

Bella Pasta, Roosky, Co Roscommon
Tel: 078 6705556 A taste of Italy in an Irish bar complex just yards from the Shannon. Pizza, pasta and many other favourites.   522

Chungs Chinese Restaurant, Boyle, Co. Roscommon
Tel: 079 62016 Fax: 079 64949 A Chinese restaurant in the Royal Hotel Boyle, with the usual long à la carte list and set menus for two or more.

Hillside House, Doon, Corrigeenroe, Boyle, Co Roscommon
Tel: 079 66075 Four B&B rooms in an attractive country home beside Lough Key with its forest, fishing and boating. Great views.

Lisroyne Inn, Strokestown, Co Roscommon
Tel: 078 33214 The smartest pub in town - neat and spotless. A warm welcome, good drinking and snacking.   521

Longford Arms Hotel, Longford, Co Longford
Tel: 043 46296 Comfortable family-run hotel in the main street. Well-appointed Accommodation includes 18 executive rooms with both bath and shower en suite. Coffee shop.   481

Regans, Market Square, Roscommon, Co Roscommon
Tel: 090 325339/326373 14 en suite bedrooms, day-long restaurant, bar, nightclub and function room - under one roof in the town centre.   524

The Royal Hotel, Boyle, Co Roscommon
Tel: 079 62016 Sixteen en suite bedrooms in a town centre hotel with a large car park, cosy bars and a riverside restaurant.   520

Viewmount House, Longford, Co Longford
Tel: 043 41919 High-quality Accommodation in a former farmhouse a mile from the town centre. En suite bedrooms, lovely gardens, fine dining.   480

TIPPERARY

The careers of leading Irish amateur golfers are quite revealing for the way they emphasise the extent to which modest, playing facilities can be overcome as a possible barrier to success at the highest level. Indeed one would be tempted to conclude that clear benefits could be derived from tightly-conceived, nine-hole layouts.

We think of Walker Cup representatives Joe Carr and his son Roddy at Sutton GC; of Tom Craddock and Philip Walton at Malahide and of three-times Irish Amateur Close champion Martin O'Brien from New Ross. And we think of Arthur Pierse, a Walker Cup player in 1983 and winner of four important championships. Pierse learned the game on the nine-hole stretch at

Tipperary GC which, though measuring a reasonably testing 6,386 yards when played twice around the medal tees, had the rather basic deficiency of having no bunkers. Yet it is interesting that Pierse became one of the finest bunker players of his time, by sharpening his sand-skills on "away" courses. Along with Malahide (27 holes) and New Ross, Tipperary GC has since graduated to bigger things. Extended to 18 holes in 1993, it measures

Rock of Cashel, Cashel, Co Tipperary

6,488 yards off the medal tees. All of which makes it rather ironic that Pierse now lives down the road, directly beside the Ballykisteen club, where he is a member.

Tipperary is acknowledged as an important sporting county not least for the fact that it was the birthplace of the Gaelic Athletic Association - the world's biggest amateur sports body. It is also the home of 11 golf clubs - Ballykisteen, Cahir Park, Carrick-on-Suir, Clonmel, Co Tipperary, Nenagh, Rockwell, Roscrea, Templemore, Thurles and Tipperary. Co Tipperary. located six miles from Cashel on the road to Dundrum village, should not be confused with its abbreviated namesake. It is part of the Dundrum House Hotel complex in the heart of the county, where Philip Walton did an admirable design job. Since it came into being in 1993, the 6,000 trees which were planted at that time have begun to blend in seamlessly with a long-established selection of majestic oak, beech and lime. The county also has reason to be proud of Thurles GC with its magnificent, 18th century clubhouse. Thanks to the stubborn insistence of a group of enlightened members, the decision was made to restore rather than demolish the one-time Turulla House, at a cost of £200,000. The finished product has become a model for other clubs confronted by a similar dilemma.

Tipperary can boast other, considerably older buildings. Indeed while travelling through the so-called Premier County, there can be few more inspiring sights in the gathering dusk than the floodlit Rock of Cashel, glowing in her ancient splendour. Roscrea also has a castle, dating back to the 13th century and Nenagh Castle was built circa 1200 by Theobald FitzWalter, the Norman who received large grants of land in Co Tipperary. As with Cashel, much of Nenagh Castle survives, notably the gatehouse and the roofless, circular keep, which has reasonably well-preserved features such as the stairs, machicolation (parapet), loops, fireplaces, corbels and the original wall-walk. The Clare Glens, named after the Clare River which was responsible for their creation, straddle the Limerick/Tipperary border, south of the charming agricultural town of Newport. Managed by both the Limerick and Tipperary county councils, they constitute an outstanding amenity area with picnic sites, a two-mile nature trail and natural rock pools.

Meanwhile, nestling along Lough Derg is the county's lakeside area where 32,000 acres of calm, clear water abound with fish. The area stretches from Killalow/Ballina to Portumna and includes several miles of inland villages offering excellent accommodation and restaurants.

Then there are the horses. Indeed thoroughbreds have become synonymous with Tipperary, mainly through the spectacular success achieved on both the flat and in national hunt, by the distinguished trainer, Vincent O'Brien. And a wonderful tradition has now become accessible to the general public through the Charlie Swan Equestrian Centre at Cloughjordan, close to Lough Derg. The centre offers daily sessions, which include individual lessons, cross-country riding, show-jumping, schooling and general horsemanship classes for enthusiasts of all levels of skill, from the absolute beginner to the accomplished rider. Instruction is supervised by Swan, an Irish national hunt champion jockey who has also become familiar to punters in Britain, particularly from riding J P McManus-owned horses at the Cheltenham National Hunt Festival.

The north of the county is dominated by its distinctive mountains and hill ranges, offering panoramic views of lush plains dotted with forest, bog and patchwork fields. Keeper, which is in the Silvermines range, south of Nenagh, is the highest peek at 2,279 feet and it is possible to drive right to the top on one of the many forest roads which traverse these foothills. South of Keeper is the Slieve Felim range, with Mauherslieve as the highest peak. For the antiquarian, there are some 20 megalithic

Bridge on the River Suir, Co Tipperary

tombs, dating back 4,000 years and surviving in varying fragmentary condition. Then, over the north-western plain of Ormond, in O'Kennedy country, the fairy hill of Knockshigowna can be seen for miles. It's quite a gentle climb up its pastured slopes to view the countless shades of green, dominating the Tipperary landscape.

Yet for all its natural splendour, Tipperary is probably best known internationally through the celebrated World War I song which became a particular favourite with British troops.

"It's a long way to Tipperary; it's a long way to go
To the sweetest girl I know
Goodbye Piccadilly; farewell Leicester Square
It's a long, long way to Tipperary, but my heart lies there."

Location of Golf Courses

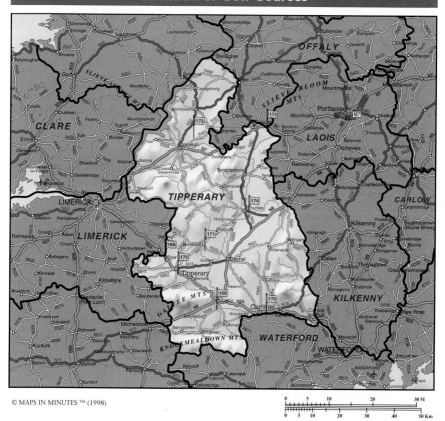

© MAPS IN MINUTES ™ (1998)

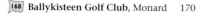

Ballykisteen

Ballykisteen Golf Club, Monard, Co Tipperary

Tel: 062 33333

Back in 1991, when land prices were depressed, Noel and Josephine Ryan paid £530,000 for what had been a major stud farm off the N24, just past Limerick Junction and three miles from Tipperary Town. "I'm not daft, but this is the daftest thing I have done in my life," said Josephine, recalling the deal.

Date Founded:	1994
No of Holes:	18
Length:	6765 yds (6185 mtrs)
Par:	72
SSS:	74
Green Fees:	Weekdays: £20 Weekends & Bank Holidays: £22
Visitors:	Welcome: Book in advance
Societies:	Welcome: Special concessions, Contact Club for details
Facilities:	Chipping/Putting Area, Practice Area, Driving Range, Golf Clubs for hire, Trolley hire, Electric Buggy hire, Bar, Restaurant, Caddy service by arrangement

Accommodation, Food and Drink

Reference numbers below refer to detailed information provided in section 2

Accommodation

Ashmore House, Co Tipperary
Tel: 062 61286 Fax: 062 62789 Town-centre Georgian house with six letting B&B bedrooms including a family room. Extensive breakfast menu. Private parking. Garden. 548

Ballinacounty House, Glen of Aherlow, Co Tipperary
Tel/Fax: 062 56000 Flexible B&B and self-catering Accommodation in 5 rooms and 2 cottages in a lovely rural setting. Restaurant with wine licence. 550

Hawthorn View, Thurles, Co Tipperary
Tel: 050 421710 4 en suite Bed & Breakfast rooms in a modern bungalow set back from the N62. Very close to Thurles Golf Course. Equestrian Centre nearby. 540

Rectory House Hotel, Dundrum, Co Tipperary
Tel: 062 71266 Fax: 062 71115 Large en suite bedrooms in a secluded 19th-century house. Intimate restaurant, spacious bar and lounge. 547

Food and Drink

Ballinacounty House, Glen of Aherlow, Co Tipperary
Tel/Fax: 062 56000 Flexible B&B and self-catering Accommodation in 5 rooms and 2 cottages in a lovely rural setting. Restaurant with wine licence. 550

Donovan's, Tipperary, Co Tipperary
Tel: 062 51384 Close to the town centre, a warm and welcoming bar and restaurant with a strong sporting theme. Beer garden. 551

Rectory House Hotel, Dundrum, Co Tipperary
Tel: 062 71266 Fax: 062 71115 Large en suite bedrooms in a secluded 19th-century house. Intimate restaurant, spacious bar and lounge. 547

Two years later, the Ryans' moment of daftness became Ballykisteen GC, a proprietary club, named after the stud farm. Their thinking was that there was scope for another course in the area, given that Tipperary GC was only nine holes (it has since been extended to 18).

On a generous site of 176 acres, the design team of Des Smyth and Declan Branigan came up with a layout worthy of the spectacularly rolling terrain and beautiful location. In fact the course is set in the heart of the Golden Vale, only half an hour's drive from the Glen of Aherlow and surrounded by the majestic Galtee Mountains and picturesque hills.

Apart from the planting of 30,000 trees, construction work at Ballykisteen was carried out to admirable standards, characterised by the beautifully-built, cut-stone wall behind the water fronting the eighth green. And to the left, is an equally attractive bridge, about 10 yards short of the first green.

Other features to delight the membership of 200, are the stream meandering across the centre of the course and a small burn, strategically placed 80 yards short of the green at the 546-yard 18th.

Sec/Manager:	Josephine Ryan
Professional:	David Reddan
Directions:	2 miles North West of Tipperary Town on N24 to Limerick
Type of Course:	Parkland

Cahir Park

Cahir Park, Kilcommon, Cahir, Co Tipperary

Tel: 052 41474

Sec/Manager:	John Costigan
Professional:	None
Directions:	1 mile South of Cahir on the R668 to Kilcommen
Type of Course:	Parkland
Date Founded:	1968
No of Holes:	18
Length:	6348 yds (5805 mtrs)
Par:	71
SSS:	71
Green Fees:	£15
Visitors:	Welcome : Any Day

Societies:	Welcome: Special concessions, Contact Club for details
Facilities:	Chipping/Putting Area, Practice Area, Trolley hire, Electric Buggy hire, Bar, Restaurant

Accommodation, Food and Drink

Reference numbers below refer to detailed information provided in section 2

Accommodation

Annagh Lodge, Coolbawn, Nenagh, Co Tipperary
Tel/Fax: 067 24225 Five comfortably appointed B&B rooms in a period country house on a 200-acre working farm. Dinner by arrangement. 545

Arden Lodge, Cahir, Co Tipperary
Tel: 052 42338 An exclusive modern bungalow offering four very comfortable B&B bedrooms a short walk from the town centre. 552

Ballinacounty House, Glen of Aherlow, Co Tipperary
Tel/Fax: 062 56000 Flexible B&B and self-catering Accommodation in 5 rooms and 2 cottages in a lovely rural setting. Restaurant with wine licence. 550

Benuala, Clonmel, Co Tipperary
Tel: 052 22158 En suite Accommodation in six good-sized rooms in a modern bungalow close to town. Private car park. 559

Fennessy's Hotel, Clonmel, Co Tipperary
Tel: 052 23680 Fax: 052 23783 Ten-bedroomed hotel offering flexible en suite Accommodation in a prime site off the main street. Leisure centre next door. 554

Indaville, Cashel, Co Tipperary
Tel: 062 62075 Built as a country lodge around 1750, now a comfortable, civilised Bed & Breakfast with five large letting bedrooms. 556

Knocklofty House, Knocklofty, Clonmel, Co Tipperary
Tel: 052 25444 Fax: 052 26444 A gracious country house set in 35 acres of gardens. 14 beautifully appointed bedrooms. Restaurant. Also self-catering. 557

Marlfield House, Clonmel, Co Tipperary
Tel: 052 25444 12 self-contained self-catering apartments in a late 18th-century residence on the banks of the Suir. 558

Tír Na Nóg, Dualla, Cashel, Co Tipperary
Tel: 062 61350 Fax: 062 62411 A warm, friendly country home on the R691. Six en suite bedrooms with orthopaedic beds. B&B, packed lunch, snacks, dinner by arrangement. 555

Food and Drink

Ballinacounty House, Glen of Aherlow, Co Tipperary
Tel/Fax: 062 56000 Flexible B&B and self-catering Accommodation in 5 rooms and 2 cottages in a lovely rural setting. Restaurant with wine licence. 550

Fennessy's Hotel, Clonmel, Co Tipperary
Tel: 052 23680 Fax: 052 23783 Ten-bedroomed hotel offering flexible en suite Accommodation in a prime site off the main street. Leisure centre next door. 554

Knocklofty House, Knocklofty, Clonmel, Co Tipperary
Tel: 052 25444 Fax: 052 26444 A gracious country house set in 35 acres of gardens. 14 beautifully appointed bedrooms. Restaurant. Also self-catering. 557

Clonmel

Clonmel Golf Club, Lyneaneala, Mountain Road, Clonmel, Co Tipperary
Tel: 052 21138

Sec/Manager:	Aine Myles-Keating
Professional:	Robert Hayes
Directions:	2½ miles South East of Clonmel off the R678 to Rathgormuck
Type of Course:	Parkland
Date Founded:	1911
No of Holes:	18

Length:	6392 yds (5845 mtrs)
Par:	72
SSS:	71
Green Fees:	Weekdays: £18 Weekends & Bank Holidays: £20
Visitors:	Welcome: Contact Club in advance
Societies:	Welcome: Prior booking required
Facilities:	Chipping/Putting Area, Practice Area Golf Clubs for hire, Trolley hire, Electric Buggy hire, Bar, plus Bar Food

Accommodation, Food and Drink

Reference numbers below refer to detailed information provided in section 2

Accommodation

Arden Lodge, Cahir, Co Tipperary
Tel: 052 42338 An exclusive modern bungalow offering four very comfortable B&B bedrooms a short walk from the town centre. 552

Benuala, Clonmel, Co Tipperary
Tel: 052 22158 En suite Accommodation in six good-sized rooms in a modern bungalow close to town. Private car park. 559

Fennessy's Hotel, Clonmel, Co Tipperary
Tel: 052 23680 Fax: 052 23783 Ten-bedroomed hotel offering flexible en suite Accommodation in a prime site off the main street. Leisure centre next door. 554

Indaville, Cashel, Co Tipperary
Tel: 062 62075 Built as a country lodge around 1750, now a comfortable, civilised Bed & Breakfast with five large letting bedrooms. 556

Knocklofty House, Knocklofty, Clonmel, Co Tipperary
Tel: 052 25444 Fax: 052 26444 A gracious country house set in 35 acres of gardens. 14 beautifully appointed bedrooms. Restaurant. Also self-catering. 557

Marlfield House, Clonmel, Co Tipperary
Tel: 052 25444 12 self-contained self-catering apartments in a late 18th-century residence on the banks of the Suir. 558

Tír Na Nóg, Dualla, Cashel, Co Tipperary
Tel: 062 61350 Fax: 062 62411 A warm, friendly country home on the R691. Six en suite bedrooms with orthopaedic beds. B&B, packed lunch, snacks, dinner by arrangement. 555

Food and Drink

Fennessy's Hotel, Clonmel, Co Tipperary
Tel: 052 23680 Fax: 052 23783 Ten-bedroomed hotel offering flexible en suite Accommodation in a prime site off the main street. Leisure centre next door. 554

Knocklofty House, Knocklofty, Clonmel, Co Tipperary
Tel: 052 25444 Fax: 052 26444 A gracious country house set in 35 acres of gardens. 14 beautifully appointed bedrooms. Restaurant. Also self-catering. 557

Orpens Bar & Estuary Restaurant, Knockboy, Co Waterford
Tel: 051 873082 Fax: 051 874180 90-cover family restaurant with lounge and bar. Informal lunchtime menu, all-day bar meals, evening à la carte. Disabled access. 576

County Tipperary

County Tipperary Golf & Country Club, Dundrum, Co Tipperary
Tel: 062 71116

Sec/Manager:	William Crowe
Professional:	None
Directions:	6 miles North West of Cashel off the R505 on the outskirts of Dundrum
Type of Course:	Parkland
Date Founded:	1993
No of Holes:	18

Length:	6725 yds (6150 mtrs)
Par:	72
SSS:	72
Green Fees:	Weekdays: £25 Weekends & Bank Holidays: £28
Visitors:	Welcome: Any Day, Prior booking required
Societies:	Welcome: Special concessions, Contact Club for details
Facilities:	Chipping/Putting Area, Golf Clubs for hire, Trolley hire, Electric Buggy hire, Bar, Restaurant, Caddy service by arrangement

Accommodation, Food and Drink

Reference numbers below refer to detailed information provided in section 2

Accommodation

Ashmore House, Co Tipperary

Tel: 062 61286 Fax: 062 62789 Town-centre Georgian house with six letting B&B bedrooms including a family room. Extensive breakfast menu. Private parking. Garden.   548

Ballinacounty House, Glen of Aherlow, Co Tipperary

Tel/Fax: 062 56000 Flexible B&B and self-catering Accommodation in 5 rooms and 2 cottages in a lovely rural setting. Restaurant with wine licence.   550

Cappamura House, Dundrum, Co Tipperary

Tel: 062 71127 Bed and Breakfast and an equestrian centre in and around a 300-year-old farmhouse. 7 bedrooms, 3 en suite.   546

Hawthorn View, Thurles, Co Tipperary

Tel: 050 421710 4 en suite Bed & Breakfast rooms in a modern bungalow set back from the N62. Very close to Thurles Golf Course. Equestrian Centre nearby.   540

Indaville, Cashel, Co Tipperary

Tel: 062 62075 Built as a country lodge around 1750, now a comfortable, civilised Bed & Breakfast with five large letting bedrooms.   556

Rectory House Hotel, Dundrum, Co Tipperary

Tel: 062 71266 Fax: 062 71115 Large en suite bedrooms in a secluded 19th-century house. Intimate restaurant, spacious bar and lounge.   547

Tír Na Nóg, Dualla, Cashel, Co Tipperary

Tel: 062 61350 Fax: 062 62411 A warm, friendly country home on the R691. Six en suite bedrooms with orthopaedic beds. B&B, packed lunch, snacks, dinner by arrangement.   555

Food and Drink

Ballinacounty House, Glen of Aherlow, Co Tipperary

Tel/Fax: 062 56000 Flexible B&B and self-catering Accommodation in 5 rooms and 2 cottages in a lovely rural setting. Restaurant with wine licence.   550

Fennessy's Hotel, Clonmel, Co Tipperary

Tel: 052 23680 Fax: 052 23783 Ten-bedroomed hotel offering flexible en suite Accommodation in a prime site off the main street. Leisure centre next door.   554

Knocklofty House, Knocklofty, Clonmel, Co Tipperary

Tel: 052 25444 Fax: 052 26444 A gracious country house set in 35 acres of gardens. 14 beautifully appointed bedrooms. Restaurant. Also self-catering.   557

Rectory House Hotel, Dundrum, Co Tipperary

Tel: 062 71266 Fax: 062 71115 Large en suite bedrooms in a secluded 19th-century house. Intimate restaurant, spacious bar and lounge.   547

Nenagh

Nenagh Golf Club, Beechwood, Nenagh, Co Tipperary

Tel: 067 31476

Sec/Manager:	Teresa Starr
Professional:	Gordon Morrison

Directions:	4 miles North East of Nenagh off the R491 to Birt
Type of Course:	Parkland
Date Founded:	1929
No of Holes:	18
Length:	6004 yds (5491 mtrs)
Par:	69
SSS:	68
Green Fees:	£15
Visitors:	Welcome: Prior Booking required
Societies:	Welcome: Prior booking, Contact Club for details
Facilities:	Chipping/Putting Area, Practice Area, Golf Clubs for hire, Trolley hire, Bar, Restaurant

Accommodation, Food and Drink

Reference numbers below refer to detailed information provided in section 2

Accommodation

Annagh Lodge, Coolbawn, Nenagh, Co Tipperary

Tel/Fax: 067 24225 Five comfortably appointed B&B rooms in a period country house on a 200-acre working farm. Dinner by arrangement.   545

Ashley Park House, Ardcroney, Nenagh, Co Tipperary

Tel: 067 38223 Fax: 067 38223 Six twin bedrooms, all en suite, in a handsome early 18th-century residence with a private lake. Bed & Breakfast.   549

Ballinacounty House, Glen of Aherlow, Co Tipperary

Tel/Fax: 062 56000 Flexible B&B and self-catering Accommodation in 5 rooms and 2 cottages in a lovely rural setting. Restaurant with wine licence.   550

Bridget's Bed & Breakfast, Coolbawn, Co Tipperary

Tel: 067 28098 Bed and Breakfast in five en suite rooms in a smart modern bungalow. 5 minutes' walk from Lough Derg.   544

Otway Lodge, Dromineer, Nenagh, Co Tipperary

Tel: 067 24133/24273 Six-bedroomed B&B guest house (all rooms en suite) on the edge of Lough Derg. Boat hire, fishing trips.   542

Riverrun Cottages, Terryglass, Nenagh, Co Tipperary

Tel: 067 22125 4-star self-catering Accommodation in five units, each sleeping 4. Quiet village setting by Lough Derg.   543

Food and Drink

Ballinacounty House, Glen of Aherlow, Co Tipperary

Tel/Fax: 062 56000 Flexible B&B and self-catering Accommodation in 5 rooms and 2 cottages in a lovely rural setting. Restaurant with wine licence.   550

Donovan's, Tipperary, Co Tipperary

Tel: 062 51384 Close to the town centre, a warm and welcoming bar and restaurant with a strong sporting theme. Beer garden.   551

The Beehive, Portumna, Co Galway

Tel: 050 941830 Irish and Italian cuisine in a pleasant oasis just off the main street. Bring your own wine. Last orders 9.30.   267

Roscrea

Roscrea Golf Club, Derryvale, Roscrea, Co Tipperary

Tel: 050 521130

During the 1970s, two Roscrea members made history through some decidedly interesting golfing exploits. With a view to raising funds for local churches, Alfie Clarke played 157 holes in the one day and a year later, he extended the record to 201 holes.

Then, on August 4th 1978, colleague Dan

Since then, one assumes that the members have been too busy enjoying their new surroundings to even contemplate further record attempts.

Sec/Manager:	Steve Crofton
Professional:	None
Directions:	2 miles East of Roscrea off the N7 to Borris in Ossory
Type of Course:	Parkland
Date Founded:	1892
No of Holes:	18
Length:	6323 yds (5782 mtrs)
Par:	71
SSS:	70
Green Fees:	Weekdays: £14 Weekends & Bank Holidays: £17
Visitors:	Welcome: Any Day, Restrictions on Sunday
Societies:	Welcome: Special concessions, Contact the Club in writing
Facilities:	Chipping/Putting Area, Practice Area Golf Clubs for hire, Trolley hire, Bar, Restaurant, Caddy service by arrangement

Hogan took up the challenge. Setting out at 5.45am, he proceeded to play 204 holes in 17 hours - 11 completed rounds of 18 holes and an additional six holes. In the process, he carded an eagle and 30 birdies and had only five double-bogeys, two as a result of lost balls.

These exploits were on a nine-hole layout, largely unchanged since the club had moved to Derryvale in 1911, 19 years after its foundation. Long-held ambitions to extend to 18 eventually became possible, however, through the purchase of 40 acres of bogland in 1978. And further parcels of nine and a half acres and 18 acres were later acquired at a combined cost of £96,000.

"The gentle, rolling terrain was ideal golfing land and I was aware on first inspection that the final product was going to be an exciting challenge for golfers of all handicap categories," recalls Arthur Spring, who was given the contract as course designer.

Work involved the construction of 11 holes and, with perfect timing, was effectively completed for the centenary celebrations in 1992.

Accommodation, Food and Drink

Reference numbers below refer to detailed information provided in section 2

Accommodation

Annagh Lodge, Coolbawn, Nenagh, Co Tipperary
Tel/Fax: 067 24225 Five comfortably appointed B&B rooms in a period country house on a 200-acre working farm. Dinner by arrangement. 545

Ashley Park House, Ardcroney, Nenagh, Co Tipperary
Tel: 067 38223 Fax: 067 38223 Six twin bedrooms, all en suite, in a handsome early 18th-century residence with a private lake. Bed & Breakfast. 549

Bridget's Bed & Breakfast, Coolbawn, Co Tipperary
Tel: 067 28098 Bed and Breakfast in five en suite rooms in a smart modern bungalow. 5 minutes' walk from Lough Derg. 544

Hawthorn View, Thurles, Co Tipperary
Tel: 050 421710 4 en suite Bed & Breakfast rooms in a modern bungalow set back from the N62. Very close to Thurles Golf Course. Equestrian Centre nearby. 540

Otway Lodge, Dromineer, Nenagh, Co Tipperary
Tel: 067 24133/24273 Six-bedroomed B&B guest house (all rooms en suite) on the edge of Lough Derg. Boat hire, fishing trips. 542

Rectory House Hotel, Dundrum, Co Tipperary
Tel: 062 71266 Fax: 062 71115 Large en suite bedrooms in a secluded 19th-century house. Intimate restaurant, spacious bar and lounge. 547

Riverrun Cottages, Terryglass, Nenagh, Co Tipperary
Tel: 067 22125 4-star self-catering Accommodation in five units, each sleeping 4. Quiet village setting by Lough Derg. 543

Food and Drink

Rectory House Hotel, Dundrum, Co Tipperary
Tel: 062 71266 Fax: 062 71115 Large en suite bedrooms in a secluded 19th-century house. Intimate restaurant, spacious bar and lounge. 547

The Beehive, Portumna, Co Galway
Tel: 050 941830 Irish and Italian cuisine in a pleasant oasis just off the main street. Bring your own wine. Last orders 9.30. 267

The Waterfront, Roscrea, Co Tipperary
Tel: 050 522431 Family restaurant catering for all tastes. Snacks, full meals, takeaways. Open from 9.30 till 9. 541

Thurles

Thurles Golf Club, Turtulla, Thurles, Co Tipperary

Tel: 0504 21983 / 24599

Sec/Manager:	Linda Ryan
Professional:	Sean Hunt
Directions:	I mile South of Thurles off the N62 to Cashel
Type of Course:	Parkland
Date Founded:	1909
No of Holes:	18
Length:	6465 yds (5911 mtrs)
Par:	72
SSS:	71
Green Fees:	£20
Visitors:	Welcome: Any Day except Tuesday, Restrictions at weekends
Societies:	Welcome: Contact Club direct for details
Facilities:	Chipping/Putting Area, Practice Area, Driving Range, Golf Clubs for hire, Trolley hire, Bar, Restaurant

Accommodation, Food and Drink

Reference numbers below refer to detailed information provided in section 2

Accommodation

Cappamura House, Dundrum, Co Tipperary

Tel: 062 71127 Bed and Breakfast and an equestrian centre in and around a 300-year-old farmhouse. 7 bedrooms, 3 en suite. 546

Hawthorn View, Thurles, Co Tipperary

Tel: 050 421710 4 en suite Bed & Breakfast rooms in a modern bungalow set back from the N62. Very close to Thurles Golf Course. Equestrian Centre nearby. 540

Rectory House Hotel, Dundrum, Co Tipperary

Tel: 062 71266 Fax: 062 71115 Large en suite bedrooms in a secluded 19th-century house. Intimate restaurant, spacious bar and lounge. 547

Food and Drink

Donovan's, Tipperary, Co Tipperary

Tel: 062 51384 Close to the town centre, a warm and welcoming bar and restaurant with a strong sporting theme. Beer garden. 551

Rectory House Hotel, Dundrum, Co Tipperary

Tel: 062 71266 Fax: 062 71115 Large en suite bedrooms in a secluded 19th-century house. Intimate restaurant, spacious bar and lounge. 547

The Waterfront, Roscrea, Co Tipperary

Tel: 050 522431 Family restaurant catering for all tastes. Snacks, full meals, takeaways. Open from 9.30 till 9. 541

Tipperary

Tipperary Golf Club, Rathanny, Tipperary, County Tipperary

Tel: 062 51119

Sec/Manager:	Joe Considene
Professional:	None
Directions:	I mile south of Tipperary Town off the R664 to Newtown

Type of Course:	Parkland
Date Founded:	1896
No of Holes:	18
Length:	6380 yds (5843 mtrs)
Par:	71
SSS:	71
Green Fees:	Weekdays: £15 Weekends & Bank Holidays: £18
Visitors:	Welcome: Book in advance
Societies:	Welcome: Book in advance
Facilities:	Chipping/Putting Area, Golf Clubs for hire, Trolley hire, Electric Buggy hire, Bar

Accommodation, Food and Drink

Reference numbers below refer to detailed information provided in section 2

Accommodation

Ashmore House, Co Tipperary

Tel: 062 61286 Fax: 062 62789 Town-centre Georgian house with six letting B&B bedrooms including a family room. Extensive breakfast menu. Private parking. Garden. 548

Ballinacounty House, Glen of Aherlow, Co Tipperary

Tel/Fax: 062 56000 Flexible B&B and self-catering Accommodation in 5 rooms and 2 cottages in a lovely rural setting. Restaurant with wine licence. 550

Cappamura House, Dundrum, Co Tipperary

Tel: 062 71127 Bed and Breakfast and an equestrian centre in and around a 300-year-old farmhouse. 7 bedrooms, 3 en suite. 546

Indaville, Cashel, Co Tipperary

Tel: 062 62075 Built as a country lodge around 1750, now a comfortable, civilised Bed & Breakfast with five large letting bedrooms. 556

Rectory House Hotel, Dundrum, Co Tipperary

Tel: 062 71266 Fax: 062 71115 Large en suite bedrooms in a secluded 19th-century house. Intimate restaurant, spacious bar and lounge. 547

Tir Na Nóg, Dualla, Cashel, Co Tipperary

Tel: 062 61350 Fax: 062 62411 A warm, friendly country home on the R691. Six en suite bedrooms with orthopaedic beds. B&B, packed lunch, snacks, dinner by arrangement. 555

Food and Drink

Ballinacounty House, Glen of Aherlow, Co Tipperary

Tel/Fax: 062 56000 Flexible B&B and self-catering Accommodation in 5 rooms and 2 cottages in a lovely rural setting. Restaurant with wine licence. 550

Donovan's, Tipperary, Co Tipperary

Tel: 062 51384 Close to the town centre, a warm and welcoming bar and restaurant with a strong sporting theme. Beer garden. 551

Rectory House Hotel, Dundrum, Co Tipperary

Tel: 062 71266 Fax: 062 71115 Large en suite bedrooms in a secluded 19th-century house. Intimate restaurant, spacious bar and lounge. 547

WATERFORD

During the 1980s, one of my favourite golfing haunts was the charming, nine-hole stretch of Dungarvan GC at Ballinacourty. A group of us from Dublin would travel down there every September, with the result that lasting friendships were made with the local members over the years. The place held such an appeal for us that we wondered whether there could be a more enjoyable nine holes anywhere else in golf. Now it is gone. But as a reflection of the amazing development which has taken place in the game in Waterford over the last 10 years, the town of

Dungarvan now has three 18-hole courses where it once had only those nine holes. Dungarvan GC moved to an 18-hole location at Knockgranagh; the West Waterford club was founded in 1993 and the delightful stretch at Ballinacourty has since been extended to 18 holes, adopting new life as the exotically-named Gold Coast GC.

Similar expansion has taken place in Waterford City. From a situation 10 years ago when Waterford GC was its only club, the city can now

Night View, Waterford City

boast the addition of clubs at Waterford Castle and Faithlegg, along with a fine Municipal course. Curiously, Waterford GC is actually situated in Co Kilkenny, so the county's nine courses are: Dungarvan, Dunmore East, Faithlegg, Gold Coast, Lismore, Tramore, Waterford Castle, West Waterford and Waterford Municipal. The Faithlegg course is attached to the Faithlegg House Hotel, an 18th century mansion which has been completely refurbished and recently acquired by the Tower Hotel Group. Designed by Patrick Merrigan, the course is located about 10 minutes' drive from Waterford City in a mature estate on the banks of the Suir. All are parkland but a number of them adopt an especially challenging quality through their proximity to the sea. Dunmore East GC is so blessed. And when standing on the high ground closeby the 16th green during a recent visit, I could look down on the charming little cove where the US ambassador's curiosity was aroused, 100 feet below.

In such a delightful setting, it wasn't difficult to understand how the sight of golfers celebrating the annual captains' drive-in, became an irresistible attraction for Jean Kennedy Smith, when she visited the fishing village situated about seven miles from Waterford City. They still talk with great affection down at the club of that red-letter day in February 1998. There is special pride in a framed letter on the clubhouse wall. On the official notepaper of the US ambassador, Mrs Kennedy Smith wrote to the club captain: "Dear Mr Hurley. Thank you very much for hosting my friends and me during my recent visit to Dunmore East. I thoroughly enjoyed meeting with you and the other members of the club. How fortunate that we arrived just in time for your party!

Metal Man, Tramore

"I would also like to thank you for the lovely blue golfing sweater you gave me. It fits perfectly and I will be sure to wear it the next time I'm golfing, which I hope is very soon. I am also looking forward to returning to your club for a game, so be sure to practise your swing. With my best wishes, sincerely, Jean Kennedy Smith, Ambassador."

Waterford has established strong links with the US through the years. In fact locals claim to have won the heart of Bing Crosby - through the beauty of their famous crystal. So, a visit to the Kilbarry factory is a must, especially for the golf tourist. In September 1975, the factory received the following letter: "Dear Sirs, I am interested in securing some trophies for a golf tournament I put on in California every year. Something similar to the items that you gave to the participants at the recent Match Play television golf function up at Gleneagles.

"I believe it consisted of a decanter and six glasses. We would have to have some engraving on the decanter - something like 'Bing Crosby National Pro-Am First Prize' and a depiction of our logo - a copy of which I am sending along. Of course, I can appreciate the fact that colour would be impossible but maybe it would be just as pretty in the clear crystal. I don't even know whether it can be done - hence this letter. I'm also interested in the price of these items. I'd probably want a dozen or so sets in varying sizes - from the Championship

Waterford Crystal, Co Waterford

down to the lesser players. You might want to submit some designs of some other type decanters, because I would like an appreciable difference between the first prize, second prize, third prize and so on down, and rather than do this in size, it might be better to let the difference be determined by quality or some other such measurement. Could I hear from you when you have a chance to answer the letter with prices etc, whether or not there'd be any duty bringing them into the States and how much time you would need to prepare these items. The tournament itself takes place the third week in January 1976. With very best regards, believe me to be - Sincerely yours, (signed) Bing Crosby."

Sixteen months after that letter was written, a superb array of Waterford crystal prizes were on display in the window of the golf shop at Pebble Beach. Waterford Crystal had broken through to the American golf scene in the showpiece of pro-am events. "It was a tremendous breakthrough," said the then production director, Colm O'Connell. "Quite apart from the marvellous field of professionals and amateurs who were being introduced to our product, we received some priceless television exposure."

When the vikings sailed up the Suir Estuary in 914 and 915, they establihed a settlement on the banks of the river, upstream, which they named Verthrafjorthr. Though legend claims the origin of the city to date as far back as the second century AD, the Norse name is preserved in English as Waterford. As it happened, the Scandinavians had become christians by the time Waterford fell victim to the next major invasion from overseas. On August 25th, 1170, the city was taken at the third assault by an Anglo Norman force led by Strongbow and Raymond le Gros. Strongbow had landed close to Reginald's Tower, a relic of the Scandinavians, which still survives at the end of the quay at the eastern corner of the fortifying walls of the city. Shortly after his conquest of Waterford, Strongbow was married to Aoife, daughter of Diarmuid Mac Murrough, the king of Leinster, in the local cathedral.

Against that background, and a later onslaught by Cromwell's army, Waterford is clearly a city rich in history. It is also rich in culture, notably as the birthplace of William Vincent Wallace, composer of the light opera Maritana among other musical works, and of the actors Dorothy Jordan and Charles Kean, and the artist, Robert West. To those diverse talents have been added the latter-day skills of the glass-blowers and crystal cutters. And what of those early trophies at Pebble Beach? In January 1977, only months before he died, Bing Crosby wrote from the US: "I think its the finest set of trophies that have ever been offered in this country for any kind of a competition and I'm sure everyone will concur with me in that belief." One could hardly wish for a more glowing endorsement.

Location of Golf Courses

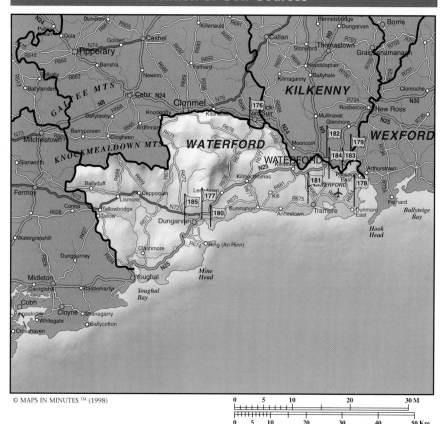

© MAPS IN MINUTES ™ (1998)

Carrick-on-Suir

Carrick-on Suir, Garravoone, Carrick-on Suir, Co Waterford

Tel: 051 640047

Sec/Manager:	Aidan Murphy
Professional:	None
Directions:	I mile South of Carrick-on-Suir off the R676 to Dungarvan
Type of Course:	Parkland
Date Founded:	1939
No of Holes:	18
Length:	6628 yds (6061 mtrs)
Par:	72
SSS:	70
Green Fees:	Weekdays: £15 Weekends & Bank Holidays: £17
Visitors:	Welcome: Any Day, Restrictions on Sunday, Contact Club in advance
Societies:	Welcome: Special concessions, Contact club for details
Facilities:	Chipping/Putting Area, Golf Clubs for hire, Trolley hire, Electric Buggy hire, Bar, Restaurant

Accommodation, Food and Drink

Reference numbers below refer to detailed
information provided in section 2

Accommodation

Arden Lodge, Cahir, Co Tipperary
Tel: 052 42338 An exclusive modern bungalow offering four very comfortable B&B
bedrooms a short walk from the town centre. 552

Benuala, Clonmel, Co Tipperary
Tel: 052 22158 En suite Accommodation in six good-sized rooms in a modern
bungalow close to town. Private car park. 559

Fennessy's Hotel, Clonmel, Co Tipperary
Tel: 052 23680 Fax: 052 23783 Ten-bedroomed hotel offering flexible en suite
Accommodation in a prime site off the main street. Leisure centre next door. 554

Knocklofty House, Knocklofty, Clonmel, Co Tipperary
Tel: 052 25444 Fax: 052 26444 A gracious country house set in 35 acres of
gardens. 14 beautifully appointed bedrooms. Restaurant. Also self-catering. 557

Marlfield House, Clonmel, Co Tipperary
Tel: 052 25444 12 self-contained self-catering apartments in a late 18th-century
residence on the banks of the Suir. 558

Food and Drink

Fennessy's Hotel, Clonmel, Co Tipperary
Tel: 052 23680 Fax: 052 23783 Ten-bedroomed hotel offering flexible en suite
Accommodation in a prime site off the main street. Leisure centre next door. 554

Knocklofty House, Knocklofty, Clonmel, Co Tipperary
Tel: 052 25444 Fax: 052 26444 A gracious country house set in 35 acres of
gardens. 14 beautifully appointed bedrooms. Restaurant. Also self-catering. 557

The Belfry Hotel, Waterford, Co Waterford
Tel: 051 844800 Fax: 051 843719 Waterford's newest hotel, due to open early
summer 2000. 45 superbly appointed en suite bedrooms, some of family size, in the
city centre. 575

Dungarvan

Dungarvan Golf Club, Knocknagranagh, Co Waterford

Tel: 058 41605/43310

Sec/Manager:	Tom Whelan
Professional:	David Hayes
Directions:	2 miles North East of Dungarvan off the N25 to Waterford
Type of Course:	Parkland
Date Founded:	1993
No of Holes:	18
Length:	6708 yds (6134 mtrs)
Par:	72
SSS:	73
Green Fees:	Weekdays; £20 Weekends & Bank Holidays: £25
Visitors:	Welcome: Any Day, Contact club in advance at weekends
Societies:	Welcome: Special concessions, Contact club for details
Facilities:	Chipping/Putting Area, Practice Area, Golf Clubs for hire, Trolley hire, Electric Buggy hire, Bar, Restaurant

Accommodation, Food and Drink

Reference numbers below refer to detailed
information provided in section 2

Accommodation

Carn-na-Radharc, Youghal, Co Cork
Tel: 024 92703 Four B&B bedrooms, 2 en suite. Private car park. Tea/coffee on
arrival. Quiet setting, great views. 168

Fortwilliam Estate, Glencairn, Co Waterford
Tel: 058 54135 Fax: 058 54306 4 self-catering houses sleeping 2, 4, 5-6 & 6. Bed
linen supplied. Several local golf courses. No credit cards.

Glenribbeen Lodge, Glenribbeen, Lismore, Co Waterford
Tel: 058 54499 or 0872 825997 Fax: 058 54499 e-mail:
glenribbeenbnb@oceanfree.net One double bedroom and two en suite family rooms.
B&B; Traditional Irish fiddle lessons & sessions. Website with Irishtourism.com

Orpens Bar & Estuary Restaurant, Knockboy, Co Waterford
Tel: 051 873082 Fax: 051 874180 90-cover family restaurant with lounge and bar.
Informal lunchtime menu, all-day bar meals, full evening à la carte. Disabled access.
576

Roseville, Youghal, Co Cork
Tel: 024 92571 Bed & Breakfast in a distinctive late 18th-century house on the N25.
4 double rooms and a twin. Very friendly. 142

Walter Raleigh Hotel, Youghal, Co Cork
Tel: 024 92011/92314 Fax: 024 93560 40 rooms, including 15 Executives, all en
suite, on the seafront. Victorian elegance, space, full menus. 180

Food and Drink

Coakley's Bar, Youghal, Co Cork
Tel: 024 93161 Liam Coakley's convivial pub in an 1820s building in the centre of
town. Good cheer and good drinking. 169

Orpens Bar & Estuary Restaurant, Knockboy, Co Waterford
Tel: 051 873082 Fax: 051 874180 90-cover family restaurant with lounge and bar.
Informal lunchtime menu, all-day bar meals, evening à la carte. Disabled access. 576

Walter Raleigh Hotel, Youghal, Co Cork
Tel: 024 92011/92314 Fax: 024 93560 40 rooms, including 15 Executives, all en
suite, on the seafront. Victorian elegance, space, full menus. 180

Dunmore East

Dunmore East Golf & Country Club, Dunmore East, Co Waterford

Tel: 051 383151

Sec/Manager:	Mary Skehan
Professional:	Derry Kiely
Directions:	10 miles South East of Waterford off the R684
Type of Course:	Parkland
Date Founded:	1993
No of Holes:	18
Length:	6655 yds (6085 mtrs)
Par:	72
SSS:	72
Green Fees:	Weekdays: £12 Weekends & Bank Holidays: £16
Visitors:	Welcome: Any Day
Societies:	Welcome: Special concessions, Contact club for details
Facilities:	Practice Area, Golf Clubs for hire, Trolley hire, Electric Buggy hire, Bar, Restaurant

Accommodation, Food and Drink

Reference numbers below refer to detailed information provided in section 2

Accommodation

"Janeville", Newtown Park, Waterford, Co Waterford
Tel/Fax: 051 874653 Quiet restful home with private car park. Early breakfasts and late evening meals on request. Four en suite rooms, sitting room, tv, beverages.

Belair Guesthouse, Tramore, Co Waterford
Tel: 051 381605 Fax: 051 386688 Georgian-style house with six letting bedrooms - four family rooms and two doubles, all en suite. Near the racecourse.

Carey's Bridge B&B, Passage East, Co Waterford
Tel: 051 382581 3 en suite double rooms for B&B at Crook, in a village by Waterford Harbour. Several local golf courses. No credit cards.

Cluain Aoibhinn, Newtown, Tramore, Co Waterford
Tel: 051 381153 E-mail: junewalsh@esatclear.ie Bed and Breakfast Accommodation in three double bedrooms, two of them en suite. No credit cards.

Dunmore Holiday Villas, Dunmore East, Co Waterford
Tel: 051 383699 Fax: 051 383787 e-mail: jkellydhv@tinet.ie 17 four star self-catering villas, each sleeping up to 6. Golf close by. Tennis court. Access, Mastercard, Visa. Excellent pubs and restaurants within walking distance.

Martina Murphy's Self-Catering, Cappoquin, Co Waterford
Tel: 058 54813 Self-catering Accommodation for up to five guests. Two bedrooms, bathroom, kitchen/diner, sitting room. No credit cards.

West Cliffe, Tramore, Co Waterford
Tel: 051 381365 Two twin rooms and a triple in a smart modern B&B two minutes from Tramore Golf Course. All en suite with tv. Private parking.

Woodstown House Country Estate, Woodstown, Co Waterford
Tel: 051 382611 Fax: 051 382644 Luxury self-catering holiday houses converted from stables and other outbuildings of Woodstown House. Most have private patios. Tennis. Beach. 573

Food and Drink

Jack Meade's Pub, Waterford, Co Waterford
Tel: 051 873187 Good cheer and good food in an 18th-century pub that's open every lunchtime and evening. Bird sanctuary & farming museum nearby. Access, Mastercard, Visa.

McAlpin's Suir Inn, Cheekpoint, Co Waterford
Tel: 051 382220 17th-century riverside inn 7 miles from Waterford. Evening meals Tues-Sat, also Mon in high season. Seafood a speciality. 570

The Ship, Dunmore East, Co Waterford
Tel: 051 383141/383144 Roadside restaurant and bar with a nautical look and a mouthwatering menu specialising in seafood. Full drinks licence. 571

Faithlegg

Faithlegg Golf Club, Faithlegg, Co Waterford

Tel: 051 382241

Sec/Manager:	J. Lambe
Professional:	Ted Higgins
Directions:	6 miles East of Waterford off the R683 to Dunmore East
Type of Course:	Parkland
Date Founded:	1993
No of Holes:	18
Length:	6872 yds (6284 mtrs)
Par:	72
SSS:	70
Green Fees:	Mon.-Thurs. : £22 Fri. Sat. & Sun. : £27
Visitors:	Welcome: Any Day
Societies:	Welcome: Special concessions, Contact club for details
Facilities:	Chipping/Putting Area, Practice Area, Golf Clubs for hire, Trolley hire, Electric Buggy hire, Bar, Restaurant, Caddy service by arrangement

Accommodation, Food and Drink

Reference numbers below refer to detailed information provided in section 2

Accommodation

"Janeville", Newtown Park, Waterford, Co Waterford
Tel/Fax: 051 874653 Quiet restful home with private car park. Early breakfasts and late evening meals on request. Four en suite rooms, sitting room, tv, beverages.

Arthur's Rest, Arthurstown, Co Wexford
Tel: 051 389192 Fax: 051 389362 A choice between Bed & Breakfast and self-catering Accommodation in a charming house near the Ballyhack car ferry. 651

Carey's Bridge B&B, Passage East, Co Waterford
Tel: 051 382581 3 en suite double rooms for B&B at Crook, in a village by Waterford Harbour. Several local golf courses. No credit cards.

Dunmore Holiday Villas, Dunmore East, Co Waterford
Tel: 051 383699 Fax: 051 383787 e-mail: jkellydhv@tinet.ie 17 four star self-catering villas, each sleeping up to 6. Golf close by. Tennis court. Access, Mastercard, Visa. Excellent pubs and restaurants within walking distance.

Glendower House, New Ross, Co Wexford
Tel/Fax: 051 421989 Eight en suite bedrooms in a modern B&B on the main road into town from Wexford. Also evening meals. 650

The Belfry Hotel, Waterford, Co Waterford
Tel: 051 844800 Fax: 051 843719 Waterford's newest hotel, due to open early summer 2000. 45 superbly appointed en suite bedrooms, some of family size, in the city centre. 575

The Horse & Hound, Ballinaboola, New Ross, Co Wexford
Tel: 051 428323 Restaurant, bar and 12 rooms for Bed & Breakfast in a friendly family-run hotel on the N25, four miles from New Ross. 653

The Old Rectory, Kilmeaden House, Kilmeaden, Co Waterford
Tel: 051 384254 1840 rectory in 12 peaceful acres. 5 antique-furnished rooms with luxury bathrooms en suite. No smoking. Open May-September. Access, Mastercard, Visa.

Food and Drink

Egans Bar and Restaurant, Waterford, Co Waterford
Tel: 051 875619 A popular bar and restaurant serving traditional Irish and English food. Roasts; daily specials. Open every day, lunchtime and evening.

McAlpin's Suir Inn, Cheekpoint, Co Waterford
Tel: 051 382220 17th-century riverside inn 7 miles from Waterford. Evening meals Tues-Sat, also Mon in high season. Seafood a speciality. 570

The Belfry Hotel, Waterford, Co Waterford
Tel: 051 844800 Fax: 051 843719 Waterford's newest hotel, due to open early summer 2000. 45 superbly appointed en suite bedrooms, some of family size, in the city centre. 575

The Horse & Hound, Ballinaboola, New Ross, Co Wexford
Tel: 051 428323 Restaurant, bar and 12 rooms for Bed & Breakfast in a friendly family-run hotel on the N25, four miles from New Ross. 653

Goldcoast

Gold Coast Golf Club, Ballinacourty, Dungarvan, County Waterford

Tel: 058 44055

Gradually, nine-hole courses are vanishing from the Irish golf scene, most of them experiencing a re-birth as a part of bigger things. So it is with the Gold Coast, formerly the nine-hole home of Dungarvan GC in Ballinacourty and now a proprietary establishment, combining membership with green-fees.

Given its modest 46 acres, it seems unlikely the site would have a golfing future when Dungarvan GC sold it for £290,000 and moved elsewhere in 1993. But fate took a hand a year later when an adjoining 54 acres became available, offering the new owner, John McGrath, the opportunity of a full, 18-hole development.

It is unquestionably a delightful site, overlooking the Atlantic from the mouth of Dungarvan Bay. And at the far end of the new land is the lighthouse, dominating the entire scene. Work started in September 1995 and the course was officially opened in 1997.

The designer, Maurice Fives, had the good sense to retain six of the old Dungarvan holes, which were noted for their magnificent greens. They are the new first (old fourth), second (fifth), third (sixth), 16th (ninth), 17th (first), 18th (second). Down around the turn is a particularly

charming area where the short seventh looks out towards Ballyvoyle Head and Tramore beyond, while the ninth green has Helvick Head as a backdrop.

In fact the course could be divided into three sections - the original holes of Ballinacourty, the seventh, eighth and ninth down by the lighthouse and those holes in between.

Sec/Manager:	Tom Considine
Professional:	None
Directions:	4 miles East of Dungarvan off the R675 to Tramore
Type of Course:	Parkland/Links
Date Founded:	1993
No of Holes:	18
Length:	6749 yds (6171 mtrs)
Par:	72
SSS:	72
Green Fees:	Weekdays: £20 Weekends & Bank Holidays: £25
Visitors:	Welcome: Book in advance
Societies:	Welcome: Book in advance
Facilities:	Chipping/Putting Area, Practice Area, Driving Range, Golf Clubs for hire, Trolley hire, Electric Buggy hire, Bar, Restaurant, Caddy service by arrangement, Swimming Pool, Sauna

Accommodation, Food and Drink

Reference numbers below refer to detailed information provided in section 2

Accommodation

Carn-na-Radharc, Youghal, Co Cork
Tel: 024 92703 Four B&B bedrooms, 2 en suite. Private car park. Tea/coffee on arrival. Quiet setting, great views. 168

Fortwilliam Estate, Glencairn, Co Waterford
Tel: 058 54135 Fax: 058 54306 4 self-catering houses sleeping 2, 4, 5-6 & 6. Bed linen supplied. Several local golf courses. No credit cards.

Glenribbeen Lodge, Glenribbeen, Lismore, Co Waterford
Tel: 058 54499 or 0872 825997 Fax: 058 54499 e-mail: glenribbeenbnb@oceanfree.net One double bedroom and two en suite family rooms. B&B; Traditional Irish fiddle lessons & sessions. Website with Irishtourism.com

Martina Murphy's Self-Catering, Cappoquin, Co Waterford
Tel: 058 54813 Self-catering Accommodation for up to five guests. Two bedrooms, bathroom, kitchen/diner, sitting room. No credit cards.

Orpens Bar & Estuary Restaurant, Knockboy, Co Waterford
Tel: 051 873082 Fax: 051 874180 90-cover family restaurant with lounge and bar. Informal lunchtime menu, all-day bar meals, evening à la carte. Disabled access. 576

Walter Raleigh Hotel, Youghal, Co Cork
Tel: 024 92011/92314 Fax: 024 93560 40 rooms, including 15 Executives, all en suite, on the seafront. Victorian elegance, space, full menus. 180

Food and Drink

Coakley's Bar, Youghal, Co Cork
Tel: 024 93161 Liam Coakley's convivial pub in an 1820s building in the centre of town. Good cheer and good drinking. 169

Orpens Bar & Estuary Restaurant, Knockboy, Co Waterford
Tel: 051 873082 Fax: 051 874180 90-cover family restaurant with lounge and bar. Informal lunchtime menu, all-day bar meals, evening à la carte. Disabled access. 576

Walter Raleigh Hotel, Youghal, Co Cork
Tel: 024 92011/92314 Fax: 024 93560 40 rooms, including 15 Executives, all en suite, on the seafront. Victorian elegance, space, full menus. 180

Tramore

Tramore Golf Club, Newtown Hill, Tramore, Co Waterford

Tel: 051 386170

In 1939, "The Irish Golfers Blue Book" reported the construction of a new 18-hole course at Tramore, to a design by Capt H L C Tippet of Walton Heath, on "130 acres of natural golfing country." The site, as elevated as its address of Newtown Hill would suggest, is, in effect, parkland by the sea.

Worthy of a club which came into being in 1894, the course had its official opening on June 25th when three of the country's leading amateurs of the time, John Burke, J C Brown and Redmond Simcox, were joined in an exhibition by professional Paddy Mahon. And the day was crowned by a dance: admission four shillings.

Gradually extending to an overall length of nearly 6,700 yards off the back tees, Tramore has been used regularly as a men's and women's championship venue. It also played host to the Irish Dunlop Professional tournament won by Christy O'Connor Snr in 1967 and the Carrolls Irish Matchplay Championship in 1971 and 1976, both of which were captured by Peter Townsend.

The venue's popularity owes much to a fine clubhouse, officially opened in May 1970. And its proximity to the sea is reflected in the club crest of an ill-fated man-of-war, framed by two sea horses. This commemorates the "Sea Horse" which was wrecked in Tramore Bay in 1816.

Its most distinguished woman player was Pat O'Sullivan, Irish champion at Killarney in 1956, while the membership has included outstanding men in Michael Burns and Eddie Power, both internationals.

Sec/Manager:	James Cox
Professional:	Derry Kiely
Directions:	Half mile West of Tramore off The R675 to Dungarvan
Type of Course:	Parkland
Date Founded:	1894
No of Holes:	18
Length:	6621 yds (6055 mtrs)
Par:	72
SSS:	73
Green Fees:	Weekdays: £27 Weekends & Bank Holidays: £33
Visitors:	Welcome: Any Day, Contact Club in advance
Societies:	Welcome: Special concessions, Contact club for details
Facilities:	Chipping/Putting Area, Practice Area, Trolley hire, Bar, (Restaurant, catering available if pre-booked)

Accommodation, Food and Drink

Reference numbers below refer to detailed information provided in section 2

Accommodation

"Janeville", Newtown Park, Waterford, Co Waterford
Tel/Fax: 051 874653 Quiet restful home with private car park. Early breakfasts and late evening meals on request. Four en suite rooms, sitting room, tv, beverages.

Belair Guesthouse, Tramore, Co Waterford
Tel: 051 381605 Fax: 051 386688 Georgian-style house with six letting bedrooms - four family rooms and two doubles, all en suite. Near the racecourse.

Cluain Aoibhinn, Newtown, Tramore, Co Waterford
Tel: 051 381153 E-mail: junewalsh@esatclear.ie Bed and Breakfast Accommodation in three double bedrooms, two of them en suite. No credit cards.

Dunmore Holiday Villas, Dunmore East, Co Waterford
Tel: 051 383569 Fax: 051 383787 e-mail: jkellydhv@tinet.ie 17 four star self-catering villas, each sleeping up to 6. Golf close by. Tennis court. Access, Mastercard, Visa. Excellent pubs and restaurants within walking distance.

St Albans Guest House, Waterford, Co Waterford
Tel/Fax: 051 358171 A spacious detached villa with eight en suite guest bedrooms and a huge garden. Half a mile from city centre.   572

The Belfry Hotel, Waterford, Co Waterford
Tel: 051 844800 Fax: 051 843719 Waterford's newest hotel, due to open early summer 2000. 45 superbly appointed en suite bedrooms, some of family size, in the city centre.   575

The Coach House, Butlerstown, Co Waterford
Tel: 051 384656 Fax: 051 384751 e-mail: coachhse@iol.ie Elegant, well-equipped en suite Accommodation in a small country house in the grounds of Butlerstown Castle. Wine licence. All the major credit cards. AA 4 diamonds. 3 star Irish Tourist Board.

West Cliffe, Tramore, Co Waterford
Tel: 051 381365 Two twin rooms and a triple in a smart modern B&B two minutes from Tramore Golf Course. All en suite with tv. Private parking.

Food and Drink

Egans Bar and Restaurant, Waterford, Co Waterford
Tel: 051 875619 A popular bar and restaurant serving traditional Irish and English food. Roasts; daily specials. Open every day, lunchtime and evening.

The Belfry Hotel, Waterford, Co Waterford
Tel: 051 844800 Fax: 051 843719 Waterford's newest hotel, due to open early summer 2000. 45 superbly appointed en suite bedrooms, some of family size, in the city centre.   575

The Ship, Dunmore East, Co Waterford
Tel: 051 383141/383144 Roadside restaurant and bar with a nautical look and a
mouthwatering menu specialising in seafood. Full drinks licence.   571

Waterford

Waterford Golf Club, Newrath, Waterford

Tel: 051 876748

Sec/Manager:	Joseph Condon
Professional:	None
Directions:	On the Northern outskirts of Waterford off the N9 North of the River Suir
Type of Course:	Parkland
Date Founded:	1912
No of Holes:	18
Length:	6257 yds (5722 mtrs)
Par:	71
SSS:	70
Green Fees:	Weekdays: £22 Weekends & Bank Holidays: £25
Visitors:	Welcome: Prior booking required
Societies:	Welcome: Special concessions, Contact club for details
Facilities:	Chipping/Putting Area, Practice Area, Golf Clubs for hire, Trolley hire, Electric Buggy hire, Bar, Restaurant

Accommodation, Food and Drink

Reference numbers below refer to detailed
information provided in section 2

Accommodation

"Janeville", Newtown Park, Waterford, Co Waterford
Tel/Fax: 051 874653 Quiet restful home with private car park. Early breakfasts and
late evening meals on request. Four en suite rooms, sitting room, tv, beverages.

Belair Guesthouse, Tramore, Co Waterford
Tel: 051 381605 Fax: 051 386688 Georgian-style house with six letting bedrooms -
four family rooms and two doubles, all en suite. Near the racecourse.

Cluain Aoibhinn, Newtown, Tramore, Co Waterford
Tel: 051 381153 E-mail: junewalsh@esatclear.ie Bed and Breakfast Accommodation
in three double bedrooms, two of them en suite. No credit cards.

Dunmore Holiday Villas, Dunmore East, Co Waterford
Tel: 051 383699 Fax: 051 383787 e-mail: jkellydhv@tinet.ie 17 four star self-
catering villas, each sleeping up to 6. Golf close by. Tennis court. Access, Mastercard,
Visa. Excellent pubs and restaurants within walking distance.

Granville Hotel, Waterford, Co Waterford
Tel: 051 305555 100 stylish en suite bedrooms in a tip-top traditional hotel on the
quay by the River Suir. Fine eating. Civilised bar for drinks & snacks.   574

St Albans Guest House, Waterford, Co Waterford
Tel/Fax: 051 358171 A spacious detached villa with eight en suite guest bedrooms
and a huge garden. Half a mile from city centre.   572

The Belfry Hotel, Waterford, Co Waterford
Tel: 051 844800 Fax: 051 843719 Waterford's newest hotel, due to open early
summer 2000. 45 superbly appointed en suite bedrooms, some of family size, in the
city centre.   575

The Coach House, Butlerstown, Co Waterford
Tel: 051 384656 Fax: 051 384751 e-mail: coachhse@iol.ie Elegant, well-equipped en
suite Accommodation in a small country house in the grounds of Butlerstown Castle.
Wine licence. All the major credit cards. AA 4 diamonds. 3 star Irish Tourist Board.

The Old Rectory, Kilmeaden House, Kilmeaden, Co Waterford
Tel: 051 384254 1840 rectory in 12 peaceful acres. 5 antique-furnished rooms with
luxury bathrooms en suite. No smoking. Open May-September. Mastercard, Visa.

Food and Drink

Egans Bar and Restaurant, Waterford, Co Waterford
Tel: 051 875619 A popular bar and restaurant serving traditional Irish and English
food. Roasts; daily specials. Open every day, lunchtime and evening.

Granville Hotel, Waterford, Co Waterford
Tel: 051 305555 100 stylish en suite bedrooms in a tip-top traditional hotel on the
quay by the River Suir. Fine eating. Civilised bar for drinks & snacks.   574

Jack Meade's Pub, Waterford, Co Waterford
Tel: 051 873187 Good cheer and good food in an 18th-century pub that's open
every lunchtime and evening. Bird sanctuary & farming museum nearby. Access,
Mastercard, Visa.

The Belfry Hotel, Waterford, Co Waterford
Tel: 051 844800 Fax: 051 843719 Waterford's newest hotel, due to open early
summer 2000. 45 superbly appointed en suite bedrooms, some of family size, in the
city centre.   575

The Silver Fox, Kilmore Quay, Co Wexford
Tel: 053 29888 A seafood restaurant of renown in a picture-postcard fishing village.
Lemon sole not to be missed! Classical guitar midweek.   649

Waterford Castle

Waterford Castle Golf Club, The Island, Ballinakill, Waterford

Tel: 051 871633

Sec/Manager:	Dick Brennan
Professional:	None
Directions:	3 miles East of Waterford City Centre via the R683 to Dunmore East. Situated on Little Island reached by ferry
Type of Course:	Parkland
Date Founded:	1992
No of Holes:	18
Length:	6814 yds (6230 mtrs)
Par:	72
SSS:	73
Green Fees:	Weekdays: £27 Weekends & Bank Holidays: £30
Visitors:	Welcome: Contact Club in advance
Societies:	Welcome: Special concessions, Contact club for details
Facilities:	Chipping/Putting Area, Practice Area, Driving Range, Golf Clubs for hire, Trolley hire, Electric Buggy hire, Bar, Restaurant, Caddy service by arrangement

Accommodation, Food and Drink

Reference numbers below refer to detailed
information provided in section 2

Accommodation

"Janeville", Newtown Park, Waterford, Co Waterford
Tel/Fax: 051 874653 Quiet restful home with private car park. Early breakfasts and
late evening meals on request. Four en suite rooms, sitting room, tv, beverages.

Carey's Bridge B&B, Passage East, Co Waterford
Tel: 051 382581 3 en suite double rooms for B&B at Crook, in a village by
Waterford Harbour. Several local golf courses. No credit cards.

Cluain Aoibhinn, Newtown, Tramore, Co Waterford
Tel: 051 381153 E-mail: junewalsh@esatclear.ie Bed and Breakfast Accommodation
in three double bedrooms, two of them en suite. No credit cards.

Dunmore Holiday Villas, Dunmore East, Co Waterford
Tel: 051 383699 Fax: 051 383787 e-mail: jkellydhv@tinet.ie 17 four star self-

catering villas, each sleeping up to 6. Golf close by. Tennis court. Access, Mastercard, Visa. Excellent pubs and restaurants within walking distance.

Granville Hotel, Waterford, Co Waterford

Tel: 051 305555 100 stylish en suite bedrooms in a tip-top traditional hotel on the quay by the River Suir. Fine eating. Civilised bar for drinks & snacks. 574

The Coach House, Butlerstown, Co Waterford

Tel: 051 384656 Fax: 051 384751 e-mail: coachhse@iol.ie Elegant, well-equipped en suite Accommodation in a small country house in the grounds of Butlerstown Castle. Wine licence. All the major credit cards. AA 4 diamonds. 3 star Irish Tourist Board.

The Old Rectory, Kilmeaden House, Kilmeaden, Co Waterford

Tel: 051 384254 1840 rectory in 12 peaceful acres. 5 antique-furnished rooms with luxury bathrooms en suite. No smoking. Open May-September. Mastercard, Visa.

Woodstown House Country Estate, Woodstown, Co Waterford

Tel: 051 382611 Fax: 051 382644 Luxury self-catering holiday houses converted from stables and other outbuildings of Woodstown House. Most have private patios. Tennis. Beach. 573

Food and Drink

Egans Bar and Restaurant, Waterford, Co Waterford

Tel: 051 875619 A popular bar and restaurant serving traditional Irish and English food. Roasts; daily specials. Open every day, lunchtime and evening.

Granville Hotel, Waterford, Co Waterford

Tel: 051 305555 100 stylish en suite bedrooms in a tip-top traditional hotel on the quay by the River Suir. Fine eating. Civilised bar for drinks & snacks. 574

Jack Meade's Pub, Waterford, Co Waterford

Tel: 051 873187 Good cheer and good food in an 18th-century pub that's open every lunchtime and evening. Bird sanctuary & farming museum nearby. Access, Mastercard, Visa.

McAlpin's Suir Inn, Cheekpoint, Co Waterford

Tel: 051 382220 17th-century riverside inn 7 miles from Waterford. Evening meals Tues-Sat, also Mon in high season. Seafood a speciality. 570

The Ship, Dunmore East, Co Waterford

Tel: 051 383141/383144 Roadside restaurant and bar with a nautical look and a mouthwatering menu specialising in seafood. Full drinks licence. 571

Waterford Municipal

Waterford Municipal Golf Club, Williamstown, Waterford, County Waterford

Tel: 051 853131

Not for the first time in Irish golf, Christy O'Connor Snr did the honours at the official opening of the Waterford Municipal course at Williamstown, three miles from the city, in 1997. The brainchild of retired city manager Michael Doody, it has the distinction of being the last, full 18 to be designed by the late Eddie Hackett.

First impressions of the layout are of generous dimensions and quality of finish, reflecting

the care and attention of the general manager, Tom Sheridan. "Eddie (Hackett) did the original design in 1992 and made his last visit here towards the end of 1996, about six weeks before he died," said Sheridan. "In my view it represents some of his finest work."

Municipal courses are sometimes viewed as the bargain basement of golfing facilities, with all that such a designation entails. If that be so, Waterford have most definitely broken the mould, except from a financial standpoint. As a low-budget project, the course was built for the remarkably modest price of £700,000.

But price didn't inhibit quality. The impressive, 130-acre site of gently rolling terrain, has a distinctly rural character to it, despite its proximity to the city centre. Course construction was done under a community scheme with 24 workmen employed on a week-on, week-off basis.

Excellent variety has been achieved in the par fours through a design wherby the 13th and 14th are the only successive holes played side-by-side, albeit in opposite directions. It makes for a surprisingly strong test.

Sec/Manager:	Tom Sheridan
Professional:	None
Directions:	2 miles south of Waterford off the R708 to Airport
Type of Course:	Parkland
Date Founded:	1997
No of Holes:	18
Length:	6700 yds (6127 mtrs)
Par:	72
SSS:	71
Green Fees:	Weekdays: £10 Weekends & Bank Holidays: £12
Visitors:	Welcome: Book in advance
Societies:	Welcome: Book in advance
Facilities:	Chipping/Putting Area, Golf Clubs for hire, Trolley hire, Caddy service by arrangement

Accommodation, Food and Drink

Reference numbers below refer to detailed information provided in section 2

Accommodation

Belair Guesthouse, Tramore, Co Waterford

Tel: 051 381605 Fax: 051 386688 Georgian-style house with six letting bedrooms - four family rooms and two doubles, all en suite. Near the racecourse.

Granville Hotel, Waterford, Co Waterford

Tel: 051 305555 100 stylish en suite bedrooms in a tip-top traditional hotel on the quay by the River Suir. Fine eating. Civilised bar for drinks & snacks. 574

St Albans Guest House, Waterford, Co Waterford

Tel/Fax: 051 358171 A spacious detached villa with eight en suite guest bedrooms and a huge garden. Half a mile from city centre. 572

The Belfry Hotel, Waterford, Co Waterford

Tel: 051 844800 Fax: 051 843719 Waterford's newest hotel, due to open early summer 2000. 45 superbly appointed en suite bedrooms, some of family size, in the city centre. 575

Woodstown House Country Estate, Woodstown, Co Waterford

Tel: 051 382611 Fax: 051 382644 Luxury self-catering holiday houses converted from stables and other outbuildings of Woodstown House. Most have private patios. Tennis. Beach. 573

Food and Drink

Granville Hotel, Waterford, Co Waterford

Tel: 051 305555 100 stylish en suite bedrooms in a tip-top traditional hotel on the quay by the River Suir. Fine eating. Civilised bar for drinks & snacks. 574

Jack Meade's Pub, Waterford, Co Waterford

Tel: 051 873187 Good cheer and good food in an 18th-century pub that's open every lunchtime and evening. Bird sanctuary & farming museum nearby. Access, Mastercard, Visa.

The Belfry Hotel, Waterford, Co Waterford

Tel: 051 844800 Fax: 051 843719 Waterford's newest hotel, due to open early summer 2000. 45 superbly appointed en suite bedrooms, some of family size, in the city centre. 575

The Ship, Dunmore East, Co Waterford

Tel: 051 383141/383144 Roadside restaurant and bar with a nautical look and a mouthwatering menu specialising in seafood. Full drinks licence. 571

West Waterford

West Waterford Golf & Country Club, Dungarvan, Co Waterford

Tel: 058 43216

Seven years ago, this was the 100th creation of Eddie Hackett, the most influential architect in the development of Irish golf over the last three decades. And for the Spratt family, it represented the realisation of a dream.

Under the management of Austin Spratt, West Waterford has developed into one of the finest courses in the south-east, with due care taken not to disturb the wildlife of the area. Meanwhile, the sound, business instincts which guided its development, can be seen in the fine properties flanking the 18th fairway.

The club is located three miles from Dungarvan in the Brickey Valley, where the Comeragh and Knockmealdown mountains form a delightful backdrop to beautifully rolling terrain. Built on a generous site of 150 acres, its par-72 layout can stretch to 6,900 yards off the back markers, but the average player will find more forward tees sufficiently challenging.

Quality construction includes sand-based greens. And in their determination to maintain these standard overall, the owners recently spent £200,000 on a sanding programme for the so-called river holes. These include the third and

fourth on the front nine and the stretch from the 12th to the 16th on the homeward journey.

Overall, West Waterford can be ranked with some of Hackett's finest work. And after a round, there is the appeal of the Tuscany-style clubhouse offering the best of home cooking. And yes, they are open for membership at what was described to me at "an attractive deal."

Sec/Manager:	Austin Spratt
Professional:	None
Directions:	3 miles West of Dungarvan off the N25 by the River Brickey
Type of Course:	Parkland
Date Founded:	1993
No of Holes:	18
Length:	6802 yds (6219 mtrs)
Par:	72
SSS:	74
Green Fees:	Weekdays: £20 Weekends & Bank Holidays: £25
Visitors:	Welcome: Prior booking required
Societies:	Welcome: Special concessions, Contact club for details
Facilities:	Chipping/Putting Area, Practice Area, Golf Clubs for hire, Trolley hire, Bar, Restaurant

Accommodation, Food and Drink

Reference numbers below refer to detailed information provided in section 2

Accommodation

Carn-na-Radharc, Youghal, Co Cork

Tel: 024 92703 Four B&B bedrooms, 2 en suite. Private car park. Tea/coffee on arrival. Quiet setting, great views. 168

Fortwilliam Estate, Glencairn, Co Waterford

Tel: 058 54135 Fax: 058 54306 4 self-catering houses sleeping 2, 4, 5-6 & 6. Bed linen supplied. Several local golf courses. No credit cards.

Glenribbeen Lodge, Glenribbeen, Lismore, Co Waterford

Tel: 058 54499 or 0872 825997 Fax: 058 54499 e-mail: glenribbeenbnb@oceanfree.net One double bedroom and two en suite family rooms. B&B; Traditional Irish fiddle lessons & sessions. Website with Irishtourism.com

Martina Murphy's Self-Catering, Cappoquin, Co Waterford

Tel: 058 54813 Self-catering Accommodation for up to five guests. Two bedrooms, bathroom, kitchen/diner, sitting room. No credit cards.

Orpens Bar & Estuary Restaurant, Knockboy, Co Waterford

Tel: 051 873082 Fax: 051 874180 90-cover family restaurant with lounge and bar. Informal lunchtime menu, all-day bar meals, evening à la carte. Disabled access. 576

Roseville, Youghal, Co Cork

Tel: 024 92571 Bed & Breakfast in a distinctive late 18th-century house on the N25. 4 double rooms and a twin. Very friendly. 142

Walter Raleigh Hotel, Youghal, Co Cork

Tel: 024 92011/92314 Fax: 024 93560 40 rooms, including 15 Executives, all en suite, on the seafront. Victorian elegance, space, full menus. 180

Food and Drink

Coakley's Bar, Youghal, Co Cork

Tel: 024 93161 Liam Coakley's convivial pub in an 1820s building in the centre of town. Good cheer and good drinking. 169

Orpens Bar & Estuary Restaurant, Knockboy, Co Waterford

Tel: 051 873082 Fax: 051 874180 90-cover family restaurant with lounge and bar. Informal lunchtime menu, all-day bar meals, evening à la carte. Disabled access. 576

Walter Raleigh Hotel, Youghal, Co Cork

Tel: 024 92011/92314 Fax: 024 93560 40 rooms, including 15 Executives, all en suite, on the seafront. Victorian elegance, space, full menus. 180

WESTMEATH

As centenary captain, Joe Healy was anxious there should be no doubt about the hospitality which golfing tourists to Westmeath could expect at his club. So it was that he claimed immodestly: "Visitors to Mullingar readily agree that the welcome mat seems to trip you immediately you turn the gate."

Before encountering genuine hospitality, however, the tourist first has to overcome the surprise of discovering that while Athlone is the largest town in Westmeath, its golf club is actually in another county - Roscommon. Indeed the situation is not unlike that in Waterford City, where Waterford GC happens to be in County Kilkenny. It has to do with the River Shannon, which defines the border between the provinces of Leinster and Connacht. So, where the river opens out into the majestic Lough Ree, we have Glasson GC on the eastern side in Leinster and Athlone GC on its western bank, in Connacht.

Athlone, Co Westmeath

Athlone is steeped in history, having had a key role in the Williamite wars. So, it is hardly surprising to discover that the first nine-hole golf-course there was built around an old fortification where the hazards included walls, moats and ditches. And we are told that it was essentially a military club, though the founding officers could not be named for security reasons. Predictably, the town is dominated by the Shannon, which offers splendid opportunities for angling, cruising, sailing and snorkelling. And in from its shores, the holidaymaker can enjoy horse-riding, cycling, walking or climbing, while savouring the special atmosphere of the local hostelries.

There are six courses in Westmeath: Delvin Castle, Glasson, Moate, Mount Temple, Mullingar and the recently developed Ballinlough Castle. Of these, Glasson and Mount Temple, which are seperated by only seven miles, work closely together. Glasson is located six miles north of Athlone via the N55 to Cavan/Longford, while Mount Temple is in the village of the same name, off the N6, five miles from Athlone and four miles from Moate. An American golfing colleague, once expressed the view that Ireland's great attraction lay in its wonderful links terrain. "We have so many fine parkland courses in the States that we expect something special when we go overseas," he said.

Glasson could certainly fit that particular bill, while Mount Temple also has its own, unique appeal. The brainchild of its owners, Michael and Margaret Dolan, it is modest in concept while providing an important, complementary element to golf in the Athlone area. It was there that I learned about a rather special golfing hazard. Noting the non-strategic nature of certain sand traps, I wondered why they have been built. "Oh, they're rabbit bunkers," said Michael Dolan. "Ah, for high-handicappers," I suggested. "No, for rabbits, to keep them quiet," the owner insisted. He then explained that the four-legged creatures with a penchant for multiplication were such a menace, that he built bunkers for them to "play in", so that they wouldn't damage the greens. And the greens at Mount Temple are interesting, to say the least. While all around him are liable to be quoting USGA specifications, Dolan takes an eminently simple approach to green-construction. "There was no building on them; we just cut the grass," he said. So it was that golf was being played at Mount Temple only three months after work started on the site. "I chose locations for the greens, mowed them and later spread about 70 tons of sea-sand on them over a period of four years," Dolan went on. "They're not easy. Which is probably why we haven't had many sub-par rounds here since we opened in October 1991."

Mount Temple is delightfully quaint, from the rudimentary design of the course, to the charming clubhouse. Here, the men's locker-room is a former byre where 13 feeding stalls have been converted into lockers. And the runner mats for winter tees are hard-wearing cow mats into which peg-holes have been bored. "Maintaining a golf course is essentially about growing grass," said Dolan. "So, a farmer like myself must have a headstart." He concluded: "In 145 acres, I built tee-boxes and removed three ditches. That was it. Nature did the rest." All of which makes for a fascinating golfing experience - utterly different.

Lough Ree, Co Westmeath

By comparison, Mullingar could claim a somewhat loftier status in the Royal and Ancient game, not least for the launching of its annual Scratch Cup in 1963. That was when Joe Carr became the distinguished, inaugural winner and he was followed by other luminaries of the amateur game such as Tom Craddock, Peter Townsend and Peter Benka. Martin O'Brien triumphed in 1971, but most attention that year focused on Roddy Carr, who shot a sparkling 64 to beat Townsend's course record by two strokes. Recalling the round, Carr talked of walking from the ninth green to the 10th tee after an outward 32 and being handed a £10 note by two club members. "What's that for?" Carr enquired. "Never mind. Just hand it back," he was instructed. So the player did as he was told and was promptly informed that he had £100 to a tenner on breaking the course record. Covering the last five holes in four under par, Carr delivered the goods. "I was a kid and a £10 note was a lot of money, while £100 was a fortune," he said. "It was a bit of an incentive and the boys (members) were as good as their word." Since then, the event has been won by Philip Walton, Darren Clarke, Paul McGinley and Padraig Harrington, all of whom have made a significant impact as professionals on the European Tour.

Cruising on the River Shannon, Co Westmeath

Craddock, who died in 1998 after a long illness, spoke of his love of the place. "I played the Scratch Cup every year up to 1986 when I had a spinal fushion, and I have played a couple of times since then," he said. "Whether I won or lost, every moment spent down there is now a happy memory. Of all the clubs I visited, Mullingar was home from home for me." Healy is right: that's the way they are down in the midlands.

Location of Golf Courses

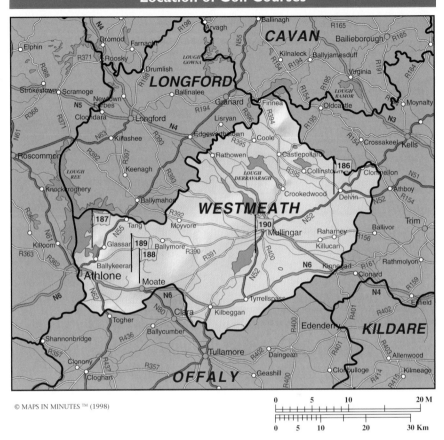

© MAPS IN MINUTES ™ (1998)

Delvin

Delvin Golf Club, Clonyn, Delvin, Co Westmeath

Tel: 044 64315

Sec/Manager:	Fiona Dillon
Professional:	David Keenaghan
Directions:	1 mile South West of Delvin off the N52 to Mullingar
Type of Course:	Parkland
Date Founded:	1992
No of Holes:	18
Length:	6019 yds (5503 mtrs)
Par:	70
SSS:	68
Green Fees:	Weekdays: £16 Weekends & Bank Holidays: £18
Visitors:	Welcome: Any Day except Wednesday and weekends, Prior booking advisable
Societies:	Welcome: Special concessions, Contact club for details
Facilities:	Chipping/Putting Area, Practice Area, Golf Clubs for hire, Trolley hire, Bar, Restaurant, Caddy service by arrangement

Accommodation, Food and Drink

Reference numbers below refer to detailed information provided in section 2

Accommodation

Catstone Lodge, Ballymore, Co. Westmeath
Tel: 044 56494 Fax: 044 56196 www.catstone.net Luxurious en suite bedrooms (60 sq m each) in a restored period-style farmhouse. Tv, sitting area, kitchenette. B&B or self-catering.

Lynnbury, Mullingar, Co Westmeath
Tel: 044 48432/40444 Country home Accommodation in a handsome house on the main Tullamore Road, very near the golf course.

Mearescourt House, Rathconrath, Mullingar, Co Westmeath
Tel: 044 55112 Four en suite guest bedrooms, each sleeping up to four, in a magnificent Georgian mansion set in sweeping parkland. Dinner by arrangement. 604

Mornington House, Multyfarnham, Co Westmeath
Tel: 044 72191 Superior Accommodation in four bedrooms, all with private bathrooms, in a lovely country house on its own estate. Superb evening meals. 603

The Fairways, Bloomfield, Mullingar, Co Westmeath
Tel: 044 42584 Four en suite rooms (one family size) with tv in a B&B guest house opposite Mullingar Golf Club.

White Gables, Headfort Place, Kells, Co Meath
Tel: 046 40322 Three double rooms and a twin, all en suite, with tv. B&B, packed lunches on request, dinner by arrangement for parties of 8 or more. 441

Food and Drink

Jack's Railway Bar, Kells, Co Meath
Tel/Fax: 046 40215 A grand pub with log fires in winter and barbecues in the beer garden in summer. Lunchtime carvery; evening meals with notice. Games room. 434

The Haggard Inn, Trim, Co Meath
Tel: 046 31110 Restaurant, carvery and bar food in an atmospheric 19th-century hostelry. Traditional music Friday and Saturday. 440

The Pollard Arms Hotel, Castlepollard, Co Westmeath
Tel: 044 61194 Recently refurbished hotel in the centre of Castlepollard. Fifteen en suite bedrooms, bar, restaurant and function room. 600

Glasson

Glasson Golf & Country Club, Glasson, Athlone, Co Westmeath

Tel: 090 285120

It would be difficult to imagine a more arresting setting than Glasson, with Lough Ree and the River Shannon visible from almost every part of the course. Indeed Breda Reid, who runs the enterprise with her husband Tom, captured its magic when she said: "I always considered this place to be heaven, even when it wasn't a golf course."

The designer, Christy O'Connor Jnr, has not done better work than this. After being provided with a wonderful site of generous, 175-acre proportions, he used the land to excellent effect, through extensive earthmoving on the front nine and the enhancement of rolling terrain on the homeward journey.

Having farmed the land like his father before him, Reid had intimate knowledge of the site, especially with regard to drainage. This and O'Connor's design skills combined to deliver a 7,120-yard stretch of which the partners could be proud.

American golfing visitors often insist that Ireland's attraction lies in its wonderful links terrain and that parkland stretches have to be very special to command their attention. Glasson is such

a gem. Indeed the short 15th, where the green juts out into the lake, is a particular gem.

A considerable bonus is its accessibility by boat, all the way from Enniskillen, since the completion of the Ballinamore Canal, linking the Shannon with Lough Erne. And golfers come from other areas of the river. Indeed hardly a day passes during the summer when a few cruisers aren't berthed at the jetty to the back of 17th.

Sec/Manager:	Fidelma Reid
Professional:	None
Directions:	6 miles North of Athlone off the N55 to Ballymahon
Type of Course:	Parkland
Date Founded:	1993
No of Holes:	18
Length:	7120 yds (6510 mtrs)
Par:	72
SSS:	74
Green Fees:	Mon.-Thurs.: £30 Fri. & Sun.: £32 Saturday: £35
Visitors:	Welcome: Any Day, Prior booking advisable
Societies:	Welcome: Special concessions, Contact club for details
Facilities:	Chipping/Putting Area, Practice Area, Golf Clubs for hire, Trolley hire, Electric Buggy hire, Bar, Restaurant, Caddy service by arrangement

Accommodation, Food and Drink

Reference numbers below refer to detailed information provided in section 2

Accommodation

Bloomfield House, Mullingar, Co Westmeath
Tel: 044 40894 Fax: 044 43767 Sixty-five en suite bedrooms, including executive suites, in a high-quality hotel on the Tullamore road (N52) by Lough Ennell. Leisure Club on site.   602

Catstone Lodge, Ballymore, Co. Westmeath
Tel: 044 56494 Fax: 044 56196 www.catstone.net Luxurious en suite bedrooms (60 sq m each) in a restored period-style farmhouse. Tv, sitting area, kitchenette. B&B or self-catering.

Creagduff House, Coosan, Athlone, Co Westmeath
Tel: 090 275891 Two self-catering apartments, each sleeping up to 4, on a 300-year-old estate. Easy parking. Tv. No credit cards.

Lacken House, Rahara, Athleague, Co Roscommon
Tel/Fax: 090 323449 Choose between B&B in the handsome 1820s manor and self-catering lodges in the grounds. Peaceful rural setting.   523

Mornington House, Multyfarnham, Co Westmeath
Tel: 044 72191 Superior Accommodation in five bedrooms, all with private bathrooms, in a lovely country house on its own estate. Superb evening meals.   603

Regans, Market Square, Roscommon, Co Roscommon
Tel: 090 325339/326373 14 en suite bedrooms, day-long restaurant, bar, nightclub and function room - under one roof in the town centre.   524

Shelmalier House, Cartrontroy, Athlone, Co Westmeath
Tel: 090 272145 Fax: 0902 73190 Quiet Accommodation in seven en suite B&B rooms with tv and phone. Award-winning breakfasts. Signposted off the N6.   606

The Gardens, The Walk, Roscommon, Co Roscommon
Tel/Fax: 090 326828 Four simply-appointed en suite bedrooms in a Bed & Breakfast house near the main roundabout in Roscommon. Parking available.

Villa St John, Athlone, Co Westmeath
Tel/Fax: 090 292490 Eight bedrooms, five en suite, in a smart modern Bed & Breakfast house half a mile out of Athlone. Large terrace. Easy parking.   601

Food and Drink

Bloomfield House, Mullingar, Co Westmeath
Tel: 044 40894 Fax: 044 43767 Sixty-five en suite bedrooms, including executive suites, in a high-quality hotel on the Tullamore road (N52) by Lough Ennell. Leisure Club on site.   602

Chungs Chinese Restaurant, Boyle, Co. Roscommon
Tel: 079 62016 Fax: 079 64949 A Chinese restaurant in the Royal Hotel Boyle, with the usual long à la carte list and set menus for two or more.

Hillside House, Doon, Corrigeenroe, Boyle, Co Roscommon
Tel: 079 66075 Four B&B rooms in an attractive country home beside Lough Key with its forest, fishing and boating. Great views.

Lisroyne Inn, Strokestown, Co Roscommon
Tel: 078 33214 The smartest pub in town - neat and spotless. A warm welcome, good drinking and snacking.   521

Regans, Market Square, Roscommon, Co Roscommon
Tel: 090 325339/326373 14 en suite bedrooms, day-long restaurant, bar, nightclub and function room - under one roof in the town centre.   524

Moate

Moate Golf Club, Aghanargit, Moate, Co Westmeath
Tel: 090 281271

Sec/Manager:	P. J. Higgins
Professional:	None
Directions:	7 miles East of Athlone of the N6 to Kilbeggan
Type of Course:	Parkland
Date Founded:	1900
No of Holes:	18
Length:	6287 yds (5748 mtrs)
Par:	72
SSS:	70
Green Fees:	Weekdays: £12 Weekends & Bank Holidays: £15
Visitors:	Welcome: Any Day, Contact Club in advance
Societies:	Welcome: Special concessions, Contact Club for details
Facilities:	Chipping/Putting Area, Trolley hire, Bar, Restaurant

Accommodation, Food and Drink

Reference numbers below refer to detailed information provided in section 2

Accommodation

Bloomfield House, Mullingar, Co Westmeath
Tel: 044 40894 Fax: 044 43767 Sixty-five en suite bedrooms, including executive suites, in a high-quality hotel on the Tullamore road (N52) by Lough Ennell. Leisure Club on site.   602

Catstone Lodge, Ballymore, Co. Westmeath
Tel: 044 56494 Fax: 044 56196 www.catstone.net Luxurious en suite bedrooms (60 sq m each) in a restored period-style farmhouse. Tv, sitting area, kitchenette. B&B or self-catering.

Creagduff House, Coosan, Athlone, Co Westmeath
Tel: 090 275891 Two self-catering apartments, each sleeping up to 4, on a 300-year-old estate. Easy parking. Tv. No credit cards.

Mearescourt House, Rathconrath, Mullingar, Co Westmeath
Tel: 044 55112 Four en suite guest bedrooms, each sleeping up to four, in a magnificent Georgian mansion set in sweeping parkland. Dinner by arrangement.   604

Shelmalier House, Cartrontroy, Athlone, Co Westmeath
Tel: 090 272145 Fax: 090 273190 Quiet Accommodation in seven en suite B&B rooms with tv and phone. Award-winning breakfasts. Signposted off the N6. 606

The Fairways, Bloomfield, Mullingar, Co Westmeath
Tel: 044 42584 Four en suite rooms (one family size) with tv in a B&B guest house opposite Mullingar Golf Club.

Villa St John, Athlone, Co Westmeath
Tel/Fax: 090 292490 Eight bedrooms, five en suite, in a smart modern Bed & Breakfast house half a mile out of Athlone. Large terrace. Easy parking. 601

Food and Drink

Bloomfield House, Mullingar, Co Westmeath
Tel: 044 40894 Fax: 044 43767 Sixty-five en suite bedrooms, including executive suites, in a high-quality hotel on the Tullamore road (N52) by Lough Ennell. Leisure Club on site. 602

Oscars, Mullingar, Co Westmeath
Tel: 044 44909 A charming town-centre restaurant with a cosmopolitan menu catering for all tastes. Full drinks licence. 605

Regans, Market Square, Roscommon, Co Roscommon
Tel: 090 325339/326373 14 en suite bedrooms, day-long restaurant, bar, nightclub and function room - under one roof in the town centre. 524

Mount Temple

Mount Temple Golf Club, Mount Temple Village, Moate, Co Westmeath

Tel: 090 281841/281545

Sec/Manager:	Michelle Allen
Professional:	David Kinahan
Directions:	5 miles East of Athlone near village of Mount Temple to the North of the N6 to Moate
Type of Course:	Parkland
Date Founded:	1991
No of Holes:	18
Length:	6481 yds (5927 mtrs)
Par:	72
SSS:	72
Green Fees:	Weekdays: £16 Weekends & Bank Holidays: £20
Visitors:	Welcome: Any Day, Contact Club for weekend restrictions
Societies:	Welcome: Contact Club in advance
Facilities:	Chipping/Putting Area, Practice Area, Golf Clubs for hire, Trolley hire, Electric Buggy hire, Restaurant

Accommodation, Food and Drink

Reference numbers below refer to detailed information provided in section 2

Accommodation

Bloomfield House, Mullingar, Co Westmeath
Tel: 044 40894 Fax: 044 43767 Sixty-five en suite bedrooms, including executive suites, in a high-quality hotel on the Tullamore road (N52) by Lough Ennell. Leisure Club on site. 602

Catstone Lodge, Ballymore, Co. Westmeath
Tel: 044 56494 Fax: 044 56196 www.catstone.net Luxurious en suite bedrooms (60 sq m each) in a restored period-style farmhouse. Tv, sitting area, kitchenette. B&B or self-catering.

Creaghduff House, Coosan, Athlone, Co Westmeath
Tel: 090 275891 Two self-catering apartments, each sleeping up to 4, on a 300-year-old estate. Easy parking. Tv. No credit cards.

Mearescourt House, Rathconrath, Mullingar, Co Westmeath
Tel: 044 55112 Four en suite guest bedrooms, each sleeping up to four, in a magnificent Georgian mansion set in sweeping parkland. Dinner by arrangement. 604

Shelmalier House, Cartrontroy, Athlone, Co Westmeath
Tel: 090 272145 Fax: 090 273190 Quiet Accommodation in seven en suite B&B rooms with tv and phone. Award-winning breakfasts. Signposted off the N6. 606

The Fairways, Bloomfield, Mullingar, Co Westmeath
Tel: 044 42584 Four en suite rooms (one family size) with tv in a B&B guest house opposite Mullingar Golf Club.

Villa St John, Athlone, Co Westmeath
Tel/Fax: 090 292490 Eight bedrooms, five en suite, in a smart modern Bed & Breakfast house half a mile out of Athlone. Large terrace. Easy parking. 601

Food and Drink

Bloomfield House, Mullingar, Co Westmeath
Tel: 044 40894 Fax: 044 43767 Sixty-five en suite bedrooms, including executive suites, in a high-quality hotel on the Tullamore road (N52) by Lough Ennell. Leisure Club on site. 602

Oscars, Mullingar, Co Westmeath
Tel: 044 44909 A charming town-centre restaurant with a cosmopolitan menu catering for all tastes. Full drinks licence. 605

Regans, Market Square, Roscommon, Co Roscommon
Tel: 090 325339/326373 14 en suite bedrooms, day-long restaurant, bar, nightclub and function room - under one roof in the town centre. 524

Mullingar

Mullingar Golf Club, Belvedere, Mullingar, Co Westmeath

Tel: 044 48629

On hitting a short-iron approach to the first green at Mullingar, a category-one player might well think himself set for a gentle test, particularly having heard that the sixth was almost driveable. But his notions about the challenge of this classic, parkland stretch, would change the moment he stepped onto the second tee.

There is no doubt but that in common with other creations of its time, Mullingar has suffered somewhat from the frenzied advances in golf equipment. Yet it has survived better than most, because of its location in the heavily wooded, Belvedere demesne.

That was where James Braid, five times winner of the British Open, came on the morning of June 5th, 1935. Amid tremendous, excitement locally, Braid stepped off the Dublin-Sligo train and set about transforming an overgrown, 120-acre site into a golf course as we now know it.

Club officials such as Dermot Shaw, Joe Downes, Fr Mulvin and P J Keelan, had their own ideas as to how the terrain could best be exploited. Indeed they offered advice which Braid gently declined. All the great man required were 18 pegs and 18 stakes; he would meet them back at the site at 5.0 pm.

They were somewhat syurprised that he was planning to do in one day what had defied their best efforts for almost two years, but they had the good sense not to question. In recalling that momentous day, the late Paddy Shaw referred, among other things, to the famous tree which stands sentinel on the right of the 10th fairway.

"Braid wanted it left there but most members wanted it cut, as it stood in the direct line to the hole," he recalled. "They discussed it at length. Most were for removing it. I felt that James Braid was right but I was in a minority. Braid won out in the end." It was unlikely, however, that the designer ever imagined the more powerful hitters flying their drives over that tree with ease.

In the event, Braid appeared to be generally pleased with what he saw. So it was that on returning to his position as the club professional at Walton Heath, he wrote to Mullingar on June 8th assuring them: "Gentlemen, I have much pleasure in stating that a first class and most interesting course could be constructed on the site. Practically every hole would be different in character, the contour being sufficiently undulating to provide some splendid positions for greens, whilst the turf is excellent for fairways....."

His final letter came 30 months later, on December 11th 1937. In it he wrote: "Although I was favourably impressed by the site during my first visit, I was far more so this time. I consider you have done remarkable work during the short time and will be much surprised if the course does not make a name for itself in the near future."

As a living thing, however, a golf course is never finished. And the popularity of the Mullingar stretch, allied to an unusually heavy rainfall in recent years, has led to drainage problems.

They are to be confronted next spring when, according to captain Aidan Egan, the club will be embarking on a "drainage programme" to prepare the course for the 21st century. It will mean deferring planned changes to the grouping of the first, eighth and 16th greens, specifically by moving the 16th green to the right, closer to the trees.

Meanwhile, Braid was absolutely correct in his prediction about great things for the course, notably in terms of its distinguished visitors. The cream of British and Irish amateur talent, who gathered for the Mullingar Scratch Trophy each August bank holiday weekend, quickly discovered the menace that lay beyond the gentle first hole.

They had seen a round become a struggle as a result of problems encountered at the magnificent, par-three second which, at 200 yards off the back tee, could require a well-hit fairway wood, depending on conditions.

Indeed one of the great strengths of the course is the quality of its short holes. And it is highly significant that when Philip Walton set a course-record 63 in the final round of the 1982 Scratch Trophy, he was level par for the four short holes, with a bogey at the 15th countering a birdie at the 12th.

Another critical aspect of Walton's round is that he had only 25 putts and carded birdies at the sixth, eighth, ninth, 10th, 12th, 13th, 16th and 18th, while reducing the 495-yard par-five fourth to an eagle three.

Mullingar had earlier been the scene of comparable excitement generated by the spectacular scoring of a Scratch Trophy competitor. It meant that on the evening of Sunday, August 7th 1966, the great Joe Carr was forced to settle an intriguing wager he had struck three days previously.

The other party to the deal was a brilliant young Englishman by the name of Peter Michael Paul Townsend. As it happened, the transaction, which took place in the clubhouse bar, involved the payment by Carr of £13 - £1 for every stroke that Townsend finished ahead of him in that weekend's Scratch Trophy.

The fact that Carr had finished runner-up in the 72-holes event spoke volumes for the majesty of Townsend's performance. With rounds of 66,74,68 and 66 for a 14-under-par aggregate of 274, the 19-year-old had set a dazzling new standard for amateur strokeplay competition in this country.

A contemporary of Townsend's, Peter Benka, became another English winner of the Scratch Trophy in 1970, a year after he had partnered Peter Oosterhuis to victory in the Sunningdale Foursomes. Then there were the Gannon brothers, Mark and Frank, who made a major impact on the event by winning it twice each.

Indeed when considering a roll of honour, it would be difficult to surpass the sequence of Mullingar Scratch Trophy winners starting in 1989. That was when Darren Clarke triumphed, to be followed by British Boys' champion Leslie

Walker, then Paul McGinley, Raymond Burns, Eddie Power and Padraig Harrington.

Meanwhile, Mullingar's prominence as a club owes as much to its remarkable members as to the quality of its course. And who could forget the scenes at Rosses Point in 1982 when victory in the Irish Junior Cup gave the club its first all-Ireland pennant.

Celebrations started as early as 2.0 in the afternoon, led by the club captain, the inimitable Joe Healy. Indeed all the familiar faces were there - Albert Lee, Roche T, Martin Mulligan, Mickey Duffy, Jim Wims, the Dunner, Seamus Casey, Bill Tormey, Larry Gavin, Eileen O'Mahony, Frank Shaw, Ita Wallace and Doreen Casey - characters all.

As Healy put it: "Visitors to Mullingar readily agree that the welcome mat seems to trip you immediately you turn the gate." Long may it remain that way.

Sec/Manager:	Anne Scully
Professional:	None
Directions:	3 miles South of Mullingar off the N52 to Tyrrellspass
Type of Course:	Parkland
Date Founded:	1894
No of Holes:	18
Length:	6778 yds (6198 mtrs)
Par:	72
SSS:	71
Green Fees:	Weekdays: £20 Weekends & Bank Holidays: £25
Visitors:	Welcome: Any Day except Wednesday and Saturday, Prior booking required
Societies:	Welcome: Contact Club direct for details
Facilities:	Chipping/Putting Area, Practice Area, Golf Clubs for hire, Trolley hire, Electric Buggy hire, Bar, Restaurant, Caddy service by arrangement

Accommodation, Food and Drink

Reference numbers below refer to detailed information provided in section 2

Accommodation

Bloomfield House, Mullingar, Co Westmeath
Tel: 044 40894 Fax: 044 43767 Sixty-five en suite bedrooms, including executive suites, in a high-quality hotel on the Tullamore road (N52) by Lough Ennell. Leisure Club on site.   602

Catstone Lodge, Ballymore, Co. Westmeath
Tel: 044 56494 Fax: 044 56196 www.catstone.net Luxurious en suite bedrooms (60 sq m each) in a restored period-style farmhouse. Tv, sitting area, kitchenette. B&B or self-catering.

Lackan Lodge, Edgeworthstown, Co Longford
Tel: 043 71299 Four guest bedrooms (2 en suite) in a peacefully located modern farmhouse on the Longford side of Edgeworthstown. No smoking.   482

Lynnbury, Mullingar, Co Westmeath
Tel: 044 48432/40444 Country home Accommodation in a handsome house on the main Tullamore Road, very near the golf course.

Mearescourt House, Rathconrath, Mullingar, Co Westmeath

Tel: 044 55112 Four en suite guest bedrooms, each sleeping up to four, in a magnificent Georgian mansion set in sweeping parkland. Dinner by arrangement.   604

Mornington House, Multyfarnham, Co Westmeath
Tel: 044 72191 Superior Accommodation in five bedrooms, all with private bathrooms, in a lovely country house on its own estate. Superb evening meals.   603

The Fairways, Bloomfield, Mullingar, Co Westmeath
Tel: 044 42584 Four en suite rooms (one family size) with tv in a B&B guest house opposite Mullingar Golf Club.

Viewmount House, Longford, Co Longford
Tel: 043 41919 High-quality Accommodation in a former farmhouse a mile from the town centre. En suite bedrooms, lovely gardens, fine dining.   480

Food and Drink

Bloomfield House, Mullingar, Co Westmeath
Tel: 044 40894 Fax: 044 43767 Sixty-five en suite bedrooms, including executive suites, in a high-quality hotel on the Tullamore road (N52) by Lough Ennell. Leisure Club on site.   602

Oscars, Mullingar, Co Westmeath
Tel: 044 44909 A charming town-centre restaurant with a cosmopolitan menu catering for all tastes. Full drinks licence.   605

The Pollard Arms Hotel, Castlepollard, Co Westmeath
Tel: 044 61194 Recently refurbished hotel in the centre of Castlepollard. Fifteen en suite bedrooms, bar, restaurant and function room.   600

Viewmount House, Longford, Co Longford
Tel: 043 41919 High-quality Accommodation in a former farmhouse a mile from the town centre. En suite bedrooms, lovely gardens, fine dining.   480

WEXFORD

During a casual meeting with golfer Tony Pierce, our conversation drifted, almost inevitably, to his beloved Rosslare. "You must pay a visit and see the great work being done down there," urged this highly knowledgeable man of Irish golf. After extracting from me what must have seemed like a fairly amaemic promise, we parted.

A few months later, before my departure from Boston after the Ryder Cup, I met up with Eric O'Brien whose main claim to golfing fame was to be beaten by Joe Carr at Killarney in 1963, in the last 36-hole final of the Irish Close Championship. But he had another distinction: he won the Rosslare Scratch Cup in 1962. Now, we're all familiar with the remarkably small world which golfers inhabit. So it was no more than mildly surprising to discover that O'Brien's victory at Rosslare came after an 18-hole play-off with R A Howlett of Tramore and who else, only the bold Tony Pierce.

Arising from those meetings, my most recent visit to Rosslare occurred on a morning when it seemed the height of lunacy to even think about playing golf, much less put on the wet gear. But in the company of two other lunatics, I did. And by the time we had left the

Wexford Wildfowl Reserve, Co Wexford

sodden green of the short second, the rain had begun to ease. One hole later, the sun had broken through, miraculously. I would later discover that Rosslare was probably the only course in the country where it was possible to have an enjoyable game of golf that day: golfers flocked from all over Wexford to take advantage of the freak weather. And in my middle years, I came to believe that the sunny south-east was not a figment of the imagination.

Statistically, the south-east corner of Ireland enjoys the longest hours of sunshine anywhere in the country, a factor which is not ignored by the many city dwellers who flock there during the summer months. And while Wexford would not be noted as a significant golfing county, it has outstanding resort courses in Rosslare, Courtown and St Helen's Bay, along with Enniscorthy, New Ross, Tara Glen and Wexford GC. Of the county's seven courses, Rosslare in the only pure links, though the finishing two holes at St Helen's Bay are set in traditional duneland. Otherwise, the challenge is parkland, even at Courtown which is by the sea.

Known as the "Model County" because of its neat, tilled fields and industrious farmers, Wexford is an agricultural area, dominated by crop and fruit production, with a secondary dependence on fishing and tourism. Among other things, it has its own Tintern Abbey. Named after its more famous counterpart in Wales, which supplied its first monks, the abbey was built about 1200 and was occupied by the Cistercians for about 300 years. After the dissolution of the monasteries in 1536, the power base became more temporal, as the family home of the Colcloughs. It was eventually donated to the nation in 1959 and the abbey is now a national monument and the Heritage Division. Indeed it has recently been extensively restored by the Department of Arts, Culture and the Gaeltacht.

On travelling through Wexford, many memorials of the 1798 Rebellion will be encountered. Indeed the uprising, which dominates the county's history and folklore, has a section to itself

*Commodore John Barry Memorial,
Wexford Quay*

in the Enniscorthy Castle Museum. Strong links are also evident with the US, not least with the presidency of John F Kennedy whose visit in 1962 is commemorated by a park and arboretum which were opened six years later at Dunganstown, his ancestral home. The great-grandfather of the assassinated president lived there before emigrating to the US during the 19th century. In the process, he was following a pattern of emigration to the New World which developed at times into something approaching an exodus. For instance, in the year 1833 alone, no fewer than 250 families, drawn mainly from the townlands around Ballygarrett, set out for Texas via Liverpool and New Orleans. They had been recruited by James Power, an intrepid local entrepreneur, who, having prospered in America, had won a contract from the Mexican government to colonise parts of Texas, which was then a federal province of Mexico. Another link is the John Barry Memorial opposite the tourist office in Wexford Town. This commemorates the acknowledged father of the American Navy, who was born in Wexford, went to sea and ultimately settled in America. During the War of Independence there, he became a naval hero and was made commander-in-chief of the navy in 1797. He is buried in St Mary's churchyard in Pennsylvania and a grateful US government presented the bronze statue to Ireland to honour the outstanding contribution which Barry made to his adopted country.

From a cultural standpoint, Wexford is justifiably proud of its annual Opera Festival. This was the brainchild of Dr Tom Walsh who, in 1951, set about reviving the Theatre Royal through the staging of little known but beautiful operas. Held each year in late October/early November, the chemistry established between the enthusiastic locals and the famous or aspiring operatic artists has become legendary. Three operas are staged over a hectic 18 days, along with an imaginative programme of fringe events, including art exhibitions, threatrical happenings, traditional music sessions and craft and antique fairs.

From the Blackstairs Mountains in the west to the low-lying sloblands in the east, Wexford has a large variety of ideal wildlife habitats. Which explains why nearly half the world's population of white-fronted Greenland geese, spend the winter on the Wexford Wildfowl Reserve, North Slobs. During the 19th century, the north and south bays of the Slaney estuary were cut off from the tide by the building of dykes, thus forming an enchanting wild-fowl repository. Other species found there include more than two-dozen varities of duck, Brent and barnacle geese, whooper and Berwick's swans, along with almost 40 species of wader.

Wexford Town, Co Wexford

Against that background, it is clear that Wexford offers an ideal environment to those students of nature, who, unlike their golfing brethern, insist on their birdies having genuine feathers.

Location of Golf Courses

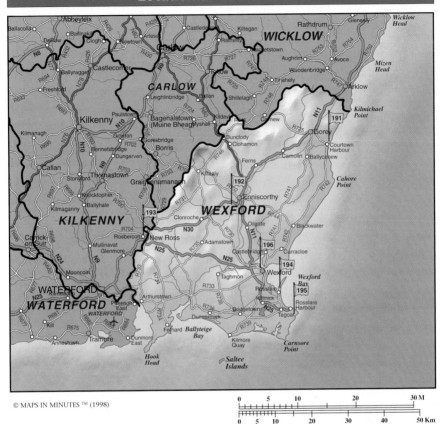

© MAPS IN MINUTES ™ (1998)

|191| Courtown Golf Club, Gorey   196

|192| Enniscorthy Golf Club, Enniscorthy   196

|193| New Ross Golf Club, New Ross   197

|194| Rosslare Golf Club, Rosslare   197

|195| St Helens Bay Golf Club, Rosslare Harbour   199

|196| Wexford Golf Club, Mulgannon   200

Courtown

Courtown Golf Club, Kiltennel, Gorey, Co Wexford

Tel: 055 25166

Sec/Manager:	David Cleere
Professional:	John Coone
Directions:	3 miles South East of Gorey off the R742 to Courtown
Type of Course:	Parkland
Date Founded:	1936
No of Holes:	18
Length:	6428 yds (5878 mtrs)
Par:	71
SSS:	71
Green Fees:	Oct - Apr: Weekdays: £17 Weekends: £22: May-Sept: Weekdays: £27 Weekends: £32
Visitors:	Welcome: Any Day, Contact Club in advance
Societies:	Welcome: Special concessions, Contact club for details
Facilities:	Chipping/Putting Area, Practice Area, Golf Clubs for hire, Trolley hire, Electric Buggy hire, Bar, Restaurant

Accommodation, Food and Drink

Reference numbers below refer to detailed information provided in section 2

Accommodation

Ballinkeele House, Ballymurn, Enniscorthy, Co Wexford
Tel: 053 38105 Fax: 053 38468 In a handsome mid 19th-century country mansion with a striking pillared portico, five en suite bedrooms provide exceptional comfort, stryle and character. Dinner at 7.30. 628

Cill Aodáin, Kiltimagh, Co Mayo
Tel: 094 81761 A friendly hotel in a small town in the heart of the county. Standard or superior rooms available. Continental and country cuisine. Bar. 424

Don Carr House, Enniscorthy, Co Wexford
Tel: 054 33458 Quietly located two-storey house with four en suite rooms for Bed and Breakfast. Five-minute walk from the town centre. 632

Harbour House, Courtown Harbour, Co Wexford
Tel/Fax: 055 25117 Family-run guest house in a renowned seaside resort. 13 en suite bedrooms with tv. Also self-catering in mobile homes. 623

Murphy's Bar & Restaurant, Arklow, Co Wicklow
Tel/Fax: 040 232781 Spacious, well-appointed main-street pub with restaurant. Self-catering Accommodation also offered. 662

Ostan Beag Hotel, Arklow, Co Wicklow
Tel: 040 233044 A hospitable hotel with 20 elegant en suite bedrooms, two bars, a restaurant and a lively nightclub. 666

PJ Murphys, Enniscorthy, Co Wexford
Tel: 054 33522/37837 Eight rooms offer versatile Bed and Breakfast Accommodation. Attached to a lively pub in the main street. 645

St Thereses, Mount Alexander, Gorey, Co Wexford
Tel: 055 21793 Fax: 055 21443 Good old-fashioned Irish hospitality in a brand new house with six letting bedrooms. Bed and Breakfast. 621

The Beehive, Coolbeg Cross, N11 Wexford Road, Co Wicklow
Tel: 040 469745 Bar, restaurant and Bed & Breakfast Accommodation in a family-run establishment on the N11. Weekend music. 664

The Loft Restaurant, Navan, Co Meath
Tel: 046 71755 A 70-cover restaurant with a continental feel and a wide-ranging menu that includes popular classics, Oriental flavours and fresh seafood. 430

Valley Lodge, Face Field, Claremorris, Co Mayo

Tel: 094 65180 Five letting rooms offer flexible Accommodation in a modern B&B farmhouse 5 miles outside Claremorris on the Castlebar road (N60). 420

Woodlands Farmhouse, Killinierin, Gorey, Co Wexford
Tel: 040 237125 Fax: 040 237133 Six tastefully decorated en suite bedrooms in a Georgian-style 19th-century residence. Large gardens. Dinner from 7.30. 627

Food and Drink

Murphy's Bar & Restaurant, Arklow, Co Wicklow
Tel/Fax: 040 232781 Spacious, well-appointed main-street pub with restaurant. Self-catering Accommodation also offered. 662

Ostan Beag Hotel, Arklow, Co Wicklow
Tel: 040 233044 A hospitable hotel with 20 elegant en suite bedrooms, two bars, a restaurant and a lively nightclub. 666

PJ Murphys, Enniscorthy, Co Wexford
Tel: 054 33522/37837 Eight rooms offer versatile Bed and Breakfast Accommodation. Attached to a lively pub in the main street. 645

Quinn's Lounge, Gorey, Co Wexford
Tel: 055 21810 Fax: 055 21819 All the Irish beers and plenty of others in a charming old-world lounge on the main street. Lunchtime snacks. 622

Taravie Hotel, Courtown Harbour, Co Wexford
Tel: 055 25208/25305 Ten en suite bedrooms in a family-run hotel by the beach. Families very welcome. 624

The Beehive, Coolbeg Cross, N11 Wexford Road, Co Wicklow
Tel: 040 469745 Bar, restaurant and Bed & Breakfast Accommodation in a family-run establishment on the N11. Weekend music. 664

The Courtyard, Ferns, Enniscorthy, Co Wexford
Tel: 054 66531 Fax: 054 66666 Top-class pub and bistro-style restaurant in the ancient capital of Leinster. Steaks are a speciality. 636

The Crosses, Kilmuckridge, Gorey, Co Wexford
Tel: 053 30458 A sporting pub (darts, pool) with live music at the weekend and an all-day menu of home-cooked food. 625

Enniscorthy

Enniscorthy Golf Club, Knockmarshall, Enniscorthy, Co Wexford

Tel: 054 33191

Sec/Manager:	Brian Kenny
Professional:	Martin Sludds
Directions:	2 miles South West of Enniscorthy off the N30 to New Ross
Type of Course:	Parkland
Date Founded:	1906
No of Holes:	18
Length:	6687 yds (6115 mtrs)
Par:	72
SSS:	72
Green Fees:	Oct-Apr: Weekdays: £15 Weekends & Bank Holidays: £20: May-Sep - : Weekdays: £20 Weekends & Bank Holidays: £25
Visitors:	Welcome: Contact Club in advance
Societies:	Welcome: Special concessions available, Contact club for details
Facilities:	Chipping/Putting Area, Practice Area, Driving Range, Golf Clubs for hire, Trolley hire, Electric Buggy hire, Bar, Restaurant

Accommodation, Food and Drink

Reference numbers below refer to detailed information provided in section 2

Accommodation

Ballinkeele House, Ballymurn, Enniscorthy, Co Wexford
Tel: 053 38105 Fax: 053 38468 In a handsome mid 19th-century country mansion with a striking pillared portico, five en suite bedrooms provide exceptional comfort, stryle and character. Dinner at 7.30. 628

Courts Hotel, Drinagh, Wexford, Co Wexford
Tel: 053 43295 Fax: 053 45827 A friendly family-run hotel with 21 en suite bedrooms, a restaurant and bars. Two miles from Wexford town centre. 639

Don Carr House, Enniscorthy, Co Wexford
Tel: 054 33458 Quietly located two-storey house with four en suite rooms for Bed and Breakfast. Five-minute walk from the town centre. 632

Hillside House, Tubberduff, Gorey, Co Wexford
Tel: 055 21793 Fax: 055 21443 A modern house in an elevated setting with views of the Tara Hills. Six en suite bedrooms, some family size. Home cooking. 620

Lemongrove House, Blackstoops, Enniscorthy, Co Wexford
Tel: 054 36115 A fine modern Bed and Breakfast guest house in attractive gardens. Nine bedrooms, all with en suite facilities and tv. A mile north of Enniscorthy. 630

PJ Murphys, Enniscorthy, Co Wexford
Tel: 054 33522/37837 Eight rooms offer versatile Bed and Breakfast Accommodation. Attached to a lively pub in the main street. 645

St Thereses, Mount Alexander, Gorey, Co Wexford
Tel: 055 21793 Fax: 055 21443 Good old-fashioned Irish hospitality in a brand new house with six letting bedrooms. Bed and Breakfast. 621

Woodville Farm, Ballyhogue, Enniscorthy, Co Wexford
Tel: 054 47810 Flexible Bed & Breakfast Accommodation in five en suite bedrooms in a late 19th-century farmhouse. Mature gardens. 638

Food and Drink

Courts Hotel, Drinagh, Wexford, Co Wexford
Tel: 053 43295 Fax: 053 45827 A friendly family-run hotel with 21 en suite bedrooms, a restaurant and bars. Two miles from Wexford town centre. 639

PJ Murphys, Enniscorthy, Co Wexford
Tel: 054 33522/37837 Eight rooms offer versatile Bed and Breakfast Accommodation. Attached to a lively pub in the main street. 645

Quinn's Lounge, Gorey, Co Wexford
Tel: 055 21810 Fax: 055 21819 All the Irish beers and plenty of others in a charming old-world lounge on the main street. Lunchtime snacks. 622

The Courtyard, Ferns, Enniscorthy, Co Wexford
Tel: 054 66531 Fax: 054 66666 Top-class pub and bistro-style restaurant in the ancient capital of Leinster. Steaks are a speciality. 636

The Crosses, Kilmuckridge, Gorey, Co Wexford
Tel: 053 30458 A sporting pub (darts, pool) with live music at the weekend and an all-day menu of home-cooked food. 625

New Ross

New Ross Golf Club, Tinneranny, New Ross, Co Wexford

Tel: 051 421433

Sec/Manager:	Kathleen Daly
Professional:	None
Directions:	1 mile West of New Ross off the R704 to Listerlin
Type of Course:	Parkland
Date Founded:	1905
No of Holes:	18
Length:	6289 yds (5751 mtrs)
Par:	71
SSS:	70
Green Fees:	Weekdays: £14 Weekends & Bank Holidays: £16
Visitors:	Welcome: Any Day
Societies:	Welcome: Special concessions available, Contact club for details

Facilities: Chipping/Putting Area, Trolley hire, Bar, Restaurant

Accommodation, Food and Drink

Reference numbers below refer to detailed information provided in section 2

Accommodation

Arthur's Rest, Arthurstown, Co Wexford
Tel: 051 389192 Fax: 051 389362 A choice between Bed & Breakfast and self-catering Accommodation in a charming house near the Ballyhack car ferry. 651

Ballinkeele House, Ballymurn, Enniscorthy, Co Wexford
Tel: 053 38105 Fax: 053 38468 In a handsome mid 19th-century country mansion with a striking pillared portico, five en suite bedrooms provide exceptional comfort, stryle and character. Dinner at 7.30. 628

Don Carr House, Enniscorthy, Co Wexford
Tel: 054 33458 Quietly located two-storey house with four en suite rooms for Bed and Breakfast. Five-minute walk from the town centre. 632

Glendower House, New Ross, Co Wexford
Tel/Fax: 051 421989 Eight en suite bedrooms in a modern B&B on the main road into town from Wexford. Also evening meals. 650

Grove Farmhouse, Ballycocksuist, Inistioge, Co Kilkenny
Tel: 056 58467 Four generously sized B&B rooms in a 200-year-old country house on a working beef farm. All rooms en suite. 363

Keppel's Farmhouse, Avoca, Co Wicklow
Tel/Fax: 040 235168 Five bright, comfortable B&B rooms in a handsome 19th-century farmhouse. Also a self-catering bungalow. 673

Lemongrove House, Blackstoops, Enniscorthy, Co Wexford
Tel: 054 36115 A fine modern Bed and Breakfast guest house in attractive gardens. Nine bedrooms, all with en suite facilities and tv. A mile north of Enniscorthy. 630

PJ Murphys, Enniscorthy, Co Wexford
Tel: 054 33522/37837 Eight rooms offer versatile Bed and Breakfast Accommodation. Attached to a lively pub in the main street. 645

Woodville Farm, Ballyhogue, Enniscorthy, Co Wexford
Tel: 054 47810 Flexible Bed & Breakfast Accommodation in five en suite bedrooms in a late 19th-century farmhouse. Mature gardens. 638

Food and Drink

Circle of Friends, Inistioge, Co Kilkenny
Tel: 056 58800 High-quality traditional and modern Irish cuisine in a picture-postcard village setting. Open every evening. 364

PJ Murphys, Enniscorthy, Co Wexford
Tel: 054 33522/37837 Eight rooms offer versatile Bed and Breakfast Accommodation. Attached to a lively pub in the main street. 645

The Courtyard, Ferns, Enniscorthy, Co Wexford
Tel: 054 66531 Fax: 054 66666 Top-class pub and bistro-style restaurant in the ancient capital of Leinster. Steaks are a speciality. 636

The Horse & Hound, Ballinaboola, New Ross, Co Wexford
Tel: 051 428323 Restaurant, bar and 12 rooms for Bed & Breakfast in a friendly family-run hotel on the N25, four miles from New Ross. 653

Rosslare

Rosslare Golf Club, Rosslare, Co Wexford

Tel: 053 32203/32032

Famed for its location in the sunny South-East, Rosslare recently carried out major refurbishment on the main, championship layout of their 27-hole complex. It involved remarkable rock-revetment work, in an endless battle at containing the forces of nature along their one and a half miles of coastline.

According to secretary/manager Jim Hall, they acted on advice from the Hydraulic Institute in

Date Founded:	1905
No of Holes:	18 (plus 12)
Length:	6601 yds (6035 mtrs)
Par:	72
SSS:	72
Green Fees:	Weekdays: £25 Weekends & Bank Holidays: £35
Visitors:	Welcome: Prior booking required
Societies:	Welcome: Contact Club in advance
Facilities:	Chipping/Putting Area, Practice Area, Driving Range, Golf Clubs for hire, Trolley hire, Bar, Restaurant

Accommodation, Food and Drink

Reference numbers below refer to detailed
information provided in section 2

Accommodation

Ailsa Lodge, Rosslare Harbour, Co Wexford
Tel: 053 33230 Fax: 053 33581 Ten large en suite bedrooms, most with sea views,
in a mid-Victorian mansion with many fine features. 648

Ballybro Lodge, Tagoat, Killinick, Co Wexford
Tel/Fax: 053 32333 Five en suite bedrooms in a large detached house run by a
golfing couple. Large gardens with varied wildlife. 652

Ballycowan Lodge, Rosslare Harbour, Co Wexford
Tel/Fax: 053 31596 Four en suite Bed & Breakfast rooms in a handsome new
detached house on the R736 road to Kilmore. Private parking. 647

Clonard House, Clonard Great, Wexford, Co Wexford
Tel/Fax: 053 43141 Nine en suite bedrooms, six with four-posters, in a Georgian
house on a working dairy farm overlooking Wexford town and harbour. 626

Coral Gables, Tagoat, Rosslare Harbour
Tel: 053 31213 Fax: 053 31414 Purpose-built, striking guest house on a hilltop
above the Wexford-Rosslare road. Seven of the 15 bedrooms have verandas. 643

Courts Hotel, Drinagh, Wexford, Co Wexford
Tel: 053 43295 Fax: 053 45827 A friendly family-run hotel with 21 en suite
bedrooms, a restaurant and bars. Two miles from Wexford town centre. 639

Faythe House, Wexford, Co Wexford
Tel: 053 22249 Fax: 053 21680 Wexford's oldest guest house, with ten en suite
bedrooms, some with views of Wexford Harbour. Quiet location in the old town. 640

O'Leary's Farmhouse, Kilrane, Rosslare Harbour, Co Wexford
Tel: 053 33134 Nine bedrooms – seven en suite - on a working farm overlooking
the sea. True Irish hospitality. Also self-catering cottages. 646

Oldcourt House, Rosslare Harbour, Co Wexford
Tel: 053 33895 A large modern house in classical style, with six en suite bedrooms
for B&B. Private car park. Next to beach. 642

Slaney Manor, Ferrycarrig, Wexford, Co Wexford
Tel: 053 20051 Fax: 053 20510 1820s manor offering superior Accommodation in
the main house, the courtyard block and a thatched mud-walled cabin. Home
cooking. Woodland walks. 629

The Saint George Guest House, Wexford, Co Wexford
Tel: 053 43474 Fax: 053 21680 Ten bedrooms, all with bathrooms en suite, in a
family-run guest house in the centre of town. Lock-up car park. 637

Woodville Farm, Ballyhogue, Enniscorthy, Co Wexford
Tel: 054 47810 Flexible Bed & Breakfast Accommodation in five en suite bedrooms
in a late 19th-century farmhouse. Mature gardens. 638

Food and Drink

Courts Hotel, Drinagh, Wexford, Co Wexford
Tel: 053 43295 Fax: 053 45827 A friendly family-run hotel with 21 en suite
bedrooms, a restaurant and bars. Two miles from Wexford town centre. 639

Slaney Manor, Ferrycarrig, Wexford, Co Wexford
Tel: 053 20051 Fax: 053 20510 1820s manor offering superior Accommodation in
the main house, the courtyard block and a thatched mud-walled cabin. Home
cooking. Woodland walks. 629

The Kilrane Inn, Kilrane, Co Wexford
Tel: 053 33661 A cheerful, family-run pub-cum-restaurant on the N25 near Rosslare
Harbour. Sunday lunch and evening meals a speciality. 631

The Oak Tavern, Ferrycarrig, Co Wexford

Wallingford, England, in undertaking this process of protecting their boundaries. It has cost the club more than £1 million since it began in 1982.

Work on the course itself, to be completed this year, will extend its overall length to 6,760 yards. And a mile down the road, an extension of the New Course from nine to 12 holes, has been officially opened in April 2000

The nine-hole stretch, which has been in play since 1992, has been a tremendous asset to the club, generating green-fee revenue of £100,000 last year at modest rates of £10 for nine holes and £15 for 18. It is extremely popular with visitors from Wales, who, with the benefit of rapid ferry crossings, can travel, play and return home in one day.

On the main course new greens and tees have been constructed at the first, third, eighth and 16th; the greens at the fourth and seventh have been upgraded and modifications have also been made to the tees at the second, ninth, 12th and 14th. Work on the sixth and 15th tees was completed during the winter.

Sec/Manager:	Jim Hall
Professional:	Johnny Young
Directions:	8 miles South East of Wexford off the N25 to Rosslare Harbour. 6 miles North of Rosslare Harbour
Type of Course:	Links

Tel: 053 20922 Fax: 053 20945 A friendly tavern on the River Slaney, serving traditional Irish food seven days a week. Next to the National Heritage Centre. 641
The Oyster, Rosslare Strand, Co Wexford
Tel: 053 32439 A charming little restaurant in the heart of a well-known seaside resort. Fresh local seafood is the speciality. 644
The Silver Fox, Kilmore Quay, Co Wexford
Tel: 053 29888 A seafood restaurant of renown in a picture-postcard fishing village. Lemon sole not to be missed! Classical guitar midweek. 649

St Helens Bay

St. Helen's Bay Golf Resort, St. Helen's, Kilrane, Rosslare Harbour, Co Wexford

Tel: 053 33234

Given the location closeby the Tuskar Lighthouse, there is an awareness that the sea can't be far away. Yet the fact that it is revealed in a golfing context only on the last two holes, has the effect of giving St Helen's Bay one of the most dramatic finishes on the Irish scene.

Designed by Ryder Cup player Philip Walton, this charming holiday course has a decidedly parkland flavour, with nine water features and 5,000 trees employed to the best strategic effect. On the more demanding homeward journey, the 190-yard 11th and 210-yard 17th offer rather special, par-three challenges.

Then there are appealing details such as stone walls dating back to the days of the Great Famine; an area of the beach known as Pirates Cove, which was once a haven for 19th century smugglers, and a tower-house near the 12th hole, dating from the 13th century.

But almost inevitably, reflections on Helen's Bay are dominated by the two finishing holes, which would not be out of place on any of the country's premier links courses. The 17th is a particularly testing par three, where, except with a helping wind, a fairway wood will be necessary to reach the tightly-trapped target.

On the other hand, the par-four 18th, at 280 yards, is almost driveable. Power had better be matched with precision, however, if major grief is to be avoided from the beckoning dunes. Overall, Walton has reason to be well pleased with his handiwork, especially as an achitectural debut.

Sec/Manager:	Larry Byrne
Professional:	None
Directions:	2 miles South of Rosslare Harbour off the N25 to Kilrane
Type of Course:	Links & Parkland
Date Founded:	1993
No of Holes:	18
Length:	6661 yds (6091 mtrs)
Par:	72
SSS:	72
Green Fees:	Weekdays: £22 Weekends & Bank Holidays: £25 Low season: Weekdays £20 Weekends & Bank Holidays : £18
Visitors:	Welcome: Any day, Prior booking advisable
Societies:	Welcome: Special rates packages available, Contact club for details
Facilities:	Chipping/Putting Area, Practice Area, Golf Clubs for hire, Trolley hire, Electric Buggy hire, Bar, Restaurant, Caddy service by arrangement, plus Accommodation on site in four Lovely Irish Cottages. Beautiful Beach

Accommodation, Food and Drink

Reference numbers below refer to detailed information provided in section 2

Accommodation

Ailsa Lodge, Rosslare Harbour, Co Wexford
Tel: 053 33230 Fax: 053 33581 Ten large en suite bedrooms, most with sea views, in a mid-Victorian mansion with many fine features. 648
Ballybro Lodge, Tagoat, Killinick, Co Wexford
Tel/Fax: 053 32333 Five en suite bedrooms in a large detached house run by a golfing couple. Large gardens with varied wildlife. 652
Ballycowan Lodge, Rosslare Harbour, Co Wexford
Tel/Fax: 053 31596 Four en suite Bed & Breakfast rooms in a handsome new detached house on the R736 road to Kilmore. Private parking. 647
Clonard House, Clonard Great, Wexford, Co Wexford
Tel/Fax: 053 43141 Nine en suite bedrooms, six with four-posters, in a Georgian house on a working dairy farm overlooking Wexford town and harbour. 626
Coral Gables, Tagoat, Rosslare Harbour
Tel: 053 31213 Fax: 053 31414 Purpose-built, striking guest house on a hilltop above the Wexford-Rosslare road. Seven of the 15 bedrooms have verandas. 643
Faythe House, Wexford, Co Wexford
Tel: 053 22249 Fax: 053 21680 Wexford's oldest guest house, with ten en suite bedrooms, some with views of Wexford Harbour. Quiet location in the old town. 640
O'Leary's Farmhouse, Kilrane, Rosslare Harbour, Co Wexford
Tel: 053 33134 Nine bedrooms – seven en suite - on a working farm overlooking the sea. True Irish hospitality. Also self-catering cottages. 646
Oldcourt House, Rosslare Harbour, Co Wexford
Tel: 053 33895 A large modern house in classical style, with six en suite bedrooms for B&B. Private car park. Next to beach. 642
Slaney Manor, Ferrycarrig, Wexford, Co Wexford
Tel: 053 20051 Fax: 053 20510 1820s manor offering superior Accommodation in the main house, the courtyard block and a thatched mud-walled cabin. Home cooking. Woodland walks. 629
The Saint George Guest House, Wexford, Co Wexford
Tel: 053 43474 Fax: 053 24814 Ten bedrooms, all with bathrooms en suite, in a family-run guest house in the centre of town. Lock-up car park. 637

Food and Drink

Slaney Manor, Ferrycarrig, Wexford, Co Wexford
Tel: 053 20051 Fax: 053 20510 1820s manor offering superior Accommodation in the main house, the courtyard block and a thatched mud-walled cabin. Home cooking. Woodland walks. 629

The Kilrane Inn, Kilrane, Co Wexford

Tel: 053 33661 A cheerful, family-run pub-cum-restaurant on the N25 near Rosslare Harbour. Sunday lunch and evening meals a speciality. 631

The Oak Tavern, Ferrycarrig, Co Wexford

Tel: 053 20922 Fax: 053 20945 A friendly tavern on the River Slaney, serving traditional Irish food seven days a week. Next to the National Heritage Centre. 641

The Oyster, Rosslare Strand, Co Wexford

Tel: 053 32439 A charming little restaurant in the heart of a well-known seaside resort. Fresh local seafood is the speciality. 644

The Silver Fox, Kilmore Quay, Co Wexford

Tel: 053 29888 A seafood restaurant of renown in a picture-postcard fishing village. Lemon sole not to be missed! Classical guitar midweek. 649

Wexford

Wexford Golf Club, Mulgannon, Co Wexford

Tel: 053 42238

Sec/Manager:	Pat Daly
Professional:	None
Directions:	Within Wexford Town down the side road by The Talbot Hotel
Type of Course:	Parkland
Date Founded:	1961
No of Holes:	18
Length:	6306 yds (5766 mtrs)
Par:	72
SSS:	71
Green Fees:	Weekdays: £18 Weekends & Bank Holidays: £22
Visitors:	Welcome: Any day except Thursday and weekends
Societies:	Welcome: Special rates packages available. Contact club for details
Facilities:	Chipping/Putting Area, Practice Area, Golf Clubs for hire, Trolley hire, Electric Buggy hire, Bar, Restaurant, Caddy service by arrangement

Accommodation, Food and Drink

Reference numbers below refer to detailed information provided in section 2

Accommodation

Ailsa Lodge, Rosslare Harbour, Co Wexford

Tel: 053 33230 Fax: 053 33581 Ten large en suite bedrooms, most with sea views, in a mid-Victorian mansion with many fine features. 648

Ballinkeele House, Ballymurn, Enniscorthy, Co Wexford

Tel: 053 38105 Fax: 053 38468 In a handsome mid 19th-century country mansion with a striking pillared portico, five en suite bedrooms provide exceptional comfort, stryle and character. Dinner at 7.30. 628

Ballybro Lodge, Tagoat, Killinick, Co Wexford

Tel/Fax: 053 32333 Five en suite bedrooms in a large detached house run by a golfing couple. Large gardens with varied wildlife. 652

Ballycowan Lodge, Rosslare Harbour, Co Wexford

Tel/Fax: 053 31596 Four en suite Bed & Breakfast rooms in a handsome new detached house on the R736 road to Kilmore. Private parking. 647

Clonard House, Clonard Great, Wexford, Co Wexford

Tel/Fax: 053 43141 Nine en suite bedrooms, six with four-posters, in a Georgian house on a working dairy farm overlooking Wexford town and harbour. 626

Coral Gables, Tagoat, Rosslare Harbour

Tel: 053 31213 Fax: 053 31414 Purpose-built, striking guest house on a hilltop above the Wexford-Rosslare road. Seven of the 15 bedrooms have verandas. 643

Courts Hotel, Drinagh, Wexford, Co Wexford

Tel: 053 43295 Fax: 053 45827 A friendly family-run hotel with 21 en suite bedrooms, a restaurant and bars. Two miles from Wexford town centre. 639

Don Carr House, Enniscorthy, Co Wexford

Tel: 054 33458 Quietly located two-storey house with four en suite rooms for Bed and Breakfast. Five-minute walk from the town centre. 632

Faythe House, Wexford, Co Wexford

Tel: 053 22249 Fax: 053 21680 Wexford's oldest guest house, with ten en suite bedrooms, some with views of Wexford Harbour. Quiet location in the old town. 640

Lemongrove House, Blackstoops, Enniscorthy, Co Wexford

Tel: 054 36115 A fine modern Bed and Breakfast guest house in attractive gardens. Nine bedrooms, all with en suite facilities and tv. A mile north of Enniscorthy. 630

O'Leary's Farmhouse, Kilrane, Rosslare Harbour, Co Wexford

Tel: 053 33134 Nine bedrooms – seven en suite - on a working farm overlooking the sea. True Irish hospitality. Also self-catering cottages. 646

Oldcourt House, Rosslare Harbour, Co Wexford

Tel: 053 33895 A large modern house in classical style, with six en suite bedrooms for B&B. Private car park. Next to beach. 642

PJ Murphys, Enniscorthy, Co Wexford

Tel: 054 33522/37837 Eight rooms offer versatile Bed and Breakfast Accommodation. Attached to a lively pub in the main street. 645

Slaney Manor, Ferrycarrig, Wexford, Co Wexford

Tel: 053 20051 Fax: 053 20510 1820s manor offering superior Accommodation in the main house, the courtyard block and a thatched mud-walled cabin. Home cooking. Woodland walks. 629

The Saint George Guest House, Wexford, Co Wexford

Tel: 053 43474 Fax: 053 24814 Ten bedrooms, all with bathrooms en suite, in a family-run guest house in the centre of town. Lock-up car park. 637

Woodville Farm, Ballyhogue, Enniscorthy, Co Wexford

Tel: 054 47810 Flexible Bed & Breakfast Accommodation in five en suite bedrooms in a late 19th-century farmhouse. Mature gardens. 638

Food and Drink

Don Carr House, Enniscorthy, Co Wexford

Tel: 054 33458 Quietly located two-storey house with four en suite rooms for Bed and Breakfast. Five-minute walk from the town centre. 632

PJ Murphys, Enniscorthy, Co Wexford

Tel: 054 33522/37837 Eight rooms offer versatile Bed and Breakfast Accommodation. Attached to a lively pub in the main street. 645

Slaney Manor, Ferrycarrig, Wexford, Co Wexford

Tel: 053 20051 Fax: 053 20510 1820s manor offering superior Accommodation in the main house, the courtyard block and a thatched mud-walled cabin. Home cooking. Woodland walks. 629

The Courtyard, Ferns, Enniscorthy, Co Wexford

Tel: 054 66531 Fax: 054 66666 Top-class pub and bistro-style restaurant in the ancient capital of Leinster. Steaks are a speciality. 636

The Kilrane Inn, Kilrane, Co Wexford

Tel: 053 33661 A cheerful, family-run pub-cum-restaurant on the N25 near Rosslare Harbour. Sunday lunch and evening meals a speciality. 631

The Oak Tavern, Ferrycarrig, Co Wexford

Tel: 053 20922 Fax: 053 20945 A friendly tavern on the River Slaney, serving traditional Irish food seven days a week. Next to the National Heritage Centre. 641

The Oyster, Rosslare Strand, Co Wexford

Tel: 053 32439 A charming little restaurant in the heart of a well-known seaside resort. Fresh local seafood is the speciality. 644

WICKLOW

In 1953, the Delgany Artisans' Golfing Society staged their annual dance at the Horse and Hound Hotel, where the guest of honour was Harry Bradshaw, whom they were proud to consider one of their own. Essentially, the objective was to pay tribute to a local hero on his triumph in the Dunlop Masters that year and a fine, debut performance in the Ryder Cup at Wentworth. After Charles Byrne, secretary of the society, had proposed the toast to The Brad, the player replied: "I look forward to the time when some other Delgany golfer will bring much greater honours to the area than I ever could." Listed among the organising committee for what proved to be a memorable function was the name C Darcy. Thirty-four years later, on October 31st 1987, Christy Darcy's son, Eamonn, was honoured with life membership by Delgany GC for the distinction he had brought his country, his former club and the whole of County Wicklow in the Ryder Cup matches at Muirfield Village, Ohio, the previous month. At the same

Wicklow Town, Co Wicklow

function, The Brad was also honoured with life membership of a club where he had learned the game and where his father, Ned, was the one-time professional and his brother, Jimmy, was the then incumbent.

County Wicklow has a wonderful golfing tradition of which the Delgany club has particular reason to be proud. Out of the 16 players who have represented Ireland in the Ryder Cup, four - Bradshaw, Jimmy Martin, John O'Leary and Darcy - were closely associated with Delgany at some stage of their career. And they learned to accept their golfing successes with a modesty, synonymous with the times in which they lived. For instance, when Bradshaw

gained his first important tournament victory in the Irish Open at Royal Portrush in 1947, the captain of the Kilcroney club, where he was the resident professional, sent a motor-car to Belfast. The idea was to intercept the newly-crowned champion en route from Portrush. Quite oblivious to all this activity, however, Bradshaw took the afternoon train from Belfast, by which stage the Kilcroney car was speeding over the Border in the opposite direction. Then, when Harry arrived in Dublin, he caught the St Kevin's bus and made his way home quietly to his wife and family in Kilmancanogue, the Irish Open trophy cradled in his arms. Meanwhile, telephone calls to Northern Ireland had established that Harry had left Belfast by train. So, search parties were sent out from Kilcroney, only to draw a blank at Amiens St railway station in Dublin.

Fortunately, Harry's father, Ned, and his brother Eddie, who were also invited to the party, guessed what the reluctant hero had done. The upshot was that a scouting party took up position at the Kilmacanogue crossroads and when the bus eventually arrived, there was The Brad, complete with his clubs and trophy, making his way homeward, as coolly as if he had been returning from a fourball at Portmarnock. It was fairly late in the day when they arrived at Kilcroney, which, incidentally, was arguably the most luxurious golf and country club in Ireland at that time. And it was considerably later before the merrymaking finally came to an end.

Against such a rich background, it is hardly surprising that Wicklow has become one of the country's most progressive, golfing areas. By the Millennium, it could boast 21 clubs, with the immediate prospect of further expansion: Eamonn Darcy is planning to design his first course at the famous beauty spot of Avoca and Bray will soon be moving from their existing nine holes to a new, 18-hole layout on the other side of the Head. Known as "The Garden of Ireland" because of its stunning scenery, Wicklow's courses vary from the modest links terrain of Arklow to the delightful parkland of Druids Glen and the towering dunes of The European Club. Its full list of courses is: Arklow, Baltinglass, Blainroe, Bray, Charlesland, Coollattin, Delgany, Djouce Mountain. Druids Glen, The European Club, Glen of the Downs, Glenmalure, Greystones, Kilcoole, Powerscourt, Rathsallagh, Roundwood, Tulfarris, Vartry Lakes, Wicklow, Woodenbridge.

Wicklow Gap, Co Wicklow

The beauty of the county is probably best captured by the utterly charming Woodenbridge course, located four miles inland from Arklow town. Extended recently from nine to 18 holes, it is situated in the Vale of Avoca immortalised by the poet, Thomas Moore, who wrote of it: "There is not in this wide world a valley so sweet; as the vale in whose bosom the bright waters meet ...." Nestling in the shadow of hill and forests and encircled by the meandering Avoca and Aughrim rivers which captivated Moore, Woodenbridge extends to 6,344 yards off the back tees for an admirably testing par of 71. So charming are the surroundings, however, that the challenge of keeping one's eye on the ball takes on quite a challenging dimension here. As it happened, County Wicklow received a splendid lift in the Hertz International Golf Travel Awards 2000, in which Druids Glen was voted "European Golf Course of the Year." A measure of that achievement is that the beaten rivals included Valderrama, Wentworth, Turnberry and the San Lorenzo course in Portugal.

It is hardly surprising that several of Ireland's leading golf-course architects, along with some of their English brethren, have jumped at the chance of working with County Wicklow terrain. Charles Hawtree was responsible for Blainroe, which is parkland by the sea, and Peter McEvoy designed Powerscourt, while collaborating with Christy O'Connor Jnr on the Rathsallagh layout. Meanwhile, Ireland's Patrick Merrigan re-designed much of the front nine at Greystones and completed a wonderful layout for the new Tulfarris course. Then there were Eddie Hackett's designs of Djouce Mountain and of the Charlesland course, where the Evans brothers decided it made sound business sense to turn half the family farm of 300 acres, over to golf.

But County Wicklow's dominant architect is undoubtedly Pat Ruddy who, after moulding a wonderful stretch of duneland near Brittas into one of the country's finest courses at The European Club, was equally successful with the parkland development of Druids Glen. However, there is no doubting where Ruddy's heart lies, as a course designer. "The European Club has been designed to perpetuate and modernise the traditional values of links golf," he said. And few would dispute that he has been successful in this grand objective, where the combination of rugged dunes, deep bunkers, sea breezes and large, undulating greens, set a searching examination of character and shotmaking skills, for the discerning golfer. Though it is claimed that golf was played at Bray in the latter part of the 18th century, Greystones, with an institution date of 1895, can claim to be the oldest club in County Wicklow. And at a time when the Dublin, Wicklow and Wexford Railway Co was more than anxious to increase its passenger traffic, Greystones had a willing sponsor for some of its more ambitious competitions. In the event, "The Irish Times" of March, 1895, reported: "This club (Greystones) has been formed under the most favourable auspices. There are about 100 members. The links are very convenient to the station on the Burnaby estate, being a nine-hole course."

From those early days of steam, visitors through Wicklow are now likely to set off on the M11 Motorway at Bray and head southwards through the Glen of the Downs. And all around, there will be breathtaking views of hill, dale and woodland. Indeed the venerable Hackett captured the magic of Wicklow when, on first looking over the site at Djouce Mountain, he observed: "The combination of pleasant and varying gradients and scenically attractive countryside, offer excellent golfing potential." And when the clubs are packed away, there could hardly be a better location for sightseeing.

Location of Golf Courses

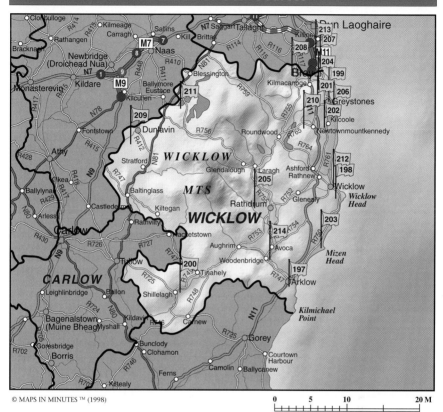

© MAPS IN MINUTES ™ (1998)

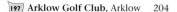

Arklow

**Arklow Golf Club, Abbeylands, Arklow,
County Wicklow**

Tel: 040 232492

Sec/Manager:	B Timmons
Professional:	None
Directions:	½ mile south of arklow off the N11 to Gorey
Type of Course:	Links
Date Founded:	1927
No of Holes:	18
Length:	6195 yds (5665 mtrs)
Par:	69
SSS:	67
Green Fees:	Weekdays: £20 Weekends & Bank Holidays: £20
Visitors:	Welcome: Restrictions, Ring in advance
Societies:	Welcome: Book in advance
Facilities:	Chipping/Putting Area, Practice Area, Driving Range, Golf Clubs for hire, Trolley hire, Electric Buggy hire, Bar, Restaurant, Caddy service by arrangement

Accommodation, Food and Drink

Reference numbers below refer to detailed
information provided in section 2

Accommodation

Ballykilty Farmhouse, Coolgreany, Arklow, Co Wicklow
Tel: 040 237111 Fax: 040 237272 Five en suite bedrooms in an old-world farmhouse on a 200-acre dairy farm. Fine gardens, tennis court. 660

Harbour House, Courtown Harbour, Co Wexford
Tel/Fax: 055 25117 Family-run guest house in a renowned seaside resort. 13 en suite bedrooms with tv. Also self-catering in mobile homes. 623

Highfield House, Woodenbridge, Arklow, Co Wicklow
Tel: 040 235262 Three immaculate bedrooms, two en suite and one with private bath, in a large modern farmhouse. Bed & Breakfast, packed lunches. 661

Hillside House, Tubberduff, Gorey, Co Wexford
Tel: 055 21726/22036 Fax: 055 22567 A modern house in an elevated setting with views of the Tara Hills. Six en suite bedrooms, some family size. Home cooking. 620

Keppel's Farmhouse, Avoca, Co Wicklow
Tel/Fax: 040 235168 Five bright, comfortable B&B rooms in a handsome 19th-century farmhouse. Also a self-catering bungalow. 673

Murphy's Bar & Restaurant, Arklow, Co Wicklow
Tel/Fax: 040 232781 Spacious, well-appointed main-street pub with restaurant. Self-catering Accommodation also offered. 662

Ostan Beag Hotel, Arklow, Co Wicklow
Tel: 040 233044 A hospitable hotel with 20 elegant en suite bedrooms, two bars, a restaurant and a lively nightclub. 666

St Thereses, Mount Alexander, Gorey, Co Wexford
Tel: 055 21793 Fax: 055 21443 Good old-fashioned Irish hospitality in a brand new house with six letting bedrooms. Bed and Breakfast. 621

Taravie Hotel, Courtown Harbour, Co Wexford
Tel: 055 25208/25305 Ten en suite bedrooms in a family-run hotel by the beach. Families very welcome. 624

The Beehive, Coolbeg Cross, N11 Wexford Road, Co Wicklow
Tel: 040 469745 Bar, restaurant and Bed & Breakfast Accommodation in a family-run establishment on the N11. Weekend music. 664

Woodlands Farmhouse, Killinierin, Gorey, Co Wexford
Tel: 040 237125 Fax: 040 237133 Six tastefully decorated en suite bedrooms in a

Georgian-style 19th-century residence. Large gardens. Dinner from 7.30.　627

Food and Drink

Murphy's Bar & Restaurant, Arklow, Co Wicklow
Tel/Fax: 040 232781 Spacious, well-appointed main-street pub with restaurant. Self-catering Accommodation also offered. 662

Ostan Beag Hotel, Arklow, Co Wicklow
Tel: 040 233044 A hospitable hotel with 20 elegant en suite bedrooms, two bars, a restaurant and a lively nightclub. 666

Quinn's Lounge, Gorey, Co Wexford
Tel: 055 21810 Fax: 055 21819 All the Irish beers and plenty of others in a charming old-world lounge on the main street. Lunchtime snacks. 622

Taravie Hotel, Courtown Harbour, Co Wexford
Tel: 055 25208/25305 Ten en suite bedrooms in a family-run hotel by the beach. Families very welcome. 624

The Avoca Inn & Greek Vine Restaurant, Avoca, Co Wicklow
Tel: 040 235774 A winning combination of convivial pub and charming Greek restaurant in a delightful setting by the Avoca river. 663

The Beehive, Coolbeg Cross, N11 Wexford Road, Co Wicklow
Tel: 040 469745 Bar, restaurant and Bed & Breakfast Accommodation in a family-run establishment on the N11. Weekend music. 664

The Crosses, Kilmuckridge, Gorey, Co Wexford
Tel: 053 30458 A sporting pub (darts, pool) with live music at the weekend and an all-day menu of home-cooked food. 625

Blainroe

Blainroe Golf Club, Blainroe, Co Wicklow

Tel: 040 468168

Sec/Manager:	W. O'Sullivan
Professional:	J. Mc Donald
Directions:	2½ miles South of Wicklow off the R750 to Arklow
Type of Course:	Parkland
Date Founded:	1978
No of Holes:	18
Length:	6752 yds (6175 mtrs)
Par:	72
SSS:	72
Green Fees:	Weekdays: £29 Weekends & Bank Holidays: £39
Visitors:	Welcome: Any day, Contact Club in advance
Societies:	Welcome: Special Group Rates available, Contact Club for details
Facilities:	Chipping/Putting Area, Practice Area, Golf Clubs for hire, Trolley hire, Bar, Restaurant, Caddy service by arrangement

Accommodation, Food and Drink

Reference numbers below refer to detailed
information provided in section 2

Accommodation

Ballykilty Farmhouse, Coolgreany, Arklow, Co Wicklow
Tel: 040 237111 Fax: 040 237272 Five en suite bedrooms in an old-world farmhouse on a 200-acre dairy farm. Fine gardens, tennis court. 660

Druid's House, Newtownmountkennedy, Co Wicklow
Tel: 01 2819477 Three recently refurbished bedrooms in a handsome modern Bed & Breakfast house standing in stepped gardens. 670

The Avoca Inn & Greek Vine Restaurant, Avoca, Co Wicklow

Tel: 040 235774 A winning combination of convivial pub and charming Greek restaurant in a delightful setting by the Avoca river.

The Beehive, Coolbeg Cross, N11 Wexford Road, Co Wicklow
Tel: 040 469745 Bar, restaurant and Bed & Breakfast Accommodation in a family-run establishment on the N11. Weekend music. 664

The Coach House, Roundwood, Co Wicklow
Tel: 01 2818157 Fourteen en suite bedrooms in a super country inn dating from the 1820s. Restaurant, 2 bars, beer garden. 671

Food and Drink

The Avoca Inn & Greek Vine Restaurant, Avoca, Co Wicklow
Tel: 040 235774 A winning combination of convivial pub and charming Greek restaurant in a delightful setting by the Avoca river. 663

The Coach House, Roundwood, Co Wicklow
Tel: 01 2818157 Fourteen en suite bedrooms in a super country inn dating from the 1820s. Restaurant, 2 bars, beer garden. 671

The Oyster, Rosslare Strand, Co Wexford
Tel: 053 32439 A charming little restaurant in the heart of a well-known seaside resort. Fresh local seafood is the speciality. 644

Charlesland

Charlesland Golf Centre, Greystones, Co Wicklow
Tel: 01 2874350

Sec/Manager:	Tim Hazelton
Professional:	Paul Heany & Gillian Burell
Directions:	5 miles South of Bray off the R761
Type of Course:	Parkland Seaside
Date Founded:	1992
No of Holes:	18
Length:	6746 yds (6169 mtrs)
Par:	72
SSS:	72
Green Fees:	Weekdays: £30 Weekends & Bank Holidays: £35 'Early Bird' Mon.-Fri. before 10.00am £20
Visitors:	Welcome: Any Day, Contact Club in advance
Societies:	Welcome: Special Group Rates available, Contact club for details
Facilities:	Chipping/Putting Area, Practice Area, Driving Range, Golf Clubs for hire, Trolley hire, Electric Buggy hire, Bar, Restaurant

Accommodation, Food and Drink

Reference numbers below refer to detailed information provided in section 2

Accommodation

Carraig House, Greystones, Co Wicklow
Tel: 01 2873273 Four rooms with tv in a charming B&B opposite the harbour on the main road through the village. Also self-catering. 669

Druid's House, Newtownmountkennedy, Co Wicklow
Tel: 01 2819477 Three recently refurbished bedrooms in a handsome modern Bed & Breakfast house standing in stepped gardens. 670

La Touche Hotel, Greystones, Co Wicklow
Tel: 01 2874401 29 en suite bedrooms with tv and telephone in a handsome hotel overlooking the sea. Restaurant, bars, nightclub. 665

Summerhill House Hotel, Enniskerry, Co Wicklow
Tel: 01 2867928 Fifty-seven bright, spacious airy bedrooms with en suite facilities, tv

and telephone in a friendly, well-situated hotel. 668

Woodland Court Hotel, Southern Cross, Bray, Co Wicklow
Tel: 01 2760258 Sixty five en suite bedrooms with all the modern comforts in a characterful hotel at the southern end of the town. Restaurant and lounge. 667

Food and Drink

La Touche Hotel, Greystones, Co Wicklow
Tel: 01 2874401 29 en suite bedrooms with tv and telephone in a handsome hotel overlooking the sea. Restaurant, bars, nightclub. 665

Summerhill House Hotel, Enniskerry, Co Wicklow
Tel: 01 2867928 Fifty-seven bright, spacious airy bedrooms with en suite facilities, tv and telephone in a friendly, well-situated hotel. 668

Woodland Court Hotel, Southern Cross, Bray, Co Wicklow
Tel: 01 2760258 Sixty five en suite bedrooms with all the modern comforts in a characterful hotel at the southern end of the town. Restaurant and lounge. 667

Coollattin

Coollattin Golf Club, Shillelagh, Co Wicklow
Tel: 055 29125

Sec/Manager:	Patrick Cleere
Professional:	Peter Jones
Directions:	4 miles South West of Tinahely off the R749 to Shillelagh
Type of Course:	Parkland
Date Founded:	1962
No of Holes:	18
Length:	6148 yds (5621 mtrs)
Par:	70
SSS:	69
Green Fees:	Weekdays: £20 Weekends & Bank Holidays: £25
Visitors:	Welcome: Weekdays, Contact Club in advance
Societies:	Welcome Special Group Rates available, Contact Club for details
Facilities:	Chipping/Putting Area, Practice Area, Golf Clubs for hire, Trolley hire, Electric Buggy hire, Bar, Restaurant, Caddy service by arrangement

Accommodation, Food and Drink

Reference numbers below refer to detailed information provided in section 2

Accommodation

Harbour House, Courtown Harbour, Co Wexford
Tel/Fax: 055 25117 Family-run guest house in a renowned seaside resort. 13 en suite bedrooms with tv. Also self-catering in mobile homes. 623

Hillside House, Tubberduff, Gorey, Co Wexford
Tel: 055 21726/22036 Fax: 055 22567 A modern house in an elevated setting with views of the Tara Hills. Six en suite bedrooms, some family size. Home cooking. 620

Sherwood Park House, Kilbride, Ballon, Co Carlow
Tel: 050 359117 Five en suite rooms in a superb Georgian house on its own working estate. B&B, evening meals on request. 371

St Thereses, Mount Alexander, Gorey, Co Wexford
Tel: 055 21793 Fax: 055 21443 Good old-fashioned Irish hospitality in a brand new house with six letting bedrooms. Bed and Breakfast. 621

Taravie Hotel, Courtown Harbour, Co Wexford
Tel: 055 25208/25305 Ten en suite bedrooms in a family-run hotel by the beach. Families very welcome. 624

Woodlands Farmhouse, Killinierin, Gorey, Co Wexford
Tel: 040 237125 Fax: 040 237133 Six tastefully decorated en suite bedrooms in a

Georgian-style 19th-century residence. Large gardens. Dinner from 7.30. *627*

Food and Drink

Quinn's Lounge, Gorey, Co Wexford

Tel: 055 21810 Fax: 055 21819 All the Irish beers and plenty of others in a charming old-world lounge on the main street. Lunchtime snacks. *622*

Taravie Hotel, Courtown Harbour, Co Wexford

Tel: 055 25208/25305 Ten en suite bedrooms in a family-run hotel by the beach. Families very welcome. *624*

The Crosses, Kilmuckridge, Gorey, Co Wexford

Tel: 053 30458 A sporting pub (darts, pool) with live music at the weekend and an all-day menu of home-cooked food. *625*

Delgany

Delgany Golf Club, Delgany, Co Wicklow

Tel: 01 2874536

Sec/Manager:	Robbie Kelly
Professional:	Gavin Kavanagh
Directions:	2 miles West of Greystones off the N11 from Dublin
Type of Course:	Parkland
Date Founded:	1908
No of Holes:	18
Length:	5986 yds (5474 mtrs)
Par:	69
SSS:	68
Green Fees:	Weekdays: £25 Weekends & Bank Holidays: £29
Visitors:	Welcome: Midweek restrictions, Contact the Club in advance
Societies:	Welcome: Special Group Rates for more than 40 players available, Contact Club for details
Facilities:	Chipping/Putting Area, Practice Area, Golf Clubs for hire, Trolley hire, Bar, Restaurant, Caddy service by arrangement

Accommodation, Food and Drink

Reference numbers below refer to detailed information provided in section 2

Accommodation

Derrybaun Mountain Lodge, Derrybaun, Laragh, Co Wicklow

Tel: 040 445644 A magnificent modern lodge at the foot of Derrybaun Mountain, with eight excellent en suite bedrooms. B&B & dinner. *672*

La Touche Hotel, Greystones, Co Wicklow

Tel: 01 2874401 29 en suite bedrooms with tv and telephone in a handsome hotel overlooking the sea. Restaurant, bars, nightclub. *665*

Lynnbury, Mullingar, Co Westmeath

Tel: 044 48432/40444 Country home Accommodation in a handsome house on the main Tullamore Road, very near the golf course.

The Coach House, Roundwood, Co Wicklow

Tel: 01 2818157 Fourteen en suite bedrooms in a super country inn dating from the 1820s. Restaurant, 2 bars, beer garden. *671*

Woodland Court Hotel, Southern Cross, Bray, Co Wicklow

Tel: 01 2760258 Sixty five en suite bedrooms with all the modern comforts in a characterful hotel at the southern end of the town. Restaurant and lounge. *667*

Food and Drink

La Touche Hotel, Greystones, Co Wicklow

Tel: 01 2874401 29 en suite bedrooms with tv and telephone in a handsome hotel overlooking the sea. Restaurant, bars, nightclub. *665*

The Coach House, Roundwood, Co Wicklow

Tel: 01 2818157 Fourteen en suite bedrooms in a super country inn dating from the 1820s. Restaurant, 2 bars, beer garden. *671*

Woodland Court Hotel, Southern Cross, Bray, Co Wicklow

Tel: 01 2760258 Sixty five en suite bedrooms with all the modern comforts in a characterful hotel at the southern end of the town. Restaurant and lounge. *667*

Druid's Glen

Druids Glen Golf Club,
Newtownmountkennedy, Co Wicklow

Tel: 01 2873600

It was a challenge no self-respecting architect could resist. "Build me the most beautiful parkland course in Ireland, and never mind the expense." This was how Hugo Flinn, the owner of Druids Glen, instructed his designer, Pat Ruddy.

The quality of Ruddy's response was evident to international audiences, when Druids Glen became home to the Murphy's Irish Open from 1996 to 1999. Viewers became familiar with such breathtaking features as the charming, short 12th at the Druid's Altar, the punishing, par-four 13th from its towering tee, and the water cascading into three small lakes at the majestic, par-four 18th.

Colin Montgomerie seemed determined to make his own of the place, when winning the Irish Open in 1996 and then retaining the title the following year with a course-record final round of 62. Indeed it took a play-off defeat by David Carter, to deprive the Scot of a hat-trick of victories in 1998.

The elaborately-refurbished, three-storey clubhouse, which was originally the 1770 home of Sir Thomas Wentworth, complements the course beautifully. Indeed quality has been synonymous with the entire development from the outset, and is reflected not only in its visual impact, as in the sand-based greens.

Given the difficulty of holes such as the 13th,

where even accomplished professionals have come to grief, and the 205-yard 17th (back tee) with its island green, it is not a course for beginners. But even moderately competent players will enjoy it enormously, not least because of the delightful setting.

Sec/Manager:	Denis Kane
Professional:	Eamonn Darcy
Directions:	2 miles East of Newtorn Mt. Kennedy off the N11 from Dublin
Type of Course:	Parkland
Date Founded:	1995
No of Holes:	18
Length:	7058 yds (6453 mtrs)
Par:	71
SSS:	74
Green Fees:	£85 per round
Visitors:	Welcome: Prebook tee times
Societies:	Welcome: Special Group Rates, Contact club for details
Facilities:	Chipping/Putting Area, Practice Area, Driving Range, Golf Clubs for hire, Trolley hire, Electric Buggy hire, Bar, Restaurant, Caddy service by arrangement, (Trolleys are complimentary)

Accommodation, Food and Drink

Reference numbers below refer to detailed information provided in section 2

Accommodation

Carraig House, Greystones, Co Wicklow
Tel: 01 2873273 Four rooms with tv in a charming B&B opposite the harbour on the main road through the village. Also self-catering. *669*

Derrybaun Mountain Lodge, Derrybaun, Laragh, Co Wicklow
Tel: 040 445644 A magnificent modern lodge at the foot of Derrybaun Mountain, with eight excellent en suite bedrooms. B&B & dinner. *672*

Druid's House, Newtownmountkennedy, Co Wicklow
Tel: 01 2819477 Three recently refurbished bedrooms in a handsome modern Bed & Breakfast house standing in stepped gardens. *670*

La Touche Hotel, Greystones, Co Wicklow
Tel: 01 2874401 29 en suite bedrooms with tv and telephone in a handsome hotel overlooking the sea. Restaurant, bars, nightclub. *665*

Summerhill House Hotel, Enniskerry, Co Wicklow
Tel: 01 2867928 Fifty-seven bright, spacious airy bedrooms with en suite facilities, tv and telephone in a friendly, well-situated hotel. *668*

Woodland Court Hotel, Southern Cross, Bray, Co Wicklow
Tel: 01 2760258 Sixty five en suite bedrooms with all the modern comforts in a characterful hotel at the southern end of the town. Restaurant and lounge. *667*

Food and Drink

La Touche Hotel, Greystones, Co Wicklow
Tel: 01 2874401 29 en suite bedrooms with tv and telephone in a handsome hotel overlooking the sea. Restaurant, bars, nightclub. *665*

Summerhill House Hotel, Enniskerry, Co Wicklow
Tel: 01 2867928 Fifty-seven bright, spacious airy bedrooms with en suite facilities, tv and telephone in a friendly, well-situated hotel. *668*

The Coach House, Roundwood, Co Wicklow
Tel: 01 2818157 Fourteen en suite bedrooms in a super country inn dating from the 1820s. Restaurant, 2 bars, beer garden. *671*

Woodland Court Hotel, Southern Cross, Bray, Co Wicklow
Tel: 01 2760258 Sixty five en suite bedrooms with all the modern comforts in a characterful hotel at the southern end of the town. Restaurant and lounge. *667*

European

The European Club, Brittas Bay, Wicklow, Co Wicklow

Tel: 040 447415

Few of us succeed in living out our wild dreams. But golf journalist Pat Ruddy did so in some style, through the development of The European Club. He took it every stage of the way from buying the land to designing the course and ultimately bringing the project to fruition in 1993.

Nobody, certainly no golf developer, seemed to be aware of the majestic links site of 200 acres near Brittas Bay, until Ruddy came upon it. His experience of travelling the golfing world in pursuit of his craft as a writer, imbued him with the knowledge and good sense to treat it gently.

The result is an outstanding links which has already claimed a place among the top-10 of the country's leading venues. And the key lies in the designer's obvious empathy with nature, though there were times when he must have cursed the damage wrought by an angry Irish Sea on his exposed 15th green.

After a relatively gentle start, characterised by the reachable, par-five third of 477 yards, the challenge heightens significantly. Indeed play-

Tel: 040 469745 Bar, restaurant and Bed & Breakfast Accommodation in a family-run establishment on the N11. Weekend music. 664

Food and Drink

Murphy's Bar & Restaurant, Arklow, Co Wicklow
Tel/Fax: 040 232781 Spacious, well-appointed main-street pub with restaurant. Self-catering Accommodation also offered. 662

Ostan Beag Hotel, Arklow, Co Wicklow
Tel: 040 233044 A hospitable hotel with 20 elegant en suite bedrooms, two bars, a restaurant and a lively nightclub. 666

The Avoca Inn & Greek Vine Restaurant, Avoca, Co Wicklow
Tel: 040 235774 A winning combination of convivial pub and charming Greek restaurant in a delightful setting by the Avoca river. 663

The Beehive, Coolbeg Cross, N11 Wexford Road, Co Wicklow
Tel: 040 469745 Bar, restaurant and Bed & Breakfast Accommodation in a family-run establishment on the N11. Weekend music. 664

ers could find their supply of golf balls seriously depleted through timid tangling with the forbidding seventh, where danger beckons right and left, all the way from tee to green.

Then comes the beguiling eighth, already one of most photographed holes in Irish golf. And from then on, the standard never wavers. Small wonder that Johnny Miller, in common with other distinguished visitors, was thoroughly enchanted by the place when he played there recently.

Sec/Manager:	Pat & Sidon Ruddy
Professional:	None
Directions:	8 miles South of Wicklow and 5 miles North of Arklow off the N11 from Dublin or off the R750 from Wicklow
Type of Course:	Links
Date Founded:	1993
No of Holes:	18
Length:	6690 yds (6117 mtrs)
Par:	71
SSS:	72
Green Fees:	£60 per round £80 per day
Visitors:	Welcome: Any day, Prior booking advisable
Societies:	Welcome: Contact Club in advance
Facilities:	Chipping/Putting Area, Practice Area, Golf Clubs for hire, Trolley hire, Electric Buggy hire, Restaurant

Accommodation, Food and Drink

Reference numbers below refer to detailed information provided in section 2

Accommodation

Ballykilty Farmhouse, Coolgreany, Arklow, Co Wicklow
Tel: 040 237111 Fax: 040 237272 Five en suite bedrooms in an old-world farmhouse on a 200-acre dairy farm. Fine gardens, tennis court. 660

Highfield House, Woodenbridge, Arklow, Co Wicklow
Tel: 040 235262 Three immaculate bedrooms, two en suite and one with private bath, in a large modern farmhouse. Bed & Breakfast, packed lunches. 661

Murphy's Bar & Restaurant, Arklow, Co Wicklow
Tel/Fax: 040 232781 Spacious, well-appointed main-street pub with restaurant. Self-catering Accommodation also offered. 662

The Beehive, Coolbeg Cross, N11 Wexford Road, Co Wicklow

Glen of the Downs

Glen of the Downs Golf Club, Coolnaskeagh, Delgany, Co Wicklow

Tel: 01 2876240

Sec/Manager:	Richard O'Hanrahan
Professional:	Patrick Geraghty
Directions:	Off the N11 Dublin to Wexford road. Approx 30 mins from Dublin City Centre
Type of Course:	Parkland
Date Founded:	1998
No of Holes:	18
Length:	6443 yds (6082 mtrs)
Par:	71
SSS:	71
Green Fees:	Winter: Weekdays: £30 Weekends & Bank Holidays: £40 Earlybird before 11am £25 Summer: Weekdays: £40 Weekends & Bank Holidays: £50
Visitors:	Welcome: Any Day, Restrictions on Thursday, Wednesday and Saturday
Societies:	Welcome: Special Group Rates, Contact Club for details
Facilities:	Chipping/Putting Area, Golf Clubs for hire, Trolley hire, Electric Buggy hire

Accommodation, Food and Drink

Reference numbers below refer to detailed information provided in section 2

Accommodation

Carraig House, Greystones, Co Wicklow
Tel: 01 2873273 Four rooms with tv in a charming B&B opposite the harbour on the main road through the village. Also self-catering. 669

Druid's House, Newtownmountkennedy, Co Wicklow
Tel: 01 2819477 Three recently refurbished bedrooms in a handsome modern Bed & Breakfast house standing in stepped gardens. 670

Keppel's Farmhouse, Avoca, Co Wicklow
Tel/Fax: 040 235168 Five bright, comfortable B&B rooms in a handsome 19th-century farmhouse. Also a self-catering bungalow. 673

La Touche Hotel, Greystones, Co Wicklow
Tel: 01 2874401 29 en suite bedrooms with tv and telephone in a handsome hotel overlooking the sea. Restaurant, bars, nightclub. 665

Summerhill House Hotel, Enniskerry, Co Wicklow
Tel: 01 2867928 Fifty-seven bright, spacious airy bedrooms with en suite facilities, tv and telephone in a friendly, well-situated hotel. 668

Woodland Court Hotel, Southern Cross, Bray, Co Wicklow
Tel: 01 2760258 Sixty five en suite bedrooms with all the modern comforts in a characterful hotel at the southern end of the town. Restaurant and lounge. 667

Food and Drink

La Touche Hotel, Greystones, Co Wicklow
Tel: 01 2874401 29 en suite bedrooms with tv and telephone in a handsome hotel overlooking the sea. Restaurant, bars, nightclub. 665

Summerhill House Hotel, Enniskerry, Co Wicklow
Tel: 01 2867928 Fifty-seven bright, spacious airy bedrooms with en suite facilities, tv and telephone in a friendly, well-situated hotel. 668

Woodland Court Hotel, Southern Cross, Bray, Co Wicklow
Tel: 01 2760258 Sixty five en suite bedrooms with all the modern comforts in a characterful hotel at the southern end of the town. Restaurant and lounge. 667

Highfield House, Woodenbridge, Arklow, Co Wicklow
Tel: 040 235262 Three immaculate bedrooms, two en suite and one with private bath, in a large modern farmhouse. Bed & Breakfast, packed lunches. 661

Keppel's Farmhouse, Avoca, Co Wicklow
Tel/Fax: 040 235168 Five bright, comfortable B&B rooms in a handsome 19th-century farmhouse. Also a self-catering bungalow. 673

The Beehive, Coolbeg Cross, N11 Wexford Road, Co Wicklow
Tel: 040 469745 Bar, restaurant and Bed & Breakfast Accommodation in a family-run establishment on the N11. Weekend music. 664

The Coach House, Roundwood, Co Wicklow
Tel: 01 2818157 Fourteen en suite bedrooms in a super country inn dating from the 1820s. Restaurant, 2 bars, beer garden. 671

Food and Drink

The Avoca Inn & Greek Vine Restaurant, Avoca, Co Wicklow
Tel: 040 235774 A winning combination of convivial pub and charming Greek restaurant in a delightful setting by the Avoca river. 663

The Beehive, Coolbeg Cross, N11 Wexford Road, Co Wicklow
Tel: 040 469745 Bar, restaurant and Bed & Breakfast Accommodation in a family-run establishment on the N11. Weekend music. 664

The Coach House, Roundwood, Co Wicklow
Tel: 01 2818157 Fourteen en suite bedrooms in a super country inn dating from the 1820s. Restaurant, 2 bars, beer garden. 671

Greystones

Greystones Golf Club, Greystones, Co Wicklow
Tel: 01 2876624

Glenmalure

Glenmalure Golf Club, Greenane, Rathdrum, Co Wicklow
Tel: 040 446679

Sec/Manager:	None
Professional:	None
Directions:	3 miles West of Rathdrum off the R752 at Greenane
Type of Course:	Parkland
Date Founded:	1993
No of Holes:	18
Length:	5700 yds (5212 mtrs)
Par:	71
SSS:	67
Green Fees:	Weekdays: £15 Weekends & Bank Holidays: £20
Visitors:	Welcome: Any Day, Restrictions on Sunday
Societies:	Welcome: Contact Club in advance
Facilities:	Chipping/Putting Area, Golf Clubs for hire, Trolley hire, Bar, Restaurant

Sec/Manager:	Oliver Walsh
Professional:	None
Directions:	Half mile South of Greystones off the R762
Type of Course:	Parkland
Date Founded:	1895
No of Holes:	18
Length:	5820 yds (5322 mtrs)
Par:	69
SSS:	69
Green Fees:	£25 per round weekdays only, Friday £30
Visitors:	Welcome: Restrictions apply, Contact Club in advance
Societies:	Welcome: Special Group Rates, Contact club for details
Facilities:	Chipping/Putting Area, Practice Area, Golf Clubs for hire, Trolley hire, Electric Buggy hire, Bar, Restaurant, Caddy service by arrangement

Accommodation, Food and Drink

Reference numbers below refer to detailed information provided in section 2

Accommodation

Derrybaun Mountain Lodge, Derrybaun, Laragh, Co Wicklow
Tel: 040 445644 A magnificent modern lodge at the foot of Derrybaun Mountain, with eight excellent en suite bedrooms. B&B & dinner. 672

Accommodation, Food and Drink

Reference numbers below refer to detailed
information provided in section 2

Accommodation

Carraig House, Greystones, Co Wicklow

Tel: 01 2873273 Four rooms with tv in a charming B&B opposite the harbour on
the main road through the village. Also self-catering.   669

Druid's House, Newtownmountkennedy, Co Wicklow

Tel: 01 2819477 Three recently refurbished bedrooms in a handsome modern Bed &
Breakfast house standing in stepped gardens.   670

La Touche Hotel, Greystones, Co Wicklow

Tel: 01 2874401 29 en suite bedrooms with tv and telephone in a handsome hotel
overlooking the sea.   665

Summerhill House Hotel, Enniskerry, Co Wicklow

Tel: 01 2867928 Fifty-seven bright, spacious airy bedrooms with en suite facilities, tv
and telephone in a friendly, well-situated hotel.   668

Woodland Court Hotel, Southern Cross, Bray, Co Wicklow

Tel: 01 2760258 Sixty five en suite bedrooms with all the modern comforts in a
characterful hotel at the southern end of the town. Restaurant and lounge. 667

Food and Drink

La Touche Hotel, Greystones, Co Wicklow

Tel: 01 2874401 29 en suite bedrooms with tv and telephone in a handsome hotel
overlooking the sea. Restaurant, bars, nightclub.   665

Summerhill House Hotel, Enniskerry, Co Wicklow

Tel: 01 2867928 Fifty-seven bright, spacious airy bedrooms with en suite facilities, tv
and telephone in a friendly, well-situated hotel.   668

Woodland Court Hotel, Southern Cross, Bray, Co Wicklow

Tel: 01 2760258 Sixty five en suite bedrooms with all the modern comforts in a
characterful hotel at the southern end of the town. Restaurant and lounge. 667

Old Conna

Old Conna Golf Club, Ferndale Road, Bray, Co
Wicklow

Tel: 01 2826055/2826766

Sec/Manager:	Dave Diviney
Professional:	Paul McDaid
Directions:	Half mile North of Bray off the R119
Type of Course:	Parkland
Date Founded:	1987
No of Holes:	18
Length:	6551 yds (5990 mtrs)
Par:	72
SSS:	71
Green Fees:	£30 per round
Visitors:	Welcome: Restrictions at weekend
Societies:	Welcome: Special Group Rates, Contact club for details
Facilities:	Chipping/Putting Area, Practice Area, Golf Clubs for hire, Trolley hire, Electric Buggy hire, Bar, Restaurant, Caddy service by arrangement

Accommodation, Food and Drink

Reference numbers below refer to detailed
information provided in section 2

Accommodation

Ariemond, Dun Laoghaire, Co Dublin

Tel: 01 2801664 Five Bed & Breakfast rooms, three en suite, two with private baths,
in a lovely house two minutes walk from the centre.   235

Ferry House, Dun Laoghaire, Co Dublin

Tel: 01 2808301 Four en suite Bed & Breakfast rooms in a handsome town house
an easy walk from the centre of Dun Laoghaire.   228

Ophira, Dun Laoghaire, Co Dublin

Tel/Fax: 01 2800997 Town-centre Bed & Breakfast Accommodation in a mid-19th
century house. Four en suite bedrooms. Tv lounge.   225

Summerhill House Hotel, Enniskerry, Co Wicklow

Tel: 01 2867928 Fifty-seven bright, spacious airy bedrooms with en suite facilities, tv
and telephone in a friendly, well-situated hotel.   668

The Kingston Hotel, Dun Laoghaire, Co Dublin

Tel: 01 2801810 Fifty-three well-equipped en suite bedrooms — singles, doubles,
twins and triples — in a family-run hotel on the seafront.   236

Woodland Court Hotel, Southern Cross, Bray, Co Wicklow

Tel: 01 2760258 Sixty five en suite bedrooms with all the modern comforts in a
characterful hotel at the southern end of the town. Restaurant and lounge. 667

Food and Drink

Summerhill House Hotel, Enniskerry, Co Wicklow

Tel: 01 2867928 Fifty-seven bright, spacious airy bedrooms with en suite facilities, tv
and telephone in a friendly, well-situated hotel.   668

The Kingston Hotel, Dun Laoghaire, Co Dublin

Tel: 01 2801810 Fifty-three well-equipped en suite bedrooms — singles, doubles,
twins and triples — in a family-run hotel on the seafront.   236

Walters, Dun Laoghaire, Co Dublin

Tel: 01 2807442 Elegant, trendy bar-café-restaurant serving anything from a coffee
or a drink to a three-course meal.   229

Woodland Court Hotel, Southern Cross, Bray, Co Wicklow

Tel: 01 2760258 Sixty five en suite bedrooms with all the modern comforts in a
characterful hotel at the southern end of the town. Restaurant and lounge. 667

Powerscourt

Powerscourt Golf Club, Powerscourt Estate,
Enniskerry, Co Wicklow

Tel: 01 2046033

Wicklow's much-envied reputation, embodied in
references to it as the "Garden County", must
have had much to do with the area where Peter
McEvoy designed the Powerscourt course.
Blessed with an abundance of mature trees and
natural features, its stunning views are dominated by the majestic, Sugarloaf Mountain.

Only four years after it was opened, the course
played host to the Smurfit Irish Professional
Championship in 1998 when Padraig Harrington
captured the title in hostile conditions, which
caused it to be curtailed to 54 holes. In the event,
McEvoy's handiwork presented a strong field
with an appropriately searching test.

Built on free-draining soil which gives it the
texture of heathland, the course is part of the

1,000-acre Powerscourt Estate which dates back to the 14th century and has been in the possession of the Slazeger family since 1961. Future plans include an additional 18-hole course and a five-star hotel.

Meanwhile, a generous site allowed the designer to create a varied examination, from genuine, three-shot par fives, to the tantalising, 150-yard downhill 16th, where club selection becomes absolutely critical. And all the while, there is the challenge of wickedly tricky, tiered greens which place a premium on accurate approach play.

Off the back tees, the course stretches to more than 7,000 yards, but the average player should be happy to settle for a more modest test. And even if the performance should slip below expectations - which is likely, certainly on the first visit - there is always the scenery.

Sec/Manager:	Bernard Gibbons
Professional:	Paul Thompson
Directions:	Set in the Powerscourt Estate 4 miles South West of Bray off the R760
Type of Course:	Parkland
Date Founded:	1996
No of Holes:	18
Length:	6485 yds (5930 mtrs)
Par:	72
SSS:	74
Green Fees:	£60 Summer rates
Visitors:	Welcome: Restrictions, Contact Club for details
Societies:	Welcome: Special Group Rates, Contact Club for details
Facilities:	Chipping/Putting Area, Practice Area, Driving Range, Golf Clubs for hire, Trolley hire, Electric Buggy hire, Bar, Restaurant, Caddy service by arrangement

Accommodation, Food and Drink

Reference numbers below refer to detailed information provided in section 2

Accommodation

La Touche Hotel, Greystones, Co Wicklow
Tel: 01287 4401 29 en suite bedrooms with tv and telephone in a handsome hotel overlooking the sea. Restaurant, bars, nightclub. 665

Summerhill House Hotel, Enniskerry, Co Wicklow
Tel: 01 2867928 Fifty-seven bright, spacious airy bedrooms with en suite facilities, tv and telephone in a friendly, well-situated hotel. 668

Woodland Court Hotel, Southern Cross, Bray, Co Wicklow
Tel: 01 2760258 Sixty five en suite bedrooms with all the modern comforts in a characterful hotel at the southern end of the town. Restaurant and lounge. 667

Food and Drink

La Touche Hotel, Greystones, Co Wicklow
Tel: 01 2874401 29 en suite bedrooms with tv and telephone in a handsome hotel overlooking the sea. Restaurant, bars, nightclub. 665

Summerhill House Hotel, Enniskerry, Co Wicklow
Tel: 01 2867928 Fifty-seven bright, spacious airy bedrooms with en suite facilities, tv and telephone in a friendly, well-situated hotel. 668

Woodland Court Hotel, Southern Cross, Bray, Co Wicklow

Tel: 01 2760258 Sixty five en suite bedrooms with all the modern comforts in a characterful hotel at the southern end of the town. Restaurant and lounge. 667

Rathsallagh

Rathsallagh Golf Club, Dunlavin, Co Wicklow
Tel: 045 403316

Rathsallagh GC sent out a clear signal of quality, by the nature of their official opening in June 1996. Doing the honours was five times British Open winner Peter Thomson, whose presence, among other things, was designed at making the owners believe they could compete with the best.

Nestling beneath the Wicklow mountains, two miles from Dunlavin, the club have since added a function room with a seating capacity of 150. And early drainage problems have been overcome by investing more than £25,000 in remedial work.

Construction work on the 252-acre site, began in February 1993 to a design by Christy O'Connor Jnr and former British Amateur champion, Peter McEvoy. Their work is especially notable for the way the layout follows the lie of beautifully rolling terrain. And it is also to the designers' credit that many fine trees were preserved.

The result is a classic parkland stretch which rises and falls in the shadow of giant beech trees, oaks and limes. Indeed certain holes such as the par-four second, are played through an avenue of trees. Water, which is used liberally, comes into play for the first time at the 170-yard fourth.

The challenge reaches an appropriate climax at the devilishly difficult finishing hole - a rising par-four of 450 yards off the back tee. Out of bounds beckons on the left off the tee, but the real test here is the long, slender, three-tier green, where birdies are as rare as a slow putt at Augusta National.

Sec/Manager:	Joe O'Flynn
Professional:	Brendan McDaid
Directions:	15 miles South of Naas off the R412 near Dunlavin
Type of Course:	Parkland
Date Founded:	1995
No of Holes:	18
Length:	6499 yds (5942 mtrs)
Par:	72
SSS:	72
Green Fees:	Weekdays: £40 Weekends & Bank Holidays: £50
Visitors:	Welcome : Restrictions at weekend, Contact Club for prior bookings
Societies:	Welcome: Special Group Rates, Contact Club for details
Facilities:	Chipping/Putting Area, Practice Area, Driving Range, Golf Clubs for hire, Trolley hire, Electric Buggy hire, Bar, Restaurant, Caddy service by arrangement

Accommodation, Food and Drink

Reference numbers below refer to detailed information provided in section 2

Accommodation

Annagh Lodge, Newbridge, Co Kildare
Tel: 045 433518 Nine excellent Bed & Breakfast rooms in a striking modern bungalow on the Dublin side of Newbridge. Sauna, conservatory.   345

Bushfield Lodge, Ballymore Eustace, Co Kildare
Tel: 045 864389/864972 A substantial modern house in a quiet rural location, with high-quality en suite bedrooms. Also a cookery school.   344

Woodcourte House, Timolin, Moone, Athy, Co Kildare
Tel: 050 724167 Six spacious bedrooms (two en suite) in a modern B&B house in a picturesque village just off the main N9 Dublin-Kilkenny road.   340

Food and Drink

Rushes, Fairgreen Street, Naas, Co Kildare
Tel: 045 433234 Classic bar food in Rushes and international cuisine in its neighbour Cicero on a prime site in Naas. Steaks a speciality.   343

Swifts, Newbridge, Co Kildare
Tel: 045 433234 All-day menus in Newbridge's trendiest bar, with a long, elegant bar and several spacious lounges.   346

The Manor Inn, Naas, Co Kildare
Tel: 045 897471 Warmth, hospitality and good food in a smartly modernised pub on the main street of Naas. Lots of racing memorabilia.   347

Roundwood

Roundwood Golf Club,
Newtownmountkennedy, Co Wicklow
Tel: 01 2818488

Sec/Manager:	Michael McGuirk
Professional:	(available by appointment)
Directions:	Off the N11 from Dublin two and a half miles West of Newtown Mt.Kennedy off the R765 to Roundwood
Type of Course:	Heathland
Date Founded:	1995
No of Holes:	18
Length:	6685 yds (6112 mtrs)
Par:	72
SSS:	72
Green Fees:	Weekdays: £22.50 Weekends & Bank Holidays: £27.50
Visitors:	Welcome: Any Day, Contact Club in advance
Societies:	Welcome: Special Group Rates, Contact Club for details
Facilities:	Chipping/Putting Area, Practice Area, Golf Clubs for hire, Trolley hire, Electric Buggy hire, (light snacks available)

Accommodation, Food and Drink

Reference numbers below refer to detailed information provided in section 2

Accommodation

Derrybaun Mountain Lodge, Derrybaun, Laragh, Co Wicklow
Tel: 040 445644 A magnificent modern lodge at the foot of Derrybaun Mountain, with eight excellent en suite bedrooms. B&B & dinner.   672

Druid's House, Newtownmountkennedy, Co Wicklow
Tel: 01 2819477 Three recently refurbished bedrooms in a handsome modern Bed & Breakfast house standing in stepped gardens.   670

La Touche Hotel, Greystones, Co Wicklow
Tel: 01 2874401 29 en suite bedrooms with tv and telephone in a handsome hotel overlooking the sea. Restaurant, bars, nightclub.   665

Summerhill House Hotel, Enniskerry, Co Wicklow
Tel: 01 2867928 Fifty-seven bright, spacious airy bedrooms with en suite facilities, tv and telephone in a friendly, well-situated hotel.   668

The Coach House, Roundwood, Co Wicklow
Tel: 01 2818157 Fourteen en suite bedrooms in a super country inn dating from the 1820s. Restaurant, 2 bars, beer garden.   671

Food and Drink

La Touche Hotel, Greystones, Co Wicklow
Tel: 01 2874401 29 en suite bedrooms with tv and telephone in a handsome hotel overlooking the sea. Restaurant, bars, nightclub.   665

Summerhill House Hotel, Enniskerry, Co Wicklow
Tel: 01 2867928 Fifty-seven bright, spacious airy bedrooms with en suite facilities, tv and telephone in a friendly, well-situated hotel.   668

The Coach House, Roundwood, Co Wicklow
Tel: 01 2818157 Fourteen en suite bedrooms in a super country inn dating from the 1820s. Restaurant, 2 bars, beer garden.   671

Tulfarris

Tulfarris Golf & Country Club, Blessington Lakes, Co Wicklow

Tel: 045 864574

Directions:	5 miles South of Blessington off N81 to Baltinglass
Type of Course:	Parkland
Date Founded:	1989
No of Holes:	18
Length:	6737 yds (6160 mtrs)
Par:	72
SSS:	74
Green Fees:	Weekdays: £40 Weekends & Bank Holidays : £50
Visitors:	Welcome: book in advance
Societies:	Welcome: Special Group Rates, Contact Club for details
Facilities:	Chipping/Putting Area, Practice Area, Driving Range, Golf Clubs for hire, Trolley hire, Electric Buggy hire, Bar, Restaurant, Caddy service by arrangement, plus two hotels and holiday village. Hotel residents have access to leisure centre

Accommodation, Food and Drink

Reference numbers below refer to detailed information provided in section 2

Accommodation

Bushfield Lodge, Ballymore Eustace, Co Kildare
Tel: 045 864389/864972 A substantial modern house in a quiet rural location, with high-quality en suite bedrooms. Also a cookery school. 344

Monaghan's Harbour Hotel, Naas, Co Kildare
Tel: 045 879145 A real home from home feel in a family-run hotel with well-equipped bedrooms, restaurant, coffee shop and bar. 349

Westown Farm, Johnstown, Naas, Co Kildare
Tel/Fax: 045 897006 Farmhouse Bed & Breakfast Accommodation run by a mother-and-daughter team. Five bedrooms, three of them en suite.

Food and Drink

Monaghan's Harbour Hotel, Naas, Co Kildare
Tel: 045 879145 A real home from home feel in a family-run hotel with well-equipped bedrooms, restaurant, coffee shop and bar. 349

Rushes, Fairgreen Street, Naas, Co Kildare
Tel: 045 898400 Classic bar food in Rushes and international cuisine in its neighbour Cicero on a prime site in Naas. Steaks a speciality. 343

The Manor Inn, Naas, Co Kildare
Tel: 045 897471 Warmth, hospitality and good food in a smartly modernised pub on the main street of Naas. Lots of racing memorabilia. 347

When looking over expensive golf-course developments, the critic's natural tendency is to tread gently, in the knowledge that much anxiety and pain have been invested in the project, apart from, obviously, the cash. One feels no such constraints on visiting Tulfarris GC.

This is unquestionably the best work by Patrick Merrigan, one of Ireland's leading golf-course architects. "It was a long, arduous exercise, but I'm pleased with the way it has turned out," said the designer.

It came about through the purchase, eight years ago, of the old, nine-hole Tulfarris course by Cork businessman Jim Hayes. And by the time a 64-bedroom hotel opened in 2000, the investment from him and his wife Maeve reached £15 million. So it merits comparison with the best.

Merrigan has resisted a previous liking for severely sloping greens. As a consequence, the putting surfaces are as good at Mount Juliet's at the same stage of maturity, which is praise indeed. Meanwhile, the location, on a 200-acre site five miles beyond Blessington and overlooking Poulaphuca Lake, is nothing short of stunning. And it has been enhanced by the planting of several thousand broadleaf trees, from oak to ash, lime, pine and beech.

Five years in the making, the course had its official opening in the spring of 2000. It is a strong challenge in every sense, measuring 7,116 yards off the back tees and 6,737 off the men's medals, while the long seventh can be stretched to a formidable 608 yards.

Sec/Manager:	Adrian Williams
Professional:	None

Wicklow

Wicklow Golf Club, Dunbur Road, Wicklow

Tel: 040 467379

Sec/Manager:	Joe Kelly
Professional:	David Daly
Directions:	On the southern outskirts of Wicklow on the coast off the R750
Type of Course:	Parkland
Date Founded:	1904
No of Holes:	18
Length:	6228 yds (5695 mtrs)
Par:	71
SSS:	70
Green Fees:	£22 per round

Visitors:	Welcome: Restrictions apply; Contact Club in advance
Societies:	Welcome: Special Group Rates, Contact Club for details
Facilities:	Chipping/Putting Area, Golf Clubs for hire, Trolley hire, Bar, Restaurant, Caddy service by arrangement

Accommodation, Food and Drink

Reference numbers below refer to detailed information provided in section 2

Accommodation

Ballykilty Farmhouse, Coolgreany, Arklow, Co Wicklow
Tel: 040 237111 Fax: 040 237272 Five en suite bedrooms in an old-world farmhouse on a 200-acre dairy farm. Fine gardens, tennis court.   660

Druid's House, Newtownmountkennedy, Co Wicklow
Tel: 01 2819477 Three recently refurbished bedrooms in a handsome modern Bed & Breakfast house standing in stepped gardens.   670

The Avoca Inn & Greek Vine Restaurant, Avoca, Co Wicklow
Tel: 040 235774 A winning combination of convivial pub and charming Greek restaurant in a delightful setting by the Avoca river.   663

The Beehive, Coolbeg Cross, N11 Wexford Road, Co Wicklow
Tel: 040 469745 Bar, restaurant and Bed & Breakfast Accommodation in a family-run establishment on the N11. Weekend music.   664

The Coach House, Roundwood, Co Wicklow
Tel: 01 2818157 Fourteen en suite bedrooms in a super country inn dating from the 1820s. Restaurant, 2 bars, beer garden.   671

Food and Drink

The Avoca Inn & Greek Vine Restaurant, Avoca, Co Wicklow
Tel: 040 235774 A winning combination of convivial pub and charming Greek restaurant in a delightful setting by the Avoca river.   663

The Beehive, Coolbeg Cross, N11 Wexford Road, Co Wicklow
Tel: 040 469745 Bar, restaurant and Bed & Breakfast Accommodation in a family-run establishment on the N11. Weekend music.   664

The Coach House, Roundwood, Co Wicklow
Tel: 01 2818157 Fourteen en suite bedrooms in a super country inn dating from the 1820s. Restaurant, 2 bars, beer garden.   671

Woodbrook

Woodbrook Golf Club, Bray, Co Wicklow
Tel: 01 2824799

Sec/Manager:	Jim Melody
Professional:	Billy Kinsella
Directions:	2 miles North of Bray off the R119
Type of Course:	Parkland
Date Founded:	1927
No of Holes:	18
Length:	6863 yds (6275 mtrs)
Par:	72
SSS:	72
Green Fees:	Weekdays: £50 Weekends & Bank Holidays: £60 Earlybird rate before 10am £40
Visitors:	Welcome: Contact Club in advance
Societies:	Welcome: Contact Club for details
Facilities:	Chipping/Putting Area, Practice Area, Golf Clubs for hire, Trolley hire, Bar, Restaurant

Accommodation, Food and Drink

Reference numbers below refer to detailed information provided in section 2

Accommodation

Ariemond, Dun Laoghaire, Co Dublin
Tel: 01 2801664 Five en suite Bed & Breakfast rooms, two with private baths, in a lovely house two minutes walk from the centre.   235

Ferry House, Dun Laoghaire, Co Dublin
Tel: 01 2808301 Four en suite Bed & Breakfast rooms in a handsome town house an easy walk from the centre of Dun Laoghaire.   228

Ophira, Dun Laoghaire, Co Dublin
Tel/Fax: 01 2800997 Town-centre Bed & Breakfast Accommodation in a mid-19th century house. Four en suite bedrooms. Tv lounge.   225

Summerhill House Hotel, Enniskerry, Co Wicklow
Tel: 01 2867928 Fifty-seven bright, spacious airy bedrooms with en suite facilities, tv and telephone in a friendly, well-situated hotel.   668

The Kingston Hotel, Dun Laoghaire, Co Dublin
Tel: 01 2801810 Fifty-three well-equipped en suite bedrooms – singles, doubles, twins and triples – in a family-run hotel on the seafront.   236

Woodland Court Hotel, Southern Cross, Bray, Co Wicklow
Tel: 01 2760258 Sixty five en suite bedrooms with all the modern comforts in a characterful hotel at the southern end of the town. Restaurant and lounge.   667

Food and Drink

Summerhill House Hotel, Enniskerry, Co Wicklow
Tel: 01 2867928 Fifty-seven bright, spacious airy bedrooms with en suite facilities, tv and telephone in a friendly, well-situated hotel.   668

The Kingston Hotel, Dun Laoghaire, Co Dublin
Tel: 01 2801810 Fifty-three well-equipped en suite bedrooms – singles, doubles, twins and triples – in a family-run hotel on the seafront.   236

Walters, Dun Laoghaire, Co Dublin
Tel: 01 2807442 Elegant, trendy bar-café-restaurant serving anything from a coffee or a drink to a three-course meal.   229

Woodland Court Hotel, Southern Cross, Bray, Co Wicklow
Tel: 01 2760258 Sixty five en suite bedrooms with all the modern comforts in a characterful hotel at the southern end of the town. Restaurant and lounge.   667

Woodenbridge

Woodenbridge Golf Club, Woodenbridge, Arklow, Co Wicklow
Tel: 040 235202

Sec/Manager:	Henry Crummy
Professional:	None
Directions:	4 miles North West of Arklow off the R747 to Avoca
Type of Course:	Parkland
Date Founded:	1884
No of Holes:	18
Length:	6400 yds (5852 mtrs)
Par:	71
SSS:	70
Green Fees:	Weekdays: £30 Weekends & Bank Holidays: £35
Visitors:	Welcome: Any Day except Thursday and Saturday, Prior booking required
Societies:	Welcome: Contact Club in advance
Facilities:	Chipping/Putting Area, Practice Area, Trolley hire, Bar, Restaurant, Caddy service by arrangement

Accommodation, Food and Drink

Reference numbers below refer to detailed
information provided in section 2

Accommodation

Ballykilty Farmhouse, Coolgreany, Arklow, Co Wicklow

Tel: 040 237111 Fax: 040 237272 Five en suite bedrooms in an old-world farmhouse
on a 200-acre dairy farm. Fine gardens, tennis court.   660

Harbour House, Courtown Harbour, Co Wexford

Tel/Fax: 055 25117 Family-run guest house in a renowned seaside resort. 13 en
suite bedrooms with tv. Also self-catering in mobile homes.   623

Highfield House, Woodenbridge, Arklow, Co Wicklow

Tel: 040 235262 Three immaculate bedrooms, two en suite and one with private
bath, in a large modern farmhouse. Bed & Breakfast, packed lunches.   661

Keppel's Farmhouse, Avoca, Co Wicklow

Tel/Fax: 040 235168 Five bright, comfortable B&B rooms in a handsome 19th-
century farmhouse. Also a self-catering bungalow.   673

Murphy's Bar & Restaurant, Arklow, Co Wicklow

Tel/Fax: 040 232781 Spacious, well-appointed main-street pub with restaurant. Self-
catering Accommodation also offered.   662

Ostan Beag Hotel, Arklow, Co Wicklow

Tel: 040 233044 A hospitable hotel with 20 elegant en suite bedrooms, two bars, a
restaurant and a lively nightclub.   666

The Beehive, Coolbeg Cross, N11 Wexford Road, Co Wicklow

Tel: 040 469745 Bar, restaurant and Bed & Breakfast Accommodation in a family-
run establishment on the N11. Weekend music.   664

Woodlands Farmhouse, Killinierin, Gorey, Co Wexford

Tel: 040 237125 Fax: 040 237133 Six tastefully decorated en suite bedrooms in a
Georgian-style 19th-century residence. Large gardens. Dinner from 7.30.   627

Food and Drink

Murphy's Bar & Restaurant, Arklow, Co Wicklow

Tel/Fax: 040 232781 Spacious, well-appointed main-street pub with restaurant. Self-
catering Accommodation also offered.   662

Ostan Beag Hotel, Arklow, Co Wicklow

Tel: 040 233044 A hospitable hotel with 20 elegant en suite bedrooms, two bars, a
restaurant and a lively nightclub.   666

The Avoca Inn & Greek Vine Restaurant, Avoca, Co
Wicklow

Tel: 040 235774 A winning combination of convivial pub and charming Greek
restaurant in a delightful setting by the Avoca river.   663

The Beehive, Coolbeg Cross, N11 Wexford Road, Co Wicklow

Tel: 040 469745 Bar, restaurant and Bed & Breakfast Accommodation in a family-
run establishment on the N11. Weekend music.   664

This page is intentionally blank

Golf Course Information

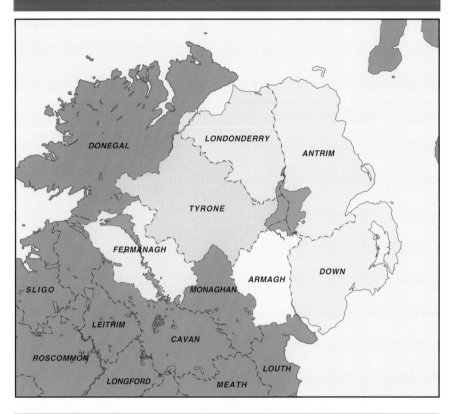

Contents - Northern Ireland

This page is intentionally blank

ANTRIM

Reflecting on his British Senior Open win of 1999 at Royal Portrush, Christy O'Connor Jnr said wistfully: "It's the sort of course I would love to go back to again and again." Visitors to County Antrim are generally of similar mind, as they contemplate a seductive land of green glens and majestic coastline. The county's greatest claim to golfing fame is, of course, the fact that it played host to the British Open at Portrush in 1951, when England's Max Faulkner captured the title. It was, and remains, the only occasion when the event was staged outside Scotland and England and when it was all over, the organisers had reason to be pleased with their decision. As the eminent writer turned golf-course architect Frank Pennink reported afterwards: "It (the Open) was played on a truly magnificent links - perhaps the finest test of all our great courses." He went on: "Colonel Hezlet (of the host club) had often extolled the virtues and charm of Royal Portrush to me with unbridled enthusiasm. I had accepted his glowing descriptions with politeness, but with a grain of salt as well. I feel I must now apologise to him and acknowledge with gratitude that his lauding of his Dunluce course was not fulsome praise; and, indeed, his rhetoric does it scant justice." Like St Andrews draws visitors to the region of Fife in Scotland, Portrush attracts enthusiasts to the varied golfing terrain of County Antrim. And many club devotees throughout Britain, have savoured the delights of the region by competing in the annual Black Bush Amateur Tournament, not least because it gave them access to Royal Portrush, apart from Ballycastle and the County Derry courses of Portstewart and Castlerock.

There are 22 courses in County Antrim - Antrim, Ballycastle, Ballyclare, Ballymena, Burnfield House, Bushfoot, Cairndhu, Carrickfergus, Cushendall, Down Royal, Galgorm Castle, Gracehill, Greenacres, Greenisland, Lambeg, Larne, Lisburn, Mallusk, Massereene, Royal Portrush, Hilton Templepatrick and Whitehead. Hilton Templepatrick, which was designed by the Bangor-born professional David Jones, is the most recent addition. Only slightly more mature, however, is another fine, parkland stretch which has been created by the English architect Simon Gidman in the grounds of Galgorm Castle, just outside Ballymena. Then there is the contrasting, parkland challenge of Cairndhu, which was built on the face of Ballygally Head, in Larne. As its location would suggest, it offers some charming views of the Antrim Hills and Carnlough, while the west coast of Scotland can be seen in the distance. In fact the tee at the 383-yard third hole is 200 feet above sea level and apart from the distraction of the stunning views, it presents a daunting carry of more than 175 yards to the fairway. Massereene offers further variety in that the outward journey is clearly parkland, while the back nine, overlooking Lough Neagh, has a sandy texture more associated with heathland. Measuring 6,614 yards off the back tees, it was considered a sufficiently strong challenge for the Irish Professional Championship of 1970, when Ulster's Hugh Jackson captured the title with an aggregate of 283.

Away from the world of golf, however, thoughts of Antrim are almost inevitably dominated by The Giant's Causeway, whose lunar landscape, lurking below the gaunt sea wall when the land ends, must have struck wonder into the hearts of the ancient Irish. William Makepeace Thackeray wrote of it: "When the world was moulded and fashioned out of formless chaos, this must have been the bit over - a remnant of chaos." Like the early people of North Antrim, Thackeray

Giants Causeway, Co Antrim

was impressed by the strangeness of a place which had been described as a geological freak, whereby the lava from volcanic eruptions was cooled into extraordinary shapes. The ancient Irish took the rather more appealing view that this was giants' work. Indeed they went so far as to suggest that it was specifically the work of legendary giant Fionn McCool, the Ulster warrior and commander of the king's armies. Capable of enormous strength, Fionn could pick thorns out of his heels while running. And we're told that once, during a fight with a Scottish giant, he scooped up a huge clod of earth and flung it at his fleeing rival. Falling short of the target, it finished in the sea to become the Isle of Man, while the divot left behind was filled with water to become Lough Neagh.

Glenarm, Co Antrim

The first historical accounts of the Causeway appeared in the late 17th century. In fact the Bishop of Derry made one of the first recorded visits to the place in 1692 and we're told that the Chevalier De La Tocnaye, who had the good sense to bring along his umbrella, galloped up to the cliff edge in 1797, when both he and his horse were enraptured by the view before them. Before the famous coast road was built in the 1830s, visitors complained about the ruggedness of the trip. Still, there was a notable compensation in that the town where tourists made their last stop before the final advance to the Causeway, was Bushmills. Since 1608, saddle-sore travellers were revived by blessed mouthfulls of the King's whiskey at the world's oldest, legal distillery. And, of course, it is still very much in business. The Causeway proper is a mass of basalt columns packed tightly together. The tops of these columns form stepping-stones which lead from the foot of the cliff and disappear under the sea. In all, there are 40,000 of these stone columns, mostly hexagonal in shape, though some have four, five, seven or eight sides. The tallest are about 40 feet and the solidified lava in the cliffs is 90 feet thick in places.

Antrim is also famous for its nine glens, which have been celebrated in song and story. Stretching from Larne up to Ballycastle, their names, south to north, are: Glenarm, Glencloy, Glenariff, Glenbalyeamon, Glenaan, Glencorp, Glendun, Glenshesk and Glentaisie. Historians tell us that around the middle of the 18th century, their remoteness was quite daunting, with

rushing rivers bisecting the land from west to east. That was when the inland track from Cushendun to Ballycastle crossed Loughareema, which was known as the vanishing lake because it could be full of water one day and empty the next. Indeed it was not unknown for coach horses to gallop into this watery grave, taking hapless passengers with them. Gaelic is still spoken there and for the most part, the current inhabitants of the glens are descendants of both the ancient Irish and the Hebridean Scots. They are noted storytellers who will regale visitors with tales of the "wee folk" who inhabit Lurigethan Mountain and Tiveragh Hill.

In 1911, Fred Daly was born in Causeway Street, Portrush. He was only nine when he started caddying at the club for the princely sum of nine-pence a round, plus a three-pence tip. Thirty six years later, he would gain the distinction at Hoylake of becoming Ireland's only winner of the British Open. Fred died in 1990, but not before donating his Open medal to the club where he had learned his craft. They, in turn, made him an honorary life member. A long association with greatness, seems to fit Portrush like a glove.

Carrick-a-Rede Rope Bridge, Co Antrim

Location of Golf Courses

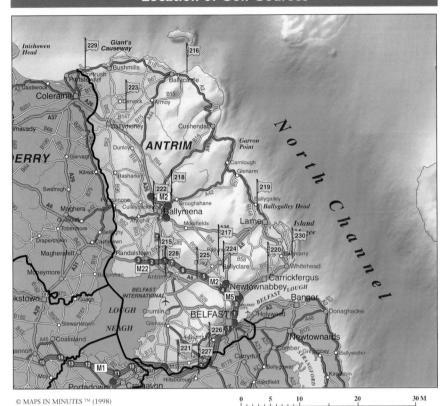

© MAPS IN MINUTES ™ (1998)

```
0        5        10              20                    30 M
|++++++++|++++++++|+++++++|+++++++|++++++++|
0    5   10       20       30       40       50 Km
```

Allen Park

Allen Park Golf Centre, 45 Castle Road,
Randalstown Road, Antrim, BT41 4NA
Tel: 028 9442 9001

Sec/Manager:	Marie Agnew
Professional:	Stephen Hamill
Directions:	Aprox. 2 miles from Antrim on Antrim to Randalstown Road.
Type of Course:	Parkland
Date Founded:	1996
No of Holes:	18
Length:	6683 yds (6110 mtrs)
Par:	72
SSS:	72
Green Fees:	Weekdays: £13 Weekends and Bank Holidays: £15
Visitors:	Welcome: Monday to Friday, Check weekend availability
Societies:	Welcome: Book in advance
Facilities:	Chipping/Putting Area, Driving Range, Golf Clubs for hire, Trolley hire

Accommodation, Food and Drink

Reference numbers below refer to detailed
information provided in section 2

Accommodation

Caldhame House, Nutts Corner, Crumlin, Co Antrim
Tel/Fax: 028 9442 2378 A splendid guest house just minutes from Belfast
International Airport. All rooms en suite, with tv.   800

Glengannon Hotel, Dungannon, Co Tyrone
Tel/Fax: 028 8772 7311 En suite bedrooms, good choice of menus and weekend live
entertainment in a low-rise modern hotel off the M1 (J15).   897

Muleany House, Moy, Dungannon, Co Tyrone
Tel: 028 8778 4183 Family-run, family-friendly home from home with nine en suite
bedrooms, drawing room, tv room, games room and traditional home cooking. 890

Reahs, Dungannon, Co tyrone
Tel: 028 8772 5575 Top-class food and luxurious overnight accomodation in a smart
detached house half a mile out of town.   891

The Ryandale, Moy, Co Tyrone
Tel/Fax: 028 8778 4629 A fine Listed building in the centre of a small village. The
Ryandale offers en suite bedrooms, restaurant, bar and nightclub. 900

Food and Drink

Glengannon Hotel, Dungannon, Co Tyrone
Tel/Fax: 028 8772 7311 En suite bedrooms, good choice of menus and weekend live
entertainment in a low-rise modern hotel off the M1 (J15).   897

Reahs, Dungannon, Co tyrone
Tel: 028 8772 5575 Top-class food and luxurious overnight accomodation in a smart
detached house half a mile out of town.   891

The Ryandale, Moy, Co Tyrone
Tel/Fax: 028 8778 4629 A fine Listed building in the centre of a small village. The
Ryandale offers en suite bedrooms, restaurant, bar and nightclub. 900

Ballycastle

Ballcastle Golf Club, 2 Cushen Dall Road,
Ballycastle, Co Antrim, BT54 6QP
Tel: 028 2076 2536

Originally referred to somewhat pejoratively as
"The Warren", because of the number of rabbit
holes on the site, Ballycastle could still boast the
distinction of being one of the founder clubs of
the Golfing Union of Ireland. As for its prolific
inhabitants: we are informed that "the trouble-
some bunny has been sufficiently dealt with."

Founded in 1891, it is situated at the eastern
end of the Causeway Coast and offers beautiful
views of the Atlantic. And though modest in
length by modern standards, the course comprises a fascinating combination of links and
parkland.

In fact the name Warren is retained for the
area of four holes from the sixth to the ninth,
which are pure links, in contrast to the distinctly
parkland, opening five holes. That early stretch,
played around the ruins of a 13th century friary,
is bordered by the Margy and Carey rivers which
provide natural hazards, especially to the right
of the first.

The homeward journey, with its crossover
15th and 16th holes and where a premium is
placed on accurate iron play, is on an adjacent
upland offering panoramic views of the Mull of
Kintyre, Rathlin Island and Ballycastle Bay.

In its early, nine-hole incarnation, the course
was described as "small and bordering a bay, half
a mile from Ballycastle Railway Station." One
hundred years on, however, and having grown
to 18 holes, it has become familiar terrain to hun-
dreds of handicap golfers in these islands, as one
of the courses used in the annual Black Bush
Tournament.

Sec/Manager:	B. J. Dillon
Professional:	Ian McLaughlin
Directions:	On the coast, 1 mile east of Ballycastle off the A2 to Ballyroy
Type of Course:	Combination: Parkland – Links- Uplands

Date Founded:	1890
No of Holes:	18
Length:	5940 yds (5406 mtrs)
Par:	71
SSS:	70
Green Fees:	Weekdays £20 Weekends and Bank Holidays £28
Visitors:	Welcome: Weekdays, Ladies Day Friday
Societies:	Welcome: Weekdays and Weekends by prior arrangement
Facilities:	Chipping/Putting Area, Practice area, Trolley hire, Bar, Restaurant, Caddy service by arrangement

Accommodation, Food and Drink

Reference numbers below refer to detailed information provided in section 2

Accommodation

Antrim Arms, Ballycastle, Co Antrim

Tel: 028 2076 2284 Good food, good beer and good times in one of Ireland's oldest hostelries, dating back to 1767. The old-world feel is allied to modern comforts, and the bedrooms, all en suite, are well furnished and decorated. Restaurant open to non-residents. 803

Brookhaven, Portrush, Co Antrim

Tel: 028 7082 4164 The bedrooms, 2 twin and 1 double en suite, are beautifully decorated and furnished. Spacious gardens for guests to stroll in. There is a superb choice of local golf courses - Royal Portrush is only a five-minute drive away. 802

Chris-Mull, Bushmills, Co Antrim

Tel: 028 2073 1154 En suite Bed & Breakfast Accommodation in double or single rooms. 200 yards from the A2. Visa, Mastercard

Clarmont, Portrush, Co Antrim

Tel/Fax: 028 7082 2397 All the bedrooms at this three-storey town house have en suite facilities. From the patio seating area there are super views out onto the Atlantic Ocean and Royal Portrush Golf. 804

Craig Park Country House, Bushmills, Co Antrim

Tel: 028 2073 2496 Fax: 028 2073 2479 B&B guest house with three letting bedrooms. Tvs and telephones. No smoking. 809

Fullerton Arms, Ballintoy, Co Antrim

Tel: 028 2076 9613 The 19th-century building, a little way inland from picturesque Ballintoy harbour, has been extensively renovated and modernised to house 11 en suite bedrooms, a lively bar and restaurant that's open to non-residents. 808

Galgorm, Portrush, Co Antrim

Tel: 028 7082 3787 This town house attracts many return visitors with its warm, easygoing atmosphere and excellent Accommodation: 12 en suite bedrooms. Drew is a keen golfer and can give advice about the local courses. 807

Glenmore House, Ballycastle, Co Antrim

Tel/Fax: 028 2076 3548 A large purpose-built country house hotel affords superb views of the Antrim coast and the Atlantic. Within easy reach of some of the top golf courses in Northern Ireland. Every aspect of a golfing holiday is catered for, including reservations and a club cleaning service. 801

Food and Drink

Antrim Arms, Ballycastle, Co Antrim

Tel: 028 2076 2284 Good food, good beer and good times in one of Ireland's oldest hostelries, dating back to 1767. The old-world feel is allied to modern comforts, and the bedrooms, all en suite, are well furnished and decorated. Restaurant open to non-residents. 803

Fullerton Arms, Ballintoy, Co Antrim

Tel: 028 2076 9613 The 19th-century building, a little way inland from picturesque Ballintoy harbour, has been extensively renovated and modernised to house 11 en suite bedrooms, a lively bar and restaurant that's open to non-residents. 808

Glenmore House, Ballycastle, Co Antrim

Tel/Fax: 028 2076 3548 A large purpose-built country house hotel affords superb views of the Antrim coast and the Atlantic. Within easy reach of some of the top golf courses in Northern Ireland. Every aspect of a golfing holiday is catered for, including reservations and a club cleaning service. 801

The Skerrys Inn, Newtowncrommelin, Co Antrim

Tel: 028 2175 8669 The Skerrys Inn is a long, low building in a small village with a big name. Traditional Irish music on Wednesday to Saturday nights. 805

Ballyclare

Ballyclare, 25 Springvale Road, Ballyclare, Co Antrim

Tel: 028 9332 2696

Sec/Manager:	Harry McConnell
Professional:	None
Directions:	Two miles north of Ballyclare
Type of Course:	Parkland
Date Founded:	1923
No of Holes:	18
Length:	5745 yds (5253 mtrs)
Par:	72
SSS:	71
Green Fees:	Weekdays: £16 Weekends & Bank Holidays: £22
Visitors:	Welcome: Any Day except Saturday & Sunday a.m.
Societies:	Welcome: Reductions for parties of 20 plus, Contact Club for details
Facilities:	Chipping/Putting Area, Practice Area, Golf Clubs for hire, Trolley hire, Bar, Restaurant

Accommodation, Food and Drink

Reference numbers below refer to detailed information provided in section 2

Accommodation

Shanleigh House, Ballymena, Co Antrim

Tel/Fax: 028 2564 4851 B&B in four bedrooms; 2 double, 1 twin, 1 family. En suite available. A warm welcome awaits all guests. No credit cards - travellers cheques only. Very close to Galgorm Castle.

The 5 Corners Inn, Ballyclare, Co Antrim

Tel: 028 9332 2657 Fax: 028 9334 9769 A white stone building that's easy to spot. The spacious bedrooms are all en suite. All the usual golfing services are offered. 806

Tully B&B, Ballymena, Co Antrim

Tel: 028 2564 6088 Two acres of lawns make an attractive, secluded setting for a large hacienda-style house. The bedrooms are all en suite and Tully has the unusual amenity of a snooker room with a full-size table. 811

Food and Drink

The 5 Corners Inn, Ballyclare, Co Antrim

Tel: 028 9332 2657 Fax: 028 9334 9769 A white stone building that's easy to spot. The spacious bedrooms are all en suite. All the usual golfing services are offered. 806

The Glensway Tavern, Martinstown, Co Antrim

Tel/Fax: 028 2175 8534 The white-painted tavern has a very warm atmosphere that has made it a favourite with the locals. Colm is a keen golfer who is more than happy to help plan golfing. 810

The Meeting House, Cairncastle, Larne, Co Antrim

Tel: 028 2858 3252 Established in the 1700's, and currently listed as an Irish Pub of Distinction, a place to relax over a good meal complimented by a fine selection of beers, wines and spirits. Restaurant open lunch and dinner, bar food served 12-8pm.

Ballymena

Ballymena, 128 Raceview Road, Ballymena, BT42 4HY

Tel: 028 2568 61487

Sec/Manager:	Carl McAuley
Professional:	Ken Revie
Directions:	Three miles East of Ballymena off the A42
Type of Course:	Heathland
Date Founded:	1902
No of Holes:	18
Length:	5798 yds (5299 mtrs)
Par:	68
SSS:	68
Green Fees:	Weekdays: £17 Weekends and Bank Holidays: £22
Visitors:	Welcome: Any day except Tuesday
Societies:	Welcome: Book in advance
Facilities:	Chipping/Putting Area, Practice Area, Golf Clubs for hire, Bar, Restaurant, Caddy service by arrangement

Accommodation, Food and Drink

Reference numbers below refer to detailed information provided in section 2

Accommodation

Four Winds, 146 Crankhill Road, Slangford, Ballymena, Co Antrim, BT44 9HA,
Tel: 028 2568 5360 The Four Winds is the farmhouse for a mixed working farm which offers bed & breakfast Accommodation. The modern building has been recently refurbished and now provides 3 letting rooms, (2 family and 1 double, all with hot and cold).

Shanleigh House, Ballymena, Co Antrim
Tel/Fax: 028 2564 4851 B&B in four bedrooms; 2 double, 1 twin, 1 family. En suite available. A warm welcome awaits all guests. No credit cards - travellers cheques only. Very close to Galgorm Castle.

The 5 Corners Inn, Ballyclare, Co Antrim
Tel: 028 9332 2657 Fax: 028 9334 9769 A white stone building that's easy to spot. The spacious bedrooms are all en suite. All the usual golfing services are offered. 806

Tully B&B, Ballymena, Co Antrim
Tel: 028 2564 6088 Two acres of lawns make an attractive, secluded setting for a large hacienda-style house. The bedrooms are all en suite and Tully has the unusual amenity of a snooker room with a full-size table. 811

Food and Drink

The 5 Corners Inn, Ballyclare, Co Antrim
Tel: 028 9332 2657 Fax: 028 9334 9769 A white stone building that's easy to spot. The spacious bedrooms are all en suite. All the usual golfing services are offered. 806

The Glensway Tavern, Martinstown, Co Antrim
Tel/Fax: 028 2175 8534 The white-painted tavern has a very warm atmosphere that has made it a favourite with the locals. Colm is a keen golfer who is more than happy to help plan golfing. 810

The Skerrys Inn, Newtowncrommelin, Co Antrim
Tel: 028 2175 8669 The Skerrys Inn is a long, low building in a small village with a big name. Traditional Irish music on Wednesday to Saturday nights. 805

Cairndhu

Cairndhu, 192 Coast Road, Ballygally, Larne,

Co Antrim, BT40 2QG
Tel: 028 2858 3324

Sec/Manager:	Nat Moore
Professional:	R. Walker
Directions:	Four miles North of Larne off the A2
Type of Course:	Parkland
Date Founded:	1928
No of Holes:	18
Length:	6136 yds (5611 mtrs)
Par:	70
SSS:	69
Green Fees:	Monday – Thursday: £15 Friday: £20 Weekends: £24
Visitors:	Welcome: Not Saturdays
Societies:	Welcome: Not Saturdays
Facilities:	Chipping/Putting Area, Practice Area, Driving Range, Golf Clubs for hire, Trolley hire, Bar, Restaurant

Accommodation, Food and Drink

Reference numbers below refer to detailed information provided in section 2

Accommodation

Shanleigh House, Ballymena, Co Antrim
Tel/Fax: 028 2564 4851 B&B in four bedrooms; 2 double, 1 twin, 1 family. En suite available. A warm welcome awaits all guests. No credit cards - travellers cheques only. Very close to Galgorm Castle.

The 5 Corners Inn, Ballyclare, Co Antrim
Tel: 028 9332 2657 Fax: 028 9334 9769 A white stone building that's easy to spot. The spacious bedrooms are all en suite. All the usual golfing services are offered. 806

Tully B&B, Ballymena, Co Antrim
Tel: 028 2564 6088 Two acres of lawns make an attractive, secluded setting for a large hacienda-style house. The bedrooms are all en suite and Tully has the unusual amenity of a snooker room with a full-size table. 811

Food and Drink

The 5 Corners Inn, Ballyclare, Co Antrim
Tel: 028 9332 2657 Fax: 028 93349769 A white stone building that's easy to spot. The spacious bedrooms are all en suite. All the usual golfing services are offered. 806

The Meeting House, Cairncastle, Larne, Co Antrim
Tel: 028 2858 3252 Established in the 1700's, and currently listed as an Irish Pub of Distinction, a place to relax over a good meal complimented by a fine selection of beers, wines and spirits. Restaurant open lunch and dinner, bar food served 12-8pm.

The Skerrys Inn, Newtowncrommelin, Co Antrim
Tel: 028 2175 8669 The Skerrys Inn is a long, low building in a small village with a big name. Traditional Irish music on Wednesday to Saturday nights. 805

Carrickfergus

Carrickfergus, 35 North Road, Carrickfergus, BT38 8LP

Tel: 019 6036 3713

Sec/Manager:	John Thomson
Professional:	Mark Johnson
Directions:	On the outskirts of Carrickfergus off the A2
Type of Course:	Parkland
Date Founded:	1926

No of Holes:	18
Length:	5752 yds (5259 mtrs)
Par:	68
SSS:	68
Green Fees:	Weekdays: £15 Weekends: £21
Visitors:	Welcome: Not Saturdays
Societies:	Welcome: Not Saturdays
Facilities:	Chipping/Putting Area, Trolley hire, Bar, Restaurant

Accommodation, Food and Drink

Reference numbers below refer to detailed
information provided in section 2

Accommodation

Shanleigh House, Ballymena, Co Antrim

Tel/Fax: 028 2564 4851 B&B in four bedrooms; 2 double, 1 twin, 1 family. En suite available. A warm welcome awaits all guests. No credit cards - travellers cheques only. Very close to Galgorm Castle.

The 5 Corners Inn, Ballyclare, Co Antrim

Tel: 028 9332 2657 Fax: 028 9334 9769 A white stone building that's easy to spot. The spacious bedrooms are all en suite. All the usual golfing services are offered. 806

Tully B&B, Ballymena, Co Antrim

Tel: 028 2564 6088 Two acres of lawns make an attractive, secluded setting for a large hacienda-style house. The bedrooms are all en suite and Tully has the unusual amenity of a snooker room with a full-size table.   811

Food and Drink

Motte 'n' Bailey, 131-3 Kingsway, Dunmurry, Co Antrim

Tel: 028 9060 3790 A round tower look for this establishment with three bars, one serving as a restaurant: pub grub plus à la carte menu.

The 5 Corners Inn, Ballyclare, Co Antrim

Tel: 028 9332 2657 Fax: 028 9334 9769 A white stone building that's easy to spot. The spacious bedrooms are all en suite. All the usual golfing services are offered. 806

The Meeting House, Cairncastle, Larne, Co Antrim

Tel: 028 2858 3252 Established in the 1700's, and currently listed as an Irish Pub of Distinction, a place to relax over a good meal complimented by a fine selection of beers, wines and spirits. Restaurant open lunch and dinner, bar food served 12-8pm.

Down Royal Park

Down Royal Park, Dunygarton Road, Maze,
Lisburn, BT27 5RT

Tel: 028 9262 1339

Sec/Manager:	J. Tinnion
Professional:	None
Directions:	South East of Lisburn within the Maze racecourse
Type of Course:	Parkland
Date Founded:	1989
No of Holes:	18
Length:	6824 yds (6239 mtrs)
Par:	72
SSS:	72
Green Fees:	Weekdays: £15 Saturday: £17 Sundays & Bank Holidays: £20 Off-peak: £12
Visitors:	Welcome: Book in advance
Societies:	Welcome: Book in advance
Facilities:	Trolley hire, Bar, Restaurant, Hotel/ Accommodation on site

Accommodation, Food and Drink

Reference numbers below refer to detailed
information provided in section 2

Accommodation

Caldhame House, Nutts Corner, Crumlin, Co Antrim

Tel/Fax: 028 9442 2378 A splendid guest house just minutes from Belfast International Airport. All rooms en suite, with tv.   800

Oakfield Guest House, 9 Crumlin Road, Lower Ballinderry, Lisburn, Co Antrim, BT28 2JU,

Tel: 028 9265 1307 Large, modernised farmhouse is surrounded by well-presented gardens, with plenty of parking space, and has 4 guest bedrooms, all en suite. Convenient for the disabled.

Win - Staff House, 45 Banbridge Rd, Dromore, Co Down, BT25 1NE,

Tel: 028 9269 2252 Surrounded by spacious gardens, (complete with a barbecue area), Win-Staff House enjoys a well-deserved reputation for friendliness, hospitality, excellent cuisine and comfortable, relaxing Accommodation. Evening meals are available on request.

Food and Drink

Motte 'n' Bailey, 131-3 Kingsway, Dunmurry, Co Antrim

Tel: 028 9060 3790 A round tower look for this establishment with three bars, one serving as a restaurant: pub grub plus à la carte menu.

Seven Stars Restaurant, Loughbrickland, Co Down

Tel: 028 4062 6461 A bright, cheerful bar-restaurant serving a good range of dishes from 11.30 to 7.30. Just off the main A1.   833

The Primrose Bar, Ballynahinch, Co Down

Tel: 028 9756 3177 Fax: 028 9756 5954 Bar and restaurant on the main street of town. Local ales, worldwide wines, bar menu and various restaurant menus.   837

Galgorm Castle

Galgorm Castle Golf Club, Galgorm Castle,
Galgorm Road, Ballymena, BT42 1HL

Tel: 028 2564 6161

Memories of a 1943 movie called "The Ox-Bow Incident", with Henry Fonda in the starring role, would be revived by a visit to Galgorm Castle, owned by the Hon Christopher Brooke and situated a mile and a half outside Ballymena. With it will come enlightenment as to the meaning of the term.

Out on the course, set in 220 acres and designed by Britain's Simon Gidman, there is a horseshoe bend in the River Braid (what a charming coincidence that it should carry the name of a five-times British Open champion). It is first encountered on the opening nine where the river has to be traversed to reach the green at the 323-yard fourth.

Then, on the homeward journey, the inside of the horseshoe contains the 15th tee which is reached by crossing a 30-metre galvanised bridge over the fast-running current. That is your ox-bow.

Overall, it would be difficult to imagine a more ideal, self-contained site, bordered as it is by the River Main to the right and the River Braid to the left, forming two sides of a triangle until they meet at the back of the 13th green. Apart from the two rivers, there are mature trees and five lakes, all of which Gidman uses to strategic effect.

Particularly impressive is the short seventh (141 yards) where the irregular-shaped lake to the front and right of the green, looked as if it might have been a part of the original landscape. Thoroughly captivating.

Sec/Manager:	Bill Hawthorne
Professional:	Lesley Callan
Directions:	I mile South West of Ballymena on the A42
Type of Course:	Parkland
Date Founded:	1997
No of Holes:	18
Length:	6724 yds (6148 mtrs)
Par:	72
SSS:	72
Green Fees:	Weekdays: £18 Weekends: £24
Visitors:	Welcome: Book in advance
Societies:	Welcome: Not Saturdays, Contact Club for details
Facilities:	Practice Area, Driving Range, Golf Clubs for hire, Trolley hire, Electric Buggy hire, Bar, Restaurant

Accommodation, Food and Drink

Reference numbers below refer to detailed information provided in section 2

Accommodation

Four Winds, 146 Crankhill Road, Slangford, Ballymena, Co Antrim, BT44 9HA,

Tel: 028 2568 5360 The Four Winds is the farmhouse for a mixed working farm which offers bed & breakfast Accommodation. The modern building has been recently refurbished and now provides 3 letting rooms, (2 family and 1 double, all with hot and cold).

Garron View, 14 Cloghs Road, Cushendall, Co Antrim, BT44 OSP.

Tel: 028 2177 1018 The house is surrounded by large, well laid out gardens and enjoys splendid views across to Lurig and the Fairy Mountains at Tieverah. 5 letting rooms (1 family room, 1 twin, and 3 doubles), 3 of which are en suite.

Shanleigh House, Ballymena, Co Antrim

Tel/Fax: 028 2564 4851 B&B in four bedrooms; 2 double, 1 twin, 1 family. En suite available. A warm welcome awaits all guests. No credit cards - travellers cheques only. Very close to Galgorm Castle.

Thornlea Hotel, 6 Coast Road, Cushendall, Co Antrim, BT 44,

Tel: 028 2177 1223 The hotel is family run so visitors are assured of a warm and friendly welcome. All 14 bedrooms are en suite and fully equipped. The Thornlea's restaurant is well known for its quality food.

Tully B&B, Ballymena, Co Antrim

Tel: 028 2564 6088 Two acres of lawns make an attractive, secluded setting for a large hacienda-style house. The bedrooms are all en suite and Tully has the unusual amenity of a snooker room with a full-size table.   811

Food and Drink

McNally's Inn, Castledawson, Co Londonderry

Tel: 028 7965 0095 A small, unpretentious modern country inn well known to golfers and others for its traditional Irish welcome. The extensive menu runs from light snacks to three-course meals. Regular live music sessions.   922

The Glensway Tavern, Martinstown, Co Antrim

Tel/Fax: 028 2175 8534 The white-painted tavern has a very warm atmosphere that has made it a favourite with the locals. Colm is a keen golfer who is more than happy to help plan golfing.   810

Thornlea Hotel, 6 Coast Road, Cushendall, Co Antrim, BT 44,

Tel: 028 2177 1223 The hotel is family run so visitors are assured of a warm and friendly welcome. All 14 bedrooms are en suite and fully equipped. The Thornlea's restaurant is well known for its quality food.

Gracehill

Gracehill, 141 Ballinlea Road, Stranocum, Ballymoney, Co Antrim, BT53 8PX

Tel: 028 7075 1209

Sec/Manager:	Mrs. M McClure
Professional:	None
Directions:	Seven miles north of Ballymoney on B147 near Stranocum
Type of Course:	Parkland
Date Founded:	1995
No of Holes:	18
Length:	6155 yds (5628 (mtrs)
Par:	72
SSS:	71
Green Fees:	Monday & Tuesday: £15 Wednesday – Friday: £20 Weekends: £25
Visitors:	Welcome: Monday – Friday and Saturday after 2.00pm
Societies:	Welcome: Monday – Friday, Check weekend availability

Facilities: Practice Area, Golf Clubs for hire, Trolley hire, Bar, Restaurant

Accommodation, Food and Drink

Reference numbers below refer to detailed information provided in section 2

Accommodation

Antrim Arms, Ballycastle, Co Antrim

Tel: 028 2076 2284 Good food, good beer and good times in one of Ireland's oldest hostelries, dating back to 1767. The old-world feel is allied to modern comforts, and the bedrooms, all en suite, are well furnished and decorated. Restaurant open to non-residents. 803

Craig Park Country House, Bushmills, Co Antrim

Tel: 028 2073 2496 Fax: 028 2073 2479 B&B guest house with three letting bedrooms. Tvs and telephones. No smoking. 809

Fullerton Arms, Ballintoy, Co Antrim

Tel: 028 2076 9613 The 19th-century building, a little way inland from picturesque Ballintoy harbour, has been extensively renovated and modernised to house 11 en suite bedrooms, a lively bar and restaurant that's open to non-residents. 808

Glenmore House, Ballycastle, Co Antrim

Tel/Fax: 028 2076 3548 A large purpose-built country house hotel affords superb views of the Antrim coast and the Atlantic. Within easy reach of some of the top golf courses in Northern Ireland. Every aspect of a golfing holiday is catered for, including reservations and a club cleaning service. 801

Food and Drink

Antrim Arms, Ballycastle, Co Antrim

Tel: 028 2076 2284 Good food, good beer and good times in one of Ireland's oldest hostelries, dating back to 1767. The old-world feel is allied to modern comforts, and the bedrooms, all en suite, are well furnished and decorated. Restaurant open to non-residents. 803

Fullerton Arms, Ballintoy, Co Antrim

Tel: 028 2076 9613 The 19th-century building, a little way inland from picturesque Ballintoy harbour, has been extensively renovated and modernised to house 11 en suite bedrooms, a lively bar and restaurant that's open to non-residents. 808

Glenmore House, Ballycastle, Co Antrim

Tel/Fax: 028 2076 3548 A large purpose-built country house hotel affords superb views of the Antrim coast and the Atlantic. Within easy reach of some of the top golf courses in Northern Ireland. Every aspect of a golfing holiday is catered for, including reservations and a club cleaning service. 801

Greenacres

Greenacres Golf Club, 153 Ballyrobert Road, Ballyclare, Co Antrim, BT39 9RT

Tel: 028 9335 4111

Sec/Manager:	Michael Brown
Professional:	Ken Revie
Directions:	3 miles from Corrs Corner on B56 towards Ballyclare near Ballyrobert
Type of Course:	Parkland
Date Founded:	1995
No of Holes:	18
Length:	6021 yds (5505 mtrs)
Par:	72
SSS:	69
Green Fees:	Weekdays: £12 Weekends: £16
Visitors:	Welcome: Any time, Saturdays after 1.30pm
Societies:	Welcome: Not Saturdays
Facilities:	Chipping/Putting Area, Driving Range, Trolley hire, Bar, Restaurant

Accommodation, Food and Drink

Reference numbers below refer to detailed information provided in section 2

Accommodation

Manor Guest House, 23 Olderfleet Rd, The Harbour Highway, Larne, Co Antrim, BT40 1AS,

Tel: 028 2827 3305 Manor Guest House is an imposing Victorian villa to which Miss J. A. Graham has been welcoming bed and breakfast guests for almost 40 years. The house has 8 bedrooms, all en suite, one of which is a full Bridal Suite complete with 4-poster bed.

The 5 Corners Inn, Ballyclare, Co Antrim

Tel: 028 9332 2657 Fax: 028 9334 9769 A white stone building that's easy to spot. The spacious bedrooms are all en suite. All the usual golfing services are offered. 806

Tully B&B, Ballymena, Co Antrim

Tel: 028 2564 6088 Two acres of lawns make an attractive, secluded setting for a large hacienda-style house. The bedrooms are all en suite and Tully has the unusual amenity of a snooker room with a full-size table. 811

Food and Drink

Craigs Cellar, Craig Cellars Ltd, 15 Main Street, Larne, Co Antrim, BT40 1JQ,

Tel: 028 2827 2861 Built in 1840, the pub was originally a Manse House. Its popularity is enhanced by the atmospheric interior and by friendly and courteous staff who really do provide service with a smile.

The 5 Corners Inn, Ballyclare, Co Antrim

Tel: 028 9332 2657 Fax: 028 9334 9769 A white stone building that's easy to spot. The spacious bedrooms are all en suite. All the usual golfing services are offered. 806

The Meeting House, Cairncastle, Co Antrim

Tel: 028 2858 3252 Established in the 1700's, and currently listed as an Irish Pub of Distinction, a place to relax over a good meal complimented by a fine selection of beers, wines and spirits. Restaurant open lunch and dinner, bar food served 12-8pm.

Hilton Templepatrick

Hilton Templepatrick Golf Club, Castle Upton Estate, Templepatrick, County Antrim, BT39 0DD

Tel: 028 9443 5500

It is said than more than 1,500 years ago, St Patrick blessed a well at Castle Upton - which accounts for the fact that it has never run dry. The area is better known these days, however, for the steady flow of golfers savouring the delights of the new, Hilton Templepatrick course.

Seven years in the making, from plans to completion, the course was designed by David Jones. In the process, the former Irish Professional champion imposed his own, individual stamp

No of Holes:	18
Length:	7300 yds (6675 mtrs)
Par:	71
SSS:	71
Green Fees:	Weekdays: £35 Weekends & Bank Holidays: £40
Visitors:	Welcome: Ring in advance
Societies:	Welcome: Book in advance
Facilities:	Chipping/Putting Area, Practice Area, Driving Range, Golf Clubs for hire, Trolley hire, Electric Buggy hire, Bar, Restaurant, Caddy service by arrangement, Swimming Pool, Sauna, Hotel/Accommodation on site

Accommodation, Food and Drink

Reference numbers below refer to detailed
information provided in section 2

Accommodation

Caldhame House, Nutts Corner, Crumlin, Co Antrim

Tel/Fax: 028 9442 2378 A splendid guest house just minutes from Belfast International Airport. All rooms en suite, with tv.   800

Shanleigh House, Ballymena, Co Antrim

Tel/Fax: 028 2564 4851 B&B in four bedrooms; 2 double, 1 twin, 1 family. En suite available. A warm welcome awaits all guests. No credit cards - travellers cheques only. Very close to Galgorm Castle.

The 5 Corners Inn, Ballyclare, Co Antrim

Tel: 028 9332 2657 Fax: 028 9334 9769 A white stone building that's easy to spot. The spacious bedrooms are all en suite. All the usual golfing services are offered. 806

Tully B&B, Ballymena, Co Antrim

Tel: 028 2564 6088 Two acres of lawns make an attractive, secluded setting for a large hacienda-style house. The bedrooms are all en suite and Tully has the unusual amenity of a snooker room with a full-size table.   811

Food and Drink

Craigs Cellar, Craig Cellars Ltd, 15 Main Street, Larne, Co Antrim, BT40 1JQ,

Tel: 028 2827 2861 Built in 1840, the pub was originally a Manse House. Its popularity is enhanced by the atmospheric interior and by friendly and courteous staff who really do provide service with a smile.

The 5 Corners Inn, Ballyclare, Co Antrim

Tel: 028 9332 2657 Fax: 028 9334 9769 A white stone building that's easy to spot. The spacious bedrooms are all en suite. All the usual golfing services are offered. 806

The Meeting House, Cairncastle, Larne, Co Antrim

Tel: 028 2858 3252 Established in the 1700's, and currently listed as an Irish Pub of Distinction, a place to relax over a good meal complimented by a fine selection of beers, wines and spirits. Restaurant open lunch and dinner, bar food served 12-8pm.

on the splendid Castle Upton estate, which is located off the M2 motorway, close to Belfast's International Airport.

"As a relative newcomer to golf-course architecture, I was thrilled, not only to be chosen as the designer, but to have been allowed full expression for my ideas," said Jones. "I have seen new courses in Ireland which look as though they have been transplanted from the States, and I was determined to avoid that."

He succeeded admirably, with a par-71 layout which stretches to a formidable 7,300 yards off the back tees. In the process, he made excellent use of the classic, parkland features one associates with mature terrain, which overlooks the County Antrim hills.

As one would expect from a modern development, a broad selection of tees makes the course adaptable to players of all standards. It also reflects the invaluable experience Jones gained from the various up-grading work he did in Ireland and from his collaboration with David Feherty on designing the Klassis course in Turkey.

Sec/Manager:	Bill Donald
Professional:	Eamon Logue
Directions:	½ mile south west of junction 5 of the M2 motorway between Belfast and Antrim
Type of Course:	Parkland
Date Founded:	1999

Lambeg

Lambeg, Aberdelghy, Bells Lane, Lambeg,
Lisburn, BT27 4QH

Tel: 028 9266 2738

Sec/Manager:	Brian Jackson
Professional:	Ian Murdock
Directions:	Two miles from Lisburn off the Lisburn/Belfast Road
Type of Course:	Parkland
Date Founded:	1987
No of Holes:	18
Length:	4526 yds (4139 mtrs)

Par:	66
SSS:	62
Green Fees:	Weekdays: £7 Weekends £9
Visitors:	Welcome: Any time, Saturdays up to 1.00pm
Societies:	Welcome: Contact club for details.
Facilities:	Practice Area, Golf Clubs for hire, Trolley hire

Accommodation, Food and Drink

Reference numbers below refer to detailed information provided in section 2

Accommodation

Bushymead Country House, 86 Drumaness Rd, Ballynahinch, Co Down, BT24 8LT,

Tel: 028 9756 1171 The house stands in spacious grounds with extensive gardens, a children's play area, barbecue site and a large pond. The house has 8 attractively furnished guest bedrooms, 7 of them en suite.

Caldhame House, Nutts Corner, Crumlin, Co Antrim

Tel/Fax: 028 9442 2378 A splendid guest house just minutes from Belfast International Airport. All rooms en suite, with tv. 800

Oakfield Guest House, 9 Crumlin Road, Lower Ballinderry, Lisburn, Co Antrim, BT28 2JU,

Tel: 028 9265 1307 Large, modernised farmhouse is surrounded by well-presented gardens, with plenty of parking space, and has 4 guest bedrooms, all en suite. Convenient for the disabled.

Win - Staff House, 45 Banbridge Rd, Dromore, Co Down, BT25 1NE,

Tel: 028 9269 2252 Surrounded by spacious gardens, (complete with a barbecue area), Win-Staff House enjoys a well-deserved reputation for friendliness, hospitality, excellent cuisine and comfortable, relaxing Accommodation. Evening meals are available on request.

Food and Drink

Maghaberry Arms, 23 Maghaberry Rd, Moira, Craigavon, Co Armagh, BT67 0JF,

Tel: 028 9261 1852 The Maghaberry Arms is a large imposing building which has been recently renovated to the very highest standard - a free house where the craic is good, the food appetising and very good value for money.

Motte 'n' Bailey, 131-3 Kingsway, Dunmurry, Co Antrim

Tel: 028 9060 3790 A round tower look for this establishment with three bars, one serving as a restaurant: pub grub plus à la carte menu.

The Primrose Bar, Ballynahinch, Co Down

Tel: 028 9756 3177 Fax: 028 9756 5954 Bar and restaurant on the main street of town. Local ales, worldwide wines, bar menu and various restaurant menus. 837

Visitors:	Welcome: Monday to Friday Saturdays after 5.00pm, Not Sundays
Societies:	Welcome: Monday to Friday up to 3.00pm, Not weekends, Book in advance
Facilities:	Practice Area, Golf Clubs for hire, Trolley hire, Bar, Restaurant

Accommodation, Food and Drink

Reference numbers below refer to detailed information provided in section 2

Accommodation

Bushymead Country House, 86 Drumaness Rd, Ballynahinch, Co Down, BT24 8LT,

Tel: 028 9756 1171 The house stands in spacious grounds with extensive gardens, a children's play area and a large pond. The house has 8 attractively furnished guest bedrooms, 7 of them en suite.

Caldhame House, Nutts Corner, Crumlin, Co Antrim

Tel/Fax: 028 9442 2378 A splendid guest house just minutes from Belfast International Airport. All rooms en suite, with tv. 800

Oakfield Guest House, 9 Crumlin Road, Lower Ballinderry, Lisburn, Co Antrim, BT28 2JU,

Tel: 028 9265 1307 Large, modernised farmhouse is surrounded by well-presented gardens, with plenty of parking space, and has 4 guest bedrooms, all en suite. Convenient for the disabled.

Win - Staff House, 45 Banbridge Rd, Dromore, Co Down, BT25 1NE,

Tel: 028 9269 2252 Surrounded by spacious gardens, (complete with a barbecue area), Win-Staff House enjoys a well-deserved reputation for friendliness, hospitality, excellent cuisine and comfortable, relaxing Accommodation. Evening meals available on request.

Food and Drink

Maghaberry Arms, 23 Maghaberry Rd, Moira, Craigavon, Co Armagh, BT67 0JF,

Tel: 028 9261 1852 The Maghaberry Arms is a large imposing building which has been recently renovated to the very highest standard - a free house where the craic is good, the food appetising and very good value for money.

Motte 'n' Bailey, 131-3 Kingsway, Dunmurry, Co Antrim

Tel: 028 9060 3790 A round tower look for this establishment with three bars, one serving as a restaurant: pub grub plus à la carte menu.

The Primrose Bar, Ballynahinch, Co Down

Tel: 028 9756 3177 Fax: 028 9756 5954 Bar and restaurant on the main street of town. Local ales, worldwide wines, bar menu and various restaurant menus. 837

Lisburn

68 Eglantine Road, Lisburn, Co. Antrim, BT27 5RQ

Tel: 028 9267 7216

Sec/Manager:	George McVeigh
Professional:	Blake Campbell
Directions:	Two miles south of Lisburn off A1 to Hillsborough
Type of Course:	Parkland & Meadowland
Date Founded:	1905
No of Holes:	18
Length:	6647 yds (6078 mtrs)
Par:	72
SSS:	72
Green Fees:	Weekdays: £25 Weekends: £30

Massereene

Massereene, St Lough Road, Antrim, BT41 4DQ

Tel: 028 9442 8096

Sec/Manager:	Mrs. S. Greene
Professional:	Jim Smyth
Directions:	Two miles South West of Antrim Town Centre by the shore of Lough Neagh
Type of Course:	Parkland
Date Founded:	1895
No of Holes:	18
Length:	6577 yds (6014 mtrs)
Par:	72
SSS:	71
Green Fees:	Weekdays: £25 Weekends: £30
Visitors:	Welcome: Any time except Saturday

Societies: Welcome: Monday, Tuesday, Thursday & Sunday, Book in advance

Facilities: Golf Clubs for hire, Trolley hire, Bar, Restaurant

Accommodation, Food and Drink

Reference numbers below refer to detailed information provided in section 2

Accommodation

Caldhame House, Nutts Corner, Crumlin, Co Antrim

Tel/Fax: 028 9442 2378 A splendid guest house just minutes from Belfast International Airport. All rooms en suite, with tv.   800

Shanleigh House, Ballymena, Co Antrim

Tel/Fax: 028 2564 4851 B&B in four bedrooms; 2 double, 1 twin, 1 family. En suite available. A warm welcome awaits all guests. No credit cards - travellers cheques only. Very close to Galgorm Castle.

The 5 Corners Inn, Ballyclare, Co Antrim

Tel: 028 9332 2657 Fax: 028 9334 9769 A white stone building that's easy to spot. The spacious bedrooms are all en suite. All the usual golfing services are offered. 806

Tully B&B, Ballymena, Co Antrim

Tel: 028 2564 6088 Two acres of lawns make an attractive, secluded setting for a large hacienda-style house. The bedrooms are all en suite and Tully has the unusual amenity of a snooker room with a full-size table.   811

Food and Drink

Dry Dock, 34 - 36 Rawey Street, Magherafelt, Co Londonderry, BT45 5AQ

Tel: 028 7963 4129 The Dry Dock pub in Rainey Street, with its bow-windowed upper storey, suggests the bridge of a ship and when you step inside the resemblance is even stronger. The Dry Dock its meeting place

McNally's Inn, Castledawson, Co Londonderry

Tel: 028 7965 0095 A small, unpretentious modern country inn well known to golfers and others for its traditional Irish welcome. The extensive menu runs from light snacks to three-course meals. Regular live music sessions.   922

The 5 Corners Inn, Ballymena, Co Antrim

Tel: 028 9332 2657 Fax: 028 9334 9769 A white stone building that's easy to spot. The spacious bedrooms are all en suite. All the usual golfing services are offered. 806

Royal Portrush

Royal Portrush, Bushmills Road, Portrush, Co Antrim, BT56 8QJ

Tel: 028 7082 2311

On discovering, almost incidentally, that Tommy Armour played in the 1919 Irish Amateur Open Championship at Royal Portrush, it is difficult not to be impressed. The fact is that most of the

world's great players, men and women, have savoured the delights of this superb links for more than 100 years.

Founded in 1888, it was known simply as the County Club. Four years later, royal patronage elevated it to the Royal County GC and in 1895 it became Royal Portrush, with the Prince of Wales, later King Edward VII, as its patron.

The championship, Dunluce Course and neighbouring Valley Course were designed by the eminent English architect, Harry Colt, in 1932. Colt indicated that the work would cost £7,000, though he would prefer to spend £10,000. In the event, the club insisted that it should cost no more than £3,200.

On being opened for play at Easter 1933, the Dunluce stretch seemed destined for greatness. And as things turned out, it was to become the only course outside England and Scotland to play host to the British Open, which was captured there by Max Faulkner in 1951.

Christy O'Connor Snr once described it as Ireland's best second-shot course. So it is ironic that it should possess arguably the toughest one-shotter in Irish golf - the 210-yard 14th, appropriately named "Calamity." In the event, the O'Connor clan had cause for celebration there in July 1999 when Christy Jnr became the first Irish winner of the British Senior Open.

Sec/Manager: Wilma Erskine

Professional: Gary McNeill

Directions: One mile from Portrush towards Bushmills off the A2

Dunluce

Type of Course: Links

Date Founded: 1888

No of Holes: 18

Length:	6772 yds (6192 mtrs)
Par:	73
SSS:	73
Green Fees:	Weekdays: £65 Weekends: £75

The Valley

Type of Course:	Links
Date Founded:	1888
No of Holes:	18
Length:	6273 yds (5736 mtrs)
Par:	70
SSS:	71
Green Fees:	Weekdays: £25 Weekends: £32

Visitors:	Welcome: Weekdays except Wed and Fri pm, Weekend restrictions, Contact Club in advance
Societies:	Welcome: Restrictions, Contact Club in advance
Facilities:	Practice Area, Golf Clubs for hire, Trolley hire, Bar, Restaurant

Accommodation, Food and Drink

Reference numbers below refer to detailed information provided in section 2

Accommodation

Antrim Arms, Ballycastle, Co Antrim
Tel: 028 2076 2284 Good food, good beer and good times in one of Ireland's oldest hostelries, dating back to 1767. The old-world feel is allied to modern comforts, and the bedrooms, all en suite, are well furnished and decorated. Restaurant open to non-residents. 803

Ashleigh House, Portstewart, Co Londonderry
Tel: 028 7083 4452 The heart of the building is a large bungalow, to which several extensions have been made to provide first-class Accommodation in six bedrooms (doubles, twins, a family room), all with en suite facilities. Lunch and dinner available by arrangement. 913

Brookhaven, Portrush, Co Antrim
Tel: 028 7082 4164 The bedrooms, 2 twin and 1 double en suite, are beautifully decorated and furnished. Spacious gardens for guests to stroll in. There is a superb choice of local golf courses - Royal Portrush is only a five-minute drive away. 802

Chris-Mull, Bushmills, Co Antrim
Tel: 028 2073 1154 En suite Bed & Breakfast Accommodation in double or single rooms. 200 yards from the A2. Visa, Mastercard

Clarmont, Portrush, Co Antrim
Tel/Fax: 028 7082 2397 All the bedrooms at this three-storey town house have en suite facilities. From the patio seating area there are super views out onto the Atlantic Ocean and Royal Portrush Golf. 804

Craig Park Country House, Bushmills, Co Antrim
Tel: 028 2073 2496 Fax: 028 2073 2479 B&B guest house with three letting bedrooms. Tvs and telephones. No smoking. 809

Fullerton Arms, Ballintoy, Co Antrim
Tel: 028 2076 9613 The 19th-century building, a little way inland from picturesque Ballintoy harbour, has been extensively renovated and modernised to house 11 en suite bedrooms, a lively bar and restaurant that's open to non-residents. 808

Galgorm, Portrush, Co Antrim
Tel: 028 7082 3787 This town house attracts many return visitors with its warm, easygoing atmosphere and excellent Accommodation: 12 en suite bedrooms. Drew is a keen golfer and can give advice about the local courses. 807

Leander House, Portrush, Co Antrim
Tel: 028 7082 2147 e-mail: leander@ni.network.com Bed & Breakfast Accommodation in a town house off Lansdowne Crescent. 8 doubles, 4 family rooms; 2 en suite.

O'Malley's Wateredge Hotel, Portstewart, Co Londonderry
Tel: 028 7083 3314 Fax: 028 7083 2224 O'Malley's Edgewater Hotel is situated on the Strand Beach, a perfect vantage point for enjoying views of the Donegal Hills and the Atlantic Ocean. The hotel has 28 bedrooms, all with en suite bathrooms. 911

Shanleigh House, Ballymena, Co Antrim
Tel/Fax: 028 2564 4851 B&B in four bedrooms; 2 double, 1 twin, 1 family. En suite available. A warm welcome awaits all guests. No credit cards - travellers cheques only. Very close to Galgorm Castle.

The Anchorage Inn, Portstewart, Co Londonderry
Tel: 028 7083 4401 Fax: 028 7083 4508 Twenty double bedrooms, all with en suite facilities. The inn incorporates Skippers Bar and Restaurant, where seafood is a speciality. Transport can be arranged to and from the golf courses. 914

Food and Drink

Antrim Arms, Ballycastle, Co Antrim
Tel: 028 2076 2284 Good food, good beer and good times in one of Ireland's oldest hostelries, dating back to 1767. The old-world feel is allied to modern comforts, and the bedrooms, all en suite, are well furnished and decorated. Restaurant open to non-residents. 803

Fullerton Arms, Ballintoy, Co Antrim
Tel: 028 2076 9613 The 19th-century building, a little way inland from picturesque Ballintoy harbour, has been extensively renovated and modernised to house 11 en suite bedrooms, a lively bar and restaurant that's open to non-residents. 808

O'Malley's Wateredge Hotel, Portstewart, Co Londonderry
Tel: 028 7083 3314 Fax: 028 7083 2224 O'Malley's Edgewater Hotel is situated on the Strand Beach, a perfect vantage point for enjoying views of the Donegal Hills and the Atlantic Ocean. The hotel has 28 bedrooms, all with en suite bathrooms. 911

The Anchorage Inn, Portstewart, Co Londonderry
Tel: 028 7083 4401 Fax: 028 7083 4508 Twenty double bedrooms, all with en suite facilities. The inn incorporates Skippers Bar and Restaurant, where seafood is a speciality. Transport can be arranged to and from the golf courses. 914

Whitehead

Whitehead Golf Club, McCrea's Brae, Whitehead, Carrickfergus, BT38 9NZ
Tel: 028 9337 0820

Sec/Manager:	J. M. Niblock
Professional:	Colin Farr
Directions:	On Co Antrim Coast off the B150 between Carrickfergus and Larne
Type of Course:	Parkland
Date Founded:	1904
No of Holes:	18
Length:	6050 yds (5332 mtrs)
Par:	70
SSS:	69
Green Fees:	Weekdays: £15 Weekends and Bank Holidays: £20
Visitors:	Welcome: Monday – Friday, Not Saturday, Sunday with Member only
Societies:	Welcome: Book in advance
Facilities:	Chipping/Putting Area, Practice Area, Trolley hire, Bar, Restaurant

Accommodation, Food and Drink

Reference numbers below refer to detailed information provided in section 2

Accommodation

Manor Guest House, 23 Olderfleet Rd, The Harbour Highway, Larne, Co Antrim, BT40 1AS,
Tel: 028 2827 3305 Manor Guest House is an imposing Victorian villa to which Miss J. A. Graham has been welcoming bed and breakfast guests for almost 40 years. The house has 8 bedrooms, all en suite, one of which is a full Bridal Suite complete with 4-poster bed.

The 5 Corners Inn, Ballyclare, Co Antrim
Tel: 028 9332 2657 Fax: 028 9334 9769 A white stone building that's easy to spot. The spacious bedrooms are all en suite. All the usual golfing services are offered. 806

Food and Drink

Craigs Cellar, Craig Cellars Ltd, 15 Main Street, Larne, Co Antrim, BT40 1JQ,

Tel: 028 2827 2861 Built in 1840, the pub was originally a Manse House. Its popularity is enhanced by the atmospheric interior and by friendly and courteous staff who really do provide service with a smile.

The 5 Corners Inn, Ballyclare, Co Antrim

Tel: 028 9332 2657 Fax: 028 9334 9769 A white stone building that's easy to spot. The spacious bedrooms are all en suite. All the usual golfing services are offered. 806

The Meeting House, Cairncastle, Larne, Co Antrim

Tel: 028 2858 3252 Established in the 1700's, and currently listed as an Irish Pub of Distinction, a place to relax over a good meal complimented by a fine selection of beers, wines and spirits. Restaurant open lunch and dinner, bar food served 12-8pm.

ARMAGH

The British aristocracy had a significant impact on the development of golf in County Armagh. We see their hand at Trandragee and at Lurgan. And the location of Co Armagh GC reminds us that the famous obelisk was built to commemorate the friendship between the one-time Protestant Archbishop Richard Robinson and the Duke of Northumberland.

County Armagh's eight courses are: Ashfield, Co Armagh, Cloverhill, Edenmore, Lurgan, Portadown, Silverwood and Tandragee. Naturally, all are parkland, but Portadown is especially interesting for its location beside the River Bann. Indeed a brave line for the second shot to the

long ninth is over a bend in the river. Portadown also has an interesting history. During World War II, nine holes were given over to the growing of flax and potatoes and it wasn't until 1974 that the course was restored to 18 holes. At Tandragee, we are informed that in 1911, the Duke of Manchester brought over John Stone, the then professional at Sandy Lodge GC, to lay out a course on his estate. Green-fees were permitted and were collected by Stone, his wife and two daughters. But the present club was formally instituted in 1920.

All of which is decidedly modern in the context of Armagh's illustrious history. The city has been the spiritual capital of Ireland for 1,500 years and remains the seat of both the Protestant and Catholic Archbishops. And Brian Boru, who defeated the Danes at the Battle of Clontarf in 1014, is buried there. St Patrick's Church of Ireland Cathedral, with its squat tower, is mostly a

The Mall, Armagh City, Co Armagh

19th-century restoration around a 13th century shell. Tradition has it that this was where St Patrick established his church in the fifth century on what he described as "my sweet hill." The celebrated English writer, William Makepeace Thackeray, admired the new building when he passed that way in 1842 and he especially liked the monuments by Roubiliac, Chantrey, Rysbrack and Nollekens. Among his observations was: "It wants a hundred years at least to cool the raw colours of the stones, and to dull the brightness of the gilding, all which benefits, no doubt, time will bring to pass ..."

The Archbishop Robinson to whom we referred in connection with the Co Armagh GC, built the famous Armagh Observatory. And in 1771, he also founded the cathedral library which contains a copy of Jonathan Swift's "Gulliver's Travels", corrected by the author's own hand. On the opposite hill is the twin-spired Catholic Cathedral, also named after St Patrick and for which the foundation stone was laid in 1840. J J McCarthy, who also designed St Macartan's Cathedral in Monaghan, was responsible for the Gothic design and graceful spires, but another architect and three bishops laboured over it before the building was finally dedicated in 1873. Archbishop Crolly, who laid the foundation stone, died during the Great Famine and it was left to Dr Dixon and

The Navan Centre, Armagh

Dr McGettigan to see the task through to a conclusion. The first Catholic Archbishop of Armagh to be appointed a cardinal was Michael Logue, whose hand can be seen in the beautiful Italianate interior decoration. Just off the city's Mall is the Planetarium and Eartharium, in the grounds of the Observatory on College Hill. The Planetarium features star shows in a domed theatre, a full-scale mock-up of the Gemini spacecraft and original equipment used by US astronauts. For its part, the Eartharium gives a global view of the planet and includesda multi-media encyclopaedia of earth and space facts. The complex also included an astro park.

Two miles west of Armagh City is the great mound of Navan Fort, stronghold of the kings of Ulster since 700 BC. It occupies a key place in Heroic Age legend, notably in tales about Cuchulain, who is mentioned in the Down chapter of this book as possibly Ireland's first golfer. Through the use of dynamic audio-visual techniques, the Navan Centre transports the visitor into the past, which is scientifically interpreted by experts. And visitors are urged not to depart the Centre without following the track to the top of the hill which commands beautiful views of the surrounding countryside. Near the fort are the King's Stables, an artificial pool where, according to tradition, the king's horses were watered. Other sites of archaeological interest nearby include Haughey's Fort which, incidentally, is in no way connected with the former Taoiseach of the Republic of Ireland. Then there is an iron-age ring fort and Loughnashade, a lake where ritualistic deposits were found.

View from Slieve Gullion, Co Armagh

Apart from its golf, its rugby players and Gaelic footballers, Armagh is also notable in a sporting context for its road-bowling. Indeed it is remarkable that the only two counties in which this particular activity survives are itself and Cork, which are on either side of the Border and separated by 250 miles. It is played in leafy lanes where competitors send a metal bowl, weighing one-and-threequarter pounds, hurtling along the tarmac, cutting corners and flying over hedges. The objective is to get from one place to another in the fewest number of shots. Just like golf, you might say.

Location of Golf Courses

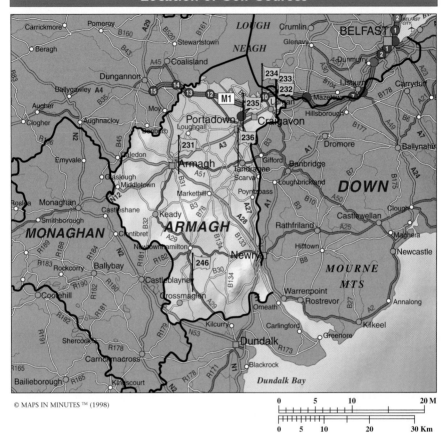

© MAPS IN MINUTES ™ (1998)

Ashfield

Ashfield Golf Club, Freeduff, Cullyhanna, Co Armagh

Tel: 028 3086 8180

Sec/Manager:	James & Elizabeth Quinn
Professional:	Erill Maney
Directions:	2 miles North East of Crossmaglen off the B30
Type of Course:	Parkland
Date Founded:	1990
No of Holes:	18
Length:	5616 yds (5135 Mtrs)
Par:	69
SSS:	70
Green Fees:	Weekdays: £10 Weekends & Bank Holidays: £12
Visitors:	Welcome: Ring in advance
Societies:	Welcome: **Book in advance**
Facilities:	Chipping/Putting Area, Practice Area, Driving Range, Golf Clubs for hire, Trolley hire, Electric Buggy hire, Bar, Restaurant, Caddy service by arrangement

Accommodation, Food and Drink

Reference numbers below refer to detailed information provided in section 2

Accommodation

Arradale House, Carrickmacross, Co Monaghan

Tel: 042 9661941 Ten en suite bedrooms for full or part board Accommodation on a working farm in a beautiful setting of woods and lakes. 461

The Heritage, Dundalk, Co Louth

Tel: 042 9335850 Keen golfers run this B&B house in a rural setting 1½ miles from Dundalk. Five letting bedrooms, 3 en suite. 401

Village Inn & Buttery, 103-105 Main Street, Markethill, Co Armagh, BT6 1PJ,

Tel: 028 3755 1237 The Village Inn is a popular venue where locals and visitors alike savour the welcoming atmosphere of a traditional Irish inn. Based on local produce, the menu offers a wide choice of high class food.

Food and Drink

Seven Stars Restaurant, Loughbrickland, Co Down

Tel: 028 4062 6461 A bright, cheerful bar-restaurant serving a good range of dishes from 11.30 to 7.30. Just off the main A1. 833

The Kilbroney Bar and Restaurant, Rostrevor, Co Down

Tel: 028 4173 8390 Town-centre restaurant, bar and beer garden. Food is served all day, every day from an à la carte menu. 830

Yellow Door, 2 Bridge Street, Gilford, Co Armagh, BT63 6EP,

Tel: 028 3883 1543 The Yellow Door restaurant has two dining-rooms - the larger one non-smoking Menus are always based on fresh local produce.

County Armagh

County Armagh, The Demense, Newry Road, Armagh, BT10 1EN

Tel: 028 3752 5861

It's not many clubs who can boast a visit by a Russian chess grandmaster. But Co Armagh suc-

ceeded in getting Victor Korchnoi to play simultaneous chess matches against three club representatives in 1982.

Needless to remark, he polished them off with no great difficulty. Still, the club benefited significantly from the attendant publicity at a time when they had endured severe hardship, stemming from a terrorist fire-bomb attack which destroyed the old clubhouse on March 25th 1980.

A measure of the members' resilience, however, was that a new clubhouse was built and operational by Christmas of the following year. And it was formally opened in May 1982 by the then president of the GUI, Fred Perry.

Founded in 1883, Co Armagh is one of Ireland's oldest clubs. Originally a nine-hole stretch, which, we are informed was unplayable during the summer "owing to the length of the grass," it was extended to its present 18-holes in 1975. A year later, Christy O'Connor Snr played an exhibition there, when he had to give best to the recently-appointed professional, Billy Todd, who had a one-under-par 68.

The layout is dominated by the Obelisk, situated between the 10th and 13th greens. This dates back to 1783 when it was built by the protestant Archbishop of Armagh, Dr Richard Robinson, to mark the friendship with his patron, the Duke of Northumberland. It stands 114 feet and, we are informed, was built of the same stone used for the episcopal palace in 1770.

Sec/Manager:	June McParland
Professional:	Alan Rankin
Directions:	¼ mile from the City Centre Off the A28 to Newry
Type of Course:	Parkland
Date Founded:	1893
No of Holes:	18

Length:	6212 yds (5680 Mtrs)
Par:	70
SSS:	69
Green Fees:	Weekdays: £15 Weekends: £20
Visitors:	Welcome: Monday, Tuesday and Friday, Check weekend availability direct with club, Ring to book.
Societies:	Welcome: Contact club in advance
Facilities:	Chipping/Putting Area, Practice Area, Golf Clubs for hire, Trolley hire, Bar, Restaurant

Accommodation, Food and Drink

Reference numbers below refer to detailed information provided in section 2

Accommodation

Muleany House, Moy, Dungannon, Co Tyrone

Tel: 028 8778 4183 Family-run, family-friendly home from home with nine en suite bedrooms, drawing room, tv room, games room and traditional home cooking. 890

Ni Eoghain Lodge, 32 Ennislare Rd, Armagh, Co Armagh, BT60 2AX,

Tel: 028 3752 5633 Set in the heart of the countryside, just 5 minutes from the centre of Armagh City, Ni Eoghain Lodge offers visitors a choice of either bed and breakfast or self-catering Accommodation. All the rooms are en suite.

The Ryandale, Moy, Co Tyrone

Tel/Fax: 028 8778 4629 A fine Listed building in the centre of a small village. The Ryandale offers en suite bedrooms, restaurant, bar and nightclub. 900

Village Inn & Buttery, 103-105 Main Street, Markethill, Co Armagh, BT6 1PJ,

Tel: 028 3755 1237 The Village Inn is a popular venue where locals and visitors alike savour the welcoming atmosphere of a traditional Irish inn. Based on local produce, the menu offers a wide choice of high class food.

Food and Drink

Chandlers Cafe, 10 Market Street, Portadown, Co Armagh, BT62 3PB,

Tel: 028 3839 2998 This stylish eatery is also a delicatessen selling a wide range of tasty delicacies. Diners are welcome to bring their own wine - there's no extra charge for corkage.

The Ryandale, Moy, Co Tyrone

Tel/Fax: 028 8778 4629 A fine Listed building in the centre of a small village. The Ryandale offers en suite bedrooms, restaurant, bar and nightclub. 900

Yellow Door, 2 Bridge Street, Gilford, Co Armagh, BT63 6EP,

Tel: 028 3883 1543 The Yellow Door restaurant has two dining-rooms - the larger one non-smoking Menus are always based on fresh local produce.

Edenmore

Edenmore, Drumnabreeze Road, Magheralin, Craigavon, Co Armagh, BT67 0RH

Tel: 028 9261 1310

Sec/Manager:	Robert McDonell
Professional:	None
Directions:	On M1 from Belfast take Moira turnoff (Junction 9). Follow A3 towards Lurgan. At Magheralin follow signposts to the course
Type of Course:	Parkland
Date Founded:	1992
No of Holes:	18
Length:	6244 yds (5709 Mtrs)
Par:	71
SSS:	70

Green Fees:	Monday – Thursday: £12 Friday: £13 Weekends & Bank Holidays: £15
Visitors:	Welcome: Any time except Saturday am
Societies:	Welcome: Any time except Saturday am, Book in advance
Facilities:	Chipping/Putting Area, Practice Area, Golf Clubs for hire, Trolley hire, Restaurant

Accommodation, Food and Drink

Reference numbers below refer to detailed information provided in section 2

Accommodation

McGirr's, Coalisland, Co Tyrone

Tel: 028 8774 7324 A large pub with 12 rooms for budget Bed & Breakfast Accommodation, a no-frills bar, lounge and off licence. 892

Oakfield Guest House, 9 Crumlin Road, Lower Ballinderry, Lisburn, Co Antrim, BT28 2JU,

Tel: 028 9265 1307 Large, modernised farmhouse is surrounded by well-presented gardens, with plenty of parking space, and has 4 guest bedrooms, all en suite. Convenient for the disabled.

Win - Staff House, 45 Banbridge Rd, Dromore, Co Down, BT25 1NE,

Tel: 028 9269 2252 Surrounded by spacious gardens, (complete with a barbecue area), Win-Staff House enjoys a well-deserved reputation for friendliness, hospitality, excellent cuisine and comfortable, relaxing Accommodation. Evening meals are available on request.

Food and Drink

Maghaberry Arms, 23 Maghaberry Rd, Moira, Craigavon, Co Armagh, BT67 0JF,

Tel: 028 9261 1852 The Maghaberry Arms is a large imposing building which has been recently renovated to the very highest standard - a free house where the craic is good, the food appetising and very good value for money.

McGirr's, Coalisland, Co Tyrone

Tel: 028 8774 7324 A large pub with 12 rooms for budget Bed & Breakfast Accommodation, a no-frills bar, lounge and off licence. 892

Yellow Door, 2 Bridge Street, Gilford, Co Armagh, BT63 6EP,

Tel: 028 3883 1543 The Yellow Door restaurant has two dining-rooms - the larger one non-smoking Menus are always based on fresh local produce.

Lurgan

Lurgan, The Demense, Lurgan, BT67 9BN

Tel: 028 3832 2087

Sec/Manager:	Mrs Gail Turkington
Professional:	Des Paul
Directions:	Short distance from Town Centre close to the Castle
Type of Course:	Parkland
Date Founded:	1893
No of Holes:	18
Length:	6257 yds (5721 Mtrs)
Par:	70
SSS:	70
Green Fees:	Weekdays: £15 Weekends: £20
Visitors:	Welcome: Mon, Thu & Fri, 50% disc. with member.
Societies:	Welcome: Book in advance
Facilities:	Chipping/Putting Area, Practice Area, Trolley hire, Bar, Restaurant.

Accommodation, Food and Drink

Reference numbers below refer to detailed information provided in section 2

Accommodation

Ivanhoe, 10 Valley Lane, Waringstown, Craigavon, Co Armagh, BT66 7SR,

Tel: 028 3888 1287 This inviting house is set in quiet, peaceful surroundings facing a wood. There are 3 spacious guest bedrooms, (2 doubles and 1 twin.

Ni Eoghain Lodge, 32 Ennislare Rd, Armagh, Co Armagh, BT60 2AX,

Tel: 028 3752 5633 Set in the heart of the countryside, just 5 minutes from the centre of Armagh City, Ni Eoghain Lodge offers visitors a choice of either bed and breakfast or self-catering Accommodation. All the rooms are en suite.

Win - Staff House, 45 Banbridge Rd, Dromore, Co Down, BT25 1NE,

Tel: 028 9269 2252 Surrounded by spacious gardens, (complete with a barbecue area), Win-Staff House enjoys a well-deserved reputation for friendliness, hospitality, excellent cuisine and comfortable, relaxing Accommodation. Evening meals are available on request.

Food and Drink

Chandlers Cafe, 10 Market Street, Portadown, Co Armagh, BT62 3PB,

Tel: 028 3839 2998 This stylish eatery is also a delicatessen selling a wide range of tasty delicacies. Diners are welcome to bring their own wine - there's no extra charge for corkage.

Maghaberry Arms, 23 Maghaberry Rd, Moira, Craigavon, Co Armagh, BT67 0JF,

Tel: 028 9261 1852 The Maghaberry Arms is a large imposing building which has been recently renovated to the very highest standard - a free house where the craic is good, the food appetising and very good value for money.

Yellow Door, 2 Bridge Street, Gilford, Co Armagh, BT63 6EP,

Tel: 028 3883 1543 The Yellow Door restaurant has two dining-rooms - the larger one non-smoking Menus are always based on fresh local produce.

Portadown

Portadown, 192 Gilford Road, Portadown, Co Armagh, BT63 5LF

Tel: 028 3835 5356

Sec/Manager:	Mrs Lily Holloway
Professional:	Paul Stevenson
Directions:	2 miles South East of Portadown off the A50 road to Gilford
Type of Course:	Parkland
Date Founded:	1900
No of Holes:	18
Length:	6147 yds (5621 Mtrs)
Par:	70
SSS:	70
Green Fees:	Weekdays: £17 Weekends and Bank Holidays: £22
Visitors:	Welcome: Not Tuesday or Saturday
Societies:	Welcome: Not Tuesday or Saturday, Book in advance
Facilities:	Practice Area, Golf Clubs for hire, Trolley hire, Bar, Restaurant

Accommodation, Food and Drink

Reference numbers below refer to detailed information provided in section 2

Accommodation

Caldhame House, Nutts Corner, Crumlin, Co Antrim

Tel/Fax: 028 9442 2378 A splendid guest house just minutes from Belfast International Airport. All rooms en suite, with tv.   800

Ivanhoe, 10 Valley Lane, Waringstown, Craigavon, Co Armagh, BT66 7SR,

Tel: 028 3888 1287 This inviting house is set in quiet, peaceful surroundings facing a wood. There are 3 spacious guest bedrooms, (2 doubles and 1 twin.

Oakfield Guest House, 9 Crumlin Road, Lower Ballinderry, Lisburn, Co Antrim, BT28 2JU,

Tel: 028 9265 1307 Large, modernised farmhouse is surrounded by well-presented gardens, with plenty of parking space, and has 4 guest bedrooms, all en suite. Convenient for the disabled.

Food and Drink

Chandlers Cafe, 10 Market Street, Portadown, Co Armagh, BT62 3PB,

Tel: 028 3839 2998 This stylish eatery is also a delicatessen selling a wide range of tasty delicacies. Diners are welcome to bring their own wine - there's no extra charge for corkage.

Maghaberry Arms, 23 Maghaberry Rd, Moira, Craigavon, Co Armagh, BT67 0JF,

Tel: 028 9261 1852 The Maghaberry Arms is a large imposing building which has been recently renovated to the very highest standard - a free house where the craic is good, the food appetising and very good value for money.

Yellow Door, 2 Bridge Street, Gilford, Co Armagh, BT63 6EP,

Tel: 028 3883 1543 The Yellow Door restaurant has two dining-rooms - the larger one non-smoking Menus are always based on fresh local produce.

Silverwood

Silverwood Golf & Ski Centre, Tormoyra Lane, Silverwood, Lurgan, BT66 6NG

Tel: 028 3832 6606

Sec/Manager:	Geoff Coupland
Professional:	Dave Paul
Directions:	Close to roundabout at Junctin 10 off M1
Type of Course:	Woodland & Parkland with lakes
Date Founded:	1984
No of Holes:	18
Length:	6496 yds (5939 Mtrs)
Par:	72
SSS:	72
Green Fees:	Weekdays: £12 Weekends and Bank Holidays: £15
Visitors:	Welcome: Not Saturday
Societies:	Welcome: Not Saturday, Book in advance
Facilities:	Chipping/Putting Area, Practice Area, Driving Range, Golf Clubs for hire, Trolley hire, Restaurant

Accommodation, Food and Drink

Reference numbers below refer to detailed information provided in section 2

Accommodation

Glengannon Hotel, Dungannon, Co Tyrone

Tel/Fax: 028 8772 7311 En suite bedrooms, good choice of menus and weekend live entertainment in a low-rise modern hotel off the M1 (J15).   897

McGirr's, Coalisland, Co Tyrone

Tel: 028 8774 7324 A large pub with 12 rooms for budget Bed & Breakfast

Accommodation, a no-frills bar, lounge and off licence.   892

Muleany House, Moy, Dungannon, Co Tyrone

Tel: 028 8778 4183 Family-run, family-friendly home from home with nine en suite bedrooms, drawing room, tv room, games room and traditional home cooking.   890

Oaklin House Hotel, Dungannon, Co Tyrone

Tel: 028 8772 5151 A fine modern hotel set in extensive grounds, with superbly appointed en suite bedrooms, and a choice of restaurants and bars.   902

Reahs, Dungannon, Co Tyrone

Tel: 028 8772 5575 Top-class food and luxurious overnight accomodation in a smart detached house half a mile out of town.   891

The Ryandale, Moy, Co Tyrone

Tel/Fax: 028 8778 4629 A fine Listed building in the centre of a small village. The Ryandale offers en suite bedrooms, restaurant, bar and nightclub.   900

Food and Drink

Glengannon Hotel, Dungannon, Co Tyrone

Tel/Fax: 028 8772 7311 En suite bedrooms, good choice of menus and weekend live entertainment in a low-rise modern hotel off the M1 (J15).   897

McGirr's, Coalisland, Co Tyrone

Tel: 028 8774 7324 A large pub with 12 rooms for budget Bed & Breakfast Accommodation, a no-frills bar, lounge and off licence.   892

Oaklin House Hotel, Dungannon, Co Tyrone

Tel: 028 877 25151 A fine modern hotel set in extensive grounds, with superbly appointed en suite bedrooms, and a choice of restaurants and bars.   902

Reahs, Dungannon, Co Tyrone

Tel: 028 8772 5575 Top-class food and luxurious overnight accomodation in a smart detached house half a mile out of town.   891

The Ryandale, Moy, Co Tyrone

Tel/Fax: 028 8778 4629 A fine Listed building in the centre of a small village. The Ryandale offers en suite bedrooms, restaurant, bar and nightclub.   900

Ni Eoghain Lodge, 32 Ennislare Rd, Armagh, Co Armagh, BT60 2AX,

Tel: 028 3752 5633 Set in the heart of the countryside, just 5 minutes from the centre of Armagh City, Ni Eoghain Lodge offers visitors a choice of either bed and breakfast or self-catering Accommodation. All the rooms are en suite.

Village Inn & Buttery, 103-105 Main Street, Markethill, Co Armagh, BT6 1PJ,

Tel: 028 3755 1237 The Village Inn is a popular venue where locals and visitors alike savour the welcoming atmosphere of a traditional Irish inn. Based on local produce, the menu offers a wide choice of high class food.

Food and Drink

Chandlers Cafe, 10 Market Street, Portadown, Co Armagh, BT62 3PB,

Tel: 028 3839 2998 This stylish eatery is also a delicatessen selling a wide range of tasty delicacies. Diners are welcome to bring their own wine - there's no extra charge for corkage.

Maghaberry Arms, 23 Maghaberry Rd, Moira, Craigavon, Co Armagh, BT67 0JF,

Tel: 028 9261 1852 The Maghaberry Arms is a large imposing building which has been recently renovated to the very highest standard - a free house where the craic is good, the food appetising and very good value for money.

Seven Stars Restaurant, Loughbrickland, Co Down

Tel: 028 4062 6461 A bright, cheerful bar-restaurant serving a good range of dishes from 11.30 to 7.30. Just off the main A1.   833

Yellow Door, 2 Bridge Street, Gilford, Co Armagh, BT63 6EP,

Tel: 028 3883 1543 The Yellow Door restaurant has two dining-rooms - the larger one non-smoking Menus are always based on fresh local produce.

Tandragee

Tandragee, Markethill Road, Tandragee, BT62 2ER

Tel: 028 3884 1272

Sec/Manager:	David Clayton
Professional:	Paul Stevenson
Directions:	1 mile South West of Trandragee off the B3
Type of Course:	Parkland
Date Founded:	1920
No of Holes:	18
Length:	6112 yds (5589 Mtrs)
Par:	71
SSS:	70
Green Fees:	Weekdays: £15 Weekends & Bank Holidays: £20
Visitors:	Welcome: Book in Advance
Societies:	Welcome: Book in Advance
Facilities:	Chipping/Putting Area, Practice Area, Golf Clubs for hire, Trolley hire, Bar, Restaurant

Accommodation, Food and Drink

Reference numbers below refer to detailed information provided in section 2

Accommodation

Ivanhoe, 10 Valley Lane, Waringstown, Craigavon, Co Armagh, BT66 7SR,

Tel: 028 3888 1287 This inviting house is set in quiet, peaceful surroundings facing a wood. There are 3 spacious guest bedrooms, (2 doubles and 1 twin.

BELFAST

Before Northern Ireland was racked by the so-called Troubles, Belfast had established a proud foothold on the international stage of professional tournament golf. It happened through the Gallaher Ulster Open, which brought Europe's leading players to Shandon Park over a period of six years. The inaugural winner in 1965 was Ryder Cup representative Bernard Hunt and he was followed, almost inevitably, by Christy O'Connor Snr. Then came another victory by Hunt in 1967 before O'Connor hit back by winning two in a row. Sadly, the tournament was discontinued after Tommy Horton won its last staging in 1971. By then, it had moved from its regular home at Shandon to the Dunmurry area where competitors savoured the special appeal of Malone GC.

Indications of a return to happier times, came in 1995 when the Dublin-based Smurfit organisation decided to bring the Irish Professional Championship to Belvoir Park (pronounced beaver). There at Newtownbreda, on a lay-out largely unchanged from the splendid, original design by Harry Colt, Philip Walton captured the title in a thrilling battle with fellow Dubliner, Paul McGinley. From the patio of Belvoir's imposing clubhouse, the green fingers of Colt's fairways fan out like pastoral avenues, while on the right can be seen the twin cranes of the Harland and Wolff shipyard, whose workers gave the P&O liner "Canberra" to the world, along with the ill-fated "Titanic."

Shandon, situated in the eastern suburbs of the city, has an enviable reputation for its lush parkland on which the 453-yard, par-four sixth, is a very worthy index one. It is also envied for the competitive qualities of its category-one members, who have established a wonderful record in national, inter-club competitions. Malone holds the distinction of having had its original course

Donegal Place, Belfast

laid out on a former popo field in 1895. Its most recent move to the Ballydrain Estate in 1962, however, brings it to within only four miles of the centre of Belfast. With 27 holes, it is the most richly-endowed of the city's courses which include nine-hole stretches at Cliftonville, Gilnahirk and Ormeau.

In all, Belfast has 11 courses, all of them parkland: They are: Balmoral, Belvoir Park, Cliftonville, Dunmurry, Fortwilliam, Gilnahirk, Knock, Malone, Mount Ober, Ormeau and Shandon Park. Interestingly, they don't include Royal Belfast, which is actually situated on the shores of Belfast Lough at Holywood, Co Down, but its very name almost demands that it be included in such a list. The wonderful hospitality one experiences in Belfast, could have something to do with the long years of suffering, endured by its inhabitants. Either way, the visitor is always made welcome, whether on its golfing terrain at the many other attractions within its ring of high hills, sea lough and river valley. Its population of almost half a million is about a third of the entire population of the province. And from being the focal point of Ulster's industrial revolution, it has been transformed into pleasantly pedestrianised areas where one can sit on benches, listening to street musicians.

The City Hall, dating back to 1903, dominates the main shopping area and could be mistaken for one of those imposing buildings in Washington DC, but for the big statue of Queen

Victoria at the front. She visited Belfast in 1849 and was clearly held in high esteem by the citizens, given that they named a hospital, a university, a park, a man-made island and several streets after her. Indeed Queen's University was built during the year of her visit and its area is dull of charming Edwardian terraces, fronted by magnolia trees. The university was designed by Charles Lanyon who was also responsible for other fine buildings in the Belfast area.

The southern part of the city is noted for its moderately-priced restaurants, pubs and accommodation, for shopping and threatre and for the Ulster Museum. And the citizens are justifiably proud of the Waterfront Hall, arguably the finest concert venue in Ireland. With the election of a new Northern Ireland assembly, the imposing, former parliament building of Stormont, five miles from the city, takes on fresh historical importance. Meanwhile, 10 miles south of Belfast is Hillsborough, one of Ulster's most delightful, small towns, whose castle will be familiar to television viewers as the focal point of political talks en route to the peace process. The town grew up around a fort built by Colonel Arthur Hill in 1650, to command the road from Dublin to Carrickfergus. We are told that the first member of the Hill family arrived in Ireland as an officer in the army of the Earl of Essex, who was sent by Queen Elizabeth I to subdue the rebellious

Belfast City Hall

O'Neill. As it happened, he stayed on and married the sister of Sorley Boy MacDonnell. From the ramparts of the fort which was remodelled in the 18th century, there are views over the park's artificial lake and across to the absolutely delightful parish church, framed by trees. Among other things, the church is notable for its stained glass windows by Joshua Reynolds and its two, magnificent, 18th century organs. Hamilton Harty (1879-1941), who was born in Hillsborough where his father was church organist for 40 years, earned the sobriquet of "The Irish Toscanini" because of his brilliance in interpreting and arranging native music. Appropriately, he is buried in the church graveyard.

Then there is the town of Carrickfergus, which thrived while Belfast was still a sandbank. In 1180, the Norman, John de Courcy, built a massive keep at Carrickfergus to guard the approach to Belfast Lough and this is now acknowledged as having been the first real Irish castle. Interestingly, when Gaelic was still the common language of Ulster in the early 17th century, Carrickfergus was the only area of the province where English was spoken. The parents of 19th century American president, Andrew Jackson, emigrated from Carrickfergus in 1765, a fact which is commemorated at the Andrew Jackson Centre, a thatched cottage close to the original home. And Jonathan Swift, author of "Gulliver's Travels" was prebendary of a church nearby.

International tournament golf returned to Belfast in 1992, with the staging of the Belfast Telegraph Irish Senior Masters at Malone. South African John Fourie took the inaugural title and was succeeded in 1993 by compatriot Gary Player. But after Tommy Horton won in 1994, the tournament was discontinued, just as happened in 1971, when he won the last staging of the Gallaher Ulster Open. If such an event were to be revived in Belfast, it is clearly unthinkable that Horton should be banned from competing. Given the Channel Islander's unfortunate record, however, the organisers might consider asking him to play under an assumed name!

Location of Golf Courses

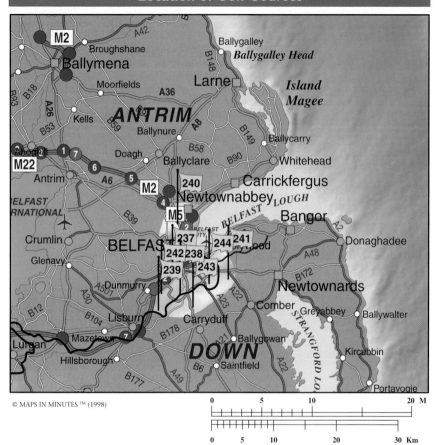

© MAPS IN MINUTES ™ (1998)

Balmoral

Balmoral, 518 Lisburn Road, Belfast, BT9 6GX

Tel: 028 9038 1514

Sec/Manager:	Robert McConkey
Professional:	Geoff Bleakley
Directions:	2 miles South of Belfast City Centre off Lisburn Rd next to Kings Hall
Type of Course:	Parkland
Date Founded:	1914
No of Holes:	18
Length:	6598 yds (6033 mtrs)
Par:	69
SSS:	70
Green Fees:	Weekdays: £20 Weekends and Bank Holidays: £30
Visitors:	Welcome: Any Day but Saturday, Book in Advance
Societies:	Welcome: Monday to Friday: Sundays before 9.00am, Contact Club for details
Facilities:	Practice Area, Golf Clubs for hire, Trolley hire, Bar, Restaurant

Accommodation, Food and Drink

Reference numbers below refer to detailed information provided in section 2

Accommodation

Carnwood Country House, 85 Victoria Rd, Holywood, Co Armagh, BT18 9BG,

Tel: 028 9042 1745 Approached by a long driveway lined with rare species of trees, Carnwood House enjoys a tranquil environment despite being conveniently located for Belfast and the local City Airport. The 4 bedrooms include the Country Suite with 4-poster bed.

Tara Guest House, 51 Princetown Rd, Bangor, Co Down, BT20 3TA,

Tel: 028 9146 8924 The Tara has 10 comfortable guest bedrooms, all of them en suite and all furnished to a high standard. An evening meal is available.

The 5 Corners Inn, Ballyclare, Co Antrim

Tel: 028 9332 2657 Fax: 028 9334 9769 A white stone building that's easy to spot. The spacious bedrooms are all en suite. All the usual golfing services are offered. 806

Food and Drink

Motte 'n' Bailey, 131-3 Kingsway, Dunmurry, Co Antrim

Tel: 028 9060 3790 A round tower look for this establishment with three bars, one serving as a restaurant: pub grub plus à la carte menu.

The 5 Corners Inn, Ballyclare, Co Antrim

Tel: 028 9332 2657 Fax: 028 9334 9769 A white stone building that's easy to spot. The spacious bedrooms are all en suite. All the usual golfing services are offered. 806

The Old Cross Inn, Newtownards, Co Down

Tel: 028 9182 0212 The oldest pub-restaurant in town, and one of the best in the region. Food served lunch and dinner & all day Sunday till 7.30. 832

Belvoir Park

Belvoir Park, 73 Church Road,

Newtownbreda, Belfast, BT8 7AN

Tel: 028 9049 1693

Nothing could have compensated for the disappointment of Royal St George's. Still, the pain of Harry Bradshaw's 1949 British Open defeat by Bobby Locke, was eased considerably by victory over his South African rival for the Irish Open title the following week.

The venue was Belvoir Park, which illustrates just how adaptable Harry Colt's design skills were to both links and parkland terrain. Indeed a measure of Colt's success at the Belfast venue that it remains one of the best courses of its kind, North or South.

Further, memorable exploits were witnessed there in 1953, when Scotland's Eric Brown had a hole-in-one at the short 16th en route to victory in the Irish Open. And even with the advances of modern golf equipment, Philip Walton found it to be no less challenging when he won the Irish Professional Championship there in 1995, with an aggregate of 273, one stroke more than Brown.

Belvoir (pronounced beaver) is classic parkland, but unlike the West Course at Wentworth, which is another of Colt's great designs, it has two loops of nine, both of which are similarly difficult. But inevitably, the toughness of the finishing holes increases the challenge of protecting a score.

All holes are strong, even by today's standards. The 16th is a formidable, 204-yard par three; the 17th is an undulating, 449-yard par four, while on the 18th, a 397-yard dog-leg to the right, the drive must be precise if the approach is not to be blocked by trees.

Sec/Manager:	Brian Campbell
Professional:	Maurice Kelly
Directions:	4 miles South of Belfast City Centre off Newcastle Road
Type of Course:	Parkland

Date Founded:	1927
No of Holes:	18
Length:	7082 yds (6476 mtrs)
Par:	71
SSS:	71
Green Fees:	Weekdays: £33 Weekends, Wednesdays and Bank Holidays £38
Visitors:	Welcome: Book in advance
Societies:	Welcome: Contact Club in writing in advance
Facilities:	Practice Area, Golf Clubs for hire, Trolley hire, Bar, Restaurant

Accommodation, Food and Drink

Reference numbers below refer to detailed information provided in section 2

Accommodation

Carnwood Country House, 85 Victoria Rd, Holywood, Co Armagh, BT18 9BG,

Tel: 028 9042 1745 Approached by a long driveway lined with rare species of trees, Carnwood House enjoys a tranquil environment despite being conveniently located for Belfast and the local City Airport. The 4 bedrooms include the Country Suite with 4-poster bed.

Oakfield Guest House, 9 Crumlin Road, Lower Ballinderry, Lisburn, Co Antrim, BT28 2JU

Tel: 028 9265 1307 Large, modernised farmhouse is surrounded by well-presented gardens, with plenty of parking space, and has 4 guest bedrooms, all en suite. Convenient for the disabled.

Tara Guest House, 51 Princetown Rd, Bangor, Co Down, BT20 3TA,

Tel: 028 9146 8924 The Tara has 10 comfortable guest bedrooms, all of them en suite and all furnished to a high standard. An evening meal is available.

Food and Drink

Motte 'n' Bailey, 131-3 Kingsway, Dunmurry, Co Antrim

Tel: 028 9060 3790 A round tower look for this establishment with three bars, one serving as a restaurant: pub grub plus à la carte menu.

The Old Cross Inn, Newtownards, Co Down

Tel: 028 9182 0212 The oldest pub-restaurant in town, and one of the best in the region. Food served lunch and dinner & all day Sunday till 7.30.   832

The Primrose Bar, Ballynahinch, Co Down

Tel: 028 9756 3177 Fax: 028 9756 5954 Bar and restaurant on the main street of town. Local ales, worldwide wines, bar menu and various restaurant menus.   837

Dunmurry

Dunmurry Golf Club, 91 Dunmurry Lane, Dunmurry, Belfast BT17 9JS

Tel: 028 9061 0834

Sec/Manager:	Ian McBride
Professional:	John Dolan
Directions:	Between Upper Malone Rd. and Lisburn Rd off the B103
Type of Course:	Parkland
Date Founded:	1905
No of Holes:	18
Length:	5832 yds (5332 mtrs)
Par:	69
SSS:	69
Green Fees:	Weekdays: £17 Weekends: £26.50
Visitors:	Welcome: Riong in advance

| Societies: | Welcome: Contact Club in writing in advance |
| Facilities: | Chipping/Putting Area, Practice Area, Golf Clubs for hire, Trolley hire, Bar, Restaurant |

Accommodation, Food and Drink

Reference numbers below refer to detailed information provided in section 2

Accommodation

Bushymead Country House, 86 Drumaness Rd, Ballynahinch, Co Down, BT24 8LT,

Tel: 028 9756 1171 The house stands in spacious grounds with extensive gardens, a children's play area, barbecue site and a large pond. The house has 8 attractively furnished guest bedrooms, 7 of them en suite.

Caldhame House, Nutts Corner, Crumlin, Co Antrim

Tel/Fax: 028 9442 2378 A splendid guest house just minutes from Belfast International Airport. All rooms en suite, with tv.   800

Oakfield Guest House, 9 Crumlin Road, Lower Ballinderry, Lisburn, Co Antrim, BT28 2JU

Tel: 028 9265 1307 Large, modernised farmhouse is surrounded by well-presented gardens, with plenty of parking space, and has 4 guest bedrooms, all en suite. Convenient for the disabled.

Food and Drink

Maghaberry Arms, 23 Maghaberry Rd, Moira, Craigavon, Co Armagh, BT67 0JF,

Tel: 028 9261 1852 The Maghaberry Arms is a large imposing building which has been recently renovated to the very highest standard - a free house where the craic is good, the food appetising and very good value for money.

Motte 'n' Bailey, 131-3 Kingsway, Dunmurry, Co Antrim

Tel: 028 9060 3790 A round tower look for this establishment with three bars, one serving as a restaurant: pub grub plus à la carte menu.

The Primrose Bar, Ballynahinch, Co Down

Tel: 028 9756 3177 Fax: 028 9756 5954 Bar and restaurant on the main street of town. Local ales, worldwide wines, bar menu and various restaurant menus.   837

Fortwilliam

Fortwilliam, Downview Avenue, Belfast BT15 4EZ

Tel: 028 9037 0770

Sec/Manager:	Michael Purdy
Professional:	Peter Hanna
Directions:	From Juntion 3 of M2 take Antrim Road south. After 1 mile turn left into Downview Avenue. Golf Course on left hand side
Type of Course:	Parkland
Date Founded:	1891
No of Holes:	18
Length:	5973 yds (5461 mtrs)
Par:	70
SSS:	69
Green Fees:	Weekdays: £21 Weekends & Bank Holidays: £28
Visitors:	Welcome: Book in advance
Societies:	Welcome: Contact Club in advance
Facilities:	Chipping/Putting Area, Practice Area, Golf Clubs for hire, Trolley hire, Bar, Restaurant

Accommodation, Food and Drink

Reference numbers below refer to detailed
information provided in section 2

Accommodation

Carnwood Country House, 85 Victoria Rd, Holywood, Co
Armagh, BT18 9BG,

Tel: 028 9042 1745 Approached by a long driveway lined with rare species of trees,
Carnwood House enjoys a tranquil environment despite being conveniently located
for Belfast and the local City Airport. The 4 bedrooms include the Country Suite
with 4-poster bed.

Manor Guest House, 23 Olderfleet Rd, The Harbour Highway,
Larne, Co Antrim, BT40 1AS,

Tel: 028 2827 3305 Manor Guest House is an imposing Victorian villa to which Miss
J. A. Graham has been welcoming bed and breakfast guests for almost 40 years. The
house has 8 bedrooms, all en suite, one of which is a full Bridal Suite complete
with 4-poster bed.

The 5 Corners Inn, Ballyclare, Co Antrim

Tel: 028 9332 2657 Fax: 028 9334 9769 A white stone building that's easy to spot.
The spacious bedrooms are all en suite. All the usual golfing services are offered. 806

Food and Drink

Craigs Cellar, Craig Cellars Ltd, 15 Main Street, Larne, Co
Antrim, BT40 1JQ,

Tel: 028 2827 2861 Built in 1840, the pub was originally a Manse House. Its
popularity is enhanced by the atmospheric interior and by friendly and courteous
staff who really do provide service with a smile.

The 5 Corners Inn, Ballyclare, Co Antrim

Tel: 028 9332 2657 Fax: 028 9334 9769 A white stone building that's easy to spot.
The spacious bedrooms are all en suite. All the usual golfing services are offered. 806

The Meeting House, Cairncastle, Larne, Co Antrim

Tel: 028 2858 3252 Established in the 1700's, and currently listed as an Irish Pub
of Distinction, a place to relax over a good meal complimented by a fine selection
of beers, wines and spirits. Restaurant open lunch and dinner, bar food served 12-
8pm.

Knock

The Knock, Summerfield, Dundonald, Belfast,
BT16 0QX

Tel: 028 9048 2249

According to an issue of "The Irish Golfer" in
1900, Knock GC was formed five years previously "when the golf fever in Ulster was at its
height." And we are told that the official opening ceremony attracted the "largest gathering of
golfers ever held at a function of this kind in
Ireland."

After such a launch, success was seemed assured. And among other things, Knock can claim

credit for fine missionary work, given that their
original nine-hole course was located in the
Shandon Park estate which went on to spawn a
club of that name, in 1926.

By that stage, the Knock members had moved
to their present location of Summerfield on the
Upper Newtownards Road, where the course was
laid out by Harry Colt. Characterised by a
wonderful variety of large and small trees, the
6,435-yard layout is arguably the most demanding par 70 in Irish golf.

A measure of its quality is that Ernie Jones
captured the Irish Professional Championship
there with an aggregate of 279 and Christy
Greene won with 282, four years later. It was
also where Christy O'Connor Snr gained his first
important tournament success, by capturing the
Ulster Professional title in 1953.

At 453 yards, the sixth is one of Knock's
strongest par fours. But the hole is more notable
as the location of what is reputedly the oldest
araucaria, or monkey-puzzle tree, in these islands. Standing 72 feet and still thriving, it is
believed to have been in existence before the
club came into being.

Sec/Manager:	Mr Managh
Professional:	Gordon Fairweather
Directions:	1 mile East of Stormont off A20 to Dondonald
Type of Course:	Parkland
Date Founded:	1895
No of Holes:	18
Length:	6435 yds 5884 mtrs
Par:	70
SSS:	71
Green Fees:	Weekdays £20 Weekends & Bank Holidays £25
Visitors:	Welcome: Except Saturdays and up to 4.00pm on Wednesday
Societies:	Welcome: Mon & Thu only, Book in advance
Facilities:	Chipping/Putting Area, Practice Area, Golf Clubs for hire, Trolley hire, Bar, Restaurant, Caddy service by arrangement

Accommodation, Food and Drink

Reference numbers below refer to detailed
information provided in section 2

Accommodation

108 Seacliff Road, Bangor, Co Down

Tel: 028 9146 1077 e-mail: heathermbell@compuserve.com website: www.bandb-bangor.couk B&B with sea views. 2 singles, 1 en suite double. No smoking. No credit cards.

Carnwood Country House, 85 Victoria Rd, Holywood, Co Armagh, BT18 9BG,

Tel: 028 9042 1745 Approached by a long driveway lined with rare species of trees, Carnwood House enjoys a tranquil environment despite being conveniently located for Belfast and the local City Airport. The 4 bedrooms include the Country Suite with 4-poster bed.

Clandeboye Lodge Hotel, Bangor, Co Down

Tel: 028 9185 2500 e-mail: info@clandeboyelodge.com 3 star hotel with 43 bedrooms, all en suite. Bar and restaurant. Adjacent to Blackwood and Clandeboye golf clubs with 7 further courses within 10 minutes. 3 RAC merit awards. Consort Crown Regional Hotel of the Year 1997, 1998 & 1999

Tara Guest House, 51 Princetown Rd, Bangor, Co Down, BT20 3TA,

Tel: 028 9146 8924 The Tara has 10 comfortable guest bedrooms, all of them en suite and all furnished to a high standard. An evening meal is available.

Food and Drink

Clandeboye Lodge Hotel, Bangor, Co Down

Tel: 028 9185 2500 e-mail: info@clandeboyelodge.com 3 star hotel with 43 bedrooms, all en suite. Bar and restaurant. Adjacent to Blackwood and Clandeboye golf clubs with 7 further courses within 10 minutes. 3 RAC merit awards. Consort Crown Regional Hotel of the Year 1997, 1998 & 1999

Papa's, Bangor, Co Down

Tel: 028 9145 3747 Espresso and ice cream bar, sandwiches and light snacks. Open 10am to 10pm 7 days a week. No credit cards.

The Old Cross Inn, Newtownards, Co Down

Tel: 028 9182 0212 The oldest pub-restaurant in town, and one of the best in the region. Food served lunch and dinner & all day Sunday till 7.30.   832

Malone

Malone Golf Club, 240 Upper Malone Road, Dunmurry, Belfast, BT17 9LB

Tel: 028 9061 2758

With the staging of the Irish Amateur Close Championship along with several, important professional tournaments, Malone could be said to have done rather well for a club which began life without a course. Yet, from their foundation in 1895, it was only 14 months until their new layout was officially opened.

But they were to change location in 1919, before eventually arriving at their present home

in 1962, when designer John Harris was presented with a beautiful location at Ballydrain, Upper Malone. Later revisions by one of the club's most distinguished members, Billy Ferguson, were endorsed through the staging of the Close Championship in 1984.

That was when Brian Hoey, from nearby Shandon Park GC, captured the title on fast-running terrain, with a tie-hole victory over Liam MacNamara in the final. In their former home on the Barberton Estate, Moses O'Neill captured the Irish Professional Championship in 1924 and 70 years later, Ballydrain played host to the Irish Senior Masters, won by Tommy Horton in 1994.

With an overall measurement of 6,599 yards, Malone would be considered relatively short by modern standards. But what it lacks in length is more than offset by a searching emphasis on accuracy, presented by flowering shrubs, tree-lined fairways and a large lake dominating the homeward journey.

A feature hole in this stretch is the 136-yard 15th, where the lake on the left is never out of the player's eye-line. This and other, classic parkland elements, combine in one of the most varied and picturesque courses imaginable.

Sec/Manager:	J. N. S. Agate
Professional:	Michael McGee
Directions:	2 miles South East of Junction 2 of the M1 Motorway to Belfast. Opposite Lady Dixon Park
Type of Course:	Parkland
Date Founded:	1895
No of Holes:	18 (plus 9 holes)
Length:	6599 yds (6034 mtrs)

Par:	72
SSS:	71
Green Fees:	Weekdays: £35 Weekends and Bank Holidays: £40
Visitors:	Welcome: Book in advance
Societies:	Welcome: Mon-Thu, Book in advance
Facilities:	Chipping/Putting Area, Practice Area, Driving Range, Golf Clubs for hire, Trolley hire, Electric Buggy hire, Bar, Restaurant, Caddy service by arrangement

Accommodation, Food and Drink

Reference numbers below refer to detailed information provided in section 2

Accommodation

Bushymead Country House, 86 Drumaness Rd, Ballynahinch, Co Down, BT24 8LT,

Tel: 028 9756 1171 The house stands in spacious grounds with extensive gardens, a children's play area, barbecue site and a large pond. The house has 8 attractively furnished guest bedrooms, 7 of them en suite.

Caldhame House, Nutts Corner, Crumlin, Co Antrim

Tel/Fax: 028 9442 2378 A splendid guest house just minutes from Belfast International Airport. All rooms en suite, with tv.   800

Oakfield Guest House, 9 Crumlin Road, Lower Ballinderry, Lisburn, Co Antrim, BT28 2JU,

Tel: 028 9265 1307 Large, modernised farmhouse is surrounded by well-presented gardens, with plenty of parking space, and has 4 guest bedrooms, all en suite. Convenient for the disabled.

Food and Drink

Motte 'n' Bailey, 131-3 Kingsway, Dunmurry, Co Antrim

Tel: 028 9060 3790 A round tower look for this establishment with three bars, one serving as a restaurant: pub grub plus à la carte menu.

The Old Cross Inn, Newtownards, Co Down

Tel: 028 9182 0212 The oldest pub-restaurant in town, and one of the best in the region. Food served lunch and dinner & all day Sunday till 7.30.   832

The Primrose Bar, Ballynahinch, Co Down

Tel: 028 9756 3177 Fax: 028 9756 5954 Bar and restaurant on the main street of town. Local ales, worldwide wines, bar menu and various restaurant menus.   837

Mount Ober

Mount Ober Golf & Country Club, 24 Ballymaconaghy Road, Knockbracken, Belfast, BT8 4SB

Tel: 028 9079 2108

Sec/Manager:	D. Macnamarra
Professional:	Geoff Loughrey
Directions:	3 miles from City Centre. Take A24, Southfield Road towards Carryduff. Just past junction with A55 turn left.
Type of Course:	Parkland
Date Founded:	1998
No of Holes:	18
Length:	5436 yds (4971mtrs)
Par:	67
SSS:	67
Green Fees:	Weekdays: £12 Weekends and Bank Holidays: £14
Visitors:	Welcome: Book in advance

Societies:	Welcome: Book in advance
Facilities:	Chipping/Putting Area Practice Area, Driving Range, Golf Clubs for hire, Bar, Restaurant, Caddy service by arrangement

Accommodation, Food and Drink

Reference numbers below refer to detailed information provided in section 2

Accommodation

Bushymead Country House, 86 Drumaness Rd, Ballynahinch, Co Down, BT24 8LT,

Tel: 028 9756 1171 The house stands in spacious grounds with extensive gardens, a children's play area, barbecue site and a large pond. The house has 8 attractively furnished guest bedrooms, 7 of them en suite.

Carnwood Country House, 85 Victoria Rd, Holywood, Co Armagh, BT18 9BG,

Tel: 028 9042 1745 Approached by a long driveway lined with rare species of trees, Carnwood House enjoys a tranquil environment despite being conveniently located for Belfast and the local City Airport. The 4 bedrooms include the Country Suite with 4-poster bed.

Oakfield Guest House, 9 Crumlin Road, Lower Ballinderry, Lisburn, Co Antrim, BT28 2JU,

Tel: 028 9265 1307 Large, modernised farmhouse is surrounded by well-presented gardens, with plenty of parking space, and has 4 guest bedrooms, all en suite. Convenient for the disabled.

Food and Drink

Motte 'n' Bailey, 131-3 Kingsway, Dunmurry, Co Antrim

Tel: 028 9060 3790 A round tower look for this establishment with three bars, one serving as a restaurant: pub grub plus à la carte menu.

The Old Cross Inn, Newtownards, Co Down

Tel: 028 9182 0212 The oldest pub-restaurant in town, and one of the best in the region. Food served lunch and dinner & all day Sunday till 7.30.   832

The Primrose Bar, Ballynahinch, Co Down

Tel: 028 9756 3177 Fax: 028 9756 5954 Bar and restaurant on the main street of town. Local ales, worldwide wines, bar menu and various restaurant menus.   837

Shandon Park

Shandon, 73 Shandon Park, Belfast, BT5 6NY

Tel: 028 9079 7859

Sec/Manager:	David Jenkins
Professional:	Barry Wilson
Directions:	3 miles from City Centre off the A55 Knockbreda Road
Type of Course:	Parkland
Date Founded:	1926
No of Holes:	18
Length:	6282 yds (5744 mtrs)
Par:	70
SSS:	70
Green Fees:	Weekdays: £22 Weekends and Bank Holidays: £27
Visitors:	Welcome: Any day, Sat after 4.00pm
Societies:	Welcome: Weekdays only, Book in advance
Facilities:	Chipping/Putting Area, Practice Area, Golf Clubs for hire, Trolley hire, Bar, Restaurant

Accommodation, Food and Drink

Reference numbers below refer to detailed
information provided in section 2

Accommodation

Carnwood Country House, 85 Victoria Rd, Holywood, Co
Armagh, BT18 9BG,

Tel: 028 9042 1745 Approached by a long driveway lined with rare species of trees,
Carnwood House enjoys a tranquil environment despite being conveniently located
for Belfast and the local City Airport. The 4 bedrooms include the Country Suite
with 4-poster bed.

Rockhaven B&B, 79 Mountain Road, Newtoonards, Co Down,
BT33 4UL,

Tel: 028 9182 3987 The 2 guest bedrooms at Rockhaven are stylishly furnished and
the house is surrounded by superb large gardens, (complete with barbecue area),
which reindeer visit on a regular basis.

Tara Guest House, 51 Princetown Rd, Bangor, Co Down, BT20
3TA,

Tel: 028 9146 8924 The Tara has 10 comfortable guest bedrooms, all of them en
suite and all furnished to a high standard. An evening meal is available.

Food and Drink

Motte 'n' Bailey, 131-3 Kingsway, Dunmurry, Co Antrim

Tel: 028 9060 3790 A round tower look for this establishment with three bars, one
serving as a restaurant: pub grub plus à la carte menu.

Papa's, Bangor, Co Down

Tel: 028 9145 3747 Espresso and ice cream bar, sandwiches and light snacks. Open
10am to 10pm 7 days a week. No credit cards.

The Old Cross Inn, Newtownards, Co Down

Tel: 028 9182 0212 The oldest pub-restaurant in town, and one of the best in the
region. Food served lunch and dinner & all day Sunday till 7.30.   832

DOWN

On leaving Dundalk for the Border town of Newry, the Cooley Mountains beckon to the right, out towards Carlingford Lough. According to legend, that is where the mythical hero Cuchulainn, of whom there is an evocative sculpture in the General Post Office in Dublin, is said to have displayed extraordinary dexterity with stick and ball, in what could have been an ancient Irish form of golf. So, it seems delightfully appropriate that latter-day golfing pilgrims should pass this way en route to one of the world's greatest links courses. Indeed when the Irish Open was staged at Portmarnock from 1976 to 1982 and again from 1986 to 1990, many a visiting practitioner took the opportunity of travelling north for a look at Royal Co Down. One could see it becoming an invaluable reference for prospective golf-course architects. Which would explain the visit of American Mark McCumber on the Saturday of the Irish Open in 1979 when he returned, refreshed to finish third behind Mark James the following day. Tom Watson has also savoured its stunning location "where the Mountains of Mourne sweep down to the sea." And several of his countrymen will be happy to follow suit, now that it has become home to the British Senior Open, for the immediate future.

The Mournes, Co Down

Distinctive and self-contained, the Mournes are tucked away in the south-east corner of Northern Ireland, with 12 shapely summits rising more than 2,000 feet on the eastern side. As it happens, the barren peak of Slieve Donard, which climbs steeply to 2,796 feet, presents a stunning backdrop to the wonderfully difficult par-four ninth at Royal Co Down. For those more interested in climbing than golfing, it represents an energic afternoon's climb from the carpark at Bloody Bridge near the holiday town of Newcastle. And from the top, one can see the Isle of Man and the full length of Strangford Lough. Then, to the north-west, lies the pale outline of Lough Neagh, a vast inland sea covering 153 square miles and famous for its eels.

Back in the 18th century, the coast from Newcastle around to the hamlet of Greencastle was notorious for smuggling. Old coastguard lookout points are redolent of a time when liquor and tobacco, tea, silk and soap were landed by boat from the Isle of Man and taken along the so-called Brandy Pad and other smugglers' trails, into the safety of the mountains. The two, large artificial lakes in the Silent Valley, which are responsible for Belfast's water supply, are surrounded by a huge, dry stone wall over 22 miles long. At Newcastle itself, there is yachting and pleasure fishing from the old harbour and walks in the sand dunes of Murlough. For a delightfully scenic drive to Newcastle, visitors travelling north from Dublin should turn east at Newry on the A2 which runs along the north shore of Carlingford Lough, between the mountains and the sea.

County Down has 24 golf courses, which is more than any other county in Northern Ireland. They are: Ardglass, Ardminnan, Banbridge, Bangor, Blackwood, Bright Castle, Carnalea, Clandeboye, Crossgar, Donaghadee, Downpatrick, Helen's Bay, Holywood, Kilkeel, Kirkistown Castle, Mahee Island, Ringdufferrin, Rockmount, Royal Belfast, Royal Co Down, Scrabo, Spa, Temple, Warrenpoint. It would be difficult to imagine a more varied selection. Contrasting size is offered by the charming nine holes at Helen's Bay and the 36 holes at Clandeboye. Then there is the hilly parkland of Holywood and the seaside challenge of Ardglass. Often overlooked by visitors to the area is the fine course at Kilkeel, situated on the main Newry Road, three miles from Newcastle. Its location made it an ideal choice as a second course for the strokeplay qualifying stage of the British Amateur Championship at Royal Co Down in 1999, when competitors found its tight, dog-leg par fours especially testing. Ringed by woodlands and a riot of rhododendron shrubs, the course, which was upgraded in 1993, is in an area which has been described, with some justification, as the Garden of Mourne. When the Irish Professional Championship was staged at Bangor in 1962, Christy O'Connor Snr, then at the peak of his formidable powers, captured the title with a stunning, 20-under-par aggregate of 264. More recently, the course has proved to be a splendid nursery for the skills of Garth McGimpsey, Ireland's most successful amateur since Joe Carr and winner of the British Amateur Championship at Royal Dornoch in 1985.

Castlewellan Forest Park, Co Down

The real attraction of County Down, however, is the wonderful variety if offers the tourist. For instance, there is the Rathfriland's Bronte Interpretative Centre, which was formerly a church and schoolhouse where Patrick Bronte, father of Charlotte and Emily, preached and taught. Then there is the Scarva Visitor Centre at Banbridge, adjacent to the Newry/Portadown Canal, which was constructed in 1742, making it the oldest summit canal in these islands. And Newtownards is home to the Somme Heritage Centre, where Ireland's contribution to the First World War can be examined, through the 10th and 16th (Irish) Divisions and the 36th (Ulster) Division. The centre features a reconstructed trench system, museum and a unique, audio/visual re-creation of the Battle of the Somme.

Folk Museum, Co Down

When St Patrick came to Ireland in 432 AD, the intention was to sail up the coast to County Antrim where, as a young slave, he tended flocks for six years on Slemish Mountain. Strong currents, however, swept his boat through the tidal narrows of Strangford Lough and he landed at the estuary of the Slaney river. So it was that County Down became known as St Patrick's country. Downpatrick's Down Cathedral, built in 1183 and with the saint's grave in its grounds, rises above the Quoile river and remains a fitting monument to his enormous impact on Irish life.

On the other side of the Lough is the Ards Peninsula, which is one of Northern Ireland's most popular holiday resort areas. Fierce currents, tidal narrows and reefs off the coast have claimed many ships through the years, which explains why the Vikings named it "violent fjord" (Strangford). Only Donaghadee, south-east of Bangor, offers a safe refuge. In 1818, the poet John Keats made the short crossing from Portpatrick in Scotland and having landed in Donaghadee, he proceeded to walk to Belfast and back. Fellow poet William Wordsworth and the composer Franz Liszt were other notable visitors. Indeed we are told that Liszt ended a grand Irish tour there, complete with baggage, including a piano. The Lough is a great bird sanctuary and wildlife reserve. Thousands of Brent geese spend the winter there and greylag and white-fronted geese visit from the Downpatrick marshes. Of the three Cistercian monasteries in medieval County Down, three were located there - Inch Abbey, Grey Abbey and Comber. The fourth was at Newry, the town which guarded the strategically important Gap of the North and is nowadays a gateway to rich golfing delights.

Location of Golf Courses

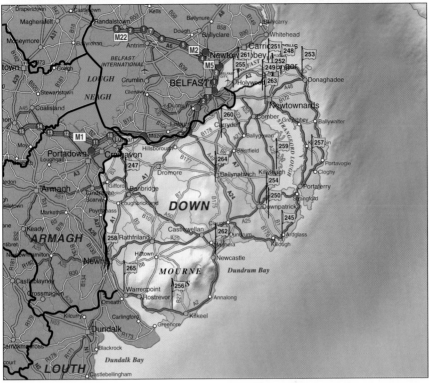

© MAPS IN MINUTES ™ (1998)

Ardglass

Ardglass Golf Club, Castle Place, Ardglass, Co
Down, BT30 7TP

Tel: 028 4484 1219

Sec/Manager:	Debbie Polly
Professional:	Philip Farrell
Directions:	Approx. seven miles South East of Downpatrick on BI
Type of Course:	Seaside
Date Founded:	1896
No of Holes:	18
Length:	5776 yds (5281 mtrs)
Par:	70
SSS:	69
Green Fees:	Weekdays: £18 Weekends & Bank Holidays; £24
Visitors:	Welcome: Any Day except Wednesday & Saturday, Restrictions on Sunday
Societies:	Welcome: Restirictions apply, Contact Club for details
Facilities:	Chipping/Putting Area, Practice Area, Golf Clubs for hire, Trolley hire, Bar, Restaurant, Caddy service by arrangement

Accommodation, Food and Drink

Reference numbers below refer to detailed
information provided in section 2

Accommodation

Burford Lodge, Ardglass, Co Down
Tel: 028 4484 1141 A friendly, family-run guest house on the seafront. Breakfast and

evening meals. 2 minutes from Ardglass Golf Club.   835

Dacara, 47 South Promenade, Newcastle, Co. Down
Tel: 028 4372 6745 e-mail: dacara@the chefshop.com Bed & Breakfast
accommodation in a homely turn-of-the-century house on the A2. Great sea views.
Golf and restaurant nearby.

Denvirs Hotel, Downpatrick, Co Down
Tel: 028 4461 2012 Hotel, bar and licensed restaurant. 2 star Accommodation
comprises 6 en suite double bedrooms.

Drumrawn House, 139 Central Promenade, Newcastle, Co.
Down
Tel: 028 4372 6847 Three large en suite bedrooms with tv and tea-makers. Private
parking. Good Irish breakfast. Royal County Down golf course nearby.

Quay Lodge, 31 South Promenade, Newcastle, Co. Down
Tel: 028 4372 3054 Bed & Breakfast accommodation in two en suite double rooms.
Private parking; sea view; two minutes drive to golf course.

Swan Lodge, 30 St Patricks Road, Saul, Co Down
Tel/Fax: 028 4461 5542 A modern B&B house with views of Strangford Lough and
St Patricks Monument. En suite rooms, tv, dinner on request.

Food and Drink

Brendan's Bar & Bistro, Downpatrick, Co Down
Tel: 028 4461 5311 Traditional Irish lunches and daily specials. Licensed. Open seven
days a week.

Courtside Bistro, Downpatrick, Co Down
Tel: 028 4461 7886 Fax: 028 4461 7191 An informal bistro that shares premises
with a more formal restaurant in the former Assembly Rooms.   838

Denvirs Hotel, Downpatrick, Co Down
Tel: 028 4461 2012 Hotel, bar and licensed restaurant. 2 star Accommodation
comprises 6 en suite double bedrooms.

Roadhouse Inn, Dundrum, Co Down
Tel: 028 4375 1209 Inn, dating from 1800, with bistro and à la carte restaurant. 7
double bedrooms. Live music every Friday, Saturday and Sunday.   851

The Anchor, Newcastle, Co Down
Tel: 028 4372 3344 A family-owned, old-world pub-restaurant just yards from the
sea. Snacks, lunches, full menu of good home cooking.   836

The Kilbroney Bar and Restaurant, Rostrevor, Co Down
Tel: 028 4173 8390 Town-centre restaurant, bar and beer garden. Food is served all
day, every day from an à la carte menu.   830

Banbridge

Banbridge Golf Club, Huntly Road,
Banbridge, Co Down, BT32 3UR

Tel: 028 4066 2211

Sec/Manager:	Thomas Mulholland
Professional:	None
Directions:	1 mile North West from centre of Banbridge off the A50
Type of Course:	Parkland
Date Founded:	1912
No of Holes:	18
Length:	5471 yds (5003 mtrs)
Par:	69
SSS:	67
Green Fees:	Weekdays: £15 Weekends & Bank Holidays: £20
Visitors:	Welcome: Any Day except Tuesday or Saturday
Societies:	Welcome: Book in advance
Facilities:	Chipping/Putting Area, Practice Area, Trolley hire, Bar, Restaurant

Accommodation, Food and Drink

Reference numbers below refer to detailed
information provided in section 2

Accommodation

Ivanhoe, 10 Valley Lane, Waringstown, Craigavon, Co Armagh, BT66 7SR,

Tel: 028 3888 1287 This inviting house is set in quiet, peaceful surroundings facing a wood. There are 3 spacious guest bedrooms, (2 doubles and 1 twin.

Village Inn & Buttery, 103-105 Main Street, Markethill, Co Armagh, BT6 1PJ,

Tel: 028 3755 1237 The Village Inn is a popular venue where locals and visitors alike savour the welcoming atmosphere of a traditional Irish inn. Based on local produce, the menu offers a wide choice of high class food.

Win - Staff House, 45 Banbridge Rd, Dromore, Co Down, BT25 1NE,

Tel: 028 9269 2252 Surrounded by spacious gardens, (complete with a barbecue area), Win-Staff House enjoys a well-deserved reputation for friendliness, hospitality, excellent cuisine and comfortable, relaxing Accommodation. Evening meals are available on request.

Food and Drink

Maghaberry Arms, 23 Maghaberry Rd, Moira, Craigavon, Co Armagh, BT67 0JF,

Tel: 028 9261 1852 The Maghaberry Arms is a large imposing building which has been recently renovated to the very highest standard - a free house where the craic is good, the food appetising and very good value for money.

Seven Stars Restaurant, Loughbrickland, Co Down

Tel: 028 4062 6461 A bright, cheerful bar-restaurant serving a good range of dishes from 11.30 to 7.30. Just off the main A1. 833

Yellow Door, 2 Bridge Street, Gilford, Co Armagh, BT63 6EP,

Tel: 028 3883 1543 The Yellow Door restaurant has two dining-rooms - the larger one non-smoking Menus are always based on fresh local produce.

Bangor

Bangor Golf Club, Broadway, Bangor, Co
Down, BT20 4RH

Tel: 028 9127 0922

Sec/Manager:	David Ryan
Professional:	Michael Barron
Directions:	1 mile from Centre of Bangor off the B21 towards Donaghadee
Type of Course:	Parkland
Date Founded:	1903
No of Holes:	18
Length:	6410 yds (5861 mtrs)
Par:	71
SSS:	71

Green Fees:	Weekdays: £20 Weekends and Bank Holidays: £25
Visitors:	Welcome: Any Day except Tuesday or Saturday
Societies:	Welcome: Book in advance
Facilities:	Chipping/Putting Area, Practice Area, Golf Clubs for hire, Trolley hire, Bar, Restaurant

Accommodation, Food and Drink

Reference numbers below refer to detailed
information provided in section 2

Accommodation

108 Seacliff Road, Bangor, Co Down

Tel: 028 9146 1077 e-mail: heathermbell@compuserve.com website: www.bandb-bangor.Co.uk B&B with sea views. 2 singles, 1 en suite double. No smoking. No credit cards.

Clandeboye Lodge Hotel, Bangor, Co Down

Tel: 028 9185 2500 e-mail: info@clandeboyelodge.com 3 star hotel with 43 bedrooms, all en suite. Bar and restaurant. Adjacent to Blackwood and Clandeboye golf clubs with 7 further courses within 10 minutes. 3 RAC merit awards. Consort Crown Regional Hotel of the Year 1997, 1998 & 1999

Mervue, Greyabbey, Co Down

Tel/Fax: 028 4278 8619 Bed and Breakfast Accommodation in a well-served golf area. 3 rooms, all en suite. No credit cards.

Tara Guest House, 51 Princetown Rd, Bangor, Co Down, BT20 3TA,

Tel: 028 9146 8924 The Tara has 10 comfortable guest bedrooms, all of them en suite and all furnished to a high standard. An evening meal is available.

Food and Drink

Clandeboye Lodge Hotel, Bangor, Co Down

Tel: 028 9185 2500 e-mail: info@clandeboyelodge.com 3 star hotel with 43 bedrooms, all en suite. Bar and restaurant. Adjacent to Blackwood and Clandeboye golf clubs with 7 further courses within 10 minutes. 3 RAC merit awards. Consort Crown Regional Hotel of the Year 1997, 1998 & 1999

Papa's, Bangor, Co Down

Tel: 028 9145 3747 Espresso and ice cream bar, sandwiches and light snacks. Open 10am to 10pm 7 days a week. No credit cards.

The Old Cross Inn, Newtownards, Co Down

Tel: 028 9182 0212 The oldest pub-restaurant in town, and one of the best in the region. Food served lunch and dinner & all day Sunday till 7.30. 832

Blackwood

Blackwood Golf Centre (Hamilton Course),
Crawfordsburn Road, Clandeboye, Co Down,
BT19 1GB

Tel: 028 9185 2706

Sec/Manager:	Richard Gibson
Professional:	Debbie Hanna & Roy Skillen
Directions:	From Belfast City Airport follow A2 towards Bangor. 2 miles before Bangor turn right to Clandeboye along the B170. Course is signposted

Hamilton

Type of Course:	Heathland & Parkland
Date Founded:	1993
No of Holes:	18
Length:	6392 yds (5844 mtrs)
Par:	71
SSS:	70

Green Fees:	Weekdays: £15 Weekends & Bank Holidays: £20
Visitors:	Welcome: Book one week ahead
Societies:	Welcome: Prior bookings required well in advance

Temple

Type of Course:	Heathland & Parkland
Date Founded:	1993
No of Holes:	18 (par 3 course)
Length:	2492 yds (2279 mtrs)
Par:	54
SSS:	54
Green Fees:	Weekdays: £8 Weekends & Bank Holidays: £10
Visitors:	Welcome: Pay and Play
Societies:	Welcome: Book in advance
Facilities:	Chipping/Putting Area, Practice Area, Driving Range, Golf Clubs for hire, Trolley hire, Bar, Restaurant, Caddy service by arrangement Hotel opposite

Accommodation, Food and Drink

Reference numbers below refer to detailed information provided in section 2

Accommodation

108 Seacliff Road, Bangor, Co Down

Tel: 028 9146 1077 e-mail: heathermbell@compuserve.com website: www.bandb-bangor.Couk B&B with sea views. 2 singles, 1 en suite double. No smoking. No credit cards.

Carnwood Country House, 85 Victoria Rd, Holywood, Co Armagh, BT18 9BG,

Tel: 028 9042 1745 Approached by a long driveway lined with rare species of trees, Carnwood House enjoys a tranquil environment despite being conveniently located for Belfast and the local City Airport. The 4 bedrooms include the Country Suite with 4-poster bed.

Clandeboye Lodge Hotel, Bangor, Co Down

Tel: 028 9185 2500 e-mail: info@clandeboyelodge.com 3 star hotel with 43 bedrooms, all en suite. Bar and restaurant. Adjacent to Blackwood and Clandeboye golf clubs with 7 further courses within 10 minutes. 3 RAC merit awards. Consort Crown Regional Hotel of the Year 1997, 1998 & 1999

Tara Guest House, 51 Princetown Rd, Bangor, Co Down, BT20 3TA,

Tel: 028 9146 8924 The Tara has 10 comfortable guest bedrooms, all of them en suite and all furnished to a high standard. An evening meal is available.

Food and Drink

Clandeboye Lodge Hotel, Bangor, Co Down

Tel: 028 9185 2500 e-mail: info@clandeboyelodge.com 3 star hotel with 43 bedrooms, all en suite. Bar and restaurant. Adjacent to Blackwood and Clandeboye golf clubs with 7 further courses within 10 minutes. 3 RAC merit awards. Consort Crown Regional Hotel of the Year 1997, 1998 & 1999

Papa's, Bangor, Co Down

Tel: 028 9145 3747 Espresso and ice cream bar, sandwiches and light snacks. Open 10am to 10pm 7 days a week. No credit cards.

The Old Cross Inn, Newtownards, Co Down

Tel: 028 9182 0212 The oldest pub-restaurant in town, and one of the best in the region. Food served lunch and dinner & all day Sunday till 7.30.   832

Bright Castle

Bright Castle Golf Club, 14 Coniamstown Road, Bright, Downpatrick, Co Down

Tel: **028 4484 1319**

Sec/Manager:	John McCaul
Professional:	None
Directions:	4 miles South of Downpatrick off the B1 towards Ardglass
Type of Course:	Parkland
Date Founded:	1979
No of Holes:	18
Length:	7143 yds (6531 mtrs)
Par:	73
SSS:	73
Green Fees:	Weekdays: £10 Weekends & Bank Holidays: £12
Visitors:	Welcome: Anytime
Societies:	Welcome: Book in advance
Facilities:	Chipping/Putting Area, Trolley hire, Electric Buggy hire Hotel opposite

Accommodation, Food and Drink

Reference numbers below refer to detailed information provided in section 2

Accommodation

Burford Lodge, Ardglass, Co Down

Tel: 028 4484 1141 A friendly, family-run guest house on the seafront. Breakfast and evening meals. 2 minutes from Ardglass Golf Club.   835

Denvir's Hotel, Downpatrick, Co Down

Tel: 028 4461 2012 Next to the major sights in the oldest street in town, a hotel that uses fresh local produce in its menus.   831

Drumrawn House, 139 Central Promenade, Newcastle, Co. Down

Tel: 028 4372 6847 Three large en suite bedrooms with tv and tea-makers. Private parking. Good Irish breakfast. Royal County Down golf course nearby.

Swan Lodge, 30 St Patricks Road, Saul, Co Down

Tel/Fax: 028 4461 5542 A modern B&B house with views of Strangford Lough and St Patricks Monument. En suite rooms, tv, dinner on request.

Food and Drink

Brendan's Bar & Bistro, Downpatrick, Co Down

Tel: 028 4461 5311 Traditional Irish lunches and daily specials. Licensed. Open seven days a week.

Courtside Bistro, Downpatrick, Co Down

Tel: 028 4461 7886 Fax: 028 4461 7191 An informal bistro that shares premises with a more formal restaurant in the former Assembly Rooms.   838

Denvir's Hotel, Downpatrick, Co Down

Tel: 028 4461 2012 Next to the major sights in the oldest street in town, a hotel that uses fresh local produce in its menus.   831

Mario's Restaurant, Newcastle, Co Down

Tel: 028 4372 3912 A friendly restaurant with a menu of Italian and Continental dishes. Open Tues-Sat evenings (Monday in summer) and Sunday lunch, tea and dinner.   850

Roadhouse Inn, Dundrum, Co Down

Tel: 028 4375 1209 Inn, dating from 1800, with bistro and à la carte restaurant. 7 double bedrooms. Live music every Friday, Saturday and Sunday.   851

The Anchor, Newcastle, Co Down

Tel: 028 4372 3344 A family-owned, old-world pub-restaurant just yards from the sea. Snacks, lunches, full menu of good home cooking.   836

Carnalea

Carnalea Golf Club, Station Road, Bangor, Co Down, BT19 1RZ

Tel: **028 9127 1767**

Sec/Manager:	Gary Steele
Professional:	Tom Loughran
Directions:	I mile West of Bangor. From A2 take B20 through Crawfordsburn then follow signs for Carnalea Station
Type of Course:	Seaside Meadowland
Date Founded:	1927
No of Holes:	18
Length:	5574 yds (5096 mtrs)
Par:	69
SSS:	66
Green Fees:	Weekdays: £15 Weekends & Bank Holidays: £19
Visitors:	Welcome: Any Day except restrictions on Saturday
Societies:	Welcome: Book in advance
Facilities:	Chipping/Putting Area, Golf Clubs for hire, Trolley hire, Bar, Restaurant

Accommodation, Food and Drink

Reference numbers below refer to detailed information provided in section 2

Accommodation

108 Seacliff Road, Bangor, Co Down

Tel: 028 9146 1077 e-mail: heathermbell@compuserve.com website: www.bandb-bangor.Couk B&B with sea views. 2 singles, I en suite double. No smoking. No credit cards.

Clandeboye Lodge Hotel, Bangor, Co Down

Tel: 028 9185 2500 e-mail: info@clandeboyelodge.com 3 star hotel with 43 bedrooms, all en suite. Bar and restaurant. Adjacent to Blackwood and Clandeboye golf clubs with 7 further courses within 10 minutes. 3 RAC merit awards. Consort Crown Regional Hotel of the Year 1997, 1998 & 1999

Copelands Hotel, Donaghadee, Co Down

Tel: 028 9188 8189 Fax: 028 9188 8344 Hotel and licensed restaurant with a bar. 2 star Accommodation in 5 en suite doubles and 11 en suite twins.

Tara Guest House, 51 Princetown Rd, Bangor, Co Down, BT20 3TA,

Tel: 028 9146 8924 The Tara has 10 comfortable guest bedrooms, all of them en suite and all furnished to a high standard. An evening meal is available.

Food and Drink

Clandeboye Lodge Hotel, Bangor, Co Down

Tel: 028 9185 2500 e-mail: info@clandeboyelodge.com 3 star hotel with 43 bedrooms, all en suite. Bar and restaurant. Adjacent to Blackwood and Clandeboye golf clubs with 7 further courses within 10 minutes. 3 RAC merit awards. Consort Crown Regional Hotel of the Year 1997, 1998 & 1999

Copelands Hotel, Donaghadee, Co Down

Tel: 028 9188 8189 Fax: 028 91888344 Hotel and licensed restaurant with a bar. 2 star Accommodation in 5 en suite doubles and 11 en suite twins.

Papa's, Bangor, Co Down

Tel: 028 9145 3747 Espresso and ice cream bar, sandwiches and light snacks. Open 10am to 10pm 7 days a week. No credit cards.

Clandeboye

Clandeboye, 51 Tower Road, Conlig, Newtownards, BT23 3PN

Tel: 028 9127 1767

In October 1984, Clandeboye played host to the greatest field of women professionals ever assembled in this country. They were competing in the Smirnoff Irish Open in which the prize fund of £100,000 was only £10,728 less than was on offer to their male counterparts at Royal Dublin.

As it happened, America's Kathy Whitworth beat distinguished compatriots Pat Bradley, Donna Caponi and Betsy King, along with Australian Jan Stephenson, to capture the top prize of £22,500. With a three-under-par aggregate of 285, Whitworth recorded the 87th victory of her career.

Founded in 1933, the 36-hole facility comprising the Dufferin and Ava courses are complemented by a new clubhouse, built at a cost of £1.5 million. The premier, Dufferin stretch, called after the estate bearing that name, has an overall length of 6,469 yards compared with 5,755 for its more modest neighbour.

Laid out on classic heathland on the hills above Conlig Village, the championship stretch offers breathtaking views of Belfast Lough and the Irish Sea. It had its origins in a design by Bangor linen merchant, William Rennick Robinson. Then came the imput of Dr Von Limburger of the Alliss and Thomas design company, 30 years ago.

While the Dufferin is memorable for its strong par fours, notably the 467-yard eighth and the 427-yard 18th, the challenges on the Ava have more to do with precision than power. Still, the 524-yard second, is considered to be one of the most demanding par fives on the Irish scene.

Sec/Manager:	Ken Waham
Professional:	None
Directions:	Half mile north west of Conlig off

the A21 between Newtownlands and Bangor

Dufferin

Type of Course:	Parkland and Heathland
Date Founded:	1933
No of Holes:	18
Length:	6469 yds (5915 mtrs)
Par:	71
SSS:	71
Green Fees:	Weekdays £25 Weekends and Bank Holidays £30

Ava

Type of Course:	Parkland and Moorland
Date Founded:	1933
No of Holes:	18; 18
Length:	5755 yds (5262 mtrs)
Par:	71
SSS:	68
Green Fees:	Weekdays £20 Weekends and Bank Holidays £25

Visitors:	Welcome: Pre booking essential, Restrictions at weekends
Societies:	Welcome: Mon, Wed, Fri and Sat pm, Prior booking advisable
Facilities:	Golf Clubs for hire, Trolley hire, Electric Buggy hire, Bar, Restaurant

Accommodation, Food and Drink

Reference numbers below refer to detailed information provided in section 2

Accommodation

108 Seacliff Road, Bangor, Co Down

Tel: 028 9146 1077 e-mail: heathermbell@compuserve.com website: www.bandb-bangor.Couk B&B with sea views. 2 singles, 1 en suite double. No smoking. No credit cards.

Clandeboye Lodge Hotel, Bangor, Co Down

Tel: 028 9185 2500 e-mail: info@clandeboyelodge.com 3 star hotel with 43 bedrooms, all en suite. Bar and restaurant. Adjacent to Blackwood and Clandeboye golf clubs with 7 further courses within 10 minutes. 3 RAC merit awards. Consort Crown Regional Hotel of the Year 1997, 1998 & 1999

Copelands Hotel, Donaghadee, Co Down

Tel: 028 9188 8189 Fax: 028 91888344 Hotel and licensed restaurant with a bar. 2 star Accommodation in 5 en suite doubles and 11 en suite twins.

Mervue, Greyabbey, Co Down

Tel/Fax: 028 4278 8619 Bed and Breakfast Accommodation in a well-served golf area. 3 rooms, all en suite. No credit cards.

Food and Drink

Clandeboye Lodge Hotel, Bangor, Co Down

Tel: 028 9185 2500 e-mail: info@clandeboyelodge.com 3 star hotel with 43 bedrooms, all en suite. Bar and restaurant. Adjacent to Blackwood and Clandeboye golf clubs with 7 further courses within 10 minutes. 3 RAC merit awards. Consort Crown Regional Hotel of the Year 1997, 1998 & 1999

Copelands Hotel, Donaghadee, Co Down

Tel: 028 9188 8189 Fax: 028 91888344 Hotel and licensed restaurant with a bar. 2 star Accommodation in 5 en suite doubles and 11 en suite twins.

The Old Cross Inn, Newtownards, Co Down

Tel: 028 9182 0212 The oldest pub-restaurant in town, and one of the best in the region. Food served lunch and dinner & all day Sunday till 7.30.   832

Donaghadee

Donaghadee Golf Club, 84 Warren Road, Donaghadee, Co Down, BT21 OPQ

Tel: 028 9188 3624

Sec/Manager:	Kenneth Patton
Professional:	Gordon Drew
Directions:	4 miles East of Bangor to the North of Donaghadee off the A2
Type of Course:	Links & Parkland
Date Founded:	1899
No of Holes:	18
Length:	6091 yds (5570 mtrs)
Par:	71
SSS:	69
Green Fees:	Weekdays: £16 Weekends & Bank Holidays: £22
Visitors:	Welcome: Any Day except Saturday
Societies:	Welcome: Book in advance
Facilities:	Chipping/Putting Area, Practice Area, Golf Clubs for hire, Trolley hire, Electric Buggy hire, Bar, Restaurant

Accommodation, Food and Drink

Reference numbers below refer to detailed information provided in section 2

Accommodation

108 Seacliff Road, Bangor, Co Down

Tel: 028 9146 1077 e-mail: heathermbell@compuserve.com website: www.bandb-bangor.Couk B&B with sea views. 2 singles, 1 en suite double. No smoking. No credit cards.

Clandeboye Lodge Hotel, Bangor, Co Down

Tel: 028 9185 2500 e-mail: info@clandeboyelodge.com 3 star hotel with 43 bedrooms, all en suite. Bar and restaurant. Adjacent to Blackwood and Clandeboye golf clubs with 7 further courses within 10 minutes. 3 RAC merit awards. Consort Crown Regional Hotel of the Year 1997, 1998 & 1999

Copelands Hotel, Donaghadee, Co Down

Tel: 028 9188 8189 Fax: 028 9188 8344 Hotel and licensed restaurant with a bar. 2 star Accommodation in 5 en suite doubles and 11 en suite twins.

Mervue, Greyabbey, Co Down

Tel/Fax: 028 4278 8619 Bed and Breakfast Accommodation in a well-served golf area. 3 rooms, all en suite. No credit cards.

Food and Drink

Clandeboye Lodge Hotel, Bangor, Co Down

Tel: 028 9185 2500 e-mail: info@clandeboyelodge.com 3 star hotel with 43 bedrooms, all en suite. Bar and restaurant. Adjacent to Blackwood and Clandeboye golf clubs with 7 further courses within 10 minutes. 3 RAC merit awards. Consort Crown Regional Hotel of the Year 1997, 1998 & 1999

Copelands Hotel, Donaghadee, Co Down

Tel: 028 9188 8189 Fax: 028 9188 8344 Hotel and licensed restaurant with a bar. 2 star Accommodation in 5 en suite doubles and 11 en suite twins.

The Old Cross Inn, Newtownards, Co Down

Tel: 028 9182 0212 The oldest pub-restaurant in town, and one of the best in the region. Food served lunch and dinner & all day Sunday till 7.30.   832

Downpatrick

Downpatrick Golf Club, 43 Saul Road, Downpatrick, Co Down, BT30 6AL

Tel: 028 4461 5947

Sec/Manager:	Mr. McCoubrey
Professional:	None
Directions:	Course signposted from Downpatrick Town Centre and located 1 mile East of town near Saul
Type of Course:	Parkland
Date Founded:	1930
No of Holes:	18
Length:	6100 yds (5577 mtrs)
Par:	69
SSS:	69
Green Fees:	Weekdays: £15 Weekends & Bank Holidays: £20
Visitors:	Welcome: Book in advance
Societies:	Welcome: Book in advance
Facilities:	Chipping/Putting Area, Practice Area, Golf Clubs for hire, Trolley hire, Electric Buggy hire, Bar, Restaurant

Accommodation, Food and Drink

Reference numbers below refer to detailed information provided in section 2

Accommodation

Adairs B&B, Portaferry, Co Down

Tel: 028 4272 8412 B&B Accommodation near the sea and Strangford Lough. 1 single, 1 en suite double, 1 en suite family room. No credit cards.

Burford Lodge, Ardglass, Co Down

Tel: 028 4484 1141 A friendly, family-run guest house on the seafront. Breakfast and evening meals. 2 minutes from Ardglass Golf Club. 835

Denvir's Hotel, Downpatrick, Co Down

Tel: 028 4461 2012 Next to the major sights in the oldest street in town, a hotel that uses fresh local produce in its menus. 831

Drumrawn House, 139 Central Promenade, Newcastle, Co. Down

Tel: 028 4372 6847 Three large en suite bedrooms with tv and tea-makers. Private parking. Good Irish breakfast. Royal County Down golf course nearby.

Swan Lodge, 30 St Patricks Road, Saul, Co Down

Tel/Fax: 028 4461 5542 A modern B&B house with views of Strangford Lough and St Patricks Monument. En suite rooms, tv, dinner on request.

Food and Drink

Brendan's Bar & Bistro, Downpatrick, Co Down

Tel: 028 4461 5311 Traditional Irish lunches and daily specials. Licensed. Open seven days a week.

Courtside Bistro, Downpatrick, Co Down

Tel: 028 4461 7886 Fax: 028 4461 7191 An informal bistro that shares premises with a more formal restaurant in the former Assembly Rooms. 838

Denvir's Hotel, Downpatrick, Co Down

Tel: 028 4461 2012 Next to the major sights in the oldest street in town, a hotel that uses fresh local produce in its menus. 831

Roadhouse Inn, Dundrum, Co Down

Tel: 028 4375 1209 Inn, dating from 1800, with bistro and à la carte restaurant. 7 double bedrooms. Live music every Friday, Saturday and Sunday. 851

Holywood

Holywood, Demense Road, Holywood, Co Down, BT18 9LE

Tel: 028 9042 3135

Sec/Manager:	None
Professional:	Paul Gray
Directions:	1 mile South of Holywood off the A2 from Belfast
Type of Course:	Undulating Parkland
Date Founded:	1904
No of Holes:	18
Length:	5932 yds (5425 mtrs)
Par:	69
SSS:	68
Green Fees:	Weekdays: £16 Weekends & Bank Holidays: £21
Visitors:	Welcome: Any Day, Restistrictions Thursday & Saturday
Societies:	Welcome: Prebook, Restrictions Thursday & Saturday
Facilities:	Chipping/Putting Area, Practice Area, Golf Clubs for hire, Trolley hire Bar, Restaurant, Caddy service by arrangement

Accommodation, Food and Drink

Reference numbers below refer to detailed information provided in section 2

Accommodation

108 Seacliff Road, Bangor, Co Down

Tel: 028 9146 1077 e-mail: heathermbell@compuserve.com website: www.bandb-bangor.Couk B&B with sea views. 2 singles, 1 en suite double. No smoking. No credit cards.

Carnwood Country House, 85 Victoria Rd, Holywood, Co Armagh, BT18 9BG,

Tel: 028 9042 1745 Approached by a long driveway lined with rare species of trees, Carnwood House enjoys a tranquil environment despite being conveniently located for Belfast and the local City Airport. The 4 bedrooms include the Country Suite with 4-poster bed.

Tara Guest House, 51 Princetown Rd, Bangor, Co Down, BT20 3TA,

Tel: 028 9146 8924 The Tara has 10 comfortable guest bedrooms, all of them en suite and all furnished to a high standard. An evening meal is available.

Food and Drink

Clandeboye Lodge Hotel, Bangor, Co Down

Tel: 028 9185 2500 e-mail: info@clandeboyelodge.com 3 star hotel with 43 bedrooms, all en suite. Bar and restaurant. Adjacent to Blackwood and Clandeboye golf clubs with 7 further courses within 10 minutes. 3 RAC merit awards. Consort Crown Regional Hotel of the Year 1997, 1998 & 1999

Copelands Hotel, Donaghadee, Co Down

Tel: 028 9188 8189 Fax: 028 9188 8344 Hotel and licensed restaurant with a bar. 2 star Accommodation in 5 en suite doubles and 11 en suite twins.

The Old Cross Inn, Newtownards, Co Down

Tel: 028 9182 0212 The oldest pub-restaurant in town, and one of the best in the region. Food served lunch and dinner & all day Sunday till 7.30. 832

Kilkeel

Kilkeel Golf Club, Mourne Park, Ballyardle, Kilkeel, Co Down, BT34 4LB

Tel: 028 4176 5095

Sec/Manager:	George Graham
Professional:	None
Directions:	3 miles West of Kilkeel off the A2 to Newry

Type of Course:	Parkland
Date Founded:	1949
No of Holes:	18
Length:	6615 yds (6048 mtrs)
Par:	72
SSS:	72
Green Fees:	Weekdays: £16 Weekends & Bank Holidays: £20
Visitors:	Welcome: Any Day except before 4.30 pm on Saturdays
Societies:	Welcome: Weekdays, Weekend restrictions
Facilities:	Chipping/Putting Area, Practice Area, Trolley hire, Electric Buggy hire, Bar, Restaurant, Caddy service by arrangement

Accommodation, Food and Drink

Reference numbers below refer to detailed information provided in section 2

Accommodation

Avoca Hotel, 93-97 Central promenade, Newcastle, Co Down, BT33 OHH,

Tel: 028 4372 2253 Overlooking the Promenade and Dundrum Bay, the Avoca Hotel's two bars offer a good choice of bar snacks and a very good restaurant. The hotel has 16 guest bedrooms of which 8 are en suite.

Dacara, 47 South Promenade, Newcastle, Co. Down

Tel: 028 4372 6745 e-mail: dacara@the chefshop.com Bed & Breakfast accommodation in a homely turn-of-the-century house on the A2. Great sea views. Golf and restaurant nearby.

Quay Lodge, 31 South Promenade, Newcastle, Co. Down

Tel: 028 4372 3054 Bed & Breakfast accommodation in two en suite double rooms. Private parking; sea view; two minutes drive to golf course.

Food and Drink

Archways, Kilkeel, Co Down

Tel: 028 4176 4112 A spacious restaurant with bar and lounge. Daily lunches, evening à la carte; entertainment.   834

Avoca Hotel, 93-97 Central promenade, Newcastle, Co Down, BT33 OHH,

Tel: 028 4372 2253 Overlooking the Promenade and Dundrum Bay, the Avoca Hotel's two bars offer a good choice of bar snacks and a very good restaurant. The hotel has 16 guest bedrooms of which 8 are en suite.

The Kilbroney Bar and Restaurant, Rostrevor, Co Down

Tel: 028 4173 8390 Town-centre restaurant, bar and beer garden. Food is served all day, every day from an à la carte menu.   830

Kirkistown Castle

Kirkistown Castle Golf Club, 142 Main road, Cloughey, Newtownards, Co Down

Tel: 028 4277 1233

Sec/Manager:	Rosemary Coultery
Professional:	J. Peden
Directions:	4 miles North of Portaferry off the A2 near Cloghy
Type of Course:	Links
Date Founded:	1902
No of Holes:	18
Length:	6119 yds (5596 mtrs)
Par:	69
SSS:	69
Green Fees:	Weekdays: £15 Weekends & Bank Holidays: £20
Visitors:	Welcome: All Days except Saturdays
Societies:	Welcome: Special concessions, Contact Club for details
Facilities:	Chipping/Putting Area, Practice Area, Golf Clubs for hire, Trolley hire, Bar, Restaurant

Accommodation, Food and Drink

Reference numbers below refer to detailed information provided in section 2

Accommodation

Adairs B&B, Portaferry, Co Down

Tel: 028 4272 8412 B&B Accommodation near the sea and Strangford Lough. I single, I en suite double, I en suite family room. No credit cards.

Fiddlers Green, 10-12 Church Street, Portaferry, Co Down, BT22 ILS,

Tel: 028 4272 8393 Fiddlers Green was christened by landlord and folk singer Frank McCarthy who, together with his wife Maureen, runs this lively, friendly pub which also offers B & B.

Lough Cowey Lodge, 9 Lough Cowey Road, Portaferry, Co Down, BT22 IPJ,

Tel: 028 4272 8263 This modern, purpose-built lodge offers guests a choice of bed and breakfast in the main building or self-catering Accommodation in the adjoining modern villa. The Lodge's peaceful garden enjoys magnificent views over Lough Cowey.

Food and Drink

Brendan's Bar & Bistro, Downpatrick, Co Down

Tel: 028 4461 5311 Traditional Irish lunches and daily specials. Licensed. Open seven days a week.

Fiddlers Green, 10-12 Church Street, Portaferry, Co Down, BT22 ILS,

Tel: 028 4272 8393 Fiddlers Green was christened by landlord and folk singer Frank McCarthy who, together with his wife Maureen, runs this lively, friendly pub which also offers B & B.

The Old Cross Inn, Newtownards, Co Down

Tel: 028 9182 0212 The oldest pub-restaurant in town, and one of the best in the region. Food served lunch and dinner & all day Sunday till 7.30.   832

Newry

Newry, 11 Forkhill Road, Co Down, BT35 8LZ

Tel: 028 3026 3871

Sec/Manager:	None
Professional:	None
Directions:	3 miles south of Newry on the B113 to Meigh
Type of Course:	Parkland

Date Founded:	1969
No of Holes:	18 (par 3 course)
Length:	4800 yds (4389 mtrs)
Par:	54
SSS:	54
Green Fees:	Weekdays £5: Weekends £6
Visitors:	Welcome: no restrictions
Societies:	Welcome: no restrictions
Facilities:	Trolley hire, Electric Buggy hire, Bar, Restaurant

Accommodation, Food and Drink

Reference numbers below refer to detailed
information provided in section 2

Accommodation

Arradale House, Carrickmacross, Co Monaghan

Tel: 042 9661941 Ten en suite bedrooms for full or part board Accommodation on a working farm in a beautiful setting of woods and lakes. 461

Avoca Hotel, 93-97 Central promenade, Newcastle, Co Down, BT33 OHH,

Tel: 028 4372 2253 Overlooking the Promenade and Dundrum Bay, the Avoca Hotel's two bars offer a good choice of bar snacks and a very good restaurant. The hotel has 16 guest bedrooms of which 8 are en suite.

The Heritage, Dundalk, Co Louth

Tel: 042 9335850 Keen golfers run this B&B house in a rural setting 1½ miles from Dundalk. Five letting bedrooms, 3 en suite. 401

Village Inn & Buttery, 103-105 Main Street, Markethill, Co Armagh, BT6 1PJ,

Tel: 028 3755 1237 The Village Inn is a popular venue where locals and visitors alike savour the welcoming atmosphere of a traditional Irish inn. Based on local produce, the menu offers a wide choice of high class food.

Food and Drink

Avoca Hotel, 93-97 Central promenade, Newcastle, Co Down, BT33 OHH,

Tel: 028 4372 2253 Overlooking the Promenade and Dundrum Bay, the Avoca Hotel's two bars offer a good choice of bar snacks and a very good restaurant. The hotel has 16 guest bedrooms of which 8 are en suite.

Seven Stars Restaurant, Loughbrickland, Co Down

Tel: 028 4062 6461 A bright, cheerful bar-restaurant serving a good range of dishes from 11.30 to 7.30. Just off the main A1. 833

The Kilbroney Bar and Restaurant, Rostrevor, Co Down

Tel: 028 4173 8390 Town-centre restaurant, bar and beer garden. Food is served all day, every day from an à la carte menu. 830

Ringdufferin

Ringdufferin Golf Club, Ringdufferin Road, Toye, Killyleagh, Co Down, BT30 9PH

Tel: 028 4482 2812

Sec/Manager:	Helen Lindsay
Professional:	Mark Lavery
Directions:	Three miles North of Killyleagh off the A22 Comber Road
Type of Course:	Drumlin
Date Founded:	1993
No of Holes:	18 (plus 9)
Length:	4652 yds (4253 mtrs)
Par:	68
SSS:	66
Green Fees:	Weekdays: £9 Weekends & Bank Holidays: £10

Visitors:	Welcome: Book in advance
Societies:	Welcome: Book in advance
Facilities:	Chipping/Putting Area, Practice Area, Driving Range, Golf Clubs for hire, Trolley hire, Bar, Restaurant

Accommodation, Food and Drink

Reference numbers below refer to detailed
information provided in section 2

Accommodation

Adairs B&B, Portaferry, Co Down

Tel: 028 4272 8412 B&B Accommodation near the sea and Strangford Lough. 1 single, 1 en suite double, 1 en suite family room. No credit cards.

Denvir's Hotel, Downpatrick, Co Down

Tel: 028 4461 2012 Next to the major sights in the oldest street in town, a hotel that uses fresh local produce in its menus. 831

Dufferin Arms, 35 High Street, Killyleagh, Co Down, BT30 9QF,

Tel: 028 4482 8229 This is a traditional country pub renowned throughout Ulster for its excellent food, drink and friendly atmosphere. Recommended by Taste of Ulster. There are 7 luxury en suite bedrooms, some with four-poster beds.

Food and Drink

Courtside Bistro, Downpatrick, Co Down

Tel: 028 4461 7886 Fax: 028 4461 7191 An informal bistro that shares premises with a more formal restaurant in the former Assembly Rooms. 838

Denvir's Hotel, Downpatrick, Co Down

Tel: 028 4461 2012 Next to the major sights in the oldest street in town, a hotel that uses fresh local produce in its menus. 831

Dufferin Arms, 35 High Street, Killyleagh, Co Down, BT30 9QF,

Tel: 028 4482 8229 This is a traditional country pub renowned throughout Ulster for its excellent food, drink and friendly atmosphere. Recommended by Taste of Ulster. There are 7 luxury en suite bedrooms, some with four-poster beds.

The Primrose Bar, Ballynahinch, Co Down

Tel: 028 9756 3177 Fax: 028 9756 5954 Bar and restaurant on the main street of town. Local ales, worldwide wines, bar menu and various restaurant menus. 837

Rockmount

Rockmount Golf Club, 27 Drumalig Road, Carryduff, Co Down, BT8 8EQ

Tel: 028 9081 2279

Sec/Manager:	D. Patterson
Professional:	None
Directions:	1 mile South of Carryduff off the A24
Type of Course:	Parkland
Date Founded:	1995
No of Holes:	18
Length:	6373yds (5827 mtrs)
Par:	72
SSS:	71

Green Fees:	Weekdays: £20 Weekends & Bank Holidays: £24
Visitors:	Welcome: Any Day except Saturday, Pay and Play
Societies:	Welcome: Any Day except Saturday, Book in advance
Facilities:	Chipping/Putting Area, Practice Area, Trolley hire, Electric Buggy hire, Bar, Restaurant

Accommodation, Food and Drink

Reference numbers below refer to detailed information provided in section 2

Accommodation

Bushymead Country House, 86 Drumaness Rd, Ballynahinch, Co Down, BT24 8LT,

Tel: 028 9756 1171 The house stands in spacious grounds with extensive gardens, a children's play area, barbecue site and a large pond. The house has 8 attractively furnished guest bedrooms, 7 of them en suite.

Carnwood Country House, 85 Victoria Rd, Holywood, Co Armagh, BT18 9BG,

Tel: 028 9042 1745 Approached by a long driveway lined with rare species of trees, Carnwood House enjoys a tranquil environment despite being conveniently located for Belfast and the local City Airport. The 4 bedrooms include the Country Suite with 4-poster bed.

Oakfield Guest House, 9 Crumlin Road, Lower Ballinderry, Lisburn, Co Antrim, BT28 2JU,

Tel: 028 9265 1307 Large, modernised farmhouse is surrounded by well-presented gardens, with plenty of parking space, and has 4 guest bedrooms, all en suite. Convenient for the disabled.

Food and Drink

Motte 'n' Bailey, 131-3 Kingsway, Dunmurry, Co Antrim

Tel: 028 9060 3790 A round tower look for this establishment with three bars, one serving as a restaurant: pub grub plus à la carte menu.

The Old Cross Inn, Newtownards, Co Down

Tel: 028 9182 0212 The oldest pub-restaurant in town, and one of the best in the region. Food served lunch and dinner & all day Sunday till 7.30.   832

The Primrose Bar, Ballynahinch, Co Down

Tel: 028 9756 3177 Fax: 028 9756 5954 Bar and restaurant on the main street of town. Local ales, worldwide wines, bar menu and various restaurant menus.   837

Royal Belfast

Royal Belfast Golf Club, Station Road, Craigavad, Holywood, Co Down, BT18 0BP

Tel: 028 9042 8165

Founded in 1881, Royal Belfast has the distinction of being Ireland's oldest club. Four years later, it became the first Irish club to be granted

the royal charter. But in common with a number of other establishments, it was forced to move from its original home.

The club's original location was at The Kinnegar, Hollywood Co Down which, a military training area and rifle-range, later led to problems. And there were further difficulties after a move to Carnalea where, according to contemporary reports, the "encroachment by the public on holidays and weekends had caused a major nuisance for the club", in 1925.

So it was that the members made the decision to purchase the 140-acre estate and house at Craigavad alongside Belfast Lough, for £11,500. And to a design by Harry Colt, immediately prior to his involvement at Co Sligo and Royal Portrush, the course was opened for play in May 1927.

As might be expected, Colt made the most of a picturesque location. Mature trees were complemented by the strategic placements of bunkers to create a 6,306-yard par-70 challenge of championship standard. Indeed Colt also gave the members some decidedly tricky greens which, according to local knowledge, mostly slope towards the Lough.

When the Irish Professional Championship was staged there in 1958, Christy O'Connor Snr captured the title with a four-round aggregate of 279. And more recently, Darren Clarke shot rounds of 65 and 67 to capture the 36-hole Ulster Professional Championship with an eight-under-par aggregate of 132.

Sec/Manager:	Susanna Morrison
Professional:	Chris Spence
Directions:	2 miles East of Holywood off the A2
Type of Course:	Parkland
Date Founded:	1881
No of Holes:	18
Length:	6306 yds (5766 mtrs)
Par:	70
SSS:	71
Green Fees:	Weekdays: £35 Weekends & Bank

Holidays: £45

Visitors:	Welcome: Avoid Wed. & Sat, Book in advance
Societies:	Welcome: Book in advance
Facilities:	Chipping/Putting Area, Practice Area, Driving Range, Golf Clubs for hire, Trolley hire, Bar, Restaurant, Caddy service by arrangement, plus Tennis & Squash

Accommodation, Food and Drink

Reference numbers below refer to detailed information provided in section 2

Accommodation

108 Seacliff Road, Bangor, Co Down

Tel: 028 9146 1077 e-mail: heathermbell@compuserve.com website: www.bandb-bangor.Couk B&B with sea views. 2 singles, I en suite double. No smoking. No credit cards.

Carnwood Country House, 85 Victoria Rd, Holywood, Co Armagh, BT18 9BG,

Tel: 028 9042 1745 Approached by a long driveway lined with rare species of trees, Carnwood House enjoys a tranquil environment despite being conveniently located for Belfast and the local City Airport. The 4 bedrooms include the Country Suite with 4-poster bed.

Tara Guest House, 51 Princetown Rd, Bangor, Co Down, BT20 3TA,

Tel: 028 9146 8924 The Tara has 10 comfortable guest bedrooms, all of them en suite and all furnished to a high standard. An evening meal is available.

Food and Drink

Clandeboye Lodge Hotel, Bangor, Co Down

Tel: 028 9185 2500 e-mail: info@clandeboyelodge.com 3 star hotel with 43 bedrooms, all en suite. Bar and restaurant. Adjacent to Blackwood and Clandeboye golf clubs with 7 further courses within 10 minutes. 3 RAC merit awards. Consort Crown Regional Hotel of the Year 1997, 1998 & 1999

Papa's, Bangor, Co Down

Tel: 028 9145 3747 Espresso and ice cream bar, sandwiches and light snacks. Open 10am to 10pm 7 days a week. No credit cards.

The Old Cross Inn, Newtownards, Co Down

Tel: 028 9182 0212 The oldest pub-restaurant in town, and one of the best in the region. Food served lunch and dinner & all day Sunday till 7.30. 832

Royal County Down

Royal County Down Golf Club, Newcastle, Co Down, BT33 OAN

Tel: 028 4372 3314

In compiling his fine book, "Classic Golf Links of Great Britain and Ireland", Donald Steel made predictably glowing reference to Royal Co Down.

But if not a sting, there was a gentle barb in the tail, especially with regard to the 547-yard 18th hole, which he suggested was somewhat weak. Not any more.

Since the book's publication in 1992, Steel has been back to Royal Co Down, wearing his golf course architect's hat. And he was given the key assignment of reshaping a finishing hole more in keeping with the celebrated quality of the remainder of the course. This he did through softening the domed fairway at driving distance and through strategic bunkering on the right.

His handiwork has already become a crucial element of such major events as the British Amateur and Home International championships of 1999. And it will be further tested in the British Senior Open to be played there in 2000. Meanwhile, the verdict so far is that competitors nervously protecting a lead, will find no sanctuary down the last.

In the shadow of the majestic Mourne Mountains, Old Tom Morris designed this incomparable links for the princely fee of four guineas back in 1889. And those who would argue that it contains too many blind shots to be considered a great test of golf, should note Tommy Armour's observation that "there is no such thing as a blind shot to any player with a memory."

As for Steel: he has succeeded in gilding the lily.

Sec/Manager:	P. E. Rolph
Professional:	Kevan J. Whitson
Directions:	Seaside Course off the A2 just to the North of Newcastle

Championship

Type of Course:	Links
Date Founded:	1889
No of Holes:	18
Length:	7037 yds (6434 mtrs)
Par:	71
SSS:	74
Green Fees:	Weekdays: £70 Weekends & Bank Holidays: £80

Annesley

Type of Course:	Links - Championship Course
Date Founded:	1889
No of Holes:	18
Length:	4681 yds (4280 mtrs)
Par:	63
SSS:	63
Green Fees:	Weekdays: £15 Weekends & Bank Holidays: £25
Visitors:	Welcome: Any Day except Wed and Sat, Book in advance
Societies:	Welcome: Book in advance
Facilities:	Chipping/Putting Area, Practice Area, Golf Clubs for hire, Trolley hire, Bar, Restaurant, Caddy service by arrangement

Accommodation, Food and Drink

Reference numbers below refer to detailed information provided in section 2

Accommodation

Avoca Hotel, 93-97 Central promenade, Newcastle, Co Down, BT33 OHH,

Tel: 028 4372 2253 Overlooking the Promenade and Dundrum Bay, the Avoca Hotel's two bars offer a good choice of bar snacks and a very good restaurant. The hotel has 16 guest bedrooms of which 8 are en suite.

Dacara, 47 South Promenade, Newcastle, Co. Down

Tel: 028 4372 6745 e-mail: dacara@the chefshop.com Bed & Breakfast accommodation in a homely turn-of-the-century house on the A2. Great sea views. Golf and restaurant nearby.

Drumrawn House, 139 Central Promenade, Newcastle, Co. Down

Tel: 028 4372 6847 Three large en suite bedrooms with tv and tea-makers. Private parking. Good Irish breakfast. Royal County Down golf course nearby.

Quay Lodge, 31 South Promenade, Newcastle, Co. Down

Tel: 028 4372 3054 Bed & Breakfast accommodation in two en suite double rooms. Private parking; sea view; two minutes drive to golf course.

Food and Drink

Archways, Kilkeel, Co Down

Tel: 028 4176 4112 A spacious restaurant with bar and lounge. Daily lunches, evening à la carte; entertainment. 834

Avoca Hotel, 93-97 Central promenade, Newcastle, Co Down, BT33 OHH,

Tel: 028 4372 2253 Overlooking the Promenade and Dundrum Bay, the Avoca Hotel's two bars offer a good choice of bar snacks and a very good restaurant. The hotel has 16 guest bedrooms of which 8 are en suite.

Mario's Restaurant, Newcastle, Co Down

Tel: 028 4372 3912 A friendly restaurant with a menu of Italian and Continental dishes. Open Tues-Sat evenings (Monday in summer) and Sunday lunch, tea and dinner. 850

Roadhouse Inn, Dundrum, Co Down

Tel: 028 4375 1209 Inn, dating from 1800, with bistro and à la carte restaurant. 7 double bedrooms. Live music every Friday, Saturday and Sunday. 851

Seven Stars Restaurant, Loughbrickland, Co Down

Tel: 028 4062 6461 A bright, cheerful bar-restaurant serving a good range of dishes from 11.30 to 7.30. Just off the main A1. 833

The Anchor, Newcastle, Co Down

Tel: 028 4372 3344 A family-owned, old-world pub-restaurant just yards from the sea. Snacks, lunches, full menu of good home cooking. 836

Scrabo

Scrabo Golf Club, 233 Scrabo Road,
Newtownards, Co Down, BT23 4SL

Tel: 028 9181 2355

Sec/Manager:	Christine Hamill
Professional:	Paul McCrystal
Directions:	1 mile South of Newtownards off the A21. Follow signs to Scrabo Country Park
Type of Course:	Parkland
Date Founded:	1907
No of Holes:	18
Length:	6232 yds (5699 mtrs)
Par:	71
SSS:	71
Green Fees:	Weekdays: £15 Weekends & Bank Holidays: £20
Visitors:	Welcome: Any Day except Wed. & Sat.
Societies:	Welcome: Special concessions available, Contact Club for details
Facilities:	Practice Area, Golf Clubs for hire, Trolley hire, Bar, Restaurant

Accommodation, Food and Drink

Reference numbers below refer to detailed information provided in section 2

Accommodation

Carnwood Country House, 85 Victoria Rd, Holywood, Co Armagh, BT18 9BG,

Tel: 028 9042 1745 Approached by a long driveway lined with rare species of trees, Carnwood House enjoys a tranquil environment despite being conveniently located for Belfast and the local City Airport. The 4 bedrooms include the Country Suite with 4-poster bed.

Clandeboye Lodge Hotel, Bangor, Co Down

Tel: 028 9185 2500 e-mail: info@clandeboyelodge.com 3 star hotel with 43 bedrooms, all en suite. Bar and restaurant. Adjacent to Blackwood and Clandeboye golf clubs with 7 further courses within 10 minutes. 4 RAC merit awards. Consort Crown Regional Hotel of the Year 1997, 1998 & 1999

Rockhaven B&B, 79 Mountain Road, Newtoonards, Co Down, BT33 4UL,

Tel: 028 9182 3987 The 2 guest bedrooms at Rockhaven are stylishly furnished and the house is surrounded by superb large gardens, (complete with barbecue area), which reindeer visit on a regular basis.

Swan Lodge, 30 St Patricks Road, Saul, Co Down

Tel/Fax: 028 4461 5542 A modern B&B house with views of Strangford Lough and St Patricks Monument. En suite rooms, tv, dinner on request.

Food and Drink

Clandeboye Lodge Hotel, Bangor, Co Down

Tel: 028 9185 2500 e-mail: info@clandeboyelodge.com 3 star hotel with 43 bedrooms, all en suite. Bar and restaurant. Adjacent to Blackwood and Clandeboye golf clubs with 7 further courses within 10 minutes. 4 RAC merit awards. Consort Crown Regional Hotel of the Year 1997, 1998 & 1999

Papa's, Bangor, Co Down

Tel: 028 9145 3747 Espresso and ice cream bar, sandwiches and light snacks. Open 10am to 10pm 7 days a week. No credit cards.

The Old Cross Inn, Newtownards, Co Down

Tel: 028 9182 0212 The oldest pub-restaurant in town, and one of the best in the region. Food served lunch and dinner & all day Sunday till 7.30. 832

Spa

Warrenpoint

Spa Golf Club, 20 Grove Road, Ballynahinch, Co Down, BT24 8PN

Tel: 028 9756 2363

Sec/Manager:	Mr. T. Magee
Professional:	None
Directions:	1 mile South of Ballynahinch off the B175
Type of Course:	Parkland
Date Founded:	1907
No of Holes:	18
Length:	6564 yds (6003 mtrs)
Par:	72
SSS:	72
Green Fees:	Weekdays: £15 Weekends & Bank Holidays: £20
Visitors:	Welcome: Book in advance
Societies:	Welcome: Special concessions available, Contact Club for details
Facilities:	Chipping/Putting Area, Practice Area, Golf Clubs for hire, Trolley hire, Bar, Restaurant

Warrenpoint Golf Club, Lower Dromore Road, Warrenpoint, Co Down, BT34 3LN

Tel: 028 3075 3695

Sec/Manager:	Marion Trainor
Professional:	Nigel Shaw
Directions:	1 mile West of Warrenpoint off the A2 to Newry
Type of Course:	Parkland
Date Founded:	1893
No of Holes:	18
Length:	6161 yds (5633 mtrs)
Par:	71
SSS:	70
Green Fees:	Weekdays: £25 Weekends & Bank Holidays: £30
Visitors:	Welcome: Book in advance
Societies:	Welcome: Book in advance
Facilities:	Chipping/Putting Area, Practice Area, Golf Clubs for hire, Trolley hire, Bar, Restaurant Caddy service by arrangement

Accommodation, Food and Drink

Reference numbers below refer to detailed information provided in section 2

Accommodation

Bushymead Country House, 86 Drumaness Rd, Ballynahinch, Co Down, BT24 8LT,
Tel: 028 9756 1171 The house stands in spacious grounds with extensive gardens, a children's play area, barbecue site and a large pond. The house has 8 attractively furnished guest bedrooms, 7 of them en suite.

Dacara, 47 South Promenade, Newcastle, Co. Down
Tel: 028 4372 6745 e-mail: dacara@the chefshop.com Bed & Breakfast accommodation in a homely turn-of-the-century house on the A2. Great sea views. Golf and restaurant nearby.

Dufferin Arms, 35 High Street, Killyleagh, Co Down, BT30 9QF,
Tel: 028 4482 8229 This is a traditional country pub renowned throughout Ulster for its excellent food, drink and friendly atmosphere. Recommended by Taste of Ulster. There are 7 luxury en suite bedrooms, some with four-poster beds.

Quay Lodge, 31 South Promenade, Newcastle, Co. Down
Tel: 028 4372 3054 Bed & Breakfast accommodation in two en suite double rooms. Private parking; sea view; two minutes drive to golf course.

Food and Drink

Avoca Hotel, 93-97 Central promenade, Newcastle, Co Down, BT33 OHH,
Tel: 028 4372 2253 Overlooking the Promenade and Dundrum Bay, the Avoca Hotel's two bars offer a good choice of bar snacks and a very good restaurant. The hotel has 16 guest bedrooms of which 8 are en suite.

Dufferin Arms, 35 High Street, Killyleagh, Co Down, BT30 9QF,
Tel: 028 4482 8229 This is a traditional country pub renowned throughout Ulster for its excellent food, drink and friendly atmosphere. Recommended by Taste of Ulster. There are 7 luxury en suite bedrooms, some with four-poster beds.

The Primrose Bar, Ballynahinch, Co Down
Tel: 028 9756 3177 Fax: 028 9756 5954 Bar and restaurant on the main street of town. Local ales, worldwide wines, bar menu and various restaurant menus.   837

Accommodation, Food and Drink

Reference numbers below refer to detailed information provided in section 2

Accommodation

Arradale House, Carrickmacross, Co Monaghan
Tel: 042 9661941 Ten en suite bedrooms for full or part board Accommodation on a working farm in a beautiful setting of woods and lakes.   461

Dacara, 47 South Promenade, Newcastle, Co. Down
Tel: 028 4372 6745 e-mail: dacara@the chefshop.com Bed & Breakfast accommodation in a homely turn-of-the-century house on the A2. Great sea views. Golf and restaurant nearby.

Quay Lodge, 31 South Promenade, Newcastle, Co. Down
Tel: 028 4372 3054 Bed & Breakfast accommodation in two en suite double rooms. Private parking; sea view; two minutes drive to golf course.

The Heritage, Dundalk, Co Louth
Tel: 042 9335850 This B&B house in a rural setting 1½ miles from Dundalk. Five letting bedrooms, 3 en suite.   401

Village Inn & Buttery, 103-105 Main Street, Markethill, Co Armagh, BT6 1PJ,
Tel: 028 3755 1237 The Village Inn is a popular venue where locals and visitors alike savour the welcoming atmosphere of a traditional Irish inn. Based on local produce, the menu offers a wide choice of high class food.

Food and Drink

Archways, Kilkeel, Co Down
Tel: 028 4176 4112 A spacious restaurant with bar and lounge. Daily lunches, evening à la carte; entertainment.   834

Roadhouse Inn, Dundrum, Co Down
Tel: 028 4375 1209 Inn, dating from 1800, with bistro and à la carte restaurant. 7 double bedrooms. Live music every Friday, Saturday and Sunday.   851

Seven Stars Restaurant, Loughbrickland, Co Down
Tel: 028 4062 6461 A bright, cheerful bar-restaurant serving a good range of dishes from 11.30 to 7.30. Just off the main A1.   833

The Kilbroney Bar and Restaurant, Rostrevor, Co Down
Tel: 028 4173 8390 Town-centre restaurant, bar and beer garden. Food is served all day, every day from an à la carte menu.   830

FERMANAGH & TYRONE

During the 1990 season, County Tyrone, or more specifically, Dungannon GC, received a level of publicity that it has never enjoyed before or since. And it all had to go with the superb performances of its most distinguished golfer, Darren Clarke, who captured the Spanish Open, Irish Close, North of Ireland and South of Ireland championships that year, before turning professional. Since then, Clarke has gone on to other, significant honours in the game. Indeed he has emulated Fred Daly by becoming only the second professional to be given honorary life membership of Royal Portrush GC. But that has been as an exile from County Tyrone, where he learned the craft of stick and ball.

Folk Park, Co Tyrone

Dominated to the east by Lough Neagh, Tyrone has Donegal and Fermanagh as its western and south-western neighbours. And in this, the most rural area of Northern Ireland, it is considerably better-endowed than Fermanagh, where golf-course developments are concerned. The 10 courses in the area are: Tyrone - Aughnacloy, Benburb Valley, Dungannon, Fintona, Killymoon, Newtownstewart, Omagh, Strabane; Fermanagh - Castle Hume, Enniskillen. Of these, Augnacloy, Benburb Valley and Fintona are nine-hole facilities; the remainder are 18 holes. Killymoon GC, situated on the outskirts of Cookstown, is named after Killymoon Castle, which was designed by the celebrated English architect, John Nash, in 1804 and was reputedly owned at one time by King George IV. We are informed that his majesty won it on the throw of a dice. Though the club is happy to settle for an institution date of 1889, there are good reasons to believe that golf was played there at least a year earlier. In the event, the course was later extended to 18 holes of which the first is especially picturesque, skirting as it does the woods of the Castle.

Indeed Tyrone offers some charming parkland terrain. Like, for instance, at Fintona, when a trout stream meanders through the layout, traversing the fairway at the short fourth and separating the par-four third from the long fifth holes. Omagh has an even finer golf course, bordering the River Drumragh on the Dublin road. Sadly, the town made international news for all the wrong reasons in August 1998, when its centre was devastated by a terrorist bomb which caused an appalling loss of life. But the remarkable resilience of the residents was soon evident in the way they rebuilt their lives.

The town, located at the meeting of two rivers, the Camowen and the Drumragh, is a popular angling centre for both game and coarse fish. And it also happens to be the birthplace of the gifted Irish playwright Brian Friel, whose latest play, "Dancing at Lughnasa", has been turned into a movie starring Meryl Streep. South-east of Omagh, near the town of

Water Gate, Enniskillen, Co Fermanagh

Ballygawley, is the homestead of Ulysses Simpson Grant, who was born there in 1838. After serving with distinction in the American Civil War as a general in the union army, Grant was elected president of the US and served two terms, from 1869 to 1877. After completing his stint in the White House, he made a sentimental visit to his County Tyrone home in 1878 and the rebuilt, thatched cottage is now the focus for an interpretative centre and souvenir shop.

In golf, Fermanagh's practitioners had reason to feel somewhat deprived, compared with their Tyrone brethren, in that their facilities were limited to the Enniskillen club until Castle Hume came on stream in 1991. It, too, is in the county town, which is dominated by the Erne and its two lakes. Indeed it has a delightful location in the grounds of the old Ely Estate on the shores of Castle Hume Lough and the Lower Lough Erne. Built to championship standards, it became a regular venue for the Ulster Professional Championship in 1996, when former European Tour player, Jimmy Heggarty, captured the title with a 36-hole total of 142 - two under par.

Meanwhile, apart from being a paradise for birds, flowers and fishermen, Lough Erne is a superb waterway for unrestricted cruising and boating. The lakeside is high and rocky in parts and in addition to its 154 islands, there are countless coves and inlets to explore. Lower Lough Erne, which is 26-miles long, is separated from the Atlantic only by a narrow strip of County Leitrim. Navigation can be quite a challenge when the wind blows, with waves surging to open-sea dimensions. For its part, the shallower, Upper Lough Erne, flowing south-east, is characterised by a maze of islands. One of the most interesting of these is Devenish, where a 12th century round tower stands sentinel as a relic of medieval monastic life. From its high windows, monks had a clear view of approaching strangers, while within its cool cavities, they rang their bells and hid their sacred relics. The island also has a tiny church of similar vintage. Then, on Boa Island, a two-faced Celtic idol in a christian graveyard provides a fascinating reminder of the

Marble Arch Caves, Co Fermanagh

old gods of ancient Ireland. Swans are a common sight on Lough Erne, while terns and common scoters breed on the low-lying islands and sandpipers, nightjars and garden warblers are to be found nesting around the shore. And closer ties with the Republic of Ireland are reflected in the Ballinamore Canal, which now links the Erne with the River Shannon, so creating a 500-mile waterway all the way to Limerick.

Elsewhere, for those not especially interested in acquatic activities, attractions include the Marble Arch Caves, along with two, rather special stately homes, both in National Trust care. Castle Coole, the Palladian mansion designed at Enniskillen by James Wyatt for the Earl of Belmore, was completed in 1796 and contains magnificent woodwork, fireplaces, furniture and a library. The other home is Enniskillen Castle, which was the seat of the Maguires, the medieval chieftains of Fermanagh, who are said to have policed the lough with a private navy of 1,500 boats. The castle now houses the county museum and trophies of the Inniskilling regiments who fought against Napoleon at Waterloo.

As we have suggested, Fermanagh may have been neglected somewhat in terms of golfing development. But Enniskillen could claim quite an elevated place in literature, given that it received honourable mention in the writings of Edmund Spenser, while Oscar Wilde and Samuel Beckett both had early schooling there.

Location of Golf Courses

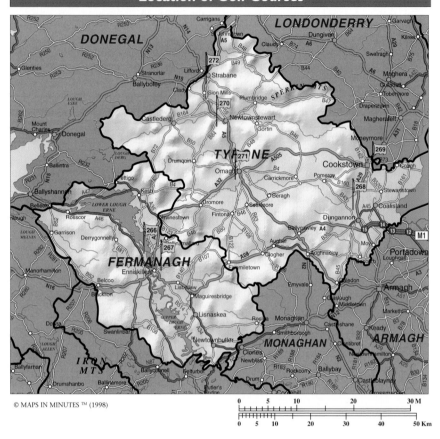

© MAPS IN MINUTES ™ (1998)

Castle Hume

Castle Hume Golf Course, Enniskillen, Co
Fermanagh, BT93 7ED

Tel: 028 6632 7077

Sec/Manager:	Austin Frazer
Professional:	Gareth McShea
Directions:	Four miles from Enniskillen off the A46 to Belleek
Type of Course:	Parkland
Date Founded:	1992
No of Holes:	18
Length:	6487 yds (5932 mtrs)
Par:	72
SSS:	71
Green Fees:	Weekdays: £15 Weekends & Bank Holidays: £20
Visitors:	Welcome: Book in advance
Societies:	Welcome: Contact Club for details
Facilities:	Chipping/Putting Area, Practice Area, Golf Clubs for hire, Trolley hire, Electric Buggy hire, Bar

Accommodation, Food and Drink

Reference numbers below refer to detailed
information provided in section 2

Accommodation

Brooklands, Ballinamallard, Co Fermanagh

Tel: 028 6638 8099 A two-storey period building on the main street of a village 5 miles from Enniskillen. 14 en suite bedrooms include singles and family rooms. 877

Clanabogan House, Omagh, Co Tyrone

Tel/Fax: 028 8224 1171 Eight large, traditionally styled bedrooms in a 17th-century house set in extensive gardens. B&B, also evening meals for parties of 8 plus. 896

Donn Carragh Hotel, Lisnaskea, Co Fermanagh

Tel: 028 6772 1206 A newly refurbished hotel in the heart of town by Upper Lough Erne. 18 en suite bedrooms with tv and phone. Bar, lounge, restaurant. 871

Fort Lodge Hotel, Enniskillen, Co Fermanagh

Tel: 028 6632 3275 A comfortable, friendly hotel with well-equipped en suite bedrooms, traditional bar-lounge and intimate restaurant. 872

Greenwood Lodge, Ederney, Enniskillen, Co Fermanagh

Tel: 028 6663 1366 B&B in one single, two twins and four doubles, most en suite. No credit cards. e-mail: greenwoodlodge@hotmail.com

Hotel Carlton, Belleek, Co Fermanagh

Tel: 028 6865 8282 19 en suite bedrooms in a handsomely renovated hotel in the centre of a pottery town on the banks of Lough Erne. 874

Moohans Fiddlestone, Belleek, Co Fermanagh

Tel: 028 6865 8008 Traditional pub and licensed guesthouse in the centre of town. Five en suite bedrooms with tv. Bar with snacks. 876

The Railway Hotel, Enniskillen, Co Fermanagh

Tel: 028 6632 2084 19 individually appointed bedrooms in a carefully renovated Victorian hotel on the Omagh road just away from the centre. 875

The Three Way Inn, Ashwood, Enniskillen, Co Fermanagh

Tel: 028 6632 7414 On the main Sligo road out of Enniskillen, very welcoming inn with an all-day menu. Self-catering Accommodation; more under way. 873

The Valley Hotel, Fivemiletown, Co Tyrone

Tel: 028 8952 1505 A modern hotel on the main Belfast-Enniskillen road (A4), with 22 comprehensively equipped en suite bedrooms. Bar, restaurant. 899

Food and Drink

Brooklands, Ballinamallard, Co Fermanagh

Tel: 028 6638 8099 A two-storey period building on the main street of a village 5 miles from Enniskillen. 14 en suite bedrooms include singles and family rooms. 877

Donn Carragh Hotel, Lisnaskea, Co Fermanagh

Tel: 028 6772 1206 A newly refurbished hotel in the heart of town by Upper Lough Erne. 18 en suite bedrooms with tv and phone. Bar, lounge, restaurant. 871

Fort Lodge Hotel, Enniskillen, Co Fermanagh

Tel: 028 6632 3275 A comfortable, friendly hotel with well-equipped en suite bedrooms, traditional bar-lounge and intimate restaurant. 872

Hotel Carlton, Belleek, Co Fermanagh

Tel: 028 6865 8282 19 en suite bedrooms in a handsomely renovated hotel in the centre of a pottery town on the banks of Lough Erne. 874

Moohans Fiddlestone, Belleek, Co Fermanagh

Tel: 028 6865 8008 Traditional pub and licensed guesthouse in the centre of town. Five en suite bedrooms with tv. Bar with snacks. 876

Pat's Bar and Restaurant, Enniskillen, Co Fermanagh

Tel: 028 6632 7462 Four bars and a 150-cover restaurant in a prime corner site on the main thoroughfare. Excellent value menus. 870

The Horseshoe & Saddlers, Enniskillen, Co Fermanagh

Tel/Fax: 028 6632 6223 Pub-cum-restaurant serving traditional Irish cuisine. A la carte menu. Open every day. Access, Mastercard, Visa.

The Railway Hotel, Enniskillen, Co Fermanagh

Tel: 028 6632 2084 19 individually appointed bedrooms in a carefully renovated Victorian hotel on the Omagh road just away from the centre. 875

The Three Way Inn, Ashwood, Enniskillen, Co Fermanagh

Tel: 028 6632 7414 On the main Sligo road out of Enniskillen, welcoming inn with an all-day menu. Self-catering Accommodation; more under way. 873

The Valley Hotel, Fivemiletown, Co Tyrone

Tel: 028 8952 1505 A modern hotel on the main Belfast-Enniskillen road (A4), with 22 comprehensively equipped en suite bedrooms. Bar, restaurant. 899

Enniskillen

Enniskillen Golf Club, Castlecoole Road,
Enniskillen, Co Fermanagh, BT74 7JY

Tel: 028 6632 5250

When Enniskillen GC gained 18-hole status
through the opening of their new front-nine in
1989, some of the older members made gentle
enquiries as to where the club planned to store
its oxygen supply. Its hilly nature certainly con-
trasted with the original nine, which has now
become the homeward journey.

Founded in 1896, the club started with a nine-
hole course at Killyhevlin before moving in 1944
to its present home at Castlecoole. Then, about
40 years later, the chance for further development
arose with the purchase of an adjoining 54 acres
from Fermanagh District Council.

Natural features include a stream which
traverses the first, seventh, eighth and ninth fair-

ways. Then there is a lake to the right of the 321-yard seventh, where the left to right dog-leg configuration brings the green within reach of a drive from a really long hitter.

Meanwhile, both nines, divided by an access road, are dominated by trees at varying stages of maturity. Indeed when a large oak on the old nine was felled in a recent storm, a tree doctor calculated that it dated back to medieval times.

The 343-yard opening hole presents a test both of skill and stamina. But there is a handsome reward two holes later when, from the elevated third green, the player is offered majestic views of Upper Lough Erne beyond the Killyhevlin Hotel. And the hope among the membership is that the latest Northern Ireland peace initiative will see a return of tourists to this delightfully picturesque county.

Sec/Manager:	William McBrein
Professional:	None
Directions:	Next to Castlecoole Estate
Type of Course:	Parkland
Date Founded:	1896
No of Holes:	18
Length:	6111 yds (5588 mtrs)
Par:	71
SSS:	69
Green Fees:	Weekdays: £15 Weekends & Bank Holidays: £18
Visitors:	Welcome : Any Day
Societies:	Welcome : Special concessions, Book in advance
Facilities:	Chipping/Putting Area, Golf Clubs for hire, Trolley hire, Electric Buggy hire, Bar

Accommodation, Food and Drink

Reference numbers below refer to detailed information provided in section 2

Accommodation

Brooklands, Ballinamallard, Co Fermanagh
Tel: 028 6638 8099 A two-storey period building on the main street of a village 5 miles from Enniskillen. 14 en suite bedrooms include singles and family rooms. 877

Clanabogan House, Omagh, Co Tyrone
Tel/Fax: 028 8224 1171 Eight large, traditionally styled bedrooms in a 17th-century house set in extensive gardens. B&B, also evening meals for parties of 8 plus. 896

Donn Carragh Hotel, Lisnaskea, Co Fermanagh
Tel: 028 6772 1206 A newly refurbished hotel in the heart of town by Upper Lough Erne. 18 en suite bedrooms with tv and phone. Bar, lounge, restaurant.   871

Fort Lodge Hotel, Enniskillen, Co Fermanagh
Tel: 028 6632 3275 A comfortable, friendly hotel with well-equipped en suite bedrooms, traditional bar-lounge and intimate restaurant.   872

Greenwood Lodge, Ederney, Enniskillen, Co Fermanagh
Tel: 028 6663 1366 B&B in one single, two twins and four doubles, most en suite. No credit cards. e-mail: greenwoodlodge@hotmail.com

Hotel Carlton, Belleek, Co Fermanagh
Tel: 028 6865 8282 19 en suite bedrooms in a handsomely renovated hotel in the centre of a pottery town on the banks of Lough Erne.   874

Kellys Inn, Omagh, Co Tyrone
Tel: 028 8556 8218 Motel-style Accommodation, spacious restaurant and cosy bars in a long modern single-storey complex on the main A5.   903

Lackaboy Farm Guest House, Enniskillen, Co Fermanagh
Tel: 028 6632 2488 2-star Accommodation in 3 singles, a twin, a double and a family room, all en suite. Evening meals for residents. Access, Visa.

Moohans Fiddlestone, Belleek, Co Fermanagh
Tel: 028 6865 8008 Traditional pub and licensed guesthouse in the centre of town. Five en suite bedrooms with tv. Bar with snacks.   876

The Old School House, Killadeas, Enniskillen, Co Fermanagh
Tel: 028 6862 1688 Joan Moore offers B&B Accommodation in three doubles, a twin and two family rooms, all en suite, in a former schoolhouse.

The Railway Hotel, Enniskillen, Co Fermanagh
Tel: 028 6632 2084 19 individually appointed bedrooms in a carefully renovated Victorian hotel on the Omagh road just away from the centre.   875

The Three Way Inn, Ashwood, Enniskillen, Co Fermanagh
Tel: 028 6632 7414 On the main Sligo road out of Enniskillen, very welcoming inn with an all-day menu. Self-catering Accommodation; more under way.   873

The Valley Hotel, Fivemiletown, Co Tyrone
Tel: 028 8952 1505 A modern hotel on the main Belfast-Enniskillen road (A4), with 22 comprehensively equipped en suite bedrooms. Bar, restaurant.   899

Food and Drink

Brooklands, Ballinamallard, Co Fermanagh
Tel: 028 6638 8099 A two-storey period building on the main street of a village 5 miles from Enniskillen. 14 en suite bedrooms include singles and family rooms. 877

Donn Carragh Hotel, Lisnaskea, Co Fermanagh
Tel: 028 6772 1206 A newly refurbished hotel in the heart of town by Upper Lough Erne. 18 en suite bedrooms with tv and phone. Bar, lounge, restaurant.   871

Fort Lodge Hotel, Enniskillen, Co Fermanagh
Tel: 028 6632 3275 A comfortable, friendly hotel with well-equipped en suite bedrooms, traditional bar-lounge and intimate restaurant.   872

Hotel Carlton, Belleek, Co Fermanagh
Tel: 028 6865 8282 19 en suite bedrooms in a handsomely renovated hotel in the centre of a pottery town on the banks of Lough Erne.   874

Kellys Inn, Omagh, Co Tyrone
Tel: 028 8556 8218 Motel-style Accommodation, spacious restaurant and cosy bars in a long modern single-storey complex on the main A5.   903

Moohans Fiddlestone, Belleek, Co Fermanagh
Tel: 028 6865 8008 Traditional pub and licensed guesthouse in the centre of town. Five en suite bedrooms with tv. Bar with snacks.   876

Pat's Bar and Restaurant, Enniskillen, Co Fermanagh
Tel: 028 6632 7462 Four bars and a 150-cover restaurant in a prime corner site on the main thoroughfare. Excellent value menus.   870

The Horseshoe & Saddlers, Enniskillen, Co Fermanagh
Tel/Fax: 028 6632 6223 Pub-cum-restaurant serving traditional Irish cuisine. A la carte menu. Open every day. Access, Mastercard, Visa.

The Railway Hotel, Enniskillen, Co Fermanagh
Tel: 028 6632 2084 19 individually appointed bedrooms in a carefully renovated Victorian hotel on the Omagh road just away from the centre.   875

The Three Way Inn, Ashwood, Enniskillen, Co Fermanagh
Tel: 028 6632 7414 On the main Sligo road out of Enniskillen, very welcoming inn with an all-day menu. Self-catering Accommodation; more under way.   873

The Valley Hotel, Fivemiletown, Co Tyrone
Tel: 028 8952 1505 A modern hotel on the main Belfast-Enniskillen road (A4), with 22 comprehensively equipped en suite bedrooms. Bar, restaurant.   899

Dungannon

Dungannon Golf Club, 34 Springfield Lane,
Dungannon, Co Tyrone, BT70 1QX

Tel: 028 8772 2098

During his early years on the European Tour,
Darren Clarke's exploits would be followed with
considerable interest in the Dungannon clubhouse. And there were special occasions when
his mother, Hettie, would be instructed to offer
celebratory drinks to the player's former
clubmates.

Apart from giving the Irish game one of its
most successful players of recent years,
Dungannon also holds the distinction of being
a founder-member of the GUI in 1891. It was
founded a year previously on land provided by
the Earl of Ranfurly, who became the first president of the national union.

Characterised by tree-lined fairways and outstanding greens, the classic, parkland course has
recently been upgraded to a design by Clarke. It
has a particularly interesting finish. Closeby the
clubhouse is a 90-yard, par-three 16th, followed
by a formidable, 554-yard 17th, before the 358-
yard 18th provides a fitting climax.

In common with a few other courses of its
vintage, Dungannon set out as a 12-hole layout.
And lest anyone be confused as to the club's
notion of a round of golf, we are informed that
"by taking in six of the holes in a second round,
the orthodox 18 are secured."

As it happened, the club reverted to nine holes
in 1896 and there was no change until the
present 18 were formed at Mullaghmore, in 1963.

Interestingly, two of the most difficult holes on
the course are two par fives, the 558-yard third
and the 17th. But they are partially offset by the
relatively easy, 492-yard 12th.

Sec/Manager:	Noel McGrath
Professional:	None
Directions:	1 mile North West of Dungannon off the B43 to Donaghmore
Type of Course:	Parkland
Date Founded:	1890
No of Holes:	18
Length:	5941 yds (5433 mtrs)
Par:	72
SSS:	69
Green Fees:	Weekdays: £15 Weekends & Bank Holidays: £18
Visitors:	Welcome: Any Day, Restrictions on Saturday, Contact Club in advance
Societies:	Welcome: Contact Club for details
Facilities:	Chipping/Putting Area, Practice Area, Trolley hire, Bar, Restaurant

Accommodation, Food and Drink

Reference numbers below refer to detailed
information provided in section 2

Accommodation

Glengannon Hotel, Dungannon, Co Tyrone

Tel/Fax: 028 8772 7311 En suite bedrooms, good choice of menus and weekend live entertainment in a low-rise modern hotel off the M1 (J15).   897

Greenvale Hotel, Cookstown, Co Tyrone

Tel: 028 8676 2243 An extended Victorian house on the outskirts of Cookstown, with 12 comfortable bedrooms and value-for-money cuisine.   893

Hawthorn House, Omagh, Co Tyrone

Tel: 028 8225 2005 Eight spacious en suite bedrooms and a high-quality restaurant in a period residence just outside town. Leisure centre very near.   901

Kellys Inn, Omagh, Co Tyrone

Tel: 028 8556 8218 Motel-style Accommodation, spacious restaurant and cosy bars in a long modern single-storey complex on the main A5.   903

McGirr's, Coalisland, Co Tyrone

Tel: 028 8774 7324 A large pub with 12 rooms for budget Bed & Breakfast Accommodation, a no-frills bar, lounge and off licence.   892

Muleany House, Moy, Dungannon, Co Tyrone

Tel: 028 8778 4183 Family-run, family-friendly home from home with nine en suite bedrooms, drawing room, tv room, games room and traditional home cooking.   890

Oaklin House Hotel, Dungannon, Co Tyrone

Tel: 028 8772 5151 A fine modern hotel set in extensive grounds, with superbly

appointed en suite bedrooms, and a choice of restaurants and bars. 902

Reahs, Dungannon, Co Tyrone

Tel: 028 8772 5575 Top-class food and luxurious overnight accomodation in a smart detached house half a mile out of town. 891

The Ryandale, Moy, Co Tyrone

Tel/Fax: 028 8778 4629 A fine Listed building in the centre of a small village. The Ryandale offers en suite bedrooms, restaurant, bar and nightclub. 900

The Valley Hotel, Fivemiletown, Co Tyrone

Tel: 028 8952 1505 A modern hotel on the main Belfast-Enniskillen road (A4), with 22 comprehensively equipped en suite bedrooms. Bar, restaurant. 899

Food and Drink

Glengannon Hotel, Dungannon, Co Tyrone

Tel/Fax: 028 8772 7311 En suite bedrooms, good choice of menus and weekend live entertainment in a low-rise modern hotel off the M1 (J15). 897

Grants Bar and Restaurant, Omagh, Co Tyrone

Tel: 028 8225 0900 A grand pub at the top end of town, with decor of reclaimed pine. On offer is the best in Food and Drink. 898

Greenvale Hotel, Cookstown, Co Tyrone

Tel: 028 8676 2243 An extended Victorian house on the outskirts of Cookstown, with 12 comfortable bedrooms and value-for-money cuisine. 893

Hawthorn House, Omagh, Co Tyrone

Tel: 028 8225 2005 Eight spacious en suite bedrooms and a high-quality restaurant in a period residence just outside town. Leisure centre very near. 901

Kellys Inn, Omagh, Co Tyrone

Tel: 028 8556 8218 Motel-style Accommodation, spacious restaurant and cosy bars in a long modern single-storey complex on the main A5. 903

McGirr's of Gortnagarn, Omagh, Co Tyrone

Tel: 028 8224 2462 A long, low modern pub-restaurant in a rural setting. All-day eating, snooker, darts, weekend entertainment. 894

McGirr's, Coalisland, Co Tyrone

Tel: 028 8774 7324 A large pub with 12 rooms for budget Bed & Breakfast Accommodation, a no-frills bar, lounge and off licence. 892

Oaklin House Hotel, Dungannon, Co Tyrone

Tel: 028 8772 5151 A fine modern hotel set in extensive grounds, with superbly appointed en suite bedrooms, and a choice of restaurants and bars. 902

Reahs, Dungannon, Co Tyrone

Tel: 028 8772 5575 Top-class food and luxurious overnight accomodation in a smart detached house half a mile out of town. 891

The Ryandale, Moy, Co Tyrone

Tel/Fax: 028 8778 4629 A fine Listed building in the centre of a small village. The Ryandale offers en suite bedrooms, restaurant, bar and nightclub. 900

The Valley Hotel, Fivemiletown, Co Tyrone

Tel: 028 8952 1505 A modern hotel on the main Belfast-Enniskillen road (A4), with 22 comprehensively equipped en suite bedrooms. Bar, restaurant. 899

Killymoon

Killymoon Golf Club, 200 Killymoon Road, Cookstown, Co Tyrone, BT80 8TW

Tel: 028 8676 3762/8676 3460

Sec/Manager:	Tom Doonan
Professional:	Garry Chambers
Directions:	1 mile South East of Cookstown off the B520 to Tullyhogue
Type of Course:	Parkland
Date Founded:	1889
No of Holes:	18
Length:	6010 yds (5496 mtrs)
Par:	70
SSS:	69
Green Fees:	Weekdays: £18 Weekends & Bank Holidays: £22

Visitors:	Welcome : Any Day, Contact Club in advance
Societies:	Welcome: Special concessions, Contact Club for details
Facilities:	Chipping/Putting Area, Practice Area, Trolley hire, Bar, Restaurant

Accommodation, Food and Drink

Reference numbers below refer to detailed information provided in section 2

Accommodation

Glengannon Hotel, Dungannon, Co Tyrone

Tel/Fax: 028 8772 7311 En suite bedrooms, good choice of menus and weekend live entertainment in a low-rise modern hotel off the M1 (J15). 897

Greenvale Hotel, Cookstown, Co Tyrone

Tel: 028 8676 2243 An extended Victorian house on the outskirts of Cookstown, with 12 comfortable bedrooms and value-for-money cuisine. 893

McGirr's, Coalisland, Co Tyrone

Tel: 028 8774 7324 A large pub with 12 rooms for budget Bed & Breakfast Accommodation, a no-frills bar, lounge and off licence. 892

Muleany House, Moy, Dungannon, Co Tyrone

Tel: 028 8778 4183 Family-run, family-friendly home from home with nine en suite bedrooms, drawing room, tv room, games room and traditional home cooking. 890

Oaklin House Hotel, Dungannon, Co Tyrone

Tel: 028 8772 5151 A fine modern hotel set in extensive grounds, with superbly appointed en suite bedrooms, and a choice of restaurants and bars. 902

Reahs, Dungannon, Co Tyrone

Tel: 028 8772 5575 Top-class food and luxurious overnight accomodation in a smart detached house half a mile out of town. 891

The Ryandale, Moy, Co Tyrone

Tel/Fax: 028 8778 4629 A fine Listed building in the centre of a small village. The Ryandale offers en suite bedrooms, restaurant, bar and nightclub. 900

Food and Drink

Glengannon Hotel, Dungannon, Co Tyrone

Tel/Fax: 028 8772 7311 En suite bedrooms, good choice of menus and weekend live entertainment in a low-rise modern hotel off the M1 (J15). 897

Greenvale Hotel, Cookstown, Co Tyrone

Tel: 028 8676 2243 An extended Victorian house on the outskirts of Cookstown, with 12 comfortable bedrooms and value-for-money cuisine. 893

McGirr's, Coalisland, Co Tyrone

Tel: 028 8774 7324 A large pub with 12 rooms for budget Bed & Breakfast Accommodation, a no-frills bar, lounge and off licence. 892

McNally's Inn, Castledawson, Co Londonderry

Tel: 028 7965 0095 A small, unpretentious modern country inn well known to golfers and others for its traditional Irish welcome. The extensive menu runs from light snacks to three-course meals. Regular live music sessions. 922

Oaklin House Hotel, Dungannon, Co Tyrone

Tel: 028 8772 5151 A fine modern hotel set in extensive grounds, with superbly appointed en suite bedrooms, and a choice of restaurants and bars. 902

Reahs, Dungannon, Co Tyrone

Tel: 028 8772 5575 Top-class food and luxurious overnight accomodation in a smart detached house half a mile out of town. 891

The Ryandale, Moy, Co Tyrone

Tel/Fax: 028 8778 4629 A fine Listed building in the centre of a small village. The Ryandale offers en suite bedrooms, restaurant, bar and nightclub. 900

Newtownstewart

Newtownstewart Golf Club, 38 Golf Course Road, Newtownstewart, Omagh, Co Tyrone, BT78 4HU

Tel: 028 8166 1466

McGirr's of Gortnagarn, Omagh, Co Tyrone
Tel: 028 8224 2462 A long, low modern pub-restaurant in a rural setting. All-day
eating, snooker, darts, weekend entertainment.   894
The Pink Elephant, 19 High Street, Omagh, Co Tyrone
Tel: 028 8224 9805 High-street café-restaurant with a menu that incorporates Irish,
European and transatlantic influences.

Omagh

Omagh Golf Club, 83a Dublin Road, Omagh, Co Tyrone, BT78 1HQ
Tel: 028 8223 4160

Sec/Manager:	Dianne Cooke
Professional:	None
Directions:	2 miles South West of Newtownstewart off the B84 to Drumquin
Type of Course:	Parkland
Date Founded:	1910
No of Holes:	18
Length:	5840 yds (5341 mtrs)
Par:	70
SSS:	69
Green Fees:	Weekdays: £12 Weekends & Bank Holidays: £17
Visitors:	Welcome: Any day, Contact Club in advance
Societies:	Welcome: Special concessions available, Contact Club for details
Facilities:	Chipping/Putting Area, Practice Area, Golf Clubs for hire, Trolley hire, Electric Buggy hire, Bar, Restaurant, Caddy service by arrangement

Sec/Manager:	Florence Caldwell
Professional:	None
Directions:	1 mile South of Omagh off the A5 to Dublin
Type of Course:	Parkland
Date Founded:	1910
No of Holes:	18
Length:	6205 yds (5674 mtrs)
Par:	71
SSS:	70
Green Fees:	Weekdays: £10 Weekends & Bank Holidays: £15
Visitors:	Welcome: Any Day, Restrictions on Saturday
Societies:	Welcome: Special concessions, Contact Club for details
Facilities:	Chipping/Putting Area, Bar

Accommodation, Food and Drink

Reference numbers below refer to detailed information provided in section 2

Accommodation

Brooklands, Ballinamallard, Co Fermanagh
Tel: 028 6638 8099 A two-storey period building on the main street of a village 5
miles from Enniskillen. 14 en suite bedrooms include singles and family rooms.   877
Clanabogan House, Omagh, Co Tyrone
Tel/Fax: 028 8224 1171 Eight large, traditionally styled bedrooms in a 17th-century
house set in extensive gardens. B&B, also evening meals for parties of 8 plus.   896
Fir Trees Hotel, Strabane, Co Tyrone
Tel: 028 7138 2382 A bright, practical modern complex on the outskirts of town,
with 25 well-equipped en suite bedrooms, a restaurant and bar-bistro.   895
Greenvale Hotel, Cookstown, Co Tyrone
Tel: 028 8676 2243 An extended Victorian house on the outskirts of Cookstown, with
12 comfortable bedrooms and value-for-money cuisine.   893
Greenwood Lodge, Ederney, Enniskillen, Co Fermanagh
Tel: 028 6663 1366 B&B in one single, two twins and four doubles, most en suite.
No credit cards. e-mail: greenwoodlodge@hotmail.com
Hawthorn House, Omagh, Co Tyrone
Tel: 028 8225 2005 Eight spacious en suite bedrooms and a high-quality restaurant
in a period residence just outside town. Leisure centre very near.   901
Kellys Inn, Omagh, Co Tyrone
Tel: 028 8556 8218 Motel-style Accommodation, spacious restaurant and cosy bars in
a long modern single-storey complex on the main A5.   903
Oaklin House Hotel, Dungannon, Co Tyrone
Tel: 028 8772 5151 A fine modern hotel set in extensive grounds, with superbly
appointed en suite bedrooms, and a choice of restaurants and bars.   902
The Old School House, Killadeas, Enniskillen, Co Fermanagh
Tel: 028 6862 1688 Joan Moore offers B&B Accommodation in three doubles, a twin
and two family rooms, all en suite, in a former schoolhouse.

Accommodation, Food and Drink

Reference numbers below refer to detailed information provided in section 2

Accommodation

Clanabogan House, Omagh, Co Tyrone
Tel/Fax: 028 8224 1171 Eight large, traditionally styled bedrooms in a 17th-century
house set in extensive gardens. B&B, also evening meals for parties of 8 plus.   896
Fir Trees Hotel, Strabane, Co Tyrone
Tel: 028 7138 2382 A bright, practical modern complex on the outskirts of town,
with 25 well-equipped en suite bedrooms, a restaurant and bar-bistro.   895
Hawthorn House, Omagh, Co Tyrone
Tel: 028 8225 2005 Eight spacious en suite bedrooms and a high-quality restaurant
in a period residence just outside town. Leisure centre very near.   901

Food and Drink

Clanabogan House, Omagh, Co Tyrone
Tel/Fax: 028 8224 1171 Eight large, traditionally styled bedrooms in a 17th-century
house set in extensive gardens. B&B, also evening meals for parties of 8 plus.   896
Fir Trees Hotel, Strabane, Co Tyrone
Tel: 028 7138 2382 A bright, practical modern complex on the outskirts of town,
with 25 well-equipped en suite bedrooms, a restaurant and bar-bistro.   895
Grants Bar and Restaurant, Omagh, Co Tyrone
Tel: 028 8225 0900 A grand pub at the top end of town, with decor of reclaimed
pine. On offer is the best in Food and Drink.   898
Hawthorn House, Omagh, Co Tyrone
Tel: 028 8225 2005 Eight spacious en suite bedrooms and a high-quality restaurant
in a period residence just outside town. Leisure centre very near.   901

The Valley Hotel, Fivemiletown, Co Tyrone

Tel: 028 8952 1505 A modern hotel on the main Belfast-Enniskillen road (A4), with 22 comprehensively equipped en suite bedrooms. Bar, restaurant.   899

Food and Drink

Brooklands, Ballinamallard, Co Fermanagh

Tel: 028 6638 8099 A two-storey period building on the main street of a village 5 miles from Enniskillen. 14 en suite bedrooms include singles and family rooms.   877

Fir Trees Hotel, Strabane, Co Tyrone

Tel: 028 7138 2382 A bright, practical modern complex on the outskirts of town, with 25 well-equipped en suite bedrooms, a restaurant and bar-bistro.   895

Grants Bar and Restaurant, Omagh, Co Tyrone

Tel: 028 8225 0900 A grand pub at the top end of town, with decor of reclaimed pine. On offer is the best in Food and Drink.   898

Greenvale Hotel, Cookstown, Co Tyrone

Tel: 028 8676 2243 An extended Victorian house on the outskirts of Cookstown, with 12 comfortable bedrooms and value-for-money cuisine.   893

Hawthorn House, Omagh, Co Tyrone

Tel: 028 8225 2005 Eight spacious en suite bedrooms and a high-quality restaurant in a period residence just outside town. Leisure centre very near.   901

Kellys Inn, Omagh, Co Tyrone

Tel: 028 8556 8218 Motel-style Accommodation, spacious restaurant and cosy bars in a long modern single-storey complex on the main A5.   903

McGirr's of Gortnagarn, Omagh, Co Tyrone

Tel: 028 8224 2462 A long, low modern pub-restaurant in a rural setting. All-day eating, snooker, darts, weekend entertainment.   894

Oaklin House Hotel, Dungannon, Co Tyrone

Tel: 028 877 25151 A fine modern hotel set in extensive grounds, with superbly appointed en suite bedrooms, and a choice of restaurants and bars.   902

The Pink Elephant, 19 High Street, Omagh, Co Tyrone

Tel: 028 8224 9805 High-street café-restaurant with a menu that incorporates Irish, European and transatlantic influences.

The Valley Hotel, Fivemiletown, Co Tyrone

Tel: 028 8952 1505 A modern hotel on the main Belfast-Enniskillen road (A4), with 22 comprehensively equipped en suite bedrooms. Bar, restaurant.   899

Strabane

Strabane Golf Club, 33 Ballycolman Road, Strabane, Co Tyrone, BT82 9PH

Tel: 028 7138 2271

Sec/Manager:	Collette Kelly
Professional:	None
Directions:	1 mile South of Strabane on the A5 to Omagh
Type of Course:	Parkland
Date Founded:	1908
No of Holes:	18
Length:	6135 yds (5610 mtrs)
Par:	69
SSS:	69
Green Fees:	Weekdays: £15 Weekends & Bank Holidays: £17
Visitors:	Welcome: Any Day, Contact Club in advance
Societies:	Welcome: Special concessions available, Contact Club for details
Facilities:	Chipping/Putting Area, Practice Area, Trolley hire, Electric Buggy hire, Bar, Restaurant, Caddy service by arrangement

Accommodation, Food and Drink

Reference numbers below refer to detailed information provided in section 2

Accommodation

Clanabogan House, Omagh, Co Tyrone

Tel/Fax: 028 8224 1171 Eight large, traditionally styled bedrooms in a 17th-century house set in extensive gardens. B&B, also evening meals for parties of 8 plus.   896

Dirgefield House, Ballybofey, Co Donegal

Tel: 074 32775 Six en suite Bed & Breakfast rooms in a beautiful house on the main road half a mile from the centre of Ballybofey.   200

Fir Trees Hotel, Strabane, Co Tyrone

Tel: 028 7138 2382 A bright, practical modern complex on the outskirts of town, with 25 well-equipped en suite bedrooms, a restaurant and bar-bistro.   895

Hawthorn House, Omagh, Co Tyrone

Tel: 028 8225 2005 Eight spacious en suite bedrooms and a high-quality restaurant in a period residence just outside town. Leisure centre very near.   901

Kellys Inn, Omagh, Co Tyrone

Tel: 028 8556 8218 Motel-style Accommodation, spacious restaurant and cosy bars in a long modern single-storey complex on the main A5.   903

Food and Drink

Fir Trees Hotel, Strabane, Co Tyrone

Tel: 028 7138 2382 A bright, practical modern complex on the outskirts of town, with 25 well-equipped en suite bedrooms, a restaurant and bar-bistro.   895

Grants Bar and Restaurant, Omagh, Co Tyrone

Tel: 028 8225 0900 A grand pub at the top end of town, with decor of reclaimed pine. On offer is the best in Food and Drink.   898

Hawthorn House, Omagh, Co Tyrone

Tel: 028 8225 2005 Eight spacious en suite bedrooms and a high-quality restaurant in a period residence just outside town. Leisure centre very near.   901

Kellys Inn, Omagh, Co Tyrone

Tel: 028 8556 8218 Motel-style Accommodation, spacious restaurant and cosy bars in a long modern single-storey complex on the main A5.   903

The Pink Elephant, 19 High Street, Omagh, Co Tyrone

Tel: 028 8224 9805 High-street café-restaurant with a menu that incorporates Irish, European and transatlantic influences.

LONDONDERRY

Not many players earn inclusion in the "Golfer's Handbook" for a remarkable golfing feat. But the City of Derry club can boast such a player. And he had the distinction of doing in on the game's most celebrated turf.

In 1966, when he was a student at Queen's University, Belfast, Frank McCarroll won the Boyd Quaich on the Old Course at St Andrews. And his 291st and last shot, which was played with a sandwedge, finished in the 18th hole for an eagle two. But in fairness, McCarroll couldn't be considered an ordinary club golfer.

In fact he was an Irish amateur international and, more recently, an international selector. And, as it happens, he was made an honorary life member of City of Derry GC in 1999. When one thinks of representative golf in Derry, the McCarroll family automatically spring to mind. And Frank's brother Colm will be remembered as runner-up to Mick Morris in the South of Ireland Championship of 1982 at Lahinch.

Interestingly, of County Derry's nine clubs, only two - Moyola Park and Roe Park - have 18-hole courses. Yet the county is better served than most, insofar as Portstewart GC has no fewer than 45 holes, with the prospect of another nine by 2003, while Castlerock, City of Derry and Foyle all have 27. On being informed of the county's golfing terrain, the first adjustment the unfamiliar visitor has to make is that the superb links at Portstewart GC happens to be in Derry and not in neighbouring Antrim. The confusion is understandable, given Portstewart's proximity to Royal Portrush. Indeed when the British Open was staged by its distinguished neighbour in 1951, Portstewart was used for the qualifying stage.

The Foyle at Night, Londonderry

With its small, sheltered harbour, promenade and three miles of strand, Portstewart is a delightful resort which was much loved by 19th century society. Indeed they guarded the place so jealously that they prohibited the building of a railway station, for fear of bringing what they deemed to be vulgar people to the town. Travelling east to west, Castlerock is the last in a series of outstanding links courses on what is known as the Causeway Coast. Apart from the main course, culminating in an 18th hole known as "Bad Boys' Corner" and where the men's Irish Amateur Close Championship was first staged as far back as 1912, Castlerock also has a seperate, nine-hole stretch. Castlerock's most famous hole is the 184-yard par-three fourth, known as the "Leg of Mutton" because of its shape. One of golf's most treacherous holes, it has out-of-bounds right, with the railway line, and also on the left. And if that weren't enough, a stream cuts diagonally across the fairway in front of the tee.

Meanwhile, the county's golfing facilities have undergone a significant expansion in recent years through the development of Foyle International Golf Centre and Roe Park, both of which were designed by Frank Ainsworth.

Mussenden Temple, Co Londonderry

Foyle has a championship-standard, par-72 parkland layout of 6,678 yards and a nine-hole, par-three stretch, all at Alder Road on the outskirts of Derry City. Ainsworth's design takes full advantage of a charming, natural setting, in the shadow of Donegal's famous purple hills. And the sixth green is overlooked by the Amelia Earhart Centre, which marks the landing place on May 21st, 1932, of the first woman aviator to make a solo flight across the Atlantic. The facility also incorporates a 19-bay, covered and floodlit driving range and a licensed restaurant. And it has the bonus of being convenient to the City of Derry Airport.

Apart from all these golfing delights, County Derry can claim to be the home of the distinguished poet, Seamus Heaney, who has won the Nobel Prize for literature. Immensely proud of his roots on the edge of the Sperrin Mountains, Heaney has written movingly about its mossy places where, during a mild winter, the whin or gorse is in perpetual flower. Threaded by streams and small roads, the Sperrins are bounded by the towns of Strabane, Dungiven, Magherafelt and Newtownstewart. And a section of the gently-contoured range spills southwards over the Owenkillew River and on towards Omagh in Co Tyrone.

It was in Georgian Limavady - from the Gaelic, Leim an Mhadra, the jump of the dog - in the beautiful Roe Valley, that Jane Ross, on hearing a passing fiddler play, wrote down a tune that is synonymous with Derry. Indeed it would be difficult to imagine any song that evokes such sentiment as "Danny Boy". A woman's song, it is essentially sad and plaintive, very much in keeping with the strife-torn history of Derry City and its famous walls. Set on a hill on the banks of the Foyle Estuary, the strategic closeness of Northern Ireland's second city to the open sea, led to it coming under repeated attack and siege over a period of 1,000 years. Still unbroken and complete, the great, 17th-century walls are 18 feet thick and about a mile in circumference. And it is still possible to

Derry City Walls, Co Londonderry

walk along them, observing old cannon still pointing their black noses over the ramparts. And thoughts are drawn back inevitably to the great siege which lasted for 105 days. Colonel Baker, a governer of the city who died on the 74th day of the siege, shares a memorial with Captain Browning in St Columb's Cathedral, a magnificent, Gothic structure dating back to 1633. We are told that Browning was killed as his ship, the "Mountjoy", broke the boom across the Foyle River and relieved the city in July 1689. The chapterhouse displays the keys to the gates which were shut against King James II, when he came there in December 1688 in an attempt at restoring his authority.

Just outside the walls is the Guildhall, looking very much like its London counterpart. Its stained-glass windows, through which light is filtered into all of the chambers, illustrate almost every significant episode of note in the city's history. Some of Derry's more prosperous citizens built themselves gracious country houses outside the walls. Indeed an eccentric, 18th century bishop of Derry, Frederick Harvey, created a palace for himself on a windswept headland at Downhill. The palace now lies in ruins, but among the landmarks on the approaches to Castlerock GC is the so-called Mussenden Temple, still intact. Perched precariously on a cliff edge, the domed rotunda was once used as the bishop's summer library.

According to the club records, City of Derry GC paid Willie Park the princely sum of £10 for designing their original course in 1912, but it has undergone significant changes since then. And like the city of its name, all of them have been for the good.

Location of Golf Courses

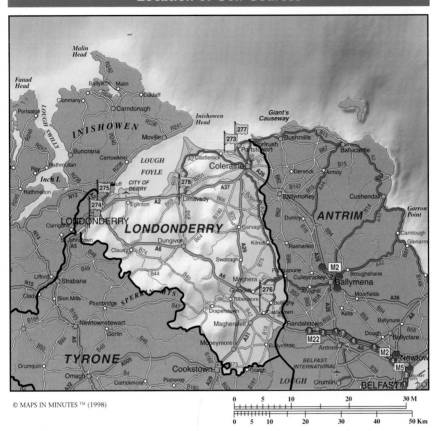

© MAPS IN MINUTES ™ (1998)

Castlerock

Castlerock Golf Club, 65 Circular Road,
Castlerock, Co Londonderry, BT51 4TJ

Tel: 028 7084 8314

Sec/Manager:	Geoffrey McBride
Professional:	Bobby Kelly
Directions:	6 miles North West of Coleraine off A2
Type of Course:	Links
Date Founded:	1901
No of Holes:	18 (plus 9)
Length:	6499 yds (5942 mtrs)
Par:	73
SSS:	71
Green Fees:	Weekdays: £30 Weekends & Bank Holidays: £40
Visitors:	Welcome: Book in advance
Societies:	Welcome: Book in advance
Facilities:	Chipping/Putting Area, Practice Area, Golf Clubs for hire, Trolley hire, Bar, Restaurant, Caddy service by arrangement

Accommodation, Food and Drink

Reference numbers below refer to detailed
information provided in section 2

Accommodation

Akaroa Guest House, Portstewart, Co Londonderry
Tel: 028 7083 2067 A model B&B guest house run with all the care and discipline of an old-fashioned family home. Accommodation comprises 11 rooms, five of them with en suite facilities. 910

Ashleigh House, Portstewart, Co Londonderry
Tel: 028 7083 4452 The heart of the building is a large bungalow, to which several extensions have been made to provide first-class Accommodation in six bedrooms (doubles, twins, a family room), all with en suite facilities. Lunch and dinner available by arrangement. 913

O'Malley's Wateredge Hotel, Portstewart, Co Londonderry
Tel: 028 7083 3314 Fax: 028 7083 2224 O'Malley's Edgewater Hotel is situated on the Strand Beach, a perfect vantage point for enjoying views of the Donegal Hills and the Atlantic Ocean. The hotel has 28 bedrooms, all with en suite bathrooms. 911

Streeve Hill, Limavady, Co Londonderry
Tel: 028 7176 6563 Fax: 028 7776 8285 Three bedrooms with private bathrooms provide superior Accommodation in an 18th-century country house. Great breakfasts; gourmet dinners. 917

The Anchorage Inn, Portstewart, Co Londonderry
Tel: 028 7083 4401 Fax: 028 7083 4508 Twenty double bedrooms, all with en suite facilities. The inn incorporates Skippers Bar and Restaurant, where seafood is a speciality. Transport can be arranged to and from the golf courses. 914

The Poplars, Ballerina, Limavady, Co Londonderry
Tel: 028 7775 0360 Six bedrooms, all with en suite facilities. Excellent walking country, halfway between Castlerock and Limavady, and there are stunning views of the massive cliffs from the lounge. 915

Food and Drink

O'Malley's Wateredge Hotel, Portstewart, Co Londonderry
Tel: 028 7083 3314 Fax: 028 7083 2224 O'Malley's Edgewater Hotel is situated on the Strand Beach, a perfect vantage point for enjoying views of the Donegal Hills and the Atlantic Ocean. The hotel has 28 bedrooms, all with en suite bathrooms. 911

Portstewart Arms, Portstewart, Co Londonderry
Tel: 028 7183 2046 Well-established public house that's long been a favorite with golfers. Built in 1840, it is the oldest pub in town, with many quaint period features. A golfing society meets regularly in the pub. 916

Streeve Hill, Limavady, Co Londonderry
Tel: 028 7176 6563 Fax: 028 7776 8285 Three bedrooms with private bathrooms provide superior Accommodation in an 18th-century country house. Great breakfasts; gourmet dinners. 917

The Anchorage Inn, Portstewart, Co Londonderry
Tel: 028 7083 4401 Fax: 028 7083 4508 Twenty double bedrooms, all with en suite facilities. The inn incorporates Skippers Bar and Restaurant, where seafood is a speciality. Transport can be arranged to and from the golf courses. 914

City of Derry

City of Derry Golf Club, 49 Victoria Road,
Londonderry, BT47 2PU

Tel: 028 7331 1610

When Willie Park Jnr designed the City of Derry course in 1911, he pronounced the nine-hole layout to be "a capable test of the skill of any player." His efforts later gained endorsement from no less an architect than the great Harry Colt, who described the par-four second as "one of the best drive and pitch holes I have ever seen."

The club now have 27 holes, comprising a championship stretch measuring 6,429 yards and a more modest, nine-hole Dunhugh stretch. The Prehen course, where former British Amateur champion, Peter McEvoy, twice won the local Scratch Cup, meanders through clumps of gorse and mature woodland.

With impressive views of the wide sweep of the River Foyle, both courses enjoy a delightfully picturesque location. Indeed Colt, who submitted a plan for bunkering after inspecting the layout, was moved to remark: "It is difficult to imagine a more charming setting for a golf course."

Walter Hagen was a distinguished visitor in 1937 and Ireland's Canada Cup winning duo, Christy O'Connor Snr and Harry Bradshaw, also played the course. Meanwhile, Fred Daly served as professional there from 1939 to 1944, before going on to capture the British Open of 1947.

Sadly, the club suffered the loss of their clubhouse in an explosion and fire in 1982, when all the minute-books and various other records were lost. Within two years, however, they had not only replaced the clubhouse with a splendid, new structure overlooking the 18th green, but had completed the additional nine holes.

Sec/Manager:	Hugh Doherty
Professional:	Michael Doherty
Directions:	3 miles South of Derry off the A5 to Strabane
Type of Course:	Parkland
Date Founded:	1912
No of Holes:	18 (plus 9)
Length:	6429 yds (5878 mtrs)
Par:	71

SSS:	71
Green Fees:	Weekdays: £20 Weekends & Bank Holidays: £25
Visitors:	Welcome: Book in advance
Societies:	Welcome: Special concessions, Contact Club for details
Facilities:	Chipping/Putting Area, Practice Area, Driving Range, Golf Clubs for hire, Trolley hire, Bar, Restaurant, Caddy service by arrangement

Accommodation, Food and Drink

Reference numbers below refer to detailed information provided in section 2

Accommodation

Banks of the Faughan Motel, Campsie, Co Londonderry

Tel/Fax: 028 7186 0242 Twelve bedrooms, seven with en suite. City of Derry Airport is a very short drive away, and there are several golf and leisure centres nearby. Groups of up to 25 can be accommodated. 918

Beechwood House, Londonderry, Co Londonderry

Tel: 028 7126 4900 A block of stables has been converted into self-contained self-catering Accommodation in five chalets which together can sleep 20 in comfort. Everything is provided for families and groups. 921

Fir Trees Hotel, Strabane, Co Tyrone

Tel: 028 7138 2382 A bright, practical modern complex on the outskirts of town, with 25 well-equipped en suite bedrooms, a restaurant and bar-bistro. 895

The Inn at the Cross, Londonderry, Co Londonderry

Tel: 028 7130 1480 Fax: 02871 301940 Views over the countryside to the Faughan river valley. Bedrooms are all en suite. Varied menus, with both à la carte and table d'hote options, in the Fireside Restaurant; less formal eating in Sally Elliot's Bar. 919

Food and Drink

Badger's, Londonderry, Co Londonderry

Tel/Fax: 028 7136 0763 Three floors of bars and restaurant. Lunchtime specials and the Sunday carvery are particularly popular. 920

Fir Trees Hotel, Strabane, Co Tyrone

Tel: 028 7138 2382 A bright, practical modern complex on the outskirts of town, with 25 well-equipped en suite bedrooms, a restaurant and bar-bistro. 895

The Inn at the Cross, Londonderry, Co Londonderry

Tel: 028 7130 1480 Fax: 02871 301940 Views over the countryside to the Faughan river valley. Bedrooms are all en suite. Varied menus, with both à la carte and table d'hote options, in the Fireside Restaurant; less formal eating in Sally Elliot's Bar. 919

Foyle

Foyle International Golf Centre, 12 Alder Road, Londonderry, BT48 8DB

Tel: 028 7135 2222

Sec/Manager:	Margaret Lapsley
Professional:	Kieran McLaughlin
Directions:	Follow A2 one and a half miles North of Foyle Bridge towards Moville and turn left into club
Type of Course:	Parkland
Date Founded:	1995
No of Holes:	18 (plus 9)
Length:	6678 yds (6106 mtrs)
Par:	72
SSS:	71
Green Fees:	Weekdays: £11 Weekends & Bank Holidays: £14
Visitors:	Welcome: Any Day, Book in advance

Societies:	Welcome: Special Society Packages, Contact Club for details
Facilities:	Chipping/Putting Area, Practice Area, Driving Range, Golf Clubs for hire, Trolley hire, Bar, Restaurant, Caddy service by arrangement

Accommodation, Food and Drink

Reference numbers below refer to detailed information provided in section 2

Accommodation

Banks of the Faughan Motel, Campsie, Co Londonderry

Tel/Fax: 028 7186 0242 Twelve bedrooms, seven with en suite. City of Derry Airport is a very short drive away, and there are several golf and leisure centres nearby. Groups of up to 25 can be accommodated. 918

Beechwood House, Londonderry, Co Londonderry

Tel: 028 7126 4900 A block of stables has been converted into self-contained self-catering Accommodation in five chalets which together can sleep 20 in comfort. Everything is provided for families and groups. 921

Fir Trees Hotel, Strabane, Co Tyrone

Tel: 028 7138 2382 A bright, practical modern complex on the outskirts of town, with 25 well-equipped en suite bedrooms, a restaurant and bar-bistro. 895

The Inn at the Cross, Londonderry, Co Londonderry

Tel: 028 7130 1480 Fax: 028 7130 1394 Views over the countryside to the Faughan river valley. Bedrooms are all en suite. Varied menus, with both à la carte and table d'hote options, in the Fireside Restaurant; less formal eating in Sally Elliot's Bar. 919

Food and Drink

Badger's, Londonderry, Co Londonderry

Tel/Fax: 028 7136 0763 Three floors of bars and restaurant. Lunchtime specials and the Sunday carvery are particularly popular. 920

Fir Trees Hotel, Strabane, Co Tyrone

Tel: 028 7138 2382 A bright, practical modern complex on the outskirts of town, with 25 well-equipped en suite bedrooms, a restaurant and bar-bistro. 895

The Inn at the Cross, Londonderry, Co Londonderry

Tel: 028 7130 1480 Fax: 028 7130 1394 Views over the countryside to the Faughan river valley. Bedrooms are all en suite. Varied menus, with both à la carte and table d'hote options, in the Fireside Restaurant; less formal eating in Sally Elliot's Bar. 919

Moyola Park

Moyola Park Golf Club, 15 Curran Road, Shanemullagh, Castledawson, Co Londonderry, BT45 8DG

Tel: 028 7946 8468

Sec/Manager:	Laurence Hastings
Professional:	Bob Cockcroft
Directions:	Half mile West of Castledawson on Curran Road
Type of Course:	Parkland
Date Founded:	1976
No of Holes:	18
Length:	6062 yds (5543 mtrs)
Par:	71
SSS:	71
Green Fees:	Weekdays: £17 Weekends & Bank Holidays: £25
Visitors:	Welcome: Book in advance
Societies:	Welcome: Special concessions, Contact Club in advance
Facilities:	Chipping/Putting Area, Practice Area Golf Clubs for hire, Trolley hire,

Electric Buggy hire, Bar, Restaurant,
Caddy service by arrangement

Accommodation, Food and Drink

Reference numbers below refer to detailed
information provided in section 2

Accommodation

Four Winds, 146 Crankhill Road, Slangford, Ballymena, Co
Antrim, BT44 9HA,

Tel: 028 2568 5360 The Four Winds is the farmhouse for a mixed working farm
which offers bed & breakfast Accommodation. The modern building has been
recently refurbished and now provides 3 letting rooms, (2 family and 1 double, all
with hot and cold).

Greenvale Hotel, Cookstown, Co Tyrone

Tel: 028 8676 2243 An extended Victorian house on the outskirts of Cookstown, with
12 comfortable bedrooms and value-for-money cuisine.   893

Shanleigh House, Ballymena, Co Antrim

Tel/Fax: 028 2564 4851 B&B in four bedrooms; 2 double, 1 twin, 1 family. En suite
available. A warm welcome awaits all guests. No credit cards - travellers cheques
only. Very close to Galgorm Castle.

Food and Drink

Dry Dock, 34 - 36 Rawey Street, Magherafelt, Co Londonderry,
BT45 5AQ

Tel: 028 7963 4129 The Dry Dock pub in Rainey Street, with its bow-windowed
upper storey, suggests the bridge of a ship and when you step inside the
resemblance is even stronger. The Dry Dock its meeting place

Greenvale Hotel, Cookstown, Co Tyrone

Tel: 028 8676 2243 An extended Victorian house on the outskirts of Cookstown, with
12 comfortable bedrooms and value-for-money cuisine.   893

McNally's Inn, Castledawson, Co Londonderry

Tel: 028 7965 0095 A small, unpretentious modern country inn well known to golfers
and others for its traditional Irish welcome. The extensive menu runs from light
snacks to three-course meals. Regular live music sessions.   922

Portstewart

**Portstewart Golf Club, 117 Strand Road, Co
Londonderry, BT55 7PG**

Tel: 028 7083 2015

Going back to 1951, when it was a qualifying
links for the British Open at Royal Portrush, it
seemed that Portstewart was destined to be for-
ever cast in the shadow of its celebrated
neigbhour. But not any more. Everything
changed utterly when Portstewart's restructured
championship layout played host to the Irish
Close Championship in 1992.

Now, it is set to emulate Killarney as only the
second Irish club with 54 holes. Through the
recent purchase of 47 acres sweeping down to
the River Bann, an extension of the Riverside
Course, from nine to 18 holes, is planned for
completion in 2003.

Envisaged as a 6,000-yard parkland stretch
with a par 68, the development will contrast with
the majestic duneland of the main course. And
it is certain to enhance the popularity of this
leading venue, which celebrated its centenary
in 1984.

So, over the years, it could be seen to have
responded admirably to a barb in the "Coleraine

Chronicle" of 1884, which reported: "Portstewart
is at length bestirring itself. It, too, is to have a
golf links. In Scotland, almost every seaside town
of any pretension has its golf course and there is
no reason why Portstewart should not provide
an attraction of this kind."

While more than meeting the demands of a
disgruntled, 19th century scribe, the club have
made a significant contribution to the game. It
was there that Maureen Madill acquired the skills
which brought her the British Women's
matchplay and strokeplay titles, along with
Curtis Cup status.

Sec/Manager:	Michael Moss
Professional:	Alan Hunter
Directions:	3 miles North West of Coleraine off
the A2 on the North Coast.

Strand

Type of Course:	Links
Date Founded:	1894
No of Holes:	18
Length:	6779 yds (6198 mtrs)
Par:	72
SSS:	73
Green Fees:	Weekdays: £50 Weekends & Bank
Holidays: £70 Weekday 36 holes
special for £70

Old Course

Type of Course:	Links
Date Founded:	1894
No of Holes:	18 (plus 9)
Length:	4730 yds (4325 mtrs)
Par:	64

SSS:	62
Green Fees:	Weekdays: £10 Weekends & Bank Holidays: £14
Visitors:	Welcome: Any Weekday, Contact Club for weekend availability
Societies:	Welcome: Book in advance
Facilities:	Practice Area, Driving Range, Golf Clubs for hire, Trolley hire, Bar, Restaurant, Caddy service by arrangement

Accommodation, Food and Drink

Reference numbers below refer to detailed information provided in section 2

Accommodation

Akaroa Guest House, Portstewart, Co Londonderry

Tel: 028 7083 2067 A model B&B guest house run with all the care and discipline of an old-fashioned family home. Accommodation comprises 11 rooms, five of them with en suite facilities.   910

Antrim Arms, Ballycastle, Co Antrim

Tel: 028 2076 2284 Good food, good beer and good times in one of Ireland's oldest hostelries, dating back to 1767. The old-world feel is allied to modern comforts, and the bedrooms, all en suite, are well furnished and decorated. Restaurant open to non-residents.   803

Ashleigh House, Portstewart, Co Londonderry

Tel: 028 7083 4452 The heart of the building is a large bungalow, to which several extensions have been made to provide first-class Accommodation in six bedrooms (doubles, twins, a family room), all with en suite facilities. Lunch and dinner available by arrangement.   913

Brookhaven, Portrush, Co Antrim

Tel: 028 7082 4164 The bedrooms, 2 twin and 1 double en suite, are beautifully decorated and furnished. Spacious gardens for guests to stroll in. There is a superb choice of local golf courses - Royal Portrush is only a five-minute drive away.   802

Chris-Mull, Bushmills, Co Antrim

Tel: 028 2073 1154 En suite Bed & Breakfast Accommodation in double or single rooms. 200 yards from the A2. Visa, Mastercard

Clarmont, Portrush, Co Antrim

Tel/Fax: 028 7082 2397 All the bedrooms at this three-storey town house have en suite facilities. From the patio seating area there are super views out onto the Atlantic Ocean and Royal Portrush Golf.   804

Fullerton Arms, Ballintoy, Co Antrim

Tel: 028 2076 9613 The 19th-century building, a little way inland from picturesque Ballintoy harbour, has been extensively renovated and modernised to house 11 en suite bedrooms, a lively bar and restaurant that's open to non-residents.   808

Galgorm, Portrush, Co Antrim

Tel: 028 7082 3787 This town house attracts many return visitors with its warm, easygoing atmosphere and excellent Accommodation: 12 en suite bedrooms. Drew is a keen golfer and can give advice about the local courses.   807

Glenmore House, Ballycastle, Co Antrim

Tel/Fax: 028 2076 3548 A large purpose-built country house hotel affords superb views of the Antrim coast and the Atlantic. Within easy reach of some of the top golf courses in Northern Ireland. Every aspect of a golfing holiday is catered for, including reservations and a club cleaning service.   801

Leander House, Portrush, Co Antrim

Tel: 028 7082 2147 e-mail: leander@ni.network.com Bed & Breakfast Accommodation in a town house off Lansdowne Crescent. 8 doubles, 4 family rooms; 2 en suite.

O'Malley's Wateredge Hotel, Portstewart, Co Londonderry

Tel: 028 7083 3314 Fax: 028 7083 2224 O'Malley's Edgewater Hotel is situated on the Strand Beach, a perfect vantage point for enjoying views of the Donegal Hills and the Atlantic Ocean. The hotel has 28 bedrooms, all with en suite bathrooms. 911

Streeve Hill, Limavady, Co Londonderry

Tel: 028 7176 6563 Fax: 028 7776 8285 Three bedrooms with private bathrooms provide superior Accommodation in an 18th-century country house. Great breakfasts; gourmet dinners.   917

The Anchorage Inn, Portstewart, Co Londonderry

Tel: 028 7083 4401 Fax: 028 7083 4508 Twenty double bedrooms, all with en suite

facilities. The inn incorporates Skippers Bar and Restaurant, where seafood is a speciality. Transport can be arranged to and from the golf courses.   914

Food and Drink

Antrim Arms, Ballycastle, Co Antrim

Tel: 028 2076 2284 Good food, good beer and good times in one of Ireland's oldest hostelries, dating back to 1767. The old-world feel is allied to modern comforts, and the bedrooms, all en suite, are well furnished and decorated. Restaurant open to non-residents.   803

Fullerton Arms, Ballintoy, Co Antrim

Tel: 028 2076 9613 The 19th-century building, a little way inland from picturesque Ballintoy harbour, has been extensively renovated and modernised to house 11 en suite bedrooms, a lively bar and restaurant that's open to non-residents.   808

Glenmore House, Ballycastle, Co Antrim

Tel/Fax: 028 2076 3548 A large purpose-built country house hotel affords superb views of the Antrim coast and the Atlantic. Within easy reach of some of the top golf courses in Northern Ireland. Every aspect of a golfing holiday is catered for, including reservations and a club cleaning service.   801

O'Malley's Wateredge Hotel, Portstewart, Co Londonderry

Tel: 028 7083 3314 Fax: 028 7083 2224 O'Malley's Edgewater Hotel is situated on the Strand Beach, a perfect vantage point for enjoying views of the Donegal Hills and the Atlantic Ocean. The hotel has 28 bedrooms, all with en suite bathrooms. 911

Portstewart Arms, Portstewart, Co Londonderry

Tel: 028 7183 2046 Well-established public house that's long been a favorite with golfers. Built in 1840, it is the oldest pub in town, with many quaint period features. A golfing society meets regularly in the pub.   916

Streeve Hill, Limavady, Co Londonderry

Tel: 028 7176 6563 Fax: 028 7776 8285 Three bedrooms with private bathrooms provide superior Accommodation in an 18th-century country house. Great breakfasts; gourmet dinners.   917

The Anchorage Inn, Portstewart, Co Londonderry

Tel: 028 7083 4401 Fax: 028 7083 4508 Twenty double bedrooms, all with en suite facilities. The inn incorporates Skippers Bar and Restaurant, where seafood is a speciality. Transport can be arranged to and from the golf courses.   914

Radisson Roe Park

Radisson Roe Park Hotel & Golf Resort, Roe Park, Limavady, Co Londonderry, BT49 9LB

Tel: 028 7172 2222

Roe Park has a charming setting within the long, encircling arm of the Sperrin Mountains and the spectacular Eagle Rock to the north and the Inishowen Peninsula in the distance. It is also in the area of Limavady where, it is claimed, 30 per cent of the golfers are left-handers.

Remarkably, this is nearly three times the average for the Royal and Ancient game, world-wide. "It's true," said golf administrator Don Brockerton. "It's not unusual around these parts to see a fourball entirely of left-handers. I think it may have something to do with a strong cricketing tradition in the area. After all, there's nothing unusual about playing cricket left-handed."

Armed with this little vignette, there is a temptation to see whether Roe Park would be more suited to faded shots, thereby making it ideal for left-handers drawing the ball. But the ultimate conclusion is that its designer, Frank Ainsworth, has done a fine, architectural job.

He started work there, three years before the four-star Radisson Hotel became a dominant element of the complex, in 1996. It is now a proprietary course with 500 members and a thriving green-fee business.

With three ponds and an overal length of 6,318 yards, the course is dominated by Mullagh Hill at its centre and has two sections, starting with the so-called Lower Five. And valuable help in course presentation was given by Ed Seay, while his design partner, Arnold Palmer, stayed at the hotel during the British Seniors' at nearby Royal Portrush in 1996.

Sec/Manager:	Don Brockerton
Professional:	Seamus Duffy
Directions:	One mile West of Limavady off B192 adjacent to Roe Valley Country Park.
Type of Course:	Links
Date Founded:	1993
No of Holes:	18
Length:	6318 yds (5777 mtrs)
Par:	70
SSS:	71
Green Fees:	£ 20 Special rates for hotel guests
Visitors:	Welcome: Book in advance
Societies:	Welcome: Special Society Packages, Contact Club for details
Facilities:	Chipping/Putting Area, Practice Area, Driving Range, Golf Clubs for hire, Trolley hire, Electric Buggy hire, Bar, Restaurant, Caddy service by arrangement, plus Visitors to the Golf Club are welcome to use the Hotel facilities for an additional charge plus Newly established Golf Academy – Book in advance

Accommodation, Food and Drink

Reference numbers below refer to detailed information provided in section 2

Accommodation

Drumcovitt House & Barn, 704 Feeny Road, Feeny, Co Londonderry, BT47 4SU,

Tel: 028 7778 12241 Drumcovitt House & Barn offers a choice of top quality bed & breakfast or self-catering Accommodation. This handsome, ivy-clad house has 3 guest bedrooms.

Streeve Hill, Limavady, Co Londonderry

Tel: 028 7176 6563 Fax: 028 7776 8285 Three bedrooms with private bathrooms provide superior Accommodation in an 18th-century country house. Great breakfasts; gourmet dinners.   917

The Poplars, Ballerina, Limavady, Co Londonderry

Tel: 028 7775 0360 Six double bedrooms, three with en suite facilities. Excellent walking country, halfway between Castlerock and Limavady, and there are stunning views of the massive cliffs from the lounge.   915

Food and Drink

Portstewart Arms, Portstewart, Co Londonderry

Tel: 028 7183 2046 Well-established public house that's long been a favorite with golfers. Built in 1840, it is the oldest pub in town, with many quaint period features. A golfing society meets regularly in the pub.   916

Roe View Inn, Limavady, Co Londonderry

Tel: 028 7776 2555 A handsome half-timbered building near the River Roe. Open fires blaze a welcome in both bars, where pool and darts are played and there's live music at weekends.   912

Streeve Hill, Limavady, Co Londonderry

Tel: 028 7176 6563 Fax: 028 7776 8285 Three bedrooms with private bathrooms
provide superior Accommodation in an 18th-century country house. Great breakfasts; gourmet dinners.   917

Accommodation, Food and Drink

Contents - Republic of Ireland

Bed & Breakfast

Six en suite rooms; super breakfasts; free fishing

Credit Cards: None

TULLAMORE FARMHOUSE | 110

Kilshanny, Ennistymon, Co Clare
Tel: 065 7071187 Fax: 065 7072023
e-mail: eileenc@tinet.ie

'We promise you something special and a hearty Irish welcome'. The words of Eileen Carroll, the delightful hostess at this elegant modern house on a 100-acre working beef farm. Bed & Breakfast accommodation is provided in six en suite bedrooms, all spacious and individually styled. The views are absolutely superb, and the house is an ideal base for touring the Burren. Award-winning breakfasts set guests up perfectly for a day's golf, fishing or sightseeing. At the end of the lane, Tullamore Cottage offers alternative self-catering accommodation for six.

Local Golf Courses: Lahinch, Ennis, Kilkee, Gort

B&B and Self-catering

Four B&B rooms; great views; off-road parking. New 3 bed self catering home.

Credit Cards: All the major cards

MULCARR HOUSE | 111

Ennistymon Road, Lahinch, Co Clare
Tel: 065 7081123 Fax: 065 7081123
e-mail: mulcarrhouse@esatclear.ie

This striking modern home is full of innovation, with different levels and extensions, and a lovely conservatory lounge for enjoying the marvellous views. There are four letting bedrooms with tea and coffee making facilities. The house stands a short walk from the golf club and main street of Lahinch, a seaside resort with one of the best surfing beaches in the land. It is only 10 kilometres to the Cliffs of Moher and 15 kilometres to Doolin. Close by and in the same ownership is a self catering new 3 bedroom home with all mod cons.

Local Golf Courses: Lahinch, Ennis, Kilkee, Gort

Country Guest House

Six large en suite rooms; some canopy beds. Dinner by arrangement.

Credit Cards: None

NEWPARK HOUSE | 112

Ennis, Co Clare
Tel: 065 6821233
e-mail: newparkhouse.ennis@tinet.ie

Newpark House is an imposing 300-year-old house set in extensive parkland off the R352 Tulla road, less than two miles from the centre of Ennis. The house has been in the Barron family since 1904 and has been operating as a guest house since the 1960s. There are six generously-sized en suite bedrooms, some with canopy beds. Antiques abound, and the owners have a large collection of books relating to Irish genealogy, so they can help you trace your Irish ancestry. A full Irish breakfast starts the day, and dinner is available by arrangement.

Local Golf Courses: Ennis, Woodstock, Dromoland Castle

Irelands oldest family-owned Pub

Pub with bar food and music. Open fire which has been burning for 200 years.

Credit Cards: All the major cards

FANNY O'DEA'S | 113

Kilrush Road, Lissycasey, Co Clare
Tel: 065 6834143

One of Ireland's oldest (1695) and most delightful hostelries, 15 minutes from Ennis on the road to Kilrush. Behind the long, low thatched roof and orange-washed walls is an interior that's equally inviting and appealing. There's a clock which featured in the pub scene in the film "Ryans Daughter" and an open fire which has been burning continuously for 200 years. Today, Fanny O'Dea's is the perfect place to stop for a drink, enjoy some wholesome bar food and listen to impromptu sessions of traditional Irish music. The current owners are direct descendants of Fanny O'Dea's.

Local Golf Courses: Ennis, Woodstock, Kilrush

MOYVILLE 114

Lahinch Road, Ennis, Co Clare
Tel: 065 6828278

A mile from the town centre, on the N85 road to Lahinch, stands this very smart modern house run as a B&B by Mary Finucane and her family. Mary is the most relaxed and charming hostess, and a stay here is like being in your own home. There are four very spacious letting bedrooms, all en suite, good parking at the front, a tv lounge for guests and excellent lawns at the back. Ennis, with its shops and restaurants and Friary, is a two-minute drive away, while in the other direction lies the Atlantic Ocean and the resort village of Lahinch.

Bed & Breakfast

4 large rooms en suite. tv lounge, lawned garden

Credit Cards: Visa

Local Golf Courses: Ennis, Woodstock, Lahinch

THE SHAMROCK INN HOTEL 115

Slipper Street, Lahinch, Co Clare
Tel: 065 7081700 Fax: 065 7081829

There's always a warm welcome at Alan Logue's family-run hotel, which stands on the main street of a resort village on the Atlantic coast. Completely renovated and refurbished, the hotel has ten letting bedrooms, all en suite, with tv, telephone and hairdryer. There's a stylish oak-panelled bar with home-cooked bar food and evening entertainment, and excellent cuisine is served in the restaurant. There's secure off-street parking, and it's only a short stroll to the mile-long golden beach. An easy drive away are the Ailwee Caves and the spectacular Cliffs of Moher. The owners of the Shamrock also have the neighbouring Atlantic Hotel (Tel: 065 7081049).

Hotel with Bar and Restaurant

Ten en suite rooms, tv, phone, hairdryer. Bar ands restaurant

Credit Cards: Access,Mastercard,Visa

Local Golf Courses: Ennis, Woodstock, Lahinch

TUDOR LODGE 116

Ennistymon Road, Lahinch, Co Clare
Tel: 065 7081270

Five hundred yards from the village centre, Anita Gallery's neat modern B&B house is a cosy place with a real home-from-home feel. Furnished throughout with real attention to detail, it has four letting bedrooms, all with en suite facilities, and a residents' lounge with tv where tea and coffee can be taken. There's good off-road parking. Early morning golfer's breakfasts are a speciality before a round at the local course, sometimes called the St Andrews of Ireland.. Lahinch is very quiet out of season, with a population of around 500, but in the summer it becomes a thriving, bustling holiday resort famous for its wonderful surfing beach.

Bed & Breakfast

Four en suite rooms, tv lounge; early morning golfer's breakfasts

Credit Cards: All the major cards

Local Golf Courses: Lahinch, Ennis, Kilkee, Gort

MAGOWNA HOUSE HOTEL 117

Inch, Ennis, Co Clare
Tel: 065 6839009 Fax: 065 6839258
e-mail: magowna@iol.ie

Magowna House Hotel is a 3* family-run country house hotel in 12 acres of gardens and grounds four miles from Ennis, Clare's bustling county town. The hotel offers very comfortable accommodation in ten en suite bedrooms, all with tv, phone and tea/coffee making facilities. The Norah Daly bar is a pleasant spot to relax with a drink, and there's an excellent restaurant. A large function room can be hired for parties or special events. There are several excellent local golf courses. The hotel has boats for hire for anglers. The Mid-Clare Way is close by for walkers. This is the ideal location for either a totally relaxing or an active break

Hotel and Restaurant

Country hotel with 10 en suite rooms with phone, tv. Bar and restaurant

Credit Cards: All the major cards

Local Golf Courses: Ennis, Woodstock, Dromoland Castle, Lahinch

County Clare

VILLA NOVA 118

1 Woodlawn, Lahinch Road, Ennis, Co Clare
Tel: 065 6828570
e-Mail: villanovaennis@tinet.ie

Mareaid O'Connor offers excellent Bed & Breakfast accommodation in her cheerfully decorated modern detached bungalow on the western side of Ennis. There are four letting bedrooms, of which two are en suite, with tv, and the house has a very friendly, welcoming feel. At the back is a splendid garden with stone tables and chairs and other ornamental features. Mareaid worked for many years at Lahinch Golf Club and has a strong kinship with golfers! Visitors to Ennis should not miss the chance to look at the imposing and substantial ruins of Ennis Friary with its marvellous sculptures and decorated tombs.

Bed & Breakfast

Four bedrooms, 2 en suite and 2 standard. Large garden. Easy parking

Credit Cards: None

Local Golf Courses: Ennis, Woodstock, Lahinch

THE BARON MCQ'S 119

78 Pannell Street, Ennis, Co Clare
Tel: 065 6824608

In a town-centre street among a maze of little lanes, Baron McQ's is a welcoming hostelry behind a traditional cheerfully painted frontage. It offers both refreshment and overnight accommodation. In the small, intimate bar, where two old black iron stoves take the eye, snacks are available throughout the day, with extra dishes at lunchtime, and they can be enjoyed with a first-class pint of Guinness. Upstairs are 11 letting bedrooms with en suite facilities and tv - not grand, but certainly well-kept and surprisingly roomy. Nearby, in Merchants Square, is a sister establishment, Ruby Tuesdays, serving a wide range of food in pleasant, informal surroundings.

Inn, Accommodation and Food

11 en suite bedrooms with tv. All-day bar snacks

Credit Cards: Access, Mastercard, Visa

Local Golf Courses: Ennis, Woodstock, Dromoland Castle

WESTCLIFF HOUSE 120

Kilkee, Co Clare
Tel: 065 9056108

Diana Martin's characterful B&B establishment is a fine 1840s terraced house that was once home to the governess of the last czar of Russia. Today's visitors can stay in seven spacious bedrooms, five of them en suite. There's a guest lounge with a piano, and the front rooms afford spectacular views over Moore Bay. Kilkee has been a popular seaside resort since the 18th century, and its traditional attractions - the sea, the beaches, the fishing, walks - are joined by the modern thallasotherapy centre and Kilkee Waterworld, where the whole family can spend the day having fun.

Bed & Breakfast

Town house B&B with seven rooms, five en suite. Great sea views

Credit Cards: None

Local Golf Courses: Kilkee, Kilrush, Ballybunion

FORTFIELD FARM 121

Donail, Killimer, Co Clare Tel: 065 9051457 Fax: 065 9052908
e-mail: fortfield@tinet.ie

An award-winning family farm and house with many unique features. The house itself, a striking modern building with a full-length conservatory, offers five B&B rooms, three of them en suite, and a very roomy tv lounge. Full Irish breakfast, family traditional music on request. Guests have the house to themselves, as hosts Sean and Bríd Cunningham have separate accommodation. The working dairy farm incorporates a terrific new attraction in the shape of an agricultural zoo with a wide variety of domesticated rare animals and birds including llamas, wallabies, pot-bellied pigs, swans and ostriches. Ideally located only 3 mins drive from Killimer/Tarbert car ferry which goes to North Kerry (20 mins crossing).

Farmhouse Bed & Breakfast

Five B&B rooms, three en suite; tv lounge. On a working farm with zoo

Credit Cards: All the major cards

Local Golf Courses: Kilrush, Kilkee, Ballybunion, Shannon

THE HAVEN ARMS | 122

Henry Street, Kilrush, Co Clare
Tel: 065 9051267 Fax: 065 9051218

A prime site on the main street for the Malone family's super pub-restaurant. Always busy and with a great atmosphere, it has a huge lounge bar and a public bar, and the bar food has won several awards. The lite bite menu offers a mouthwatering range of sandwiches, and the lunchtime list also includes a fish dish and roast of the day, chicken curry and seasonal salads. The evening menu served in the restaurant also changes daily. Live music is a feature, and many of the regulars are happy to strike up an impromptu session! A really happy place where visitors are always welcome.

Bar & Restaurant

Lunchtime and evening menus; regular live music

Credit Cards: Access, Mastercard, Visa

Local Golf Courses: Kilrush, Kilkee, Ballybunion, Lahinch

COIS NA SIONNA | 123

Killimer (Ferry Junction), Kilrush, Co Clare
Tel/Fax: 065 9053073
e-mail: coisnasionna@eircom.net

A striking modern house done out in black and white, with a giant red B&B sign on its facade. Seamus and Imy Kerrigan offer excellent overnight accommodation in four rooms with en suite facilities, tv and glorious views over the Shannon estuary. Seamus also operates a bus service which can collect or deliver guests using Shannon Airport and transport golfers to and from the local courses. The house sits opposite the ferry that runs hourly across the estuary to Tarbert in Co Kerry, a 20-minute trip which avoids an 85-mile road journey.

Bed & Breakfast

Four en suite rooms with tv; glorious views

Credit Cards: Access, Mastercard, Visa

Local Golf Courses: Kilrush, Kilkee, Ballybunion, Lahinch

CARRAIG HOUSE | 124

Liscannor, Co Clare
Tel/Fax: 065 7081260

An impressive modern house in a lovely secluded setting a short walk from the famous fishing village of Liscannor. Agnes and Noel Andrews are the most delightful of hosts, and their six letting bedrooms, all en suite, offer peace, comfort and superb views. The house is a great place to escape from it all, or for visiting the numerous sights in the region. Liscannor itself is the site of the Holy Well of St Brigid, a major place of pilgrimage, and, on the highest cliff, O'Brien's Tower, built in the early 19th century as a viewing point for tourists.

Bed & Breakfast

Six en suite bedrooms; secluded setting, superb views

Credit Cards: None

Local Golf Courses: Lahinch, Kilkee, Gort, Ennis

KELLY'S BAR & RESTAURANT | 125

26 Henry Street, Kilrush, Co Clare
Tel: 065 9051811 Fax: 065 9051856
e-mail: kellys.kilrush@oceanfree.net

The reputation of Mark Reidy's splendid pub stretches far beyond the boundaries of Kilrush and a visit to this 'Pub of the Year' is a must for anyone touring this lovely part of Ireland. Open from 10.30am Kelly's is the most welcoming of places, and the good food and drink are accompanied from Wednesday to Saturday by live music. All food is sourced locally where possible and the seafood menu changes daily to reflect the days catch. Other attractions at Kilrush include a Blue Flag beach, 120 berth purpose built marina and a 420-acre woodland park; the dolphins in the Shannon estuary are also a great draw.

Bar and Restaurant

Good food and drink all day long; live music most evenings

Credit Cards: Access, Mastercard, Visa

Local Golf Courses: Kilrush, Kilkee, Ballybunion, Lahinch

County Clare

GLASHA MEADOWS 126

Glasha, Doolin, Co Clare
Tel: 065 7074443
e-mail: glameadows@tinet.ie

Marian and Martin McDonagh and their family run a delightful Bed & Breakfast business in their smart modern house set in its own grounds on the coast road into Doolin. The six en suite bedrooms, all on the ground floor, are roomy, bright and comfortable. Home-made scones greet guests on arrival, and the tv lounge is a good place to relax after a day on the links or visiting the many places of interest in the region. Doolin is famous for its traditional Irish song and dance, and the Doolin ferry crosses to the atmospheric Aran islands.

Bed & Breakfast

Six en suite bedrooms, tv lounge. Close to Aran Islands

Credit Cards: Access, Mastercard, Visa

Local Golf Courses: Lahinch, Kilkee, Gort, Ennis

CRAGGY ISLAND 127

Ardeamush, Doolin, Co Clare
Tel: 065 7074595
e-mail: cragisle@gofree.indigo.ie

On the edge of the wonderful Burren, two miles from Doolin and two miles from the spa town of Lisdoonvarna, the O'Connor family's traditionally-styled house offers en suite Bed & Breakfast accommodation in cheerful, relaxed surroundings. Breakfast provides plenty of choice, and there are several good pubs and restaurants in the area. Doolin is famous as the music capital of Ireland, and Adrian O'Connor, a musician and singer, will entertain guests by the fireside or invite them to the local pubs when he and his band are playing. Guests are requested not to smoke in the house.

Bed & Breakfast

En suite bedrooms; good breakfast choice; lots of live music!

Credit Cards: Access, Mastercard, Visa

Local Golf Courses: Lahinch, Kilkee, Gort, Ennis

CASTLE VIEW LODGE 128

Ennistymon Road, Lahinch, Co Clare
Tel: 065 7081648

Pat and Margaret Donovan, a young couple well in tune with the needs of golfers, run a high-quality Bed & Breakfast business in their modern home on the main road from Lahinch to Ennistymon (N67). The house is exceptionally well appointed throughout, and the six letting bedrooms are individually designed, all with en suite facilities and multi-channel tv. The house overlooks the two Lahinch golf courses, and players wanting a quick morning start can arrange for an early breakfast to send them on their way. Lahinch is a pleasant coastal resort, and the surrounding area is full of interesting things to see and do.

Bed & Breakfast

Six en suite bedrooms with tv. House overlooks golf courses

Credit Cards: None

Local Golf Courses: Lahinch, Kilkee, Gort, Ennis

Co Cork

THE BRAMBLES 140

Ballyrichard, Midleton, Co Cork
Tel/Fax: 021 633758
web: moira@sportingtoursireland.ie

Look for the sign off the Midleton-Cork road (N25) to find this modern house set in capacious gardens sheltering behind mature conifers. Vincent and Theresa Connolly provide abundant comfort for their guests in five en suite bedrooms - four doubles and a single - all with multi-channel tv. No smoking in the bedrooms. Full Irish breakfast to start the day. Wheelchair accessible. Local activities and attractions include Fota Wildlife Park, Trabolgan Holiday Centre and the Jameson Heritage Centre - all well worth a visit in between rounds. Fishing and riding are also available in the vicinity.

Bed and Breakfast

5 non-smoking rooms, all en suite, tv. Easy place to find just off N25. Large gardens
Credit Cards:

Local Golf Courses: Fota Island, East Cork, Harbour Point, Cork

VICTORIA HOTEL 141

Macroom, Co Cork
Tel: 026 41082 Fax: 026 42148

On the main square of a town that's famous for its castle, the Victoria is a fine base for tourists and sportsmen. The hotel has 16 bedrooms, all en suite, with satellite tvs and telephones. The restaurant offers a wide dining choice on à la carte and prix fixe menus, and an equally extensive choice is available all day on the lighter bar menu. Local amenities include boating, water-skiing and angling on the huge man-made lakes two miles east of Macroom.

Hotel & Restaurant

16 rooms, all en suite. Telephone, tv. Town-centre location. Restaurant & bar menus
Credit Cards: All the major cards

Local Golf Courses: Macroom, Kanturk, Lee Valley, Bandon

ROSEVILLE 142

New Catherine Street, Youghal, Co Cork
Tel: 024 92571

Old-fashioned comfort and hospitality are keynotes at this late 18th-century residence of distinction near the middle of town on a one-way stretch of the N25. Phyllis Foley is the most welcoming and friendly of owners, and a stay in the Foley home is a wonderfully relaxing experience. Overnight Bed & Breakfast accommodation consists of four doubles and one twin bedroom, all with en suite facilities and tv. A full Irish breakfast is served in a spacious, comfortable dining room, and guests have the use of an equally appealing lounge. The renowned Aherne seafood restaurant is a three-minute walk away, and Roseville is also well placed for Youghal's varied attractions and its Blue Flag beaches.

Bed & Breakfast

5 rooms, all en suite. Tv. Plenty of parking space. Convenient location

Credit Cards: All the major cards

Local Golf Courses: Youghal, East Cork, West Waterford, Dungarvan

GLENVIEW HOUSE 143

Ballinaclasha, Midleton, East Cork
Tel: 021 631680 Fax: 021 634680
e-mail: glenviewhouse@esatclear.ie
web: www.dragnet-systems.ie/dira/glenview

Glenview House, a Georgian house dating from 1780, stands three miles west of Midleton in acres of private land surrounded by beautiful forest. In this ideal spot for escaping the bustle of daily life, visitors can opt for B&B in the four main-house rooms or 2 luxury apartments in the coach house. The bedrooms are all en suite, with super king-size beds. Evening meals by arrangement. Ample safe parking, wheelchair friendly, guide dogs welcome. Various local activities, including no fewer than 16 golf courses within a 30-minute drive!

Bed & Breakfast

7 en suite B&B rooms. Extensive grounds. Ample parking. Dinner by arrangement.
Credit Cards: All the major cards

Local Golf Courses: Cork, Fota Island, Harbour Point, East Cork

LYNWEN LODGE 144

Cork Road, N25, Midleton, Co Cork
Tel: 021 631934

One mile west of Midleton on the N25, Lynwen Lodge is a large, well-appointed house standing in two acres of gardens and grounds that include a practice area for golfers. Guests are very well provided for in ten luxurious en suite bedrooms (all at least doubles) with tvs and telephones. A full Irish breakfast is provided, and five-course dinners or lighter evening meals can be pre-booked; the guest house has a wine licence. Meeting rooms are available, and the private car park has space for 40 cars. Local amenities and attractions include fishing and a wild-life park. Book your rooms well in advance. Credit cards are welcome.

Guest House

10 rooms, all en suite, tv, telephone. Evening meals, with wine licnece, by arrangement. Plenty of parking.
Credit Cards: All the major cards

Local Golf Courses: Cork, East Cork, Fota Island, Harbour Point

LOUGH MAHON HOUSE 145

Lower Glanmire Road, Tivoli, Co Cork
Tel: 021 502142 Fax: 021 501804
e-mail: loughmahonhse@eircom.net

In an imposing early-Victorian house among well-designed adjacent properties, Margot Meagher offers high-class B&B accommodation in seven well-decorated en suite bedrooms that provide flexible permutations for families or groups. It's a popular base for golfing or touring holidays and lies only a mile or so from Cork city centre on the Waterford/Dublin road. A full choice is offered for breakfast. The house retains many original features - the windows and the doors, the high ceilings and the wide hallways. There's plenty of car parking space.

Bed & Breakfast

7 rooms, all en suite, tv. Private car park. Close to Cork city centre

Credit Cards: All major credit cards

Local Golf Courses: Cork , Harbour Point, Fota Island

THE OLD THATCH 146

Killeagh, Co Cork
Tel: 024 95116/95108

Character and continuity are two words that really mean something at this remarkable pub on the main Cork-Youghal road (N25). The long, low building is a great sight with its beautiful thatched roof, and no less amazing inside, where Irish willow twig has been used to roof the bar and lounge. Beech and spruce, cedar and oak were used for the furnishings, and old Guinness barrels adorn the back of the bar. A varied menu is available throughout the day, with steaks a renowned speciality. As to continuity, the pub has been in the same family for over 300 years; it is currently in the safe hands of brother and sister Eamonn and Marian Sweeney.

Pub and Restaurant

Character and history aplenty in a striking thatched pub. All-day service of food and drink.
Credit Cards:

Local Golf Courses: Youghal, East Cork, Harbour Point, Cork

THE MILLS INN 147

Ballyvourney, Macroom, Co Cork
Tel: 026 45237 Fax: 026 45454

Set in landscaped gardens 20 miles from Killarney on the N22 Cork-Killarney road, this is one of the oldest and finest inns in Ireland. Period charm combines with modern amenities in the 12 beautifully-appointed en suite bedrooms. All rooms have tvs and phones, and Superior rooms boast jacuzzi baths. Fresh seafood is a speciality in the restaurant and hot food is served all day in the bars. Great walking and cycling country (bicycles can be provided), and fishing and riding are available nearby.

Hotel & Restaurant

12 rooms, all en suite. Tv, telephone. Seafood speciality restaurant. Cycling
Credit Cards: All the major cards

Local Golf Courses: Macroom, Killarney, Kenmare

GLEBE HOUSE 148

Tay Road, Cobh, Co Cork
Tel/Fax: 021 811373
e-mail: glebehouse@eircom.net
web: dragnet-systems.ie/dira/glebehouse

In the centre of Cobh Island, in a location that is at once quietly secluded and easy to find, four bedrooms provide visitors with a very comfortable stay. The rooms are all of a very good size, and the recent addition of en suite bath and shower is just one of several improvements put in train by owner Georgina Coughlan and her husband, who run an aquatic business in adjacent premises. Breakfast with all the options is served in a very spacious dining room leading to a sun lounge. Plenty of parking. Family run.

Bed & Breakfast

4 rooms, all with en suite bath and shower, tv, hair dryers. Easy parking.

Credit Cards: Mastercard, Visa

Local Golf Courses: Fota Island, Harbour Point, Cork, East Cork

County Cork

DE BARRA 149

55 Pearse Street, Clonakilty, Co Cork
Tel: 023 33381

No visit to Clonakilty would be complete without looking in at this wonderful pub on the town's main thoroughfare. The building's green-painted frontage adorned with plant boxes and hanging baskets, is an award winner in the Bord Na Gaeilge National Shopfront Competition, and stepping through the door is like walking straight back to the 1950s. A wide range of beers and stouts is served, and there's live entertainment every night. The pub has its own folk club, and traditional Irish folk music brings in the crowds from all walks of life. Other attractions in tidy Clonakilty include the West Cork Model Railway Village.

Public House

A Clonakilty institution: a delightful old-fashioned pub with folk music
Credit Cards: None

Local Golf Courses: Bandon, Skibbereen, Old Head, Bantry

SPRINGFORT HALL HOTEL 150

New Two-Pot-House, Mallow, Co Cork
Tel: 022 21278 Fax: 022 21557
e-mail: stay@springfort-hall.com web: springfort-hall.com

The Walsh family's 18th-century country mansion four miles north of Mallow off the N20 provides a haven of peace and quiet combined with a generous helping of old-world charm and hospitality. The 50 bedrooms - 30 doubles and 20 twins - are appointed to a very high standard, with en suite bathroom, tv, telephone, hairdryer, garment press, iron and ironing board. Four highly qualified chefs prepare fine Irish cuisine to enjoy in the delightful restaurant (also open to non-residents). The drawing room, with its blazing log fire and inviting armchairs, is a perfect place to unwind. Salmon fishing on the Blackwater can be arranged.

Hotel and Restaurant

30 double rooms, 20 twins, all en suite. Telephone, tv. Restaurant open to non-residents. Fishing
Credit Cards: All the major cards

Local Golf Courses: Mallow, Kanturk, Charleville, Fermoy

SPRINGMOUNT HOUSE 151

Cork Road, Fermoy, Co Cork
Tel: 025 31623

Michael and Helen Lyons, both keen golfers, offer very comfortable Bed & Breakfast accommodation in their modern town house in Fermoy on the N8 Cork to Dublin road. Each of the rooms - seven twins, a double and a family room - has tv and en suite facilities with power showers, and decor and furnishings are of high quality. Packed lunches are available. The house has an extensive walled garden, and there's plenty of off-road parking. Local attractions include a leisure centre, cinemas, bars, and restaurants, all within walking distance, as well as fishing on the River Blackwater and pony trekking.

Bed & Breakfast

Seven twins, 1 double, 1 family room, all en suite. Tv. Packed lunches can be provided
Credit Cards: All the major cards

Local Golf Courses: Fermoy, Mallow, Mitchelstown, East Cork

WESTFIELD HOUSE 152

West Village, Ballincollig, Co Cork
Tel: 021 871824 Fax: 021 877415
e-mail: rosecotter@inet.ie

Rose Cotter's detached modern villa on the N22 provides warm, comfortable accommodation (no smoking) in four spacious, well-furnished double bedrooms, three ensuite, the other with a private bathroom, all with tvs. All the options are available for breakfast, packed lunches can be provided, and tea and coffee are on hand in the lounge. There's off-road parking for six cars. Local attractions include an equestrian centre and the famous gunpowder mills.

Bed & Breakfast

4 rooms, 3 en suite. Off-road parking. Packed lunch option.

Credit Cards: Visa, Mastercard

Local Golf Courses: Cork City, Lee Valley, Muskerry, Mahon

County Cork

TRADE WINDS 153

16 Casement Square, Cobh, Co Cork
Tel: 021 813754
e-mail: sandrao'shea@eircom.net

A delightfully intimate and elegant 40-cover restaurant in a three-storey Victorian terrace. Locally caught fish ('not caught by the chef but exquisitely cooked by her') is always a favourite on a wide-ranging menu that offers something for everyone, with a fine wine list to accompany the fine food. There's plenty to do to work up an appetite in historic Cobh, whose museum tells the moving story of the period when 2½ million Irish adults and children emigrated from Cobh on coffin ships, steamers and ocean liners.

Restaurant

Elegant licensed restaurant in the main square overlooking the sea. Seafood a speciality
Credit Cards: Mastercard, Visa

Local Golf Courses: Fota Island, Harbour Point, Cork, East Cork

---

PHELANS WOODVIEW HOUSE 154

Tweedmount, Blarney, Co Cork
Tel: 021 385197

On the C1283 a mile from Blarney and four miles from Cork, this roomy modern low-rise house is a great place for either a meal or an overnight stay. Billie and Catherine Phelan are the hands-on owners and Billie is also the chef, offering a tempting menu highlighted by the best fresh fish available on the day. The restaurant has a full drinks licence for diners and guests. Accommodation comprises eight bedrooms, all en suite, with tvs. Private car park.

Restaurant and B&B

8 rooms, all en suite. Tv. Restaurant open to non-residents. Bar

Credit Cards: All the major cards

Local Golf Courses: Muskerry, Lee Valley, Mahon, Douglas

SHANNONPARK HOUSE 155

Carrigaline, Co Cork
Tel: 021 372091 Fax: 021 371632 Mobile: 087 2942307

All-action hostess Nora Hyland offers superb bed & breakfast accommodation in a roomy bungalow set in large gardens just outside the village. The six bedrooms, all en suite and with tvs,tea and coffee making facilities are exceptionally well furnished, as are the dining room, where a full Irish breakfast is served, and the very comfortable lounge next to it. Fishing, golfing, riding and aquatic sports are available nearby. A really lovely place to stay, thanks in no small measure to the warm, caring attitude of the owner. Car Ferry 3 miles, Cork Airport 7 miles, Beaches 2 miles, Carrigaline ¼ mile

Bed & Breakfast

6 rooms, all en suite, tv. Well placed for car ferry and air connections. Fishing, riding nearby.
Credit Cards: All major credit cards

Local Golf Courses: Fernhill, Kinsale, Douglas, Monkstown

THE BOSUN 156

Monkstown, Co Cork
Tel: 021 842172 Fax: 021 842008

A versatile spot in an exceptionally scenic area with a wealth of history and all kinds of leisure activities. The Bosun offers overnight accommodation in bright, cheerful en suite bedrooms with tv, phone, trouser press and hairdryer. Fine food, featuring the freshest of local country, river and sea produce, is available throughout the day in the bar. The restaurant is open for Sunday lunch and nightly for dinner from 6.30 pm.

Guest House, Restaurant, Bar

En suite bedrooms, tv, telephone. A la carte menu in bar all day.

Credit Cards: All the major cards

Local Golf Courses: Monkstown, Fota Island, Harbour Point, Cork

ASHGROVE LODGE 157

Ashgrove, Cobh, Co Cork
Tel/Fax: 021 812483

Four miles from historic Cobh (Queenstown) on the north channel of
Cork harbour, a 17th-century stone-built coach house has been skilfully
converted to provide ultra-modern self-catering accommodation of comfort and character, available on a weekly or monthly basis. The house
comprises two double bedrooms, one with shower and toilet en suite,
the other with twin beds and an adjoining bathroom; a fully-equipped
kitchen/dining room; and a large sitting room with french windows
opening on to a patio and fields beyond. Oil-fired central heating, garage, gardens front and back, and a little castle in the grounds that dates
from the 12th century. The area is one of great scenic beauty.

Self-Catering

2 double rooms, kitchen-diner, sitting room, tv, payphone, garage.

Credit Cards:

Local Golf Courses: Fota Island, Harbour Point, Cork, East Cork

COOLIM 158

Coolflugh, Tower, Blarney, Co Cork
Tel: 021 382848
e-mail: nugent.coolim@oceanfree.net

A large modern house with a steeply-pitched roof and a Scandinavian
look - lots of pine for floors and doors. The three bedrooms - a double
with king-size bed and two triples (each containing a double and single
bed which can be used for either twin or triple occupancy) all have en
suite facilities. The residents' lounge is a real delight: roomy, comfortable and exquisitely furnished. Breakfast is served with home-made bread
and pancakes. Coolim stands on the main Killarney-Blarney road beside Muskerry Golf Club and Blarney Castle.

Bed & Breakfast

3 rooms, all en suite. Home baking.
Golf Club adjacent

Credit Cards: All major credit cards

Local Golf Courses: Muskerry, Lee Valley, Mahon, Douglas

BLAIRS INN 159

Cloghroe, Blarney, Co Cork
Tel: 021 381470

A typical Irish country pub, set well back from the R579 in a secluded
riverside position. John and Anne Blair have won many awards for their
hospitality and friendliness and have also earned high praise for the
cuisine, which puts an Irish twist on international dishes. Fish, freshly
landed at Dingle and Kenmare, is always a favourite, so too the terrific
Irish stew. Traditional music Mondays in season; fireside guitar sessions
Sunday evenings. The pub is equally popular with locals and visitors to
the area.

Pub & Restaurant

Extensive menus. Live music

Credit Cards: All the major cards

Local Golf Courses: Muskerry, Lee Valley, Mahon, Mallow

AN CUASÁN 160

Coolavokig, Macroom, Co Cork
Tel: 026 40018

Proprietors: Sean & Margaret Moynihan

A fine country house enjoying a tranquil setting in spacious mature
gardens on the main Macroom-Killarney road. A drive leads up to the
house, which has a large, handsome conservatory. Inside, all is spick
and span, with good taste evident in the decor and furnishings. The six
bedrooms, three doubles and three twins, all have en suite facilities;
some have balconies to make the most of the views. The scenery in
these parts is ruggedly beautiful and country walks are very much on
the agenda as well as walking the fairways. Fishing, riding and water
sports are available nearby.

Bed & Breakfast

6 rooms, all en suite. Extensive gardens. Country walks

Credit Cards: Mastercard, Visa

Local Golf Courses: Macroom, Bantry, Bandon, Lee Valley

County Cork

GLANWORTH MILL | 161

Glanworth, Co Cork
Tel: 025 38555 Fax: 025 38560
e-mail: glanworth@1ol.ie web: iol.ie/glanworth

A 4-star guesthouse with a sense of history and a unique appeal. The old mill wheel swishes gently in the mill race, while a Norman castle keeps watch above. The restored watermill enjoys a lovely setting by the River Funcheon in the lush Blackwater Valley. Each of the ten en suite bedrooms has the style of the writer whose name it takes, from Elizabeth Bowen to Edmund Spenser, from Anthony Trollope to William Trevor. Fine dining in the Fleece 'n' Loom restaurant, lighter fare in the tea rooms. Fishing, walking.

Country Inn and Restaurant

10 en suite bedrooms in a beautifully restored watermill. Restaurant & tea rooms. Fishing
Credit Cards:

Local Golf Courses: Fermoy, Mallow, Mitchelstown

BERNARD'S BAR | 162

29 Main Street, Skibbereen, Co Cork
Tel: 028 21772

Life-long publicans Bernard and Mary O'Brien run one of Skibbereen's most renowned and well-situated pubs. Their very large off-licence has a vast selection of wines, beers and spirits displayed alongside Irish made pipes, Swiss army knives, Maglite torches and accessories - a browsers paradise.

Bernard's Bar is an Irish Pub of Distinction and an oasis for relaxing and for good dining, serving the best of West Cork fare on weekdays and summer evenings. To discover Bernard's use the laneway from Main Street with art works on famous Irish writers or the main entrance from the town car park. A warm welcome awaits you.

Bar and Restaurant

Licensed premises: bar and restaurant, all-day menu. Plus off licence

Credit Cards: All the major cards

Local Golf Courses: Skibbereen

COOLIGREENANE HOUSE | 163

Inchigeela, Co Cork
Tel: 026 49344

Nora Herlihy offers accommodation of character in three separate locations. At scenically set Cooligreenane House there are three bedrooms, one of which is en suite, with tvs, farmhouse breakfasts and private access to coarse fishing. Rose Cottage, beside Lough Allua, is a cosy two-bedroomed bungalow equipped for a self-catering holiday, and nearby Tigh Mhuire offers similar facilities in a three-bedroomed bungalow. Both places are centrally heated, with large gardens. Plenty of lake fishing, with no close season and no need for a licence.

B&B and Self-catering

3 B&B rooms, 1 en suite. Self-catering lakeside bungalows

Credit Cards: None

Local Golf Courses: Macroom, Lee Valley

QUAYSIDE HOUSE | 164

The Park, Kinsale, Co Cork
Tel: 021 772188 Fax: 021 772664

A family-run guest house in a picturesque seafront setting overlooking Kinsale harbour adjacent to the town centre, yachting marina and all the amenities. All the bedrooms are en suite, with tv and telephone. They comprise four doubles, four twin rooms and a family room; they have great charm and character, and the house, originally a boathouse but much extended, has three verandas that offer relaxation and lovely views. Kinsale's gourmet restaurants are close by, and the golf course is a short drive away. Sea angling trips, sailing and riding can be arranged. Mary Cotter is the proprietor, and her own home, Teppswood House, is used for B&B overspill. Both Quayside House and Teppswood House are 3 star registered guest houses with the Irish Tourist Board (Bord Failte).

Guest House

9 bedrooms including a family room, all en suite, tv, telephone. 3 star registered
Credit Cards: Visa, Mastercard

Local Golf Courses: Kinsale, Old Head, Fernhill, Monkstown

HILL TOP FARM 165

Ballyvoige, Cill-na-Martra, Macroom, Co Cork
Tel: 026 40154

A lovely secluded setting in the hills, up off the N22 between Macroom and Killarney. The house has extensive gardens and a large conservatory. Four bedrooms, three en suite, include one suitable for family occupation. Full breakfasts; packed lunches can be provided, also evening meals by arrangement, or there's a traditional Irish pub 100 yards away. The farm is an ideal base for touring Cork and Kerry, and many sporting facilities are available nearby.

Bed & Breakfast

4 rooms, 3 en suite. Dinner by arrangement.

Credit Cards: None

Local Golf Courses: Macroom, Kanturk, Bantry, Lee Valley

ECO DOUGLAS 166

1-2 Eastville, Douglas, Co Cork
Tel: 021 892522 Fax: 021 895354 web: eco.ie

Behind the long street frontage this is a most appealing, intimate restaurant with 80 covers. The menu is as well conceived as the room itself, with an excellent choice of meat, poultry, fish and vegetarian dishes including some with Oriental and Scandinavian influences. The wine list is a veritable who's who of fine wines from around the globe. Take the Cork South Ring Road (N25/N8) and follow signs for Douglas.

Restaurant

Inviting 80-cover restaurant with globally-influenced menu and wine list

Credit Cards: All the major cards

Local Golf Courses: Douglas, Mahon, Monkstown, Fernhill

ASHLEE LODGE 167

Tower, Blarney, Co Cork
Tel: 021 385346 Fax: 021 385726
e-mail: ashlee@iol.ie web: welcome.to/ashleelodge

A striking Mediterranean-style bungalow set in prize-winning landscaped gardens four miles from Blarney village on the R617 Blarney-Killarney road. Hosts Ann and John O'Leary offer high standards of hospitality, comfort and service: well-chosen antiques and modern fabrics match well in the public rooms and in the six charming guest bedrooms, five en suite, all with satellite tvs, phones and hairdryers. Good breakfast menu. Packed lunches on request. No smoking.

Bed & Breakfast

6 rooms, 5 en suite. Tv, telephone. Packed lunch

Credit Cards: Mastercard, Visa

Local Golf Courses: Muskerry, Mallow, Mahon, Douglas

CARN-NA-RADHARC 168

Ardsallagh, Youghal, Co Cork
Tel: 024 92703

Situated 1½ miles off the N25 at Youghal Bridge, a splendid detached bungalow in private gardens in a cul-de-sac. It enjoys magnificent views of woodland, river and mountains from its elevated position. Overnight Bed & Breakfast accommodation comprises two single bedrooms, a double and a twin; each room has its own individual appeal, and special orthopaedic beds guarantee a good night's sleep. Two rooms have en suite facilities. Plenty of parking space. Good walking, cycling and fishing in the area. Hosts are Maura and Pat Coughlan.

Bed & Breakfast

4 bedrooms, 2 of them en suite. Quiet location; grand views

Credit Cards: None

Local Golf Courses: Youghal, Dungarvan, Goldcoast, West Waterford

COAKLEY'S BAR   169

1 Grattan Street, Youghal, Co Cork
Tel: 024 93161

Liam Coakley, a native of Youghal, returned home after many years working in London to open his cheerful pub in the centre of town on a one-way stretch of the N25. Behind the smart green-and-red facade of the 1820s building, the pub is cosy and welcoming, and simply oozes atmosphere. A winner of the coveted James Joyce award, it serves a good selection of beers and the best Guinness in town. Close to the harbour and other places of interest in a town full of history and with a wealth of archaeological delights; also Blue Flag beaches. Easy parking.

Public House

Small and welcoming pub with no food but a good range of thirst-quenchers
Credit Cards: None

Local Golf Courses: Youghal, Dungarvan, West Waterford, East Cork

AN SÚGÁN   170

41 Strand Road, Clonakilty, Co Cork
Tel: 023 33498

On a corner site in the old quays area of Clonakilty, this renowned pub-restaurant is colourful, characterful and invariably welcoming. Above the famous bar is a more formal restaurant; seafood is a speciality in both. The mouthwatering restaurant menu ranges from seafood chowder and Rossmore oysters to crab mornay, lobster and seafood platters of various sizes and content; there's also plenty for meat-eaters. Adjacent to the pub, Strand House is an old merchant's house offering high-quality B&B accommodation in five guest bedrooms, and self-catering rooms are available in nearby Mill Lane Cottages.

Pub, Restaurant, B&B, Self-Catering

Pub and restaurant specialising in seafood. B&B and self-catering
Credit Cards: All the major cards

Local Golf Courses: Bandon, Skibbereen, Old Head, Kinsale

WOODLEIGH   171

Carrigadrohid, Macroom, Co Cork
Tel: 026 48119

Plain and simple home-from-home accommodation in a semi-detached house with a conservatory and gardens. The owners have four letting bedrooms, all en suite, with tvs. A good breakfast starts the day, and evening meals can be provided with advance notice. Just off the R618, between Blarney and Macroom, Woodleigh is an ideal base for touring West Cork. Good coarse fishing is available nearby, also water-skiing, great walking and cycling. Easy parking.

Bed & Breakfast

4 rooms, all en suite, tv

Credit Cards: None

Local Golf Courses: Macroom, Bandon, Lee Valley, Bantry

HILLVIEW HOUSE   172

Killard, Blarney, Co Cork
Tel: 021 385161 e-mail: hillview_blarney@yahoo.co.uk
Website: www.geocities.com/TheTropics/Coast/1491/index.html

An attractive house with lots of character and a setting of peaceful, colourful gardens and grounds. Its a particularly convivial relaxed place where Tony and Fran Cronin offer comfortable B&B accommodation in four recently renovated bedrooms, all en suite with tv's, pressurised showers and tea/coffee making facilities. There is also a sun lounge for reading and relaxing on fair weather days as well as a large private car park. Fran also supplies an extensive breakfast menu, help with itineraries and warm hospitality. The house lies off the N20 on the outskirts of Blarney village close to the castle, shops and hotels. Cork city is only 4 miles away.

Bed & Breakfast

4 rooms, all en suite. Easy parking. Close to castle and Cork city.

Credit Cards: None

Local Golf Courses: Muskerry, Mallow, Lee Valley, Mahon

Country Guest House

18th-century mansion, 6 rooms, all en suite. Tv. B&B, packed lunch, dinner by arrangement. Fishing
Credit Cards: All the major cards

BALLYVOLANE HOUSE   173

Castlelyons, Co Cork
Tel: 025 36349 Fax: 025 36781
e-mail: ballyvol@iol.ie web: ballyvolanehouse.ie

A private driveway leads through wooded grounds up to a mansion of distinction, built in 1728 and later modified in Italianate style. The pillared hall and well-proportioned reception rooms are impressive, but owners Jeremy and Merrie Green generate a relaxed, informal feel. The six letting bedrooms are warm and comfortable, with antiques and en suite bathrooms - one has an Edwardian bath reached by mahogany steps. Packed lunches; dinner with notice. Fishing is available on a private 10-mile stretch of the River Blackwater, a 20-minute drive away. AA QQQQQ.

Local Golf Courses: Fermoy, Mitchelstown, Mallow, East Cork

Bed & Breakfast

6 rooms, 5 en suite. Tv. Fishing

Credit Cards: None

BIRCH HILL HOUSE   174

Grenagh, Blarney, Co Cork
Tel: 021 886106

A grand and imposing grey-painted farmhouse, part of a working dairy and beef farm, at the top of a long lane, signposted off the N20 and from Blarney (4 miles). Built in 1874, it's all on quite a grand scale, with big chairs and long tables in the day rooms. B&B accommodation is in six rooms, all but one with en suite facilities. The house overlooks the River Martin, where trout fishing is available. There are pleasant riverside walks and a picnic area.

Local Golf Courses: Muskerry, Mallow, Kanturk, Fermoy

Hotel and Restaurant

100 en suite bedrooms, satellite tv, telephone. 5 rooms for disabled guests. Restaurant, lounge bar
Credit Cards: All the major cards

IBIS HOTEL   175

Lee Tunnel Roundabout, Dunkettle, Cork, Co Cork
Tel: 021 354354 Fax: 021 354002

Off the N8 at the entrance to Cork City, this is part of a worldwide chain of more than 500 well-equipped, functional modern hotels. This one has 100 bright, well-kept bedrooms, all en suite, with satellite tv, telephones with voice-mail/modem points, hairdryers and tea-makers. Five bedrooms are equipped for disabled guests. Other amenities include 24-hour reception, 24-hour snacks, a buffet breakfast and full à la carte menus.

Local Golf Courses: Cork, Fota Island, Harbour Point, Douglas

Bar and Restaurant

Main-street bar and restaurant with a choice of bars and a tempting lunchtime menu
Credit Cards: Visa

THE FOUR WINDS   176

Main Street, Charleville, Co Cork
Tel: 063 89285

Pat Cronin's delightful bar and restaurant stands on a prominent corner site on the N20 Mallow-Limerick road. It's very much at the centre of Charleville's social life, and behind its cheerful yellow and black frontage adorned with old-fashioned street lamps there's an abundance of life and atmosphere. Besides the comfortable lounge bar there's an 80-cover restaurant where food is served between noon and 3pm (average price about £8 per head). The Four Winds is a popular choice for parties and discos, and would be a great spot for celebrating a hole-in-one at nearby Charleville golf course. Street parking.

Local Golf Courses: Charleville, Kanturk, Killeline, Mitchelstown

County Cork

Bed & Breakfast

6 rooms, all en suite. Extensive private grounds
Credit Cards: Visa, Mastercard, Eurocard, Access

MARANATHA COUNTRY HOUSE 177

Tower, Blarney, Co Cork
Tel: 021 385102 Fax: 021 382978
e-mail: maranatha@cork-guide.ie
web: cork-guide.ie/blarney/maranatha/welcome.html

Outstanding accommodation in a distinguished 1880's Victorian home nestled in 27 acres of lawns and gardens. The six en suite bedrooms are nothing short of stunning, all on a grand scale, with huge mirrors, masses of drapery and each room with its own decorative theme. The Rose room has two canopy beds, while the Claddagh room has a 7 foot four-poster and the Regal suite comes with a two person jacuzzi. With lots to do here and locally being near to Blarney castle, it is a good base to try out the 3 local golf courses and the 5 courses in nearby towns.

Local Golf Courses: Muskerry, Lee Valley, Mallow, Macroom

Restaurant & Accommodation

Speciality seafood restaurant above a beach. 3 double rooms, 2 twins, all en suite. Tv, telephone
Credit Cards: All the major cards

SPANISH POINT 178

Ballycotton, Co Cork
Tel: 021 646177 Fax: 021 646179

A speciality seafood with guest accommodation in a dramatic setting above the beach in a village signposted off the N25 Cork-Waterford road. The owner has two trawlers and fishes just off the coast, so the produce that goes into his kitchen could not be fresher. What comes out is splendid dishes such as roast cod with asparagus and a chive butter sauce, or grilled turbot with potato scales on a bed of wilted tomatoes and scallions. For overnight guests there are three doubles and two twin rooms, all en suite, with tv and telephone. Sea angling. Cliff and beach walks.

Local Golf Courses: Youghal, East Cork, Fota Island, Cork

Bed & Breakfast

5 rooms, 3 rooms en suite. Tv. Riding nearby. Local pub with same owner
Credit Cards: Visa, Mastercard, Euro

BOHERNAMONA HOUSE 179

Courtbrack, Blarney, Co Cork
Tel: 021 385181 Fax: 021 382443

The welcome is warm and the beds comfortable in this strikingly designed modern house signposted on the R617 five miles north of Blarney. The whole place is bright and cheerful, with a lot of flair evident in the colourful decor. There are five letting bedrooms, three of which are en suite. Large gardens; plenty of parking space. Owner Noreen Murray also runs a nearby traditional Irish pub where the craic is always good.

Local Golf Courses: Muskerry, Lee Valle, Macroom, Kanturk

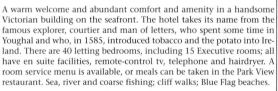

Hotel and Restaurant

40 en suite rooms including 15 Executives; tv, telephone. Room service menu plus full restaurant menus
Credit Cards: All the major cards

WALTER RALEIGH HOTEL 180

Youghal, Co.Cork
Tel: 024 92011/92314 Fax: 024 93560

A warm welcome and abundant comfort and amenity in a handsome Victorian building on the seafront. The hotel takes its name from the famous explorer, courtier and man of letters, who spent some time in Youghal and who, in 1585, introduced tobacco and the potato into Ireland. There are 40 letting bedrooms, including 15 Executive rooms; all have en suite facilities, remote-control tv, telephone and hairdryer. A room service menu is available, or meals can be taken in the Park View restaurant. Sea, river and coarse fishing; cliff walks; Blue Flag beaches.

Local Golf Courses: Youghal, West Waterford, Goldcoast, Dungarvan

SPRINGFIELD HOUSE 181

Kilkern, Rathbarry, Castlefreke, Clonakilty, Co Cork
Tel/Fax: 023 40622

Leave the N71 between Clonakilty and Rosscarbery to find this delightful Georgian framhouse, where John and Maureen Callanan cater for all their guests' needs in a warm, friendly setting. The select farmhouse accommodation consists of four bedrooms, all en suite, some with tv. There are outstanding views over green fields to the ocean beyond, and amenities/attractions in the area include sandy beaches, riding, birdwatching, fishing and the model village. Fresh farm produce, tea on arrival, home cooking a speciality. The house is 1 km from Rathbarry, 5 km west of Clonakilty. AA 3 Diamonds rated.

Bed & Breakfast

Four bedrooms, all en suite. Tea on arrival. Home cooking.
AA 3 Diamonds
Credit Cards: None

Local Golf Courses: Bandon, Skibbereen, Bantry, Macroom

THE CASTLE INN 182

Buttevant, Co Cork
Tel: 022 23044

On the N20 Mallow-Limerick road, this is one of the atmospheric pubs around, full of character and characters. Behind its long, brightly painted facade (note the huge Guinness pelican) the bars are roomy and comfortable, with a separate 40-cover restaurant area and a good-sized games room with pool and darts. Atmosphere and colour are provided by Maria McAuliffe, who runs the whole operation almost singlehanded, and the cheerful band of loyal local customers. Irish stew is an all-time favourite on the appetising menu, which always includes some daily lunchtime specials. Bus tours are catered for with 12 hours notice.

Bar and Restaurant

Lots of local colour, games room with pool and darts, menu with lunchtime specials
Credit Cards: Visa

Local Golf Courses: Charleville, Mallow, Kanturk, Mitchelstown

LITTLE ACRE 183

Cork Road, Skibbereen, Co Cork
Tel/Fax: 028 22528 e-mail: lilacre@indigo.ie

A leisurely stroll or a very short drive out of Skibbereen on the Cork Road, Little Acre is a substantial detached house with impressively large gardens and plenty of off-road parking space. Behind its cheerful yellow-painted facade, the house is very warm and welcoming, and owner Fiona Sheane offers five letting bedrooms for Bed and Breakfast accommodation, all of them en suite twins/doubles with tv and tea/coffee making facilities. Good breakfast choice. Fiona is a former tour guide, so she can put guests in the picture with authority concerning the local places of interest; she is also an expert scuba diver, and anyone willing to have a go will find excellent facilities nearby.

Bed and Breakfast

5 en suite double/twin bedrooms. Tv, tea and coffee facilities. Plenty of parking
Credit Cards: Visa, Mastercard

Local Golf Courses: Skibbereen, Bantry, Bandon

ROSALITHIR 184

Frehanes, Rosscarbery, Co Cork
Tel/Fax: 023 48136

A large and handsome bungalow within easy distance of the main N71 West Cork road. Newly built on a working dairy farm, it offers impressive standards of decor in its four en suite bedrooms, which comprise two doubles and two twins. A full breakfast starts the day, and packed lunches are available - a useful service for all-day golfers or tourists making the most of the wonderful beaches and the cliff and countryside walks. Tea or coffee is offered on arrival. Plenty of off-road parking. In the house next door to Rosalithir, self-catering accommodation is available for up to six guests (see separate entry). Both establishments are owned by Catherine O'Sullivan and her husband.

Bed & Breakfast

4 bedrooms, doubles and twins, all en suite. Easy parking. Packed lunches
Credit Cards: None

Local Golf Courses: Skibbereen, Bandon, Bantry Bay, Old Head

County Cork

County Cork

ROSALITHIR FARM COTTAGE · 185

Frehanes, Rosscarbery, Co Cork
Tel/Fax: 023 48136

Self-catering accommodation in a charming, carefully renovated two-storey farmhouse set in a private garden on a working dairy farm. Furnished and maintained to a very high standard, the accommodation consists of a sitting room with open fire, dining room, separate large kitchen, ground-floor bathroom and shower, master double bedroom with en suite bathroom, a room with a double and a single bed, and a single room. Facilities include central heating, dishwasher, microwave, tumbledryer, fridge, freezer, colour tv, video/radio/cassette player, garden furniture, barbecue, bed linen, towels, highchair - babysitting by arrangement. A lovely sandy beach is a 3-minute drive away. B&B in owner Catherine O'Sullivan's neighbouring home (see separate entry).

Self-Catering

3 bedrooms and all other rooms/equipment for self-catering. B&B next door
Credit Cards: None

Local Golf Courses: Skibbereen, Bantry, Bandon

AN GARRÁN COÍR · 187

Castlefreke, Clonakilty, Co Cork Tel: 023 48236

A lovely detached house off the N71 between Clonakilty and Ross Carbery. The name means 'a plentiful grove', and the Calnan family welcome guests to their select Bed & Breakfast residence, which enjoys panoramic views of beautiful rolling countryside on the rugged West Cork coastline. The comfortable en suite bedrooms - one with jacuzzi - are elegantly co-ordinated, and each has a tv and hairdryer. Award-winning breakfasts served in the spacious dining room offer a wealth of choice that includes the famous Clonakilty black and white pudding. A separate snack area in the reception room has use-as-you-please tea/coffee-making facilities. Guest lounge. Tennis court. The house is part of a working dairy farm and guests can watch the morning and evening milking. Dinner by arrangement. The award winning village of Rathbarry is only 1 mile away.

Bed and Breakfast

En suite bedrooms with tv. Renowned breakfasts. Tennis. AA recommended QQQQ
Credit Cards: None

Local Golf Courses: Bandon, Skibbereen, Old Head, Kinsale

County Donegal

DERGFIELD HOUSE · 200

Ballybofey, Co Donegal
Tel: 074 32775 Fax: 074 32593
e-mail: derghouse@eircom.net

Peter and Miranda Byrne, a friendly, welcoming young couple, run a most delightful Bed & Breakfast business in their beautiful house, which stands on the main N15 road half a mile from the town centre and a mile from the golf course. Overnight accommodation consists of six comfortable bedrooms, all of them with en suite facilities. The Finn Valley, where the twin towns of Ballybofey and Stranorlar stand, is a really lovely part of the world, with some spectacular mountain scenery. At nearby Raphoe is the Beltony Stone Circle, known as the 'Stonehenge of Donegal' and actually even older than Stonehenge.

Bed & Breakfast

Six en suite bedrooms, tea/coffee making facilities. Excellent touring base. Wonderful scenery
Credit Cards: All the major cards

Local Golf Courses: Ballybofey, Donegal, Letterkenny, Strabane

THE HARBOUR RESTAURANT · 201

Quay Street, Donegal, Co Donegal
Tel: 073 21703 Fax: 073 22697

"Pizza, seafood, coffee, steaks, chicken, wines, spuds, pasta." That's what is written outside this splendid family-owned-and-run restaurant with views of the quays. Brian and Margaret Neilan have built up a good reputation over ten years with locals, and visitors are as welcome as the flowers in May to dear old Donegal. The speciality is seafood, locally caught and zingy-fresh, but there are also succulent steaks, pizzas, and baked potatoes with a variety of fillings. The restaurant, with 60+ covers, is roomy and comfortable, and the layout, on different levels, gives it great character and atmosphere. A long-time favourite with golfers, on a par with the best in the area.

Restaurant

Well-established restaurant near Donegal's quays. Seafood, steaks, pizza, baked potatoes
Credit Cards: All the major cards

Local Golf Courses: Donegal, Bundoran, Ballybofey, Narin & Portnoo

PORTNASON HOUSE 202

Ballyshannon, Co Donegal
Tel:072 52016 Fax: 073 31739

Portnason House is a handsome, well-proportioned house of great charcater standing alone in 54 acres of a charming country estate on the Erne estuary. Madge and Barry Sharkey offer B&B accommodation in ten spacious, airy en suite bedrooms, and guests also have the use of elegant, inviting reception rooms warmed in winter by log fires in antique marble fireplaces. The estate has 700 metres of frontage on the N15 Donegal-Sligo road, and from the courtyard there is direct private access to the beach. Other features include a spring-fed boating pond, two old stone piers and a walled garden and orchard. Connemara ponies are bred on the estate, and there's stabling for guests' horses.

Bed & Breakfast

Characterful accommodation in 10 en suite bedrooms. Access to beach, fishing, stabling
Credit Cards: All the major cards

Local Golf Courses: Bundoran, Donegal, County Sligo, Strandhill

ATLANTIC VIEW HOUSE 203

West End, Bundoran, Co Donegal
Tel: 072 41403

This two-storey period house on the N15 at the southern end of town is an ideal base for golfers. Frank and Claire McGloin are both very keen players, and Frank, an ex-club professional will be happy to organise reduced-rate bookings at some local courses. The Bed & Breakfast accommodation is all en suite, and most of the rooms live up to the name of the house by offering splendid views of the ocean and the coastline. The rooms are spacious yet cosy, and the residents' lounge is just the place for swapping golfing tales. Claire's excellent home cooking includes the bread and preserves that are part of a super breakfast.

Bed & Breakfast

En suite accommodation with sea views. Tv. Full Irish breakfast with home cooking
Credit Cards: None

Local Golf Courses: Bundoran, Donegal, County Sligo, Strandhill

THE STRAND HOTEL 204

Ballyliffin, Inishowen, Co Donegal
Tel: 077 76107 Fax: 077 76486

Many hotels will make similar claims, but the Strand Hotel can very accurately be called a golfer's paradise. Friendly and intimate, with a welcome for all the family, it offers professional, unobtrusive service and all the modern comforts. It is ideally located beside two of Ireland's leading golf courses, the classic Ballyliffin Old Links and the Glashedy Links, which opened for play in August 1995. The hotel offers midweek and weekend golf breaks, and non-golfers will find plenty of alternative activities in and around Ballyliffin, including nature walks, pony trekking, sandy beaches, fishing and wildlife watching.

Hotel and Restaurant

Hotel with modern facilities and restaurant. Beside two golf courses

Credit Cards: All the major cards

Local Golf Courses: Ballyliffin, Greencastle, North West, Portsalon

MEVAGH HOUSE 205

Carrigart, Co Donegal
Tel: 074 55693/55512

A charming modern house on the B245 a short walk west of Carrigart. Visitors are greeted with tea or coffee on arrival, and owners Fidelma and Donald Cullen make sure that all their guests' needs are taken care of. All the bedrooms have en suite facilities and tv. Beyond the garden there's a broad sweep of lovely open countryside to explore. The owners also run a taxi, minibus and coach service, so there is never a problem in organising transport to and from the golf courses and the many local places of interest. Packed lunches can be provided. This place is a real favourite with golfers, many of whom return year after year.

Bed and Breakfast

En suite bedrooms, tv. Off-road parking. Taxi service on the premises
Credit Cards: All the major cards

Local Golf Courses: Rosapenna, Portsalon, Letterkenny, Dunfanaghy

County Donegal

Co Donegal

COASTGUARD HOLIDAY COTTAGES 206

Downings, Co Donegal
Tel: 074 25660/25666 Fax: 074 24788

Three-bedroomed cottages in a truly magnificent setting provide a perfect base for a self-catering holiday. Each cottage has a spacious lounge, a fully-fitted modern kitchen, a master bedroom with shower/toilet en suite and two other bedrooms served by a fully-tiled shower/toilet. Oil-fired central heating keeps things cosy, and there's a utility room with a washing machine and dryer. Downings is a picturesque fishing port famous for the production of traditional Donegal tweed. Lots of spectacular scenery, wonderful walks and the exciting Atlantic Drive. Rosapenna Golf Course is beside the cottages.

Self-Catering Cottages

Three-bedroomed cottages in a picturesque fishing port. Fully equipped for self-catering holidays
Credit cards: All the major cards

Local Golf Courses: Rosapenna, Portsalon, Letterkenny, Dunfanaghy

---

County Dublin

MARINE HOTEL 220

Sutton Cross, Dublin 13, Co Dublin
Tel: 01 839 0000 Fax: 01 839 0442
e-mail: sstone@thegrand.ie

A high-quality hotel which has been welcoming visitors since 1887. The city is an easy drive away, but the setting is very peaceful, with lawns rolling down to the shore of Dublin Bay. Well-appointed en suite accommodation offers either Standard or Superior rooms, both very comfortable, many with sea views. Fine cuisine in the Meridian Restaurant, informal eating in the bar. Amenities include swimming pool, sauna and steam room, while Sutton Strand and the coastal walk provide scenic surroundings for a spot of gentle exercise off the premises.

Hotel with Restaurant

High-class en suite bedrooms; fine cuisine; pool and sauna

Credit Cards: All the major cards

Local Golf Courses: Deer Park, Howth, Portmarnock, St Anne's

ESTUARY HOUSE 221

Estuary Road, Seatown East, Malahide, Co Dublin
Tel/Fax: 01 890 0242
e-mail: info@estuaryhouse.com

The address gives a big clue about the location! This striking modern brick-and-timber house, designed to the very highest standards by owners Pauline and Michael Dawson, has a frontage that overlooks the Malahide Estuary, and most of the rooms enjoy sea views. The well-travelled host offers four superb en suite bedrooms all fitted out to the highest standards, and guests have the use of a huge lounge and classic dining room, where the day gets off to the best start with a great choice for breakfast: the full Irish naturally includes black and white pudding. The house stands a mile out of Malahide.

Bed & Breakfast

Four rooms, all en suite; sea views; great breakfast choice

Credit Cards: Access, Mastercard, Visa

Local Golf Courses: Malahide, Portmarnock, Island, Donabate

ARRANMORE HOUSE 222

104 Lower Drumcondra Road, Dublin 9, Co Dublin
Tel/Fax: 01 8300009/8300558
e-mail: arranmore9@eircom.ie website: arranmorehouse.com

Period charm and modern amenities combine in Sean Paul and Anne Mahon's Bed & Breakfast establishment in a Victorian terrace. The four bedrooms are all different in detail but all are very spacious, with high ceilings and original doors and windows. All have en suite facilities, clock radio, tv, trouser press and hairdryer, and guests have the use of a comfortable lounge with tv. There's private off-street parking, and a bus service to the city centre passes the door - alternatively, it's a leisurely 20-minute walk to the main sights. Fine pubs and restaurants nearby.

Town House Bed & Breakfast

Four large B&B rooms en suite. Off-street parking

Credit Cards: Access, Mastercard, Visa

Local Golf Courses: Clontarf, Royal Dublin, St Anne's, St Margaret's

THE BRIAN BORU | 223

Prospect Road, Glasnevin, Dublin 9
Tel: 01 830 4527

A public house has stood on this site for over 200 years, and the present grand building dates from the 1850s, with the front part virtually unaltered since. Michael Hedigan is the latest member of the family who have owned it for 100 years, and in the conservatory-style restaurant a full carvery lunch is served Monday to Friday from 12 to 3, and Sunday from 12.30 to 18.00. In the evening, an à la carte menu operates Mon-Sat until 8 o'clock. The premises are full of atmosphere, and in the summer the beer garden is a popular bonus. Plenty of car parking space.

Public House with Restaurant

Pub with carvery lunch and evening à la carte.

Credit Cards: Access, Mastercard, Visa

Local Golf Courses: Royal Dublin, Clontarf, St Margaret's

EMMERDALE | 224

8 Killininny Cottages, Firhouse Road, Dublin 24, Co Dublin
Tel: 01 4516270
e-mail: emmerdale@eircom.net

Mary and Edward Quinn are the charming owners of a Bed & Breakfast establishment of real character. Though recently built, Emmerdale has the look and feel of an old-style cottage, and the three letting bedrooms with tv, one of which is en suite, are at ground level, making for very easy access. There's plenty of parking at the rear of the house, where a superb conservatory leads to lovely landscaped gardens. The house is close to an excellent pub-restaurant and only one mile from The Square Shopping Centre at Tallaght village. Buses to Dublin City.

Bed & Breakfast

Three B&B rooms with tv, 1 en suite. Extensive gardens

Credit Cards: None

Local Golf Courses: Newlands, Edmondstown, Castle, Grange, Stackstown

OPHIRA | 225

10 Corrig Avenue, Dun Laoghaire, Co Dublin
Tel/Fax: 01 2800997
e-mail: johnandcathy@ophira.ie web: www.ophira.ie

The home of Cathy and John O'Connor and their family dates from 1849 and was the first house in Corrig Avenue. It retains many original features in its four well-proportioned bedrooms, all of which have en suite facilities. There are tea-makers in the rooms, and breakfast offers a choice that includes Clonakilty pudding. Residents have a comfortable lounge with tv. Secure parking is available at the house, which is in the centre of town less than a five-minute walk from the ferry port or DART station for Dublin. Alternatively, a frequent bus service to Dublin stops less than a minute away.

Bed & Breakfast

Four en suite bedrooms. Tv lounge; secure parking

Credit Cards: Access, Mastercard, Visa

Local Golf Courses: Dun Laoghaire, Elm Park, Woodbrook, Kilternan

GIBNEYS | 226

Malahide, Co Dublin
Tel: 01 845 0606 Fax: 01 845 4289
e-mail: gibneys@tinet.ie web: www.gibneys.com

A fantastic 17th-century pub run with great charm by a family of keen golfers. Behind its quaint facade there's loads of character, with stone floors, archways, intimate little sections and plenty of room to enjoy a drink and a snack or to settle down to a full meal. The bar menu, served all day until 8pm, runs from made-to-order sandwiches, pizza and filled baked potatoes to beefburgers, smoked salmon, battered cod, steak, shepherds pie, barbecued chicken wings and a hearty breakfast grill. The wine list has a selection from both Old and New Worlds.

Public House with Food

Pub with all-day menu and wine list, 17th Century, run by keen golfers

Credit Cards: Access, Mastercard, Visa

Local Golf Courses: Malahide, Portmarnock, Island, Forest Little

County Dublin

THE MILESTONE 227

Ballydowd, Lucan, Co Dublin
Tel: 01 6241818

Cait and Simon Cunningham's recently built detached house has many splendid features, including a lovely peaceful setting among trim lawns, abundant parking space and a good bus connection to Dublin City. The four letting bedrooms, all with en suite facilities, are very spacious, with superb decor and some eyecatching antiques. Tea and coffee are available in the tv lounge, and breakfast is served in the exquisite dining room. The house is located approximately a mile on the Dublin side of Lucan village (hence the name) in a very pleasant, upmarket part of the city suburbs. The owners are happy to supply information on the local transport facilities and the places of interest in Dublin.

Bed & Breakfast

Four en suite bedrooms; tv lounge, spacious garden

Credit Cards: None

Local Golf Courses: Lucan, Hermitage, Luttrellstown, Westmanstown

FERRY HOUSE 228

15 Clarinda Park North, Dun Laoghaire, Co Dublin
Tel: 01 2808301 Fax: 01 2846530
e-mail: ferry_house@hotmail.com

Eamon and Pauline Teehan, from a family of international sporting renown, are the hosts at Ferry House, which stands in a prime location a short walk from the town centre and the ferry terminal. The house was built in the 1860s and retains many fine original features. There are four letting bedrooms for Bed & Breakfast accommodation, all with en suite facilities and tv. Dun Laoghaire has easy connections to Dublin but also has many attractions of its own, including the National Maritime Museum and, at nearby Sandycove, the James Joyce Martello Tower.

Bed & Breakfast

Four en suite bedrooms in 1860s house; tv and tea-makers

Credit Cards: Access, Mastercard, Visa

Local Golf Courses: Dun Laoghaire, Elm Park, Woodbrook, Kilternan

WALTERS 229

68 Upper George Street, Dun Laoghaire, Co Dublin
Tel: 01 2807442

One of the smartest and most fashionable spots in Dun Laoghaire – a bar, café and restaurant where the ambience is lively and relaxing, making it an ideal place to unwind after a round of golf or a spell of sightseeing. Light oak and stainless steel feature strongly in the stylish modern decor of John Coughlan's establishment, where customers are served by elegant girls who look like models. The bar-café is the place for a convivial drink and a snack, while upstairs is a more formal restaurant with a tempting menu of excellent dishes. Last orders are at 11 o'clock.

Bar, Café and Restaurant

Drinks, snacks and full meals served until 11pm

Credit Cards: Access, Mastercard, Visa

Local Golf Courses: Dun Laoghaire, Elm Park, Woodbrook, Kilternan

WILLO'S 230

Lucan Village, Co Dublin
Tel/Fax: 01 628 3365

Nuala Jackson runs a most delightful B&B in the centre of historic Lucan Village, just off the N4 and an easy 20-minute drive or bus trip from Dublin City centre. The seven bedrooms, four of them en suite and all with tv and teamakers, have individual appeal and the owners personal attention keeps everything in perfect condition - the bedrooms, dining room and residents lounge have all recently been decorated. This would be an ideal base for golfers, holiday makers and tourists with easy access to the main road links, airport, ferry port, pubs and restaurants.

Bed and Breakfast

Seven bedrooms (4 en suite) with tv, 20 minutes from Dublin City centre

Credit Cards: None

Local Golf Courses: Lucan, Hermitage, Luttrelstown, Westmanstown

MCMENAMINS 231

74 Marlborough Road, Donnybrook, Dublin 4, Co Dublin
Tel: 01 4974405 Fax: 01 4968585
e-mail: info@irishwelcome.com web: www.irishwelcome.com

In a distinguished Georgian house in an exclusive area of the city, Pauric and Marie McMenamin offer guests a comfortable, peaceful and thoroughly enjoyable stay. The five newly refurbished letting bedrooms are all en suite, with phone and tv, and guests start the day with a breakfast that features home-made bread and preserves; there's a terrific choice, including traditional Irish, scrambled eggs with smoked salmon, a hearty Dublin Coddle and a 'vegetarian surprise'. The house has private car parking, and it's only a short walk to a great selection of pubs and restaurants.

Town House Bed & Breakfast

Five en suite rooms with phone and tv. Private car parking

Credit Cards: Access, Mastercard,Visa

Local Golf Courses: Elm Park, Castle, Milltown, Edmondstown

FAGAN'S 232

Lower Drumcondra Road, Dublin 9, Co Dublin
Tel: 01 8375309 Fax: 01 8570719

One of the great Victorian pubs, where recent renovation has spoiled none of its charm and character. There's bags of space inside, with seats for 150 and lots of cosy little alcoves for enjoying an intimate drink or a meal. An excellent carvery lunch is served every day and the main à la carte menu runs from 3 till 9 Monday to Saturday. The choice is extensive and very tempting, from paté, garlic mushrooms and prawn salad starters to basket food, scampi, steaks, lasagne and several ways with chicken. The 6oz beefburgers, served with French fries and a choice of topping, are a Fagan's speciality. Comprehensive wine list.

Pub with Restaurant

Victorian pub with restaurant; lunchtime carvery, evening à la carte

Credit Cards: All the major cards

Local Golf Courses: Clontarf, Royal Dublin, Elmgreen, Elm Park

ROSELEA 233

4 Station Road, Portmarnock, Co Dublin
Tel: 01 8460117 Fax: 01 8461044
e-mail: michaelo'casey@ireland.com

Michael and Diane O'Casey, who formerly ran a restaurant in Dublin, are in their third year of Bed & Breakfast business at a neat modern bungalow set in ample gardens and lawns about half a mile from Portmarnock Golf Club. Guest accommodation comprises two double rooms and two twins, all with en suite facilities and tv. There's plenty of car parking space, and the house is close to Portmarnock station, which is soon to be served by the efficient DART rail system. The day begins in fine style at Roselea with a splendid breakfast that includes home-made bread and preserves.

Bed & Breakfast

4 rooms en suite, with tv. Near golf course and railway station

Credit Cards: Access, Mastercard,Visa

Local Golf Courses: Portmarnock, Malahide, Howth, Deer Park

THE BLOODY STREAM 234

Howth, Co Dublin
Tel: 01 8395076

No trip to Howth would be complete without a visit to The Bloody Stream, the busiest and most atmospheric pub-restaurant in town. It takes its name from the stream which runs under the property, site of a great battle between the Danes, who were occupying the bridge, and a force under Sir Almeric Tristram, said to be a descendant of Sir Tristram, one of King Arthur's knights. So there's history aplenty here, and in the excellent restaurant seafood is a speciality on a menu that always includes dishes of the day. Other attractions include live music and a beer garden.

Pub and Restaurant

Pub with seafood speciality restaurant. Garden; live music

Credit Cards: Access, Mastercard,Visa

Local Golf Courses: Howth, Deer Park, Portmarnock, St Anne's

County Dublin

County Dublin

ARIEMOND 235

47 Mulgrave Street, Dun Laoghaire, Co Dublin
Tel/Fax: 01 2801664
e-mail: ariemond@hotmail.com

Marie Power welcomes guests with true Irish hospitality at her lovely pink-painted house, which stands just two minutes on foot from the town centre. Bed & Breakfast guests have five rooms – three of which are en suite; each room is individually styled with comfort in mind, and guests start the day with a good choice for breakfast, including a special vegetarian version. The house has its own car park. Dun Laoghaire still has something of the air of a Victorian resort, and among its many attractions is the National Maritime Museum in the former Mariners' Church.

Bed & Breakfast

Five rooms, 3 en suite. Private car park

Credit Cards: Access, Mastercard, Visa

Local Golf Courses: Dun Laoghaire, Elm Park, Woodbrook, Stackstown

THE KINGSTON HOTEL 236

Adelaide Street, Dun Laoghaire, Co Dublin
Tel: 01 2801810 Fax: 01 2801237
website: www.kingstonhotel.com

The newly refurbished Hotel is situated on the seafront of Dun Laoghaire overlooking Dublin Bay and Ireland's largest enclosed harbour. All 53 elegantly decorated bedrooms are en suite, and many enjoy views of the Bay. Singles, doubles, twins and triples are available, and all have telephone and tv. The hotel has one of the finest traditional bars in the area, and bar food is served every day. In the new restaurant "The Haddington Bistro", guests can choose between the à la carte and table d'hote menus, both of which offer an excellent range of fine cuisine. Guests with small children are welcome.

Hotel with Restaurant and Bar

53 en suite rooms with telephone and tv. Bar food and restaurant

Credit Cards: All the major cards

Local Golf Courses: Dun Laoghaire, Elm Park, Woodbrook, Stackstown

STEIERMARK 237

13 Beach Park (on Strand Road), Portmarnock, Co Dublin
Tel/Fax: 01 8462032
e-mail: grabnerg@hotmail.com

A charming 'Irish/Austrian' Bed & Breakfast house owned and run by Katherine and Gerhard Grabner. The detached property is in an excellent location opposite the golf course and enjoys sea views; there are four letting bedrooms, three en suite, the other with a private bathroom not en suite, all with cable/satellite tv and tea-makers. There's ample off-street parking, and the beach, pubs and restaurants are all in very easy reach. Bus and rail connections are good, and the many local attractions include the splendid Malahide Castle, a must for all visitors to the region.

Bed & Breakfast

4 well-appointed bedrooms; sea views, golf course opposite

Credit Cards: Mastercard, Visa

Local Golf Courses: Portmarnock, Malahide, Howth, Deer Park

THE GOLF LINKS 238

The Strand, Portmarnock, Co Dublin
Tel: 01 846 0129

The only pub in Portmarnock, and also a 100-cover restaurant serving excellent-value food with well-chosen wines. Owned and run by Gerry O'Dwyer and his mother, it stands along the Portmarnock Strand overlooking the bay and the famous golf links. The interior is elegant and very civilised, with a quiet, calm atmosphere - a great place to relax and unwind. There's a good-sized car park and a beer garden. Gerry and his mother are both golfers, and their pub hosts regular gatherings of two golfing societies. The seaside setting is a major plus at this delightful place, which serves food until 8.30.

Bar and Restaurant

Good food and wine; overlooks the bay

Credit Cards: Access, Mastercard, Visa

Local Golf Courses: Portmarnock, Malahide, St Anne's, Howth

BUTLERS TOWN HOUSE `239`

44 Lansdowne Road, Ballsbridge, Dublin 4, Co Dublin
Tel: 01 6674022 Fax: 01 6673960
e-mail: info@butlers-hotel.com

In the heart of Dublin's Embassy belt, very near the international rugby ground and a short walk from many of the city's attractions, Butlers is a fine town house that has been lovingly restored to its pristine Victorian splendour and sympathetically modernised to offer all the up-to-date conveniences. The 20 bedrooms, each individually designed, are air-conditioned, with bath or shower en suite, telephone, tv and modem ports. A gourmet Irish breakfast is served in the conservatory, and a light menu is available from room service. Secure parking for guests' cars.

Town House Bed & Breakfast

20 en suite rooms with telephone and tv. Secure car parking

Credit Cards: All the major cards

Local Golf Courses: Elm Park, Castle, Milltown, Clontarf

SOUTHDALE BED & BREAKFAST `240`

143 Heather Walk, Portmarnock, Co Dublin
Tel/Fax: 01 846 3760

A striking modern house with four good-sized en suite bedrooms and a well laid out lounge and dining area. The owner, Marie d'Emidio, has strong ties with the town, and looks forward to welcoming golfing guests to her delightful B&B home. The location is very convenient, 200 yards from Portmarnock Golf Club and a similar distance from the seafront and numerous shops and pubs; the airport link road and the Dart train to Dublin are also close at hand. The sea and the land both have much to offer, and one of the most interesting local sights is the splendid Malahide Castle, which is a short drive by the scenic coast road.

Bed & Breakfast

4 en suite bedrooms; handy for golf and sea

Credit Cards: None

Local Golf Courses: Portmarnock, Malahide, Howth, Deer Park

WHITE SANDS HOTEL `241`

Coast Road, Portmarnock, Co Dublin
Tel: 01 8460003 Fax: 01 8460420
e-mail: sandshotel@tinet.ie

High standards of comfort and service in a bright modern hotel facing the shores of Portmarnock Strand, overlooking Lambay Island and Ireland's Eye. The 32 en suite bedrooms are all equipped with tv, telephone, trouser press and hairdryer, and the sea view de luxe suite even has its own jacuzzi. Local and International cuisine is served in the evenings in the Kingsford Smyth restaurant. An informal daily carvery lunch and traditional Sunday lunch is on offer in the OAsis bar. All in all, a perfect base for a golfing or sightseeing holiday.

Hotel and Restaurant

32 well-equipped en suite bedrooms; restaurant and bar, 3 star

Credit Cards: All the major cards

Local Golf Courses: Portmarnock, Malahide, Howth, Deer Park

THE OLD FORGE `242`

Saggart, Co Dublin
Tel: 01 4589226 Fax: 01 4587592

A row of four houses built in 1747 has been converted into a single dwelling where Jim and Florence Burns offer charming Bed & Breakfast accommodation. They have taken great care to keep the place authentic, preserving the two-foot thick walls and the low ceilings. There are six letting bedrooms, three en suite, and a separate self-contained section that can sleep five; this part has all the mod cons for self-catering, but breakfast can be provided. Saggart is handily placed for a number of golf courses and is 20 minutes from Dublin City. Excellent secure parking.

B & B and Self-Catering

6 rooms (3 en suite) + self-catering for five guests

Credit Cards: Access, Mastercard, Visa

Local Golf Courses: Beech Park, Slade Valley, City West, Dublin Mountain

County Dublin

GLEANN-NA-SMOL — 243

Nashville Road, Howth, Co Dublin
Tel: 01 832 2936 e-mail: rickars@indigo.ie
website: comdestination-ireland.com.glean-na-smol

Kitty Rickard and her son and daughter share the work at their most delightful Bed & Breakfast home, a golfer's favourite where guests are treated as part of the family. The location, in the upmarket fishing port of Howth, is a great asset, and the five individually styled letting bedrooms, all well furnished and with en suite facilities, include a triple. A large patio area leads to very spacious rear gardens where guests are free to stroll, and it's an easy walk to the town centre, which has a good choice of shops and pubs and restaurants.

Bed & Breakfast

5 en suite bedrooms including a triple

Credit Cards: None

Local Golf Courses: Howth, Deer Park, Portmarnock, St Anne's

WOODVIEW FARMHOUSE — 244

Margaretstown, Skerries, Co Dublin
Tel/Fax: 01 8491528
e-mail: clintonj@indigo.ie

In a lovely secluded farmhouse 2½ miles north of Skerries Joe and Mary Clinton offer Irish hospitality at its very best. Built in 1935, the house is part of a working market garden farm; the front part of the property is practically hidden by a mass of mature trees and creepers. The owners offer Bed & Breakfast accommodation in eight letting rooms, six of them with en suite facilities; a splendid breakfast starts the day, and Mrs Clinton, an excellent cook, will prepare an evening meal given notice. Ardgillan Castle, a noted tourist attraction, is close by.

Farmhouse Bed & Breakfast

8 bedrooms, 6 en suite; B&B + evening meals on request

Credit Cards: Visa,Mastercard,Access

Local Golf Courses: Balbriggan, Skerries, Hollywood Lakes, Beaverstown

PEBBLE MILL — 245

Kinsealy, Near Malahide, Co Dublin
Tel/Fax: 01 8461792

A magnificent modern detached house set in its own grounds of four acres five minutes' drive from Malahide town centre and only 15 minutes south to Dublin (also direct bus and rail connections). In this setting in a desirable suburb Monica Fitzsimons offers three letting bedrooms, including two triples. All the rooms are en suite, with tv and tea-making equipment, and the house has a private car park. Golf, horse riding, scenic walks, pubs and restaurants are all close at hand, and not-to-be-missed attractions in Malahide include the splendid castle and the model railway museum.

Bed & Breakfast

3 B&B rooms including 2 triples. Spacious grounds, private parking

Credit Cards: None

Local Golf Courses: Malahide, Portmarnock, Forest Little, Clontarf

WILLOWBROOK HOUSE — 246

Balheary Road, Swords, Co Dublin
Tel: 01 8403843

Kay Sharkey offers select Bed & Breakfast accommodation and ample private parking in her fine modern villa set in an acre of beautiful landscaped gardens. Guests have the choice of five bedrooms, all en suite, with tv. Tea and coffee are available in the lounge. The house is a very short drive or an easy walk from Swords, where there are plenty of pubs, restaurants and interesting sights. Dublin Airport is a convenient five-minute drive away, and Dublin itself can be reached in a quarter of an hour. The house enjoys a quiet location only 400 yards from the main N1 road.

Bed & Breakfast

5 en suite bedrooms with tv; large gardens, ample parking

Credit Cards: None

Local Golf Courses: Swords, Malahide, Forest Little, Portmarnock

THE HAWTHORN HOTEL 247

Main Street, Swords, Co Dublin
Tel: 01 8401308 Fax: 01 8401398
e-mail: hawthornhotel@eircom.net

On the bustling main street of Swords, an easy drive from Dublin, Sean Duignan's recently refurbished hotel has everything a guest could want. The ten en suite bedrooms are very well appointed, the staff are friendly and efficient, and there's an excellent choice of food and drink: bar food served all day in the roomy bar, and full menus in the restaurant. There's plenty to see in and around Swords, including the five-sided ruin of the medieval Swords Castle and, at nearby Donabate, the marvellous Georgian Newbridge House, used in the film *The Spy Who Came in from the Cold*.

Hotel with Bar and Restaurant

10 en suite bedrooms; bar and restaurant menus

Credit Cards: Access, Mastercard, Visa

Local Golf Courses: Swords, Malahide, Forest Little, Portmarnock

CEDAR HOUSE 248

Jugback Lane, Swords, Co Dublin
Tel: 01 8402757 Fax: 01 8402041

A neatly kept modern house off Watery Lane, close to Swords town centre. Kathleen Keneghan is a natural hostess, and her warm personality is a major attraction of a stay here. There are five letting bedrooms, all en suite, with tv and tea-making facilities; uniform in size and decor, they are comfortable and well appointed. Packed lunches available. Swords has plenty to offer the visitor and Dublin city and airport are close by, while on the coast are the towns of Malahide, with its fine sandy beaches and splendid castle, and Portmarnock, with its magnificent golf course.

Bed & Breakfast

5 en suite rooms with tv. Packed lunches available

Credit Cards: Access, Mastercard, Visa

Local Golf Courses: Swords, Malahide, Forest Little, Portmarnock

GLENVEAGH TOWN HOUSE 249

31 Northumberland Road, Ballsbridge, Dublin 4, Co Dublin
Tel: 01 668 4612 Fax: 01 668 4559
e-mail: glenveagh@eircom. net

A stunning late-Victorian town house occupying a prime site in one of Dublin's most fashionable districts. Winnie Cunningham is the most delightful hostess, welcoming guests from all over the world to her lovely house. Bed & Breakfast accommodation comprises 13 rooms, all en suite and individually designed to the highest standards. All the rooms have tv and telephone. The house is within easy walking distance of many excellent pubs and restaurants, and also Lansdowne Road rugby ground.

Town House Bed & Breakfast

13 en suite rooms with tv and telephone

Credit Cards: Access, Mastercard, Visa

Local Golf Courses: Elm Park, Milltown, Castle

THE PLAYWRIGHT INN 250

Newtownpark Avenue, Blackrock, Co Dublin
Tel: 01 288 5155 Fax: 01 278 1989

A landmark among Irish pubs, winner of numerous awards and a must for anyone who appreciates good food, good drink, good company and the unique decor. The unique aspect starts on the outside, with the longest thatched roof in Europe over the red-painted facade, and in the traditional surroundings of the bars there is much to catch the eye, including murals, bronzes, old billboards, restored theatre seats and quotes from Irish playwrights. There's a fine choice of food, with a particularly notable carvery, and regular banquets with traditional music and dancing provide nights to remember.

Inn with restaurant

Inn with extensive menus and regular live entertainment

Credit Cards: All the major cards

Local Golf Courses: Elm Park, Milltown, Castle, Dun Laoghaire

County Dublin

Town House B&B

15 en suite rooms with tv and phone. Guest lounge

Credit Cards: Access, Mastercard, Visa

HEDIGAN'S GUEST HOUSE 251

14 Hollybrook Park, Clontarf, Dublin 3, Co Dublin
Tel: 01 853 1663 Fax: 01 833 3337
e-mail: hedigans@indigo.ie

A fine redbrick mansion with many splendid features and a golf-loving owner in Matt Hedigan. The Bed & Breakfast accommodation consists of 15 en suite rooms - singles, doubles and mini-suites - appointed to a very high standard, with tv and telephone. The day starts with a hearty Irish breakfast, and guests can relax in their own reading room and lounge. The house is in a location that provides easy access to the city centre, the ferry port and the beach, and there are three golf courses within 1½ miles.

Local Golf Courses: Clontarf, Royal Dublin, St Anne's, Elmgreen

Bed & Breakfast

Four rooms, all en suite; sea views; great breakfast choice

Credit Cards: Access, Mastercard, Visa

ESTUARY HOUSE 252

Estuary Road, Seatown East, Malahide, Co Dublin
Tel/Fax: 01 890 0242
e-mail: info@estuaryhouse.com

The address gives a big clue about the location! This striking modern brick-and-timber house, designed to the very highest standards by owners Pauline and Michael Dawson, has a frontage that overlooks the Malahide Estuary, and most of the rooms enjoy sea views. The well-travelled host offers four superb en suite bedrooms all fitted out to the highest standards, and guests have the use of a huge lounge and classic dining room, where the day gets off to the best start with a great choice for breakfast: the full Irish naturally includes black and white pudding. The house stands a mile out of Malahide.

Local Golf Courses: Malahide, Portmarnock, Island, Donabate

Hotel with bar and restaurant

Superbly appointed en suite bedrooms. Bar, bistro and restaurant.

Credit Cards: All the major cards

LUCAN SPA HOTEL 255

Lucan, Co Dublin
Tel: 01 628 0494 Fax: 01 628 0841
e-mail: info@lucanspahotel.ie website: www.lucanspahotel.ie

Originally part of the Sarsfield Estate, the hotel commemorates the legendary Irish cavalry commander, Patrick Sarsfield, and retains much of the charm of another era. Superbly appointed en suite bedrooms with tv, iron, tea/coffee making and direct dial phones. Food and drink facilities include the "Ballyneety" bar, "Earl of Lucan" bistro and "The Honora D" restaurant. Apart from championship golf coussrses there are scenic walks, the National Stud and Japanese Gardens nearby. Dublin City centre is just 7 miles.

Local Golf Courses: Elm Park, Hermitage, Lucan, Luttrellstown

Bed & Breakfast

Six spacious B&B bedrooms with tv. Riding centre next door

Credit Cards: None

FORT VIEW HOUSE 260

Kinvara, Co Galway
Tel: 091 637147

Bernadette Silke offers Bed & Breakfast accommodation of a high standard in her immaculate modern bungalow. Located three kilometres from Kinvara and signposted at Dunguaire Castle, the house has six letting bedrooms, all of a very generous size, with en suite facilities, excellent views and tv. The dining room and residents' lounge are as well appointed as the accommodation, and the rural setting and the warm family welcome are further bonuses. Next door to the house and in the same ownership is an equestrian centre where eight horses cater for both fun riders and serious competitors.

Local Golf Courses: Gort, Loghrea, Galway Bay, East Clare

LAKE HOTEL 261

The Square, Oughterard, Co Galway
Tel: 091 552275 Fax: 091 552794

Hotel with restaurant and bars

En suite bedrooms with tv and phone; bars and seafood restaurant

Credit Cards:Access, Mastercard,Visa

'A more beautiful village can scarcely be seen than Oughterard.' So said the poet William Thackeray, and this most welcoming hotel, owned by Gerry and Mary McDonnell, stands right at its heart. An ideal base for golfing, walking, fishing, boating or just lazing, the hotel has en suite bedrooms with tv and telephone. The bar is a great place for enjoying a drink and making new friends, and a good selection of dishes using local ingredients is served in the spacious restaurant (seafood a speciality). Oughterard Golf Club is a two-minute drive away, and boats and gillies can be arranged for fishing expeditions.

Local Golf Courses: Oughterard, Bearna, Galway, Tuam

ROUNDSTONE HOUSE HOTEL 262

Roundstone, Co Galway
Tel: 095 35864 Fax: 095 35944

Hotel and Restaurant

12 en suite bedrooms, dining room and bar

Credit Cards:Access, Mastercard,Visa

On the main street of a charming fishing village 12 miles south of Clifden, the Vaughan family's hotel is one of the best known in the region. Personal attention and first-class service are watchwords, and 16 en suite bedrooms provide a very comfortable night's rest. Excellent freshly prepared food is served all day in the dining room and hotel bar from extensive menus that range from traditional Irish breakfast to gourmet evening meals. Locally caught fish is a speciality. The bar, full of atmosphere and character, is popular with both locals and guests.

Local Golf Courses: Connemara, Oughterard, Westport, Ballinrobe

WILLMOUNT HOUSE 263

Ballinasloe Road, Portumna, Co Galway
Tel: 0509 41114

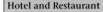

Bed & Breakfast

Four bedrooms, three en suite, in a Georgian farmhouse.

Credit Cards: None

Ann McDonagh heads a welcoming young farming family at their handsome Georgian home (1748) on a 110-acre mixed farm less than a mile from Portumna town. It's a superb setting near Lough Derg, and a long, winding drive makes an impressive approach to the house. Guest accommodation on the upper floor comprises four spacious bedrooms - three are en suite - all refurbished to a very high standard; pine floors and doors give a Scandinavian feel, and the views from the rooms are truly superb. There is a tv lounge for guest use only with tea making facilities available in the dining room. Portumna Forest Park and the Nature Reserve at Coole are among the local attractions.

Local Golf Courses: Portumna, Loughrea, Birr, Ballinasloe

THE BLACKTHORN 264

Crow Street, Gort, Co Galway
Tel/Fax: 091 632127

Public House & Restaurant

Open all day for food. Speciality seafood and steaks. Live music Saturday night

Credit Cards: All the major cards

Owner-Managers Liam and Maria Payne are justly proud of their splendid pub-restaurant, winner of Best Newcomer awards in 1998 and the Bridgstone Award for Excellence in 2000. There's an old-world atmosphere in the cosy bars and spacious restaurant with their stone floors and dressed beamed ceilings. The Blackthorn is open for food seven days a week, with service from 10am till late. Breakfast, lunch and à la carte menus provide plenty of choice throughout the day, and there are also menus for private parties. Seafood and steaks are among the specialities. Live music Saturday night. Private car park at rear.

Local Golf Courses: Gort, Loughrea, Athenry, Galway Bay

County Galway

CARNA BAY HOTEL   265

Carna, Co Galway
Tel: 095 32255 Fax: 095 32520

In the same ownership as Glynsk House Hotel and in an equally beautiful location. The Cloherty family's Carna Bay Hotel overlooks the bay from which it takes its name, and most of the 26 bedrooms enjoy splendid views of the bay and surrounding hills. All the rooms are very comfortably appointed, with en suite facilities, tv and telephone, and daytime relaxation is very easy in the lounge. The great outdoors beckons strongly here, with many sporting pursuits available nearby. A day in the fresh air will generate an appetite that the hotel's restaurant is ready to deal with: the finest local fish, Connemara lamb, home-made brown Irish soda bread.

Hotel and Restaurant

26 en suite bedrooms, tv, telephone. Restaurant specialising in local seafood and lamb
Credit Cards:Access, Mastercard,Visa

Local Golf Courses: Connemara, Oughterard, Bearna, Galway

RIVER WALK HOUSE   266

Riverside, Oughterard, Co Galway
Tel: 091 552788

Oughterard is the ideal centre for touring lovely Connemara, and Ann Kelleher's substantial modern detached house is a perfect base to begin. The six bedrooms - doubles, twins and singles - are all en suite, with tv, and guests have the use of a comfortable lounge. It's only a two-minute walk to the centre of the village, with its choice of restaurants, pubs and shops, and golf, fishing and pony-trekking are among the many activities in the vicinity. Walking and hiking are also popular: the Western Way starts in the village and skirts Lough Corrib to Maam and on to Westport.

Bed & Breakfast

Eight en suite bedrooms, tv; scenic walks and sports facilities nearby

Credit Cards: None

Local Golf Courses: Oughterard, Ballinrobe, Bearna, Galway

THE BEEHIVE   267

Patrick Street, Portumna, Co Galway
Tel: 0509 41830

Just off the main street of Portumna, The Beehive Restaurant and Pizzeria is a pleasant spot to relax over a meal. Partners Matilde Patterson and Jackie Hogan, one Italian the other Irish, cook side by side, with everything prepared and presented with great attention to detail. The pizzas are really excellent, but everything is worth trying on a menu that offers plenty of variety. Prices are kind, value for money great, and customers can bring their own wine. Opening hours are 10am to 10pm Tuesday to Saturday, 6pm to 10pm Sunday. Last orders 9.30pm. Closed Monday. All in all, a delightful little place (just 28 covers).

Restaurant

28-cover restaurant & pizzeria open all day Tues-Sat and Sun evening

Credit Cards:

Local Golf Courses: Portumna, Loughrea, Ballinasloe, Birr

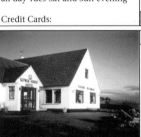

GLYNSK HOUSE HOTEL   268

Cashel Bay, Co Galway
Tel: 095 32279 Fax: 095 32342

The Cloherty family's hotel overlooks Glynsk Bay in a setting that's breathtaking even by the standards of this lovely part of the world. The view from the front looks towards the mountains in the distance, and the location has been chosen by the Irish Tourist Board for their promotional literature. 12 en suite bedrooms with tv and telephone provide restful overnight accommodation, and in the picture-windowed restaurant an extensive à la carte menu specialises in the excellent local seafood. The lounge has a peaceful, relaxed atmosphere that's perfect for making new friends and telling tales of hole-in-one near misses. Same ownership as Carna Bay Hotel.

Hotel and Restaurant

12 en suite bedrooms, tv, telephone. Seafood speciality restaurant

Credit Cards: Access,Mastercard,Visa

Local Golf Courses: Connemara, Oughterard, Westport

CREGG HOUSE 269

Galway Road, Clifden, Co Galway
Tel: 095 21326

Two miles outside Clifden on the Galway Road (N59), Mary and Hugh O'Donnell's home enjoys tremendous views of the beautiful Connemara countryside. In their attractive modern house set above and back from the road, guest accommodation comprises six en suite bedrooms with central heating. Guests have the use of a comfortable tv lounge, and there's a private car park. There's always a great family atmosphere here, and a splendid breakfast starts the day. Packed lunches are available - a boon for all-day golfers or visitors planning a day's fishing (2 minutes drive) or walking - one of many planned walks starts outside the house.

Bed & Breakfast

Six en suite bedrooms, tv lounge, private car park

Credit Cards: Visa

Local Golf Courses: Connemara, Oughterard, Westport, Castlebar

---

MEADOW COURT HOTEL 270

Clostoken, Loughrea, Co Galway
Tel: 091 841051 Fax: 091 842406
e-mail: meadowcourthotel@tinet.ie

Set in landscaped gardens two miles outside Loughrea, Meadow Court Hotel is a striking modern building offering high standards of accommodation, food and service. Our 18 bedrooms are individually designed and appointed, with en suite facilities, television, telephone, garment press, hairdryer, tea/coffee making facilities and modems. In the comfortable, award-winning restaurant, lunch and dinner are served every day and an extensive snack menu is available in between main meal times. The fine food is complemented by an extensive wine cellar. The bar, where traditional music is played throughout the week, is a good place to unwind.

Hotel with restaurant and bars

18 well-appointed en suite bedrooms; restaurant and bar-lounge

Credit Cards: All the major cards

Local Golf Courses: Loughrea, Gort, Ballinasloe, Portumna

CLIFDEN GLEN 271

Clifden, Co Galway
Tel: 095 21401 Fax: 095 21818 e-mail: clifglen@indigo.ie

John Baraguanath and Blaithin de Sachy run this unique holiday village on a 210-acre private estate just outside Clifden. Guests have a choice of accommodation: self-catering lodges or ApartHotel cottage suites. The former each have an en suite double bedroom, two other bedrooms sharing a bathroom and a large, comprehensively equipped living/dining area. The ApartHotel offers 44 semi-detached cottage suites on the banks of the Owenglen river. Each comprises en suite bedroom and open-plan living area, plus tv, fridge, telephone and many other accessories. Also on the estate are a pub, restaurant, tennis courts and children's play area.

Hotel and Self-Catering

Restaurant and pub on site

Credit Cards: All the major cards

Local Golf Courses: Connemara, Oughterard, Westport, Castlebar

---

BEN VIEW HOUSE 272

Bridge Street, Clifden, Co Galway
Tel: 095 21256 Fax: 095 21226
web: www.galway.net/pages/ben-view

Since 1926 the Morris family have been extending traditional hospitality to guests at their mid 19th-century town house in the centre of Clifden. Eileen Morris is continuing the tradition, and is also a mine of information on what to see and do in the region. She is always more than happy to plan daily excursions. The Bed & Breakfast accommodation consists of nine en suite bedrooms ranging from singles to family size, and antique furniture adds to the delightful old-world character of the place. Tv's in all rooms. Close to all the town's amenities and open all year. Registered Irish Tourist Board, RAC and AA.

Bed & Breakfast

Nine en suite bedrooms offering excellent B&B accommodation

Credit Cards: All the major cards

Local Golf Courses: Connemara, Oughterard, Westport, Castlebar

THE TWELVE PINS HOTEL 273

Coast Road, Barna Village, Co Galway
Tel: 091 592368 Fax: 091 592485
e-mail: the12pinshotel@eircom.net

Pat Lohan has recently taken over the reins at this delightful roadside hotel on the coast road five miles from Galway City and just three minutes drive from Barna Golf Club. The hotel has 18 en suite bedrooms, all with remote-control tv, telephone and trouser press. Two rooms are accessible to wheelchair users. The Pins Bar, with its traditional ambience and an open log fire, is a great place to enjoy a drink and a snack, and at weekends live music gets everyone in party mood. The excellent restaurant specialises in lobster, duck and steak.

Hotel with Restaurant and Bar

18 en suite bedrooms with tv and telephone. Restaurant, bar, live music

Credit Cards: All the major cards

Local Golf Courses: Bearna, Oughterard, Galway, Galway Bay

LOUGH FADDA HOUSE 274

Ballyconneely Road, Clifden, Co Galway
Tel: 095 21165
e-mail: feneran@gofree.indigo.ie

Tom and Breege Feneran know everything about the history and sights of the area, adding an extra dimension to a stay in their low-rise modern house. The setting, in two acres of grounds, is peaceful and secluded, yet the house is only five minutes from Clifden town centre. Guest accommodation consists of six bedrooms - two twins, two doubles and two triples - all with en suite facilities and tea making facilities (there's also a tv lounge). Breege cooks a first-class multi-choice breakfast. Private car park. Golf, fishing, pony trekking and hill walking nearby.

Bed & Breakfast

Six en suite bedrooms including triples, tea making facilities, tv

Credit Cards: None

Local Golf Courses: Connemara, Oughterard, Castlebar, Westport

TEACH AN EASARD 275

Ballyconneely, Co Galway
Tel/Fax: 095 23560

Connemara Golf Course is just a short drive from Teach an Easard, a fine farmhouse located in the picturesque little fishing village of Ballyconneely about five miles from Clifden. Carmel and Joe Joyce provide very comfortable overnight accommodation in six letting bedrooms, all with en suite facilities and tv. Their expertise and great hospitality have earned them an award for the best farmhouse accommodation in Connacht. Apart from golf, there's plenty to do in the neighbourhood, including games on the beach, angling and pony trekking.

Bed & Breakfast

Six en suite bedrooms in a farmhouse B&B

Credit Cards: None

Local Golf Courses: Connemara, Oughterard, Westport

THE BOAT INN 276

The Square, Oughterard, Co Galway
Tel: 091 552196 Fax: 091 502694
e-mail: boatinn@indigo

Occupying a prime site in the centre of Oughterard, The Boat Inn is at the very heart of village life. For overnight guests there are 11 good-sized letting bedrooms with en suite facilities, tv and telephone. The restaurant is in traditional style and offers an appetising menu and wine list; seafood is a speciality. The unique boat-shaped bar provides a friendly and relaxed atmosphere for enjoying a drink and a snack, while the continental-style terrace is a pleasant summertime alternative. Mike and Noreen O'Callaghan are your welcoming hosts, assisted by capable, congenial staff.

Hotel with Restaurant and Bar

Eleven en suite bedrooms with tv and phone. Restaurant with great seafood; bar and terrace

Credit Cards: All the major cards

Local Golf Courses: Oughterard, Ballinrobe, Galway, Bearna

County Galway

Hotel and Restaurant

11 en suite bedrooms with tv; bar and restaurant

Credit Cards: All the major cards

THE PASS INN HOTEL & RESTAURANT 277

Kylemore, Co Galway
Tel: 095 41141 Fax: 095 41377
e-mail: passinn@indigo.ie

A small family-run hotel just above the N59 Clifden-Westport road midway between the villages of Letterfrack and Leename. The 11 warm, comfortable letting bedrooms are all en suite, with tv and hairdryers. The hotel bar is open to non-residents and is equally popular with locals and guests. An excellent variety of tasty bar meals, including vegetarian main courses, is always available, and in the restaurant, which commands one of the most stunning rooms in Connemara, home-cooked meals make fine use of the best local produce. This friendly, relaxing hotel is owned and managed by Rose Rima and her family.

Local Golf Courses: Connemara, Oughterard, Westport, Castlebar

Bed & Breakfast

Nine en suite bedrooms, tv, telephone. City-centre location

Credit Cards: Access,Mastercard,Visa

ARDAWN HOUSE 278

College Road, Galway, Co Galway
Tel: 091 568833/564551 Fax: 091 563454
e-mail: ardawn@iol.ie

A handsome brick-built house of high quality located in the centre of the city by the greyhound track. The owner and hosts are Mike and Breda Guilfoyle. Mike is Captain of Galway Bay Golf and Country Club and always looks forward to welcoming golfers to his guest house. The nine bedrooms are all en suite, with cable tv, telephone, hairdryer, iron and trouser press. The day starts with a splendid breakfast featuring home-made bread and preserves, fresh fruit, additive-free bacon and sausages, free-range eggs and Atlantic wild salmon. There's private parking on site, and it's a short 4 minute walk to the train and bus depots. Irish Tourist Board approved 4* and AA 4* Guesthouse

Local Golf Courses: Galway Bay, Galway, Bearna, Athenry

Bed & Breakfast

Five en suite double bedrooms. Very close to the beach

Credit Cards: All the major cards

CILL CUANA 279

16 Grattan Park, Salthill, Galway, Co Galway
Tel: 091 585979 Fax: 091 581772

Hosts Benny and Mary Curran, who are keen players themselves, look forward to welcoming golfers to their pleasant modern Bed & Breakfast house throughout the year. The house sits off the coast road very close to the sea (Galway Bay) and Galway city centre is an easy ten-minute walk away. Cill Cuana is very well appointed, with fine antiques and collectibles spread around the house, and the five letting bedrooms all have en suite facilities, tvs and hairdryers. There's private off-road parking, and guests are greeted on arrival with complimentary tea or coffee.

Local Golf Courses: Galway Bay, Galway, Athenry, Bearna

Bed & Breakfast

Five bedrooms with en suite and tv. Near beach and city centre

Credit Cards: None

BREDAGH HOUSE 280

Ballybane Road, Ballybane, Galway, Co Galway
Tel: 091 770936 Fax: 091 770056
e-mail: bredaghhouse@hotmail.com
www.galway.net/pages/breadaghhouse

Bredagh House Bed & Breakfast is a recently constructed redbrick house located at the gateway to Galway City next to the Corrib Great Southern Hotel, where guests can enjoy a drink in the evening. Margaret Laffey's house has five letting bedrooms with en suite facilities, tv and hairdryer. It's only a short walk from the beach and the city centre, and is an ideal base for touring the Burren and Connemara by car or by coach. Margaret is a mine of information on the latest happenings in and around Galway and might also be able to help golfers with their back problems - ask about Tru-Back.

Local Golf Courses: Galway Bay, Galway, Athenry, Bearna

Co Galway

County Kerry

MAL DUA HOUSE | 281

Galway Road, Clifden, Connemara, Co Galway
Tel: 095 21171 Fax: 095 21739
e-mail: info@maldua.com website: maldua.com

In the heart of Connemara, but less than a mile from Clifden and all its amenities, Mal Dua House offers the best of both worlds. The large, handsome house provides luxury in a relaxed atmosphere, hospitality, good food and abundant peace and quiet. The 14 en suite bedrooms are tastefully furnished and have all the modern accessories - tv, telephone, hairdryer, trouser press, central heating - needed for a comfortable stay. Light meals with selected wines are served in the Dining Room overlooking the landscaped gardens, and Afternoon Tea in the drawing room is always a special occasion. Private car park, bicycles for hire and courtesy bus available.

Guest House

14 luxurious en suite bedrooms, tv, telephone. Light meals. RAC ◊◊◊◊◊, AA ◊◊◊◊◊, ITB ★★★★
Credit Cards: All the major cards

Local Golf Courses: Connemara, Oughterard, Castlebar, Westport

BROOK MANOR LODGE | 290

Fenit Road, Tralee, Co Kerry
Tel: 066 7120406 Fax: 066 7127552

On the R558 a mile and a half west of Tralee, Brook Manor Lodge is a luxury country guset house situated in 3½ acres of private grounds, with the Slieve Mish mountains forming a beautiful backdrop. Vincent and Margaret O'Sullivan are ideal hosts, at once charming and professional, and the six en suite bedrooms are provided with every comfort and accessory to guarantee a quiet, contented stay. Breakfast, with abundant choice, is served in the elegant dining hall or adjoining conservatory, while afternoon tea and friendly conversation are dispensed in the cosy guest lounge.

Bed and Breakfast

6 luxuriously appointed en suite rooms, tv, telephone. Quiet, scenic location
Credit Cards: None

Local Golf Courses: Tralee, Dooks, Killorglin, Ballybunion

WILLOW LODGE | 291

Convent Garden, Kenmare, Co Kerry
Tel: 064 42301

This is a gem of a place, built in the grounds of a nunnery and just a few minutes' walk from the centre of town. The house, beautifully decorated and furnished throughout, has a roomy lounge, a sunny dining room and five en suite bedrooms, each named after a tree and each with its own individual appeal and charm. New arrivals are greeted with a smile, a pot of tea and home baking, and the days start with a splendid breakfast that will keep the energy level high for a day's golfing or sightseeing. Ample parking. Horse riding, hill walking, water sports.

Bed & Breakfast

5 rooms, all en suite (one with jacuzzi). Tv, hair dryer, tea making facilities. 2 min from town centre.
Credit Cards: None

Local Golf Courses: Kenmare, Ring of Kerry, Bantry, Killarney

SALLYPORT HOUSE | 293

Glengariff Road, Kenmare, Co.Kerry
Tel: 064 42066 web: sallyporthouse.com

An elegant country house set in ten acres of lawns and trees overlooking the harbour and the bay. In the same family ownership since being built in 1932, it has five antique-furnished bedrooms with either king- or queen-size beds, capacious en suite bathrooms, telephones and tvs. One room has a four-poster. Guests can relax in the lounge, stroll along the river estuary or explore the charming town of Kenmare, which has recently been granted Heritage Town status.

Bed & Breakfast

5 rooms, all en suite. Telephone, tv.

Credit Cards: None

Local Golf Courses: Kenmare, Ring of Kerry, Bantry, Killarney

Bed and Breakfast

13 rooms, all en suite, tv, telephone. Opposite Killarney Golf Club

Credit Cards: All the major cards

THE 19TH GREEN `294`

Lackabane, Fossa, Killarney, Co Kerry
Tel: 064 32868 Fax: 064 32637
e-mail: 19thgreen@eircom.net
website: www.19thgreen-bb.com

A family-run guest house two miles from Killarney on the Killorglin/Ring of Kerry road. Purpose-built with comfort in mind, it has 13 en suite bedrooms with satellite tv, telephone and hairdryer. There's a spacious car park, and a putting green where guests can warm up before a round of the real thing at Killarney Golf Club just across the road. Early-morning breakfast can be arranged for those playing golf before 8am, and hosts Timothy and Bridget Foley (he's a keen golfer) will happily advise on the local sights, attractions and eating places.

Local Golf Courses: Killarney, Beaufort, Killorglin, Dooks

Hotel, Restaurant & Bar

11 rooms, all en suite. Telephone, tv

Credit Cards: Visa, Mastercard

THE WANDER INN `295`

Henry Street, Kenmare, Co Kerry
Tel: 064 42700 e-mail: wanderinn@tinet.ie

True Irish hospitality in a town-centre hostelry run by the Keane family. A hearty breakfast, lunch and dinner are served in the excellent restaurant, and in the evening everyone shares in the craic in the bar. The hotel has 11 letting bedrooms, all en suite and very well equipped. Golfing apart, there's plenty to do and see in the vicinity, including visits to the famous Stone Circle and Kenmare Lace Centre.

Local Golf Courses: Kenmare, Killarney, Ring of Kerry, Bantry

Country Home B & B

Special Golfers packages, transport provided, superb accommodation, dinners/snacks, Ensuite, Sky Tv
Credit Cards: Visa, Mastercard

THE WHITE HOUSE COUNTRY HOME B&B `296`
THE JEWEL IN THE RING GOLF & LEISURE TOURS

Cappamore, Killarney Road, Kenmare, Co Kerry
Tel: 064 42372 website: www.Kerry-insight.con/white-house

We offer all-in-one Golf & Leisure tours. Groups of 2-7 persons are catered for with a choice of 10 plus magnificent golf courses, all within 20 miles from your idyllic accommodation. The White House is 2½ miles from Kenmare and Molls Gap. All rooms have mountain views with luxury beds and there is a relaxing sun-lounge with Sky Tv. Dinners and snacks on request. Private scenic tours can be arranged at very keen prices. Irish Tourist Board approved. Open all year.

Local Golf Courses: Killarney, Kenmare, Ring of Kerry, Beaufort

Bed and Breakfast

8 rooms, all en suite, tv. Very handy for Killarney Golf Club

Credit Cards: All the major cards

WOODLANDS `297`

Ballydowney, Golf Course Road, Killarney, Co Kerry
Tel/Fax: 064 31467

Less than a mile from Killarney town on the Ring of Kerry Road, and only half a mile from Killarney Golf Club. Eight modern en suite bedrooms with tv provide all the amenities for a comfortable stay. For golfers rising with the lark early breakfasts can be ordered from an excellent menu, and hosts Paud and Julia O'Donoghue, both keen and very competent golfers, can arrange local tours for golf widows. There are many glorious sights in the region, including the Gap of Dunloe and the Killarney Lakes.

Local Golf Courses: Killarney, Beaufort, Killorglin, Dooks

County Kerry

County Kerry

KATHLEEN'S COUNTRY HOUSE | 298

Tralee Road, Killarney, Co Kerry
Tel: 064 32810 Fax: 064 32340

"Easy to Get To! Hard to Leave!" Thus the fully justified boast of this marvellous country guest house set in beautiful mature gardens a mile from town. Winner of many awards, 5 Qs AA accredited, 4 Star classified by the ITB, it is owned by Kathleen O'Regan Sheppard, a leading light in Kerry and Irish tourism. Style and comfort are keynotes, from the floral displays and original artwork to the lovely bedrooms (non-smoking), all with en suite bath and shower, antique pine, orthopaedic beds, tvs and telephones. Brilliant breakfasts are served in the dining room looking out to the garden. There's plenty to see and do in the area, and bus and boat trips can be arranged from here.

Country Guest House

Top-quality en suite bedrooms, tv, telephone. Extensive gardens. Multi-choice breakfast menu.
Credit Cards: All the major cards

Local Golf Courses: Killarney, Beaufort, Killorglin, Dooks

CRYSTAL SPRINGS | 299

Ballycasheen, Killarney, Co Kerry
Tel: 064 33272
e-mail: crystalsprings@eircom.net
web: homepage.eircom-net/~doors/

Crystal Springs, a striking mid-1990s purpose-built house, stands off the N22 or N71 on a river bank overlooking a historic mill beside a natural spring. Some of the bedrooms enjoy a river view; all are furnished to a high standard, and all have en suite facilities, tv and telephone. Breakfast proposes an exceptional choice that could include porridge with Bailey's, scrambled eggs with smoked salmon and lemon pancakes with fresh fruit. Wine licence. Private car park. Bureau de change. 10-minute walk from the town.

Bed and Breakfast

All rooms en suite, tv, telephone. Riverside location. Fishing. Bureau de change.
Credit Cards: All the major cards

Local Golf Courses: Killarney, Beaufort, Killorglin, Tralee

SHEILIN SEAFOOD RESTAURANT | 300

Waterville, Co Kerry
Tel: 066 947 4231

An intimate, relaxed, family-run bistro-style restaurant serving fresh fish and shellfish caught locally and delivered daily. Fish is not the only option, and Kerry mountain lamb is another popular choice. Owners Marie and Michael Courtney are both keen golfers, and the walls of their delightful restaurant in a terrace of business premises are covered with photographs of famous golfers, including Tiger Woods with their grandchildren. Many of their own golfing trophies are also on display, and there are some striking modern paintings in the second dining area, which is more used for groups or parties. 50 seats in total. Wine licence.

Restaurant

Seafood speciality restaurant using the best of the local catch. Also a wine bar. Owners are keen golfers.
Credit Cards: All the major cards

Local Golf Courses: Waterville, Ring of Kerry, Dooks, Kenmare

---

CASTLE VIEW HOUSE | 301

Carrig Island, Ballylongford, Co Kerry
Tel/Fax: 068 43304 e-mail: castleviewhouse@eircom.net
website: www.kerry-insight.com/castleview

Patricia and Garrett Dee provide a warm and friendly Irish welcome at their comfortable house in a peaceful setting on a scenic island (cross by the bridge) facing historic Carrigafoyle Castle. There are six letting bedrooms, three twins and three with double and single beds. All have en suite facilities. Tv in the lounge, tea and coffee always available. There's plenty of choice on the breakfast menu (full Irish or continental) and a four-course evening dinner makes excellent use of fresh local produce. The Tarbert-Killimer car ferry is close by. Vouchers and credit cards welcome

Bed and Breakfast

6 en suite bedrooms. Scenic setting. Full breakfast. Dinner by arrangement
Credit Cards: All the major cards

Local Golf Courses: Ballybunion, Kilrush, Tralee, Killeline

MEADOWLANDS HOTEL `302`

Oakpark, Tralee, Co Kerry
Tel: 066 7180444 Fax: 066 7180964
e-mail: medlands@iol.ie

A charming and intimate modern hotel set in three acres of landscaped gardens a short distance north of Tralee town centre. Overnight accommodation comprises 24 en suite bedrooms and three suites with jacuzzis. All rooms are air-conditioned, with individual heating controls, tv, trouser press and iron/ironing board. Open fires warm the day rooms, and excellent meals are served in the restaurant, where seafood is a speciality - much of it caught from the owner's fishing boats. Food is also available in Johnny Franks Bar. Plenty of private parking. The hotel facilities are suitable for disabled gusests.

Hotel, Restaurant & Bar

24 rooms & 3 suites, all en suite. Tv. Restaurant and bar meals

Credit Cards: All the major cards

Local Golf Courses: Ceann Sibeal, Ballybunion, Tralee, Dooks

TRALEE TOWNHOUSE `303`

High Street, Tralee, Co Kerry
Tel: 066 718 1111 Fax: 066 718 1112
e-mail: michaeloshea@eircom.net web: traleetownhouse.com

In the heart of Tralee, this hotel style Bed & Breakfast has a wide choice of well-appointed accommodation. Each bedroom is en suite with satellite tv, telephone, hairdryer and tea/coffee making facilities. There is an elevator to all floors. All rates are inclusive of Irish breakfast that includes home-baked breads and scones. It is also located close to an Arnold Palmer designed golf course. Come and savour this wonderful Kerry hospitality.

Bed & Breakfast

A townhouse of quality and comfort in the heart of Tralee.

Credit Cards: Visa, Mastercard

Local Golf Courses: Tralee, Ballybunion, Killorglin, Killeline

AN BOTHAR PUB `304`

Cuas, Ballydavid, Dingle, Co Kerry
Tel: 066 9155342
e-mail: botharpub@eircom.net web: botharpub.com

In an area of breathtaking scenery, An Bothar Pub stands in splendid isolation on the tiny road to Brandon Creek that links the small village of Cuas with the outside world. The pub has letting bedrooms, all en suite, some with four beds and therefore very suitable for families or groups. Prime fresh produce from land and sea plus fine home baking makes up the menu in the restaurant, which is open every evening. Food is also available in the bar, where there's live traditional music most evenings. Among the many things to see in this glorious part of Ireland are the ruins of an Iron Age fort on the slopes of Mount Brandon.

Pub, Food & Accommodation

6 en suite bedrooms, some for multiple occupation. Bar and restaurant meals. Live music

Credit Cards: Visa, Mastercard

Local Golf Courses: Ceann Sibeal, Killorglin, Dooks, Tralee

GREENMOUNT HOUSE `305`

Gortonora, Dingle, Co Kerry Tel: 066 9151414 Fax: 066 9151974
e-mail: mary@greenmounthouse.com
web: greenmounthouse.com/index.htm

Comfort, hospitality and excellent housekeeping are just some of the attractions of John and Mary Curran's neat, modern guest house a short walk from Dingle town centre. B&B accommodation comprises 12 en suite bedrooms including six superior rooms with sea views. Tv and telephone in each room. Outstanding breakfasts, a feast for which the Currans are famous, are served in a stylish conservatory that takes full advantage of the setting high above the harbour. John and Mary know all there is to know about the area and will happily tell guests what to see and do in this lovely part of Ireland. RAC Small Hotel of the Year for Ireland 1997.

Bed and Breakfast

12 well-equipped modern bedrooms, all en suite, some with sea views. Great breakfasts

Credit Cards: None

Local Golf Courses: Ceann Sibeal, Tralee, Dooks, Killorglin

THE LAUNE & TAYLOR'S 306

102-3 New Street, Killarney, Co Kerry
Tel: 064 32772 Fax: 064 37908

A double-fronted period building in the centre of town, open every day of the year for both accommodation and meals. The 20 elegantly refurbished bedrooms - singles, doubles and triples - are all en suite, with tvs. In Taylor's Restaurant, breakfast is served from 7.30 till noon, lunch until 3, then a full à la carte menu right through until 10pm. The Laune Bar, where the atmosphere is always friendly, is an ideal place for winding down after a day on the golf course or enjoying the sights and scenery of Killarney and the surrounding countryside.

Bar, Restaurant, Accommodation

20 bedrooms, singles, doubles and triples. All en suite, tv. Breakfast, lunch and dinner
Credit Cards: None

Local Golf Courses: Killarney, Beaufort, Killorglin, Kanturk

KILLFOUNTAIN FARM 307

Killfountain, Dingle, Co Kerry
Tel: 066 9151389

Kathleen Lynch runs a delightful Bed & Breakfast operation in her neatly kept modern house set in private gardens off the Ballyferriter road a mile or so west of Dingle. Six en suite bedrooms with tv provide a comfortable night's rest, and a good breakfast with home baking guarantees a good start to the day. With Ceann Sibeal (Ballyferriter) course no more than a decent pitch away, the location is ideal for golfers, and golfing breaks are a speciality. This is good walking country, and fishing, riding and tennis are also available in the vicinity, as well as access to some great beaches. Good restaurants and pubs in nearby Dingle. Easy parking.

Bed and Breakfast

6 en suite bedrooms with tv. By Ballyferriter golf course. Good breakfast with home baking
Credit Cards: All the major cards

Local Golf Courses: Ceann Sibeal, Dooks, Killorglin, Tralee

DARBY O'GILL'S COUNTRY HOUSE HOTEL 308

Lissivigeen, Killarney, Co Kerry
Tel: 064 34168 Fax: 064 36794
e-mail: darbyogill@tinet.ie

Just outside Killarney in the heart of the Kingdom of Kerry, this charming country house hotel is an ideal spot for a relaxing break. The en suite bedrooms are finished to a very high standard and furnished in country pine to give a smart yet homely feel. Dinner is served each evening in Darby's Restaurant, where Sunday lunch is a speciality. Daily plate lunches are available in the lounge bar, where entertainment is hosted nightly in the summer. Traditional pub games are played in the small, cosy public bar.

Hotel, Restaurant & Bar

En suite bedrooms, evening meals, bar lunches

Credit Cards: None

Local Golf Courses: Killarney, Beaufort, Kenmare, Macroom

WOODCOURTE HOUSE 340

Timolin, Moone, Athy, Co Kildare
Tel: 0507 24167 Fax: 0507 24326

Agnes Donoghue runs a quiet, comfortable Bed & Breakfast house 500 metres off the main N9 in the picturesque village of Timolin with a panoramic view of the plains of Kildare. The large modern house has six spacious, centrally heated bedrooms, two en suite, the others serviced by bathroom, shower room and toilet. A camping and caravan site is available in the grounds, and the house has a play area for children and a pool room. Art classes are held throughout the year. A traditional Irish breakfast is served, with other meals by arrangement. Log fires in the dining room and drawing room.

Bed & Breakfast

Six bedrooms, two en suite. Irish breakfast; other meals by arrangement
Credit Cards: None

Local Golf Courses: Athy, Carlow, Rathsallagh, Kilkea Castle

BALLYGORAN LODGE 342

Old Celbridge Road, Maynooth, Co Kildare
Tel/Fax: 01 629 1860
e-mail: ballyg@eircom.net

A mile out of Maynooth, Anne and Frank run a friendly, relaxed Bed & Breakfast business in their well-appointed modern residence with a large garden and easy parking. They bought the property in 1997 and have lavished time and money in making it what a good B&B should be: roomy, warm, comfortable, sociable. There are four splendid letting bedrooms, all en suite with tv and tea/coffee making facilities. The area is rich in golf courses and racetracks, and a local sight well worth a visit is Castletown House, a Palladian mansion at Celbridge.

Bed & Breakfast

Four en suite rooms with tv and tea/coffee facilities.

Credit Cards: None

Local Golf Courses: K Club, Knockanally, Kilcock, Castlewarden

RUSHES 343

Fairgreen Street, Naas, Co Kildare
Tel: 045 898400 Fax: 01 462 7446
e-mail: suitsyou@gofree.indigo.ie

Something for everyone in a prime site in town - restaurant, bar with food, night club. Managing Director Alan Walkin is a keen golfer and would love to see many like-minded souls in his excellent establishments. Rushes serves a good range of drinks and a classic bar menu that spans sandwiches, snacks and mains such as steaks, lasagne, curry and fish & chips. Next-door neighbour Cicero has a more formal menu running from Californian-style mussels and cabbage parcels filled with smoked cheese, leeks and pistachios to more steaks, chicken roulade, roast duck and speciality fajitas

Restaurant and Bar

Restaurant, bar, lounge; two menus, good range of drinks

Credit Cards: Access, Mastercard, Visa

Local Golf Courses: Bodenstown, Craddockstown, Naas, Killeen

BUSHFIELD LODGE 344

Bishopsland, Ballymore Eustace, Co Kildare
Tel: 045 864389/864972 Mobile: 087 677 2338
e-mail: bushfieldlodge@ireland.com

A fine modern house in a quiet rural location three miles south of Blessington off the N81. Owner Elizabeth O'Connor-Deegan and her husband, a very keen golfer, welcome overnight guests with five spacious, well-appointed en suite bedrooms, and the day starts with a splendid breakfast served in the feature dining room. Elizabeth, a highly trained chef, runs a cookery school on the premises, offering a range of classes designed to show how the experts set about preparing a meal. Local attractions include the village itself, by the Liffey, horseracing and Blessington lakes.

B & B and Cookery School

5 large, en suite bedrooms; super breakfasts. Cookery classes available

Credit Cards: None

Local Golf Courses: Naas, Rathsallagh, Tulfarris, Curragh

ANNAGH LODGE 345

Naas Road, Newbridge, Co Kildare Tel: 045 433518
Fax: 045 433538 e-mail: annaghlodge@eircom.net
web: http://homepage.eircom.net/~annaghlodge

Superior guest accommodation in a striking modern bungalow on the Naas Road in Newbridge. It has many splendid features, including tranquil gardens, a porticoed entrance, a conservatory and a sauna. Derna Wallace offers nine letting bedrooms, all beautifully furnished, with en suite facilities, tv and telephone. Full Irish breakfast with many special touches. There are many attractions for racegoers in the neighbourhood, including courses at Punchestown, Naas and The Curragh and the Irish National Stud; also what are claimed to be the finest Japanese Gardens in Europe.

Guest House

9 en suite bedrooms with tv, telephone. Sauna, conservatory

Credit Cards: Mastercard, Visa

Local Golf Courses: Curragh, Newbridge, Craddockstown, Rathsallagh

County Kildare

SWIFTS 346

Main Street, Newbridge, Co Kildare
Tel: 045 433234 Fax: 045 438845

On the main street of town, Kieran Gallagher runs the trendiest bar in town, a place that's popular with all ages. Great staff, caring management and a good atmosphere make it a favourite with locals and visitors alike, and the night club which is attached to it is guaranteed to make the evenings jolly. In the long, elegant bar and spacious lounges a regularly changing menu is served all day from 12.30 till 9 o'clock, so racegoers can enjoy a meal before or after a visit to one of the local tracks - Naas, Punchestown and The Curragh. The highlight of Punchestown's year is the three-day jumping festival held in late April.

Bar with food and Night Club

All-day menu; choice of bars and lounges. Night club attached

Credit Cards: Access, Visa

Local Golf Courses: Newbridge, Curragh, Craddockstown, Rathsallagh

THE MANOR INN 347

Main Street, Naas, Co Kildare
Tel: 045 897471 Fax: 045 898775

Warmth, hospitality, good eating and good drinking in a smartly modernised pub on a prime site on the busy main street of Naas in the heart of horse-racing territory. All-day bar meals and a great à la carte menu offer plenty of choice for the hungry punter, served either in the bar or in the Oyster Room restaurant. The bars and lounges are full of racing pictures and mementos: spot the huge bronze of horse and jockey in the main bar. The Curragh, Punchestown and Naas are all close at hand, and there's the additional attraction of motor racing at Mondello. Hands-on owner Gerry Deans is assisted by super staff. Regular live music adds to the fun.

Pub and Restaurant

All-day bar meals and restaurant menu. Live music

Credit Cards: Access, Amex, Visa

Local Golf Courses: Naas, Craddockstown, Bodenstown, Killeen

ASHLEY BED & BREAKFAST 348

Richardstown, Clane, Co Kildare
Tel/Fax: 045 868533

Evelyn Ryan run a pleasant Bed & Breakfast establishment in a quiet rural setting, with beautiful landscaped gardens,two miles out of Clane on the road to Celbridge. There are three letting bedrooms, two en suite and one standard room, as well as a self-contained unit adjacent to the main house. Ashley B&B is in the heart of golfing country but there is also horse riding, horse racing, motor car racing and many more attractions around. It is an oasis from the cares of the world and is only 18 miles from Dublin City centre.

Bed & Breakfast

3 en suite bedrooms; rural setting; many local sights

Credit Cards: None

Local Golf Courses: K Club, Bodenstown, Woodlands, Castlewarden

MONAGHAN'S HARBOUR HOTEL 349

Limerick Road, Naas, Co Kildare
Tel: 045 879145 Fax: 045 874002

There's a delightful home-from-home feel about this hotel , which stands on the Limerick Road two minutes walk from the centre of Naas. Mary Monaghan, 25 years in the business, provides excellent home comforts and really good home cooking. The modern bedrooms are well equipped and well furnished, and guests can relax in a convivial, well-stocked bar. The hotel restaurant is open for breakfast at 7.30 (breakfast is served all day), lunch sees a choice between restaurant and coffee shop menus, and a fine choice is available for dinner in the restaurant. A good place to make your base for sporting and sightseeing holidays.

Hotel with Restaurant and Bar

Well-equipped rooms; all-day breakfast; good choice for other meals

Credit Cards: All the major cards

Local Golf Courses: Naas, Newbridge, Craddockstown, Killeen

Bed & Breakfast

4 en suite bungalow rooms; huge rear garden

Credit Cards: None

STRAFFAN BED & BREAKFAST 350

Clane Road, Straffan, Co Kildare Tel: 0162 72386
e-mail: judj@gofree.indigo.ie

This very smart newly refurbished bungalow, the home of Una and Joe Healy offers four en suite bedrooms for first-class Bed & Breakfast accommodation. All guests are welcome, but this is a particularly good base for golfers, as the K Club, where the Ryder Cup is due to be staged in 2005, is only a mile away, with many other courses close by. Golfers can practise their swings without even leaving the premises, as the house has a lovely long back garden! Non-golfing delights in the neighbourhood include the wonderful Butterfly Farm and the Steam Museum with Walled Gardens. It is situated three miles from the Maynooth exit of the M4 and three miles from the Kill exit of the N7.

Local Golf Courses: K Club, Castlewarden, Killeen, Bodenstown

Country Guest House with Leisure Centre

Ten superbly equipped en suite bedrooms; on site leisure centre
Credit Cards: Access, Visa

THE GABLES GUEST HOUSE & LEISURE CENTRE 351

Kilcullen Road, Ryston, Newbridge, Co Kildare
Tel: 045 435330 Fax: 045 435355

Leave the M7 at junction 8 or 10 for Newbridge and Ray Cribbin's splendid guest house and leisure centre on the banks of the Liffey. The ten bedrooms are equipped to hotel standard, with bath and shower en suite, tv, radio-alarm clock, phone, trouser press and hairdryer. But an equally fine feature is the leisure centre, whose amenities include a 14-metre indoor pool, turbo jacuzzi, steam room, sauna and gymnasium, with a professional instructor available. Guests can fish on the Liffey almost outside the door, and there are several other fishing rivers, plus lakes and canals nearby. A great sporting base, on or off the premises.

Local Golf Courses: Newbridge, Naas, Athy, Woodlands

Bed & Breakfast

3 en suite bedrooms, 1 bedroom with private bathroom; tv lounge, large gardens
Credit Cards: Mastercard, Visa

WHITE OAKS 164

Tennypark, Callan Road (N76), Kilkenny, Co Kilkenny
Tel: 056 63295 e-mail: whiteoaks@eircom.net

Houseproud Maria Witherow and her golfing husband are the hosts at this immaculate, substantial bungalow set in trim gardens 1½ miles outside Kilkenny on the N76 road to Clonmel. Superior Bed & Breakfast accommodation consists of four spacious, individually appointed bedrooms all with pleasant views. Three are en suite and one has a private bathroom. Tv and tea-making facilities are available in the guest lounge, and a lovely conservatory has recently been added. There is much of interest in Kilkenny, sometime seat of the Confederate Parliament, including the 12th-century Castle, the 13th-century St Canice's Cathedral and several notable medieval ruins.

Local Golf Courses: Kilkenny, Mount Juliet, Callan

THE RAFTER DEMPSEY'S 361

4 Friary Street, Kilkenny, Co Kilkenny
Tel/Fax: 056 22970

In the heart of the city, just ten yards from the High Street, stands the atmospheric Rafter Dempsey's, a 1997 Pub of the Year Black & White award winner. In their large, three-storey premises Gerry and Josephine Rafter offer excellent overnight accommodation in 17 en suite bedrooms of various sizes, all comfortable and well-furnished, with tv. There's a good choice for breakfast, and the pub also has good-value lunch and dinner menus. Live music is a regular feature, and when the sun shines the beer garden is the place to be. Park in the street or nearby public car park.

Pub, Accommodation & Meals

17 en suite bedrooms with tv; lunch and dinner menus; beer garden

Credit Cards: Access, Mastercard,Visa

Local Golf Courses: Kilkenny, Mount Juliet, Callan

County Kildare

Counties Kilkenny & Carlow

BERKELEY HOUSE 362

5 Lower Patrick Street, Kilkenny, Co Kilkenny
Tel: 056 64848 Fax: 056 64829

Ten bright, spacious rooms offer flexible Bed & Breakfast accommodation in a fine three-storey terrace mansion dating from the 1780s. Granite and marble steps lead up from the pavement and, inside, the house is superbly furnished throughout, with obvious respect for the dignity of the building. But the amenities are up to date, as all rooms have en suite facilities, tv and telephone. Owner Linda Blanchfield has a wealth of experience in her field, with spells at Mount Juliet and London's Savoy, and her house is an ideal base for discovering the fascinating past and lively present day of the city of Kilkenny.

Town House Bed & Breakfast

10 en suite rooms with tv and telephone

Credit Cards: Access, Mastercard, Visa

Local Golf Courses: Kilkenny, Mount Juliet, Callan

GROVE FARMHOUSE 363

Ballycocksuist, Inistioge, Co Kilkenny
Tel: 056 58467
e-mail: grovefarmhse@unison.ie

Part of a 150-acre working beef farm, Grove Farmhouse is a beautifully restored and modernised 200-year-old country house set in mature gardens with stunning views of the countryside. Nellie Cassin and her husband are both working farmers but they also love entertaining guests, and their four en suite bedrooms are all very spacious, with exceptional decor and furnishings (lots of antiques) and great views. There's a good choice for breakfast, which sets guests up splendidly for a day walking, golfing or exploring the many places of interest in the region. The farm is signposted on the R700 between Thomastown and Inistioge.

Farmhouse Bed & Breakfast

4 huge en suite bedrooms on a working farm

Credit Cards: Visa

Local Golf Courses: Mount Juliet, Callan, New Ross

CIRCLE OF FRIENDS 364

The Bank House, High Street, Inistioge, Co Kilkenny
Tel: 056 58800 Fax: 056 58801

A special night of fine food and good company is promised at the Circle of Friends, a 42-cover restaurant in a charming period building. It is perhaps surprising to find a restaurant of such quality in such a setting, but the picture postcard village of Inistioge deserves it, and chef-owner Dave Whelan, with 20 years experience in London, certainly knows his onions. He knows everything else to do with food, too, and his splendidly varied menus offer the very best in traditional and modern Irish cuisine. Evening meals (last orders 9.30 daily), wine licence, lunchtime specials, and an informal downstairs café.

Restaurant and Café

42-cover restaurant serving fine Irish cuisine. Also informal café

Credit Cards: All the major cards

Local Golf Courses: Mount Juliet, Callan, New Ross

VIEWMOUNT HOUSE 365

Castlecomer Road, Kilkenny, Co Kilkenny
Tel/Fax: 056 62447

A comfortable country house set in attractive gardens right next to Kilkenny Golf Club and near the leading hotel in the area, the Newpark. Eamonn and Mary greet guests with a real Irish welcome, and provide excellent overnight accommodation in six well-furnished en suite bedrooms. Tea-making facilities and tv are available. This is an ideal base not only for golfers but for visitors to Kilkenny, Ireland's most famous medieval city, with its narrow streets and lanes, marvellous old buildings and a vibrant cultural life. And a short drive north of Kilkenny is Dunmore Cave, rich in atmosphere and legend.

Country Bed & Breakfast

6 en suite bedrooms; golf course adjacent

Credit Cards: Access, Mastercard, Visa

Local Golf Courses: Kilkenny, Mount Juliet, Callan

BANVILLE'S BED & BREAKFAST 366

49 Walkin Street, Kilkenny, Co Kilkenny
Tel: 056 70182

Miriam Banville, two years in the business and already with plans to expand, gives her name to her Bed & Breakfast operation in an end-of-terrace house five minutes on foot from the centre of historic Kilkenny. Newly re-pebbledashed and in pristine condition throughout, the house has four neat, bright and homely letting bedrooms, all doubles, with en suite facilities and tv. Tea and coffee are available in the guest lounge. Plenty of parking. Kilkenny, called a city though its population is only 9,000, has a long and fascinating past and a vibrant present, with a number of annual arts festivals.

Bed & Breakfast

4 en suite doubles with tv; guest lounge, easy parking

Credit Cards: None

Local Golf Courses: Kilkenny, Mount Juliet, Callan

TEACH DOLMAIN 370

Shamrock Square, Carlow Town, Co Carlow
Tel: 0503 30911 Fax: 0503 30464

Willie Rath's pub is all an Irish pub should be. The setting is delightful, the welcome warm, the food and drink spot on, and the entertainment lively and varied. Teach Dolmain comprises three bars, where traditional Irish music is a regular feature, and two restaurants. A lunchtime carvery operates between noon and 3 o'clock, and in the Carlovian Restaurant connoisseurs of fine food will appreciate the quality and variety of the à la carte menu available from 7 to 10.30 on Wednesday, Thursday, Friday and Saturday evenings. A must for anyone visiting the interesting county town of Ireland's second smallest county.

Pub and Restaurant

3 Bars and 2 restaurants. Fine cuisine, live music

Credit Cards: Access, Mastercard, Visa

Local Golf Courses: Carlow, Mount Wolseley, Kilkea Castle, Athenry

SHERWOOD PARK HOUSE 371

Kilbride, Ballon, Co Carlow Tel: 0503 59117 Fax: 0503 59355
e-mail: sherwoodpark@indigo.ie
web: www.sherwoodparkhouse.ie

'A unique Georgian residence offering luxury guest accommodation on its own working estate'. Maureen Owens and her husband look forward to welcoming golfers to their lovely home, which nestles among rolling parkland just off the main N80 midway between Dublin and Rosslare. The five bedrooms are appointed in period style, with en suite facilities and brass and canopy beds. An Irish breakfast starts the day, and evening meals can be arranged with notice (candlelit dinner served at 8, bring your own wine). Golf, fishing, riding and the renowned Altamont Gardens are among the local attractions.

Country House

Five en suite bedrooms for B&B; dinner by arrangement

Credit Cards: Access, Mastercard, Visa

Local Golf Courses: Carlow, Mount Wolseley, Kilkea Castle, Coollattin

SAN GIOVANNI 372

Killeshin, Castlecomer Road, Graigne Cullen, Co Carlow
Tel: 0503 40828

Margaret Bolger is a relative newcomer to the Bed & Breakfast business but has great plans for future expansion. Her fine modern house has extensive gardens front and rear, with a good barbecue area, easy parking and some delightful views. Overnight accommodation comprises nine individually designed bedrooms, of which seven have en suite facilities. Carlow Golf Course is a short drive away, and the local attractions in Ireland's second smallest county include the ruins of 13th-century Carlow Castle, the largest dolmen in Europe at Browne's Hill and the famous Altamont Gardens in Ballon.

Bed & Breakfast

Nine bedrooms, seven en suite. Large garden

Credit Cards: None

Local Golf Courses: Carlow, Kilkenny, Rathdowney, Mountrath

Counties Kilkenny & Carlow

CEDAR LODGE — 380

Cloughkeating, Patrickswell, Co Limerick
Tel: 061 355137

Situated in an acre of mature gardens at the end of a long lane, Noreen O'Leary's farmhouse-style home is a lovely peaceful base for touring, and both Noreen and her husband, being local people, know everything there is to know about the region. The house has five letting bedrooms, all with en suite facilities and tv, and the owners offer a good choice for breakfast, including home-made bread. The garden has a newly constructed patio, and there's a private car park. The village of Patrickswell is a nice place for a stroll, and it's only a short drive to Limerick with its many restaurants and pubs.

Bed & Breakfast

Secluded house with 5 en suite bedrooms, tv. Home baking

Credit Cards: Mastercard, Visa

Local Golf Courses: Limerick County, Limerick, Adare Manor

HANRATTY'S HOTEL — 381

5 Glenworth Street, Limerick, Co Limerick
Tel: 061 410999 Fax: 061 411077

Founded in 1796, Hanratty's Hotel is steeped in folklore and history. It stands in the centre just off the main street and is an ideal base for exploring the city and the surrounding sights. The hotel's 22 bedrooms are appointed to a very high standard, with en suite bathroom, phone, remote-control tv and hairdryer. Room service is available round the clock, and there's a private lock-up car park. Hanratty's Pub offers comfort, charm, light snacks and a warm, rustic character, and the restaurant is noted for its high standard of cuisine, offering both traditional and international dishes.

Hotel with Restaurant and Bar

22 en suite bedrooms with tv, phone. Restaurant and bar

Credit Cards: All the major cards

Local Golf Courses: Limerick County, Limerick, Rathbane, Castletroy

DEEBERT HOUSE — 382

Kilmallock, Co Limerick
Tel: 063 98106

'A place to write home about' is an apt description of Anne O'Sullivan's delightful Georgian house, which stands in award-winning gardens by the R515 (off the N20 Limerick-Cork road). Overnight accommodation comprises two double rooms, two twins and a family room, all except one double with en suite facilities. All rooms have tv and telephone, and the house has an unlicensed restaurant. Self-catering also available. It's an ideal base for touring, and in the vicinity there are several golf courses, many other sporting and outdoor opportunities and a number of historic sites, including the riverside ruins of a 13th-century Dominican friary.

Country B&B, also evening meals & self-catering

5 bedrooms (4 en suite) with tv and phone. Self-catering option

Credit Cards: Access, Mastercard, Visa

Local Golf Courses: Charleville, Mitchelstown, Killeline, Adare Manor

ASHFORD — 383

Templeglantine, Co Limerick
Tel: 069 84001 Fax: 069 84311

Near the church in a small community between Abbeyfeale and Newcastle West, Ashford is a distinguished modern detached house in red brick. It stands in beautiful gardens and features a huge conservatory and a first-floor balcony, both of which guests are free to use. Marjorie Sheehan offers Bed & Breakfast accommodation in five en suite rooms with tv. The whole place is furnished and fitted to a very high standard, with many antiques and the finest carpets and bedding. Adare is 15 minutes away, Limerick half an hour. Private car park.

Bed & Breakfast

Five en suite rooms with tv. Private car parking

Credit Cards: Mastercard, Visa

Local Golf Courses: Newcastle West, Killeline, Adare, Adare Manor

Hotel with Restaurant

19 en suite bedrooms with tv and phone. A la carte restaurant

Credit Cards: Mastercard, Visa

LEEN'S HOTEL 384

Main Street, Abbeyfeale, Co Limerick
Tel: 068 31121 Fax: 068 32550
e-mail: leenshotelabbeyfeale@eircom.net

Sheehan's three-storey hotel on a prime site in the main street represents all that's good about Irish hospitality: the welcome, the easy-going atmosphere, the comfort, the good food generously served. There are 19 good-sized letting bedrooms, all en suite, with tv and telephone. The restaurant has a great reputation for its hearty portions and excellent use of prime local produce. Typical dishes on the evening menu run from garlicky baked Cromaine mussels and goose liver paté to steaks, fried plaice, several ways with chicken and the speciality fajitas.

Local Golf Courses: Newcastle West, Killeline, Charleville, Ballybunion

Public House

Pub serving breakfast and all-day snacks

Credit Cards: None

THE DARK HORSE 385

Cork Road, Patrickswell, Co Limerick
Tel: 061 355196

Fergus Kilcoyne has recently taken over The Dark Horse, which stands on the main Limerick-Cork road four miles south of Limerick. He has made many changes, giving the place a definite sporting theme in the process. Breakfast is served from 10 o'clock till noon, and light snacks, soup and sandwiches are available throughout opening hours, to be enjoyed with a brilliant pint of Guinness. There's plenty of off-road parking, and next to the pub is a very fine restaurant that's open for dinner. Adare, one of the prettiest villages in all of Ireland, stands on the River Maigue three miles away down the N21.

Local Golf Courses: Adare Manor, Limerick, Limerick County

Bed & Breakfast

Four en suite bedrooms; tv lounge. Farm setting

Credit Cards: None

FORT ANN 386

Patrickswell, Co Limerick
Tel: 061 355162

A short distance south of Patrickswell on the main road to Adare (N21), Breda Mann's lovely country home is a peaceful and convenient base for visiting Adare, Limerick and the lesser known sights of County Limerick. Part of a 70-acre dairy farm, it has four letting bedrooms, all of a good size, with en suite facilities. There's a tv lounge where tea and coffee are served to residents. County Limerick has only one major lake, Lough Gur, which is an easy drive from the house and is at the centre of an important area of Stone Age discoveries.

Local Golf Courses: Adare, Adare Manor, Limerick, Limerick County

Farmhouse Accommodation

Four antique-furnished bedrooms, three en suite, one with private bathroom. Tv. Farm setting
Credit Cards: Mastercard, Visa

CLONUNION HOUSE 387

Limerick Road, Adare, Co Limerick
Tel/Fax: 061 396657

Mary and Michael Fitzgerald and their family are the hosts at this super 200-year-old house on a 130-acre working farm two kilometres out of Adare on the road to Limerick. Antiques are a feature throughout the house, which was home to Lord Dunraven's stud manager. The four beautiful bedrooms are spacious and well-appointed, three with en suite facilities and one with a private bathroom. There is a guest lounge with TV and many books. The views are splendid and a fine traditional breakfast gets the day off to the best of starts. Anyone wanting to sample the delights of rural Ireland would do well to make this lovely farmhouse their base.

Local Golf Courses: Adare, Adare Manor, Newcastle West, Limerick

County Limerick

County Limerick

BERKELEY LODGE

388

Station Road, Adare, Co Limerick
Tel/Fax: 061 396857
e-mail: berlodge@iol.ie

Luxurious Bed & Breakfast accommodation in a fine modern redbrick house in the centre of the village, close to restaurants, churches and all the major attractions. Pat and Bridie Donegan offer six superb en suite bedrooms with tv, and a delightful alternative in Parsley Cottage, which has all the mod cons and can sleep six. A memorable breakfast, served in the lovely dining room, provides plenty of choice, including whiskey porridge, and way you want with eggs and cinnamon French toast served with maple syrup. Private car parking.

Bed & Breakfast

Six en suite bedrooms with tv. Great breakfasts. Private car park

Credit Cards: None

Local Golf Courses: Adare, Adare Manor, Limerick, County Limerick

DUNRAVEN ARMS HOTEL

389

Adare, Co Limerick
Tel: 061 396633 Fax: 061 396541 e-mail: dunraven@iol.ie

Established in 1792, Bryan and Louis Murphy's marvellous hotel is one of Ireland's best. Set in the picturesque village of Adare, the Dunraven Arms has 76 beautifully appointed bedrooms, including eight suites, with antique furniture and en suite bathrooms. Also self-catering cottages. There are two fine restaurants, the thatched Inn Between and the Maigue, named after the river that flows through the village. The hotel is a paradise for outdoor enthusiasts, with two golf courses, fishing, archery and hunting on hand. The Clonshire Equestrian Centre is only two minutes away, while the hotel itself has a superb state-of-the-art leisure centre.

Hotel with Restaurant and Bar

76 beautifully appointed en suite bedrooms & suites; two restaurants; leisure centre

Credit Cards: All the major cards

Local Golf Courses: Adare, Adare Manor, Limerick, Limerick County

THE WILD GEESE

390

Adare, Co Limerick
Tel/Fax: 061 396451 e-mail: wildgeese@indigo.ie

Award-winning chef, David Foley and Julie Randles run this superb restaurant located in a magnificent row of pretty thatched cottages. The setting is absolutely delightful and the food is worth a lengthy detour. Local produce from small suppliers features strongly on the menu with hand-reared duck a specialty that appears in marvellous dishes like "deep-fried wontons of confit of duck on a vegetable stirfry" or "roast breast on creamed savoy cabbage with a leek and pear tartlet and a puy lentil sauce". Other notable choices include local goose, venison, Clare crab, Kenmare salmon, organic beef and a great selection of Irish cheeses. Superb wines accompany.

Restaurant

45-cover restaurant featuring local fresh produce in an innovative style.

Credit Cards: All the major cards

Local Golf Courses: Adare, Adare Manor, Limerick, Limerick County

RATHKEALE HOUSE HOTEL

391

Rathkeale, Co Limerick
Tel: 069 63333 Fax: 069 63330
e-mail: rhh@iol.ie

Purpose-built in 1997, the hotel already has a welcoming, 'lived-in' feel assisted by personal attention from family owners and spacious public areas where wood is a major feature. The O'Connor family's long, low hotel has 30 en suite bedrooms, tastefully furnished, with tv and telephone. The Orchard Restaurant is gaining a good reputation for its fine Irish-International cuisine and the Chestnut Bar is a convivial spot for a snack and a drink; live music takes place on summer weekends in the lounge. The Foynes Flying Boat Museum is one of many local attractions.

Hotel with Restaurant and Bar

30 en suite bedrooms. Bar and licensed restaurant

Credit Cards: All the major cards

Local Golf Courses: Adare, Adare Manor, Killeline, Newcastle West

THE PEPPERCORN 392

Patrickswell, Co Limerick
Tel: 061 355999

Restaurant

Licensed restaurant open for dinner
Tuesday-Sunday

Credit Cards: All the major cards

Fine food and fast, friendly service are the twin attractions of the Peppercorn run by a young couple who have high hopes for their modern, mediterranean style 60-seat restaurant. Chef-proprietor Diarmuid O'Callaghan is always on hand to see that satisfaction is guaranteed, and his comprehensive menu caters for all tastes, with steak, seafood and vegetarian options for which ingredients are sourced locally. Non smoking sections available. Private car parking at the rear of the restaurant. The Peppercorn is open Tuesday to Sunday evenings, from 5.30 to 10pm (last orders). Limerick and Adare are both within easy reach, and Lough Gur Stone Age Centre is also a short drive away.

Local Golf Courses: Adare, Adare Manor, Limerick, Limerick County

MONASTERBOICE INN 400

Monasterboice, Drogheda, Co Louth
Tel: 041 9837383 Fax: 041 9837485

Restaurant

150-cover roadhouse restaurant specialising in steaks

Credit Cards: All the major cards

Formerly an important stop on the Dublin-Belfast coaching route, Paddy Donegan's marvellous inn is one of the top roadhouse restaurants in the county. That irresistible Irish magic is there in abundance, and in the superb new conservatory or in one of the little snugs diners can tuck into a first-class meal. Prime steaks are a speciality - fillet, sirloin or minute grilled to perfection and served plain or with a choice of sauces. Other favourites on the extensive menu run from garlic mushrooms and crab paté to omelettes, sole meunière, chicken Maryland and gammon with pineapple. There are vegetarian main courses and a special children's menu. Plenty of off-road parking.

Local Golf Courses: Seapoint, County Louth, Rathbane, Laytown

THE HERITAGE 401

Mullaharlin Road, Heynestown, Dundalk, Co Louth

Tel: 042 9335850

Bed & Breakfast

Five B&B bedrooms, three en suite, tv. Rural setting

Credit Cards: None

A large end-of-terrace house in a quiet rural setting a mile and a half from the centre of Dundalk. Teresa Byrne and her husband, both keen golfers, offer Bed & Breakfast accommodation in five smartly refurbished bedrooms, three with en suite and hairdryer. The whole place is immaculate, and guests can relax in a beautiful lounge with an open fire. Pony trekking and good fishing are available nearby, and the busy town of Dundalk has much to offer. Among the attractions in the area is the Proleek Dolmen, a vast stone structure dating back more than 5,000 years.

Local Golf Courses: Dundalk, Ardee, Greenore, Killinbeg

SILLOUGUE HOUSE 402

Monasterboice, Drogheda, Co Louth
Tel: 041 9845284
website: www.sillougue.bizland.com

Bed & Breakfast

14 top-quality en suite bedrooms with tv and telephone

Credit Cards: None

A long lamp-lit lane leads from the N1 Dublin-Belfast road to Eamonn and Irene McHugh's striking modern house set in 3 acres of grounds. Purpose-built in 1998, it has 14 bedrooms offering B&B accommodation of the highest class: all rooms have en suite facilities, tv, telephone and hairdryer, and guests enjoy a fine breakfast in the handsome dining room. The location is ideal for visiting the megalithic tombs at Newgrange, and Drogheda, whose attractions include the fascinating Millmount Museum, is only four miles down the road.

Local Golf Courses: Seapoint, County Louth, Laytown, Ardee

Co Louth

County Mayo

ST GOBNAITS 403

Dublin Road, Drogheda, Co Louth
Tel: 041 983 7844 Fax: 041 983 7844

Breda Lucey and her husband make staying at their B&B home a real delight. Set by the N1, with off-road parking, their attractive house has four spacious, well-appointed letting bedrooms, all en suite, with tv. The town of Drogheda, with its sights and pubs and restaurants, is an easy walk away, and the railway station is even closer. There are several golf courses within easy reach, and it's a short drive to the beaches and to Newgrange, just over the county border in Co Meath, where the 4,000-year-old passage grave is one of many remarkable sights at the Boyne Valley Archaeological Site.

Bed & Breakfast

Four en suite rooms, tv. Off-road parking

Credit Cards: All the major cards

Local Golf Courses: Seapoint, County Louth, Laytown, Ardee

CLADDAGH HOUSE 410

Sligo Road, Ballina, Co Mayo
Tel: 096 71670 e-mail: brenclad@eircom.net
website: http://homepage.eircom.net/~clad.

Agnes and Brendan McElvanna run a quite exceptional B & B establishment on the Sligo road out of Ballina. The six guest bedrooms are all designed and furnished individually, and guests can relax in a superb lounge on the upper floor; overall, this B&B could hold its own with many hotels in terms of accommodation. There's a good choice for breakfast, and parking is easy. Several top golf courses are a short drive away, and other nearby attractions include salmon fishing on the River Moy and trout fishing on Lough Conn and Lough Cullen. The whole area is rich in scenic beauty, history and character. Excellent views of surrounding countryside.

Bed & Breakfast

Six en suite bedrooms in a detached B&B. No smoking house with full fire safety certificate.
Credit Cards: Major cards accepted

Local Golf Courses: Ballina, Enniscrone, Castlebar, Strandhill

ENNISCOE HOUSE 411

Enniscoe, Castlehill, Ballina, Crossmolina, Co Mayo
Tel: 096 31112 Fax: 096 31773
e-mail: mail@enniscoe.com web: www.enniscoe.com

An imposing Georgian mansion set in woods and parkland on the shores of Lough Conn. Log fires, antiques and portraits of owner Susan Kellett's ancestors add to the wonderful period atmosphere, and the six en suite bedrooms are full of character. Alternatively, there are three self-contained courtyard apartments. Breakfast in the dining room, lunch in the tea rooms, dinner by arrangement. The estate includes woodland walks and pleasure grounds, a Victorian walled garden, a fascinating little heritage museum and a family history research centre that researches the antecedents of Mayo families.

Historic House B & B

Six en suite bedrooms, three courtyard apartments; B&B, dinner by arrangement
Credit Cards: All the major cards

Local Golf Courses: Enniscrone, Ballina, Strandhill, Belmullet

QUIGNALEGAN HOUSE 412

Sligo Road, Ballina, Co Mayo
Tel/Fax: 096 71644

A warm welcome awaits you at Quignalegan House - a purpose built Bed and Breakfast ideally located on the N59 Sligo road and just 3 minutes drive from Ballina town centre. All five rooms are en suite with tvs and hairdryers. Tea and coffee is available in the guest lounge. There is a good breakfast choice. A large secure car park to the rear provides ample parking with storage available for Golf and Fishing equipment. The area is an ideal base for exploring the unspoilt scenery of the North Mayo/West Sligo countryside. Hill walking, golfing and fishing are all within easy reach.

Bed & Breakfast

Five en suite B&B bedrooms with tvs and hairdryers. Lounge. Large car park
Credit Cards: None

Local Golf Courses: Ballina, Enniscrone, Castlebar, Westport

DOWNHILL INN `413`

Sligo Road, Ballina, Co Mayo
Tel: 096 73444 Fax: 096 73411
e-mail: thedownhillinn@eircom.net web: www.downhillinn.ie

Forty five bedrooms in a well-designed modern hotel on the outskirts of Ballina going towards Sligo. The rooms are all of a good size (single and double bed in each), with en suite bath/power shower, tv, telephone and hairdryer, and two are accessible to guests in wheelchairs. The Terrace Restaurant provides excellent food in a relaxed dining room overlooking the gardens and patio. There are many leading golf courses within an easy drive, and the nearby River Moy is one of Ireland's top salmon rivers. The inn is run by a young, enthusiastic couple John and Nicola Raftery.

Hotel with Restaurant and Bar

45 en suite bedrooms (2 beds in each), tv, telephone. Restaurant, bar

Credit Cards: All the major cards

Local Golf Courses: Ballina, Enniscrone, Strandhill, Belmullet

---

ASHLEAM HOUSE `414`

Mount Falcon, Foxford Road, Ballina, Co Mayo
Tel: 096 22406

e-mail: helen.smyth@ireland.com

In an excellent location for touring, golf and fishing, Ashleam House stands in its own grounds four miles south of Ballina on the road to Foxford. Helen Smyth, 15 years in the hospitality business, is a splendid hostess, and her neatly kept house is a real home from home. There are six letting bedrooms, four en suite, and guests have the use of a comfortable tv lounge. The River Moy, famous for its salmon fishing, is no more than a line's cast away, and Mount Falcon Castle is just one of many historic and scenic attractions in the region.

Bed & Breakfast

Six B&B bedrooms, four en suite. Tv lounge, private car park

Credit Cards: Visa, Access, Amex

Local Golf Courses: Ballina, Enniscrone, Castlebar, Westport

DRUMSHINNAGH HOUSE `415`

Newport Road, Rahins, Castlebar, Co Mayo
Tel/Fax: 094 24211
e-mail: berniecollins@oceanfree.net

Drumshinnagh House (the name means 'the hill of the fox') is situated on an elevated site in 25 acres of countryside 2 miles from the centre of Castlebar. Owned and managed by the hospitable Collins family, the house has seven letting bedrooms, all decorated to a high standard, with en suite facilities, tv and hairdryer. Visitors can relax in the sitting room or join the family for a friendly cup of tea in the kitchen. Private car park. Taxi service on call. Packed lunches and evening meals on request. Open all year.

Bed & Breakfast

Seven en suite bedrooms for B&B. Other meals by request

Credit Cards: None

Local Golf Courses: Castlebar, Westport, Belmullet, Claremorris

---

ST ANTHONY'S `416`

Distillery Road, Westport, Co Mayo
Tel: 098 28887 Fax: 098 25172
e-mail: sk@achh.iol.ie

Built in 1820 as "The Manse" house, St Anthony's has been transformed into a Bed & Breakfast establishment of real character. Robert and Sheila Kilkelly, 30 years in the business, offer excellent accommodation in six well-appointed bedrooms, each with its own style and unique furnishings. All rooms are en suite with tea and coffee making facilities as well as tv; two are fitted with jacuzzis. At St Anthony's enjoy luxury B&B accommodation where there is also laundry and drying facilities. Internet access is also available if required. Clew Bay, a nine-hole tourist orientated golf course, is close by.

Bed & Breakfast

Six en suite bedrooms with tv; 2 with jacuzzi.

Credit Cards: Mastercard, Visa

Local Golf Courses: Westport, Castlebar, Ballinrobe, Claremorris

County Mayo

TRAVELLERS FRIEND HOTEL AND THEATRE   417

Old Westport Road, Castlebar, Co Mayo
Tel/Fax: 094 23111
e-mail: tfhotel@anu.ie web: www.castlebar.ie/tf

A unique complex of hotel/restaurant and theatre/concert hall three minutes' walk from the town centre, owned and run by the Jennings family. Warm hospitality, modern facilities and excellent cuisine are keynotes in the hotel, which has 27 letting bedrooms, all en suite, with multi-channel tv, telephone and trouser press. There's a good choice of eating, from bar food to carvery and à la carte menus offering traditional and international dishes. The hotel boasts the largest conference facility in the west of Ireland. The theatre regularly presents the cream of artists both home-grown and international.

Hotel, Restaurant and Theatre

27 en suite bedrooms, tv, telephone. Restaurants, bar, theatre

Credit Cards: All the major cards

Local Golf Courses: Castlebar, Westport, Claremorris

DROM CAOIN   418

Belmullet, Co Mayo
Tel/Fax: 097 81195
e-mail: dromcaoin@esatlink.com

A striking modern house standing in neat gardens, offering a choice of either Bed & Breakfast or self-catering accommodation. The former comprises four rooms with two beds, the latter two apartments, one for up to three guests, the other for up to five. Owner Máirín Maguire-Murphy is a qualified cook, and her award-winning breakfasts have won prizes for being the best in the county. Evening meals are available with notice - vegetarian foods are a speciality. Drom Caoin is a great base for golfers, with many special deals on offer, and it also attracts fishermen - it has a fully-fitted tackle and drying room.

Bed & Breakfast, Self-Catering

Four two-bedded B&B rooms (dinner with notice) + two self-catering apartments

Credit Cards: Mastercard, Visa

Local Golf Courses: Belmullet, Enniscrone, Westport, Castlebar

---

LAVELLE'S ERRIS BAR   419

Main Street, Belmullet, Co Mayo
Tel: 097 82222 Fax: 097 81056
e-mail: kevinryan@eircom.net

A small cream-and-white frontage on Belmullet's main thoroughfare leads into a spacious, convivial pub with rows of bar stools and sturdy wooden furnishings. Owned and run by Kevin Ryan, Lavelle's offers a great selection of drinks (an in-house brewery is planned for the near future) and a fine range of food served all day, with lunchtime specials adding to the choice. A big tv screen shows major sporting events. Kevin runs the pub's golfing society, the attached restaurant (open high season only) and the next-door coffee shop.

Pub, Coffee Shop, Restaurant

Food and drink served all day in the bar; coffee shop next door

Credit Cards: Mastercard, Visa

Local Golf Courses: Belmullet, Enniscrone, Ballina, Westport

VALLEY LODGE   420

Facefield, Claremorris, Co Mayo
Tel: 094 65180
e-mail: valleylodge@eircom.net

The Barrett family's modern Bed & Breakfast establishment is at the heart of an 80-acre working cattle and sheep farm five miles outside Claremorris on the main road (N60) to Castlebar. The five letting bedrooms are of a generous size and very well furnished; all have en suite facilities, tv and hairdryer. The setting is delightfully rural and peaceful, but a short drive brings guests to Claremorris or Castlebar, the chief town of the area. The Marian Shrine at Knock, which Pope John Paul II visited in 1979, is one of Europe's major sites of pilgrimage.

Bed & Breakfast

Five large en suite bedrooms on a working farm

Credit Cards: None

Local Golf Courses: Castlebar, Claremorris, Tuam, Ballinrobe

Hotel, Restaurant and Bars

18 well-equipped bedrooms; meals served daily; music on Wednesday

Credit Cards: All the major cards

WESTERN HOTEL 421

Main Street, Claremorris, Co Mayo
Tel: 094 62011 Fax: 094 62838

Paul Hanley's Western Hotel, a well-known landmark on the main street of town, is a great base for touring Mayo and the neighbouring counties. Behind its long, long frontage (more than 40 metres) the atmosphere is friendly and welcoming, the bars busy and full of life. The place is at its liveliest on Wednesday night, when there's a traditional music session. Overnight accommodation comprises 18 bedrooms, all with tv and phone. Breakfast, morning coffee and lunches are served daily, and in the evening an à la carte menu in the restaurant specialises in steaks. There's a 45-seat function/party room.

Local Golf Courses: Claremorris, Castlebar, Tuam, Ballinrobe

Bed & Breakfast

Six B&B bedrooms, four en suite. Super breakfasts

Credit Cards: Amex, Visa

ESKERVILLE 422

Claremorris Road, Knock, Co Mayo
Tel: 094 88413

Mary Taaffe and her son are the most delightful hosts at their low-rise modern house, the second house on the left on the main road out of Knock (N17) towards Claremorris. Bed & Breakfast accommodation is offered in six well-kept bedrooms, four of them en suite, most with tv (and guests have the use of a tv lounge). The house stands in trim lawns, with plenty of parking space. The breakfasts are renowned throughout the county. The church and basilica at Knock are a must for anyone visiting this part of the country and are an easy walk away, with shops and pubs only yards beyond. Golf, fishing and pony trekking nearby.

Local Golf Courses: Claremorris, Castlebar, Tuam, Ballinrobe

Bed & Breakfast

Five bedrooms, all en suite, for B&B. Fisherman's favourite

Credit Cards: None

SUNCROFT 423

3 Cathedral Close, Ballina, Co Mayo
Tel: 096 21573

Five en suite bedrooms in a well-appointed, very modern town house sitting in the shadow of the Cathedral within easy walking distance of the town centre. The whole house is decorated and furnished to commendably high standards, and residents have the use of a splendid lounge. With the River Moy and Lough Conn very close by, this is a favourite base for fishermen, but owner Mrs Walsh is keen also to welcome more golfers. Ballina celebrates every July with a street festival and arts week, and a little further away Ceide Field at Ballycastle gives a unique insight into prehistoric farming methods.

Local Golf Courses: Ballina, Enniscrone, Belmullet

Hotel with Restaurant and Bar

Single, double and triple rooms; restaurant; bar

Credit Cards: All the major cards

CILL AODÁIN HOTEL 424

Main Street, Kiltimagh, Co Mayo
Tel: 094 81761 Fax: 094 81838

A historic rural village in the very heart of the county is the setting for Tony McDermott's friendly hotel. Guests have the choice of standard or superior rooms, including singles, doubles and triples. The candlelit dining room specialises in Continental and Country cuisine using the best of local produce, and a carvery lunch is served daily. There's a modern residents' lounge and a convivial bar with open fires. There's plenty to see and do in the immediate vicinity (fun park, sculpture park, village museum), and The Marian Shrine at Knock is only a ten-minute drive away.

Local Golf Courses: Castlebar, Claremorris, Ballina

County Mayo

County Meath

Restaurant

70-cover restaurant with wide-ranging menus. Open 7 days a week

Credit Cards: Access, Mastercard, Visa

THE LOFT RESTAURANT 430

26 Trimgate Street, Navan, Co Meath
Tel: 046 71755 Fax: 046 28347
e-mail: theloft@tjgavigan.com

On the corner of Trimgate Street and Railway Street, The Loft has a continental feel, eyecatching artwork and an open-plan kitchen fronting the 70-seat dining area. The menu is extensive, combining the popular classics like pasta, pizza and chargrilled steaks with zingy-fresh seafood dishes and some exciting flavours of Asia. Daily blackboard specials add to the already abundant choice, and the Early Bird menu (6.00-7.30) offers particularly good value for money. Open seven days a week. Restaurant Association of Ireland and Meath Good Food Circle members. (Same ownership as The Ground Floor restaurant in Kells).

Local Golf Courses: Royal Tara, Headfort, Navan, Moor Park

Guest House

15 en suite bedrooms with tv, telephone. Private car park

Credit Cards: Mastercard, Visa

BROGANS GUEST HOUSE 431

High Street, Trim, Co Meath
Tel: 046 31237 Fax: 046 37648
e-mail: brogangh@iol.ie

Denys, Gerry and Ruth Merrick offer smiles, genuine Irish warmth and true hospitality at their guest house and bar in the historic town of Trim on the River Boyne. Accommodation offers a choice between seven rooms in the main house and eight more modern, individually designed rooms in the converted stables. All the rooms have en suite facilities, telephone and tv. The bar is a popular place to unwind after a day's golf or sightseeing, with frequent music sessions and plenty of craic. Trim Castle, a must for visitors, is the largest Anglo-Norman fortress in Ireland.

Local Golf Courses: County Meath, Royal Tara, Navan, Moor Park

Bar and Restaurant

Bar-restaurant serving sandwiches, panini and a wide range of drinks

Credit Cards: All the major cards

RYAN'S BAR AND RESTAURANT 432

22 Trimgate Street, Navan, Co Meath
Tel/Fax: 046 78333

Mick Ryan's very modern bar and restaurant is a great place to pause awhile for a drink and something to eat. Luxury is the keynote, with top-quality timber used throughout, and an open log fire keeps things cosy and comfortable. Mick is a very keen golfer, and welcomes like-minded visitors with open arms. The snack menu offers a good selection of sandwiches plain or toasted and panini with mouthwatering hot fillings; there's also soup and a hot special of the day. All the major beer brands and many exciting wines are served, and the Ryan Vine, wine shop next door in the same ownership, stocks wines from around the world.

Local Golf Courses: Navan, Royal Tara, Moor Park, County Meath

Bed & Breakfast

Five en suite B&B rooms, one family size. Telephone, tv

Credit Cards: Mastercard, Visa

KILLEENTIERNA HOUSE 433

Powderlough, Dunshaughlin, Co Meath
Tel: 01825 9722 Fax: 01825 9722
e-mail: imorris@clubi.ie

Joe and Ita Morris are the owners of this smart modern Bed & Breakfast residence in a rural setting on the N3 on the Dublin side of Dunshaughlin. Four of the rooms are en suite doubles and the fifth, also en suite, is ideal for families, with accommodation for four. All rooms have tv and telephone. A full Irish breakfast starts the day, setting guests up for a round of golf or a day at the races - Fairyhouse is a short drive away, and Navan is 15 miles up the road. Restaurants and bars are a five-minute walk away, and among the many attractions in the region is the magical Hill of Tara and New Grange medieval burial ground.

Local Golf Courses: Black Bush, Kilcock, Ashbourne, Royal Tara

Public House and Restaurant

Pub-restaurant serving lunch (dinner by arrangement). Beer garden

Credit Cards: Mastercard, Visa

JACK'S RAILWAY BAR   434

Junction of N52 and R164, Kells, Co Meath
Tel/Fax: 046 40215

Ray Olohan's super pub-restaurant at the junction of the Mullingar and Athboy roads is a favourite spot for lunch, when a tempting carvery operates. Evening meals can be provided with advance notice, and in summer the beer garden is the setting for convivial barbecues. Log fires warm the bar, which is divided into lounge-restaurant, lounge (with its own entrance) and games lounge with pool table and jukebox. Monks from Iona brought, or perhaps even wrote the renowned *Book of Kells* in this town, and a copy of it (the original is in Trinity College Dublin) is in St Columba's Church in Kells.

Local Golf Courses: Headfort, Moore Park, Navan, Delvin

Bed & Breakfast

Four bedrooms, two en suite, tv. Great breakfasts

Credit Cards: Mastercard, Visa

TEACH CUAILGNE   435

Carlanstown, Kells, Co Meath
Tel/Fax: 046 46621
e-mail: pegoreilly@eircom.net

Tea and coffee greet guests on arrival at Peggy O'Reilly's modern detached house in a pleasant rural setting by Carlanstown village, three miles north-east of Kells (N52). B&B accommodation comprises four bedrooms with orthopaedic beds. Two rooms are en suite, all have tv and hairdryer. Peggy, who is vice-captain of the nearby Headfort Golf Club, sees that guests start the day with a hearty Irish breakfast. Safe parking; private garden; afternoon teas; tv lounge. Fishing and riding are available nearby, and the house is a good base for touring the many local places of interest.

Local Golf Courses: Headfort, Moore Park, Navan, Ardee

Bed & Breakfast

Four bedrooms, all en suite, tv. Quiet, attractive setting. Tv, tea and coffee making facilities in all rooms.

Credit Cards: Access,Mastercard,Visa

DUNLAIR HOUSE   436

Old Road, Athlumney, Navan, Co Meath
Tel: 046 72551

Dunlair House is a luxurious home, sitting in 1 acre of mature gardens just off the R153 and only twenty minutes walk from the town centre. The setting is both picturesque and peaceful with good secure car parking and storage space available for golf equipment. It's convenient to Dublin airport and ferry port. Navan has plenty of restaurants, pubs shops, a multiplex cinema and many outstanding places of interest (Newgrange visitors centre, Hill of Tara etc.) The area is very popular with tourists from all over the world because of its archaeological treasures and ancient buildings and legends.

Local Golf Courses: Navan, Royal Tara, Moor Park, County Meath

Bed & Breakfast

10 en suite rooms with tv and phone. Super breakfasts

Credit Cards:Access, Mastercard,Visa

KILLYON   437

Dublin Road, Navan, Co Meath
Tel: 046 71224 Fax: 046 72766

Very popular ever since opening in 1995, Michael and Sheila Fogarty's trim modern house on the Dublin Road is an excellent Bed & Breakfast base for all sorts of activities, including golf, horse riding and visiting the numerous historic archaeological sites in the area. Fishing is also popular, and the River Boyne runs through the back garden. The ten letting bedrooms all have en suite facilities, tv and telephone, and the day starts with one of Killyon's greatest prides - an award-winning breakfast that includes home-baked bread. Packed lunches and evening meals are available with notice.

Local Golf Courses: Navan, Headfort, Moor Park, Royal Tara

County Meath

THE HEADFORT ARMS HOTEL 438

Kells, Co Meath
Tel: 046 40063 Fax: 046 40387
e-mail: headfortarms@eircom.net web: www. headfortarm.com

The Duff family have managed The Headfort Arms Hotel for more than a quarter of a century, ensuring that guests enjoy traditional standards of hospitality along with modern-day comforts. They have 18 letting bedrooms, all en suite, with telephone and tv. There's a choice of places for eating: the new bistro is for the more serious diner, while the Carvery and Coffee Shop is open from 7.30 fro breakfast right through till 10pm. The Kelltic Bar is popular with the younger set, who also love the weekend disco in the nightclub.

Hotel with Restaurant & Bar
18 en suite rooms, restaurant, coffee shop, bar, nightclub

Credit Cards:Access, Mastercard,Visa | **Local Golf Courses:** Headfort, Moor Park, Royal Tara, Navan

ROYAL VIEW HOUSE 439

Bellinter, Navan, Co Meath
Tel: 046 27893

Leonard and Colette Collins own and run Royal View House, a fine modern house in a picturesque location with large front and rear gardens. They offer four Bed & Breakfast rooms, all with en suite facilities and tv, and all decorated to the highest standards. The Royal Tara Golf Club is very close by, and the whole area is rich in delightful scenery and historic sites. Leonard is a very keen and skilled fisherman who would be glad to show golfers the local rivers and to provide them with pleasant diversions from the golf course. Taxi service on the premises.

Bed & Breakfast
4 en suite rooms with tv. Taxi service

Credit Cards: None | **Local Golf Courses:** Navan, Headfort, Moor Park, Royal Tara

THE HAGGARD INN 440

Haggard Street, Trim, Co Meath
Tel: 046 31110

A black-and-white building dating from the early part of the 19th century is the cosy, atmospheric setting for enjoying anything from a drink and a snack to a full evening meal. Pat McCarthy's welcoming hostelry has an appealingly traditional look, with thick walls, low ceilings and plush carpets. Food is available all day until 10 o'clock, with bar food, evening meals and a splendid carvery lunchtime and all day Sunday. Live traditional music is performed every Friday and Saturday. Trim is a delightful little town with a number of interesting historic ruins.

Inn with Food
Food served all day until 10pm.
Lunchtime carvery

Credit Cards:Access, Mastercard,Visa | **Local Golf Courses:** County Meath, Royal Tara, Delvin, Kilcock

WHITE GABLES 441

Headfort Place, Kells, Co Meath
Tel: 046 40322 Fax: 046 49672
e-mail: kelltic@eircom.net

In a house dating from the early 1800s, with an exceptional blend of the traditional and the contemporary, Penny McGowan offers high-quality Bed & Breakfast accommodation in four en suite bedrooms with tv. The whole house has a lovely welcoming feel, and when the sun shines the beautiful garden beckons. Penny is a classically-trained cook: her breakfasts would grace the grandest hotel and with notice she will provide packed lunches and (for parties of eight or more) evening meals. Penny is also a very keen walker, and her home is the base for tailor-made walking holidays. Sauna and drying room are added attractions.

Bed & Breakfast
4 en suite rooms with tv. Packed lunches; dinner for parties

Credit Cards: None | **Local Golf Courses:** Headfort, Navan, Ardee, Delvin

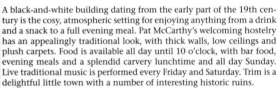

THE EVERGREENS | 442

29 Bachelors Walk, Ashbourne, Co Meath
Tel: 01 8352392
e-mail: evergreens@indigo.ie

Neat, well-presented Bed & Breakfast accommodation in a modern bungalow two minutes from the village and the N2. There are three en suite letting bedrooms and one not en suite, a delightful conservatory and a tv lounge. Good choice for breakfast. Residents' car park. A fine example of a hospitable Irish B&B, with a bubbly hostess in May Walsh and a direct recommendation from the local golf club. Riding and clay-pigeon shooting are available nearby, Fairyhouse racecourse is only six miles away, and it's an easy drive along the N2 to Dublin.

Bed & Breakfast

4 rooms, 3 en suite. Tv lounge

Credit Cards: None

Local Golf Courses: Ashbourne, Black Bush, Corrstown, St Margaret's

BLACKWATER INN | 443

Fannell Street, Kells, Co Meath
Tel: 046 40386

George Plunkett, a keen sportsman, welcomes golfers and other visitors to his atmospheric pub in the centre of town. One of 14 public houses in Kells, this one is popular with a customer base and is well known for serving one of the best pints of stout in the county. Stone floors and heavy wooden furniture give the bar a rugged look, and regular entertainment is provided by live music both traditional and modern. No food is served. There are many interesting places to visit in Kells, including St Columba's Church, which contains a facsimile of the Book of Kells.

Public House

Town-centre pub with regular live music

Credit Cards: None

Local Golf Courses: Headfort, Moor Park, Royal Tara, Navan

CASTLE VIEW HOUSE | 444

Slane, Co Meath
Tel/Fax: 041 9824510

Marie Warren's lovely chalet-style bungalow offers versatile Bed & Breakfast accommodation in quiet, scenic surroundings. The five letting bedrooms (four en suite, the other with a private bathroom) include two triples; each room has been designed with great attention to detail, and all have tv and tea-makers. The house occupies an elevated site that includes plush front lawns, massive rear gardens and a large car park. The quaint village of Slane is famous for its castle, where rock concerts are occasionally held, and the neolithic remains at Newgrange are a short drive away.

Bed & Breakfast

Five quality bedrooms including triples, 4 en suite; large garden

Credit Cards: Visa, Access

Local Golf Courses: Moor Park, Royal Tara, Navan, Headfort

BANJO SHERLOCK'S | 445

Kennedy Road, Navan, Co Meath
Tel: 046 74688 Fax: 046 74689

Above a row of shops by Navan's premier shopping centre, Banjo Sherlock's is a very cheerful and relaxed bar-restaurant with huge floor space, a distinctive pine decor and 120 covers. The menu caters for all appetites, starting with sandwiches and a cold meat platter served with home-made brown bread and tea. Other options run from Caesar salad and Thai-style chicken wings to pizza, pasta, baked trout, burgers and steaks. The owners are both keen golfers and welcome fellow players - and, of course, all other visitors to the county town. Regular live music. Last food orders 9pm.

Bar & Restaurant

Long menu of snacks and dishes served all day till 9pm.

Credit Cards:Access, Mastercard,Visa

Local Golf Courses: Navan, Headfort, Moor Park, Royal Tara

SAN GIOVANNI HOUSE   446

Dublin Road (N2), Slane, Co Meath
Tel: 041 9824147

This large modern house on the main Dublin road (N2) near Slane makes a really delightful Bed & Breakfast base for golfers and other visitors to a fascinating and picturesque part of the world. Olive and Jo Owens' house is at the heart of a mushroom farm on a prime ten-acre site. The five letting bedrooms all have en suite facilities, tv and tea/coffee kits, and residents have their own very comfortable and relaxing lounge. There are plenty of good pubs and restaurants nearby, as well as historic sites including the Hill of Slane and the Newgrange neolithic tumulus.

Farmhouse Bed & Breakfast

5 en suite rooms with tv; guest lounge

Credit Cards: None

Local Golf Courses: Moor Park, Royal Tara, Navan, Headfort

ANNESBROOK   447

Duleek, Co Meath Tel: 041 9823293 Fax: 041 9823042
e-mail: sweetman@annesbrook.com
web: www.hidden-ireland.com/annesbrook

A superb 18th-century country house set in ten acres of gardens and woodland in the lovely Boyne Valley. Interesting features include a fine portico and gothic dining room, both added for a visit by George IV. Today the atmosphere is relaxed and informal, and Kate Sweetman welcomes overnight guests with five comfortable bedrooms, all with bathrooms en suite. The walled garden and orchard provide much of the produce for the house which stands on the R152 just south of Duleek.

Country House Hotel

5 en suite bedrooms for B&B;

Credit Cards: All the major cards except American Express

Local Golf Courses: Navan, Moor Park, Laytown, Black Bush

THE GROUND FLOOR RESTAURANT   448

Bective Square, Kells, Co Meath Tel: 046 49688 Fax: 046 28347
e-mail: thegroundfloor@tjgavigan.com

One of the top eating places in the heritage town of Kells, The Ground Floor is modern, stylish and informal, with contemporary layout and design, intimate candle light and interesting art on the walls. The extensive menus in the 70-cover restaurant are varied and imaginative, spanning modern Irish cuisine and international influences. Steaks are cooked to order on the chargrill. Other choices could be a delicious, simply prepared Dover sole or Cantonese-style duck. The Early Bird menu (18.00-19.30) offers particularly good value for money. Full bar licence. Open seven days a week. Restaurant Association of Ireland and Meath Good Food Circle members. (Same ownership as The Loft restaurant in Navan.)

Restaurant

70-cover restaurant with extensive menus and full licence

Credit Cards: Access,Mastercard,Visa

Local Golf Courses: Royal Tara, Headfort, Navan, Moor Park

WELLINGTON COURT HOTEL   449

Trim, Co Meath
Tel: 046 31516 Fax: 046 36002

An imposing gate in a massive perimeter wall leads to this comfortable, well-run hotel, whose facilities include excellent accommodation, good food and considerable expertise in handling functions large and small. En suite guest bedrooms, 18 in all, are very well furnished, with tv and telephone. The lounges are ideal spots to relax for a chat with a drink and a snack, while in the intimate surroundings of the restaurant there's a choice of à la carte or fixed-price menus, with fine fresh produce used for all the dishes. The hotel is very close to Trim Castle, the setting for many scenes in the film *Braveheart*.

Hotel with Restaurant

18 well-furnished rooms with en suite, tv and phone. Restaurant and lounge menu

Credit Cards: All the major cards

Local Golf Courses: County Meath, Navan, Moor Park, Royal Tara

Country House

14 en suite bedrooms with tv. Breakfast, packed lunch, evening meals. AA ****

Credit Cards: Access, Visa

FORTSINGLETON GEORGIAN MANSION · 460

Emyvale, Monaghan, Co Monaghan
Tel: 047 86054 Fax: 047 86120 e-mail: fortsingleton@eircom.net
web: http://homepage.eircom.net/~fortsingleton

A Georgian mansion of exceptional character standing in six acres of gardens and rolling farmland a mile outside Emyvale and six miles north of Monaghan, off the N2. Ray and Ann Goodall welcome guests to their superb home, which has 14 letting bedrooms, all with en suite facilities and tv. The rooms, all decorated to the highest standard, are all different and many have distinctive themes - one has an authentic victorian railway carriage! The daughter of the house is a qualified chef, using home-grown vegetables and prime local produce in her excellent evening meals. A full breakfast starts the day, and packed lunches can be provided.

Local Golf Courses: Rossmore, Co Cavan, Slieve Russell, Nuremore

Farmhouse Accommodation

Ten en suite bedrooms with tv. B&B or full board

Credit Cards: Access, Visa

ARRADALE HOUSE · 461

Kingscourt Road, Carrickmacross, Co Monaghan
Tel/Fax: 042 9661941

Farmer's wife Christine McMahon runs this delightful establishment that's part of a working dairy farm on the Carrickmacross-Kingscourt road. The setting, among lakes and woodland, is both peaceful and beautiful, and the ten en suite bedrooms offer style and comfort. There are tvs in the rooms, and also a tv lounge available to guests. A full Irish breakfast includes home-made bread and preserves, and other meals can be arranged with notice. This is angling country, and the house has a large tackle room with a bait fridge. Boat hire can be arranged, and a tour of the lakes for first-time visitors. 50 miles from Dublin, 70 miles form Belfast.

Local Golf Courses: Nuremore, Ardee, Killinbeg

Hotel with Restaurant

Ten bedrooms, all en suite; bar lunches, à la carte dinners

Credit Cards: Access, Visa

LENNARD ARMS HOTEL · 462

The Diamond, Clones, Co Monaghan
Tel: 047 51075/51350

Sam Mealiff's family-run hotel stands just off the market place (often known in Ireland as the Diamond) in the bustling little town of Clones. Overnight accommodation is provided in ten bedrooms, some of them en suite, all offering comfort, warmth and modern facilities. The hotel offers a full meal service - breakfast, bar lunches and an evening à la carte menu using prime local produce. There's plenty to see and do in this fast-expanding town near the Fermanagh border, and the hotel, which has a long tradition of hospitality, is a good base for sightseeing and all kinds of sports. the Hilton golf club is local in Clones. At present it is 9 holes but is being extended to an 18 hole all weather course by the end of 2000.

Local Golf Courses: Rossmore, County Cavan, Slieve Russell

Farmhouse Accommodation

Five bedrooms, three en suite. B&B; evening meals with notice

Credit Cards: Access, Visa

GLYNCH HOUSE · 463

Newbliss, Near Clones, Co Monaghan
Tel: 047 54045 Fax: 047 54321
e-mail: mirth@tinet.ie

Peace in abundance in a handsome 18th-century farmhouse that's part of a 200-acre working beef farm just outside the picturesque village of Newbliss. Martha O'Grady entertains guests from all over Europe who return to this lovely tranquil retreat, which has five letting bedrooms, three of them en suite. Evening meals with prior booking are a speciality - bring your own wine. The house is a short drive from Clones, a major centre of lace-making, where the distinctive variety often features small raised dots called Clones Knots. In the market place stands the 5th century High Cross carved with biblical scenes.

Local Golf Courses: Rossmore, Nuremore, County Cavan, Slieve Russell

Counties Monaghan, Cavan & Longford

Farmhouse B&B and Self-catering bungalow

Five en suite bedrooms, tv lounges. Also self-catering bungalow for six
Credit Cards: Access, Visa

RIVERSIDE HOUSE   470

Cootehill, Co Cavan
Tel: 049 5552150/5559950 Fax: 049 5559950
e-mail: unasmith@eircom.net

The River Annalee runs through the 113-acre dairy farm where Joe and Una Smith welcome guests with a choice of accommodation. In the main house are five en suite bedrooms, two large, comfortable lounges with tv and a dining room overlooking the river. A full breakfast is served, with evening meals on request. In the grounds is a self-catering bungalow with three generously sized bedrooms, each with a double and single bed, two bathrooms, a living room, separate dining room and fully fitted kitchen. A great base for anglers, with all the facilities on site, but they'd like to see more golfers!

Local Golf Courses: Rossmore, Co Cavan, Slieve Russell, Nuremore

Hotel and Leisure Centre

13 en suite rooms, tv, phone, computer point. Restaurant; leisure centre
Credit Cards: Mastercard, Visa

BREFFNI ARMS HOTEL & LEISURE CENTRE   471

Arvagh, Co Cavan
Tel: 049 4335127 Fax: 049 4335799

Eamonn and Philomena Gray's newly refurbished hotel and leisure centre stands in an area famous for its fishing lakes, golf courses, horse-riding and leisure walks. Accommodation comprises 13 spacious en suite bedrooms, all with tv, phone, hairdryer and computer point. Food and drinks are served in both the bar and the restaurant, and there's live music on Friday and Saturday, with dancing on Sunday. The smart leisure centre has a 15-metre indoor pool, sauna, steam room, jacuzzi and a fully equipped fitness room. Attentive personal service puts the seal on a stay in this friendly, relaxed hotel.

Local Golf Courses: County Cavan, County Longford

Farmhouse B&B

Four en suite bedrooms; tv lounge. Fishing, pitch and putt and horse riding nearby
Credit Cards: Visa

LISNAMANDRA   472

Crossdoney, Co Cavan
Tel: 049 4337196

A spacious 17th-century house on a working dairy farm provides excellent en suite accommodation in four comfortable bedrooms. Bert and Iris Neill's home lies a mile north of the village of Crossdoney, 5 miles south-west of Cavan (via Cavan Golf Club) and just four miles from Killykeen Forest Park (horse-riding) and superb lake fishing. Cavan's lakes and rivers are renowned in Ireland and further afield. The house, which is rich in character and charm, is centrally heated throughout, with tea/coffee-makers in the bedrooms and tv in the lounge. Breakfast menu; flexible mealtimes.

Local Golf Courses: County Cavan, Slieve Russell, County Longford

Guest house with Restaurant

En suite bedrooms; quiet garden setting; B&B + dinner

Credit Cards: All the major cards

VIEWMOUNT HOUSE   480

Dublin Road, Longford, Co Longford
Tel: 043 41919 Telex: 043 42906
e-mail: viewmt@iol.ie website: www.viewmounthouse.com

This strikingly handsome former landlords residence adjoins Longford county golf club. Less than a mile from the town centre the house is surrounded by 4 acres of magnificent gardens. En suite bedrooms are individually styled with period furniture. Breakfast from an extensive menu can be enjoyed in the delightful dining room with its vaulted ceilings. The high class restaurant is situated in the courtyard. While touring Longford you will see some of Irelands best and unspoilt scenery. Its waterways are renowned for fishing and boating. Local attractions include Carrigglas Manor, Ardagh Village, Corlea Centre, Strokestown House and Gardens, etc.

Local Golf Courses: County Longford, Roscommon, Mullingar

LONGFORD ARMS HOTEL 481

Hotel with Restaurant

En suite rooms include 18 executives. Bar and coffee shop

Credit Cards: All the major cards

24 Main Street, Longford, Co Longford
Tel: 043 46296 Fax: 043 46244
e-mail: longfordarms@tinet.ie

A comfortable family-run on the main street of the main town in the heart of the Midlands. Bedrooms, all practically fitted out and well-furnished, include 18 executive rooms with plenty of desk space and both bath and shower. Some of the rooms are designated non-smoking. Food is available throughout the day in the bar and coffee shop. Locals sights to see include the 19th-century limestone Cathedral of St Mel, dedicated to a 5th-century local bishop. Longford comes alive in a big way each July with the summer festival of pop and rock music.

Local Golf Courses: County Cavan, County Longford, Roscommon

LACKAN LODGE 482

Farmhouse Bed & Breakfast

4 bedrooms (2 en suite) in a tranquil no-smoking farmhouse. Tv lounge

Credit Cards: Visa, Mastercard

Edgeworthstown, Co Longford
Tel/Fax: 043 71299

Charlie and June Murphy offer a warm welcome to Bed & Breakfast visitors at their peacefully located modern farmhouse on the Longford side of Edgeworthstown. Cattle, sheep and horses graze in the fields around the house, where all four bedrooms, two of them en suite, are on the ground floor. The lounge has television, an open fire and tea/coffee-making facilities and, like the rest of the house, is non-smoking. Evening meals, served in the spacious dining room, are available on request for stays of three nights or more. Outside there is ample parking space and a colourful garden.

Local Golf Courses: County Longford, Mullingar, Roscommon

TYRRELLS RESTAURANT 500

Restaurant

Modern Irish cooking and New World Wines

Credit Cards: Laser, Mastercard, Visa

Ballindoolin House & Gardens, Edenderry, Co Offaly
Tel: 0405 32400 Fax: 0405 32377
website: www.ballindoolin.com

David and Nikki Molony run a restaurant of enormous appeal in one of the old farm buildings of the complex of Ballindoolin House & Gardens. Full of atmosphere, with rough-hewn walls and slate-flagged floor, the restaurant is open all year around Wednesday to Saturday for lunch and dinner and for Sunday lunch. David's cooking is modern Irish, typified by a starter of Oriental rare lamb with bitter chicory and a main course of chicken with lime and coriander or pan-fried salmon and cod with a garlic risotto cake. New World wines. No smoking before 10.

Local Golf Courses: Edenderry, Castle Barna, Highfield

FIDDLERS CREEK 510

Rockwood Parade, Sligo, Co Sligo
Tel: 071 41866

Restaurant and Bar

Town-centre restaurant with all-day menus; bar with frequent live music.

Credit Cards: All the major cards

A well-designed, traditionally decorated bar and restaurant in the town centre, with a beautiful scenic view of the River Garavogue. The bar, with lots of nooks and snugs, is the liveliest in Sligo, especially on Wednesday, Thursday and Friday, when there's live music. Its licence runs till 1am, so there's craic aplenty. The restaurant offers an excellent all-day menu, plus hot lunches from 12 till 3; and the full à la carte menu runs from 6 till 10. Enda Scanlon, partner in this terrific place, is a keen golfer and a member at nearby Strandhill Golf Club. Both the town and the county are full of interesting things to do and places to see.

Local Golf Courses: Strandhill, County Sligo, Enniscrone

Hotel with Restaurant and Bar

27 en suite bedrooms with tv, phone & central heating. All-day restaurant; bar

Credit cards: All the major cards

CASTLE ARMS HOTEL   511

Main Street, Enniscrone, Co Sligo
Tel/Fax: 096 36156

Upholding the tradition of offering a warm and friendly welcome. Good food and comfortable accommodation.

- Family run hotel
- 27 en suite bedrooms with direct telephone and television
- Society rates available
- Ideal base to play other championship courses in the area
- Adjacent to a three mile long sandy beach
- Private car park

For further details please do not hesitate to contact Liam or Shane Grimes

Local Golf Courses: Enniscrone, Ballina, Strandhill, County Sligo

---

Bed & Breakfast

Four en suite bedrooms with tv and central heating. Large garden

Credit Cards: None

GLENVIEW B&B   512

Cummeen, Strandhill Road, Sligo, Co Sligo
Tel: 071 70401/62457 Fax: 071 62457

Veronica Kane, 25 years in the Bed & Breakfast business, welcomes golfers to her modern house set in mature gardens on the Strandhill side of Sligo (about a mile from Sligo town centre). The four letting bedrooms are all en suite, with tv and central heating, and guests start the day with a breakfast fit for a king. This is Yeats country (WB and his painter brother Jack) and the Yeats Memorial Building is one of the sights of Sligo. The county is rich in ancient monuments (megalithic tombs close by), and Strandhill, a short dive away, has one of the best surfing beaches in Europe.

Local Golf Courses: Strandhill, County Sligo, Bundoran

Bed & Breakfast

Seven B&B rooms with en suite facilities and tv

Credit Cards: None

ST MARTINS   513

Enniscrone, Co Sligo
Tel: 096 36111

Martina and Eamon Flynn have been in the business for 30 years, and their current B&B establishment is a long, single storey house in a prime site on Enniscrone's main street. At present there are seven letting bedrooms, all with en suite facilities and tv, but an extension under way as we went to press will provide a further eight rooms. Lots of plus points: great breakfasts, and a position close to fantastic beaches, the new waterfront leisure centre and the renowned seaweed baths. And Enniscrone Golf Club, where the Flynns are known and liked, is only half a mile away.

Local Golf Courses: Enniscrone, Ballina, Strandhill, County Sligo

---

Hotel and Restaurant

16 en suite rooms with phone; bars and restaurant; car park

Credit Cards: All the major cards

THE ROYAL HOTEL   520

Boyle, Co Roscommon
Tel: 079 62016 Fax: 079 64949

Originally called Freeman's Royal Hotel, this was the first major building on the south side of the Boyle river, now extended and modernised to offer up-to-date facilities for today's guests. The hotel has 16 bedrooms, all en suite, with telephone and tea-maker. The whole place is well furnished, and the day rooms include cosy bars, a coffee shop and a restaurant that looks out over the river. Also a Chinese restaurant. The hotel has its own large car park. Boyle Abbey, a magnificent 12th-century abbey ruin, is close by, and lovely Lough Key, with its forest park, boating and fishing, is a short drive away. Traditional music in the evenings in Sir Henry's bar.

Local Golf Courses: Roscommon, County Sligo, Strandhill

LISROYNE INN | 521

Strokestown, Co Roscommon
Tel: 078 33214

Behind a smart Guinness-coloured frontage, this is an immaculately kept pub with a large car park and a warm and welcoming landlord in John O'Rourke. It's very much a favourite with the locals, who meet for a drink and a chat, and perhaps a toasted sandwich or a bowl of soup. Strokestown is a handsome market town with plenty of attractions. The Irish Famine Museum, in the grounds of the Georgian Strokestown Park House, tells the story of the disastrous potato blight of the 1840s that led to millions starving to death. On a more peaceful note, the famous Walled Garden boasts the longest herbaceous border in the British Isles.

Public House

Neatly kept pub serving and light snacks

Credit Cards: None

Local Golf Courses: Roscommon, Co Longford, Glasson, Athlone

BELLA PASTA | 522

Roosky, Co Roscommon
Tel: 078 6705556

Gianini Savio has brought the flavour of Italy to a small village by the River Shannon on the border with Leitrim. His delightful little restaurant is part of the Wier Lodge complex and operates within an Irish pub. A range of pizza and pasta is the mainstay of the menu, but there's plenty more to choose from, and for lighter snacks the bar menu offers the likes of garlicky fried calamari, chicken tikka toasted sandwich and omelettes. Main dishes could include steak Diane and salmon in a creamy basil sauce. A new venture that shows great initiative and deserves to succeed.

Restaurant and Bar

Italian cuisine in an Irish pub setting by the Shannon

Credit Cards: None

Local Golf Courses: Roscommon, County Longford, County Cavan

LACKEN HOUSE HOLIDAY RESIDENCE | 523

Rahara, Athleague, Co Roscommon
Tel/Fax: 0903 23449
e-mail: info@lackenhouse.findhere.org
website: www.lackenhouse.findhere.org

A lovely rural setting in quiet countryside guarantees a peaceful stay in a unique cut-stone manor house dating back to the 1820s. Jan and Gertina Cammeraat, a Dutch couple with three young children, have completely restored the estate and offer a choice between Bed & Breakfast accommodation in the manor house (six non-smoking en suite rooms including a bridal suite) and four comfortable self-catering chalet-style lodges in the grounds. Further expansion plans include a small gym, rest room with library, gamesroom and coffee corner.

Country Holiday Residence

6 en suite rooms for B&B; 4 self-catering lodges

Credit Cards: None

Local Golf Courses: Roscommon, Ballinasloe, Glasson, Athlone

REGANS OF ROSCOMMON | 524

Market Square, Roscommon, Co Roscommon
Tel: 0903 25339/26373 Fax: 0903 27833

Brothers Eamon and Dominic Regan offer calm, comfort, character and cuisine in their well-known establishment in the centre of the pleasant county town. Accommodation comprises 14 well-appointed bedrooms, all with en suite facilities, tv and telephone. The hotel restaurant is open from 8 in the morning till 10 at night for excellent cooking using the finest local produce, and Kitty's nightclub is a popular place to spend a leisurely evening - or a lively one, with dancing on Friday and Saturday till late. There are three function rooms catering for meetings, weddings and all kinds of celebrations.

Hotel with Restaurant

14 en suite bedrooms, tv, telephone. All-day restaurant, nightclub

Credit Cards: All the major cards

Local Golf Courses: Roscommon, Co Longford, Glasson, Athlone

Counties Sligo & Roscommon

HAWTHORN VIEW   540

Horse & Jockey, Cashel Road, Thurles, Co Tipperary
Tel: 0504 21710

Set back from the main N62 between Thurles and Horse & Jockey, Hawthorn View is a modern bungalow with a generous garden and excellent parking. Noreen O'Mahony and her daughter offer very comfortable Bed and Breakfast accommodation in four bedrooms - three doubles and a twin - with en suite facilities and tv. The whole place has recently been refurbished and recarpeted, and each room has its own individual appeal. Thurles Golf Course is a two-minute drive away, there's an equestrian centre nearby, and other attractions in the vicinity include Thurles racecourse, Holy Cross Abbey and the Rock of Cashel. Thurles railway station is only 5 mintues drive away.

Bed & Breakfast

4 bungalow bedrooms, all en suite. Thurles Golf Course very near

Credit Cards: None

Local Golf Courses: Thurles, County Tipperary, Roscrea, Rathdowney

THE WATERFRONT   541

The Mall, Roscrea, Co Tipperary
Tel: 0505 22431

Behind its cheerful facade - gleaming stone with red-painted woodwork - this is a charming, friendly restaurant for all the family. First orders are at 9.30 am, last at 9pm. Breakfasts and lunches can be taken away or enjoyed in the dining area, which has three sections including one reserved for non-smokers. Snacks include sandwiches (plain, open, club, toasted), salads, omelettes and an all-day breakfast, and many of the starters are also available as main courses. The full à la carte menu comes on stream at 3pm and runs from curries and mixed grill to dill-sauced salmon and roast duck with a hoisin dipping sauce. Children's menu and portions. Wine licence.

Restaurant

Friendly family restaurant open from 9.30 till 9. Takeaway available. Wine licence

Credit Cards: All the major cards

Local Golf Courses: Roscrea, Rathdowney, Mountrath, Birr

OTWAY LODGE   542

Dromineer, Nenagh, Co Tipperary
Tel: 067 24133/24273
web: flannery@eircom.net

Ann Flannery's Otway Lodge, formerly Lord Otway's hunting lodge and before that a military barracks, is now a roomy, comfortable Bed & Breakfast guest house with six en suite letting bedrooms. The spacious premises include a table tennis room, and a laundry service is available. The owners also have a shop next to the B&B. Standing in the centre of the village beside Lough Derg, it's a great base for sporting enthusiasts, with sailing, water skiing and windsurfing on the lake. Boats can be hired and fishing trips arranged. Easy parking.

Guest House

6 en suite bedrooms. Lakeside setting. Boats, fishing, water sports

Credit Cards: None

Local Golf Courses: Nenagh, Roscrea, Portumna, Birr

RIVERRUN COTTAGES   543

Terryglass, Nenagh, Co Tipperary
Tel: 067 22125

Off the Borrisokane-Portland road (N52) at the northern end of Lough Derg, Riverrun Cottages consist of five 4-star self-catering units in modern but 'old-looking' cottages; each accommodates four guests. The units comprise two bedrooms (one with shower, one with bath), kitchen and lounge with open fire, and everything is provided for a comfortable, self-contained holiday. A barbecue is avialble, and there are several good pubs in the vicinity. The location, right by the lough, makes this a popular base for water-borne activities, including boat hire and great fishing. There's a tennis court on the premises. Easy parking. Super gardens.

Self-Catering

Five units in period-looking modern cottages. 2 bedrooms, lounge, kitchen. By Lough Derg. Tennis
Credit Cards: All the major cards

Local Golf Courses: Nenagh, Roscrea, Portumna, Birr

BRIDGET'S BED & BREAKFAST   544

Coolbawn, Nenagh, Co Tipperary
Tel: 067 28098

Off the R493 between Coolbawn and Terryglass, Bridget's Bed & Breakfast is a smart modern bungalow set in its own grounds just five minutes' walk from Lough Derg (and a mile and a half from the village of Ballinderry). Mr & Mrs Bower - she's Bridget - offer comfortable Bed and Breakfast accommodation in five en suite bedrooms - two singles, a double and two twins. Visitors are greeted with tea or coffee on arrival. Tv in the lounge. Easy parking. With the lough so close, this is a favourite base for water-borne activities, and the owners have rowing and fishing boats for hire (and indeed for sale!). Great fishing. Old-style pubs nearby.

Bed & Breakfast

Five en suite bedrooms including two singles. Fishing. Boat hire

Credit Cards:

Local Golf Courses: Nenagh, Roscrea, Portumna, Birr

ANNAGH LODGE   545

Coolbawn, Nenagh, Co Tipperary
Tel/Fax: 067 24225
e-mail: annaghlg@hotmail.com website: www.annaghlodge.com

Built in 1815 for a certain Captain Minchin, Annagh Lodge country house enjoys a secluded, scenic setting on a 200-acre working farm near Lough Derg just south of Coolbawn. The five letting bedrooms are all of a good size (one is a family room), with individual style and beautiful views. The owners are Rachel and Andrew Sterling, she a qualified hotelier and experienced cook, he a farmer who produces much of the food for Rachel's splendid dinners. Guests are free to roam across the fields or through the forest, to see the workings of the farm or just to relax in the garden or the drawing room. All sorts of sporting activities can be arranged.

Country Guest House

B&B in 5 spacious rooms, one of family size. Dinner by arrangement. Lots of sporting activities
Credit Cards: All the major cards

Local Golf Courses: Nenagh, Roscrea, Portumna, Birr

CAPPAMURA HOUSE   546

Dundrum, Co Tipperary
Tel: 062 71127

Eight miles west of Cashel off the R505, Cappamura House is a 300-year-old farmhouse which has been in the same family ever since it was built. Bed and Breakfast accommodation comprises seven beautifully decorated, amply-sized bedrooms, three of them with en suite facilities, the others with hot and cold water. Horse riding is a popular pastime in these parts, and there's an equestrian centre in the grounds, where the local point-to-point meetings are held. For non-equestrians, there are plenty of interesting walks nearby. A relaxing spot in the heart of the Golden Vale.

Bed & Breakfast

7 bedrooms including 3 en suite. Equestrian centre in the grounds

Credit Cards: None

Local Golf Courses: Tipperary, County Tipperary, Thurles, Ballykisteen

RECTORY HOUSE HOTEL   547

Dundrum, Co Tipperary
Tel: 062 71266 Fax: 062 71115
e-mail: rectoryh@iol.ie

Built as a private residence in the mid-19th century and later acquired by the Church of Ireland, Rectory House stands peacefully in secluded tree-lined grounds off the R505 at the entrance to Dundrum village. Recently converted to provide guests with all the modern conveniences and comfort, the house nonetheless retains all its old-fashioned charm, making it an ideal spot for a break from the urban hassle. There are ten letting bedrooms, all large and well-furnished, with en suite facilities, tv and telephone. A la carte restaurant, bar and lounge. Golf and leisure centre a mile from the house.

Hotel & à la carte restaurant

10 en suite bedrooms with tv and telephone. All meals available in restaurant. Bar and lounge
Credit Cards: Mastercard, Visa

Local Golf Courses: Tipperary, County Tipperary, Thurles, Ballykisteen

County Tipperary

ASHMORE HOUSE · 548

John Street, Cashel, Co Tipperary
Tel: 062 61286 Fax: 062 62789
e-mail: ashmorehouse@yahoo.iol

Right in the heart of Cashel, Ashmore House is a classical Georgian town house with spacious, high-ceilinged rooms, elegant furnishings and abundant old-world charm. Laura Ryan has been welcoming guests on a Bed & Breakfast basis for more than a decade. The six bedrooms include double, twin and family rooms, and guests start the day on the right note with a splendid multi-choice breakfast served in the dining room. The house has a lovely peaceful walled garden and private off-street parking. Next door is Bolton Library, which contains the smallest book in the world.

Guest House

Six spacious B&B rooms in a Georgian town house. Garden. Private parking. Extensive breakfast menu
Credit Cards: Mastercard, Visa

Local Golf Courses: Tipperary, County Tipperary, Ballykisteen, Cahir

ASHLEY PARK HOUSE · 549

Ashley Park, Ardcroney, Nenagh, Co Tipperary
Tel: 067 38223 Fax: 067 38013 e-mail: margaret@ashleypark.com
Website: www.ashleypark.com

In the heart of Ireland lies Ashley Park. Set in 76 acres of beech woodland, the 18th century house overlooks Lough Ourna, a private lake known for its profusion of migratory wildfowl and stocked with trout. Within five minutes drive is the newly lengthened championship course at Nenagh. The estate is centrally located on the northern route and is ideal for reaching Ireland's legendary courses such as Ballybunion and Lahinch. The house is a near museum of brilliantly preserved antiquity, far removed from any hustle and bustle, with elegant bedrooms, big bathrooms and deeply carved beds. Downstairs, there are mesmerizing peat fires and quiet rooms full of gleaming dark floors and furniture.

Bed and Breakfast

Six en suite bedrooms, tv. Peat fires, extensive grounds, private lake, boat.
Credit Cards: None

Local Golf Courses: Nenagh, Roscrea, Portumna, Birr

BALLINACOUNTY HOUSE · 550

Glen of Aherlow, Co Tipperary
Tel/Fax: 062 56000

Ballinacounty House comprises a stable complex in a lovely rural setting six miles southeast of Tipperary town. Chris Stanley's establishment comprises five Bed and Breakfast bedrooms and two self-catering cottages, each of the latter sleeping up to four. Also on the premises is a restaurant with a wine licence (advance booking essential). The accommodation is very well presented throughout, with every detail geared to the comfort of guests. This is a beautiful part of the world, and healthy walks are very much the order of the day.

Bed and Breakfast, Self-Catering, Restaurant

Five bedrooms for B&B, two cottages for self-catering. Restaurant on site
Credit Cards: Visa

Local Golf Courses: Tipperary, County Tipperary, Ballykisteen, Cahir

DONOVAN'S · 551

O'Brien Street, Tipperary, Co Tipperary
Tel: 062 51384

Off the main street, just moments from the town centre, John Donovan's inn is a warm, welcoming, roomy haven behind its long frontage. Traditional Irish music is played in the piano lounge, and the walls throughout are covered with sporting memorabilia. Hungry punters make for the elevated dining area, where the evening menu offers international classics such as deep-fried brie with a raspberry sauce, home-made beef burgers, chicken supreme with a herb sauce and escalope of salmon with Normandy sauce. Sirloin steak comes with garlic butter or a whiskey and mushroom sauce. In the summer the scene shifts to the beer garden.

Restaurant and Bar

Warm, roomy bar and restaurant with a sporting theme. Evening menu. Irish music
Credit Cards: None

Local Golf Courses: Tipperary, County Tipperary, Ballykisteen

Bed and Breakfast

Four en suite bedrooms with tv. Off-road parking. Reflexology

Credit Cards: None

ARDEN LODGE | 552

Townspark, Clonmel Road, Cahir, Co Tipperary
Tel: 052 42338

Part of an exclusive modern housing development, Arden Lodge stands off the Clonmel Road just five minutes' walk from the centre of town. The whole place was built to the highest specification, and its bungalow frontage includes a handsome pillared portico; the hard-standing parking is lit by period-style street lamps. Patricia Maguire has four letting bedrooms with en suite facilities, tv and first-class carpets and furnishings. A full-time hostess with a sound background in the hotel business, she also offers in-house reflexology treatment - an unusual extra in this delightful spot.

Local Golf Courses: Cahir Park, Carrick-on-Suir, Clonmel

Hotel and Restaurant

Town centre location, flexible accommodation. Tv, telephone, tea/coffee facilities. Restaurant and bar
Credit Cards: Amex, Mastercard, Visa

FENNESSY'S HOTEL | 554

Gladstone Street, Clonmel, Co Tipperary
Tel: 052 23680 Fax: 052 23783

Flexible accommodation is offered at Fennessy's Hotel, one of the most notable buildings in town and once the home of the mayor. Built in 1815, it occupies a prime site on the main street, and owner Richard Fennessy has recently completed a top-to-bottom refurbishment. All the rooms are individually furnished and decorated with tv, telephone and tea/coffee facilities - some of the bathrooms boast jacuzzis. A full menu of home-cooked food is available in the restaurant, and bar snacks cater for lighter appetites. The hotel is handily placed for visiting the sights of Clonmel and is next door to the library, leisure centre and the towns main shopping precinct. After your visit you are sure to want to return.

Local Golf Courses: Clonmel, Cahir Park, Carrick-on-Suir

Bed and Breakfast

Six en suite bedrooms. Landscaped gardens. B&B, packed lunches, snacks, dinner by arrangement
Credit Cards:

TÍR NA NÓG | 555

Dualla, Cashel, Co Tipperary
Tel: 062 61350 Fax: 062 62411
e-mail: tnanog@indigo.ie

Joan and Tommy Maloney offer traditional hospitality and courteous personal care at their friendly country home in a village on the R691 Cashel-Kilkenny road. The house is set in two acres of landscaped gardens, and peace and quiet are assured in the six warm, cosy en suite bedrooms, which have orthopaedic beds, tvs and other amenities designed for a comfortable stay. A good breakfast starts the day, there's a snack menu, and dinner is served with advance notice. Lots of good walks in the area, plus sights to see (Rock of Cashel 5 minutes away) and games to play. Tír Na Nóg means 'The Land of Youth'.

Local Golf Courses: Tipperary, County Tipperary, Cahir Park, Clonmel

Bed and Breakfast

Five B&B bedrooms. Quiet location just outside town. Easy parking

Credit Cards: None

INDAVILLE | 556

Boherclough Street, Cork Road, Cashel, Co Tipperary
Tel: 062 62075

No distance at all from the centre of Cashel on the Cork Road (N8), Indaville is one of the oldest dwellings in the neighbourhood and is steeped in history. Built around 1750 as a hunting lodge, is has now been made available by owners Mr and Mrs Murphy as a comfortable, characterful Bed and Breakfast establishment. The five large letting bedrooms offer flexible accommodation in the lowest part of the house, below the level of the driveway. The rooms have thick walls and abundant character, and guests have their own entrance. A really peaceful spot far enough from town to guarantee peace and quiet but near enough to all the town's many attractions. Easy parking.

Local Golf Courses: Tipperary, County Tipperary, Cahir Park, Clonmel

County Tipperary

County Tipperary

KNOCKLOFTY HOUSE 557

Knocklofty, Clonmel, Co Tipperary
Tel: 052 25444 Fax: 052 26444

Denis English, an Irishman born across the valley, has transformed the former home of the Earls of Donoughmore into a country house hotel of distinction. The setting, between Clonmel and Cahir, in beautiful gardens and parkland by the River Suir (fishing rights), is a pure delight, and the gracious, high-ceilinged en suite bedrooms, all with tv and telephone, offer everything for a comfortable stay. Our self-catering mews houses and cottages offer spacious 1, 2 and 3 bedrooms, mostly en-suite and fully furnished to the highest standard, with all the latest mod cons. Guests have full use of the on-site leisure centre with swimming pool, sauna, jacuzzi, sunbed and gym.

Hotel, Restaurant, Self-Catering

14 en suite bedrooms, tv, telephone. Leisure centre. Fishing. Restaurant. Also self-catering
Credit Cards: All the major cards

Local Golf Courses: Clonmel, Cahir Park, Carrick-on-Suir

MARLFIELD HOUSE 558

Clonmel, Co Tipperary
Tel: 052 25444 Fax: 052 26444

Marlfield House is a splendid late 18th-century residence set amid glorious parkland and forest on the banks of the River Suir about a mile and a half from Clonmel. Self-catering holiday accommodation of the highest quality is offered in 12 self-contained apartments in the house, and in the basement are a bar and restaurant. Unique features of the property include a superb conservatory designed by Richard Turner, who was also responsible for the Palm House at Kew Gardens and the botanical gardens in Dublin and Belfast. The house has fishing rights on a stretch of the Suir. Guests have full use of the leisure centre at our sister house, Knocklofty (2 miles away), with swimming pool, sauna, jacuzzi, sunbed and gym.

Self-Catering Apartments

12 self-catering apartments in 18th-century house. Restaurant and bar. Fishing
Credit Cards: All the major cards

Local Golf Courses: Clonmel, Cahir Park, Carrick-on-Suir

BENUALA 559

Marlfield Road, Clonmel, Co Tipperary
Tel: 052 22158
e-mail: benuala@indigo.ie

Nuala O'Connell, one of the nicest landladies you could hope to meet, has been in the B&B business for 25 years and offers overnight accommodation in six well-decorated bedrooms in a modern bungalow just outside town. All the rooms are of a good size, with en suite facilities and tv, and guests will have no problem parking (there's a private car park). Golf, fishing and pony trekking are all available in the vicinity, and a wildlife sanctuary is among the other local attractions. The house stands a short distance from town in the direction of Cahir.

Bed and Breakfast

Six en suite bedrooms, tv. Private parking

Credit Cards: None

Local Golf Courses: Clonmel, Cahir Park, Carrick-on-Suir

Co Waterford

MCALPIN'S SUIR INN 570

Cheekpoint, Co Waterford
Tel: 051 382220
e-mail: mcalpin@ireland. Com

A charming 17th-century black-and-white pub in Cheekpoint, once the main port for the boats from England. It's a quiet backwater now, but much of the fish and shellfish for the inn is landed at the quay opposite. The menu majors on the deep with such delights as mussels or prawns in garlic butter, crab bake, scallops in a white wine and cheese sauce and the popular cold seafood platter of salmon, smoked salmon, barbecued salmon, prawns, shrimps, mussels, crab and smoked mackerel as well as beef fillet and genuine curries. Food is served Tuesday to Saturday evenings, also Monday evenings May to August.

Pub with Food

17th-century pub with a menu majoring on seafood. Evenings only

Credit Cards: All the major cards

Local Golf Courses: Faithlegg, Waterford Castle, Dunmore East

THE SHIP RESTAURANT & BAR 571

Dunmore East, Co Waterford
Tel: 051 383141/383144

A sturdy, creeper-clad Victorian building on a prominent roadside site above the bay. Inside, the theme is strongly nautical, the furniture made from old barrels, the atmosphere inviting and informal. Fresh seafood is the speciality on a sophisticated evening menu that tempts with the likes of gratin of oysters with leeks and chardonnay with tagliatelle and parmesan crisps, or a symphony of seafood and shellfish with a saffron butter vinaigrette. Dinner every night except Sunday and Monday in winter. Less formal lunchtime menu seven days a week June to August, also Sunday April, May, September and October.

Restaurant and Bar

70-seat restaurant specialising in fresh seafood. Good-value lunches; evening à la carte
Credit Cards: Amex, Mastercard, Visa

Local Golf Courses: Dunmore East, Tramore, W'ford Castle, W'ford Municipal

---

ST ALBANS GUEST HOUSE 572

Cork Road, Waterford, Co Waterford
Tel/Fax: 051 358171

Just half a mile from the city centre, St Albans is a spacious detached villa with a huge rear garden and plenty of parking space. The home of Helen Mullaly, who moved here in the summer of 1999, St Albans has eight guest bedrooms, all of them en suite, appealingly furnished and decorated and very well equipped. Helen serves a generous breakfast with a choice of either 'the Full Irish' or continental. The house, which has a warm, welcoming atmosphere, is well placed for exploring the city and the picturesque Waterford coast with its pretty fishing villages. The Waterford Crystal factory is also nearby.

Bed and Breakfast

Eight en suite bedrooms, large garden, easy parking

Credit Cards: All the major cards

Local Golf Courses: Waterford, Waterford Municipal, Tramore

WOODSTOWN HOUSE COUNTRY ESTATE 573

Woodstown, Co Waterford
Tel: 051 382611 Fax: 051 382644
e-mail: woodstown@granvillehotel.ie

Spacious mews-style houses converted from the stables, carriage houses and dower house of Woodstown House provide top-quality self-catering holiday accommodation. Each house has a hallway, living room, kitchen/dining room, 2/3 bedrooms and bathroom. All the mod cons are provided, including central heating, telephone, cooker, microwave, washing machine & dryer, dishwasher, bed linen and multi-channel tv. Most have a private patio and the whole complex is set in beautifully landscaped gardens with tree-lined avenues leading to Woodstown beach. Tennis courts, jogging paths, barbecue area.

Self-Catering Holiday Houses

Mews-style houses with 2/3 bedrooms, living room, kitchen-diner, tv, phone. Gardens, tennis, beach
Credit Cards: All the major cards

Local Golf Courses: W'ford Municipal, W'ford Castle, Dunmore East

---

GRANVILLE HOTEL 574

The Quay, Waterford, Co Waterford
Tel: 051 305555 Fax: 051 305566
e-mail: stay@granville-hotel.ie web: www.granville-hotel.ie

Dating from the early years of the 19th century, the Granville, on the quay by the River Suir, is one of Ireland's oldest and most distinguished hotels. Owners for 20 years Liam and Ann Cusack pursue the long tradition of hospitality, warmth and comfort, and the 100 individually styled en suite bedrooms offer every extra for a stay to remember. Top-quality contemporary cuisine is served in the award-winning Bianconi Restaurant, and less formal eating is available in the civilised bar. Several function/meeting rooms, including one where Parnell made many famous speeches.

Hotel and Restaurant

100 top-class en suite bedrooms in a historic quayside hotel. Superb restaurant
Credit Cards: All the major cards

Local Golf Courses: Waterford, Waterford Castle, Waterford Municipal

County Waterford

County Waterford

County Westmeath

THE BELFRY HOTEL 575

Conduit Lane, Waterford, Co Waterford
Tel: 051 844800 Fax: 051 843719

Waterford's newest hotel, due to open early summer 2000. The Belfry, in the city centre, will have 45 beautifully decorated en suite bedrooms with the full range of accessories including a second phone line for computers and modems. Some rooms are of family size and will be available at special rates. One of the many pubs and restaurants in the vicinity is the hotel's own Egans Lounge Bar with an informal lunchtime menu and carvery and an evening à la carte. An ideal base for golfers, with many courses within easy reach and, in the hotel itself, storage and drying facilities.

Hotel with lounge bar menu

45 bedrooms, all en suite, incl some family. Tv, telephone. Lunchtime meals and carvery; evening à la carte
Credit Cards: All the major cards

Local Golf Courses: Waterford, W'ford Municipal, Faithlegg, Tramore

---

ORPENS BAR & ESTUARY RESTAURANT 576

Knockboy, Waterford, Co Waterford
Tel: 051 873082 Fax: 051 874180
e-mail: orpens@eircom.net.ie web: homepage.tinet.ie/~orpens

Pat and Mary Orpen's inviting roadside establishment is a good place to pause at any time of day. Bar food is available throughout the opening hours, and a lunchtime carvery (informal) menu is served in the lounge very day except Sunday. From 6.30pm the full evening à la carte menu is offered in the separate upstairs Estuary Restaurant, covering an impressively wide range of dishes to appeal to all tastes and appetites. Fish - all from local waters - is a popular order, while meat-eaters will be pleased with the variety of steaks. Chef's specials include tempting ways with chicken, and there's plenty of main-course choice for vegetarians.

Restaurant, Bar and Lounge

90-cover family restaurant, plus bar and lounge. Daytime bar meals; wide-ranging evening menu
Credit Cards: Mastercard, Visa

Local Golf Courses: Waterford, Dungarvan, Goldcoast, West W'ford

---

THE POLLARD ARMS HOTEL 600

The Square, Castlepollard, Co Westmeath
Tel: 044 61194
e-mail: info@pollardarms.eircom.ie

Fifteen en suite bedrooms provide an excellent base in Liam and Elizabeth Sullivan's popular hotel at the main crossroads in the centre of Castlepollard. The rooms are very well equipped, with tv, telephone and trouser press as standard accessories. The whole place has just been refurbished, and as we went to press further bedrooms were in the pipeline. Lunch and dinner are served seven days a week in the fully licensed restaurant, whose menu runs from soup and sandwiches (plain or toasted) to smoked salmon platter, lots of ways with chicken, sirloin steaks and the daily fish and roast meat specials. Separate bar.

Hotel with Restaurant

Fifteen en suite bedrooms. Fully licensed restaurant. Bar

Credit Cards: All the major cards

Local Golf Courses: Delvin, Mullingar, County Longford

VILLA ST JOHN 601

Roscommon Road, Athlone, Co Westmeath
Tel/Fax: 0902 92490

Half a mile out of Athlone on the road to Roscommon, John and Maura Duggan offer great hospitality and comfortable Bed & Breakfast accommodation in their beautifully decorated modern house. They have eight letting bedrooms, five of them en suite, all with tv, tea-makers and hairdryers. There's also a tv lounge and a pleasant terrace for taking the air. Breakfast provides plenty of choice, and evening meals can be arranged with notice. It's an easy walk to town, where there are bars, restaurants and lots of things to see. Athlone Castle, which played a military role for 700 years, has a visitor centre and museum.

Bed & Breakfast

8 rooms, 5 en suite; tv in rooms + tv lounge

Credit Cards: Access,Mastercard,Visa

Local Golf Courses: Glasson, Athlone, Moate, Mount Temple

BLOOMFIELD HOUSE HOTEL & LEISURE CLUB | 602

Tullamore Road, Mullingar, Co Westmeath Tel: 044 40894
Fax: 044 43767 e-mail: bloomfieldhouse@eircom.net
web: www.bloomfieldhouse.com

Bloomfield House Hotel, set in the heart of Ireland, enjoys an idyllic setting overlooking Lough Ennell and surrounded by acres of rich parkland. The hotel can boast 65 superbly appointed bedrooms including 4 presidential and 4 executive suites and its quietly secluded loation, only 2 miles from Mullingar on the N52, is ideal for golf and leisure breaks. There is a state of the art leisure centre with swimming pool, sauna, steamroom, jacuzzi and gym, with massage/aromatherapy and reflexology also available. Golf is available at nearby Mullingar, Glasson, Esker Hills and Tullamore.

Hotel, Restaurant, Leisure Club

65 en suite bedrooms including suites. Tv, telephone. Licensed restaurant. Leisure Club
Credit Cards: All the major cards

Local Golf Courses: Mullingar, Glasson, Esker Hills and Tullamore

---

MORNINGTON HOUSE | 603

Multyfarnham, Co Westmeath
Tel: 044 72191 Fax: 044 72338
e-mail: info@mornington.ie web: www.mornington.ie

A country house of distinction, built in 1710 and in the same family ownership for the last 140 years. The house stands in its own 50 acre estate and a pleasant 800 yd walk takes you to a 9 mile long lake. Mornington House is centrally placed for the county's golf courses. Overnight accommodation comprises a single and four double bedrooms, all with private bathrooms. There's a wide choice for breakfast, and the four-course dinner, available by prior arrangement and always based on the best and freshest seasonal produce, is not to be missed, as Anne O'Hara is a highly accomplished chef and a member of Euro-Toques.

Bed and Breakfast

One single and four double bedrooms with private bath. Dinner by arrangement
Credit Cards: All the major cards

Local Golf Courses: Mullingar, Delvin, Glasson

MEARESCOURT HOUSE | 604

Rathconrath, Mullingar, Co Westmeath
Tel: 044 55112

Country house accommodation in a magnificent Georgian mansion set in sweeping parkland with many rare trees and plants. The woodland and lakeland walks make it a perfect haven for anyone wanting to escape the urban turmoil and unwind. The letting part of the house comprises a drawing room, dining room, study and four double bedrooms with period furniture, all en suite. A warm welcome awaits from the owners, Brendan and Eithne Pendred, and guests can look forward to imaginative country cooking (dinner by arrangement). Member of Friendly Homes of Ireland. There are seven golf courses (Mullingar, Mount Temple, Glasson, Moate, Delvin, Tullamore and Longford) all within 30 minutes drive of Mearescourt House.

Bed and Breakfast

Four double bedrooms, all en suite. Dinner by arrangement

Credit Cards: Mastercard, Visa

Local Golf Courses: Mullingar, Delvin, Mount Temple, Moate

OSCARS | 605

21 Oliver Plunkett Street, Mullingar, Co Westmeath
Tel: 044 44909

Oscars is a delightful 64-cover restaurant handily located in the middle of Mullingar. Hosts Noel Kennedy and Tony Maloney present a tempting menu that ranges far and wide for its inspiration, offering something for everyone at affordable prices. Steaks and burgers (the Emperor burger is served with fried onions and a garlic sauce) are perennial favourites, along with pasta served with a choice of no fewer than ten sauces. Among the speciality dishes are prawns gratinated with Irish cheddar or chargrilled sirloin of veal with lemon-scented mushrooms and a sauce of cracked mustard seed, Irish whiskey and cream. Full drinks licence.

Restaurant

64-cover restaurant with a wideranging menu and full drinks licence
Credit Cards: Mastercard, Visa

Local Golf Courses: Mullingar, Esker Hills, Tullamore, Castle Barna

County Westmeath

Bed and Breakfast

Seven en suite bedrooms of family size. Great breakfasts

Credit Cards: All the major cards

SHELMALIER HOUSE 606

Cartrontroy, Athlone, Co Westmeath
Tel: 0902 72145 Fax: 0902 73190
e-mail: shelmal@iol.ie

Jim and Nancy Denby offer a lovely traditional atmosphere and excellent accommodation in a quiet Bed and Breakfast establishment a mile out of Athlone town (signposted on the N6 town route). The seven bedrooms are all en suite, with tv and telephone. Most are big enough for family occupation, with both double and one or two single beds. The day starts in the best possible way, as the house is a winner of a National Galtee Breakfast Award. Private car park. Secure storage for clubs.

Local Golf Courses: Glasson, Mount Temple, Moate

Guest House, B&B plus dinner

Six bedrooms, all en suite, some for up to six. Table d'hote dinner

Credit Cards: Mastercard, Visa

HILLSIDE HOUSE 620

Tubberduff, Gorey, Co Wexford
Tel: 055 21726/22036 Fax: 055 22567
e-mail: hsh@eircon.net

Set back from the N11 Rosslare-Dublin road four miles northeast of Gorey, the Sunderland family's fine modern house enjoys views of the Tara Hills from its elevated position. Tea or coffee greets guests before they are shown to one of the six en suite bedrooms, some of which can sleep up to six people. All have tv and hairdryers, and cots and high chairs can be provided. The residents' lounge is a cosy place to meet and relax, and in the comfortable dining room home-style cooking offers a varied five-course table d'hote dinner using the pick of local produce.

Local Golf Courses: Courtown, Arklow, Coollattin, Enniscorthy

Bed and Breakfast

Six en suite bedrooms with tv. Packed lunches by arrangement

Credit Cards: Mastercard, Visa

ST THERESES 621

Mount Alexander, Gorey, Co Wexford
Tel: 055 21793 Fax: 055 21443 e-mail: thereses@iol.ie

Monica Kenny's fine modern country home stands in its own grounds just off the main Gorey-Courtown road in a peaceful setting with a large, secure parking area. The six letting bedrooms all have en suite facilities, tv and hairdryer, and both they and the lounge and dining room are the last word in sumptuous style. The house is an ideal base for a quiet break or a golfing holiday (13 courses within a 30-minute drive including Woodenbridge, European Club, Courtown, Arklow, Coollattin and Enniscorthy), or for touring the area, where the numerous attractions include the 17th-century Craanford watermill and the story-telling centre in Raheen - pass the stick round and tell your story. Packed lunches can be provided.

Local Golf Courses: Courtown, Arklow, Coollattin, Enniscorthy

Bar and Lounge

Wide range of beers. Lunchtime snacks. Live music Saturday night

Credit Cards: Visa

QUINN'S LOUNGE 622

72 Main Street, Gorey, Co Wexford
Tel: 055 21810 Fax: 055 21819

All the Irish beers and stouts, including perhaps the best pint of Guinness in town, are served in a charming old-fashioned lounge in the heart of Gorey's main street. Slate floors, beamed ceilings and low lighting create just the right sort atmosphere, and in the Regency-furnished piano room a pianist plays from 8 o'clock on Saturday evenings. This room is available for private parties for up to 100. Lunchtime snacks are served in the lounge. Car parking at the rear. Arthur Quinn, a former golf club captain, is the hands-on proprietor of this convivial spot, which was formerly the Railway Hotel, established in 1890.

Local Golf Courses: Courtown, Arklow, Coollattin, Enniscorthy

HARBOUR HOUSE 623

Courtown Harbour, Gorey, Co Wexford
Tel/Fax: 055 25117

Harbour House is a family run guest house under the personal supervision of the O'Gorman family. It is ideally located just of the main Rosslare/Dublin N11 route in the renowned seaside resort of Courtown Harbour and is just four miles from Gorey. All 13 bedrooms are en suite and have tv, tea making facilities and hairdryer. Harbour House can also offer the self catering option in fully serviced, luxury mobile homes. There's plenty to do in the vicinity - golf, tenpin bowling, safe bathing, woodland walks - and in the evening there are restaurants, the theatre, Irish music, signing and discos.

Guest House, Self-Catering

Thirteen en suite B&B rooms plus self-catering in mobile homes

Credit Cards: All the major cards

Local Golf Courses: Courtown, Arklow, Coollattin, Woodenbridge

TARAVIE HOTEL 624

Courtown Harbour, Gorey, Co Wexford
Tel: 055 25208/25305

Ten en suite bedrooms in a family-run hotel on a corner site in the centre of the village, very close to the beach. The rooms are comfortable and well appointed, as are the day rooms, which comprise lounge, tv room, bar and restaurant. The last is open seven days a week for lunch and dinner; lunches are also served in the bar, and soup, sandwiches and light meals are served throughout the day. Local attractions include a Blue Flag beach, excellent fishing and Pirates Cove, a family entertainment venue with adventure, golf and tenpin bowling.

Hotel with Restaurant

Ten en suite bedrooms, tv. Restaurant and bar menus

Credit Cards: Mastercard, Visa

Local Golf Courses: Courtown, Arklow, Coollattin

THE CROSSES 625

Kilmuckridge, Gorey, Co Wexford
Tel: 053 30458

The Crosses is a modern (1985) free house in the centre of the village, due south of Gorey and two miles from the coast. It's a place of many attractions: sporting (pool and darts), musical (live music at the weekend) and, of course, food and drink. The inside is very roomy and comfortable, and visitors can enjoy good home-cooked food throughout the day. The 'pub grub' menu offers lunchtime snacks (barbecued chicken drumsticks, pasta with a beefy tomato sauce, mushrooms stuffed with cream cheese and garlic), generously filled sandwiches and 'for the hungry customer' the likes of lasagne, roasts, chicken curry and bacon with cabbage. Also 'kiddies corner' and lots of wicked desserts.

Restaurant and Bar

Food served all day. Open 11 in the morning to 11 at night

Credit Cards: All the major cards

Local Golf Courses: Courtown, Arklow, Coollattin, Enniscorthy

CLONARD HOUSE 626

Clonard Great, Wexford, Co Wexford
Tel/Fax: 053 43141
e-mail: clonardhouse@indigo.ie

John and Kathleen Hayes welcome guests to their handsome Georgian house set in parkland at the centre of a working dairy farm overlooking Wexford town and harbour. Built in 1783 by the Irish rebel leader William Hatton, it retains many of its original features, including the imposing eight-panel hall door, cornices and fireplaces. The grand stairway leads up to nine individually-styled bedrooms with en suite shower facilities and tv. Most have antique furniture, and six have four-poster beds. Wine licence. A real taste of country living with easy access to a town's amenities.

Farmhouse Bed & Breakfast

Ten en suite bedrooms with tv. Six rooms have four-posters

Credit Cards: None

Local Golf Courses: Rosslare, St Helen's Bay, Wexford

County Wexford

WOODLANDS HOUSE 627

Killinierin, Gorey, Co Wexford
Tel: 0402 37125 Fax: 0402 37133
e-mail: woodlnds@iol.ie

Philomena O'Sullivan offers six letting bedrooms in her handsome mid 19th-century residence off the N11 between Gorey (4 miles) and Arklow. The bedrooms, beautifully appointed and tastefully decorated in keeping with the civilised, traditional surroundings, all have tv, and three have balconies overlooking the award-winning gardens and the lovely countryside beyond. A full Irish breakfast starts the day and a five-course dinner is served at 7pm. On-site activities include tennis, table tennis (racquets and bats supplied) and a pool (full-size table). Tea and scones on arrival.

Country House B&B

Six en suite bedrooms with tv (3 with balconies). B&B; Dinner by arrangement
Credit Cards: None

Local Golf Courses: Courtown, Arklow, Coollattin, Woodenbridge

BALLINKEELE HOUSE 628

Ballymurn, Enniscorthy, Co Wexford
Tel: 053 38105 Fax: 053 38468
e-mail: info@ballinkeele.com   web: www.ballinkeele.com

Built in 1840 to a design of Daniel Robertson, John and Margaret Maher's distinguished country mansion with a striking pillared portico provides the most civilised and stylish base for a spell of relaxation. The whole place is pristine: original oils and prints hang on the walls, the furniture is very grand and the five en suite bedrooms (non-smoking) offer abundant space, comfort and character. Meals really are something to look forward to: Margaret is a fine cook, and her delicious dinners (book by noon) are served by candle-light in the lovely dining room. Croquet on the lawn. Fishing and riding nearby.

Country House B&B

Three double, two twin rooms with shower (1 bath) en suite. Dinner by arrangement. Croquet on the lawn.
Credit Cards: Mastercard, Visa

Local Golf Courses: Enniscorthy, New Ross, Wexford, Courtown

SLANEY MANOR 629

Ferrycarrig, Wexford, Co Wexford
Tel: 053 20051 Fax: 053 20510

Three miles west of Wexford, Slaney Manor has its entrance on the N25, near the junction with the N11. Built by the Percival family in the 1820s, it has retained all the characteristics of 19th-century affluent country living and, run by James and Esther Caulfield, it offers three types of overnight accommodation (all non-smoking): 15 Victorian-style rooms with four-posters in the main house, 25 high-quality courtyard rooms and a delightful one-bedroomed thatched, mud-walled cabin. All rooms have en suite facilities and tv; main-house rooms have telephones. Light meals and snacks, afternoon tea. Book for table d'hote dinner. Great views and exhilarating walks.

Country Manor Hotel

40 en suite bedrooms, tv, some with four-posters. Light meals, afternoon tea; dinner by arrangement
Credit Cards: All the major cards

Local Golf Courses: Wexford, Rosslare, St Helen's Bay

LEMONGROVE HOUSE 630

Blackstoops, Enniscorthy, Co Wexford
Tel: 054 36115

Colm and Ann McGibney's fine modern home is located at a roundabout on the N11 Rosslare-Dublin road less than a mile north of Enniscorthy. Built in the early 1990s with something of a continental look, it stands, along with several outbuildings, in an acre and a half of pleasant gardens. No detail has been overlooked in the decor and furnishings, and the nine en suite bedrooms are well equipped to provide a quiet, comfortable night's rest. Pugin's cathedral on the main street of Enniscorthy is a major local attraction, and a new leisure centre has opened near the house: thus mind and body are both looked after.

Bed and Breakfast

Nine rooms, all en suite, with tv. Off-road parking

Credit Cards: None

Local Golf Courses: Enniscorthy, Courtown, New Ross, Wexford

THE KILRANE INN 631

Kilrane, Co Wexford
Tel: 053 33661

Cheerfully painted in yellow and blue, this very appealing pub-restaurant stands on the main N25 just five minutes' drive from Rosslare Harbour and ferry port. Owned and run by Jim O'Donoghue and his family, it is the first and last pub in Ireland for those travelling to and from Britain and the Continent, and offers hospitality and good food in abundance. In the wood-floored bars, which have lots of intimate little corners, a wide range of drinks is served to accompany bar snacks and lunches. In the evening an extensive à la carte menu numbers salads, seafood and steaks among its specialities. Music and other live entertainment at the weekend. Beer garden.

Pub-Restaurant

Wide choice of drinks and food. Bar snacks, lunches, evening meals. Music at weekends
Credit Cards: Access, Visa

Local Golf Courses: Rosslare, St Helen's Bay, Wexford

DON CARR HOUSE 632

Bohreen Hill, Enniscorthy, Co Wexford
Tel: 054 33458

Ann Carroll's award-winning Bed and Breakfast establishment is a modern two-storey house in a quiet area off the N11 Dublin-Rosslare road. Overnight accommodation is offered in four comfortably appointed bedrooms. Two have en suite facilities and all have tv and tea/coffee making facilities. Private parking for motorists, and cyclists and walkers are very welcome. The River Slaney flows nearby. Enniscorthy, whose attractions include a leisure centre and the National 1798 Centre, is a five-minute walk away. Highlight of the Centre is a a dramatic audio-visual display simulating the Battle of Vinegar Hill.

Bed and Breakfast

Two en suite, two standard rooms, all with tv and tea/coffee facilities. Easy parking. Handy for town
Credit Cards: All the major cards

Local Golf Courses: Enniscorthy, New Ross, Wexford, Courtown

THE COURTYARD 636

Main Street, Ferns, Enniscorthy, Co Wexford
Tel: 054 66531 Fax: 054 66666

A top-class pub and bistro-style restaurant with plenty of off-road parking. The bar and lounge are spacious and smart (the whole place has recently been refurbished) and Dandy Pat's Bistro Restaurant, named in honour of Patrick Byrne offering an à la carte menu. It is particularly noted for its steak, which has a great local reputation. The Courtyard stands in a prominent position on the N11 in historic Ferns, halfway between Enniscorthy and Gorey. It won the Black & White (Newcomer) Pub of the Year Award for 1999. Open 11am to 11pm. Among the sights to see in Ferns are the Castle and the 12th-century Cathedral of St Aidan.

Pub and Restaurant

Bistro à la carte menu, carvery lunch and table d'hote menus for parties of 10 or more. Open all day.
Credit Cards: All the major cards

Local Golf Courses: Enniscorthy, New Ross, Wexford, Courtown

THE SAINT GEORGE GUEST HOUSE 637

George Street, Wexford, Co Wexford
Tel: 053 43474 Fax: 053 24814

John and Olive Doyle, with many years experience in the Bed & Breakfast business, assure guests of a warm welcome at The Saint George, a family-run guest house situated in the centre of Wexford close to shops, churches, restaurants and all the other amenities. The cream-painted brick building, on a prominent corner site, dates from 1846 and was originally home to the nuns who taught at the school which stood next door. Old-world charm aplenty survives, and the ten letting bedrooms are models of good taste. Recently refurbished, they all have bathrooms en suite, tv and telephone. Secure off-street parking.

Guest House

Ten Bed & Breakfast rooms, all en suite, with tv and telephone. Secure parking
Credit Cards:Access, Mastercard,Visa

Local Golf Courses: Wexford, Rosslare, St Helen's Bay

WOODVILLE FARM 638

Ballyhogue, Enniscorthy, Co Wexford
Tel: 054 47810 Fax: 054 47810

Four miles west of Enniscorthy off the N30 road to New Ross and 5 miles from the N11 lies Woodville Farm, a large farmhouse built in the late 19th century and in the ownership of the same family for 70 years. This is very much a working farm, and the current owner-farmer Peter Doyle is also a history buff and a great story-teller. Behind the frontage - distinctive with its complete covering of tightly knit creeper - the interior is classic Irish, relatively unadorned and very easy on the eye. Five en suite bedrooms offer flexible Bed and Breakfast accommodation. This is excellent walking country, and there's good fishing on the adjacent River Slaney.

Bed and Breakfast

Five en suite bedrooms. Large gardens & farm. Fishing

Credit Cards: None

Local Golf Courses: Enniscorthy, New Ross, Wexford, Rosslare

COURTS HOTEL & FARMERS KITCHEN 639

Rosslare Road, Drinagh, Wexford, Co Wexford
Tel: 053 43295 Fax: 053 45827 e-mail: info@farmerskitchen.com
website: www.farmerskitchen.com

A high-class roadhouse hotel 100 yards from a roundabout on the N25 two miles south of Wexford town centre. Daniel Finnerty's hotel has 21 bedrooms designed with comfort in mind and offers a choice of single, twin/double and triple occupancy. All rooms have en suite facilities, tv and telephone. The 120-seat Farmer's Kitchen Lounge Bar and Restaurant provides guests and non-residents with an extensive menu that is available daily from 12.30 to 10 o'clock. Irene Scallan's Bar is the relaxed setting for regular traditional music sessions, and there's a function room with private bar facilities.

Hotel with Restaurant and Bar

21 en suite bedrooms with tv, telephone. All-day restaurant, bar with traditional music sessions
Credit Cards: All the major cards

Local Golf Courses: Wexford, Rosslare, Enniscorthy

FAYTHE HOUSE 640

Swan View, The Faythe, Wexford, Co Wexford
Tel: 053 22249 Fax: 053 21680 e-mail: faythehse@iol.ie
web: www.iol.ie/~faythhse

Turn right and then left after the Talbot Hotel to find Faythe House, Wexford's oldest Bed & Breakfast guest house. Set back from the road in a quiet part of the old town, the building dates from 1827; it's run by Damian Lynch, who has a lifetime's experience in the hotel business. Ten letting bedrooms, all recently refurbished, provide very comfortable, well-equipped overnight accommodation. All rooms have en suite facilities (most with both bath and shower), tv, telephone and hairdryer. Some rooms enjoy fine views of Wexford Harbour, others overlook the flower and vegetable garden. Large private car park.

Bed & Breakfast Guest House

Ten bedrooms with en suite facilities, tv, telephone. Some with harbour views. Large car park
Credit Cards: Mastercard, Visa

Local Golf Courses: Wexford, Rosslare, St Helen's Bay

THE OAK TAVERN 641

Ferrycarrig, Co Wexford
Tel: 053 20922 Fax: 053 20945

The O'Reilly family provide the warmest of greetings and the best of traditional Irish cooking at their 150-year-old tavern beside Ireland's National Heritage Centre and Park. The setting, on the banks of the picturesque River Slaney, is a great asset, and when the weather is fine, riverbank dining is a pure delight. Inside, the bars are bright, warm and welcoming, with a wealth of sporting memorabilia. Bar food is available all day, supplementing morning brunch, a lunch menu from 12.30 and an evening à la carte served in the restaurant from 5.30. Wexford is a very easy drive away.

Tavern & Restaurant

Traditional Irish food served every day all year round in a riverside location
Credit Cards: All the major cards

Local Golf Courses: Wexford, Rosslare, St Helen's Bay

OLDCOURT HOUSE | 642

Rosslare Harbour, Co Wexford
Tel: 053 33895

Built in 1996 in classical style, with a smart black-and-white painted facade. The house is situated in the village of Rosslare Harbour overlooking the bay and is adjacent to beaches and the ferry port. Proprietress Mary McDonald is a keen and accomplished golfer who looks forward to welcoming other enthusiasts to her home. With six large en suite bedrooms, it is an ideal base for small golf parties and also for touring this delightful part of the country. The lounge is made for relaxation, and an early breakfast can be served in the handsome dining room for crack-of-dawn tee-off. Private car park.

Bed & Breakfast

Six en suite rooms with tv. Private car park

Credit Cards: Mastercard, Visa

Local Golf Courses: Rosslare, St Helen's Bay, Wexford

CORAL GABLES | 643

Tagoat, Rosslare Harbour, Co Wexford
Tel: 053 31213 Fax: 053 31414
e-mail: coralgables@eircom.net

An ultra-modern three-storey B&B guest house with a striking, steeply-raked roof. Situated on a hilltop overlooking the Wexford-Rosslare road, Sarah Haslam's Coral Gables provides the perfect stopover for visitors arriving or departing through Rosslare port. It's also a fine base for exploring the heritage and scenery of Wexford or for a golfing holiday. The 15 letting bedrooms offer great comfort and considerable luxury; all have en suite facilities, seven boast verandas and all have tv and telephone. Day rooms include a tv lounge. Early morning breakfast available (for non-residents also). Private car park. Competitive group rates.

Guest House

15 B&B bedrooms, all en suite, 7 with verandas. Tv, Telephones.

Credit Cards: Mastercard, Visa

Local Golf Courses: Rosslare, St Helen's Bay, Wexford

THE OYSTER | 644

Rosslare Strand, Co Wexford
Tel: 053 32439

The Oyster, a charming little seafood restaurant in the heart of one of Ireland's favourite seaside resorts, is certainly one of the best of its kind in the region. Specialities include Bannow Bay oysters, Rosslare smokies, Slaney salmon, black sole and several mouthwatering ways with prawns and crab landed daily at Kilmore Quay and Dunmore East. Owner Jimmy Delaney has many other fish to fry: he owns the pitch & putt and is a great proponent of all types of sporting activities (golf included, of course!).

Restaurant

Fully licensed restaurant specialising in local seafood

Credit Cards: Access, Visa

Local Golf Courses: Wexford, St Helens Bay, Rosslare

PJ MURPHYS | 645

9 Main Street, Enniscorthy, Co Wexford
Tel: 054 33522/37837

The location is one of the very best in the whole of Enniscorthy, opposite the Cathedral in the main street. P J Murphys has two hats, one as a Bed & Breakfast place, the other as a pub. The flexible overnight accommodation consists of eight bedrooms with their own entrance next to the pub entrance. Both the bedrooms and the pub are looking very smart after a recent top-to-toe refurbishment programme. The pub is a lively, welcoming spot to drop into after a round of golf or visiting the many places of interest in and around the town. Owner Maura Murphy has been here for 33 years.

Bed and Breakfast, Pub

Eight bedrooms for B&B; in the same building as a pub

Credit Cards: None

Local Golf Courses: Enniscorthy, Courtown, Wexford, New Ross

County Wexford

O'LEARY'S FARMHOUSE 646

Kilrane, Rosslare Harbour, Co Wexford
Tel: 053 33134

A modern home overlooking the sea with 9 letting bedrooms (7 en suite) on a farm. Guests have the perfect chance to sample the simple, delightful life of an Irish farmhouse. The decor is both warm and unadorned, with great care taken to keep things uncomplicated and unpretentious, and the welcome guests receive will not soon be forgotten.

Alternatively, guests can opt for self-catering accommodation in a cottage beside the main house, which is only a mile away from St Helen's Bay Golf Club.

Bed & Breakfast, Self-Catering

Nine bedrooms, 7 of which are en suite bedrooms, on a working farm. Tv. Also self-catering cottage
Credit Cards: None

Local Golf Courses: St Helen's Bay, Rosslare, Wexford

BALLYCOWAN LODGE 647

Tagoat, Rosslare Harbour, Co Wexford
Tel/Fax: 053 31596

1999 was the first Bed & Breakfast season for John and Catherine McHugh at their handsome new detached house in the village of Tagoat, 150 metres from the N25 and only five minutes' drive from Rosslare Ferryport. The whole place is spick and span, bright and welcoming, and the four letting bedrooms, two singles and two twins, all with en suite facilities and tv, enjoy attractive views. There's good secure off-road parking, and the house is an excellent base for touring, golf and fishing. It's also conveniently located for miles of safe, sandy beaches, and there are a number of good restaurants in the vicinity.

Bed & Breakfast

Four en suite bedrooms, tv. Private car parking

Credit Cards: None

Local Golf Courses: St Helen's Bay, Rosslare, Wexford

AILSA LODGE 648

Rosslare Harbour, Co Wexford
Tel: 053 33230 Fax: 053 33581
e-mail: ailsalodge@eircom.ie

Dominic Sheil's premier guest house is an imposing mid-Victorian residence extended and modernised but still retaining many superb features, including a fine hallway and inviting residents' lounge. The ten letting bedrooms are on a grand scale, and many of the en suite bathrooms have both bath and shower. All rooms have tv and telephone. The house occupies an elevated site overlooking Rosslare harbour, and the majority of the rooms enjoy sea views. Two acres of grounds provide a peaceful, scenic setting, and there's plenty of parking space.

Country Guest House

Ten en suite Bed & Breakfast rooms with tv and telephone. Period appeal. Sea views
Credit Cards: Mastercard, Visa

Local Golf Courses: St Helen's Bay, Rosslare, Wexford

THE SILVER FOX 649

Kilmore Quay, Co Wexford
Tel: 053 29888

Look for the signs to Kilmore Quay on the main Wexford-Rosslare road (N25) and take the R739 to the village centre and the red-painted Silver Fox. Rena and Nick Cullen have built up a big reputation at their bright, cheerful seafood restaurant with 100 covers, where most of the produce that makes up the mouthwatering menus is caught locally and landed just yards from the front door. Everything is recommended, but the house special should definitely not be missed: fillets of lemon sole grilled and served with a trio of tasty sauces - prawns, mushrooms and cheese. Classical guitar music make a classy accompaniment during the week.

Restaurant

100-cover seafood restaurant with wine licence and classical guitar music
Credit Cards: Amex, Mastercard, Visa

Local Golf Courses: St Helen's Bay, Rosslare, Waterford

Bed, Breakfast & Dinner

Eight en suite bedrooms in a modern bungalow. Evening meals by arrangement

Credit Cards: Mastercard, Visa

GLENDOWER HOUSE 650

Portersland, Wexford Road, New Ross, Co Wexford
Tel/Fax: 051 421989
e-mail: glendower@indigo.ie

Margaret Bennett's handsome modern single-storey house lies off the main road into town from Wexford and Rosslare (N25). An owner who relates very well to golfers (and to all other guests!), she offers superior overnight accommodation in eight good-sized bedrooms with en suite facilities and tv. Margaret very much enjoys cooking, and her evening meals are a treat not to be missed, the equal of most top restaurants. Value for money is excellent, and she hopes to expand on what is already a comprehensive and very tempting dinner menu. Private parking.

Local Golf Courses: New Ross, Mount Juliet, Faithlegg

Bed & Breakfast, Self-Catering

En suite bedrooms with tv plus self-catering accommodation

Credit Cards: None

ARTHUR'S REST 651

Arthurstown, Co Wexford
Tel: 051 389192 Fax: 051 389362
e-mail: arthursrest@hotmail.com

Peggy Murphy offers a choice of accommodation (B&B or self-catering) for up to 16 guests. Bed & Breakfast rooms in the main house are all en suite, with tv, while in the stone-built house opposite ('The Loft') there are three bedrooms and two bathrooms for self-catering stays. The location is ideal as a base for touring the sights of the South-East, which include the Kennedy Memorial Park and Arboretum, Dunbrody Abbey and Hook Lighthouse. The local car ferry at Ballyhack plies across the estuary to County Waterford.

Local Golf Courses: New Ross, Mount Juliet, Faithlegg

Bed & Breakfast

Five en suite bedrooms - 1 single, 1 double, 3 twin rooms. Large grounds with wildlife

Credit Cards: All the major cards

BALLYBRO LODGE 652

Tagoat, Rosslare, Co Wexford
Tel/Fax: 053 32333
e-mail: ballybrolodge@oceanfree.net

Three and a half acres of landscaped gardens and pasture are the setting for Ballybro Lodge.Home to a wide variety of wildlife - 28 species of bird were spotted last year. The lodge, a large detached house, is owned and run by Susan and Eric Stewart, a golfing couple who offer five en suite letting bedrooms. Each room has tea/coffee making facilities. There's a guest lounge for relaxing to read or watch tv. Breakfast is served from 7.30 for early-bird golfers or guests with an early ferry to catch. Nearby attractions include a riding school at Ballyhealey Beach and boat hire at Kilmore Quay Pier for diving and sea fishing.

Local Golf Courses: Rosslare, Wexford, St Helen's Bay

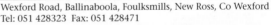

Hotel with Restaurant and Bar

12 en suite bedrooms, tv, telephone. Licensed restaurant and bar

Credit Cards: All the major cards

THE HORSE & HOUND 653

Wexford Road, Ballinaboola, Foulksmills, New Ross, Co Wexford
Tel: 051 428323 Fax: 051 428471

A friendly family-run hotel in a small crossroads village on the N25 from Rosslare. The Murphy family extend a warm welcome to guests, who will find very comfortable overnight accommodation in 12 bright en suite bedrooms with tv and telephone. The cocktail bar is a good spot to relax over a drink with friends, and the 30-cover restaurant is well known for its excellent food, service and atmosphere. Entertainment is provided in the cabaret lounge, where leading Irish artists regularly perform. Easy parking. Local sights include the Kennedy Memorial Park and Arboretum.

Local Golf Courses: New Ross, Mount Juliet, Faithlegg

County Wexford

Farmhouse B&B

5 large en suite bedrooms. Working farm. Tennis

Credit Cards: Visa, Mastercard

BALLYKILTY FARMHOUSE 660

Coolgreany, Arklow, Co Wicklow
Tel: 0402 37111 Fax: 0402 37272
e-mail: ballykiltyfarmhouse@eircom.net

Three miles out of Arklow off the N11 Dublin-Wexford road, Ballykilty Farmhouse is a substantial early 18th-century building set in extensive mature gardens on a 200-acre working dairy farm. Anne Nuzum and her sons keep the place in immaculate condition, and the house has many delightful features. Bed & Breakfast accommodation comprises five spacious, beautifully decorated bedrooms - two doubles, two twins and a triple. Sandy beaches, horse riding, pony trekking, golf and fishing are available nearby, and there are many places of interest to visit, including the Maritime Museum in Arklow and the Beit Art Collection in Russborough House, Blessington.

Local Golf Courses: Arklow, European, Blainroe, Woodenbridge

Bed & Breakfast

Three pristine bedrooms, 2 en suite. B&B and packed lunches

Credit Cards: None

HIGHFIELD HOUSE 661

Woodenbridge, Arklow, Co Wicklow
Tel: 0402 35262

Joe and Muriel Steadman are the owners of Highfield House, a large modern farmhouse at Woodenbridge, a short drive west of Arklow. Joe farms the land, while Muriel looks after the Bed & Breakfast side of the business. The three bedrooms, two en suite, the other with a private bathroom not en suite, are, like the rest of the house, kept in immaculate condition; all have tvs, and two have their own balconies. There are facilities for making tea or coffee in the comfortable, relaxing lounge, and packed lunches can be provided. The house is in sight of Woodenbridge Golf Club and the local places of interest include Avoca, where the BBC series Ballykissangel was filmed.

Local Golf Courses: Arklow, Woodenbridge, European, Glenmalure

Bar, Restaurant, Self-Catering

Bar with full restaurant menu. Also self-catering accommodation

Credit Cards: Access, Mastercard, Visa

MURPHY'S BAR & RESTAURANT 662

49 Main Street, Arklow, Co Wicklow
Tel/Fax: 0402 32781

Brian and Joan Murphy run this bright, spacious, well-appointed bar and restaurant on the main street of Arklow. Large, comfortable chairs set at sturdy tables invite visitors to stay for a meal, and the menu is full of good things, both traditional and more unusual. Grilled sole, roast lamb and fillet steak typify the former, while the more adventurous could plump for steamed fillets of red snapper served with a pesto and tarragon bouillabaisse, or pan-fried escalopes of ostrich served with a risotto of wild mushrooms and saffron tagliatelle. The owners also offer self-catering accommodation nearby.

Local Golf Courses: Arklow, Woodenbridge, European, Courtown

Riverside Pub and Restaurant

Pub with beer garden and neighbouring Greek restaurant

Credit Cards: Access, Mastercard, Visa

THE AVOCA INN & GREEK VINE BISTRO 663

Avoca, Co Wicklow
Tel: 0402 35774 Fax: 0402 35858

In a delightful setting by a bridge over the River Avoca, this is a winning combination of traditional Irish pub and charming Greek restaurant run by Michael and Carley Charalambous. The pub has plenty of entertainment - pool table, gaming machines, darts - and a beer garden by the river that comes into its own in the summer. Visitors curious to see the familiar locations of BallyK can refresh themselves here and enjoy a splendid meal from the Greek-European menu in the 90-cover restaurant. The menus provide plenty of variety, and there's an extensive wine list. Open from noon till 11.30pm.

Local Golf Courses: Arklow, Woodenbridge, European, Glenmalure

THE BEEHIVE `664`

Coolbeg Cross, N11 Wexford Road, Co Wicklow
Tel: 0404 69745
e-mail: beehive@iol.ie

On the N11 halfway between Rosslare and Dublin, The Beehive is pub, restaurant and B&B all in one. Under the new management of hardworking AB and Mary Costelloe, it offers five en suite bedrooms - singles, twins or doubles - for guests staying overnight. There are two bars, a pool room and a restaurant where quality food is served daily. A carvery operates from 12.30, and the main menu runs from chicken liver paté with Cumberland sauce and trout salad to vegetable lasagne, gammon steak or a chef's special of honey-roast duckling with traditional orange sauce.

Pub, Restaurant and B&B

5 letting bedrooms, all en suite. Bars and restaurant

Credit Cards: Access, Mastercard, Visa

Local Golf Courses: Arklow, Woodenbridge, European, Courtown

LA TOUCHE HOTEL `665`

Trafalgar Road, Greystones, Co Wicklow
Tel: 01287 4401 Fax: 01287 4504
e-mail: enquiries@latouche.net website: www.latouche.net

Comfort, convenience and true Irish hospitality combine in the 29-room La Touche Hotel, which has a superb location on the beautiful east coast overlooking the sea. All the rooms are en suite, with remote-control tv and phone. The Captain's Lounge Bar, with sea views and a bar menu, is a favourite meeting place. Bennigan's Bar has regular live entertainment and a big tv screen for sports events, and away from the main hotel building Club Life is the place for partying the night away with resident DJs and regular theme weekends.

Hotel, Restaurant and Bars

29-room hotel by the sea. Restaurant and bars

Credit Cards: All the major cards

Local Golf Courses: Druids Glen, Powerscourt, Glen of the Downs

OSTAN BEAG HOTEL `666`

Main Street, Arklow, Co Wicklow
Tel: 0402 33044 Fax: 0402 33060

At the heart of a bustling port town, Ostan Beag - the little hotel - is a cheerful, welcoming place to stay. Twenty elegant en suite bedrooms with tv and telephone provide a very comfortable night's rest, and day rooms comprise two lively bars, top-class food service and the vibrant Tunnel nightclub, where 'the pace is frantic, the music brilliant and the lighting effects spectacular'. Just the thing after a day on the golf course! The beach is a great attraction, of course, as well as the Maritime Museum, and the Vale of Avoca is just a stone's throw away.

Hotel, Restaurant & Nightclub

20 en suite rooms, two bars, restaurant and nightclub.

Credit Cards: Access, Mastercard, Visa

Local Golf Courses: Arklow, Woodenbridge, European, Courtown

WOODLAND COURT HOTEL `667`

Southern Cross, Bray, Co Wicklow
Tel: 01 276 0258 Fax: 021 276 0298

The Woodland Court Hotel, with sixty-five superior bedrooms furnished and equipped to the highest standards, offers the discerning traveller an excellent standard of accommodation and service which will make a visit to Ireland a truly memorable experience. Situated just off the M11 in 2 acres of private grounds the hotel is surrounded by a selection of the worlds finest golf courses to suit every budget. Food is served from 7.30 am daily in the "Green Room" and the lobby bar is the ideal place to relax and unwind. With Dublin city centre just 12 miles away the Woodland Court Hotel is the ideal base for your next visit to County Wicklow.

Country Hotel with Restaurant

65 superbly equipped en suite bedrooms; lounge and restaurant

Credit Cards: All the major cards

Local Golf Courses: Woodbrook, Powerscourt, Old Conna, Druids Glen

County Wicklow

County Wicklow

SUMMERHILL HOUSE HOTEL 668

Enniskerry, Co Wicklow
Tel: 01 286 7928 Fax: 01 286 7929

Ideally situated in one of the most scenically attractive parts of Ireland this friendly country house hotel is a perfect base for holidaymakers and sportsmen alike. Accommodation comprises 57 en suite bedrooms, all bright and tastefully furnished with tv, tea/coffee making facilities, telephone and hairdryer. The Copper Beech Lounge is a good place to unwind and relax, and there is excellent fare served nightly in the courtyard restaurant. The Summerhill House is a sister hotel to the Woodland Court Hotel, Bray and is situated opposite the world famous Powerscourt House and Championship golf course and just 12 miles from Dublin city centre.

Country Hotel, Bar, Restaurant

57 en suite bedrooms with tv and phone; bar and restaurant

Credit Cards: Access, Visa, Amex

Local Golf Courses: Woodbrook, Powerscourt, Old Conna,Druids Glen

CARRAIG HOUSE 669

The Harbour, Greystones, Co Wicklow
Tel: 01 287 3273

Kath and Frank Ryan run the most delightful Bed & Breakfast business in their sturdy 160-year-old house, the first two-storey residence to be built in this charming seaside village on the popular eastern coast below Dublin. They have four letting bedrooms for B&B, with tv and tea-makers, and a separate mews-style self-catering facility which can sleep up to four. The sea views are naturally superb, there's plenty of opportunity for fishing and the Blue Flag beach is great for frolicking in the summer. This is also great walking country, and there are many golf courses an easy drive away.

Bed & Breakfast , Self-Catering

4 bedrooms, tvs, tea and coffee making facilites, seperate self catering mews property

Credit Cards: None

Local Golf Courses: Charlesland, Druid's Glen, Glen of the Downs

DRUID'S HOUSE 670

Kilmacullagh, Newtownmountkennedy, Co Wicklow
Tel: 01 281 9477

Catherine Tierney, three years in the Bed & Breakfast business, has a regular golfing clientele and looks forward to welcoming more golfers to her fine modern house set among stepped gardens on an elevated site off a drive. She has three recently refurbished letting bedrooms, all with tv and tea-makers, and besides a good Irish breakfast she can provide packed lunches for guests planning a day walking, touring or playing a round on one of the many local golf courses (Druid's Glen is within walking distance). The village sits in the shadow of the Wicklow Mountains, so the house is a great base for exploring the superb scenery that County Wicklow has to offer.

Bed & Breakfast

Three rooms with tv; B&B + packed lunches

Credit Cards: None

Local Golf Courses: Druid's Glen, Roundwood, Glen of the Downs

THE COACH HOUSE 671

Roundwood, Co Wicklow
Tel: 01 281 8157 Fax: 01 281 8449
e-mail: thecoachhouse@eircom.net

A small country inn which has grown considerably from its origins in the 1820s. Behind the smart black-and-white frontage there's a winning mix of traditional and modern in the bars, restaurant and function room. The fourteen bedrooms are tastefully designed, with en suite facilities and satellite tv. It's a very sociable place, with darts played in the bars, and traditional Irish music and ballads most nights of the week. There's a pleasant beer garden. Roundwood is a wonderful hill-walking area with breathtaking mountain scenery and woodlands waiting to be explored. The Coach House can organise guides.

Country Inn, Accommodation

14 en suite bedrooms with tv; bars and restaurant

Credit Cards: All the major cards

Local Golf Courses: Druid's Glen, Roundwood, Delgany

DERRYBAWN MOUNTAIN LODGE `672`

Derrybawn, Laragh, Co Wicklow
Tel: 0404 45644 Fax: 0404 45645
website: derrybawnlodge@eircom.net

A magnificent modern lodge in an equally magnificent setting two miles south of Laragh village at the foot of Derrybawn Mountain. Teresa Kavanagh offers overnight comfort and luxury in eight superb en suite bedrooms with tv, tea/coffee facilities, hairdryer and DD phone; there are extensive menus for breakfast and dinner, plus packed lunches on request. A perfect base for walkers, climbers, golfers and tourists. A nearby place of great interest is the seven churches and monastic ruins at Glenalough, one of Ireland's most important spiritual sites; next to it is the Wicklow Mountains National Park Visitor Centre.

Mountain Lodge

Eight en suite bedrooms, B&B + dinner

Credit Cards: All the major cards

Local Golf Courses: Glenmalure, Delgany, Druid's Glen, Roundwood

KEPPEL'S FARMHOUSE `673`

Avoca, Co Wicklow
Tel/Fax: 0402 35168

Joy and Charles Keppel's 19th-century farmhouse stands near the village of Avoca, brought into prominence as the setting for the BBC series Ballykissangel. They offer Bed & Breakfast accommodation in five non-smoking bedrooms with en suite showers, tv, tea-makers and hairdryers. An alternative to the B&B is a recently refurbished bungalow with three bedrooms (double, twin and bunk room), living room with an open fireplace, fully fitted kitchen, bathroom and utility room. Fitzgerald's Pub is just a short walk away, and there are many other places to visit, including the famous Avoca Handweavers.

B & B, also Self-Catering

5 non-smoking bedrooms for B&B and self-catering bungalow

Credit Cards: None

Local Golf Courses: Arklow, Woodenbridge, European, Glenmalure

County Wicklow

This page is intentionally blank

Accommodation, Food and Drink

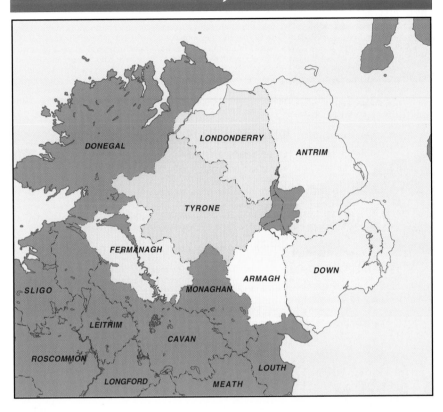

Contents - Northern Ireland

County Antrim

CALDHAME HOUSE   800

104 Moira Road, Nutts Corner, Crumlin, Co Antrim
Tel/Fax: 028 9442 2378

A splendid, comfortably appointed country house on the road between Nutts Corner and the Moira Roundabout, with Belfast International Airport just a few minutes' drive away. Owned and personally run by Amelia McKavanagh, the house has a lovely peaceful atmosphere, and the bedrooms, all en suite with tv and trouser press, offer a high standard of overnight accommodation. The place is well known in golfing circles and is in easy reach of several top courses. Every aspect of a golfing holiday is catered for, including tee-time reservations and a club-cleaning service. Ample private parking.

Bed & Breakfast

En suite bedrooms with tv. Private parking. Handy for Belfast Airport

Credit Cards: Visa, Mastercard

Local Golf Courses: Allan Park, Massereene, Hilton Templepatrick

GLENMORE HOUSE   801

Whitepark Road, Ballycastle, Co Antrim
Tel/Fax: 02820 763548
e-mail: glenmore_house3@lineone.net

A large purpose-built country house hotel whose location 2½ miles from Ballycastle on the B15 Ballintoy road affords superb views of the Antrim coast and the Atlantic. John and Valerie Brown offer high-quality accommodation within easy reach of some of the top golf courses in Northern Ireland. Every aspect of a golfing holiday is catered for, including reservations and a club cleaning service. All the bedrooms have en suite facilities and tvs. The restaurant is open to non-residents and there's a comfortable bar. Guests can enjoy a spot of trout fishing on a lake in the grounds. Plentiful parking.

Country House Hotel

All rooms en suite, tv, telephone. Fishing

Credit Cards: Visa, Euro, Mastercard

Local Golf Courses: Ballycastle, Portstewart, Royal Portrush, Gracehill

BROOKHAVEN   802

99 Coleraine Road, Portrush, Co Antrim
Tel: 02870 824164

Genuine hospitality is second nature to Trelford and Denise Coates, and in their white-painted country house on the main Portrush-Coleraine road guests can look forward to a friendly welcome and a relaxing break from the usual routine. The bedrooms are beautifully decorated and comfortably furnished, and there are spacious gardens for guests to stroll in. There is a superb choice of local golf courses - Royal Portrush is only a five-minute drive away.

Bed & Breakfast

2 twin and 1 double en suite. Guest tv lounge.

Credit Cards: None

Local Golf Courses: Ballycastle, Portstewart, Royal Portrush

ANTRIM ARMS   803

75 Castle Street, Ballycastle, Co Antrim
Tel: 028 2076 2284

Good food, good beer and good times in one of Ireland's oldest hostelries, dating back to 1767. The old-world feel is allied to modern comforts, and the bedrooms, all en suite, are well furnished and decorated. An open fire blazes a welcome in the bar, where a wide selection of ales, wines and spirits is served. Full Irish breakfast, lunch, bar snacks, high tea, à la carte suppers. Restaurant open to non-residents. A good base for touring a lovely part of the world.

Inn, Hotel & Restaurant

All rooms en suite, tv. Snacks and full menus

Credit Cards:

Local Golf Courses: Ballycastle, Portstewart, Royal Portrush

CLARMONT — 804

10 Lansdowne Crescent, Portrush, Co Antrim
Tel/Fax: 02870 822397
e-mail: clarmont@talk21.com

In a dignified terrace at the northern end of Portrush, Clarmont offers a real home from home in civilised, congenial surroundings. All the bedrooms at this beautifully kept three-storey town house have en suite facilities, and from the patio seating area there are super views out onto the Atlantic Ocean. Royal Portrush Golf Club is also in view, one of several leading courses within easy reach.

Bed & Breakfast

All rooms en suite. Tv.

Credit Cards: Visa, Mastercard

Local Golf Courses: Ballycastle, Portstewart, Royal Portrush

THE SKERRYS INN — 805

12 Old Cushendun Road, Newtowncrommelin, Ballymena,
Co Antrim
Tel: 02821 758669

The Skerrys Inn is a long, low building in a small village with a big name, off the A43 about 12 miles north of Ballymena. Third generation owner Eamon McKeown offers a real taste of Irish hospitality and his in is the perfect place to relax after a day on the fairways. An open fire warms the convivial bar, where the regulars play darts and pool, and listen to traditional Irish music on Wednesday to Saturday nights. Good selection of ales, wines and spirits. Bar food. Courtyard parking at the rear.

Country Inn

Traditional ales. Tv room, darts, pool, live music Wed-Sat. Bar food

Credit Cards: None

Local Golf Courses: Ballycastle, Ballymena

THE 5 CORNERS INN — 806

249 Rashee Road, Ballyclare, Co Antrim
Tel: 028 9332 2657 Fax:028 9334 9769
e-mail: max.max@virgin.net

A white stone building that's easy to spot on the B59 Ballyclare-Ballymena road about 10 minutes' drive from the centre of Ballyclare. The spacious bedrooms, all en suite, have tvs and telephones. The lounge area is the scene of regular live entertainment, and there's a separate games area. Excellent home cooking, with a wide choice that includes children's and vegetarian menus. All the usual golfing services are offered. The last tee of the local golf club is only a short chip away, and other sports amenities nearby include fishing, swimming and riding.

Guest Inn & Restaurant

All rooms en suite. Tv, telephone. Full restaurant menu

Credit Cards: All the major cards

Local Golf Courses: Ballyclare, Greenacres, Massereene

GALGORM — 807

117 Eglinton Street, Portrush, Co Antrim BT56 8DZ
Tel: 02870 823787

Only a five-minute walk from the town centre , Ann and Drew Semple's handily placed town house (take the one-way system for the town past the fire station and its the first house on the right) attracts many return visitors with its warm, easygoing atmosphere and excellent accommodation: the 12 en suite bedrooms are decorated and appointed to a very high standard. Drew is a keen golfer and always has time for a chat and to give advice about the local courses. The house overlooks the Strand and is central to both the bus and train terminals.

Bed & Breakfast

12 rooms, all en suite. Tv. Tea and Coffee on request.

Credit Cards: All the major cards

Local Golf Courses: Ballycastle, Portstewart, Royal Portrush

FULLERTON ARMS | 808

22-24 Main Street, Ballintoy, Ballycastle, Co Antrim
Tel: 02820 769613

A real home from home, where Les and Ann Taggart put out the welcome mat. The 19th-century building, a little way inland from picturesque Ballintoy harbour, has been extensively renovated and modernised to house 11 en suite bedrooms, a lively bar with a traditional Irish theme and a sumptuous restaurant that's open to non-residents. Extensive choice includes vegetarian and children's menus. A beer garden and barbecue facilities are at the back of the premises. Private parking. Bookings fo local courses; transport can be arranged.

Guest House and Restaurant

11 rooms all en suite. Tv. Irish-theme bar. Licensed restaurant. Private parking
Credit Cards: All the major cards

Local Golf Courses: Ballycastle, Portstewart, Royal Portrush, Gracehill

---

CRAIG PARK COUNTRY HOUSE | 809

24 Carnbore Road, Bushmills, Co Antrim BT57 8YF
Tel: 028 207 32496 Fax: 028 207 32479
e-mail: jan@craigpark.co.uk web: www.craigpark.co.uk

Jan and David Cheal have a lovely large "Georgian style" country house Bed and Breakfast just two miles from Bushmills. The three large guest bedrooms all have en suite facilities, tv and telephone. The breakfasts are both generous and splendid, and Jan and David are more than happy to tell their guests about the local golf courses and the many scenic and historic delights in the area, including the Old Bushmills Distillery, Dunluce Castle and the Giant's Causeway. The house itself enjoys distant views of the mountains of Donegal and the Antrim Hills. No smoking.

Bed and Breakfast

3 bedrooms, all ensuite, tv, telephone, no smoking

Credit Cards: Visa, Mastercard

Local Golf Courses: Gracehill, Ballycastle, Royal Portrush

THE GLENSWAY TAVERN | 810

67 Glenravel Road, Martinstown, Ballymena, Co Antrim
Tel/Fax: 02821 758534

A cheerful and popular village tavern on the main road (B45) from Ballymena to Cushendall. The white-painted tavern, with flower baskets outside and comfortable seating within, has a very warm atmosphere that has made it a favourite with the locals, who drop in for a chat, a cool Guinness and a bar snack. Colm McGlade, who owns and runs the inn with his wife Anne, is a keen golfer who is more than happy to help plan golfing tours and can guide his guests to some of the best courses in Antrim. Parking spaces at the front.

Village Inn

Happy ambience. Wide range of drinks. Golfing owner

Credit Cards: None

Local Golf Courses: Ballyclare, Ballymena, Galgorm Castle

TULLY BED & BREAKFAST | 811

102 Moorfields, Ballymena, Co Antrim
Tel: 02825 646088

Two acres of lawns make an attractive, secluded setting for a large hacienda-style house just off the A36 Ballymena-Larne road. The bedrooms are all en suite, with tvs, and Tully has the unusual amenity of a snooker room with a full-size table. A good base for golfers, tourists and anyone looking for a spot to relax in perfect peace. Owner Kate McAllister is happy to give guests a lift to local restaurants - but they have to find their own way back!

Bed & Breakfast

All rooms en suite. Snooker. Extensive gardens. Easy parking

Credit Cards: None

Local Golf Courses: Ballyclare, Ballymena, Galgorm Castle

THE KILBRONEY 830

31 Church Street, Rostrevor, Co Down
Tel: 028 417 38390 Fax: 028 302 67035

With its long opening hours (11.30am to 11pm), The Kilbroney can refresh visitors with food and drink seven days a week. It comprises restaurant, bar and beer garden, and lies handily in the centre of town. Rostrevor is on the A2, with the fishing port of Kilkeel to the east and the important commercial town of Newry on the Armagh border to the west. A little way north, the Mountains of Mourne beckon with their usually gentle slopes criss-crossed by ancient paths and great for walking or climbing - just the thing to build up an appetite for a visit to The Kilbroney.

Restaurant and Bar

Restaurant & bar; food and drink served all day, every day

Credit Cards: Access, Mastercard, Visa

Local Golf Courses: Warrenpoint, Newry, Ashfield, Kilkeel

DENVIR'S HOTEL 831

14-16 English Street, Downpatrick, Co Down
Tel: 02844 612012 Fax: 02844 617002

Ronnie Martin and Colin Magowan are partners in this centrally located hotel, which has recently been renovated to preserve the period feel of a building that dates back to 1642. Eight comfortable, cosy bedrooms, all of them en suite, cater for overnight guests, while the inner man will find satisfaction in the restaurant: food is an important attraction here, and only the freshest of local produce - fish, meat and vegetables - finds its way into the kitchen for the outstanding menus. The hotel has an enviable location close to the Cathedral, Museum, Courthouse and Heritage Centre. St Patrick's grave is a 2-minute walk away.

Hotel with Restaurant

8 en suite bedrooms; restaurant; central location

Credit Cards: No information

Local Golf Courses: Downpatrick, Bright Castle, Ringdufferin

THE OLD CROSS INN 832

4 Castle Place, Newtownards, Co Down
Tel: 028 9182 0212

Good food and friendly service are by-words at the Old Cross Inn, the oldest pub-restaurant in town and one of the best in the region. Lunches are served daily, and the bistro menu is available Monday to Saturday evening and all day Sunday till 7.30. The choice is excellent, with a range of starters followed by meat, fish, pasta and salad main courses, and a good selection of vegetarian dishes. In addition to the main menu, visitors could be tempted by the Tea Time Specials, a select choice of tasty snacks. Late licence every Friday and Saturday.

Pub and Restaurant

Pub with restaurant; food served lunch and evening + all day Sunday

Credit Cards:

Local Golf Courses: Scrabo, Bangor, Blackwood, Clandeboye

SEVEN STARS RESTAURANT 833

4 Main Street, Loughbrickland, Co Down
Tel: 028 406 26461

A friendly, helpful couple run this bright, cheerful restaurant, which stands in the centre of the village just off the main A1 road that runs from Newry up to Belfast. Bar snacks and light lunches make way for the main à la carte menu, which offers a good choice of dishes prepared with care from prime seasonal ingredients. Mr Johnstone is a very keen golfer, so he knows how important it is to have his golfing customers well satisfied after building up an appetite at one of the several local courses. Nearby attractions include Castewellan Forest Park and the Bronte Interpretive Centre at Rathfriland, along the B3.

Bar & Restaurant

Bar snacks, light lunches and full à la carte

Credit Cards: Access, Mastercard, Visa

Local Golf Courses: Banbridge, Royal County Down, Spa, Tandragee

County Down

ARCHWAYS PUB & RESTAURANT 834

23 Newry Street, Kilkeel, Co Down
Tel: 028 417 64112

In the centre of Kilkeel, five minutes from Kilkeel Golf Club, Archways is a roomy restaurant with a bar and lounge. A friendly atmosphere is generated by owner Mr Allen, and customers can look forward to a convivial drink and a meal throughout the day; informal menu for lunch, à la carte in the early evening (last orders 7 o'clock). The food and drink are not the only offerings, as there's live entertainment twice weekly, a disco at the weekend, karaoke sessions and pool tables. Every summer Kilkeel hosts a Harbour Festival, and the Nautilus Centre is a year-round attraction.

Restaurant with Bar

Meals every day and regular entertainment, disco, karaoke

Credit cards: Access, Mastercard, Visa

Local Golf Courses: Kilkeel, Warrenpoint,Royal County Down

BURFORD LODGE GUEST HOUSE 835

30 Quay Street, Ardglass, Co Down
Tel: 02844 841141

Anne Wills and her daughters put out the welcome mat at their guest house, where every visitor is greeted as a friend. The house, which stands on the seafront two minutes from Ardglass Golf Course, has six letting bedrooms, all en suite, with tea-making facilities. There's a choice for breakfast, and evening meals are also served. Ardglass is one of Northern Ireland's three main fishing ports - the others, Portavogie and Kilkeel - are also in Co Down. The attractions of the sea are considerable, but there's plenty of interest inland, too, with Downpatrick itself an easy drive away and Strangford a little way to the north.

Guest House

6 en suite bedrooms for B&B; evening meal also served

Credit Cards: None

Local Golf Courses: Ardglass, Downpatrick, Bright Castle

THE ANCHOR 836

9-11 Bryansford Road, Newcastle, Co Down
Tel: 028 437 23344 Fax: 028 437 25479

In the same family ownership for more than 40 years, The Anchor is a very friendly bar-restaurant where visitors are welcome for a drink or a meal at any time. It stands just off the central promenade a few steps from the sea, and anyone dropping anchor here will immediately be impressed by the warm, old-world atmosphere. Good honest home cooking is the order of the day, and the choice extends to bar snacks, light lunches and a full à la carte. There is always plenty to see and do in Newcastle, which is one of Northern Ireland's premier seaside resorts.

Bar & Restaurant

Home cooking in a family run bar-restaurant

Credit Cards: Access, Mastercard,Visa

Local Golf Courses: Royal County Down, Bright Castle, Ardglass

THE PRIMROSE BAR 837

30 Main Street, Ballynahinch, Co Down
Tel: 028 97 563177 Fax: 028 97 565954

Pamela Gillespie and her staff make The Primrose a very appealing place to pause after a day on the fairways. On the main street of town, just two minutes walk from the centre, they serve a wide range of local ales, along with a worldwide selection of wines and a superb choice of spirits and liqueurs. On the food side are a bar menu that changes daily and seasonal à la carte menus in the restaurant, along with vegetarian and children's options.

Restaurant and Bar

Main-street premises offering both bar and restaurant menus

Credit Cards: All the major cards

Local Golf Courses: Spa, Lisburn. Rockmount, Ringdufferin

Bistro

Informal eating in the dignified Assembly Rooms. Good wine list

Credit Cards: All the major cards

COURTSIDE BISTRO · 838

19 English Street, Downpatrick, Co Down
Tel: 028 4461 7886 Fax: 028 4461 7191

Downpatrick's Assembly Rooms, the meeting place for 200 years of the venerable Down Hunt, are the setting for a formal restaurant and this relaxing downstairs bistro. The bistro's cooking is of a very high standard on menus that run from soup of the day and panini to burgers, roast chicken and a hearty steak, mushroom and Guinness casserole. An excellent list of select wines has been chosen to complement the food, which is served all sessions except Monday and Tuesday evenings. The building is suitably grand for the former meeting place of the world's oldest Hunt Club.

Local Golf Courses: Downpatrick, Bright CAstle, Ringdufferin, Ardglass

Restaurant

Licensed Italian and Continental Restaurant open evenings and Sunday lunch
Credit Cards: All the major card

MARIO'S RESTAURANT · 850

65 South Promenade, Newcastle, Co Down
Tel: 028 437 23912

Mario Limoni's splendid restaurant enjoys a prime location at the south end of town overlooking the sea. Mario's menus offer an excellent à la carte choice of well-prepared dishes, mainly with an Italian or Continental accent. Freshly made pasta is available with a variety of sauces as either a starter or main course, and other options run from cream of mushroom soup and eggs florentina to sole, salmon, chicken, steak and veal main courses, with desserts from the trolley to finish. Open Tuesday-Saturday evenings (also Monday in summer) and Sunday for carvery lunch, high tea and à la carte dinner.

Local Golf Courses: Royal County Down, Ardglass, Bright Castle

Inn with restaurant

Seven double bedrooms with tv. Bar and restaurant

Credit Cards: All thge major cards

ROADHOUSE INN · 851

157-163 Main Street, Dundrum, Co Down
Tel: 028 437 51209 Fax: 028 437 51809

Behind a handsome black-and-white facade on the main street is a welcoming inn dating from 1800. Hungry visitors can choose between snacks served in the bar and either bistro or à la carte menus in the restaurant, and Sunday lunch is a hearty four-course affair. There's live music every Friday, Saturday and Sunday, and the inn has a function room that can accommodate up to 150. For guests staying overnight seven double bedrooms with tv provide abundant warmth and comfort. Off-road parking. Dundrum Castle is one of the finest Norman castles in Northern Ireland.

Local Golf Courses: Ardglass, Downpatrick, Royal County Down

Bar and Restaurant

Several bars, restaurant, live music in high season

Credit Cards: All the major cards

PAT'S BAR AND RESTAURANT · 870

1-5 Townhall Street, Enniskillen, Co Fermanagh
Tel: 028 66 327462 Fax: 028 66 328258

Two sporting brothers, Ronan and Owen O'Hare, are the hands-on owners of Pat's Bar and Restaurant, which occupies a prime corner site on the town's main street. Very spacious, with many unusual features in its four bars and 150-cover restaurant, it is the perfect spot for getting together for business or pleasure. The menu, which includes daily lunch specials and an à la carte option, offers excellent value for money, and the place really buzzes in high season, when live music is on the agenda every day. There's always lots to do in Enniskillen, and the Heritage Centre at the Castle is a must for visitors.

Local Golf Courses: Castle Hume, Enniskillen

County Down

Co Fermanagh

DONN CARRAGH HOTEL 871

Main Street, Lisnaskea, Co Fermanagh
Tel: 028 677 21206 Fax: 028 677 21223
e-mail: donncarraghhotel@btclick.com

Des McGovern and Gerry Reilly run a splendid hotel that's ideally situated for enjoying the scenic beauty of the Fermanagh countryside and the delights of nearby Upper Lough Erne. Reopening in 1999 after a complete refurbishment, the hotel has 18 en suite bedrooms with tv and telephone. The Benaughlin Restaurant provides a choice of à la carte or table d'hote menus, and for less formal eating and drinking Maggie May's Bar fits the bill nicely. There's live entertainment at the weekend and dancing in the nightclub. Private car park. The hotel is named after Donn Carragh Maguire, the first king of his Celtic tribe.

Hotel with Restaurant and Bar

18 en suite bedrooms; restaurant, bar, lounge, nightclub

Credit Cards: All the major cards

Local Golf Courses: Castle Hume, Enniskillen, Slieve Russell

FORT LODGE HOTEL 872

Forthill Street, Enniskillen, Co Fermanagh
Tel/Fax: 028 66 323275

Standing in the shadow of the renowned Coles Monument alongside scenic Forthill Park, this friendly, comfortable hotel is a good base for discovering the attractions of bustling, historic Enniskillen. All the bedrooms are en suite, with satellite tv + video, radio and telephone. The Crannog Lounge offers a lunchtime carvery and bar meals throughout the day in a traditional ambience, while the Bailey Restaurant is an intimate setting for enjoying fine cuisine on the à la carte or table d'hote menus. Extensive refurbishment is ongoing, and further buildings are being acquired to add still further to the hotel's scope and appeal.

Hotel with Restaurant

En suite bedrooms with tv, video, radio, telephone. Bar-lounge and restaurant

Credit Cards: Access,Mastercard,Visa

Local Golf Courses: Castle Hume, Enniskillen

THE THREE WAY INN 873

247 Sligo Road, Ashwood, Enniskillen, Co Fermanagh
Tel: 028 66 327414

Major developments are under way at the Three Way Inn, a large, welcoming building which stands two miles outside Enniskillen on the main Sligo Road (N16). Owners Gerry and Alan run this friendly, relaxed inn with an all-day menu to attract the hungry visitor, and attached to the main building is a newly constructed self-catering facility with two units each able to accommodate four to six guests. Further extensions and additions are in the pipeline, which will make the inn an excellent value-for-money base for exploring the regions' many scenic and historic attractions. The inn has a good-size car park. Live entertainment every weekend.

Inn with Self-Catering

Roadside inn with all-day menu + self-catering units

Credit Cards: None

Local Golf Courses: Castle Hume, Enniskillen

HOTEL CARLTON 874

2 Main Street, Belleek, Co Fermanagh Tel: 028 6865 8282
Fax: 028 6865 9005 e-mail: reception@hotelcarlton.co.uk
web: www.hotelcarlton.co.uk

Recently rebuilt to preserve all its traditional charm, the Carlton stands in a beautiful wooded setting by Lough Erne in the heart of town. Owner Seamus Rooney offers excellent overnight accommodation in 19 comfortable en suite bedrooms ranging from singles to triples and family rooms. Furnishings are a pleasing mixture of antique and contemporary. The cosy lounge is warm and welcoming, and fine food, based on local produce, is served in the restaurant. Belleek is famous for its distinctive decorative pottery, whose history is told in the Visitor Centre opposite the hotel.

Hotel with Restaurant

19 en suite bedrooms from singles to family rooms. Lounge, restaurant

Credit Cards: All the major cards

Local Golf Courses: Castle Hume, Enniskillen, Bundoran

THE RAILWAY HOTEL | 875

Hotel with Restaurant

19 en suite rooms from singles to triples; restaurant

Credit Cards: Access, Mastercard, Visa

34 Forthill Street, Enniskillen, Co Fermanagh
Tel: 028 66 322084 Fax: 028 66 327480

James Crozier and Owen McKenna keen golfers, bought the Railway Hotel in September 1999 and are clearly succeeding in continuing the tradition of hospitality established through 150 years of family ownership. Guests staying overnight have the choice of 19 well-appointed bedrooms ranging from singles to family rooms, all en suite, with TV and telephone. A full range of meals are available, in style in the Dining Car Restaurant, which has an excellent reputation locally for food. The hotel is well set up to cater for all kinds of functions and parties.

Local Golf Courses: Castle Hume, Enniskillen, Bundoran

MOOHANS FIDDLESTONE | 876

Pub and Guesthouse

Five en suite bedrooms with tv; bar with snacks and entertainment

Credit Cards: None

5 Main Street, Belleek, Co Fermanagh
Tel: 028 686 58008

A warm and heartfelt welcome awaits visitors to John McCann's traditional Irish pub and licensed guesthouse in the centre of Belleek, home of the famous decorative pottery. For overnight guests there are five upstairs letting bedrooms, all with en suite facilities and tv. Residents have their own lounge and secure parking for their cars. The lively bar, where snacks and light meals are served, plays host to traditional nights throughout the year, and travelling musicians are always welcome. The place has a really delightful old-world appeal, with stone floors, low ceilings and an open fire.

Local Golf Courses: Castle Hume, Enniskillen, Bundoran

BROOKLANDS | 877

Hotel with Restaurant

14 en suite bedrooms with tv and phone; lounge and restaurant

Credit Cards: All the major cards

25 Main Street, Ballinamallard, Co Fermanagh
Tel: 028 66 388099 Fax: 028 66 388947

On the main street of a village on the B46 Omagh road, this friendly hotel has been completely refurbished to add modern comfort and amenity to period character. Overnight accommodation comprises 14 tastefully decorated en suite bedrooms with tv and telephone; there are five singles and nine doubles, including two suitable for families. Day rooms consist of the Carriage Restaurant serving an evening à la carte menu, the lounge bar, where coffee and bar snacks are available throughout the day, a function room and a Saturday nightclub. Special packages include golf and cruising on Lough Erne.

Local Golf Courses: Castle Hume, Enniskillen, Omagh

MULEANY HOUSE | 890

Guest House

Nine en suite bedrooms; B&B, dinner by arrangement

Credit Cards: Access, Mastercard, Visa

86 Gorestown Road, Moy, Dungannon, Co Tyrone
Tel/Fax: 028 87 784183
e-mail: mary@muleany@freeservice.uk

A mile outside Moy on the road to Benburb stands this handsome modern family-run guest house, where Brian and Mary Mullen offer home-from-home hospitality in an atmosphere of luxury and friendship. The nine bedrooms are all en suite, with tv and a pleasing harmony of antique furniture and modern drapes. With a drawing room, games room and tv room, families are very well catered for, and for grown-ups there's a well-stocked bar. Bed & Breakfast, with dinner by arrangement for parties of 8 or more.

Local Golf Courses: Dungannon, Killymoon, Silverwood, Allen Park

Counties Fermanagh & Tyrone

Accommodation & Restaurant

12 en suite bedrooms; high-class cuisine

Credit Cards: All the major cards

REAHS RESTAURANT & ACCOMMODATION | 891

24 Killyman Road, Dungannon, Co Tyrone
Tel: 028 87 725575 Fax: 028 87 726676

In a neat detached house half a mile out of town, Nigel and Mary Reah offer the winning combination of high-class food and luxurious overnight accommodation. There are 12 en suite letting bedrooms, eight twins and four new singles, all decorated and furnished with a sure touch that shows Mary's flair for design. The 50-cover restaurant provides visitors with a variety of menu options, including bistro, grill bar and à la carte. Manchester-born Nigel is an ex-rugby player who now coaches the local youth squad. Reahs is warmly recommended by the local Golf Club.

Local Golf Courses: Dungannon, Killymoon, Silverwood, Allen Park

Pub, B&B Accommodation

12 en suite budget bedrooms for Bed & Breakfast

Credit Cards: None

MCGIRR'S | 892

The Square, Coalisland, Co Tyrone
Tel: 028 87 747324

Paul McGirr owns and runs the only public house in Coalisland, a thriving small town a short drive north-east of Dungannon on the way to Lough Neagh (a canal once linked the town, formerly a coal-mining centre, to the Lough). Stone floors and heavy oak fittings give a solid, masculine feel to the bar, and for guests staying overnight there are 12 low-priced en suite bedrooms - clean and warm and an ideal base for visitors on a tight budget. Also on the premises are a lounge and an off-licence. Breakfast only. Street parking.

Local Golf Courses: Dungannon, Killymoon, Silverwood, Edenmore

Hotel with Restaurant

12 bedrooms with tv; choice of menus in the restaurant

Credit Cards: Access,Mastercard,Visa

GREENVALE HOTEL | 893

57 Drum Road, Cookstown, Co Tyrone
Tel: 028 867 62243 Fax: 028 867 65539
e-mail: greenvaleh@iol.com

Greenvale Hotel is an extended Victorian house with a hands-on golf-loving owner in Michael McElhatton. It stands on the outskirts of Cookstown, whose main street has claims to being the longest in Ireland, close to one of the local visitor attractions, Drum Manor Forest Park. The house has 12 letting bedrooms, all with tv, hairdryer and trouser press, and a 50-cover restaurant (last orders 9.30) serving excellent cuisine and offering really good value on the à la carte, table d'hote and specials menus. Other pluses are a massive garden and car park and friendly, efficient staff.

Local Golf Courses: Killymoon, Dungannon, Moyola Park, Omagh

Pub and Restaurant

Modern country pub with restaurant and games room

Credit Cards: Access,Mastercard,Visa

MCGIRR'S OF GORTNAGARN | 894

Gortin Road, Omagh, Co Tyrone
Tel: 028 82 242462

Brother and sister Declan and Nuala McGirr have recently taken over the reins from their parents at this splendid modern pub-restaurant. Long and low, it has ample parking facilities and a shop and filling station on site. The convivial bar has a separate games room with pool and darts, and there's live entertainment at the weekend. The restaurant is open daily, serving breakfast, lunch, high teas and an extensive evening à la carte. Last food orders 9pm. Families are very welcome, and there's a special children's menu. McGirr's stands on the B48 close to a number of the top local attractions, the Ulster-American Folk Park, the Ulster History Park and the Gortin Glen Forest Park.

Local Golf Courses: Omagh, Newtownstewart, Dungannon

FIR TREES HOTEL 895

Dublin Road, Strabane, Co Tyrone
Tel: 028 71 382382 Fax: 028 71 383116

The Fir Trees is a bright modern low-rise complex on the outskirts of town on the main road (A5) to Omagh. Family-run, with a friendly, homely atmosphere, John Kelly's excellent establishment offers comfortable overnight accommodation in 25 en suite bedrooms with the full range of accessories - tv, telephone, trouser press, hairdryer, tea-making facilities. The 60-seater fully licensed restaurant offers both Irish and international cuisine, while Martha's Bar and Bistro is a good spot for enjoying a drink and a meal in less formal surroundings, with live entertainment at the weekend. Plenty of parking space.

Hotel with Restaurant & Bar

25 fully equipped en suite bedrooms. Restaurant, bistro and bar

Credit Cards: Access,Mastercard,Visa

Local Golf Courses: Omagh,Strabane, Newtownstewart, City of Derry

CLANABOGAN HOUSE 896

85 Clanabogan Road, Omagh, Co Tyrone
Tel/Fax: 028 82 241171
e-mail: r&m@clanaboganhouse.freeserve.co.uk

Clanabogan House, a family run Bed and Breakfast is a listed 17th century house set in 5 acres of woodlands and gardens. It is situated just of the A32 (Omagh - Enniskillen road) and 2½ miles from Omagh. There are 8 spacious bedrooms each with tv and tea/coffee making facilities. On site there is a golf driving range, pony trekking and a bar. Ample parking. Meals by previous arrangement.

Country House

Eight large bedrooms, six en suite. Evening meals for 8 or more

Credit Cards: Access,Mastercard,Visa

Local Golf Courses: Omagh, Castle Hume, Strabane, Enniskillen

GLENGANNON HOTEL 897

Ballygawley Road, Dungannon, Co Tyrone
Tel: 028 87 727311

A short drive from the western end of the M1 (Junction 15) is a brightly coloured low-rise modern hotel offering well-priced accommodation. The rooms are all en suite and the tariffs quote rates for single, double and triple occupation. The restaurant (last orders 9pm) has a good choice of menus, including a weekday bistro lunch, snacks, an all-day breakfast, a grill bar and a monthly table d'hote with an all-in price that includes wine. The hotel is very well known for its live music, with entertainment at the weekend in the lounge/function hall. Masses of car parking space.

Hotel with Restaurant

En suite accommodation and varied menus. Weekend entertainment

Credit Cards: Access,Mastercard,Visa

Local Golf Courses: Dungannon, Killymoon, Silverwood, Allen Park

GRANTS BAR AND RESTAURANT 898

29 George Street, Omagh, Co Tyrone
Tel: 028 82 250900 Fax: 028 82 248900

Behind an imposing frontage at the top end of town, Myles McCann's grand pub is well worth a visit for its ambience and decor as well as its food and drink. The two bars and two eating areas are clad in reclaimed old pine, with blockwood floors. The full range of drinks is on offer, along with a tempting range of dishes, from mango chicken bites and chilli tiger prawns to sea bass with pesto tagliatelle and pepper steak. As the menu says: 'Having dinner at Grants is a time of sensual delight, wit and laughter. Good food, good company and fine wine. What could be better!'

Pub with Restaurant

Spacious bars and restaurant with a wide-ranging menu
Credit Cards: Access, Visa, Amex, Mastercard

Local Golf Courses: Omagh, Newtownstewart, Dungannon, Strabane

THE VALLEY HOTEL | 899

Main Street, Fivemiletown, Co Tyrone
Tel: 028 895 21505 Fax: 028 895 21688
web: www.lakelandhotels.com

On the main Belfast-Enniskillen road (A4), John Williamson's Valley Hotel is a modern establishment with 22 luxury bedrooms, all with bath and shower en suite, tv, radio and telephone. Among the smart day rooms, the Blue Room serves food all day and provides live entertainment every Friday and Saturday night; the Blessingbourne Restaurant offers an extensive à la carte menu. Sports people and sightseers will both find plenty to do and see in Fivemiletown and the surrounding area.

Hotel with Restaurant

22 en suite bedrooms; restaurant and all-day menus

Credit Cards: All the major cards

Local Golf Courses: Enniskillen, Castle Hume, Omagh, Dungannon

THE RYANDALE | 900

16-18 the Square, Moy, Co Tyrone
Tel/Fax: 028 87 784629

Marian Daly and Collette Murtagh offer food, drink, accommodation, function facilities and regular live entertainment in their fine Listed building in the centre of the village. The bedrooms have all been refurbished to provide comfort and character, and in the restaurant an excellent selection of dishes makes good use of local produce. Food is served from 9am to 9.30pm. There's live music three nights a week and dancing every Saturday night. The garden runs down to the River Blackwater, which at this point forms the boundary with Co Armagh. The layout of the village is based on the plan of Marengo in Lombardy.

Hotel with Restaurant

Hotel with individually appointed bedrooms, restaurant, live entertainment

Credit Cards: Access,Mastercard,Visa

Local Golf Courses: Dungannon, Killymoon, Silverwood, Allen Park

HAWTHORN HOUSE | 901

72 Old Mountfield Road, Omagh, Co Tyrone
Tel/Fax: 028 82 252005
e-mail: hawthorn@lineone.net web: www.hawthornhouse.net

Nestling at the foot of the Sperrin Mountains ten minutes' walk from the town centre, Michael Gaine's Hawthorn House is a handsome period residence transformed into a high-class guesthouse and restaurant. The whole place is roomy and well planned, and the eight bedrooms are large and comfortably furnished, with en suite facilities, tv and telephone. The 60-cover restaurant provides excellent eating on menus that are a showcase for modern Irish cuisine, with seafood a speciality. The house, where more bedrooms are planned, stands very near one of the country's largest leisure centres.

Guesthouse and Restaurant

Eight en suite bedrooms with tv and phone; licensed restaurant

Credit Cards: Access,Mastercard,Visa

Local Golf Courses: Omagh, Newtownstewart, Dungannon, Strabane

OAKLIN HOUSE HOTEL | 902

Parkmount, Moy Road, Dungannon, Co Tyrone
Tel: 028 877 25151 Fax: 028 877 24953
e-mail: oaklin@aol.com

A superb modern hotel set in extensive gardens and grounds that offer peace, tranquillity and the freedom to roam without leaving the premises. The hotel, which is easily reached from exit 15 of the M1, caters equally well for the private guest as for conferences, weddings and functions, and the bedrooms - singles, doubles and twins - offer every comfort. The Derby Room and the Pickwick Bistro provide a choice of excellent eating (last orders 9.30). Dungannon is an attractive town with much to interest the visitor, including a police station that looks like a castle!

Hotel with Restaurants

Well-equipped en suite bedrooms; large grounds; choice of restaurants

Credit Cards: Visa, Access, Amex, Mastercard

Local Golf Courses: Dungannon, Killymoon, Silverwood, Omagh

Co Tyrone

County Londonderry

KELLYS INN 903

Ballygawley Road, Omagh, Co Tyrone
Tel: 028 855 68218 Fax: 028 855 67160

A long, low, modern complex a short drive south of Omagh on the main A5 road towards Belfast. Overnight accommodation is provided by 13 rooms in motel style, bright and practical, with plenty of parking space for guests' cars. Also on this site are cosy bars and a very large restaurant offering several options: self-service, carvery, lunch specials and à la carte menus. The atmosphere is relaxed and cheerful, and there are regular live music and dancing sessions. Go-ahead owner Patsy Kelly has plans to expand this successful operation.

Motel, Bars and Restaurant

13 motel-style bedrooms in a complex with bars and restaurant

Credit Cards: Access,Mastercard,Visa

Local Golf Courses: Omagh, Dungannon, Strabane, Enniskillen

AKAROA GUEST HOUSE 910

75 The Promenade, Portstewart, Co.Londonderry
Tel: 02870 832067

In the very heart of town close to the best bars and restaurants, this is a popular golfer's destination, a model B&B guest house run with all the care and discipline of an old-fashioned family home. Accommodation comprises two single rooms and nine doubles, five of them with en suite facilities. Akaroa is a modernised three-storey terraced house with excellent sea views from most rooms. Parking is not a problem.

Bed & Breakfast

2 single rooms, 9 doubles; 5 en suite. Easy parking

Credit Cards: None

Local Golf Courses: Castlerock, Portstewart, Royal Portrush

O'MALLEY'S EDGEWATER HOTEL 911

88 Strand Road, Portstewart, Co Londonderry
Tel: 02870 833314 Fax: 02870 832224
e-mail: edgewater.hotel@virgin.net

O'Malley's Edgewater Hotel is situated on the Strand Beach, a perfect vantage point for enjoying views of the Donegal Hills and the Atlantic Ocean. The hotel has 28 bedrooms, all with en suite bathrooms, satellite tvs, telephones, radios and tea-makers. Six of the rooms have been converted into spacious suites that are ideal for families. The restaurant and the comfortable lounge both enjoy sea views. Bar snacks available at any time. Function facilities. Private parking.

Hotel & Restaurant

28 rooms including 6 suites, all en suite. Satellite tv, telephone. Licensed restaurant, bar snacks

Credit Cards: All the major cards

Local Golf Courses: Castlerock, Portstewart, Royal Portrush

ROE VIEW INN 912

160 Ballyquinn Road, Limavady, Co Londonderry
Tel: 028 7776 2555

A handsome half-timbered building near the River Roe, three miles from Limavady on the B68 Dungiven road. Open fires blaze a welcome in both bars, where pool and darts are played and there's live music at weekends. Soup, burgers and pies provide light snacks, and there's a good variety of beer. A popular spot for parties, wedding receptions and celebrating holes in one, with separate function rooms and a large beer garden. Plenty of parking space.

Public House

2 bars. Beer garden. Bar snacks. Pool,darts, live music

Credit Cards: None

Local Golf Courses: Radisson Roe Park, Portstewart, Castlerock

ASHLEIGH HOUSE 913

164 Station Road, Portstewart, Co Londonderry
Tel: 02870 834452

A family-run guest house in a quiet location on the outskirts of town (B185). The heart of the building is a large bungalow, to which several extensions have been made to provide first-class accommodation in six bedrooms (doubles, twins, a family room), all with en suite facilities and tvs. Central heating, sumptuous carpeting and inviting leather chairs make for great comfort, and guests have the use of a tv lounge and spacious dining room - dinner is available by arrangement. Private car parking.

B&B Guest House

Grade A guest house. 6 rooms, all en suite. Payphone, tv. Parking

Credit Cards: None

Local Golf Courses: Castlerock, Portstewart, Royal Portrush

THE ANCHORAGE INN 914

87-89 The Promenade, Portstewart, Co Londonderry BT55 7AG
Tel: 02870 834401 Fax: 02870 834508
e-mail: theanchor@btinternet.com

Twenty double bedrooms, all with en suite facilities, underfloor heating, tvs, telephones and tea-makers, provide comfortable, relaxed accommodation on Portstewart's delightful promenade. The inn incorporates Skippers Bar and Restaurant, where seafood is a speciality and snacks are available throughout the day, and the Anchor Bar, known for its friendly, convivial atmosphere and, naturally enough, great Guinness. The bar also has one of the liveliest night clubs in the area. Transport can be arranged to and from the golf courses. A great base for golfing, boating, touring or just relaxing.

Hotel, Restaurant & Bar

20 rooms, all en suite, tv. Restaurant (seafood speciality), bar, night club

Credit Cards: All the major cards

Local Golf Courses: Castlerock, Portstewart, Royal Portrush

THE POPLARS 915

352 Seacoast Road, Ballerina, Limavady, Co Londonderry
Tel: 028 7775 0360

Comfort is the keynote at this large modern bungalow, where Helen McCracken offers bed and breakfast accommodation in six double bedrooms, three with en suite facilities, all with tvs and tea-makers. This is excellent walking country, halfway between Castlerock and Limavady, and there are stunning views of the massive cliffs from the lounge - you can gasp as the gliders fly off the ridge and disappear! The day starts with a terrific 'Ulster Fry' breakfast that includes home-made bread and jam. Easy parking.

Bed and Breakfast

6 rooms, 3 en suite. Tvs. Great scenery

Credit Cards: All the major cards

Local Golf Courses: Castlerock, Radisson Roe Park

PORTSTEWART ARMS 916

2 Coleraine Road, Portstewart, Co Londonderry
Tel: 028 7183 2046

Just off the main promenade on the Coleraine Road, this is a well-established public house that's long been a favourite with golfers. Built in 1840, it was in its early years a hotel, and is now the oldest pub in town, with many quaint period features as well as attractions such a pool table and gaming machine. A golfing society meets regularly in the pub. Licensee Pat Kelly has been in the business for 30 years and is proud of the hospitality he provides alongside the best draught Guinness in town.

Public House

Long-established pub. Period features. Pool table

Credit Cards: None

Local Golf Courses: Castlerock, Portstewart, Royal Portrush

STREEVE HILL | 917

25 Downland Road, Streeve Hill, Limavady, Co Londonderry
Tel: 028 777 66563 Fax: 028 777 68285
e-mail: streeve@hidden-ireland.com
web: www.hidden-ireland.com/streeve

From Limavady, take the Castlerock road for half a mile then follow the estate wall to reach Peter and June Welsh's superb country mansion. Built in 1730 by Conolly McCausland, it has a rose-brick Palladian façade and enjoys fine views over gardens and parkland to the distant Sperrin Mountains. The three letting bedrooms all have private bathrooms, and guests start the day with a first-class breakfast; the house is also renowned for its gourmet dinners. The famous gardens of Drenagh are one of many local attractions. Golf, tennis, riding, shooting and fishing all available nearby.

Country House Hotel

Three bedrooms with private bathrooms. Fine country setting. Gourmet dinners
Credit Cards: Access,Mastercard,Visa

Local Golf Courses: Radisson Roe Park, Portstewart, Castlerock

BANKS OF THE FAUGHAN MOTEL | 918

69 Clooney Road, Campsie, Co Londonderry
Tel/Fax: 02871 860242
e-mail: bf.motel@talk21.com

Twelve bedrooms, seven with en suite facilities, all with central heating, tvs and tea-makers, in a well-appointed bed and breakfast motel on the main Derry City/Donegal-Causeway Coast route (A2). City of Derry Airport is a very short drive away, and there are several golf and leisure centres nearby, as well as fishing facilities and a gliding centre. All ages are welcome, and individuals or groups of up to 25 can be accommodated.

Motel

12 doubles, 7 en suite, breakfast, tv, leisure centre nearby

Credit Cards: Amex, Visa

Local Golf Courses: Foyle, City of Derry

THE INN AT THE CROSS | 919

171 Glenshane Road, Londonderry, Co Londonderry
Tel: 02871 301480 Fax: 02871 301394
web: www.innat.thecross@virgin.net

A family-owned hotel three miles from Londonderry on the main A6 road to Belfast. Views over the countryside to the Faughan river valley creates a peaceful, relaxed atmosphere and guests will spend a restful night in the bedrooms, all en suite, with satellite tv and telephone. Varied menus, with both à la carte and table d'hote options, in the "Companions" Restaurant; Bar/bistro meals are available all day. Entertainment from Wednesday to Sunday.

Hotel, Restaurant & Bar

All rooms en suite. Food in bar or restaurant

Credit Cards: All the major cards

Local Golf Courses: City of Derry, Foyle

BADGER'S BAR & RESTAURANT | 920

16-18 Orchard Street, Londonderry, Co Londonderry
Tel: 028 7136 3306

Here's a bar and restaurant with plenty of atmosphere. Right in the middle of town, it was built in 1870 and was an ale house before its conversion. Three floors of bars and restaurants offer plenty of space for drinking and dining, and excellent menus provide all the choice a hungry golfer could want. Lunchtime specials and the Sunday carvery are particularly popular. All in all, a welcoming, well-run establishment with the same owner for the last 20 years.

Bar & Restaurant

3 floors of eating and drinking. Handy town-centre location

Credit Cards: No information

Local Golf Courses: City of Derry, Foyle

County Londonderry

BEECHWOOD HOUSE   921

45 Letterkenny Road, Londonderry, Co Londonderry
Tel: 028 7126 1696 Fax: 028 7126 4900

A block of stables has been skilfully and attractively converted into self-contained self-catering accommodation in four chalets which together can sleep 20 in comfort. Behind the cheerful red and white frontage everything is provided for families and groups to make their own way independently, but a full Irish breakfast is available in the main house if required. Plenty of parking space right outside. From the Craigavon Bridge (Upper Deck) take the A40 Letterkenny road. Beechwood is two miles along on the left.

Self-Catering

4 chalets, up to 4 guests per chalet.
Tv, telephone, breakfast on request

Credit Cards: All the major cards

Local Golf Courses: Foyle, City of Derry

MCNALLY'S INN   922

62 Hillhead Road, Castledawson, Co Londonderry
Tel: 028 7965 0095

A small, unpretentious modern country inn on the main road between Castledawson and Toomebridge, just above Lough Neagh. Well known to golfers and others for its traditional Irish welcome, it also scores with good food and drink. The extensive menu runs from light snacks to three-course meals, and Sunday lunch is a particular delight. Drinks include a fine selection of malt whiskeys and a great Guinness. Regular live music sessions. Off-road parking. Beer garden.

Inn

Open seven days. Car wash. Telephone

Credit Cards: None

Local Golf Courses: Moyola Park, Killymoon, Galgorm Castle

Alphabetic List of Golf Courses

A

B

C

D

List of Golf Courses by County

County Kerry

Ballybunion	Ballybunion	82
Beaufort	Beaufort	83
Ceann Sibeal	Ballyferriter	83
Dooks	Glenbeigh	84
Kenmare	Kenmare	85
Killarney	Killarney	85
Killorglin	Killorglin	87
Ring Of Kerry	Kenmare	88
Tralee	Tralee	88
Waterville	Waterville	89

County Kildare

Athy	Athy	94
Bodenstown	Sallins	94
Castlewarden	Castlewarden	94
Craddockstown	Naas	95
Curragh	Curragh	95
Highfield	Carbury	96
K Club	Straffan	97
Kilkea Castle	Castledermot	97
Killeen	Kildare	98
Knockanally	Donadea	99
Naas	Naas	99
Newbridge	Newbridge	100
Woodlands	Naas	100

County Kilkenny

Callan	Callan	104
Kilkenny	Kilkenny	104
Mount Juliet	Thomastown	105

County Laois

Heath	Portlaoise	106
Mountrath	Mountrath	107
Portarlington	Portarlington	107
Rathdowney	Rathdowney	108

County Limerick

Adare Golf Club	Adare	114
Adare Manor	Adare	115
Castletroy	Castletroy	115
Killeline	Newcastle West	116
Limerick	Limerick	116
Limerick County	Ballyneety	117
Newcastle West	Ardagh	117
Rathbane	Rathbane	118

County Longford

County Longford	Longford	150

County Louth

Ardee	Ardee	122
County Louth	Balltray	122
Dundalk	Dundalk	123
Greenaore	Greenaore	124
Killinbeg	Killinbeg	124
Seapoint	Drogheda	124

County Mayo

Ballina	Ballina	129
Ballinrobe	Ballinrobe	129
Belmullet (Carne)	Belmullet	130
Castlebar	Castlebar	131
Claremorris	Claremorris	131
Westport	Westport	133

County Meath

Ashbourne	Ashbourne	138
Black Bush	Dunshaughlin	138
County Meath	Trim	139
Headfort	Kells	139
Kilcock	Kilcock	140
Laytown & Bettystown	Bettystown	141
Moor Park	Navan	141
Navan	Navan	142
Royal Tara	Navan	143

County Monaghan

Nuremore	Nuremore	148
Rossmore	Monaghan	148

County Offaly

Birr	Birr	155
Castle Barna	Daingean	155
Edenderry	Edenderry	155
Esker Hills	Tullamore	156
Tullamore	Tullamore	157

County Roscommon

Athlone	Athlone	164
Roscommon	Roscommon	165

County Sligo

County Sligo	Rosses Point	162
Enniscrone	Enniscrone	162
Strandhill	Strandhill	163

County Tipperary

Ballykisteen	Monard	170
Cahir Park	Cahir Park	170
Clonmel	Clonmel	171
County Tipperary	Dundrum	171
Nenagh	Nenagh	172
Roscrea	Roscrea	172
Thurles	Thurles	174
Tipperary	Tipperary	174

County Waterford

Carrick-on-Suir	Carrick-on-Suir	178
Dungarvan	Dungarvan	178
Dunmore East	Dunmore East	179
Faithlegg	Faithlegg	179
Goldcoast	Dungarvan	180
Tramore	Tramore	181
Waterford	Waterford	182